WORLD PHILOSOPHY S

SCEPTICISM

HERO AND VILLAIN

WORLD PHILOSOPHY SERIES

Additional books in this series can be found on Nova's website under the Series tab.

Additional E-books in this series can be found on Nova's website under the E-book tab.

WORLD PHILOSOPHY SERIES

SCEPTICISM

HERO AND VILLAIN

SIR ROY CALNE
AND
WILLIAM O'REILLY
EDITORS

New York

Copyright © 2013 by Nova Science Publishers, Inc.

All rights reserved. No part of this book may be reproduced, stored in a retrieval system or transmitted in any form or by any means: electronic, electrostatic, magnetic, tape, mechanical photocopying, recording or otherwise without the written permission of the Publisher.

For permission to use material from this book please contact us:
Telephone 631-231-7269; Fax 631-231-8175
Web Site: http://www.novapublishers.com

NOTICE TO THE READER

The Publisher has taken reasonable care in the preparation of this book, but makes no expressed or implied warranty of any kind and assumes no responsibility for any errors or omissions. No liability is assumed for incidental or consequential damages in connection with or arising out of information contained in this book. The Publisher shall not be liable for any special, consequential, or exemplary damages resulting, in whole or in part, from the readers' use of, or reliance upon, this material. Any parts of this book based on government reports are so indicated and copyright is claimed for those parts to the extent applicable to compilations of such works.

Independent verification should be sought for any data, advice or recommendations contained in this book. In addition, no responsibility is assumed by the publisher for any injury and/or damage to persons or property arising from any methods, products, instructions, ideas or otherwise contained in this publication.

This publication is designed to provide accurate and authoritative information with regard to the subject matter covered herein. It is sold with the clear understanding that the Publisher is not engaged in rendering legal or any other professional services. If legal or any other expert assistance is required, the services of a competent person should be sought. FROM A DECLARATION OF PARTICIPANTS JOINTLY ADOPTED BY A COMMITTEE OF THE AMERICAN BAR ASSOCIATION AND A COMMITTEE OF PUBLISHERS.

Additional color graphics may be available in the e-book version of this book.

LIBRARY OF CONGRESS CATALOGING-IN-PUBLICATION DATA

Scepticism : hero and villain / editors, Sir Roy Calne and William O'Reilly.
    p. cm.
 Includes index.
 ISBN 978-1-62417-783-5 (softcover)
1. Scepticism. I. Calne, Roy, Sir. II. O'Reilly, William, 1970-
 B837.S2855 2012
 149'.73--dc23
                       2012017837

Published by Nova Science Publishers, Inc. † New York

We dedicate the book to the authors of the individual chapters.

We thank Jennifer Cummings and Jennifer Richards for their patient and extensive efforts to bring the book to completion.

We are especially grateful to Nadya and Alexandra Columbus for their support and encouragement.

CONTENTS

Preface to the Volume xi
Lord Rees

Introduction to the Volume xv
Roy Calne

SCIENCE 1

Chapter 1 Scepticism in Cosmology 3
Michael P. Hobson

Chapter 2 Doubt and Commitment in Science and Beyond 23
John Polkinghorne

Chapter 3 Scepticism and Radiation 31
Dillwyn Williams and Keith Baverstock

Chapter 4 Scepticism and Mathematics 47
Thomas William Korner

Chapter 5 Scepticism in Medical Research 57
Damian C. Crowther

Chapter 6A Introduction to Evolutionary Biology and Scepticism 67
Roy Calne

Chapter 6 Evolutionary Biology and Scepticism: The Reception of Darwinism in 19th Century German Embryology 71
Robert Asher

Chapter 7 Scepticism in Medicine, Organ Transplantation, Gene and Stem Cell Therapy 87
Roy Calne

Chapter 8	Can Medical Ethics Survive When Medicine is Commercialised? *K. O. Lee*	**99**
Chapter 9	Recovery from Brain Damage and Plasticity: Nihilism, Scepticism and Optimism *John Pickard*	**111**
Chapter 10	A Principled Climate Change Scepticism *M. J. Kelly*	**131**

HUMANITIES   **139**

Chapter 11	Ancient Scepticism and Its Challenges *Lucia Prauscello*	**141**
Chapter 12	Philosophical Scepticism: Neither Friend Nor Foe but Frenemy *Fraser MacBride*	**159**
Chapter 13A	Introduction to Religious Belief *Roy Calne*	**171**
Chapter 13	Doubting Religious Fundamentalism – The Sociologist as Sceptic *Graham Howes*	**175**
Chapter 14	Belief and Cynicism in Religion *Robert A. Hinde*	**187**
Chapter 15	Doubt in Religion and Theology *Brian Hebblethwaite*	**197**
Chapter 16	Scepticism and History *William O'Reilly*	**205**
Chapter 17	*Gotcha*: The Poetics of Linguistic Scepticism *Drew Milne*	**215**
Chapter 18	Love, Sex, Prostitution and Hypocrisy *Roy Calne*	**229**
Chapter 19A	Introduction to Art *Roy Calne*	**237**
Chapter 19	'Art Made for Strangers': Re-Thinking Inuit Art *Maria Tippett*	**243**

Chapter 20	'I Saw It With My Own Eyes' Scepticism and Photography: A Marriage Made in Heaven *Kiloran Howard*	253
Chapter 21	Scepticism and the Army *Nigel Chancellor*	263

ECONOMICS, LAW AND POLITICS — 275

Chapter 22	Economic Scepticism *Andrew Verity*	277
Chapter 23	Is Money Good or Evil, Does It Really Exist at All? *Marcus Johnson*	291
Chapter 24A	Introduction for Teaching Scepticism *Roy Calne*	297
Chapter 24	How Do We Teach Scepticism? *Daisy Christodoulou*	299
Chapter 25	Sport *Stephen Chittenden*	315
Chapter 26A	Introduction to the Law *William O'Reilly*	327
Chapter 26	Between Blind Justice and Sceptical Justice: Lynching in Brazil *Jose de Souza Martins*	329
Chapter 27	Sentencing and Punishment of Offenders *David A. Thomas*	343
Chapter 28	The Prison and the Performance Revolution: 'Virtual' or Virtuous Improvement? *Alison Liebling*	357
Chapter 29	The Reasonableness of Doubt: Scepticism and the Law *Ian Winter*	373
Chapter 30	'An Impossible Sense of Expectation': Lies and Disappointment in British Politics *Ross Hawkins*	383
Chapter 31	The Revival of Arab Scepticism: From Private to Public *Farah Dakhlallah and Adam Coutts*	395

Chapter 32	Israeli Dual Scepticism *Yonatan Mendel and Ronald Ranta*	**407**
Chapter 33	Corruption: Evil or Necessity or How I Learnt to Love Human Nature *Paul Ffolkes Davis*	**419**
Postscript		**431**
Index		**433**

PREFACE TO THE VOLUME

Lord Rees

"If a man will begin with certainties, he shall end in doubts; but if he will be content to begin with doubts, he shall end in certainties," so wrote Francis Bacon. This maxim is exemplified by many of the chapters in this book which extol the importance of scepticism.

The perspective these chapters offer is very welcome. This is especially so, because most people's attitude towards scepticism is ambivalent: it's not clear to most of us whether it is a vice or a virtue. On the one hand, it may connote such unappealing traits as lack of commitment, 'sitting on the fence' and similar stances. But on the other hand, it signals the virtues of tolerance, and a willingness to accept that one may be mistaken. For all of us engaged in science, scepticism is an essential virtue -- we mustn't be 'fooled' by nature; we mustn't become too attached to our 'pet' theories; we mustn't be influenced by wishful thinking.

Scientists should indeed be even more cautious and sceptical in their work than in everyday life. Their highest aim is to make a discovery that is unexpected and novel. And a specially compelling case has to be made before taking seriously a claim that seems intrinsically unlikely, or which seems incompatible with much of what seems firmly established. As Carl Sagan said "Extraordinary claims demand extraordinary evidence." The more remarkable a claim is, the more sceptical (and less credulous) it's appropriate to be.

Science is a 'work in progress'. Some theories are supported by overwhelming evidence; others are provisional and tentative. But, however confident we may be in a theory we should keep our minds open -- or at least ajar -- to the possibility that some intellectual revolution will overthrow it, or at least offer a drastically different perspective.

Scientists tend to be severe critics and strong skeptics of other people's work. They have more incentive than anyone else to uncover errors. That's because the greatest esteem in the scientific profession goes to those who contribute something unexpected and original -- and especially to those who can overturn a consensus. But they need to ensure that they are equally critical of their own work. And that's harder: someone who has invested years of their lives in a project is bound to be strongly committed to its importance, to the extent that it is a traumatic wrench if it the whole effort comes to nought. But it is only after intense scrutiny and criticism that initially-tentative ideas firm up -- for instance, the link between smoking and lung cancer, and between HIV and AIDS. But that's also how seductive theories get destroyed by harsh facts. The great historian Robert Merton described science as 'organised scepticism'.

Scientists don't fall into a single mould. Indeed even the greatest of all display a wide range of personalities and intellectual styles. For instance, Newton's mental powers seem to have been really 'off scale'. His concentration was as exceptional as his intellect: when asked how he cracked such deep problems, he said 'by thinking on them continually'. In contrast, Darwin was less abnormal as a personality, and more modest in his self-assessment: he wrote 'I have a fair share of invention, and of common sense or judgement, such as every fairly succcessful lawyer or doctor must have, but not, I believe, in any higher degree'.

And Darwin's statement reminds us that the thought processes of most scientists are not intrinsically different from those of other professionals – or indeed of those of a detective assessing the evidence at a crime scene.

The path towards a consensual scientific understanding is often winding – with many blind alleys being explored before reaching it. Sometimes a maverick is vindicated. We all enjoy seeing this happen - but such instances are rarer than is commonly supposed, and perhaps rarer than would be inferred from reading the popular press. And sometimes a prior consensus is overturned. But most advances transcend and generalise the concepts that went before, rather than contradicting them. For instance, Einstein didn't overthrow Newton. He transcended Newton, giving us a new perspective offering broader scope and deeper insights.

When rival theories fight it out there is eventually just one winner -- at most. Sometimes, one crucial piece of evidence clinches the case.

That happened for the big bang cosmology. It happened also for continental drift. In other cases, an idea gains only a gradual ascendancy -- alternative views get marginalised until their leading proponents die off.

Sometimes, the subject moves on, and what once seemed an epochal issue is bypassed or sidelined.

Our current scientific knowledge and capability is actually surprisingly 'patchy'. Many everyday things still baffle even the experts. In contrast, some of the best-understood phenomena are far away in the cosmos. Back in the 17th century, Newton could describe the 'clockwork of the heavens'; eclipses could be both understood and predicted. But few other events are so predictable. For instance, it's hard to forecast, even a day before, whether those who go to view an eclipse will encounter clouds or clear skies; in the far more complex fields of sociology and economics, all trends are notoriously unpredictable. And some familiar matters that interest us all -- diet and child care for instance -- are so poorly understood that 'expert' advice changes from year to year.

It may seem odd that we need to be more sceptical of a dietician's advice than of what an astronomer says about a galaxy millions of light-years away. But that's because what makes things hard to understand is not how big they are but how complex they are. Even the smallest insect, with its layer upon layer of intricate structure, is far more complex than a star. Everyday phenomena, especially those that involve entities as complicated as human beings, are far more challenging and intractable than anything in the inanimate world.

As a subject advances, new questions come into focus that couldn't previously have been posed. But old controversies get settled: there is a huge body of knowledge that (even if not certain) is firmly enough established to be confidently applied, whether in medicine or in engineering. This confidence may surprise anyone who trawls the internet.

If, for instance, you seek medical guidance to treat some ailment, a Google search will reveal a bewildering range of purported remedies. But, if your own health were at stake, you wouldn't attach equal weight to everything in the blogosphere: you'd rightly be deeply skeptical or most of it. You'd entrust yourself to someone with manifest medical credentials and a successful record of diagnosis – though, even then, you should be cautious. Likewise, we get a clearer 'steer' on other contentious issues like climate science -- though not of course a complete consensus – by attaching more weight to those with serious credentials in the subject. (Indeed in this particular subject it is often the so called 'sceptics' who are the most firmly entrenched in their views.)

Noisy controversy on a scientific topic need not signify evenly-balanced arguments. But broad and open debate is always the best route towards clarity. This is the way science advances. And the benign developments in communications mean that more people, worldwide, can participate in science -- in particular, the best scientific journalists and bloggers are plugged into an extensive network and can help to calibrate novel claims.

But what about ideas 'beyond the fringe'? Here there's less scope for debate -- both sides don't share the same methods or play by the same evidence-based rules.

To inject a personal note, I've not, as an astronomer, found it fruitful to have much dialogue with astrologers nor creationists. We shouldn't let a craving for certainty -- for the easy answers that science can seldom provide -- drive us towards the illusory comfort and reassurance that they offer.

This book ranges over the whole of science -- and indeed over the entire map of learning. It is a fascinating and eclectic 'mix' – but I'm confident that any reader will come away more convinced of the wisdom of Francis Bacon's maxim with which I began, and be grateful to the Editors for assembling such a fine and comprehensive volume.

INTRODUCTION TO THE VOLUME

Roy Calne
Departments of Surgery and Medicine, University of Cambridge, UK
Visiting Professor, Departments of Surgery and Medicine,
National University of Singapore

In ancient Greece philosophers who argued against perceived wisdom using logic were called "the sceptics" and scepticism has remained roughly definable in these terms. The sceptic would view a proposition with initial doubt and disbelief and challenge the proposer to provide sufficient evidence to promote credibility. There is an extensive historical narrative of people who stood up against the establishment, particularly the religious establishments. Many of them suffered as a result and were persecuted. The majority accepted view may be vulnerable to rational argument, but it is difficult to erect credible alternatives. Only in the last two hundred years with increasing scientific knowledge and the clarification of the scientific method, has a constructive alternative agenda become available to those with a sceptical mind. The scientific method depends on the statement of an hypothesis that has been tested experimentally and/ or careful observations of nature, which will counter alternative accepted explanations. The power of science rests on the repeatability of experiments and the demonstration that the facts of a tested hypothesis can work in practice when the science is applied. Thus we expect an aeroplane to take off and land safely, defying gravity and permitting rapid transport. The ability to fly, the design of the aircraft, the power of the engines, the control of the navigation and the continuous contact with monitors on the ground lead the passenger to have faith in the scientific inventions that were essential to produce this form of transport.

The word "faith" immediately conjures up the use of the word in the religious context and leads to discussion of religion as a form of mysterious understanding of the unknown without repeatable direct evidence. The strength of religion and the power invested in those with high hierarchical positions in religion are phenomena common to virtually all civilisations. They support the hypothesis that religion is an instinctive hard-wired attribute of *homo sapiens*. Recently the concept of "hard-wired instinct" has become a little less certain with demonstrations of the plasticity and change, which is a normal feature of the developing brain, but also a characteristic of certain functions in the brain in adult life. Powerful modification of the brain occurs in strict Jesuit and Madrassi schools for young children. The Jesuits claim that if they have care of the child from the age of three they will mould the child's belief for life. It seems that some Islamic mullahs can do the same. Prolonged and repetitive indoctrination of young children can establish unshakeable religious belief – the success of doctrinal "brainwashing" or "holy waterboarding"

Although we like to consider civilised behaviour as depending on rational choices, in fact emotion frequently overrides rationality. For a society to exist, regulation and some kind of moral code are necessary and in most societies religion has played a central part in both of these. Exhortation towards a sceptical approach to dogma has been attributed to the Buddha who is alleged to have advised his followers to believe in no statements or concepts,even if the Buddha himself had uttered them, unless they are consistent with the common sense of the individual. The human brain has evolved over millions of years and one of its singular and unique characteristics is abstract thought and self-awareness with the obvious questions demanding an answer, "where do we come from?", "why are we here?" and "where are we heading?". The sceptic would be very doubtful of the ability of religion and political systems to answer any of these questions, nor can science provide an explanation. In recent years the concept of relativity, the "big bang" origin of the universe and the world of quantum physics are difficult concepts to explain by common sense and reason. We can communicate instantly around the world via the internet and this depends on the utilisation of quantum physics in many of the relevant applications, but the quantum theory that light can be both particulate and wave in form at the same time is counter-intuitive. The evolution of the brain in primitive man would not have been subjected to moulding by quantum concepts, so one might conjecture that the evolved brain is not well suited to handle subatomic physics.

The above somewhat random observations related to the importance or irrelevance of scepticism in human endeavour. In this volume various aspects of the phenomena referred to will be challenged in more detail and the reader may judge whether scepticism is a valuable and laudable attitude and activity or whether it is likely to lead to more harm than good to our species and the rest of the planet.

Curiosity and lethal aggression are human attributes illustrated in the story of the Garden of Eden. The fruit of the Tree of Knowledge was forbidden but nevertheless was acquired with disastrous consequences. If funds are available and the ambiance suitable for academic discourse, science will progress. The acquired knowledge rides on a ratchet and cannot be unlearned. Horrific atomic weapons are here to stay. Each advance in science is subjected to rigorous and sceptical criticism, which if withstood and confirmed by experiments and observation lead to credibility, although scientists are aware that accepted scientific data are always subject to re-examination and change. It is important that scepticism is not over-zealous since the sensitivity of a really innovative lateral thinker may be crushed by an overwhelming hierarchical criticism, that may also have an agenda of competition. The evidence of credibility varies depending on the subject. There is an apocryphal story of three scientists, a biologist, a chemist and a mathematician, arriving in an unfamiliar country on a train. The biologist observes a sheep out of the window and comments that the sheep in this country are black; the chemist begs to differ that the evidence only points to one black sheep; the mathematician disagrees with both and explains that the evidence so far only suggests that at least one half of one sheep in this country is black. The degree of rigorous scepticism varies in different scientific subjects. Climate change is a field where the extreme complexity does not provide enough data for a full understanding, but this has not deterred politicians from dogmatic interpretation. The present state of knowledge supports global warming with a significant contribution resulting from human activities. Successive increasingly cold winters in northern Europe might persuade one that the case for global warming is not entirely convincing, but the experts disagree and enormous effort expense and emotion are directed towards decreasing the carbon footprint of man. Strangely, however, scarcely any attention has been directed to the explosion of population growth, which must be a significant factor adding to the human contribution to global warming. Population growth continues at an alarming rate and it seems quite likely that *homo sapiens* will saturate the available world habitat and exhaust the resources of both water and food in an effort to sustain the increasing number of people on the planet.

Evolution is accepted by most rational people; the evidence is overwhelming although circumstantial. The ever-increasing complexity of living beings has been studied in detail and the urge to reproduce is universal in all living species, otherwise there would be no evolution. The desire to maintain the species is obvious by even cursory biological observation. The gentle and obedient dog changes her nature completely during the period of being "on heat" and her sensitive hearing appears suddenly to be lost, at least when called by the owner. A more bizarre example of the wish to reproduce is the Praying Mantis, where the male, having completed the reproductive act, becomes a post-copulatory feast for the female. It is not surprising that major religions exhort their members to go forth and multiply and the religious leaders are vehemently against birth control. Modern medicine has gone a long way to reduce infant and child mortality, so that there are progressively increasing numbers of people alive involved in competition for survival of the fittest and eventually major conflict is likely. World leaders seem to be completely impotent in coping with the population increase, which is unsustainable despite the catastrophic AIDS epidemic. Most of us would like to live in peace with our families, but there has always been a small minority who detest peaceful co-existence. Previously the harm that they could unleash was limited by the weapons available, but now with the new and extraordinarily effective agents designed to kill, a small number of people who do not value their own lives are a potential major threat to civilised existence.

Much has been written of the differences between science and the arts, but there is a hinterland between the two which has been underestimated. Mathematicians are renowned for expressing the joy of the beauty of certain equations, and all people seem to have an instinct for arts in the broader sense very similar to the instinct towards a religious faith. Appreciation and enjoyment of the arts is a unique human characteristic, with the exception of certain birds, which seem to have instinctive behaviour similar to what we would regard as artistic. The rituals of the mating dance of the Bluefoot Booby is a good example, and another the sculptured architecture constructed by the Bowerbird to demonstrate to the female he is wooing, how skilful he is. Besides construction and dancing, birds communicate by singing. The purpose of the birdsong seems to be primarily to procure a mate, but also an indication of territorial possession, a warning of danger and a signal for the time to migrate. In these examples, although to call the avian pursuits artistic could be challenged, nevertheless they would seem to have survival advantage and this could also be the case with humans. The morale-improving rallying properties of music are well-known in religious ceremonies and also in battle. The bugle, drums and bagpipes can all play a part in raising spirits and frightening the enemy. The rituals of dancing, singing and especially communal enjoyment of musical rhythm are common to most humans. They are a cohesive force for society and probably have the same survival advantages as with the birds. They also raise the question of appreciation of beauty as an aesthetic pleasure. All aspects of the arts in human interaction have various degrees of utility but also an extremely powerful and totally inexplicable beauty from the simple beauty of a mathematical equation, to the subtle calming effect of a Shubert sonata.

A scientific researcher motivated by curiosity who unravels an important and difficult problem will be delighted to have achieved this advance in knowledge, but on the downside, on reflection, it is clear that the particular advance would had eventually occurred without his efforts. It has been pointed out that in this respect the arts are different. Thus if Crick and Watson had never been born the structure of DNA would still have been discovered, but if Shakespeare, Rembrandt and Beethoven had never been born their lasting majestic gifts to humanity would not have been created. No-one else could have written Beethoven's 9th Symphony. Scepticism is a healthy activity but it needs to be modulated if the sceptic is to survive. Although only democracies claim to have free speech, there are limits in every society which cannot be exceeded without the majority punishing the critical sceptic. In Britain 300 years ago the public expression of religious scepticism was dealt with by burning alive. What we feel and what we express may be quite different and lead to accusations of hypocrisy, but there can be no political system devoid of hypocrisy. Corruption and hypocrisy seem to be essential ingredients of every government. The sceptic, who may deplore the cult of the celebrity and the almost religious interest and worship of football and footballers, would be wise to heed a Yorkshire man's advice to his son "see all, hear all, say nought". The subjects which are taboo vary from country to country, in the West the mantra of politically correct behaviour and particularly vocal expression of critical comments, are now well established and anyone who contravenes the code by speaking out, is liable to persecution, as witches were in olden times.

Curiosity and scepticism are the fuel of scientific progress. Scepticism occurs in all human activity, but moving away from science, scepticism is less powerful because it does not have the advantage of experimental proof. Nevertheless in intercourse between nations historical reason for scepticism can be persuasive. Afghanistan is a vast, hilly country ruled by a proud tribesman with a warrior tradition, demonstrated by two important victories in the 19th century over the British, who at that time had the most powerful military machine. In the 1st Afghan war the British army were annihilated, apart from one British survivor who arriving at his camp on a dying horse, gave the terrible news to his comrades (Fig 1.). In the 20th century Russia, also a formidable military power, was humbled by the Afghans. There can be no doubt that the Afghan tribes, although often displaying lack of love between themselves, have an extraordinary united hatred for foreigners on their soil, especially armed invaders who wish to undermine their main trade of opium from the poppy and change their ancient and established regimes of government for an open, liberal, democratic system, which would emancipate women and reduce corruption. Such a philosophy espoused by Western governments is detested by most Afghans. It is not therefore surprising that an armed enterprise led by America, now the most powerful military country in the world, would be fiercely resisted and after eight years of the bitterest fighting the NATO leaders now seem to be agreed that they cannot win. To impose their wishes on the Afghans would probably require the use of nuclear or other devastating weapons, leaving nobody to vote democratically and no woman to be emancipated. From the history of the past 200 years a sceptical assessment of the chances of victory for the NATO forces would have been justified but the arguments of history, rational assessment and the likely outcome were brushed aside by bellicose and powerful politicians, riding a tide of irrational and unreasonable emotions. In the place of powerful emotion useful scepticism has no chance and the result was massive loss of life and treasure on both sides.

Dr. William Brydon "The only British survivor of the 1st Afghan War" painted by Lady Butler, Tate Gallery, London.

SCIENCE

In: Scepticism: Hero and Villain
Editors: R. Calne and W. O'Reilly

ISBN 978-1-62417-783-5
© 2013 Nova Science Publishers, Inc.

Chapter 1

SCEPTICISM IN COSMOLOGY

Michael P. Hobson[*]
Astrophysics Group, Cavendish Laboratory, Cambridge, CB3 0HE

The Oxford English Dictionary lists three meanings of the word 'scepticism', as follows: (1) the doctrine of Sceptics; the opinion that real knowledge of any kind is unattainable; (2) sceptical attitude in relation to some particular branch of science; doubt or incredulity as to the truth of some assertion or supposed fact; and (3) doubt or unbelief with regard to the Christian religion.

Cosmology is the pursuit of knowledge and understanding of the universe in which we live. This clearly represents the antithetical viewpoint to that expounded in the first definition, so we need not consider this meaning any further. Turning to the third definition, the study of cosmology is not necessarily driven by doubt or disbelief in the Christian religion. Indeed, the earliest cosmological models pre-date Christianity by several millennia. Nonetheless, the modern discipline of cosmology does provide a rather different perspective on creation than that put forward in the Book of Genesis. This can, and often does, lead to rather arid science-versus-religion debates that are best avoided. I will therefore not pursue this definition of scepticism any further here either. Rather, I will focus my discussion of scepticism in cosmology around the second definition, in particular the doubt and incredulity of successive generations of cosmologists as to the truth of assertions or supposed facts put forward by their predecessors, an approach that is central to the scientific method itself. A few words of warning are necessary before embarking on this discussion. Firstly, this process is far from reaching a conclusion and, secondly, as observed by the famous 20th century Russian physicist, Lev Landau, "cosmologists are often in error, but never in doubt".

Scepticism has been central to the development of our understanding of the universe since the beginning of recorded history, but there are three eras in particular

---

[*]E-mail address: amorpho@gmail.com

during which our cosmological model evolved very rapidly. These periods broadly coincide with: the ancient civilisations of the Egyptians and Mayans through to the burgeoning of ancient Greek philosophy; the Renaissance; and the industrial revolution through to the present day. In each case, the revolutionary changes in our description of the universe have been driven by doubts regarding the existing world view at the time.

Cosmology of the Ancients

The first advances in cosmology were made very early in classical antiquity, as mankind began to emerge from pre-historic beliefs in mythology and the supernatural. Most importantly, it was realised that one might develop an understanding of the universe by observing it carefully, even if that understanding was often still placed in the context of mythology or religious beliefs. There is considerable evidence that observational astronomy was central to many ancient cultures. The design and placement of the pyramids at Giza are thought to have been strongly influenced by astronomical observations, which also played a key role in setting the calendar for religious life at the time. Indeed, the early Egyptian astronomers may well have tracked the positions of stars over a long period of time to sufficient accuracy to have observed the precession of the equinoxes: the gradual movement in the orientation of Earth's axis of rotation, like that of a spinning top, during which the positions of the north and south celestial poles appear to move in circles against the fixed background of stars, completing one circuit approximately every 26,000 years. Unfortunately, all these events are too remote for there to remain a reliable record of the achievements and movitations, sceptical or otherwise, of these earliest astronomers and cosmologists.

As in mathematics and many other sciences, the Greeks mark the starting point in recorded history for astronomy and cosmology, at least in Western civilisation. In particular, one may reasonably credit the first use of sceptical thinking in the description of the universe to Thales of Miletus in the 6th century BC. Thales, who is thought by some to have himself received instruction from Egyptian priests, was the first of the Seven Sages of Greece and regarded by many, including Aristotle over two centuries later, as the first philosopher in the Greek tradition. He laid the foundations of the scientific method, by defining general principles and setting forth hypotheses, for which he is often described as the "Father of Science". He is also credited with the first application of deductive reasoning to geometry and is the earliest individual in history to whom a mathematical discovery has been attributed. Most importantly, Thales was the first to attempt to explain natural phenomena, including the existence of the world, without reference to mythology. Indeed, Thales' scepticism regarding mythological explanations of the physical world, and his ultimate rejection of them, became the central tenet of the Ionian school of philosophy, which separated scientific thinking (termed logos) from the religious or supernatural (mythos). The Ionian school, which included Anaximander and his most famous pupil, Pythagoras, was responsible for several fundamental cosmological realisations and discoveries. These included recognising the Earth as an isolated heavenly body in space, knowledge of the Earth as a sphere, and even early determinations of its radius and of the Earth-Moon distance. According to Herodotus, Thales himself once predicted a solar eclipse, which by modern methods we now know to have occurred on May 28, 585 BC. A further key notion developed by the Ionian school was that massive bodies fall towards the centre of the Earth, which was therefore reasoned to be situated at the centre of the universe.

By the 4th century BC, following further works by Plato and his student Aristotle, most educated Greeks believed in a cosmological model in which the Earth was a stationary, non-rotating, sphere at the centre of the universe, and the Sun, Moon, stars, and naked-eye planets moved around the Earth on spheres or circles, arranged in the order Moon, Sun, Venus, Mercury, Mars, Jupiter, Saturn, with the stars all located on the outermost 'celestial sphere'. In the minds of the ancient Greeks, this geocentric cosmology was supported by everyday experience. Firstly, one cannot feel the Earth moving; it seems to be completely at rest. Secondly, the Sun, planets and stars appear to revolve around the Earth each day. In particular, the trajectories of stars during the course of the night appear to move in perfectly circular trajectories around the north celestial pole. This concurred precisely with the basic tenets of Aristotilean physics, which grew out of earlier dictums by Plato, that the only allowable motions in the heavens were uniform motion either in a straight line or a circle, the two key geometrical concepts of Greek mathematics. This viewpoint was further supported observationally by the careful cataloging of the positions (and brightnesses) of several hundred stars in the Northern sky by Timocharis in the 3rd century BC, and 150 years later by Hipparcos. Indeed, the comparison by Hipparcos of these two catalogues led undeniably to the (re-)discovery of the precession of equinoxes. Perhaps most importantly, however, geocentrism also concurred with religious beliefs that placed mankind at the centre of creation.

The culmination of several centuries of Greek astronomy came with the writing of the 13 volumes of the *Almagest* by Claudius Ptolemaeus, or Ptolemy, in the 2nd century AD, which presented a synthesis of the achievements of the Greek and Babylonian astronomers up to that point, combined with new ideas and insights by Ptolemy himself. Firstly, sceptical of the existing arguments for placing the Earth at the centre of the universe, Ptolemy devised a new rationale by observing that, at any one time, roughly one-half of the total number of stars were above the horizon and the rest were below it. He reasoned simply that if the Earth were not at the centre of the universe, this division would not be equal. More importantly, however, Ptolemy added some significant new features to the basic geocentric model of Aristotle, an endeavour driven by his doubts regarding the existing model, as the divergence between its predictions and astronomical observations became increasingly apparent over time. In particular, the Aristotilean model could explain neither the observed changes in the brightness of planets, nor the increasingly accurate observations (some by Ptolemy himself) of the finer details of their complicated motion across the sky, which revealed them occasionally to slow down, stop and even reverse direction (known as retrograde motion). In response to these shortcomings, Ptolemy proposed a new model in which each planet moved via a system of two or more circles. In the simplest case, the planet moved at a uniform rate around a small circle, called the epicycle, the centre of which itself moved at a non-uniform rate around a larger circle, called the deferent. The centre of the deferent was halfway between the Earth and the equant, a point near the centre of the planet's orbit from which the centre of the planet's epicycle appears to move at a uniform rate. It is worth noting that, despite the existence of the equant point, many Greek philosophers were deeply sceptical about Ptolemy's model, since they believed it compromised Plato's dictum of uniform circular motion.

In spite of these doubts, the combined motions around the epicycle and deferent in Ptolemy's model caused a planet's distance from the Earth to change as it moved around its orbit, thereby explaining changes in its observed brightness and also allowing for retrograde motion. Indeed, the predictions of Ptolemy's model agreed relatively well with observed celestial motions, although it was necessary periodically to add further smaller epicycles to some planets' orbits to maintain agreement with observations over longer time periods. Consequently, for nearly 1400 years, Ptolemy's geocentric system was accepted as the correct cosmological model by European and Islamic astronomers, and was used to predict the positions of the Sun, Moon and planets, which were needed for the preparation of astrological charts and the determination of the correct dates for religious festivals.

Although scepticism played an important role in encouraging innovation in Greek astronomy, it is worth mentioning at this point how it also severely stifled advancement in our understanding of the universe during this period. Not all Greek philosophers agreed with the geocentric model. Indeed, as early as the 5th century BC, some Pythagoreans – most notably Philolaus – believed the Earth to be one of several planets going around a 'central fire'. It was, however, Aristarchus of Samos in the 3rd century BC who proposed the most far-sighted alternative to geocentrism. In a letter from Archimedes to King Gelon, the model of Aristarchus is described as "the hypothesis that the fixed stars and the Sun remain without motion. As for the Earth, it moves around the Sun on the circumference of a circle with centre in the Sun". Moreover, Aristarchus also suggested that the other planets also orbited the Sun and that the Earth rotated about an axis through its centre. We know now, of course, that this heliocentric model, which predated Ptolemy's cumbersome geocentric system by 5 centuries, was far closer to reality. It was, however, deeply unpopular, since it contradicted religious beliefs. According to Plutarch, Aristarchus was accused of impiety for "putting the Earth in motion". Moreover, the followers of Aristotle rejected Aristarchus' model on the following 'physical' grounds. First, heavy objects fall towards the centre of the Earth and not towards the Sun, hence they reasoned that the former must be at the centre of the universe. Second, if the Earth orbited the Sun, one ought to observe the shifting of the fixed stars as one's point of view changes over the course of a year (a phenomenon known as stellar parallax). Since no such shifts were observed, it was reasoned that either the Earth did not move, or that the stars were much further away than had previously been conceived, so that their parallax was undetectable. The Aristotileans chose the simpler explanation that the Earth did not move, which thus contradicted any non-geocentric cosmology. In fact, the stars are much more distant than the Greeks ever considered, resulting in stellar parallax being a very subtle effect, which was not verified observationally until the advent of modern telescopes in the 19th century. A final argument made against Aristarchus' model by the Aristotileans was that, if the Earth rotated, an object thrown vertically upwards should land in a different spot, contrary to every-day observation.

Renaissance Cosmology

It was not until the early 16th century, and the Renaissance in Europe, that Aristarchus' heliocentric model was revived by the great German–Polish astronomer and polymath, Nicolaus Copernicus, who is it thought may also have been ordained a Catholic priest, or at least taken minor orders. As a young man, Copernicus had made some observations of the Moon that verified certain known peculiarities in Ptolemy's theory and established his doubts regarding geocentrism. This scepticism led him to read extensively about Greek and Roman astronomy, in particular accounts by Cicero and Plutarch, and gather information about ancient astronomical calendar systems. Copernius was particularly struck by the heliocentric ideas of Philolaus and, especially, the model of Aristarchus. Based on these ideas, Copernicus wrote an initial account, the *Commentariolus* (Little Commentary), of his own heliocentric theory some time before 1514, but made only a very few manuscript copies available to his closest acquaintances. Only decades later, and late in his life, was he urged to complete and publish a mathematically detailed account of his model. By 1532, Copernicus had basically completed his major work *De revolutionibus orbium coelestium* (On the Revolutions of the Celestial Spheres), which marked the beginning of the end for the widespread belief in a geocentric, and anthropocentric, universe.

Copernicus' aim was to present a more elegant and practical alternative to Ptolemy's model, while preserving the basic notions of Aristotilean physics. He was motivated in particular by his dislike of the equant introduced by Ptolemy, in keeping with the doubts expressed by several Greek philosophers at the time of its devising. The major features of Copernicus' theory were: (1) heavenly motions are uniform, eternal, and circular, or compounded of several circles (epicycles); (2) the centre of the universe is near the Sun; (3) around the Sun, in order, are Mercury, Venus, Earth and Moon, Mars, Jupiter, Saturn, and the fixed stars; (4) the Earth has three motions: daily rotation, annual revolution, and annual tilting of its axis; (5) retrograde motion of the planets is explained by the Earth's motion; and (6) the distance from the Earth to the Sun is small compared to the distance to the stars. Thus, while introducing several pivotal innovations, Copernicus' model retained the Platonic ideal of using only uniform circular motions, correcting what was seen by many as the chief inelegance in Ptolemy's system. This did lead, however, to Copernicus' model having even more epicycles than Ptolemy's, and being only marginally more accurate in predicting celestial motions. Conversely, the move away from a geocentric model contradicted the long-held Aristotilean idea that all objects fall towards the centre of the universe. Copernicus' model constituted a profound shift in cosmological thinking.

Although *De revolutionibus orbium coelestium* was basically completed by 1532, Copernicus was nervous about publishing his work, despite urging by his closest friends. Copernicus was concerned by the potential scepticism and scorn "to which he would expose himself on account of the novelty and incomprehensibility of his theses", in particular from the Catholic Church. Nonetheless, rumours about Copernicus' theory had begun to reach educated people all over Europe, and in 1533 the papal secretary, Johann Widmannstetter, outlined Copernicus' theory in a series of lectures to Pope Clement VII and several of his cardinals. Fortunately for Copernicus, at that time the Church had a particular interest in astronomy, since a reform of the Julian Calendar was considered necessary and any system that increased the accuracy of astronomical predictions would allow the Church to develop a more accurate calendar. Consequently, in 1536, at the instruction of the Pope, Cardinal von Schönberg wrote to Copernicus making a formal request for the publication of his work. Nonetheless, perhaps still wary of astronomical, philosophical and religious objections, Copernicus further delayed publication until 1543, when, under strong pressure from his pupil Rheticus, he finally consented and sent a manuscript to the German printer Johannes Petreius in Nuremberg. The printing was supervised by Copernicus' friend and Lutheran theologian, Andreas Osiander, who added an unauthorised preface defending the work against potential criticism by presenting it simply as a calculational device that allowed simpler and more reliable astronomical predictions, but did not necessarily have implications outside the limited realm of astronomy. In the main text, however, it is clear that Copernicus himself believed his heliocentric model described the physical reality of the universe. It is reputed that, in May 1543, the first printed copy was placed into Copernicus' hands as he lay on his death-bed. Legend has it that he awoke from a stroke-induced coma, looked at his book, and then died peacefully.

Despite the publication of Copernicus' theory, there remained substantial scepticism and resistance to the notion of heliocentrism for a considerable period thereafter. Unsurprisingly, the Catholic Church was reluctant to accept a theory that did not place God's creation at the centre of the universe, since this was in conflict with many of its teachings and beliefs. Indeed, some of the Church's greatest thinkers had even folded the notion of geocentrism into their theology. St. Thomas Aquinas, for example, noted that, in the ascension of Christ, his physical body remained on Earth, but his soul rose into heaven, in keeping with the Aristotilean ideas. Even beyond the Church, however, geocentrism was simply regarded as a well-established fact, ingrained in society at every level, that should not be overturned by a new system that, owing to its adherence to circular motions, did not offer much better astronomical predictions. People and institutions were not ready for the monumental change in their view of the universe that Copernicus' model represented. Consequently, heliocentrism was widely criticised and ridiculed.

The widespread resistance to heliocentrism did not, however, deter some thinkers from embracing the new cosmological model and developing it further. In post-reformation England, for example, under the reign of Elizabeth I, the Catholic Church's discomfort with heliocentrism was of little concern, and the Coperican picture was enthusiatically adopted by a number of prominent mathematicians and astronomers. In particular, in 1576, Sir Thomas Digges published the first account of the Copernican model in English, which was a milestone in the popularisation of the idea. Moveover, Digges extended Copernicus' idea by embedding the solar system in an infinite distribution of stars, which were assumed to be objects like the Sun. This profound proposal was also championed by the Italian philosopher, mathematician, astronomer and Dominican friar, Giordano Bruno, who further suggested that the universe contained an infinite number of inhabited worlds populated by other intelligent beings. Unfortunately, such ideas placed him in ill favour with the Catholic Church, and he was burned at the stake in 1600 after the Roman Inquisition found him guilty of heresy for his pantheism.

The long road to overturning the widely-held scepticism regarding heliocentrism would require the combined efforts, over more than a century, of some of the greatest astronomers, mathematicians and physicists in mankind's history, including both Galileo and Newton. This process began with the Danish nobleman and astronomer, Tycho Brahe, who was inspired by inaccuracies in existing astronomical tables to begin a great series of observations of the stars and planets. In particular, he was motivated by errors both in the Alphonsine Tables, based on the Ptolemaic model, and the Prutenic Tables, based on the Copernican model, regarding the predicted date of a conjunction of Jupiter and Saturn in 1563. With the sponsorship of Frederick II of Denmark, Tycho constructed two observatories on the island of Hven, in which he constructed the most advanced astronomical instruments available at the time. He made numerous technical innovations, including developing the notions of systematic and random errors in measurements, and understanding the effects of bending of instruments under gravity and of refraction by the atmosphere. Using numerous clocks to measure their transits times, Tycho obtained positions accurate to about 1 arcminute (1/60th of a degree) for the Sun, Moon, planets and 777 stars over a period of 20 years, and was the last of the major naked-eye astronomers. Even Tycho, however, was not immune to the prevailing concensus in favour of geocentrism, and was also troubled by the apparent lack of any stellar parallax, which should exist in a heliocentric model. Torn between the geometrical simplicity of the Copernican model and the philosophical benefits, as he saw them, of the Ptolemaic system, he used his extensive and meticulous observations to propose a compromise between the two world views, in which the planets orbit the Sun, but the Sun and Moon orbit the Earth, which is stationary at the centre of the universe. Since Tycho's system was a religiously acceptable alternative that matched available observations, it was very influential in the late 16th and early 17th centuries, thereby muddying the waters of renaissance cosmology still further.

Fortunately for astronomy, in 1600, the year before his death, one of Tycho's final acts was to employ the young German mathematician and astronomer, Johannes Kepler, to anaylse his observations of the motion of Mars. Kepler was a mathematical genius with the necessary skills to perform a detailed analysis of Tycho's magnificent set of data on the planetary orbits. Moreover, unlike Tycho, he was a convinced Coperican from the beginning. Indeed, in 1597, Kepler's first major astronomical work, *Mysterium cosmographicum* (The Cosmographic Mystery), had been the first published defence of the Copernican system. In this work, Kepler had also advanced an extremely innovative geometrical idea to explain both the number of planets (the six naked-eye planets known at the time) and the relative sizes of their orbits, which was based on embedding the five regular Platonic solids within one another, with the Sun at the centre. In Kepler's own words: "The Earth's orbit is the measure of all things: circumscribe around it a dodecahedron and the circle containing it will be Mars; circumscribe around Mars a tetrahedron, and the circle containing this will be Jupiter; circumscribe about Jupiter a cube and the circle containing this will be Saturn. Now inscribe within the Earth an icosahedron and the circle contained in it will be Venus; inscribe within Venus an octahedron, and the circle contained in it will be Mercury. You now have the reason for the number of planets." Kepler believed he had revealed God's geometrical plan for the universe. Although we now know it to be incorrect, this simple model could, remarkably, account for the relative sizes of the planets' orbits to within an accuracy of about 5%, which was within the limits of available astronomical observations.

The publication of *Mysterium cosmographicum* had brought Kepler fame in European astronomy, and had prompted Tycho to employ him. On Tycho's death in 1601, Kepler replaced him as Imperial Mathematician in Prague and began analysing his observations. By 1603, Kepler had discovered what is now known as his 'second law', namely that a line from the Sun to a planet sweeps out equal areas in equal times. More profound, however, was Kepler's 'first law', discovered in 1605, which arose from Kepler's inability to fit the orbits of the planets using circles. Circular orbits had been a key feature of all cosmological models since Aristotle, but Kepler's deep understanding of geometry led him to make an unprecedented intuitive leap and attempt to fit other shapes. He first tried ovoids, but still could not obtain a good fit to the observations. Realising he needed closed curves with properties intermediate between those of circles and ovoids, Kepler then tried ellipses and found excellent agreement with the data. Thus, he arrived at his first law: the planetary orbits are ellipses with the Sun at one focus, although Kepler provided no physical explanation for this phenomenon. The transition from circular to elliptical planetary paths dramatically changed the accuracy of celestial predictions. Aside from minor alterations owing to relativisitic effects, this law is still considered correct today. Kepler's first and second laws were published in his 1609 work *Astronomia nova* (The New Astronomy), but the discovery of his third (and final) law did not come until a decade later, while writing a summation of all his previous work in his most influential treatise *Harmonices mundi* (Harmony of the World). According to Kepler himself, an epiphany while reviewing the observational data led him to his third law: that the period of a planetary orbit is proportional to the three-halves power of the mean distance of the planet from the Sun, although he again provided no physical explanation for this phenomenon. Nonetheless, using his three laws, which were founded on the heliocentric viewpoint, Kepler was the first astronomer to predict a transit of Venus successfully (for the year 1631), a fact not easily overturned by the geocentrists.

At the same time that Kepler was in Prague, analysing Tycho's observations and discovering his laws of planetary motion, a revolution in science was taking place in Padua, owing to the work of the great Italian physicist, mathematician, astronomer and philosopher, Galileo Galilei, who is now widely considered to be the father of modern science. Indeed, Galileo's influence on both physics and astronomy is hard to overstate. In physics, he was responsible for the overthrow of Aristotilean ideas that had dominated science for two millennia. In particular, Galileo performed a magnificent set of experiments to elucidate the nature of motion, which led to three great discoveries: (1) the law of acceleration, which states that the time required for a object moving under gravity to travel a given distance is independent of its mass and proportional to the square-root of the distance; (2) that the time for an object to fall down the diameter of a circle equals the time to for it to roll down a chord; and (3) that the period of the swing of a long pendulum is independent of its amplitude. Galileo's interest in the nature of motion prompted him to consider the Copernican cosmological model as a possible explanation of the origin of the tides in the Adriatic, and led to his many seminal contributions to astronomy.

In particular, Galileo pioneered the use of telescopes for making astronomical observations. Just a year after the invention of the telescope in 1608 by Hans Lipperhey, Galileo had constructed his own telescopes, which were ten times more powerful. With magnifying powers of up to a factor of 30, Galileo's telescopes immediately yielded many new astronomical discoveries that called into question some central tenets of geocentrism. Firstly, Galileo saw that the Moon was mountainous rather than a perfectly smooth sphere, which was the first observation of imperfections on a celestial body. The Moon's imperfections could be related to those seen on Earth and used to argue that neither was unique, but both are just celestial bodies made from everyday material. Galileo was also able to see a large number of stars invisible to the naked eye, particularly those responsible for the appearance of the smooth band of emission from the Milky Way. In early 1610, he went on to observe Jupiter's four largest moons for the first time, and showed that they orbited Jupiter rather than the Earth. This was a profound discovery since it demonstrated that not everything orbited the Earth, which flatly contradicted the orthodox geocentric view of the universe and associated theological thinking. Galileo published his findings almost immediately in his *Sidereus nuncius* (The Starry Messenger) in March 1610, much to the delight of Kepler, who boldly claimed "The conclusion is quite clear. Our moon exists for us on Earth, not for the other globes. Those four little moons exist for Jupiter, not for us. Each planet in turn, together with its occupants is served by its own satellites. From this line of reason we deduce with the highest degree of probability that Jupiter is inhabited." Galileo also observed the rings of Saturn for the first time, although he mistakenly took them also to be close satellites of the planet.

In terms of undermining geocentrism, however, Galileo's most important discovery came in December 1610, when he used his telescope to observe that Venus showed all phases, just like the Moon. This is incompatible with the Ptolemaic system. In Ptolemy's original model, Venus' deferent and epicycle lie entirely inside the sphere of the Sun, in which case the phase of Venus must always be crescent or all dark. Even if one modifies the model by placing Venus' orbit beyond that of the Sun, then the phase of Venus must always be gibbous or full. Thus, Galileo's observation of Venus at first small and full, and later large and crescent, directly contradicted Ptolemy's model, but is a natural consequence of the heliocentric system. As a result, the geocentrists finally began to abandon the Ptolemaic system as the 17th century progressed, but only in favour of the still theologically acceptable Tychonic model, which was also consistent with Galileo's observations.

Galileo himself, however, became a public champion of Copernicanism following his observations of the phases of Venus and, as a result, he met with vehement opposition from many philosophers and clerics. In 1615, in a letter to Grand Duchess Christina, Galileo set out his objections to geocentrism, and expressed the opinion that the Bible is only an authority on matters of faith and morals, not science. Unfortunately, this letter was circulated and led to Galileo being denounced to the Roman Inquistion. In 1616, Galileo was acquited, but the Catholic Church deemed Copernicanism to be "philosophically and scientifically untenable and theologically heretical" and Galileo was warned to abandon his support for it, which he promised to do. Following the death of Pope Gregory XV in 1623, Pope Urban VIII declared that Copernicanism could be discussed, provided it was only considered hypothetically. In the words of Cardinal Bellarmine: "...content yourself with speaking hypothetically and not positively, as I have always believed Copernicus did. For to say that, assuming the Earth moves and the Sun stands still serves all appearances better than eccentrics and epicycles, is to speak well. This has no danger in it, and it suffices for mathematicians. But to wish to affirm that the Sun is really fixed in the centre of the heavens... is a dangerous thing, not only by irritating all the theologians and scholastic philosophers, but also by injuring our holy faith." Emboldened by the Church's new position, Galileo began writing his most famous work, Dialogue Concerning the Two Chief World Systems, which was published in 1632. The defence of Copernicanism it contained, however, was not considered sufficiently hypothetical by the Church, and later that year Galileo was again tried by the Inquisition and found "vehemently suspect of heresy". He was forced publically to recant his support for Copernicanism, under threat of torture, and was held under house arrest until his death in 1642. Following his condemnation in 1632, Galileo did, however, write Two New Sciences, which summarised all his work on the laws of motion, which included a description of the relativity of motion and law of inertia, and the application of these laws to the motion of projectiles. This work was to provide inspiration for a rather talented young English mathematician called Isaac Newton.

Newton came up to Trinity College in Cambridge in 1661 and received his Batchelor of Arts degree in Mathematics in 1665. Later in 1665, university activities were suspended because of the Great Plague and Newton, aged just 22, returned to his native Woolsthorpe in Lincolnshire. Over the subsequent two years (a period often described as his *annus mirabilis*), Newton made the following epoch-making series of discoveries: the binomial series, differential and integral calculus, the theory of colour in optics, the unification of celestial mechanics and the law of gravity. For the last of these, Newton himself claimed that "the notion of gravitation, as I sat in contemplative mood, was occasioned by the fall of an apple". Already a confirmed Copernican, this observation led Newton to consider the possibility that the force which caused the apple to fall to the ground was the same as that which kept the planets in orbit around the Sun. Combining this idea with Kepler's third law of planetary motion, Newton very quickly arrived at his inverse square law of gravity, namely that there exists an attractive force between all massive bodies, the magnitude of which is proportional to the product of their masses divided by the square of the distance between their centres. It was not until 1679, however, that Newton returned to his work on celestial mechanics and subsequently showed that Kepler's three laws of planetary motion could all be derived from his inverse square law of gravitation. This strong vindication of heliocentrism finally led to the demise, albeit gradually, of geocentrism during the late 17th century, following its inclusion in Newton's major work *Philosophiae naturalis principia mathematica* (Mathematical Principles of Natural Philosophy), published in 1687. This work also introduced the calculus and most of classical mechanics, and is generally considered to be one of the most important scientific books ever written.

Cosmology in the Modern Era

Newton's laws of mechanics laid the foundations for many of the advances of the industrial revolution in the late 18th and early 19th centuries, which, including the period up to the present day, mark the era of modern astronomy and cosmology. A coherent theme of this latest period of great advancement in our understanding of the universe has been the continued gradual displacement of mankind from the centre of creation. The final fatal blows to the notion of geocentrism came through increasingly accurate observations of stellar positions as the quality of telescopes improved. In 1729, the third Astronomer Royal, James Bradley, discovered stellar aberration, which is an apparent motion of the stars about their actual location, resulting from the finite speed of light and the motion of Earth in its orbit around the Sun (and is independent of the distance to the object). Thereafter, Tycho's geocentric system fell out of use among scientists. Aberration should not be confused with stellar parallax, which is instead caused by a change in the position of the observer looking at a relatively nearby star, as measured against more distant objects, and is therefore dependent upon the distance to the star. Nonetheless, the long-sought-after first measurement of stellar parallax itself was eventually obtained in 1838 for the star 61 Cygni by the German astronomer Friedrich Wilhelm Bessel. This observation finally disproved Ptolemy's ancient claim that parallax motion did not exist, substantiated the heliocentric model, and demonstrated the very large distances at which the stars lie from Earth.

Even by the mid 18th century, however, it was generally accepted that the solar system was embedded in a large distribution of stars, which were similar to the Sun. In 1750, the English astronomer Thomas Wright published an amazingly insightful work entitled An Original Theory of the Universe, in which he speculated (correctly) that this collection of stars, or Galaxy (derived from the Greek word for 'milky'), had a finite extent and might be a rotating body held together by gravitational forces, similar to the solar system but on a much larger scale. Moreover, he hypothesised (again correctly) that this rotation would result in a flattened disk of stars, which we see from our position inside the disk as the band of emission known as the Milky Way. He even speculated that some of the diffuse and extended objects, termed nebulae, revealed in the night sky by telescopic observations might be separate galaxies. In 1755, Immanuel Kant expanded on Wright's ideas regarding the structure of the Galaxy and introduced the term 'island universe' for these nebulae. Nonetheless, these early cosmologies were only speculative ideas, without any quantitative support from observations.

The first quantitative estimates of the size and structure of the Galaxy were made by the German-born British astronomer William Herschel in 1785 by using his telescope in Slough to perform a careful count of the number of stars in different regions of the sky. Though groundbreaking, his attempt was rather inaccurate, however, since he assumed the solar system to be close to the centre of the Galaxy and all stars to have the same intrinsic luminosity. He also failed to take into account the absorption of light by interstellar dust present in the Galactic plane. Indeed, it was not until this effect was quantified in 1930 that the present picture of our Galaxy emerged, although our understanding of its structure has continued to evolve right up to the present day. It is now generally accepted that the Milky Way is a barred spiral galaxy with a disk approximately 100,000 light-years in diameter and about 1000 light-years thick, containing around 300 billion stars. Our solar system is located around two-thirds of the way out from the centre, on the inner edge of the Orion–Cygnus Arm, and orbits around the centre of the galaxy once every 250 million years. As a guide to relative physical scales, if the solar system out to the orbit of Pluto were one inch in diameter, the Milky Way would be about the size of France. Clearly, our view of mankind's place in the universe has changed considerably from the geocentric ideal of the Earth being at the centre of creation.

By the close of the 18th century, however, observations of the 109 brightest astronomical nebulae by Charles Messier, followed by a catalogue of a further 5000 by William Herschel, had already begun to suggest that mankind's place at the heart of creation might be usurped even further. In 1845, Lord Rosse constructed a new 72-inch aperture telescope at Birr Castle in Ireland and was able to distinguish between elliptical and spiral nebulae. He also observed individual point-like sources of light in some nebulae, which seemed to support Wright's and Kant's earlier speculations that these nebulae might not be objects in the Milky Way, but instead separate galaxies like our own. The size and quality of telescopes increased rapidly throughout the 19th century and, by the turn of the 20th century, the advent of photographic plates allowed one to make an accurate and permanent record of observations. In 1917, Heber Curtis observed a nova within the 'Great Andromeda Nebula' (Messier object M31) and found 11 more novae by searching the photographic record. Curtis noted that these novae were on average much fainter than those occurring in our own Galaxy, and was able to estimate a distance to Andromeda that placed it well outside our Galaxy. He therefore became an ardent advocate of the island universe hypothesis. This idea was, however, treated with extreme scepticism by the astronomy establishment at the time. In particular, the eminent Harvard astronomer Harlow Shapley vehemently opposed the idea, prompting the so-called 'Great Debate' between the him and Curtis concerning the nature of the spiral nebulae and the dimensions of the universe. The debate was conclusively settled in a flurry of activity in the early 1920s. Some tens years earlier, the pioneering woman astronomer, Henrietta Leavitt, had discovered a relationship between the luminosity and the period of variation for a type of variable star known as Cepheids. In 1922, Edwin Hubble used the new 100-inch aperture Mount Wilson telescope to resolve the outer parts of Andromeda into individual stars and identify some of them as Cepheids. By measuring their period of variability, he was able to infer their intrinsic luminosity and thus determine the distance to Andromeda, which he verified was far too large for it to be part of the Milky Way. Hubble repeated such observations in several other spiral nebula and, in each case, confirmed them as being entirely separate galaxies located at significant distances from our own. In 1926, Hubble published his pioneering paper describing external galaxies and a classification scheme for their morphologies that is still used today.

While observational astronomers such as Hubble were fundamentally changing the scientific view of the universe, a revolution was also taking place in theoretical physics through the work of Albert Einstein, which was founded on his scepticism of the Newtonian view of the world. Some years earlier, in 1905, while working as a patent clerk in the Patent Office in Bern, Einstein had shaken the foundations of theoretical physics by publishing four papers that changed our view of space, time and matter. In this *annus mirabilis*, oddly reminiscent of Newton's some 240 years earlier, Einstein wrote four papers that developed the theories of: the photoelectric effect (which later gave rise to quantum theory), Brownian motion, the special theory of relativity and matter–energy equivalence (embodied in his famous equation $E = mc^2$). It would require another decade of long and often tortuous calculation, however, for Einstein to formulate arguably his greatest achievement: the theory of general relativity, which overturned even more radically the notions of space and time, and led to a new relativisitic theory of gravity to replace Newton's theory. In his theory of special relativity, Einstein had replaced the Newtonian concepts of space and time, but had obtained a description valid only for observers in uniform relative motion. As early as 1907, however, he had wondered "is it conceivable that the principle of relativity also applied to systems that are accelerated relative to one another?". According to Einstein, his epiphany came in typically enigmatic style: "I was sitting in a chair in the patent office in Bern when all of a sudden a thought occurred to me: if a person falls freely he will not feel his own weight. I was startled. This simple thought made a deep impression on me. It impelled me towards a theory of gravitation." This *principle of equivalence* led Einstein henceforth to assume complete physical equivalence between a gravitational field and a corresponding acceleration of the reference system, but the mathematical formulation of this idea was a titanic struggle. By the end of 1912, Einstein realised that the unified entity of spacetime must have a non-Euclidean geometry. Fortunately, the mathematics of such geometries had already been developed by Bernhard Riemann in the late 19th century, and, after a further three years of struggle, Einstein finally published his completed theory of general relativity in November 1915. Within a month, Einstein discovered that his new theory could account precisely for a well-known 'anomaly' in the orbit of Mercury. Moreover, in 1919, his prediction for the deflection of light from distant stars by the Sun was experimentally verified by the Cambridge astronomer Arthur Eddington, and Einstein became internationally famous.

Once general relativity was formulated, Einstein realised in 1917 that he had the necessary tools with which to derive the first fully self-consistent model of the universe as a whole. He immediately faced a problem, however, in that his equations predicted the universe to expand or contract, which ran contrary to the prevailing belief at the time that the universe was static. In order to construct a static model for the universe, Einstein added to his equations an extra term that contained a new constant of nature called the 'cosmological constant'. Einstein viewed this extra term as "not justified by our actual knowledge of gravitation", but "logically consistent" and "necessary only for the purpose of making possible a quasi-static distribution of matter". Indeed, by carefully fine-tuning the value of the cosmological constant, Einstein constructed a static model for the universe. Through the mid 1920s, however, the theoretical physicists Friedmann, Lemaître and Robinson all independently obtained the general solution to Einstein's equations of general relativity for an isotropic universe, each finding that, without fine-tuning the value of the cosmological constant, the generic predicted behaviour was for the universe to expand or contract.

Theory and observation came together beautifully in 1929, when Hubble combined his distance measurements to a selection of spiral galaxies with exquisite spectrographic studies of them made nearly 20 years earlier by Vesto Slipher. Such spectra may be used as a cosmic 'bar-code' to identify particular atoms from the pattern of narrow lines in the spectrum, and also as a 'radar-gun' to determine the velocity of the emitting material along the line-of-sight by measuring the Doppler shift in the frequency of the spectral lines as compared with laboratory measurements on Earth (this effect is analogous to the changing sound of an ambulance's siren as it passes by, which changes from a high pitch, when it is moving towards you, to a low pitch, when it is moving away from you). Slipher found that the 'spiral nebulae' were made from the normal material, but also discovered that their observed spectral lines were all shifted significantly to lower frequencies (towards the red end of the visible spectrum of light). From these so-called 'redshifts' in the spectral lines, he thus deduced that the galaxies were all moving away from us at considerable speeds. When Hubble compared the speeds of recession of these galaxies with the distances that he had measured to them, he made the astonishing discovery, now known as Hubble's law, that the universe is expanding uniformly in all directions and the speed of recession of an object is proportional to its distance. It should be noted that this does not mean that the Earth is at the centre of the universe, much to the disappointment of any remaining geocentrists! Imagine, for example, baking a fruit cake containing some raisins. As the cake rises each raisin will 'see' all the other raisins moving away from it, but no raisin is 'special'. Moreover, if the cake expands uniformly as it bakes, each raisin would 'measure' a speed of recession for each of the other raisins that is proportional to its distance away. When Einstein learned of Hubble's results, he is said to have described his inclusion of the additional cosmological constant term in the equations of general relativity as "the biggest blunder" of his life. As we will see later, however, posterity may judge otherwise.

The combination of Hubble's observation that the universe is expanding and Einstein's theory of general relativity (with the simplifying assumptions of the large-scale homogeneity and isotropy of space) laid the foundations for the development of the standard Big Bang theory of cosmology, which remains to the present day our best description of the universe. The idea was first proposed in 1932 by the Belgian physicist and Roman Catholic priest, Georges Lemaître, who suggested that the observed expansion of the universe implied that, moving backwards in time, it must contract and would continue to do so until all the mass of the universe was contained in a single point, a "primeval atom", where and when the fabric of spacetime itself comes into existence. Extrapolation of the expansion of the universe backwards in time using general relativity yields an infinite density and temperature at a *finite* time in the past; this *singularity* signals the breakdown of the theory of general relativity. Based on a range of cosmological observations, it is currently thought that this occurred around 13.7 billion years ago. It is worth noting, however, that the Big Bang theory cannot and does not provide any explanation for the initial singularity, but instead describes and explains the general evolution of the universe since that instant, as it expanded from an extremely hot and dense state at very early times to the current cool and diluted state that continues to expand today.

The Big Bang theory was advocated and developed further in the late 1940s and early 1950s by George Gamow, who introduced the idea that the nucleii of the light elements, such as helium, deuterium and lithium, could be formed from nuclear processes occurring in the rapidly expanding and cooling first minutes of the universe, following the Big Bang. His colleagues, Ralph Alpher and Robert Herman, also determined the thermal history of the universe in this model and predicted the existence of the cosmic microwave background radiation (CMB), a near-uniform bath of thermal radiation, sometimes called 'the afterglow of creation', that pervades the universe. Alpher and Hermann calculated that, just 300,000 years after the Big Bang, the universe would cool sufficiently for free protons and electrons to combine to form hydrogen atoms, marking a sharp transition between an opaque charged-particle plasma to a transparent neutral gas through which photons can travel unhindered, stretching as the universe expands, until they are observed today as the CMB, a thermal blackbody radiation characterised by a temperature of just a few degrees Kelvin.

As one might imagine, such a profound an idea as the Big Bang met with extreme scepticism from many cosmologists (and it still does today). During the 1930s several other ideas were proposed to explain Hubble's observations of redshifted galaxy spectra. These included: the Milne model, which proposed a physical explosion of matter in a fixed, pre-existing special-relativistic spacetime; the Friedmann oscillatory universe (also advocated by Einstein), which exhibits cycles of expansion and contraction without any singularity; and Zwicky's tired light hypothesis, which suggested that the light particles (photons) observed from distant galaxies had merely lost energy in collisions with other particles as they travelled through the universe. All of these theories suffered, however, from theoretical difficulties and/or contradicted observations. By the late 1940s, the only serious contenders were the Big Bang theory and the steady-state model suggested by the British astrophysicist Fred Hoyle. Ironically, it was Hoyle who gave the former its name by referring to it as "this big bang idea" during a BBC Radio broadcast in March 1949. The steady-state theory asserted the 'perfect cosmological principle' that, although the universe is expanding, it nevertheless presents the same appearance at all epochs; it has no beginning and no end. As a consequence, the theory required the continous creation of new matter (mostly hydrogen) to keep the average matter density of the universe equal over time. In the mid 1950s, however, another Cambridge astronomer, Martin Ryle (who founded the group of which the author is a member!), performed a ground-breaking survey of extragalactic sources at radio wavelengths and found that there was an excess of quasars and radio-galaxies at large distances (and hence in the distant past, owing to the finite speed of light). This showed that the universe does indeed change with cosmic epoch, which contradicted the steady-state model, but was consistent with the Big Bang theory.

By the early 1960s, observations also revealed that the percentage by mass of Helium in the universe was around 23%, wherever it could be measured. This uniformity and the fact that this percentage was much greater than what could be created in the cores of stars pointed to a cosmic origin, as suggested earlier by Gamow. Indeed, Hoyle himself showed that such a percentage of Helium was indeed predicted to be synthesised in the early stages of the Big Bang. Subsequent calculations by Fowler and Wagoner showed that Big Bang nucleosynthesis also produced traces of other light elements, which were very difficult to form inside stars. The predicted abundances matched observations very well. The status of the Big Bang as our best theory for the origin and evolution of the cosmos was secured, however, by the serendipitous discovery of the CMB by Penzias and Wilson in 1964. While preparing the 20-foot horn-shaped antenna at Bell Laboratories to perform some radio-astronomical observations, they discovered an excess of radiation at a temperature of around 3 Kelvin, wherever they pointed the telescope in the sky. After exhaustive efforts to find the source of this emission, which even included scraping out bird droppings from the inside of the antenna, Penzias and Wilson realised that the signal must be cosmic microwave background predicted by Alpher and Hermann. Indeed, this oldest light in the universe has since proven to be a great gift to cosmology, since it provides an early-childhood snapshot of the universe when it was just a tiny fraction of its current age. After the discovery of the CMB, and especially when its spectrum was found to match that of thermal radiation from a black body, most cosmologists were fairly convinced that some version of the Big Bang scenario must have occurred.

Since the 1960s, most work in cosmology has been in the context of the Big Bang model, and devoted in particular to understanding how large-scale structure in the universe, such as galaxies and clusters, form in the context of the Big Bang model, and to understanding the physics of the universe at earlier and earlier times, when the universe was extremely hot and dense. This has led to many surprises and, at times, considerable scepticism in the standard Big Bang theory, which has had to evolve considerably to match increasingly accurate observations, although perhaps not yet at a level that mirrors the addition of epicycles to Ptolemy's geocentric model of the universe.

A central problem for the original Big Bang model has been to explain the formation of galaxies. As early as the 1930s and 1940s, Lemaître, Tolman and Lifshitz all independently showed that density perturbations in an expanding universe grow quite slowly under their own self-gravity, with their density contrast relative to the background increasing only in proportion to the growth of the overall scale factor of the universe. Assuming galaxies evolved from infinitesimal density fluctuations in the very early universe, they inferred that galaxies could not have formed by the current epoch, which is clearly contrary to observations, which in the 1950s and 1960s began to uncover the large-scale distribution of galaxies and clusters in the universe through the work of Neyman, Abell and Zwicky. Moreover, in 1960s and 1970s, a number of theoretical cosmologists, including Harrison, Zel'dovich, Peebles and Silk, had shown that to form these galaxies and clusters, the small density perturbations from which they evolved should leave imprints in the temperature distribution of the CMB across the sky. By 1980, however, the predicted amplitude of these temperature fluctuations exceeded observational limits on anisotropies in the CMB and clearly a fundamental change was needed in our understanding of the formation of structure in the universe. This led the American theoretical cosmologist, Jim Peebles, to suggest that the universe might be dominated by a hitherto unknown form of matter, now called dark matter, that interacts only very weakly with normal (baryonic) matter, of which we and everything we see around us is comprised. This allows for dark matter fluctuations to form, into which normal matter can later 'fall', without imprinting excess temperature variations in the CMB. Detailed numerical simulations showed this model to be remarkably successful in accounting for the large-scale distribution of structure in the universe. Most importantly, when the Cosmic Background Explorer (COBE) satellite detected anisotropies in the CMB for the first time in 1992, they were found to be at a level of about one part in 100,000 relative to the 2.73 Kelvin background, which is consistent with structure formation in the cold dark matter (CDM) scenario. During the following decade, the CMB anisotropies were measured with increasing accuracy by a large number of ground-based and balloon-borne experiments, and by the Wilkinson Microwave Anisotropy Probe (WMAP) satellite over the period 2002-2009. The observations remain consistent with the CDM model.

In the last decade, however, there has been an unexpected twist in the story of cosmology. In 1998, measurements of the redshift–magnitude relation for type Ia supernova, which can be used as 'standard candles' in cosmology, indicated that the expansion of the universe has been accelerating since the universe was about one-half its current age. This came as a complete surprise, as it was thought that the expansion should decelerate as a result of the attractive gravitational force between all objects slowing down the expansion. To explain an accelerating universe, one has to posit some additional component of the universe, known generically as 'dark energy', which has a large negative pressure and thus leads to a gravitational repulsion. Amazingly, the simplest form for such a component is provided precisely by the additional cosmological constant term (or Λ-term) that Einstein included in his equations of general relativity when trying to build a static universe model, but then rejected as his "biggest blunder" when he learned that the universe is expanding. The resulting 'ΛCDM' scenario our the best current cosmological model, which explains all existing observations. Indeed, results from WMAP, other CMB observations and galaxy surveys of large-scale structure are all consistent with a ΛCDM model, known as the 'concordance cosmology', in which the contributions to total mass/energy density in the universe today are approximately 73% dark energy, 23% dark matter, and 5% ordinary matter, and in which structure forms from the passive gravitational evolution of scale-invariant perturbations generated (somehow) in the very early universe.

Nonetheless, there remain numerous open questions, and many cosmologists view the current standard model of cosmology with considerable scepticism. In addition to the unknown physical nature of both dark matter and dark energy, which supposedly dominate our universe, our understanding of fundamental physics is only sufficient to project back to around one ten-billionth of a second after the Big Bang, at which epoch the typical densities and energies of particles are at the limit of what can be reached in the latest particle physics experiments, such as the Large Hadron Collider. At earlier times, the physics of the Big Bang is subject to considerable speculation and doubt. The most popular current model, known as the theory of inflation, proposes that, almost immediately following the Big Bang, the universe underwent a short period of exponential expansion, growing in size by a factor of a billion, billion, billion in just one million billion billion billionth of a second, during which microscopic quantum fluctuations in the matter fields at the time were stretched to macroscopic scales to generate the seeds of structure formation. Indeed, this mechanism for the origin for all the structure in the universe was proposed by Stephen Hawking, amongst others, in the early 1980s. The inflationary model also solves a number of other problems, such as explaining why the universe is so homogeneous and isotropic on the largest scales. Although an attractive proposal, inflation does, however, have some theoretical problems of its own and cosmology now finds itself again in a period rich in alternative models, the development of which is driven, once more, by scepticism in our existing description of the universe. Only time will tell whether yet another revolution in our thinking is required, but, based on the experience of the last few millennia, it seems very likely.

In closing, it must be mentioned that, for some, the evolution in cosmological thinking has been less profound than that laid out in the last few pages. Polls conducted by Gallup in the 1990s found that 16% of Germans, 18% of Americans and 19% of Britons still held that the Sun revolves around the Earth.

Chapter 2

DOUBT AND COMMITMENT IN SCIENCE AND BEYOND

John Polkinghorne
Queens' College, Cambridge, UK

People sometimes say that scientists doubt everything. In fact, such an absolute and unrelenting scepticism would be a mistaken strategy, inducing frustration and intellectual paralysis. We have to start the exploration of reality by initially embracing commitment to a particular perspective from which to view it. Of course, subsequent investigation may reveal that this point of view is plagued by obscurities and tricks of perspective, so that its revision will prove necessary. An unreasonable unwillingness to think again would be as stultifying to science as relentless scepticism, but one has to start from somewhere. In science, a delicate balance is required between simultaneously both questioning and trusting the present form of understanding. It is illusory to think that we can proceed by stepping from certainty to certainty, but it is equally illusory to suppose that every new enquiry needs to start with a totally clean slate, uninfluenced by past ideas. Einstein discovered special relativity by trusting Maxwell's equations of electromagnetism and showing that taking them seriously questioned received thinking about the nature of space and time. Neither a supine clinging to past ideas nor a restless suspicion of them is helpful to science, or indeed to any human quest for truth.

This mixed economy of doubt and commitment lends a certain air of precariousness to the scientific enterprise. One source of possible uncertainty is the presence of an ineluctable element of circularity in scientific argument. There are no interesting scientific facts that are not already interpreted facts. Raw experimental readings (registrations in counters, marks on photographic plates) only acquire significance when it is understood what the apparatus being employed is actually capable of detecting and measuring. This act of interpretation requires recourse to theoretical opinion. Experiments can confirm or disconfirm theories, but those theories themselves have to be used to interpret experiments. The long-term fruitfulness displayed by a well-winnowed scientific theory, capable of yielding understanding of a wide range of phenomena, often including some aspects which were unknown when the theory was formulated (as when Paul Dirac predicted the unsuspected existence of antimatter), strongly supports the belief held by scientists that this circularity is normally benign rather than vicious. Yet this trusting stance is a motivated act of commitment rather than the acknowledgement of an inevitable rational necessity. From this fact arise the attempts of post-modern sceptics to persuade us that contemporary scientific understanding is actually no more than a culturally induced consensus held by the members of the invisible college of scientists. Despite the great implausibility of this claim, it cannot be disposed of by logic alone.

A further subtlety in science arises from the need to exercise certain tacit skills of judgement which cannot be reduced to the following of a carefully specified protocol. For example, all experimentalists have to wrestle with the problem of 'background', the need to identify and allow for the presence of spurious events that do not arise from the phenomenon under investigation but from effects extraneous to it, as when a stray cosmic ray happens to leave a trace in a bubble chamber. There is no little black book or handy computer programme which tells the experimentalist exactly how to make the necessary allowance. Dealing with background problems requires acts of judgement by the scientist, employing skills and insights that can only be learnt from long apprenticeship in the scientific community. Sometimes these judgements turn out to be wrong and all branches of science can tell warning stories about the mistakes that this can lead to.

Theories of deep significance are not simply read out of experiments by a kind of Baconian analysis of common factors found in a wide range of particular instances. Something altogether more creative is required on the part of the theorist. Strictly speaking, theories that make universal claims are always underdetermined by the finite experimental data available. Einstein once said that deep theoretical understanding must be 'freely invented'. He was too profoundly convinced of the independent reality of the physical world to mean by this a post-modern notion of science as confabulation. Rather, he meant that deep discovery required a kind of imaginative leap, such as that which had enabled him in November 1915 to write down, fully-formed, the equations of general relativity.

Of course, having done so, he had then to work out the consequences of the equations. Within a few days he had shown that they implied what had seemed to be an anomaly in the motion of the planet Mercury which had long defied Newtonian explanation. Einstein said that this was the happiest day of his life. It was the kind of unforced success that strongly supports the belief that physics really is describing intrinsic aspects of the physical world.

Einstein, like many great theoretical physicists, was guided in his search for a new theory by a quest for beautiful equations. Mathematical beauty is a rather rarefied form of aesthetic value, but it is one that the mathematicians can recognise and agree about. It involves properties such as economy and elegance and what the mathematicians call being 'deep', that is profound consequences are found to stem from an apparently simple starting point. Like all forms of beauty, it is easier to recognise than to describe and its discernment calls for tacit acts of judgement. Its pursuit is no mere act of aesthetic indulgence on the part of the theorists, but a fertile technique for discovery. Time and again in the history of theoretical physics, such equations have furnished the key to unlocking the secrets of the universe. Dirac, one of the founding figures of quantum theory, once said that it is more important to have beauty in your equations than to have them fit experiment! Of course, he did not mean that in the end empirical adequacy could be dispensed with – no scientist could suppose that. However if your new theory did not at first sight seem to fit the facts, though that was certainly a setback, it was not necessarily absolutely fatal. No doubt you had had to solve your equations in some approximation, and maybe you had made the wrong approximation. Or maybe, the experiments were wrong. So there was at least some residual hope. But in Dirac's view, if your equations were ugly … there was no hope! The whole history of modern physics testified that profound and successful theories are always expressed in mathematically beautiful equations. He himself made his many notable discoveries by a life-long and relentlessly successful quest for mathematical beauty. This role of mathematical beauty is linked with an important aspect of physicists' experience, the sense of wonder at the marvellous order of the universe disclosed to their enquiry, thus affording a precious reward for all the labour involved in scientific research.

These considerations make it clear that science is a subtle activity that cannot claim to attain results to which one might unhesitatingly apply phrases such as 'certain proof' and 'absolutely indubitable fact', of the kind that an intransigent scepticism might require before accepting the conclusions reached. This by no means implies that science does not achieve understanding to which it is entirely rational to accord belief, but simply that an act of commitment is involved which goes beyond assent to the absolutely certain. Time and again science offers us the 'best explanation' of what is going on in the physical world, affording insights that deserve to be taken with the utmost seriousness and which prove capable of providing the basis for reliable technological exploitation. In fact the concept of proof of the logically coercive kind that would defy any possibility of sceptical challenge, is a rare category. This is true even in mathematics. Kurt Goedel showed that an axiomatic system rich enough in structure to contain the integers cannot establish its own consistency by internal argument and, if it is consistent, it can be shown to contain propositions that intuitively can be seen to be true but which cannot be proved within the system. Even belief in the consistency of arithmetic requires a (rather easy) act of commitment.

I believe that the philosopher of science who has been most helpful in discussing these issues is Michael Polanyi. . Before he turned to philosophy he had been a very distinguished physical chemist, so that Polanyi knew science from the inside, with the benefit of long experience of working in the scientific community. He called his major work *Personal Knowledge* [1] because he believed that the tacit skills of judgement needed in science are intrinsically activities of persons, having to be learnt through apprenticeship in a truth-seeking community, and that they could never properly be delegated to a well-programmed computer. 'We know more than we can tell' is an oft-repeated Polanyi maxim. The role of commitment in science was very important for him, as the basis both for scientific exploration and for trust in the results obtained. In rejecting the stance of a relentless scepticism, Polanyi said that he had written *Personal Knowledge* to show how he could commit himself to what he believed scientifically to be true, while knowing that it might be false. Science is trustworthy but not incorrigible.

Yet is not the point that, although science cannot prove a theory to be true beyond the possibility of a sceptical peradventure, surely it can show a theory to be false by producing an empirical counterexample? Contrary to the popular saying that one can never actually prove a negative, is this not precisely what science seems able to do? Such a claim forms the basis of Karl Popper's famous account of the *logic* of scientific discovery [2]. 'All swans are white' until the exploration of Western Australia reveals the existence of black swans and so the hypothesis is found to fail. However falsification is not as unproblematic as Popper seemed to suppose. Even for a very low level theory such as the colouring of swans, there are interpretative issues. Perhaps that black Australian bird is simply a long-necked duck. A deep scientific theory with extensive applications and implications will not be abandoned at the first sign of an apparent anomaly. In 1925, a respected American experimentalist, D. C. Miller, claimed to have measured a non-zero drift of the Earth through the ether, in direct contradiction to special relativity. Einstein was unperturbed, telling a friend subsequently that he had never taken Miller's result seriously, a self-confidence which, of course, proved to be justified.

Popper's former student Imre Lakatos gave a more realistic account of actual practice with his concept of a scientific research programme [3]. Such a programme is defined by its 'hard core', the set of basic assumptions which specify the character of the programme. For example, the Newtonian programme had as its hard core Newton's laws of motion and the hypothesis of universal inverse-square law gravitation. The hard core is buffered from immediate contact with empirical data by a belt of auxiliary hypotheses which specify how the core ideas are to be applied. These hypotheses can be adjusted in order to improve the fit with observations without endangering the belief in the hard core itself. For the Newtonian programme these auxiliary hypotheses included the nature and number of the planets in the solar system. When the behaviour of the newly-discovered planet Uranus was found not to be following the Newtonian predictions of the astronomers, this did not lead to the rejection of the programme. Independently, John Couch Adams and Urbain Leverrier both proposed the additional auxiliary hypothesis of the existence of a further planet lying beyond Uranus, which was perturbing its motion. The subsequent discovery of Neptune constituted a brilliant success for the Newtonian programme. Acts of judgement are involved in assessing the persuasiveness of such accommodating modifications. This strategy of adjustment cannot always be expected to succeed. A small discrepancy, observed later, in the motion of the planet Mercury could not be successfully dealt with by the supposition of another planet, Vulcan, too close to the Sun to be readily observed. As we saw earlier, at this point the Newtonian programme had to give way to the Einsteinian programme with general relativity as its hard core.

Occasions of radical revision of the core itself might seem to provide the sceptic with grounds for doubt about the assertion that science is achieving realistic knowledge of physical reality. Thomas Kuhn described such moments as ones of revolutionary paradigm shift, in which the whole character of scientific understanding changed so drastically that it produced a deep discontinuity between what had gone before and what followed [4]. Newton and Einstein were supposed to hold such conflicting views that rational discussion between them would not be possible. This claim of the incommensurability of different paradigms is highly unpersuasive and it was subsequently somewhat modified by Kuhn. A new paradigm has to be able recover the successes of its predecessor in appropriate regimes. One of the first tasks of the pioneers of relativity and quantum theory was to establish what they called correspondence principles, showing how the undoubted successes of Newtonian mechanics could be retrieved as excellent approximations to the behaviour of bodies large on the scale set by Planck's constant and moving slowly on the scale set by the velocity of light. There is a degree of reassuring continuity present within the unfolding revisions of physical theory. It does not achieve absolute truth but it can lay justified claim to the attainment of verisimilitude, a reliable account of reality on a specific scale.

A striking aspect of scientific exploration of the physical world is that quite often the character of the reality revealed is found to be very surprising, proving quite different from what prior expectation had led scientists to expect. This fact provides good ground for the belief that the character science's understanding is indeed induced by contact with the independent character of nature itself. Quantum theory is the paradigm example of encounter with the unforeseeable. In 1899, any competent student of philosophy could have 'proved' that it was impossible for something to behave sometimes like a wave and sometimes like a particle. After all, a wave is spread out and oscillating, while a particle is small and bullet-like. Nevertheless, as we all know, that is how light was found to behave. For about twenty-five years after this discovery, the physicists had to live with the seeming paradox unresolved. A sceptic might have claimed that this situation constituted a dismissal of the claims of physics to give a rational account of physical reality. However, the discovery of quantum field theory successfully dissolved the paradox. Quantum mechanics is surely the most successful scientific theory of all time, with a vast range of predictions now known to be fulfilled with exquisite accuracy. Its fundamental hard core lies in the superposition principle, allowing the intimate mixing of possibilities that Newton and commonsense would say could never be combined together. In the clear world of every day, there is a state in which a billiard ball is 'here' and another where it is somewhere else, 'there', and they are quite distinct from each other. In the quantum world, a photon can be in a state of 'here' or in a state of 'there', but there are also other states in which these two possibilities are simultaneously combined in a well-defined mathematical way (called superposition). The commonsense logic of Aristotle is based on the law of the excluded middle, which says that there is no intermediate possibility between A ('here') and not-A ('there'). For photons, and other quantum entities, a different kind of quantum logic has to apply, taking into account the existence of the range of different superpositions of those classically immiscible states A and not-A. The quantum world is cloudy and unvisualisable precisely because of this counterintuitive mixing.

Superposition provides the means for understanding wave/particle duality. In the clear world of Newtonian physics there can only be states with a definite number of particles in them (just look and count them). In the quantum world there can be states with an *indefinite* number of photons (superpositions of states with different numbers of photons). It can be shown that it is these are the states which display wave-like properties (have definite phases).

The essence of rationality is to seek to conform our thinking to the actual nature of what we are trying to think about. There can be no undue tyranny of commonsense, for matters may be quite different from what our everyday intuitions might lead us to expect. The different characters of the everyday world and the quantum world show that there is no universal form that rationality has to take, which could cover both. Aristotelian logic and quantum logic both have their appropriate roles to play. Equally, there is no universal form of epistemology. Entities can only be known in ways that respect their actual natures. Heisenberg's uncertainly principle asserts that if we know accurately the position of a quantum entity, we cannot at all know its momentum, and vice versa. It is only possible to know half as much in the quantum world as we can know in the clear world of Newtonian thinking. In the late 1920s, the biologist J. B. S. Haldane, commenting on the discoveries of his physicist colleagues, said that the universe had turned out to be not just queerer than we thought, but queerer than we could have though without the nudge of nature pushing us in counterintuitive directions.

The sceptic needs to take seriously the fact that the natural question for a scientist to ask about a proposition, both within science and beyond it, is not 'Is it reasonable?', as if we thought we knew beforehand what shape rationality had to take. No one in 1899 would have been prepared to believe wave/particle duality to be a reasonable possibility. Instead, the proper question to ask is 'What makes you think that might be the case?' In this form the question is open to the unexpected, for it does not seek to lay down beforehand the shape that an acceptable understanding has to take, but there will only be acceptance for a surprising proposal if there is motivating evidence offered in support of it. Openness to the unexpected is an essential ingredient in the quest for truth. Neither naïve credulity nor intransigent scepticism are helpful stances to take.

I believe that this kind of open but exacting approach to gaining understanding is relevant all forms of truth-seeking enquiry. In conclusion, I would like to say that, as someone who is both a physicist and a Christian believer, I believe that the quest for religious truth has to be pursued in a similar fashion of seeking well-motivated belief. Scientists are often wary of religion because they fear that it involves unquestioning submission to the dictates of some unchallengeable authority – an infallible book, an infallible community or an infallible person. Of course, they do not wish to commit intellectual suicide, but neither do I. Faith is not a leap into the dark but a leap into the light. I believe that I have motivations for my religious beliefs of a kind that persuades me to commit my life to them. This is not the place to pursue that matter further, though I have sought to do so elsewhere [5].

REFERENCES

[1] M. Polanyi, *Personal Knowledge*, Routledge and Kegan Paul, 1958.
[2] K. Popper, *The Logic of Scientific Discovery*, Hutchinson, 1959.
[3] I. Lakatos, *The Methodology of Scientific Research Programmes*, Cambridge University Press, 1978.
[4] T. Kuhn, *The Structure of Scientific Revolutions* 2 ed, University of Chicago Press, 1970.
[5] J. C. Polkinghorne, *Science and Christian Belief/The Faith of a Physicist*, SPCK, 1994/Fortress Press, 1996.

Chapter 3

SCEPTICISM AND RADIATION

Dillwyn Williams[1] and Keith Baverstock[2]

[1]Department of Public Health, University of Cambridge, UK
Emeritus Professor of Histopathology, University of Cambridge, UK
[2]Department of Environmental Sciences,
University of Eastern Finland, Kuopio Campus, Finland

INTRODUCTION

Taking a view on a science based policy can be difficult for the general public. A lack of understanding of the technical issues combined with increasing distrust of both policy makers and scientists can easily lead to widespread scepticism. Scepticism arising from a lack of knowledge is different from the critical attitude essential to science. All scientists should be sceptics, both in the original meaning of the word; they think and consider the results or facts with which they are presented; and also in the common usage of the word; they do not take statements at face value but need to see and question the evidence leading to the conclusion before they will accept it. Not all scientists are impartial, they are human, their judgements are certainly not infallible. Some may be consciously or unconsciously influenced by a variety of circumstances, including the continuing need to obtain grant support for their work, and personal financial involvement in the topic under discussion. Nuclear power is one subject which has led to extreme scepticism. The chance of a reasoned discussion between a proponent and an opponent of nuclear power ending in agreement are about as good as those of an agreement between the Pope and Richard Dawkins on religion. Agreement between atheists and believers is ultimately impossible because it depends on faith, agreement on nuclear power should be possible, based on a rigorous assessment of risks, costs and benefits. Why is it that attitudes to radiation have become so polarised that consensus now seems impossible to achieve? The discovery of radiation at the end of the 19th century and the use of x-rays to 'see' through tissue led to radiation being viewed as somehow both magical and beneficial. The healing properties of radioactive spa water were widely accepted until a few decades ago, and some still believe that exposure to low-dose radiation is beneficial. Of course the development and use of the atomic bombs played a major role in the shift in public opinion, but that experience alone does not explain the paradox between the passion with which anti-nuclear views are presented and the general acceptance that the use of X-rays and of radioactive isotopes in diagnosis and treatment are essential to modern medicine. The extreme hyperbole that surrounded the development of nuclear power together with the link with manufacture of materials for nuclear weapons set the scene for a sceptical approach to such huge undertakings. The general attitude to radiation today is one of uncertainty and unease, with a large section of the public being extremely mistrustful of the claims made about safety. We do not intend to reach conclusions about the advisability of nuclear power, and in view of the earlier comments on impartiality the authors should make it clear that they have no obligation to and have received no financial support from either pro- or anti-nuclear sources. This chapter sets out to explore how the extreme polarisation of views on the risks of radiation and of nuclear power has developed and what factors might underlie it.

A BRIEF HISTORY OF RADIATION

The discoveries of x-rays by Roentgen and radioactivity by Becquerel in 1895-6 generated considerable excitement at the time, not least because of the applications of x-rays to medicine, but it was not long before the negative aspects were discovered in terms of burns and other skin damage to those we would now call radiologists and radiographers. The Polish scientist Mme Skłodowska-Curie and her French scientist husband Pierre Curie succeeded in 1902 in extracting about 0.1 gm of radium from prodigious quantities of uranium ore (pitchblende) and separating it from barium. Despite its scarcity and cost ($120,000/g in 1910) radium quickly found application in luminising watch dials, particularly in the USA, where young women, some hardly more than girls, used brushes to paint the watch dials with radium suspended in an aqueous solution of gum arabic. The desire to create finely crafted figures on the dial led to the practice of "tipping" the brush with the tongue, which in turn led to the ingestion of radium. In 1920 the Radium Corporation alone produced 4 million luminous watches, but by 1924 nine young women luminisers had died apparently from natural causes and others were presenting to dentists with jaw deformities, due according to the company to poor dental hygiene. Radium-226 is a long half-life isotope emitting alpha and gamma radiation, when absorbed into the body it is taken up by bones, where the alpha particles with their high energy but very limited range damage or kill the bone forming cells. Years after the first exposure, bone sarcomas, normally very rare tumours were found in the dial painters. Together with radiologists, they were the first groups studied to determine the occupational effects of radiation exposure. The reluctance to accept a link between the apparently innocuous practice of painting the dials of watches that so many people wore and the serious consequences to the dial painters illustrates one of the hall-marks of the public attitude to radiation at that time, an overpowering belief in its goodness that precluded general acceptance of the possibility that it could be harmful.

Dial painting was much less practised in Europe because of the cost of the paint but at the start of WWII the UK recognised the value of luminous instruments in aircraft and set up luminising factories. Again the workers were predominantly young women but this time stringent precautions were taken to prevent ingestion of radium; sticks were used in place of brushes and the paint was organically based and therefore not good to the taste. As well as emitting alpha particles radium emits energetic gamma rays which created a higher than normal radiation level in the workplace because of the presence of paint pots and completed work. In the early years a typical luminiser would receive 0.5Gray (500 mGy) in a year, roughly 500 times the relevant dose from natural background radiation. (One Gray is a measure of the amount of radiation absorbed, 1Gy = 1Joule/gm) This level of exposure led to a reduction in white blood count so more stringent conditions were introduced. Limiting the amount of paint issued and the hours worked eventually led to a 10 fold reduction in the annual doses. In the 1960s the UK Medical Research Council instituted an epidemiological study of UK luminisers under the leadership of Richard Doll and Austin Bradford Hill. However, by 1970 it seems that Doll had concluded that detectable effects were unlikely, and proposed ditching the study. It was rescued in 1971 by Jack Vennart, then at the MRC Radiobiology Unit, who had led the determination of doses to the luminisers. The results eventually revealed the effectiveness of the use of sticks rather than brushes (very few luminisers' bodies contained radium), but an increase in breast cancer some 20 to 30 years later was linked to the level of gamma ray exposure. The finding that life expectancy was exceptionally good for those luminisers entering the profession in mid-life attracted the attention of the well known radiation expert, Alice Stewart, who believed it indicated a deep flaw in the study. However, careful investigation in the late 1980s confirmed the vital status of these ex-luminisers, by then well into their 80s. This longevity appears not to be related to radiation exposure but a consequence of comparing a group of workers originally selected to be fit with the matched but unselected general population, the so-called "healthy worker effect", found in many occupational epidemiological studies. Despite the firm scientific evidence of the carcinogenic effects of radiation from X-rays in the early radiologists and of radiation from radium in the US dial painters, the public attitude to radiation remained one of generally unquestioning trust in its use until the development and use of the atomic bomb.

ATOMIC WEAPONS

The atomic bombs dropped on Hiroshima and Nagasaki are the only atomic weapons deliberately used in war. Their use was at first widely welcomed in the West, it shortened the war and saved allied lives; the great loss of Japanese life was obscured by the dehumanisation of the enemy that seems an inevitable component of modern warfare. The results of the first investigation by a Japanese team shortly after the explosions were suppressed by the US military, but public attitudes began to change as the first accounts and pictures of the devastating effect of radiation on the human body emerged. Pictures showing adults and children with patches of skin blistering and dropping off, accounts of the agonising death over a few weeks of those receiving doses of around 5Gy, and the disfigurement of those receiving slightly lower but survivable doses were published. These, combined with the recognition of the devastating destructive power that wiped out nearly all buildings around the hypocentre led to widespread realisation that while radiation could be a power for good, it could also do immense harm. Robert Oppenheimer, one of the fathers of the bomb publicly regretted its use, and the recognition that if one nation had developed the technology others would follow, as Russia soon did, led to the creation of the Campaign for Nuclear Disarmament, and increasing scepticism about the peaceful uses of nuclear energy. To investigate the consequences of exposure to radiation from the bomb the US Government sent a mission to Hiroshima and Nagasaki shortly after peace was declared. It then established the Atomic Bomb Commission. This was very nearly closed down, but following the Francis committee's report in 1955 it became the Radiation Effects Research Foundation, jointly funded by the US and Japanese Governments. This is still active over 65 years after the bombs were dropped; over the years it has produced invaluable studies of the long-term health effects of exposure to whole body radiation from gamma rays and neutrons. These have shown highly significant increases in incidence of a wide range of cancers, most of these risks were not established until decades after exposure but still continue. For those exposed as young children, now in their 70s, the excess absolute risks have increased as the population ages. As well as the long-term cancer risk, a number of non-cancer diseases have also increased in incidence many decades after exposure. About 100,000 of those exposed to significant levels of external radiation from the atomic bombs in Japan survived. The fallout from these bombs made little contribution to the doses received, but the above ground testing of nuclear weapons over the next 15-20 years led to radioactive fallout across the world.

FALLOUT FROM NUCLEAR WEAPONS TESTS

Tests of the first atomic weapon in Nevada and their use in Hiroshima and Nagasaki were followed within a few years by the acquisition by several nations of nuclear technology. Extensive above ground testing of atomic weapons then took place in several locations worldwide, including Nevada, the Marshall Islands, Maralinga, and Semipalatinsk, leading to radioactive fallout across virtually the whole world, particularly the northern hemisphere. Radioactive isotopes of iodine, caesium and strontium were among the most important constituents because of their bioavailability in the environment. In Europe and the USA extensive efforts were made to assess the extent of fallout and the consequent radiation doses to the public. Because testing locations were generally reasonably remote from large population centres, little attention was paid to the local fallout.

One of the least remote testing centres was in Nevada USA, where above ground testing from 1951 to 1962 led to widespread contamination from fallout. Concern about the levels of fallout from the tests and increasing rates of thyroid cancer led the US Congress to pass public law 97-414 in January 1983, requiring an assessment of the exposure of the American people to iodine 131 from the Nevada tests, and an assessment of the risks of thyroid cancer from iodine 131, with a requirement to report in one year. In the event the report was not published until October 1997 shortly after a summary had been leaked by the New York Times and 14 years after public law 97-414 was passed. The US National Cancer Institute study had been largely completed by 1986 when the Chernobyl accident happened, and had found that previous estimates of doses to the public had been underestimated. Prior to 1992 the belief was that this would not matter as radioactive iodine was thought not to be carcinogenic. A possible reason for the continuing suppression of the report was the finding in 1992 of increases in childhood thyroid cancer resulting from the Chernobyl accident. Investigation in the USA in the 1990s revealed that some country dwellers with their own cows or goats might well have received thyroid doses of several Gy over those years. The study also showed that relatively high levels of Iodine 131 were deposited right up to the Canadian border and presumably beyond although that has apparently and surprisingly never been reported or the possible effects studied. An increase in thyroid cancer among those exposed to fallout from the Nevada test at very young ages has been detected in the USA.

In the United Kingdom considerable concern for the impact of global fallout on public health led to an extensive programme monitoring milk and other foodstuffs. Most isotopes of iodine have a half life of a few days or less. Isotopes of strontium with a much longer half life, a bone seeking element that also readily found its way into milk, were of concern for the health of children. This resulted in a programme to measure strontium in the bones of deceased children. By an Act of Parliament UK hospitals were obliged to send bone samples from any deceased child for analysis. Subsequently, this program has been criticised on ethical grounds, it did however result in a model for the metabolism of strontium thus providing a valuable means of assessing the full risk of radioactive fallout. The findings may have been a factor in UK and US support for a treaty banning above ground testing. The use of the Marshall Islands for weapons testing has also been controversial. In March 1954 the Bikini atoll was used to test a fission-fusion-fission weapon, Castle Bravo. This weapon uses a small atomic device to trigger a hydrogen bomb, the neutrons from which then fission a natural uranium casing: the weapon produced a yield of 15 Megatons.

This kind of weapon is particularly 'dirty' in that fission products from approximately a quarter of a ton of natural uranium are generated as well as large quantities of plutonium 239. The timing of this explosion was unfortunate in that the wind rapidly carried high levels of fallout over the adjacent atolls Rongelap and Rongerik, the former populated by native Marshallese and the latter by American service personnel responsible for weather forecasting. The then mayor of Rongelap, a schoolteacher, vividly describes that morning. Just before dawn he was amazed to see what he thought was the sun rising in the West. Some hours later what appeared to be snow fell from the sky covering the ground and anyone outside in white dust. The children who played with this radioactive coral dust quickly became ill but it was two days before an American navy vessel arrived to investigate the situation and implement a decontamination programme. It has been estimated that the dose from external whole body irradiation was up to 2Gy, with inevitably additional exposure from inhalation and ingestion of the radioactive dust, including iodine 131 and short lived isotopes. Cases of both hypothyroidism and thyroid cancer occurred in the small resident population. Marshallese with thyroid problems were taken to the USA for treatment. The US government gave assurances of safety in 1957, but in 1984 Greenpeace evacuated the atoll, relocating the population in the Kwajalein islands. They remain there today, still highly sceptical about the safety of returning to their native home. However it was exposure of Japanese citizens that gave most publicity to the Castle Bravo test: a Japanese fishing vessel, the Lucky Dragon, was only 125 km from ground zero at the time of the test and was heavily contaminated.

By the time it returned to Japan all the crew were suffering from radiation sickness and subsequently one died. The possible consequences of fallout exposure are not confined to radiation induced cancers; amongst a range of non-tumour effects radiation has been suspected to affect cognitive development. Rainfall is an important factor in fallout distribution, and heavy rainfall in the west of Norway led to much higher fallout than in the dryer eastern side of the country, allowing a comparison of the effect of low doses on school performance. It seemed to be the case that doses of a few mGy per year could be responsible for a somewhat poorer school performance. A more recent study comparing school performance of children in two regions of Sweden, one where, again due to rainfall, there were higher doses to the population from fallout, seems to confirm the earlier Norwegian study. While studies of the long term effects of exposure to the atomic bombs or to fallout from above ground nuclear tests have been closely followed by interested scientists, they have had little impact on the general public attitude to radiation. In sharp contrast the accident at Chernobyl has had a major and lasting impact.

NUCLEAR POWER PLANT ACCIDENTS

On the 26th of April 1986 the Chernobyl nuclear power plant exploded, spreading radioactivity from fallout over most of Europe. It was not the first nuclear plant accident, but it was by far the largest. Not since the cessation of atmospheric testing of atomic weapons had such a widespread exposure of the public to man-made radioactivity occurred. The Chernobyl event caused considerable public concern way beyond the immediate vicinity of the stricken reactor. Little more than 4 years after the accident increased numbers of thyroid cancer in children were reported from both Minsk in Belarus and Kiev in Ukraine; these reports were greeted with profound scepticism by both the western nuclear medicine community and the International Atomic Energy Agency. One of the main components of the fallout in Belarus and Ukraine was radioactive iodine (131I), which is concentrated in the thyroid gland. However 131I was widely used both in diagnosis and treatment of thyroid diseases, and was at that time believed not to cause thyroid cancer. It clearly irradiated the thyroid gland and external radiation was known to cause thyroid cancers but the belief in the safety of I131 was based on epidemiological evidence from studies of large numbers of patients given diagnostic tests or treated with 131I for thyrotoxicosis; these showed no excess thyroid cancer. The belief that exposure to 131I was safe was so firmly held that huge amounts (about 4×10^{14} Bq*) (* Becquerel, the unit of radioactivity, 1Bq = 1 disintegration per second) were deliberately released from the Hanford nuclear facility in the United States to follow its distribution. The scepticism with which many in the scientific and medical community greeted the initial reports of an increase in thyroid cancer shows the power of an ingrained belief to warp judgement; rather than questioning the basis of the belief the apparently contradictory evidence was disbelieved. The explanation was simple, the studies which had led to belief in the safety of 131I had been carried out almost entirely on adults. The risk of developing thyroid cancer after exposure to radiation, either from 131I or external radiation was very high in the youngest children exposed, dropping rapidly with increasing age at exposure, with little or no risk to those exposed as adults.

The increase in thyroid cancer in those exposed at a very young age to high levels of fallout is still present 25 years after the accident, although it is now seen in young adults. About 6000 cases have occurred in the most exposed populations; as this population ages an increasing proportion of the new cases is not due to the radiation. Other health consequences of Chernobyl are inadequately studied and bitterly contested, in contrast to the situation in the atomic bomb exposed population where the results of a comprehensive long-term international study are widely accepted. The dramatic nature of the accident, the secrecy in the early stages, and the finding of large numbers of thyroid carcinomas in children a few years later have made it an iconic event for those against nuclear power. The large early increase in thyroid cancers led to studies being concentrated on that topic. Some individual investigations have shown an increase in leukaemia after fallout exposure, others have not. Some have shown an increase in congenital defects, others have not. A possible increase in breast cancer has been reported. One worrying observation is the finding of DNA changes in unexposed children of exposed parents. This 'mini-satellite instability' has no apparent clinical consequences to date, but clearly this and other possible consequences require further study. A combination of social upheaval, fear of the consequences to self and family of exposure, the nature of radiation and other factors led to huge psychosocial problems in those exposed. To anti-nuclear activists the term radiophobia has become anathema, because it is regarded as trivialising the very real problems arising from fear of radiation, and indeed it has been used in this way by the pro-nuclear lobby. As well as the general public exposed to fallout only, there were many clean-up workers (liquidators) who were exposed to a mixture of external radiation and fallout, and they have shown an increase in a number of malignancies. The review of the health effects by the World Health Organisation and the International Atomic Energy Authority in 2006 marking 20 years after the accident led to a press release that was widely criticised as factually misleading. It also implied that everything was known about the health effects, despite the fact that many of the health consequences of atomic bomb exposure were not detected until more than 20 years after the event and there was evidence of continuing effects. One aim of the IAEA is to promote the peaceful use of atomic energy, and its impartiality in this important review must be questioned. The review has been quoted selectively by the Nuclear Energy Institute on behalf of the nuclear industry; its latest fact sheet on Chernobyl in 2010 states that 'only 56 deaths could be attributed to radiation exposure from the accident', while accepting that '4000 people could theoretically die from radiation induced cancers'. In contrast a 2009 book from Yablokov and Nesterenko, scientists from Moscow and Minsk, estimated that radiation from Chernobyl could lead to over 200,000 deaths from cancer in Europe, and about 20,000 in the rest of the world. Yablokov and Nesterenko's reports are based on many studies from the former USSR, largely not reviewed in the West; where they have been the methodology used has been criticised, and the conclusions regarded as unsubstantiated. The lack of an internationally supported comprehensive study similar to that set up after the atomic bombs is painfully clear.

One of the consequences of the great disparity in the reported findings is that those in favour of or opposed to nuclear energy can each find reports to support their arguments, or if you prefer bolster their prejudices, and intensify their scepticism. One western study predicts about 16,000 deaths from cancers due to Chernobyl radiation in Europe up to 2065. This number is equivalent to about 0.01% of all cancer deaths in the same population over the same time period; some groups choose to quote the figure of 16,000, others 0.01%. Deaths due to tobacco will be very much greater; the comparison illustrates one aspect of the public reaction to radiation, it is in a category of its own, a carcinogen that cannot be seen or otherwise perceived, and one over which the individual has no control. Chernobyl greatly increased scepticism about the safety of nuclear energy and of radiation in general. The events at Fukushima in 2011, with once again initial cover-up of the severity of the accident, have further reinforced those views. The long term consequences of Fukushima cannot be accurately predicted, partly because the reactors are still not stabilised. A comprehensive study of the health effects of Chernobyl would help in planning and in dispelling anxiety after Fukushima, but a proposal to the EC to set up such a study (the ARCH report) at the time of writing still appears to be in limbo in Brussels.

THE LOW DOSE PROBLEM

Most of the inhabited world has been exposed to low-dose radiation from nuclear testing and fallout from nuclear power plant accidents at Chernobyl and Fukushima. Accurate assessment of the risks from low dose exposure is clearly of high importance. In order to make secure estimations of risk arising from environmental exposures to agents such as radiation both direct human epidemiological evidence and a plausible mechanism are required. Prior to 1992 both of these criteria seemed to have been met, the epidemiological evidence was provided by studies of the survivors of the atomic bombings in Japan in 1945 and the presumed mechanism was based on physical and genetic concepts in terms of radiation tracks intersecting DNA strands. This mechanism was an elaboration of the early ideas on target theory initially proposed in 1924 by Crawford, which required that ionising radiation directly interacted with genes which were relevant to the biological effects produced. In 1992 two radiation effects that could not be accommodated within the prevailing mechanistic paradigm were published, and have been widely confirmed. Neither of the two new effects, genomic instability and the bystander effect, could be explained in terms of track DNA intersections. The basis for the assumption that the risks of low dose exposure can be predicted from the observed risks of high dose exposure (linear no threshold theory) is therefore called into question. Because these effects cannot be accommodated within the existing paradigm, long term studies of large populations exposed to low dose radiation are essential. In the absence of evidence to the contrary it remains the view of the major international radiation protection organisations that the linear no-threshold theory for the risks of low-dose radiation should be the basis for radiation protection.

Radiation induced cancers cannot at present be distinguished from those that occur spontaneously and therefore in any epidemiological study must be analysed against a background of spontaneous cancer incidence. The difficulty of using study populations above a certain size therefore creates a limit on how sensitive epidemiological techniques can be. Thus, at doses of more than one Gray the Japanese bomb survivors provide reasonably good estimates of risk but at lower doses the uncertainty increases. Typically low doses are defined as less than about 50 mGy. However, in practical terms environmental exposures to radiation of the general population are significantly less than this, typically of the order of a few mGy. Because the numbers exposed to very low doses are often large the collective dose (the sum of all the individual doses) is large and the public health effects can be important. This issue forms a battleground for the highly negative dispute between the pro-and anti-nuclear lobbies. The inherent uncertainty in the relationship between risk and dose at very low doses allows one side to claim there is a dose threshold below which there is no risk and the other side to claim that there may be a relatively increased risk at low doses, and that after a nuclear accident where many more are exposed to low doses than to high doses the overall effects of low doses are much greater than those of high doses. These claims are partly responsible for the wide discrepancies in the projected effects of Chernobyl fallout. In theory the issue could be settled by recourse to mechanistic arguments but to date there is no consensus on a mechanism that would include the classical radiobiological effects together with genomic instability and the bystander effect. The proposal that there is no threshold, the so called LNT concept, is based on physics and the fact that the sizes of damaging events at the molecular level caused by radiation vary widely. The majority are comparatively small and probably do little molecular damage in the cell but a minority, specifically the track ends of electrons, can deposit enough energy to severely damage the DNA. Furthermore, at very low doses and given the heterogeneous nature of cellular material, it is the number of cells affected that increases with dose. It is argued that this is not compatible with a threshold dose effect

Those that are sceptical of the damage that low doses of radiation can do to human health, as well as the relevant international organisations, may still maintain that it is inappropriate to base estimates of risk on collective dose, despite upholding the principle of the linear no threshold theory and acknowledging that there is no evidence for a threshold below which dose has no effect,. This is a curious position which is akin to a Chancellor of the Exchequer claiming that an increase in tax of say 0.1% for a large proportion of the public would raise no revenue because the impact on the individual was too small to be noticed. In fact the largest studies available confirm the linear no threshold theory down to increasingly low doses. Recent epidemiological studies which include greater numbers of people exposed to low doses have suggested that a direct linear extrapolation of the Japanese bomb survivor data to zero dose gives a good approximation to risk in the range 20 to 100 mGy. The lowest dose at which an effect on human health has been reported to date is 6 mGy, the effects of radiation are generally accepted to be cumulative and everyone receives at least 1 mGy from natural background radiation each year. It is therefore clear that basing consequences on collective dose is logically appropriate, at least for those above the age of six years. It should also be remembered that the risks of developing cancer after radiation exposure are in general higher for those exposed as children. A lack of certainty about the dangers of low-dose radiation leads to uncertainty over the prediction of the overall effects of Chernobyl across Europe and of the effects on the world as a whole of low-dose exposure due to nuclear tests. This lack of certainty is another factor which can be used either to fuel fears of possible radiation effects, or to support the safety of very low-dose exposure, on the dubious grounds that if an effect has not been demonstrated it can be assumed not to exist.

CONCLUSION

Over the last 100 years attitudes to radiation have changed. It was originally regarded as an unmitigated benefit but now there are deeply divided views on its dangers and its use as a source of energy. An influential and highly vocal part of society is extremely sceptical of its supposed benefits, and implacably opposed to nuclear power stations. Many politicians scientists and industrialists are committed supporters of nuclear power and see further development of new power stations as essential. Review of the evolution of attitudes to radiation; its discovery, medical applications, the development and use of nuclear bombs, the development of nuclear power, the worldwide fallout from nuclear tests, the major accidents at Chernobyl and Fukushima, and the problems associated with low-dose exposure can explain the development of different points of view, but not the depth of the level of distrust that exists between the two groups. There is some substance in the accusations that each group hurl at the other, and it is not surprising that the majority in the middle are confused. The nuclear industry and its defenders have undoubtedly exaggerated the benefits of nuclear power. They have played down the problems of nuclear waste disposal, covered up leaks and underestimated cost and build time for nuclear power stations. They have downplayed the risk of future accidents by concentrating on reassuring the public that the circumstances that gave rise to the last accident cannot possibly occur again, rather than accepting that accidents cannot be entirely eliminated and the next will be due to some other cause. They have quoted the literature selectively to create an impression that the major accidents that have occurred have had minimal effects; for example concentrating on the relatively small number of deaths that have occurred to date while not mentioning other consequences such as the many thousands of operations that have followed exposure after Chernobyl, ignoring the fact that we do not know what future effects and morbidity may occur, and that we do not know what the consequences of the DNA changes found in the unexposed offspring of exposed parents will be. Extreme antinuclear groups have undoubtedly minimised the advantages of nuclear power and exaggerated the ease with which it can be replaced by alternative green sources. They have overemphasised the health risks of nuclear power and not compared these to risks associated with other forms of energy generation, or indeed other hazards in life. They have quoted the literature selectively, often quoting only whichever paper gave the highest figure for radiation induced disease without examining its reliability or whether there was any evidence that the diseases or incidence discussed were due to radiation or might represent only the natural incidence of that disease. They have used graphic pictures of desperately deformed children or abnormal organs where the evidence that they were due to radiation was simply that they occurred in exposed areas, while tragically these conditions occur in all societies. It is only fair to say that they have rightly stressed the problems associated with nuclear waste disposal and decommissioning, and in the aftermath of Chernobyl the estimates of the consequences given by some of the 'green' organisations have been closer to those that have so far been substantiated than those given by the nuclear industry and international organisations. The contradictory publicity from these two opposed views causes confusion. There is however a more subtle effect on public consciousness, this is that almost any aspect of environmental radiation exposure causes anxiety. One eminent psychologist when asked how people could be made to be more comfortable with radiation replied that it would be necessary to make them comfortable with the concept of nuclear war. Civil nuclear power may well have benefits, particularly at a time when it seems likely that the climate will change for the worse due to increasing levels of carbon dioxide. However, the underlying anxiety about exposure to radiation, which manifested itself spectacularly in the psychosocial effect following the Chernobyl accident, makes persuading a sceptical public to accept nuclear power generation an uphill battle. Accidents like those at Chernobyl and Fukushima have added to the difficulty. An almost religious devotion to the anti-nuclear cause or a financial stake in pro-nuclear decisions, reminds one that it has to be accepted that the willingness of the human mind to be self-servingly deluded is an enduring feature and one that will adversely influence decisions, including those affecting human health, for decades to come.

Other factors that influence public opinion should be considered, in particular the roles of Government, of experts, of the media, and of education. Most governments in democracies find it difficult to deal with long-term decisions that may be unpopular with the electorate. They find it even more difficult to deal with an issue that arouses such emotion as nuclear power. Putting it crudely many politicians will give a higher priority to being re-elected in 3 or 4 years time than to take decisions which in the long term are in the best interests of the country but which in the short term are unpopular. They are pressurised by interest groups on decisions which may lead to enormous expenditure and have huge long term implications. Under these circumstances they will often turn to experts for advice. In a highly specialised subject like nuclear power many of the experts will have links with the nuclear industry, or will have had those links in the past and may have them in the future. The same situation arises in many areas of Government decision making, and regrettably Government practices seem designed to reduce the availability of truly independent experts, University funding is cut, links between universities and industry are being encouraged, with funding provided by industry, leaving few experts with no links to the industry on which they are asked to advise. In addition secondment of staff from industry to Government is supported. We believe that, before any decision as momentous as the one to determine energy policy for the next several decades is finalised, the Government should publish the full facts and assumptions on which it based its provisional decision, together with the names and commercial links of all those it consulted and the relevant donations made over the last 10 years to ministers or the party in Government. The same principles should apply to a decision to abandon nuclear power, as has recently happened in Germany, a country with a very powerful green lobby; the population needs to know how its energy supply can be maintained without importing nuclear energy or dirty coal energy from other countries. Governments have a history of a lack of openness in relation to nuclear power as was shown after both the Chernobyl and Fukushima accidents; if they are to increase trust in their decisions and reduce scepticism they must be more open, and not hide behind the façade of commercial confidentiality.

The media play a major role in the general public's attitude to nuclear power. Any accident at a nuclear power plant will be reported, 20 years of unblemished operation is unlikely even to have a passing mention. A nuclear accident sends the press into overdrive, and the more graphic the damage and the more horrific the injuries the bigger the story. Unfortunately few of those writing the stories in the mass media have the relevant knowledge. The media judges a story or programme by its impact rather than its accuracy. This was shown by an award winning emotion arousing programme on the consequences of Chernobyl, focussing on one child with deformities which could well have arisen from the use of thalidomide; available in the area at the time. There is no simple answer to this problem, but maybe a scientific media standards board could be given the power to insist on a declaration of interest by the author and in some circumstances to force the organisation to allow a right of reply with equal prominence to the original article or programme. There is a particular problem with polemicists whose whole raison d'etre is to be controversial. It would be good, if unlikely, if an article dealing with a scientific problem such as radiation could be accompanied by a health warning like a cigarette packet, perhaps 'this article presents the views of someone who knows little or nothing of the relevant scientific background, but intends to give his (her) opinion in any case'.

A deep-seated problem underlying both the scepticism of many towards radiation, and the attitude of the media and of politicians is that so few have any real understanding of the relevant science. The majority of those in the media and in politics will have had no scientific education beyond the age of 16, yet they are the opinion formers and decision makers on matters such as radiation and nuclear energy. How many of these powerful people realise for example that the official safety limit above which lamb from those few farms in Wales where fall-out from Chernobyl still lingers is regarded as not fit for human consumption is 1000 Becquerel per kilo or have any concept of the level of risk involved? How many realise that a few decades ago, before the units of measurement were changed, the limit would be 0.03 microCuries rather than 1000Bq, the same amount of radiation but to the non-expert conveying a very different impression of risk? It is natural to fear the unknown, particularly when as is the case with radiation the individual cannot detect its presence or control it, and cannot assess the risks associated with it. Becquerel per kilo is a foreign language for the great majority of the population, for the media who shape opinions and the politicians who take decisions. Scepticism flourishes in the absence of knowledge, and better science education is needed to ensure that the problems of radiation and nuclear energy are properly presented in the media, understood by the public, and that rational decisions on policy are taken by politicians.

Chapter 4

SCEPTICISM AND MATHEMATICS

Thomas William Korner
DPMMS, Cambridge University, UK

The Ancient Greeks (or at least that tiny proportion of them who interest mathematicians) loved arguing. Here is one of their arguments to show that 2 is not the square of any fraction. (I promise that this will be the only piece of actual mathematics in this essay, and the readers may skip it if they wish.)

Suppose that 2 is the square of some fraction u/v. By dividing top and bottom by 2 as many times as we need we may suppose that at least one of u and v is odd integer ('integer' is just another name for 'whole number'). Since $2 = (u/v)^2 = u^2/v^2$ we may multiply through by v^2 to get $2v^2 = u^2$. Since $2v^2$ is even u^2 is even. The square of an odd integer is odd so u must be even, that is to say $u = 2m$ where m is an integer. Thus $2v^2 = (2m)^2 = 4m^2$ and, dividing by 2, we obtain $v^2 = 2m^2$. We can now repeat our argument to show that v is even. This contradicts our earlier statement that at least one of u and v is odd. Since the assumption that 2 is the square of some fraction leads to a contradiction, 2 is not the square of some fraction

Here is another argument invented by the philosopher Zeno.

Achilles and a tortoise have a race. Since Achilles can run 10 times faster than the tortoise, he gives the tortoise a 900 metre start. Achilles runs the 900 metres but during this time the tortoise crawls 90 metres. Achilles now runs the 90 metres, but during this time the tortoise crawls 9 metres. Achilles now runs the 9 metres, but during this time the tortoise crawls 90 centimetres. Achilles now runs 90 centimetres but ... and so on. Achilles can never catch the tortoise and the idea of motion is self-contradictory.

Both arguments are very clever and lead by apparently simple steps to astonishing conclusions. If we reject both arguments, it is difficult to see how we can avoid rejecting all abstract reasoning. If we accept both arguments, we accept a complete divorce between abstract reasoning and common experience. Is possible to accept one and reject the other?

I think it is. The first argument starts from explicit premises such as 'The square of odd number is odd' and 'Any fraction can be written so that either the denominator or the numerator is odd'. Although the second argument is excellent and thought provoking, it is not clear how to write down explicit premises for it.

If this view is correct we can hope to evade (note that I do not say solve) philosophical problems of the type raised by Zeno by studying arguments which proceed from explicit premises by explicit rules of reasoning to explicit conclusions. It is not hard to see that such a study excludes all but a tiny segment of human experience, but it turns out that the study of what we might call 'Pure Mathematics' is amusing and occasionally useful.

Presented with a premise like 'the square of an odd number is odd' or 'every triangle has four sides', it is always possible to reject the premise. (The reader will probably accept the first and reject the second. The mathematician will do the same, but take rather longer about it.) Sometimes this is all that happens, but sometimes it is possible to show that premise A follows from premise B so that someone who accepts premise B will have to accept premise A. Obviously this cannot go on for ever but we might hope to start from a small set of premises presented on a 'take it or leave it' basis. Two arguers (or as we shall now call them, 'mathematicians') can agree to accept them in the same way as two chess players agree to observe the rules of chess or decide not to accept them in which case they can either agree on another set of premises (that is decide to play bridge) or just decide not to accept any (in which case they cease to be mathematicians). We know something, though only at second hand, about the origins of the two arguments with which I began. We know nothing about about how the Greeks dealt with them until we come to Euclid. We suspect that others had written texts on geometry before him but that he so completely superseded them that all trace has been lost. We do not know if he was a mathematician of genius or just a textbook writer of genius. (The distinction may be irrelevant; the writer of such a text must be a great mathematician.) What we do know is that Euclid's *Elements* presents a fully formed model of how Pure Mathematics should be done. Starting from a limited set of axioms (that is to say, premises) Euclid deduces all of geometry by means a chain of explicit arguments and sets out a model that we follow to this day.

There may be poets who feel the ghost of Homer beside them as they write. There may be politicians attended by the spirit of Pericles. I know for certain that Euclid sits at my elbow whenever I construct a long mathematical argument.

Of course, the Euclidean method is intended as a means of *testing* mathematical arguments, not of *discovering* them. In 1906, a letter came to light written by Archimedes, the greatest mathematician of antiquity. In it he describes how he discovered one of his major theorems by a process of informal reasoning, but emphasises the difference between 'heuristic' argument and formal proof.

All of mathematics involves long chains of reasoning from agreed premises, but I shall call mathematics in the style of Euclid, where we attempt to deduce everything from a single small set of agreed premises, 'Great Book' mathematics.

Greek civilisation was replaced by a line of societies which considered sharp swords as much more interesting and effectual arguments than the words of philosophers. However, the torch of Greek mathematics passed through Constantinople and Baghdad and onwards to a Europe recovering from the dark ages.

The modern history of Europe is marked, if not by the rise of learning, then certainly by the rise of teaching. Euclid's geometry lends itself to teaching, since the weak students can learn by rote and the strong students can taste the joy of discovery and puzzle solving. It is easy to persuade oneself that the study of abstract reasoning will be a good preparation for the general business of life.

> In the course of my law reading I constantly came upon the word demonstrate. I thought, at first, that I understood its meaning, but soon became satisfied that I did not. I said to myself, What do I do when I demonstrate more than when I reason or prove? How does demonstration differ from any other proof? I consulted Webster's Dictionary. They told of 'certain proof,' 'proof beyond the possibility of doubt'; but I could form no idea of what sort of proof that was. I thought a great many things were proved beyond the possibility of doubt, without recourse to any such extraordinary process of reasoning as I understood demonstration to be. I consulted all the dictionaries and books of reference I could find, but with no better results. You might as well have defined blue to a blind man. At last I said, Lincoln, you never can make a lawyer if you do not understand what demonstrate means; and I left my situation in Springfield, went home to my father's house, and stayed there till I could give any proposition in the six books of Euclid at sight. I then found out what demonstrate means, and went back to my law studies.
>
> *The Life of Abraham Lincoln* H. Ketcham

There was another reason for teaching Euclid. Just as English Churchmen valued natural history as teaching the benevolence and existence of a creator, so Euclid was valued as giving a glimpse of the absolute. Euclid's *Elements* showed that things which, at first sight, seemed implausible or even patently false, could be deduced by an unbreakable chain of reasoning from axioms which were self-evidently true. The power that this view of Euclid held over men's minds may be explicitly seen in philosophers like Spinoza, Descartes, Hobbes and Kant, but I suspect that its implicit effect was still greater for being unexamined.

The first great challenge to the 'Great Book' idea of mathematics was the invention and development of the calculus. For two centuries, mathematics was dominated by the study and application of this powerful theory, but no one was able to cast the calculus into Euclidean mode. Certainly it contained long chains of argument moving from simple premises to striking conclusions, but it seemed impossible to find a *fundamental* set of premises from which everything could be deduced.

Mathematicians are pragmatic characters and, if something is interesting and enjoyable, they let philosophical considerations alone. Some mathematicians viewed the absence of a 'Great Book' for the calculus as regrettable but inevitable. Others imitated the fox in Aesop's fable and declared 'Great Books' to be an unnecessary brake on progress. I suspect that most who thought about the matter thought of the 'Great Book' as a rather dull task for future generations.

In the end, a 'Great Book' for the calculus was written by the hands of many of the most distinguished mathematicians of the 19th century and the task turned out to be both difficult and interesting. Mathematicians discovered that certain definitions which appeared clear to the 18th century were neither clear nor definitions and certain facts, which appeared too obvious to mention, were actually profound statements about the nature of numbers. We still teach our students from this 'Great Book' on whose first page is inscribed in letters of gold 'An increasing sequence bounded above tends to a limit'.

I said earlier that most people viewed Euclid's axioms as obvious truths. However, one axiom, the so-called 'Parallel Postulate' (which states, in modern terms, that through any point there is one and only one line parallel to a given line), was felt to be a less obvious truth than the others. Several attempts were made to deduce it from the remaining axioms, but they failed and eventually several mathematicians decided that it was not an 'obvious truth' but just a particular choice of premise. Different choices gave different 'non-Euclidean' geometries. It was found that Euclidean geometry contained models of these non-Euclidean geometries so that, if these geometries were rejected as unsatisfactory, Euclid's geometry would have to be rejected too.

Slowly mathematicians came round to the view that the axioms of Euclid were not self evident truths but merely 'rules of the game'. Simplifying greatly, we may say that Gauss held this view in 1820 and that most leading mathematicians agreed by 1900. The final blow to the view of Euclidean geometry as a 'preferred' if not a 'true' vision of space was given by Einstein's General Theory of Relativity which showed that some physical laws were best understood in a non-Euclidean context.

The reader may have observed that we have discussed premises and conclusions but not the nature of the logic by which we move from one to the other. Without great exaggeration it may be said that, although many people wrote many books on logic between the time of Aristotle and the publication of Boole's *Laws of Thought* in 1854, they wrote nothing interesting. Boole's book began the investigation of logic from a mathematical point of view. As the mathematical investigation of logic proceeded, it interacted with the work on the 'Great Book' of calculus and a reinvestigation of Euclid's 'Great Book'. (The reader may be interested to learn that close investigation revealed several missing links in a chain of reasoning which previous generations had believed to be perfect, but nothing that could not be repaired.) For a moment it looked as though it would be possible to write a single 'Great Book' covering all of mathematics founded, not on intuition about space (which now appeared fallible), but on the absolute truth of logic.

The great project was brought to a halt by the problem of self-reference. What are we to do about statements like 'This statement is false'? The natural way out is to introduce the notion of grammar and declare such statements ungrammatical and so not part of our theory. Unfortunately, the plans for the new 'Great Book' involved extensive use of self-referential objects. It turned out to be impossible either to exclude them altogether or to provide a *self-evident* rule for excluding some examples of self reference and allowing others. (Weyl wrote of one famous attempt that it 'causes reason to commit hara-kiri'.)

As I have said before, mathematicians are pragmatic people and, since no *self-evident* rule could be found, they simply adopted a *convenient* rule that seemed (and still seems) to work (Zermelo–Frankl set theory). It was now possible to write the 'Great Book' of all mathematics, but mathematicians had to accept that it rested on premises which although they looked obvious were merely 'rules of the game'.

A final, and totally unexpected, blow to the concept of the 'Great Book' as representing absolute truth was given by Gödel in 1931 when he gave an argument to show that no 'Great Book' that contained certain important mathematical topics could be proved clear of contradictions in a way that mathematicians would consider satisfactory.

It is clear that, contrary to what was hoped before the crisis just described, Pure Mathematics provides no defence against absolute scepticism. None the less, mathematics is an outlier among human activities and it may be interesting for those not committed to absolute scepticism to look at how mathematicians use scepticism in their everyday practice.

The first point to notice is that mathematicians habitually work at several levels of scepticism. To see why this is so, consider Applied Mathematics where we use mathematics to describe the real world. If our theory makes predictions which turn out to be wrong, then, no matter how carefully our chains of mathematical reasoning have been constructed, our theory is wrong. If our theory makes predictions which turn out to be right, then, however many leaps of faith our mathematics contains, there must be some validity in our arguments.

If we have no such external check, then our arguments have to be watertight. Write down the odd integers in sequence $1, 3, 5, 7, \ldots$. If we add them up one at a time we get $1, 1+3=4, 1+3+5=9, 1+3+5+7=16, \ldots$ that is to say the squares $1 = 1^2, 4 = 2^2, 9 = 3^2, 16 = 4^2 \ldots$. It is not hard to guess the rule, but how do we know it always holds? We can check particular instances but we cannot check *all* the sums.

Write down the odd integers in sequence $1, 3, 5, 7, \ldots$. It looks as though none of them is divisible by any smaller number ... but when we look a little further we see that 9 is divisible by 3.

In Pure Mathematical proof, scepticism rules. If an argument has gaps then it must be rejected. In the normal world, when someone puts forward an argument, it is up to someone else to attack it. A good Pure Mathematician will do both jobs. Once she has produced an argument, she will bend all her critical faculties to finding the flaws in it. Only after she has failed to find gaps, will she consult her colleagues.

However, proof is only part of Pure Mathematics. A Pure Mathematician may wish to understand the work of an Applied Mathematician or to understand why a result (which may or may not be true) is at least plausible. She then lowers her scepticism level appropriately. Mathematicians have developed a whole vocabulary to cover this situation. 'Assume good behaviour.' 'By a hand-waving argument.' 'If things are sufficiently smooth.'

One excellent test for the correctness of an argument is to write it as a chapter in a 'Great Book'. This is not always helpful. Some parts of mathematics have little natural connection with the rest. (An example is the mathematical theory of voting. This interesting subject includes a theorem of Arrow which shows that all voting systems will produce unsatisfactory results under certain circumstances.) Others, like Newton's system of Mechanics, seem prime candidates for inclusion in a 'Great Book' but neither illuminate nor are illuminated by the other chapters.

Having said this, there are many examples where inclusion in a 'Great Book' has proved of major benefit both to the 'Great Book' and to the subject included. (Every time my readers use a computer, they use results generated when logic was written in a 'Great Book'.)

In my account of mathematics, scepticism appears merely as a working tool valued only when it produces interesting results. Carried over to philosophy, this attitude would lead to the rejection of solipsism not because it can be be refuted (and, as I have tried to show, mathematics does not provide a method for refuting extreme scepticism of this type) but because it is uninteresting.

Philosophy is very close to mathematics and the practice of the two disciplines has always been linked. Does the mathematical approach to scepticism have any wider application? Up to this point in the essay I have been expressing views on the nature of mathematics which, though not universal, are shared by many mathematicians. However, I can think of no political or religious view, however extreme or middle-of-the road, which has not been firmly held by some mathematician. The one thing that most (but by no means all) agree on is that mathematicians pursue their subject because they enjoy it and not to provide practical benefits (the geese may, very occasionally, lay golden eggs, but that is not central to their existence) or moral lessons for mankind. What follows are therefore my thoughts on the matter. If, from now on, the reader replaces 'mathematicians think' by 'the author thinks' the apparent loss of authority will be balanced by greater honesty.

There are many groups of individuals who hold strong beliefs about the nature of the world which are in direct contradiction to what we may call the *consensus* view. In the old days, we needed to consult Martin Gardner's *Fads and Fallacies in the Name of Science* to learn about these views, but we can now learn them directly from the Internet. Frequently, these groups define themselves as 'sceptical' seekers after truth, often lecturing those who hold the consensus view on the virtues of scepticism.

As might be expected, Pure Mathematicians can say little that is useful about the uses of scepticism outside their own subject. They may perhaps point out that the Pure Mathematician's scepticism is primarily directed against his or her own work. (Thus a Pure Mathematician reads his or her own work with an eye to finding flaws and other peoples' work with an eye to understanding.) They may add the observation that most self-proclaimed 'sceptics' reserve their scepticism for the ideas of other people and leave their own ideas unexamined. (Sometimes the situation is even odder. There are several schools of 'Alternative Medicine' whose principles are in direct contradiction, but whose practitioners quietly refrain from criticising each other.)

In this context we may recall Darwin's golden rule,

> ... namely, that whenever a published fact, a new observation or thought came across me, which was opposed to my general results, to make a memorandum of it without fail and at once; for I had found by experience that such facts and thoughts were far more apt to escape from the memory than favourable ones.
>
> *Autobiography*

Since Pure Mathematicians enjoy long chains of reasoning and subtle arguments, they have another objection to groups like the 'Young Earth Creation Scientists' who say that 'the all-knowing truthful Creator has given us His inerrant book' and that it is therefore unscientific to accept any other view. Pure Mathematicians feel that to engage in argument against opponents who are allowed to play Genesis as a winning card at any time they please is to take part in a rather dull game. Of course, this simply suggests that Creationist Geology is intellectually rather uninteresting and has no bearing on whether it is true.

Applied Mathematicians probably have more to say. Since, whatever their internal differences, mathematicians form a united front against the outside world, they might start by boasting that the sceptics who infest the Internet are bumbling amateurs in scepticism compared with their colleagues across the hallway in the Pure Mathematics Department. They might then say that, although mild amounts of scepticism are useful in allowing one to avoid stupid errors, the ultimate judge of a scientific theory is not argument but experiment. The only serious scientists, they would claim, are those who make testable predictions.

If you argued that, say, Geology is a 'historic science' and cannot make predictions, they would reply that, if someone found a gold watch in the middle of a coal seam, geologists would produce a plausible explanation for the discovery, but, if people continued to find gold watches in coal seams, then the entire science of geology would be overthrown. If you then tried to present String Theory as a theory without evidence, they might reply that the theory is still young and that, if it proves untestable in the long term, the most beautiful parts of it will move over to Pure Mathematics and the most physically interesting bits will be cannibalised and used in other more testable parts of Applied Mathematics. (Both processes have already started.)

Some people erect scepticism into a system and call themselves 'contrarians'. To a mathematician, it seems as intellectually lazy to deny all received opinions as to affirm them and probably even less useful. It is, of course, likely that many things which are believed as facts are actually false, but reflection suggests many reasons why it is unlikely that most of them are. It also true that it is rarely (but note that I do not say never) useful to state that something is false without suggesting what is true. It is a matter of observation that many contrarians feel that rejecting everything leaves them free to do nothing about anything. If it is better to light a candle than to curse the darkness, it is surely also better to try and light one candle than to go round counting those which are unlit.

Perhaps unfairly, the word contrarian (at least in a British context) conjures up for me the picture of a prosperous middle-aged man drinking port and exchanging paradoxes with a few friends round a comfortable fire. The Shelleys and their circle were contrarians of a more serious nature who suffered for their views at the hands both of society and each other. Mathew Arnold tells us that when Mary Shelley asked about a school for her son she was told 'I suppose you want him to learn to think for himself'. 'Teach him to think for himself?' she replied 'Oh, my God, teach him rather to think like other people!' (The story has a happy ending: her son seems to have been totally conventional.)

Mathematicians live in a very comfortable ivory tower. Those who, like journalists, lawyers and politicians, have to deal with the real world are entitled to object that the high standards of mathematical argument are irrelevant to the rough and tumble of normal life. However, I have been asked to comment on scepticism from the point of view of a mathematician and I would like to comment in particular on two arguments which are frequently used by sceptics (and many others).

The first is the argument from conviction 'I really, truly, deeply believe what I am saying'. This carries no weight whatsoever with mathematicians, almost all of whom will have constructed theorems or theories and been totally convinced of their truth only to discover a flaw in the reasoning (I would write a 'subtle flaw' but all flaws are 'blindingly obvious' when you see them) or to find that experiment does not support them ('a beautiful theory killed by an ugly fact'). Sometimes the argument from conviction is converted into an argument from authority: 'I really, truly, deeply believe what I am saying and I have a PhD', but it hardly needs to be said that mathematicians do not accept arguments from authority or democracy ('I really, truly, deeply believe what I am saying and so do the majority of Americans'). In passing, I may add that the argument from conviction always brings to my mind Emerson's observation that 'the louder he talked of his honour, the faster we counted the spoons'.

The second argument is that what seems to be the case must actually be the case. Of course, this is a good (indeed, probably the best) place to start a discussion, but it may not be the best place to finish it. The professional experience of mathematicians leads them to suspect that both the actual universe and the universe of thought are, in the words of Haldane, not only 'queerer than we suppose, but queerer than we can suppose'.

We may imagine conversations between *Common sense* and *Consensus* at various times since Jenner's introduction of vaccination.

1800

Common sense It is ridiculous to suppose that introducing poisonous material into the body can cause anything but harm.

Consensus I agree.

1900

Common sense It is ridiculous to suppose that introducing poisonous material into the body can cause anything but harm.

Consensus I know that it seems ridiculous and I have no idea how it works, but the statistics show that vaccination is effective.

2000

Common sense It is ridiculous to suppose that introducing poisonous material into the body can cause anything but harm.

Consensus The eradication of smallpox shows that vaccination worked and, although some details remain mysterious, we have a good idea of why it worked.

2100

Common sense It is ridiculous to suppose that introducing poisonous material into the body can cause anything but harm.

(But, although we know what *Common sense* will say in 2100, we will have to wait until then to discover what *Consensus* will reply.)

Nowadays when people talk of scientific sceptics, they tend to think of 'climate sceptics'. I am inclined to think that the influence of such sceptics is much overrated both by themselves and by those who seek to answer their arguments ('Who fights too long with dragons becomes a dragon themselves.') The species of clever monkeys which destroyed the Grand Banks Fisheries and builds houses on flood plains does not lack knowledge of the possible consequences of its actions, it lacks the will to apply that knowledge.

However, there is one argument used by 'climate sceptics' which readers might think would appeal to mathematicians. This is the argument from uncertainty. All scientific theories are provisional. We have seen Newtonian Mechanics modified by Special Relativity and Special Relativity by General Relativity (and it is, I think, a matter of surprise to the experts that General Relativity has survived unmodified for nearly a century). Within my lifetime, the theory of plate tectonics has overthrown all the accepted wisdom of geophysicists. The theories that underlie the expectation of continued global warming caused by human action are fairly new and the systems they describe are very complex. The science, sceptics say, is not settled and so we should take no action.

Mathematicians have studied the closely related topics of probability, gambling, insurance and decision making under uncertainty since the time of Pascal. After three and a half centuries of study, they have come to the conclusion that, when people disagree about the probability of a certain outcome, they should bet on it. The articles and blogs of climate sceptics are full of predictions of coming ice ages, imminent refreezing of the Arctic and so on. They contain full measures of cutting sarcasm and veiled or open accusations of dishonesty. The authors proclaim their absolute certainty in their own opinions and yet they refuse to 'put their money where their mouth is'. An active betting market in global warming would do more to convince me of the seriousness of the objectors' case than all the rhetoric in the world.

I conclude this essay by repeating that, for the mathematician, scepticism is a tool, not a virtue.

Chapter 5

SCEPTICISM IN MEDICAL RESEARCH

Damian C. Crowther
Trinity Hall and Cambridge Institute for Medical Research,
Department of Genetics, Cambridge, UK

If we look back with today's measures of success, it was only during the 20th century that a visit to the doctor did the average patient more good than harm. Despite the rather disappointing efficacy of ancient remedies the doctor was by no means a poor man in the community. Indeed there has been an unbroken tradition of the honourable physician, held in high esteem by the people, right back to ancient Greek times and beyond. The sick would consult their doctors, often paying handsomely for the privilege, not just for the treatment that they received but also for the empowerment and comfort that come from a formal diagnosis and the doctor's prognosis. The need to have a name for suffering and to know what an uncertain future may hold seems to be fundamentally important to us. In moments of illness and crisis we look for a source of security and for many people, over many generations, the physician has vied with the man of religion for the provision of this rock. Arguably, faith is needed in equal measure for the medical visit as for the religious service. For a patient to gain full benefit they must believe *in* their doctor; a consultation without this element of trust fast becomes a tragedy of escalating anxiety for both participants. For these reasons the patient suspends some degree of scepticism when consulting their doctor so that they can receive, at least at an emotionally level, the full benefits of the interaction.

To justify the suspense of scepticism on the part of the patient, the medical profession has developed a conservative culture and code of professional conduct that in effect takes the weight of scepticism from the shoulders of the patient and takes the burden unto itself. This role as sceptic of last resort brings with it many benefits, it explains for example the ostracising of the "quack doctor" and the "snake oil seller". Happily, and for patients' sakes it would seem, the pseudo-medical practitioners are thus placed outside the shell of institutional scepticism as their pandering of untrustworthy remedies is seen as a direct threat to the patient-doctor relationship. The rejection of bogus treatments has been an important role for the modern doctor. The question posed here is how sceptical should the profession be? If we get the balance wrong, do we risk rejecting too much?

Of the three main clinical roles described above, namely diagnostician, prognostician and therapist, it has traditionally been the last that has been most tightly regulated by the medical profession and more generally by society. Certainly doctors are bound to spend many, some say too many, years learning the arts of diagnosis and the appropriate rhetoric (these days called "communications skills") for imparting the prognosis to the patient. However it is the perception of these parts of the consultation as "arts" that renders them less easy to assess in a quantitatively sceptical manner. It is still quite acceptable for a doctor to portray his or her diagnostic skills as an innate ability, a "knack" or the result of arcane rites undertaken in beacon establishments of the profession. While there have been efforts to improve on this human art of diagnosis they have been met with remarkably little progress in recent years. On one hand, efforts to provide ever more data for doctors' decision support has been found to reduce rather than increase diagnostic accuracy. It seems that the experienced doctor can filter the noise in the consultation and use what data remains to guide the diagnosis. This largely non-conscious process appears to be disturbed when new systems of work artificially elevate the profile of all available data. On the other hand, if supporting doctors does not work how about taking them out of the diagnostic process altogether? To this end there have been efforts to development "expert systems", that is computer software, that can detect patterns in clinical data and provide rational, and formally justifiable, diagnoses. In general these systems have been particularly disappointing, being unable to generate unifying diagnoses when presented with the heterogeneous and noisy data that is characteristic of the clinic. As a result expert systems are not in widespread use in any clinical context except in the most constrained and circumscribed domains.

So it is that the arts of medicine still resist the regulation that comes from institutional scepticism, leaving the science of therapeutics to bear the brunt of scrutiny. Indeed it is the doctor as therapeutician who feels the greatest weight of the sceptical moral ethics that have been handed down from Greek times. Hippocrates' maxim "to abstain from doing harm" (paraphrased in Latin as "primum non nocere") is as powerfully applied today as it was 2500 years ago. The implication that it is morally worse to cause harm by an act than by the failure to act is ingrained in the therapeutic culture. In this analysis, there is particular disgrace for a doctor who fails in his duty of scepticism by embracing a treatment that, although promising. In such a case it is doubtless the direct link between a doctor's action and the adverse effect on the patient that makes the sceptical failure most apparent; so the doctor must only prescribe treatments that cause little or no harm, and ideally are likely to do good. So the medical profession presents itself as "nobody's fool" and a benign agent so that the patients' sceptical impulses are most effectively suppressed to the benefit of both parties.

The question that emerges is: how does the profession, and society as a whole, decide which treatments are beneficial and worthy of their "sacred" endorsement? Important steps towards a quantifiable and sceptical approach to clinical research, in support of rational therapeutic decision making, were taken in the 1970's with the publication of Professor Archie Cochrane's book *Effectiveness and Efficiency: Random Reflections on Health Services* [1]. The first institutional embodiment of this new field of study called "evidence based medicine" was at McMaster University in Canada. David Sackett and Gordon Guyatt in particular set about defining the characteristics of a clinical study that made it a reliable source of data [2]. Having defined what studies fell within their remit they then developed methods that allowed them to analyse disparate data sets in an effort to find generalisable conclusions with a greater degree of statistical certainty than could be achieved by reading any individual study. Thus were born the two icons of modern medicine namely the "randomised controlled trial (RCT)" and the discipline of "meta-analysis".

The RCT has become the cornerstone of the sceptical medical profession and like a small-time dictator has taken increasingly more titles and qualifications; so an RCT may take on epithets such as "double blind", "placebo controlled", "international", "multicentre" and so on. Each of these phrases publicly distances the physician-scientist from the generation of data, with a view to banishing subjective bias and so providing the impartiality that is required by an audience of sceptical medical professionals. The process of meta-analysis distances the scientist still further from the generation of data – now the practitioner is no longer a physician-scientist treating patients or performing laboratory experiments. Rather, the investigator is a statistician who impartially, and quantifiably, draws data together from a number of different clinical trials and determines what can be said objectively about a treatment or clinical test, and exactly how confidently we can say it.

Can it be that bias and prejudice have now been eliminated from medical research and practice? Can doctors and patients both justifiably leave behind their sceptical natures and get on with the business of keeping individuals, and the population, healthy? Or could it be that the meta-analysts are playing the same confidence games with doctors that the doctors (arguably) play with their patients. In practical terms, when faced with a meta-analysis of dozens of double blind, placebo controlled (etc) RCTs the clinician will, with perhaps a sense of resignation, feel that his/her duty to be sceptical has at last been relieved. Surely now it is the statisticians who decide which treatments stay and which should be discarded. This is what appears to be increasingly the case in socialised healthcare systems such as the UK's National Health Service and in the managed healthcare plans such as Medicare in predominantly private systems such as in the USA. In these communities institutions such as the National Institute for Health and Clinical Excellence have been charged with assessing clinical trial data and by combining this with an assessment of value for money they are generating a series of detailed clinical guidelines for doctors. So it is that the duty of the doctor to be sceptical has become institutionalised and rather divorced from the practicing physician-scientist. But I do not believe that this is end of the story. The sceptical mind must wonder who generates the clinical studies that test new treatments. What questions do these studies ask? Perhaps equally important is what questions are not being asked? How does basic medical research work and what effect does the scepticism of the bio-medical profession have on the way we progress?

Let me present what has been a widely adopted strategy for the discovery of new therapies. Typically a particular disease will have been the subject of tens of years of research with the aim of understanding its causation at a molecular level. There are a number of ways in which this may be achieved. Often it will be rare familial cases, of otherwise common diseases, that give the first clue to the causative defects. Indeed it is a particular hope of molecular medicine that by studying rare, genetically-defined, disease processes we can shed light on the vastly more common, but clinically-equivalent, disorders that appear sporadically in the population. Accordingly, it is geneticists who analyse the DNA from family members and so track down which gene is implicated and which mutations directly cause the disease in affected individuals. As genetic data is gathered, the assignment of disease causation to a particular gene, and a mutation therein, can be done with a defined level of confidence. Provided that sufficient numbers of affected and unaffected family members are available, there comes a point when it becomes statistically unreasonable to deny the link between mutation and disease; it is then that the race begins to characterise the mechanism. The gene itself and the protein that it encodes become the subjects of further research with the aim of understanding how they interact with other cellular components. It is molecular- and cell-biologists that can show how the disease-linked gene or protein fits into the web of other known biological pathways and functions. Even at this early stage the scientists may be proposing therapeutic strategies based on existing knowledge of how related proteins and cellular structures behave. Hypotheses are proposed, and experiments designed, according to a framework of biology that is often firmly established. In many cases the community will have rather fixed ideas about how particular biological pathways should be manipulated to restore the healthy functioning of tissues and indeed of the whole organism.

From these descriptions it can be seen that an accepted method for discovering therapeutic targets may start with the observation of rare cases of familial disease, with a defined molecular cause, and then proceeds to treatments based on the role of the new target in existing biological pathways. But such rare familial disorders are not the true target of the drug discovery process, rather it is the non-familial, so-called sporadic, versions of the same disease that have the greatest significance for society and for the bottom line of pharmaceutical companies. However moving from the rare and well defined cases of disease to the less understood sporadic equivalent often requires a step of inductive logic that is commonly taken but rarely, if ever, formally justified. This step should exercise the sceptical mind because it is the proposal that familial- and sporadic-forms of clinically-identical diseases have identical causes. In my particular field of interest, namely Alzheimer's disease (AD), the field has been dominated by therapeutic strategies that were proposed 10 years ago based on the molecular characterisation of rare families in which the disorder was seen to be inherited through the generations. Despite these clearly inherited cases of AD accounting for as little as 5% of the total, almost the entire drug discovery effort ever since then has been focussed on one molecular target, with very little, if any, success. Of course a lack of success so far does not prove that the strategy is a bad one, however this example serves to show how, in important areas of scientific research, a community of scientists may become subservient to a particular conceptual hegemony. In practical terms when an idea or concept becomes over-valued, the sceptical mind, rather than questioning the underlying framework, may instead become diverted into silencing discordant voices. Such dysfunctional scepticism may act at many levels within the scientific establishment, ranging from unfavourable reviews of controversial grant applications and manuscripts to institutional strategies that starve dissenting views by denying their proponents reasonable career progression. I would argue that in Alzheimer's disease, like many other fields that have developed almost monothematic research strategies, the sceptical mind should be actively doubting the dogma. Paradoxically the sceptic should be suspicious of the accepted view and welcome the new, not least because the old ideas have in the case of Alzheimer's disease yielded so few therapeutic fruits.

Potential challenges to the accepted wisdom in Alzheimer's disease and other research fields have come from experimental approaches that are often termed "hypothesis free". Of course no scientific experiment can actually be hypothesis free, and in this context the term refers to approaches that allow the investigator to test many possible causes of a particular disease without the need to generate a single specific, and possibly biased, *a priori* hypothesis. Indeed the term "hypothesis free" is a profound misnomer because technical advances in genetics and other disciplines allow us to undertake experiments that can test an exhaustive multitude (thousands or millions) of unique hypotheses. I shall describe a popular approach to so-called hypothesis-free science that is termed the genome wide association study (GWAS). In this type of genetic study investigators analyse marker sequences in the DNA from thousands of patients with a disease. The same analysis is performed on samples taken from control patients who are similar in all respects except that they do not suffer from the particular disease. Such extensive personal analysis, looking at the precise DNA sequence at each of around one million positions within the genome, has only become possible within the past few years. In simple terms the study can assess whether particular variations in DNA sequence are accompanied by a change in an individual's risk of developing a disease. It is then possible to assign, with a quantifiable degree of confidence, whether particular, usually nearby, genes are responsible for the detected increase or decrease in disease risk. In this way studies involving almost thirty thousand individuals have yielded a list of ten genes that are linked to risk [3]. Crucially, for the first time we are systematically, and without bias, determining the genetic basis for common, sporadic disease rather than the rare, and genetically simpler, familial diseases. What has been astonishing in the field of AD has been that none of the genes that have been studied so extensively for over a decade as causes of familial AD have been identified as modifying the risk of developing sporadic AD.

While the finding that there appears to be little or no genetic overlap between familial and sporadic AD does not necessarily invalidate the pre-existing pathological concepts, it has undoubtedly provided for new and refreshing discussions and hypotheses. However the genome wide association study is a limited tool for drug discovery because it can only be relied on to detect relatively common genetic variations that have a relatively strong effect on disease risk. There are likely to be important genes and proteins, that could become drug targets, that will only reveal themselves when randomly mutated in vary rare individuals; unfortunately such genes are cannot be systematically discovered either by the study of familial disease or by GWAS's. However by creating disease models that are based on a state-of-the-art understanding of the human pathological processes we can systematically search for such targets with reasonable hopes of success. By exhaustively modifying the genetic material in many individual organisms, and in my laboratory we use either the fruit fly (*Drosophila melanogaster*) or the nematode worm (*Caenorhabditis elegans*), we can trawl through all the genetic interventions that can possibly increase or decrease the severity of disease-related deficits in our models organisms. One advantage of using small, rapidly replicating organisms such as flies and worms, is that we can perform experiments cheaply and quickly and so undertake exhaustive searches for therapeutic targets that would of course be unfeasible and unethical in human subjects.

Our approach has not yet escaped entirely from the "accepted" concepts in the AD field. Our fly and worm model systems are still based on the assumption that there is an underlying similarity between familial and sporadic cases of AD. But we are now able to take a step from known, or accepted, territory into the unknown. We are systematically assessing the importance of previously neglected biological and cellular pathways in AD and by using the human GWAS data as a guide we can tell whether our exploratory steps in the model organisms are leading us to interesting new areas or into genetic wilderness. A particular example might be to use genetic tools to systematically alter the levels of individual genes in our fly or worm models of AD and then measure the consequent effects on the severity of disease-related symptoms. In this way we can assess the disease-relevant roles of *all* the genes and proteins in our organisms and so determine which may be possible drug targets. If the drug targets we discover are linked functionally to genes that are implicated by human genetic studies then that provides further validation of the approach. These powerful approaches allow the scientist to discover potential drug targets that have not been previously detected in studies of rare familial disease or using GWAS approaches for sporadic disease. However the utility of this approach is likely to depend on how faithfully the model organism replicates the disease process in the patient. This in turn is determined by the degree of biological similarity between the model organism and the human. It is at this point, I would argue, that biomedical scepticism is failing to derive the optimal utility from the available animal models of disease. For each of the various model organisms, notably the nematode worm, the fruit fly and the mouse (*Mus musculus*), there are trade-offs in terms of utility. In general the more biologically similar an organism is to humans the longer it takes and the more it costs, to perform equivalent experiments (Figure 1). For example the smallest efficacy trials for a potential drug in the clinic costs of the order of £10 million. Experiments using mice are also relatively costly and are constrained by strict ethical considerations.

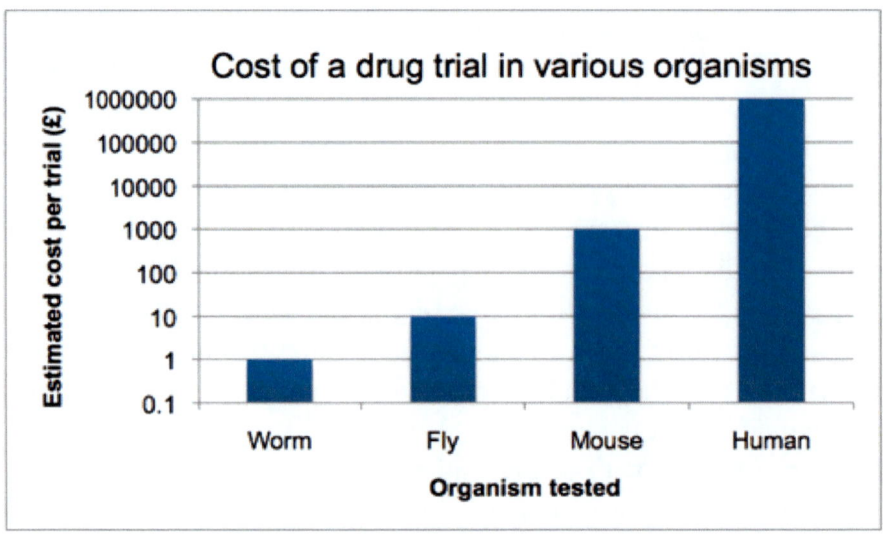

Figure 1. The cost of drug trials increases faster than exponentially as we use animal models that approach the human.

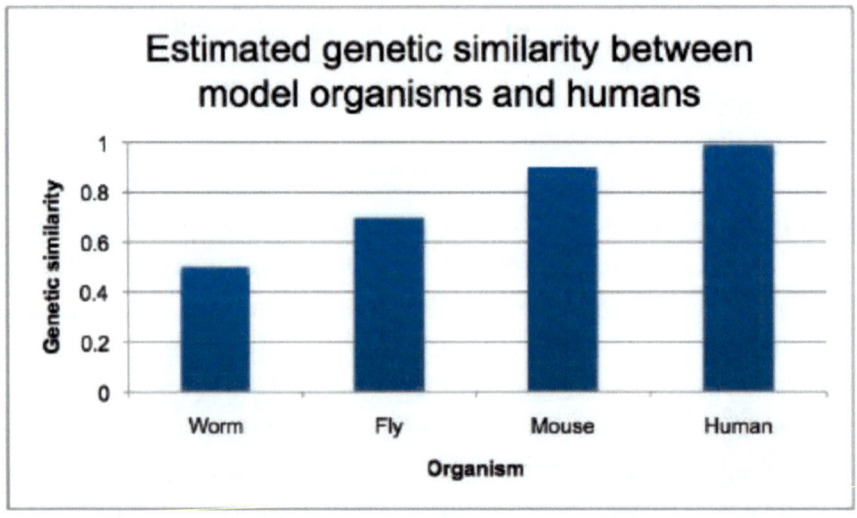

Figure 2. The genetic similarity with humans increases linearly as we approach the human.

While these factors favour the use of worms and the flies, nevertheless the biological proximity of the mouse to the human means that there is a counter-incentive to perform experiments in such "higher" organisms. It seems obvious that we should be able to find an optimum distribution of experimental burden across this spectrum of disease models. In crude terms we would expect to see many pilot and early screening experiments in lower organisms because they are cheap and quick. In an optimal world we would then move on to fewer and better-focussed experiments being performed in higher organisms such as mice. In reality this well-constructed programme of experimental approaches does not exist, indeed there is almost no uptake of invertebrate model systems in the pharmaceutical industry; current drug development strategies typically make an unseemly jump from *in vitro* experimental systems to the vastly more expensive mouse work and thereafter into the clinic. I would argue that unreasonable scepticism on the part of the biomedical community with regard to the utility of fly and worm models systems is skewing research strategy and resulting in the suboptimal usage of scientific resources.

One way to take things forward is to quantify scepticism, expressing it in terms of (un)certainty, wherever possible. Without getting into the rhetoric of "known unknowns" and "unknown unknowns" it is surely the case that any reasonable estimate of uncertainty will provide a better basis for rational scepticism than unbridled and potentially biased application of "scientific intuition". In the specific case of invertebrate models of disease and their role in medical research, it is rational to be sceptical about their applicability but this should not result in their abandonment. Rather we should see how their spectrum of strengths and weaknesses could be used optimally in a series of experiments aimed at understanding and intervening in disease.

To conclude it seems to me that the medical profession has historically adopted a highly conservative and sceptical approach with a view to maintaining credibility with its clientele. However as the profession has become more scientific, evidence-based and socially-regulated this scepticism has been institutionalised and divorced somewhat from individual doctors. In this process it has been easy for practitioners to lose the impetus to sceptical thought or to misuse the impulse for the suppression of scientific creativity. The dynamic nature of the research community should continually challenge accepted orthodoxies. In the examples discussed here there is a risk of scientific hegemony and new ideas and novel resources are exploited suboptimally because of dysfunctional scepticism. One way to facilitate new ideas and to promote the optimal use of available experimental resources is to quantify scepticism in terms of uncertainty. This may lead to a rational system for estimating the utility of the countless new hypotheses and experimental approaches that are to be the lifeblood of our future scientific communities.

REFERENCES

[1] Cochrane, A.L., Effectiveness and Efficiency: Random Reflections on Health Services. 1st edition ed. The Rock Carling Fellowship Series. 1973, Oxford: *The Nuffield Provincial Hospitals Trust.*

[2] Guyatt, G., et al., A clinician's guide for conducting randomized trials in individual patients. *CMAJ,* 1988. 139(6): p. 497-503.

[3] Hollingworth, P., et al., Common variants at ABCA7, MS4A6A/MS4A4E, EPHA1, CD33 and CD2AP are associated with Alzheimer's disease. *Nat. Genet.,* 2011.

Chapter 6A

INTRODUCTION TO EVOLUTIONARY BIOLOGY AND SCEPTICISM

Roy Calne

Evolution is a central tenant of biology and ever since the publication of the Darwin-Wallace theory during the late 1850's, their notion of "Descent with Modification" has been supported by a diverse array of evidence from both hard- and soft-tissue anatomy. Gregor Mendel, who was a contemporary of Darwin, provided a fascinating and correct explanation of the principles of inheritance based on mathematical observations. In the course of his life Mendel was not a prolific scholar, at least in terms of publishing and would not have had a chance of obtaining any kind of research grant in the present academic climate. He did discuss at local scientific meetings how he had managed to breed peas and beans so that they had certain characteristics such as tall or short. His major research paper (Mendel 1865) was sitting on one of the shelves of Darwin's library, but it is alleged that Darwin could not have read it as the pages had not yet been cut, typical of a newly printed, and unread book fresh from the publisher. If he had known of Mendel's work this might have helped him understand inheritance, a concept that remained unclear throughout the 19th century. Advances in microscopy disclosed the universal cellular nature of living matter and the physical basis of inheritance that had been suspected for many years. However a clear biochemical solution for inheritance did not arrive until decades after Darwin's (and Mendel's) death, based on the structure of the DNA double helix. This provided a linked chemical alphabet, and a means by which this alphabet was translated into the synthesis of proteins (Watson and Crick, 1953).

Palaeontology has shown in remarkable detail the anatomy and (indirectly) physiology of many creatures at different points in the tree of life going back many millions of years (picture of Coelacanth). It must have been a most extraordinary sensation of excitement when the young museum biologist, Marjorie Latimer, saw on the fishmonger's slab in East London, South Africa, a large and rather ugly fish which was to her scholarly mind the Coelacanth, thought to have been extinct for over 65 million years. Subsequently different species of Coelacanths have been found in the Indian Ocean and off the coast of Indonesia. These living fossils re-emphasised the truths of Darwin's theory which are consistent with geological and molecular biological data, currently accepted by modern scientists. The factual evidence is overwhelming but this does not deter the faith of the creationists, whose acceptance of religious myths continue to excite controversy. Most scientists would not disapprove of creationism being taught as part of history or religious studies but it is ridiculous for them to suggest that it has a place in scientific education.

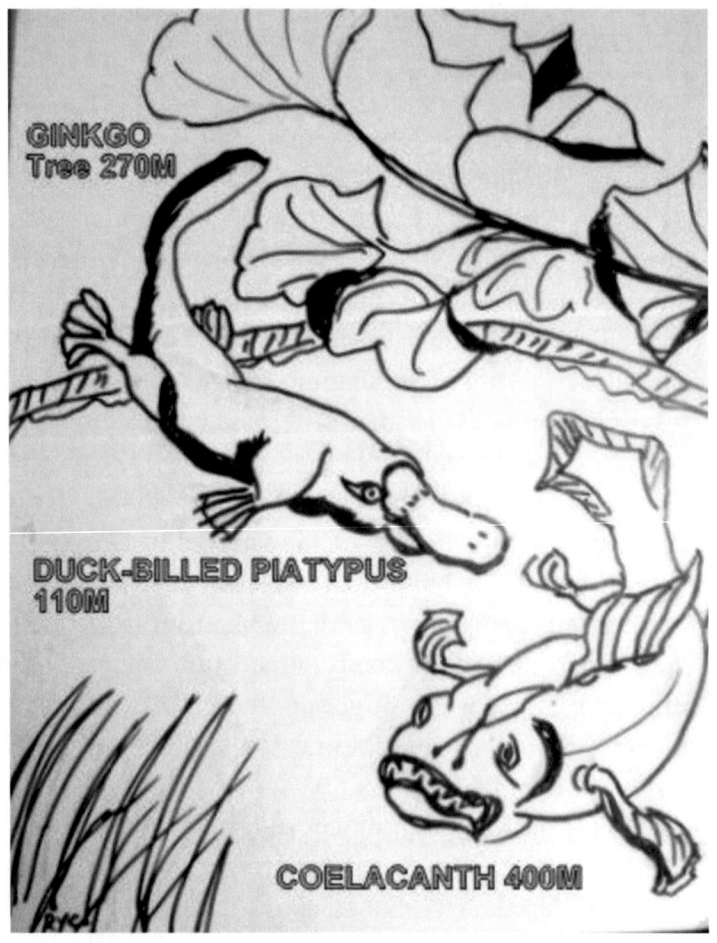

RYC drawing of Coelacanth, Gingko Tree & Platypus, and text indicating fossil age.

Robert Asher's chapter on evolution focuses on the reception of the Darwin-Wallace theory in continental Europe, in particular by Karl Reichert, a German biologist who made exceedingly important observations on the development of ossicle bones of the ear and their derivation from the branchial arches. As Asher explains, despite Reichart's remarkable discovery regarding the embryology of mammalian ear bones and reptilian jaw bones, Reichart failed to make the connection to a larger theory of evolution despite his careful work in an era when German biology was at its zenith.

REFERENCES

Meldel GJ. 1865 Versuche uber Pflanzen-Hybriden. Verhandlungen des naturforschenden Vereines in Brunn, vol. iv.

Watson JD, Crick FHC. 1953. Molecular structure of nucleic acids. Nature 4356:737-738.

In: Scepticism: Hero and Villain
Editors: R. Calne and W. O'Reilly

ISBN: 978-1-62417-783-5
© 2013 Nova Science Publishers, Inc.

Chapter 6

EVOLUTIONARY BIOLOGY AND SCEPTICISM: THE RECEPTION OF DARWINISM IN 19TH CENTURY GERMAN EMBRYOLOGY

Robert Asher[*]
Department of Zoology, University Cambridge, UK

ABSTRACT

Karl Bogislaus Reichert (1811-1883) was a German embryologist whose lifespan overlapped almost entirely with that of Charles Darwin (1809-1882). In contrast to Darwin, Reichert is relatively unknown beyond historians of science and developmental biologists. Nevertheless, Reichert was the first to make one of the most important empirical observations in vertebrate biology of the last 200 years: the homology of mammalian ear ossicles with jaw elements of other vertebrates. In a different time and place, Reichert's remarkable discovery might have led him to recognize the larger theoretical framework later articulated by Darwin and Wallace, and given him much more recognition, both during his lifetime and today. Instead, Reichert was reluctant to extrapolate theoretical generalities from biological data, consistent with the inductive climate of his time. In this chapter, I describe how Karl Reichert comprises an example of how the conservatism of early 19th century scepticism, combined with much more banal personality conflicts with younger German scientists, impeded his recognition of what is today recognized as the basis for evolutionary biology: Darwinian descent with modification.

---

[*] E-mail: r.asher[at]zoo[dot]cam.ac.uk, tel. 01223 336 680.

INTRODUCTION

The Darwin-Wallace Theory

"Evolution" as now understood is encapsulated in Darwin's phrase "descent with modification": the differential reproductive success of organisms over geological time that vary in morphology and/or behaviour in ways that are patterned by a heritable genetic programme. This simple idea has revolutionized how we understand modern organisms as genealogically related to, and diversified from, past life on Earth.

Importantly, there are many features of "evolution" attributed to Darwin over the past 150 years that he did not advocate. For example, he never proposed to explain the origin of life itself (Darwin 1860: 514; Pereto et al. 2009). Furthermore, to some of his more fervent readers, "Darwinism" implied progress, inexorable increase of complexity over time, recapitulation of "lower" stages within the embryological development of "higher" animals, and was infamously alleged to be relevant to social and political questions in the form of Social Darwinism and eugenics. Natural historians of the 19th century (e.g., von Baer 1873), and many later biologists (e.g., Simpson 1953), rightfully objected to some or all of these accoutrements, and a fair reading of any of the six editions of *On the Origin of Species* makes clear that ideas such as recapitulation or eugenics were later elaborations, peripheral to the biological theory of descent with modification.

In addition, critics of the *Origin* noted ways in which evolutionary ideas had already been proposed. The notion that living things share common ancestry long predates the first edition of *On the Origin of Species* (1859). Darwin himself gave an exhaustive account in later editions of the *Origin* of his intellectual predecessors (e.g., 1872: p. xiv), including his grandfather Erasmus Darwin, Etienne Geoffroy St Hilaire, and Johann Wolfgang von Goethe, all writing independently of each other in approximately 1794-95. Starting on p. xiii, Darwin (1872) noted further publications from Lamarck, Wells, Herbert, Grant, Matthew, von Buch, Rafinesque, d'Halloy, and some two dozen others that, to varying degrees, foreshadowed what we now understand as Darwinian evolution via the mechanism of natural selection.

Induction

For a variety of reasons, pronouncements on biological evolution (or "transmutation") prior to the first edition of the *Origin* in 1859 were largely ignored or ridiculed. The latter reception was particularly acute in Britain among naturalists and philosophers regarding the 1844 publication of the pro-"transmutation" work *Vestiges of the Natural History of Creation*. Its author, Robert Chambers, did not formally reveal his identity during his lifetime, anticipating the hostile reception his book received (see Secord 2000). Naturalists of the time noted its many factual errors, and Darwin himself wrote that its early editions showed "little accurate knowledge and a great want of scientific caution" (Darwin 1872: xvii). Stated differently, Darwin (along with the substantial majority of other 19th century British naturalists) viewed Chambers' *Vestiges* as too much speculation about Life history based on not enough data from Life itself.

The eagerness to synthesise grand biological theories without a correspondingly profound empirical basis, as evident to varying degrees in the writings of Chambers and Lamarck, was anathema to influential, early 19th century naturalists such as Georges Cuvier (Rudwick 1997). To them, the ideal "science" was inductive, with scientists themselves subordinate to the task of impartially collecting the facts of nature, long before (if at all) coming to any theoretical framework by which one might understand those facts. Cuvier lamented the scarcity of inductivism in 18th and early 19th century natural philosophy. For example, he wrote that in geological treatises of the time,

> "each [author] devised some principle, found in advance a priori, or based only on a very small number of partial ... observations, and used all the forces he could muster to submit to it--- well or badly--- all the facts made known to him. But in the midst of all these endeavors, by an almost inconceivable misfortune, the extension of factual knowledge was almost entirely neglected" (Cuvier 1807; translated by Rudwick 1997: 104).

The mathematical and physical principles of our solar system as formulated by Isaac Newton were epitomized as the ideal of inductive science, concentrating first on "factual knowledge" and only later on the formulation of more general laws (see Hull 1973). This basic conception of scientific investigation---facts first, theory later---makes sense. However, its ideal form is perhaps impossible to actually put into practice and fails to recognize that investigators always have some *a priori* expectations about the mechanics of nature. Deductivism implies this process by which theorizing may take place prior to, or during, empirical observation. Today, we recognize that data collection is inevitably performed against such a framework, and do not demand of scientific practitioners any particular chronology in their cognitive processes to qualify as "scientific". Whether it is formulated sooner or later, a given theory may properly be confirmed or rejected (in whole or in part) depending on experimentation and data scrutiny. To believe that any human could serve as an impartial judge, sufficiently patient so as to refrain from theorizing until some rubicon of empirical buttressing has been crossed, is rightfully considered to be rather naive.

Our modern perspective differs from that of Darwin and Reichert during their formative years in the 1820s and 30s. The foil against which early 19th century naturalists such as Karl Ernst von Baer, Adam Sedgwick (mentors to Reichert and Darwin, respectively), and Georges Cuvier taught their pupils was not a naive, inductive, empirical scientist, but a speculative, deductive, armchair-bound gentleman naturalist. As a student in Königsberg and Berlin during the early 1830s, Karl Reichert was weaned in a climate grounded in empirical observation, particularly given the ever-increasing application of microscopes in biology, and the endless supply of new data they provided about a previously unknown world of anatomy. Darwin's professional formulation, which also began in the 1820s, differed greatly in that he had begun (and failed at) medical study at Edinburgh. Thereafter he was supposedly in training to be an Anglican clergyman at Cambridge. However, his influences at Cambridge (e.g., the geologist Adam Sedgwick) were similarly oriented towards the then-dominant inductive philosophy of natural science. Indeed, important commentators on that philosophy--- William Whewell and John Herschel---were prominent figures in Cambridge during Darwin's undergraduate years at Christ's College. Well into his career, and many years after his stay in Cambridge, Darwin positively assessed his own work to the extent that it emulated the inductive, Newtonian model, and by the 1850s he had earned respect from his peers precisely because he had a long record of sober, inductive scholarship (Hull 1973).

Few scientific theories are as relevant across such a broad spectrum of phenomena as Darwinian natural selection. Although (as noted above) natural selection does not attempt to explain life's origins, it still has massive explanatory power in posing a mechanism by which all of modern life attained its diversity from one or few aboriginal forms. At this scale of explanation, the weight of such a theory was clearly too much for the idealized model of "theory free" inductivism. The broad historical scope of evolutionary biology made it an awkward fit to the portrayals of Newton's methodology, although, as Darwin showed, his theory was eminently amenable to rational tests of very specific predictions that it made about the natural world.

One might therefore ask, given the inductive climate of its time, what was it about Darwin's *Origin of Species* that pushed evolutionary biology from the realm of speculation and towards acceptability among sceptics? Why did the lukewarm reaction of senior continental naturalists in the immediate aftermath of 1859 gradually give way to an enthusiastic reception in the younger generation of scientists in the 1860s and beyond? Here I advocate the view (Hull 1973; Gould 1980) that the causes include not only the sophistication and compelling nature of

Darwin's scholarship, but also the increased acceptance of deductive, rather than inductive, reasoning in 19th century science. The reception of evolutionary ideas in biology, combined with the climate of inductivism that pervaded the early 19th century, helps us to understand what it meant to be a "sceptic" during the decades on either side of the Darwinian revolution in biology.

KARL REICHERT AND PRE-1859 GERMAN EMBRYOLOGY

Karl Bogislaus Reichert was born on 20 December 1811 to Karl Reichert (senior) and Leopoldina Natzmer in the East Prussian town of Rastenburg (now Katrzyn, Poland). His biological father died when Karl junior was an infant. Shortly thereafter, and fortunately for the child, his mother re-married the headmaster of the local grammar school, Justus Krüger. Reichert's stepfather was good to him in many ways, including the assurance of a place in his *Gymnasium*. Karl Reichert junior did not put that education to waste, and was an accomplished pupil throughout his childhood (Kim 2000). For his post-secondary education, Reichert attended the University of Königsberg (now Kaliningrad, Russia), again with the financial support of his stepfather (Kim 2000). His most important influence during his student years in Königsberg, particularly given the course of his later embryological career, was probably the anatomist and embryologist Karl Ernst von Baer, whose lectures Reichert attended in 1831-32. As part of his Prussian military training, Reichert was then admitted to further study at the Friedrich-Wilhelm Institute of Medicine and Surgery in Berlin, where he arrived in the autumn of 1832. Starting in 1833, Reichert attended lectures from the renowned anatomist and physiologist Johannes Müller (1801-1858), who himself had arrived in Berlin from Bonn at around that time. Müller was probably the most influential German experimental anatomist of the 1830s and 40s. Several of the world's most important students of embryology, cell biology, and comparative anatomy of the 19th century owe their academic beginnings to Müller (Otis 2007). From his time in Bonn he had already begun mentoring Jakob Henle (1809-1885) and Theodor Schwann (1810-1882), both of whom moved with Müller to Berlin in the early 1830s. Müller's other students in Berlin included (in roughly chronological order) Robert Remak (1815-1865), Rudolf Virchow (1821-1902), Hermann von Helmholtz (1821-1894), Emil DuBois-Reymond (1818-1896), and Ernst Haeckel (1834-1919).

In the midst of this august company, Reichert was solid but not intellectually outstanding. Indeed, after completing his doctoral degree in 1836, at least two of his subsequent academic positions were offered first to his more dynamic peers. From 1843 to 1853, Reichert was Professor of Anatomy in Dorpat (now Tartu,

Estonia), a position which had previously been offered to Jakob Henle. Henle regarded Dorpat as an academic "Siberia" and had little hope for any fruitful research career there (Otis 2007: 54). The highly regarded Professorship of Anatomy in Berlin, the very position vacated by the untimely death of his esteemed mentor Müller, had also been offered to Henle first. Not only had Henle declined the offer (due in part to his reluctance to take on burdensome administrative responsibilities), but when the position was made available to Reichert, it was at a fraction of the salary (Kim 2000: 84). Thus, when the *Origin of Species* was published in 1859, Reichert had just succeeded his mentor Johannes Müller as Professor of Anatomy in Berlin. Due to Müller's sterling reputation, his new job might have been the most influential seat of comparative anatomy in the world. Yet Reichert is remembered today not for his scholarship as the Professor of Anatomy in Berlin (1858-1883), Breslau (now Wroclaw, Poland; 1853-1858), or Dorpat (1842-1852), but for the careful observations of cranial development in vertebrates he made as a student of Müller in Berlin a quarter-century before.

Development and Mammalian Ear Ossicles

During the mid 1830s, Reichert made one of the most extraordinary discoveries in the history of vertebrate biology: the common developmental origins of mammalian hearing bones and posterior jaw elements of non-mammalian vertebrates. By the time he was a student, Reichert's senior colleagues Karl Ernst von Baer (1792-1876) and Martin Heinrich Rathke (1793-1860) had already established the basis of comparative embryology (Russell 1916). In particular, von Baer established that embryos, however different as adults, are very similar in their early appearance. This was superficially similar to Haeckel's concept, the "biogenetic law", formulated decades later. However, von Baer's idea differed in that he specified merely that general features of an animal appear first, specialized features later (Gould 1977; Hopwood 2006), without a necessary implication of shared ancestry. One such generalized feature was identified in the 1820s by Rathke: "Visceralbogen" or visceral arches, slit-like features located behind the embryonic head (Figure 1). There are typically six pairs of arches on either side, although not all of them are visible in a given embryo at any one time. Each arch contains tissues from which adult structures develop, including blood vessels, glands, and bones. Importantly, in very different animals, the same adult structures derive from the same visceral arches. Reichert's discovery relates to how visceral arches contribute to the anatomy of hearing in vertebrates, particularly those that hear on land such as frogs, reptiles (including birds), and mammals.

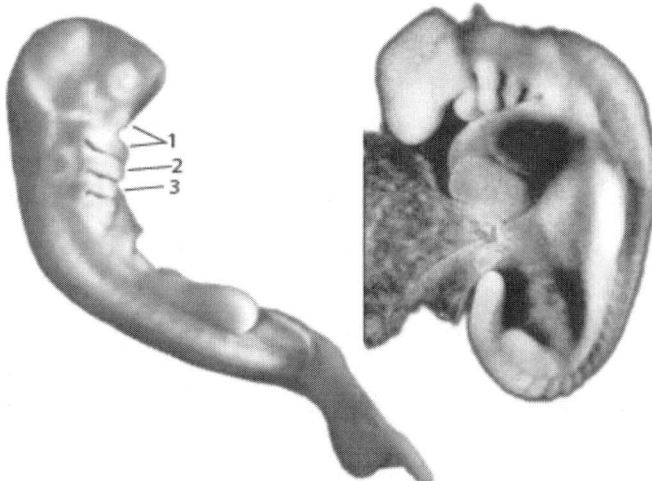

Figure 1. Photographs of early embryos of a sea turtle (*Lepidochelys olivacea*, left, courtesy of I. Werneberg and M. Sánchez-Villagra, Zürich) and human (right, courtesy of R. O'Rahilly and M. Richardson, Leiden). Numerals 1-3 adjacent to the turtle embryo correspond to visceral arches 1-3, evident immediately caudal to the head primordium (top) in both embryos (not to scale).

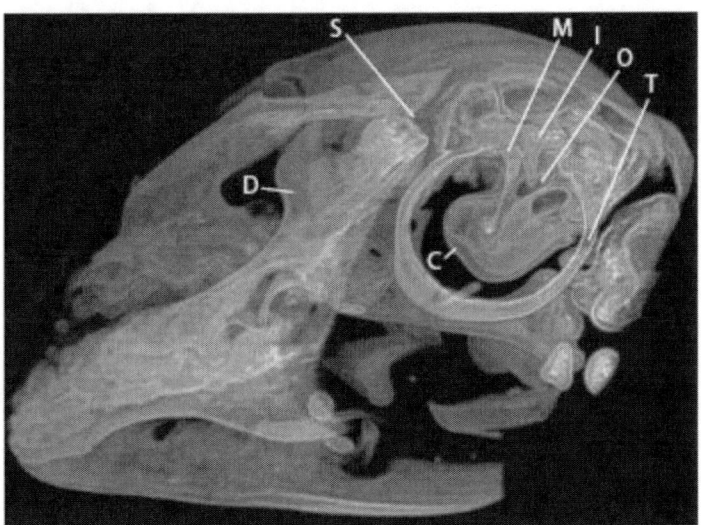

Figure 2. Computerized tomographic image of a foetal hyrax skull (*Procavia capensis*, Zoologisches Museum Berlin A1-19), viewed in ventrolateral aspect. Anterior is to the left, dorsal on top. As in all mammals, the circular tympanic bone ("T") frames the eardrum, to which the ossicular chain attaches: malleus ("M"), incus ("I"), stapes (unossified in this specimen), leading ultimately into the oval window ("O") to stimulate the organ of hearing inside the cochlea ("C"). The single jaw bone, or dentary ("D") articulates with the squamosal ("S") to form the uniquely mammalian dentary-squamosal jaw joint. Other vertebrates have just one bone connecting the eardrum to the oval window, and multiple bones in the jaw.

Hearing in most of these animals is facilitated by a tympanic membrane, against which abuts a delicate bone called the stapes or columella. This bone conveys vibrations from the membrane to a much smaller aperture in the skull called the oval window.

Although the adult appearance of a lizard and chicken are radically different, both hear via a tympanum-stapes mechanism. Reichert observed that the stapes bone in both derives from the second visceral arch, whereas the elements forming the jaw joint in reptiles derive from the first visceral arch. Mammals differ from frogs and reptiles in that they have two additional hearing bones (the malleus and incus) carrying acoustic vibrations from the tympanum to the stapes and oval window (Figure 2).

In addition, mammals have only one bone comprising the jaw, whereas other vertebrates have several. Before Reichert's dissertation work, the embryonic origins of these bones were unclear. With access to developmental series of frog, chicken, and pig, and the equipment and expertise in microscopy available from Johannes Müller in Berlin, Reichert observed that mammalian middle-ear bones begin as cartilaginous elements attached to the back of the embryonic jaw. As development proceeds, they take shape, become relatively smaller, and eventually migrate behind the jaw joint, detaching from the jaw at a relatively advanced stage. He found that as in frog and chicken, the stapes bone of the pig derives from the second visceral arch. To his astonishment, he found that the two "new" mammalian ear bones (incus and malleus) had the same embryonic origins from the first visceral arch as two bones--- the articular and quadrate--- that comprised the jaw joint in the frog and chicken. He made no mistake about the importance (and clarity) of his discovery:

> "Rarely does one find a part of the animal organism in which changes from its original formation are so clearly evident as the middle ear bones of mammals. One can hardly believe that their curious, diverse construction is comparable with simple, long-formed, cartilaginous visceral arches, or that from the latter any sort of complicated form may be derived; yet nevertheless it is in fact so. Namely, the first two visceral arches [of the embryo] comprise the structures out of which building blocks for the individual components of the middle ear bones derive" (Reichert 1837: 178).[1]

---

[1] "Selten trifft man auf einen Theil des thierischen Organismus, welcher das Urbild seines frühsten Zustandes so sehr im Verlaufe der weitern Entwickelung verändert, als die Gehörknöchelchen der Säugethiere. Kaum möchte man es glauben, so man ihren merkwürdigen, vielgeformten Bau mit der einfachen Längenform der knorpelartigen Visceralstreifen des Kopfes vergleicht, dass aus letzteren jene complizirte Form hervorgehen könne; und dennoch ist's in der That also. Die beiden ersten Visceralbogen nämlich sind es, welche aus ihren festeren Grundlagen einzelne Stücke für die Gehörknöchelchen hingeben"

Since the 19th century, advances in comparative anatomy (Gaupp 1899; Maier 1990; Sánchez et al. 2002), palaeontology (Allin 1975; Luo 2007), and developmental genetics (Tucker et al. 2004; Takechi & Kuratani 2010) have emphatically confirmed the evolutionary homology upon which Reichert had stumbled. At the close of the 19th century, Ernst Gaupp (1865-1916) revisited the study of Reichert (1837) and placed it into the evolutionary context by which it is understood today: the "Gaupp-Reichert" theory of mammalian ear ossicle homology (Gaupp 1912).

Reichert as an "Anti-Darwinian"

In making this discovery, Reichert was simply describing what he observed. He had no over-arching theory that would have predicted the continuity between the bones making up the jaw joint in a chicken (articular and quadrate) and those comprising part of the ossicular chain in a mammal (malleus and incus). The fact that they did show continuity could be connected to the vague belief that vertebrates were derived from a common plan or "archetype", but such a notion entailed no mechanism as to how or why animals as different as frog, chicken, and pig came to exhibit such an extraordinary level of anatomical similarity during their development, despite substantial differences as adults. Having accurately distilled a complicated developmental process by which mammalian ear ossicles take their shape from first and second arch-derived primordia, Reichert may have viewed his task as finished. Following the inductive ideal, he had accomplished the critical first steps of documentation and refrained from further theoretical speculation. Darwin's mechanism for explaining this remarkable homology via common descent and a shared developmental programme was over two decades away, but (as mentioned above) ideas concerning "transmutation" had occasionally surfaced in the literature, and Reichert would have been familiar with at least some of the writings of Lamarck and Goethe.

Reichert wrote little directly about evolutionary ideas. He has been described as "anti-Darwinian" (Weindling 1991: 71), and it is unlikely he would have accepted common ancestry as the basis for the shared embryonic pattern he uncovered. However, while he was not evolutionary in his theoretical outlook, it might be more accurate to recognize his hostility as "anti-Haeckelian" rather than "anti-Darwinian", in particular because of Haeckel's incorrect (and unnecessary) over-emphasis on developmental recapitulation as a part of "evolution". By the time Darwin's idea had been published in 1859, Reichert had already been drawn into a dispute with his younger rivals regarding the details of another major advance of 19th century German science: the cell theory (see below and Weindling 1991). This likely made it more difficult for Reichert to accept other theories, such as natural selection, advocated by younger scientists like Haeckel.

Reichert recognized, as did von Baer and Rathke before him, many facts of animal development that were contradictory to the proposal that "higher" organisms necessarily repeated adult stages of "lower" ones during development. This idea, what was to become Haeckel's so-called "biogenetic law", had a long history (see Russell 1916: chapter 7), and was endorsed in whole or in part by the earlier generation of philosopher-naturalists, including Etienne Geoffroy St. Hilaire (1772-1844), Lorenz Oken (1779-1851), and Johann Friedrich Meckel (1781-1833). Anchored to the data he observed in vertebrate embryos, Reichert rejected the so-called "law" of repetition or recapitulation:

> "The idea that the embryo of higher animals, in its individual development, passes through those of the lower animal world, even if we rightfully restricted the signficance attributed by an observer to the vertebrates, is not supported by the current state of science" (Reichert 1837: 143).[2]

In other words, embryos of "higher" animals do not repeat the stages of "lower" ones during their development. Reichert saw that animal embryos resembled each other greatly in early phases of their development, and that their differences became more acute as growth proceeded. However, he was cognizant of the differences across species, and that a "frog" or "fish" stage during chicken or pig development was simply absent.

This is actually a modern viewpoint (Richardson et al. 1998) and recognizes that no innate trend compels one organism during its early development to exhibit an adult stage of another. Rather, the developing embryo is just as integrated an animal as the adult; function is relevant during the entire life cycle of an animal, from fertilized egg to maturity. Thus, even ignoring for a moment the heated disputes about cell theory, Reichert rejected developmental recapitulation, conflated as it was into Haeckel's version of Darwinism. For Reichert, it was as an overly theoretical and speculative concept he and others had refuted decades before (Russell 1916).

---

[2] "so ist ... die Idee, dass der Embryo der höheren Thiere die Stufen der niedern Thierwelt in seiner individuellen Entwickelung durchlaufe, wodurch die Beobachter ihre Deutung unterstützen, selbst dann, wenn wir diesen Satz, wie mit Recht, nur auf die Wirbelthiere reduciren, nach dem jetzigen Stand der Wissenschaft nicht haltbar."

The Cell Theory and Rivalry with the Younger Generation

Reichert was sceptical of evolution and certain other innovations of 19th century biology. Other high-profile German biologists of the mid-19th century, such as Max Schultze (1825-1874), Karl Gegenbaur (1826-1903), and Ernst Haeckel (1834-1919) espoused major theoretical advances besides Darwinism, such as the cell theory, although these ideas did not represent simple points on a one-dimensional spectrum. Advocates of the cell-theory were not necessarily advocates of Darwinism (e.g., Theodor Schwann, 1810-1880). Schwann was a friend of Reichert and overlapped with him in the lab of Johannes Müller during the early 1830s. Schwann famously collaborated with the botanist Matthias Schleiden (1804-1881) to make the discovery that both animals and plants are composed of very similar building blocks: cells. Cell walls in plants were much more visible with the microscopes of the 1830s, dependent as they were on natural light. Animals lack cell walls, and their cell membranes are less obvious in poor light without proper stains or thin sections. The shared experience of a botanist (Schleiden) and a zoologist (Schwann) overcame these obstacles to recognize the continuity of animal and plant cells, which has since formed the basis for modern cell biology.

As a pioneer of microscopic anatomy and embryology, Reichert knew that living tissue was comprised of individual cells. At issue, however, was not their mere existence, but the extent to which animal and plant cells resembled each other in their composition and mode of genesis. In particular, it was not obvious if the nucleus and other cellular components were reformed in their entirety, or if there might be continuity in these elements from old to newly formed cells. Integral to the version of the cell theory championed by younger German biologists (e.g., Schultze, Haeckel, O. Hertwig) was the notion that the contents of the nucleus were carried on from one generation to the next. Reichert, in contrast, wrote of the importance of the yolk sac for cell origins, that no cell could exist without a cell-membrane, and that therefore cellular contents were not continuous across generations. Somehow, he thought, an as-yet unknown mechanism led to the complete reformation of the nucleus during cell-birth. Those who supported the continuity of the nucleus across generations, Reichert argued, did not base their conclusions on appropriate stages of developing cells. Without the relevant empirical basis for observing cell origins, i.e., sufficiently early stages, "the moment of genesis will be completely missed"[3] (Reichert 1845: 40).

As the 1860s progressed, biologists such as Haeckel, Schultze, and Gegenbaur were increasingly intolerant of older scientists, such as Reichert, who did not

---

[3] "wird das genetische Moment gänzlich vermisst".

accept either the cell theory or Darwinism (Weindling 1991). Haeckel in particular wrote scathing critiques of Reichert's views on the anatomy of marine invertebrates, noting at least one case in which Reichert mistook an artefact of lighting for a cellular organelle. Here is a sample of the tone by which Haeckel addressed Reichert in an 1869 publication:

> "I have clearly demonstrated the utter worthlessness of Reichert's assertions, and the perversity of his misrepresentations, and at the same time set forth the history of this strange controversy. Nevertheless, Reichert has not been deterred from continuing his publications on this subject ... On reading [Reichert], we seem to have retrograded about half a century" (Haeckel 1869: 225).

This particular disagreement concerned the microscopic anatomy of "rhizopodans", a diverse group of protists which includes the amoeba. Was the cell interior of these animals, what had been referred to as the "sarcode" or protoplasm, common in its composition across organisms, and was there material continuity across generations? Haeckel believed so; Reichert disagreed. Although Haeckel was correct in certain respects regarding his interpretation of the cell theory (e.g., that cellular contents were consistent in diverse animals, that a cell can exist without a membrane, and that the substance of the nucleus is passed on from parent to daughter cells), in other regards he too made mistakes (e.g., that recapitulation was a "law"). Whatever the details of their disagreement were, by the tone of their exchange it is evident that Reichert and Haeckel represented opposite poles of a major shift in German biological thought in the mid-19th century. This shift is encapsulated in the 1891 recollections of the British-born, German physiologist William Thierry Preyer regarding the contrast he observed from his perspective as a student in the early 1860s and as a professor in 1891:

> "Darwin's teachings were viewed as completely mistaken almost everywhere at that time [early 1860s], whereas today [in 1891], not a single competent natural scientist can be found who does not recognize the broadening of natural comprehension and methodological progress [of Darwin's teachings] (Preyer 1891: 357).[4]

---

[4] The (awkwardly written) German is quoted directly from a web-summary of Preyer's 1891 recollections: http://tinyurl.com/preyer-letter (accessed 29 Sept 2011). Text translated here into English is shown below in bold type. In addition, I've included the immediately preceding passage in which Preyer mentions Reichert by name as one of his university lecturers who was at best indifferent to Darwin: "Weder von meinen Altersgenossen noch von den Universitaetslehrern, deren Vorlesungen ich besuchte, Bronn, Peters, Pagenstecher, Reichert, um nur einige wenige zu nennen, hat damals, zu Anfang der sechziger Jahre ... mich auf dem betretenen Wege fortzuschreiten ermuthigt. Im Gegentheil, [fast] allgemein wurde zu jener

CONCLUSION

Karl Reichert contributed substantially to the empirical basis of biology, most famously for his recognition of the developmental homologies of the vertebrate jaw. He did so at a time when an entirely new class of facts about biology---i.e., microscopic anatomy---was just becoming broadly accessible to students of natural science at relatively low cost. Furthermore, the dominant, inductive scientific philosophy of his time (see Hull 1973) exalted empirics, not theoretics. It is therefore reasonable to expect that a capable---if not brilliant---mind such as his would hesitate to follow through on any observed, large-scale continuities between biological generations or species, however strongly his data on cranial development would have supported this.

In addition to his inductive, philosophical reluctance to stray from data collection into the realm of biological theory, Reichert had very banal, personal, and frankly unpleasant reasons to disagree with the younger generation of German embryologists, most of whom (particularly Haeckel) were fervid advocates of Darwinism and very antagonistic towards Reichert. It is possible that Reichert's cell-theory adversaries (e.g., Gegenbaur, Haeckel, Schultze, Hertwig, who themselves mischaracterized certain aspects of evolution) were even more influential in negatively forming his opinion on Darwinism than any overly inductive orientation he would have picked up as a student of von Baer and Müller in the early 1830s. Karl Reichert aptly deciphered part of the pattern of evolution; however, through a combination of personal and philosophical reasons, he left comprehension of the process behind that pattern to his younger colleagues.

ACKNOWLEDGMENTS

I thank Professor Sir Roy Calne and Dr. William O'Reilly for inviting me to participate in this volume. I thank Prof. Wolfgang Maier, Dr. Nick Hopwood, Prof. Marcelo Sánchez-Villagra, and Mr. Uwe Dörmann for comments on the text, Mr. Uwe Dörmann and Dr. Young-Ok Kim for access to Dr. Kim's medical dissertation on Karl Reichert, and Dr. Vera Warmuth for discussion of WT Preyer. Figure two is derived from a project on mammalian skeletal diversity

---

Zeit Darwin's Lehre fuer vollstaendig verfehlt angesehen, waehrend [jetzt] nicht ein einziger competenter Naturforscher gefunden werden kann, der [sie durch die] herbeigefuehrten Erweiterungen der Naturerkenntniss und methodologischen Fortschritte nicht [anerkennt]." (Preyer 1891: 357)"

made possible by the Leverhulme Trust. For further reading I would recommend the references listed in the Literature Cited, below, and *Darwin and His Critics* by David Hull (1973, University of Chicago Press), *Müller's Lab* by Laura Otis (2007, Oxford University Press), and *The Tragic Sense of Life* by Robert J. Richards (2008, University of Chicago Press).

REFERENCES

Allin, E. F. (1975) Evolution of Mammalian Middle-Ear. *Journal of Morphology, 147*, 403-437.

Chambers, R. (1844) *Vestiges of the natural history of creation.* London,: J. Churchill.

Darwin, C. (1859) *On the origin of species by means of natural selection.* London,: J. Murray.

Darwin, C. (1860) *On the origin of species by means of natural selection, or, The preservation of favoured races in the struggle for life* (5th thousand. ed.). London,: J. Murray.

Darwin, C. (1872) *On the origin of species by means of natural selection, or, The preservation of favoured races in the struggle for life* (11th thousand. ed.). London,: J. Murray.

Gaupp, E. (1899) Ontogenese und Phylogenese des Schallleitenden Apparates bei den Wirbeltieren. *Ergebnisse der Anatomie und Entwicklungsgeschichte, 8*, 990-1149.

Gaupp, E. (1912) Die Reichertsche Theorie, Hammer-, Amboss- und Kieferfrage. *Archiv für Anatomie und Entwicklungsgeschichte, 1913*, 1-416.

Gould, S. J. (1977). *Ontogeny and phylogeny.* Cambridge, Mass.: Belknap Press of Harvard University Press.

Gould, S. J. (1980) Darwin's Middle Road. *In: The panda's thumb: more reflections in natural history.* Norton, New York, pp. 59-68.

Haeckel, E. (1869) Monograph of Monera. *Quarterly Journal of Microscopical Science, s2-9*, 219-232.

Hopwood, N. (2006). Pictures of evolution and charges of fraud - Ernst Haeckel's embryological illustrations. *Isis, 97*(2), 260-301.

Hull, D. L. (1973) *Darwin and his critics; the reception of Darwin's theory of evolution by the scientific community.* Cambridge, Mass.,: Harvard University Press.

Kim, Y.-O. (2000) "Karl Bogislaus Reichert (1811-1883) Sein Leben und seine Forschungen zur Anatomie und Entwicklungsgeschichte." Medical Dissertation, Universität Mainz., Mainz.

Luo, Z. X., Chen, P. J., Li, G. & Chen, M. (2007) A new eutriconodont mammal and evolutionary development in early mammals. *Nature, 446*, 288-293.

Maier, W. (1990). Phylogeny and Ontogeny of Mammalian Middle-Ear Structures. Netherlands Journal of Zoology, 40(1-2), 55-74.

Otis, L. (2007) *Müller's lab*. Oxford ; New York: Oxford University Press.

Pereto, J., Bada, J. L. & Lazcano, A. (2009) Charles Darwin and the Origin of Life. *Origins of Life and Evolution of Biospheres, 39*, 395-406.

Preyer, W. T. (1891) Briefe von Darwin. mit Erinnerungen und Erlaeuterungen. *Deutsche Rundschau, 17*, 356-390.

Reichert, K. B. (1837) Über die Visceralbogen der Wirbelthiere im allgemeinen und deren Metamorphosen bei den Vögeln und Säugethieren. *Archiv für Anatomie, Physiologie, und wissenschaftliche Medizin, 1837*, 120-220.

Reichert, K. B. (1845) *Bemerkungen zur vergleichenden Naturforschung im Allgemeinen und vergleichende Beobachtungen über das Bindegewebe und die verwandten Gebilde*. Dorpat (Tartu): W. Gläser.

Richardson, M. K., Hanken, J., Selwood, L., Wright, G. M., Richards, R. J., Pieau, C., et al. (1998) Haeckel, embryos, and evolution. *Science, 280*, 983-+.

Rudwick, M. J. S. & Cuvier, G. (1997) *Georges Cuvier, fossil bones, and geological catastrophes: new translations & interpretations of the primary texts*. Chicago: University of Chicago Press.

Russell, E. S. (1916; reprinted 1982). *Form and Function: a Contribution to the History of Animal Morphology*. Chicago: University of Chicago Press.

Sánchez-Villagra, M. R., Gemballa, S., Nummela, S., Smith, K. K. & Maier, W. (2002) Ontogenetic and phylogenetic transformations of the ear ossicles in marsupial mammals. *Journal of Morphology, 251*, 219-238.

Secord, J. A. (2000). *Victorian sensation: the extraordinary publication, reception, and secret authorship of Vestiges of the natural history of creation*. Chicago: University of Chicago Press.

Simpson, G. G. (1953) *The major features of evolution*. New York,: Columbia University Press.

Takechi, M. & Kuratani, S. (2010) History of Studies on Mammalian Middle Ear Evolution: A Comparative Morphological and Developmental Biology Perspective. *Journal of Experimental Zoology Part B-Molecular and Developmental Evolution, 314B*, 417-433.

Tucker, A. S., Watson, R. P., Lettice, L. A., Yamada, G. & Hill, R. E. (2004) Bapx1 regulates patterning in the middle ear: altered regulatory role in the transition from the proximal jaw during vertebrate evolution. *Development, 131*, 1235-1245.

von Baer, K. E. (1873) Zum Streit über den Darwinismus. *Augsberger Allgemeine Zeitung, 130*, 1986-1988.

Weindling, P. (1991) *Darwinism and social Darwinism in imperial Germany: the contribution of the cell biologist, Oscar Hertwig, 1849-1922.* Stuttgart; New York; Mainz: G. Fischer; Akademie der Wissenschaften und der Literatur.

In: Scepticism: Hero and Villain
Editors: R. Calne and W. O'Reilly

ISBN: 978-1-62417-783-5
© 2013 Nova Science Publishers, Inc.

Chapter 7

SCEPTICISM IN MEDICINE, ORGAN TRANSPLANTATION, GENE AND STEM CELL THERAPY

Roy Calne

ABSTRACT

The journey from scepticism to acceptance has a remarkably predictable history. The initial hypothesis is treated with disbelief and dismissed by the experts and the individual responsible may be shunned or even persecuted. When the hypothesis is validated with scientific evidence, the concept is accepted and the next stage is for the previously scoffing experts to develop a specific memory loss and claim that they knew that it was true all along.

The last stage usually involves one of the most strident early sceptics to claim that he had thought of it in the first place, and the originator is ushered into obscurity. Although this is a common tale, the original scepticism is usually based on received wisdom and this raises the ambiguity of scepticism, on the one hand the questioning of received wisdom but in the example above scepticism is actually initiated and fuelled by received wisdom.

INTRODUCTION

And let it be noted that there is no more delicate matter to take in hand, nor more dangerous to conduct, nor more doubtful in its success, than to set up as a leader in the introduction of changes. For he who innovates will have for his enemies all those who are well off under the existing order of things, and only the lukewarm supporters in those who might be better off under the new. This lukewarm temper arises partly from the fear of adversaries who have the laws on their side and partly from the incredulity of mankind, who will never admit the merit of anything new, until they have seen it proved by the event.

"The Prince"
N. Machiavelli
1513

In this chapter I will attempt to examine the double-edged sword of scepticism in medicine and in the context of specific examples, organ transplantation, gene and stem cell therapy. Organ transplantation, initially the target of powerful, sceptical dismissal, having gone through a stuttering gestation, both experimentally and clinically, is now accepted as valuable therapy for people otherwise doomed to early death from untreatable destruction of vital organs. Now, although there is plenty of room for improvement in safely managing the patient's tendency to reject the graft, the treatment is now so successful that more than 1 million patients having benefitted worldwide and the main concern is the shortage of organs to transplant, from both living volunteers and the dead. The mismatch between organs available and those in need increases every year and as the results improve the shortage becomes more severe and a solution increasingly difficult. Gene and stem cell therapy became realistic goals for the management of a variety of diseases, once the structure of DNA was established in 1953 and the multi-potent, physiological roles of a variety of stem cells was observed. Media hype has waxed and waned without obvious translation from the laboratory to the clinic of both these therapeutic approaches. Gradually the important details are being clarified so that targets can be defined, for without that information it is unreasonable to expect significant progress. Nevertheless, in this interim period before evidence-based therapies can be offered, there is unfortunately room for unprincipled "quackery" to take advantage of desperately afflicted patients and provide untested and often dangerous therapies without a scientific foundation purely for financial gain. Sadly this is deserving of scepticism and also condemnation. Nevertheless once these therapies are available and prove to be of value, scepticism will vanish and the criminal market in financial exploitation of desperate hope will no longer exist.

Throughout the ages medicine has been a treasure trove for scepticism. Religious leaders of the earliest civilisations took on the responsibility of caring for the sick with a variety of empirical and often harmful actions, perhaps most striking literally, to make a hole in the skull "to let out evil spirits" The persistence of witch-doctors to this day and the belief in them by many of their followers, demonstrates blind trust and faith in diagnoses and treatments that have no scientific basis but are attended to with considerable elaborate ceremony. For thousands of years there was little real progress in medicine although some effective treatments were developed empirically. For example the painkilling effects of opium extract from the poppy have been known for 6000 years. The alleviation of distressing heart failure symptoms by a digitalis extract from the purple foxglove, resulted from careful observation by an English general practitioner, William Withering in 1785. A few years later Edward Jenner introduced vaccination to prevent smallpox, having noticed that the milder but similar disease of cowpox in milkmaids appeared to render the sufferer resistant to catching the more lethal smallpox. Other time-honoured treatments had no scientific basis. Blood-letting was extremely popular and fashionable for hundreds of years despite there being not a shred of evidence that it did any good and many observations that it usually made the patients worse. There are still many advocates and believers in homeopathy and alternative medicine. Scientific medicine required a platform of anatomy and physiology from which to understand and treat diseases with some confidence that the patient might be helped. The most important advance in medicine was the demonstration by William Harvey in 1628 that blood circulated from the lungs to the heart and then to the rest of the body. To explain this circulation Harvey had to postulate the existence of minute capillary blood vessels that could not be observed before the development of microscopy. Harvey was justifiably fearful that his colleagues would regard his observations with scepticism, but also that he might be persecuted by the Church for advocating concepts of the blood circulation that differed from the received wisdom derived from Aristotle and adopted by clerical dogma. Following Harvey and with increasing confidence in the importance of studying human anatomy and physiology, a crescendo of medical advances occurred with the understanding of bacterial, parasitic and viral causes of diseases. A huge leap forward was the development in the 1940s of an effective antibiotic, penicillin, which heralded intense and successful efforts to find new antibiotics to increase the therapeutic armoury. Safe anaesthesia allowed surgeons to operate on all parts of the body including the brain and the heart-lung machine enabled the circulation to be temporarily substituted by a pump with an oxygenator taking on the function of the lungs. The more medicine and surgery advance the greater are the expectations for successful treatment of diseases that so far have resisted the new techniques.

I will consider briefly the transplantation of vital organs which has now passed through the phase of scepticism into general acceptance and then areas of genetic engineering and stem cell treatment that have received media hype far in excess of the state of the art. The building blocks are there but there would appear to be important missing pieces that remain to be discovered. By analogy blood transfusion was attempted, both experimentally and therapeutically, in the 17th century. The polymath architect Christopher Wren was one of a group of enthusiastic experimenters who showed that the procedure of blood transfusion could be done using a sharpened feather quill instead of a hypodermic needle. But at that time there was no concept that there were important blood groups nor was there any way of preventing blood from clotting, so the results were disastrous and when attempted in patients usually fatal. It required these previously unknown factors to be clarified before blood transfusion could be done safely. This was an important lesson that the mere performance of an operation did not ensure success if there was ignorance of vital relevant physiological information. In what is now called "regenerative medicine" there have been significant advances in understanding how tissues are differentiated in the embryo, the role of genes producing specific proteins and micro-manipulation of cells would seem to justify cautious optimism that therapeutic applications will be found. No doubt stumbling blocks will also be encountered. It can be useful to be aware of one's ignorance, for example consider the following in three species, the dog, the newt and the Zebra fish; the dog and man have been together for thousands of years but the dog's lifespan is usually between 15 and 16 years. The life span of humans until recently was around 60 years with exceptions reaching beyond 100. Longevity has certainly increased, but apart from certain biblical characters, to live beyond 100 is unusual. But why is the dog's life span so much less than humans? The dog cares for its young for a much shorter period and the young become independent and in the wild hunt in packs after about 6 months, but then after 15 years ageing sets in and this process is not understood. It seems to be biologically programmed.

The newt is a primitive amphibian that has highly advanced regenerative properties, so that if it loses a tail or a limb replacements grow rapidly with remarkable accuracy. After amputation, a small number of residual stem cells cooperate to produce bone, muscle, nerves, blood vessels and skin, with joints to allow appropriate articulation in the limbs. Unfortunately there is no evidence in man that such cells with these extraordinary properties exist or could be organised as in the newt. Cell differentiation to produce the separate organs occurs in the foetus of all species, but we do not know if a similar process might be possible to engineer in an adult human. The Zebra fish is very popular in biological studies because it is small, translucent and easy to keep in the laboratory and its heart has remarkable powers of regeneration after it has been damaged. We know that stem cells are present in all tissues in the body including the heart and presumably these cells participate in the repair of the Zebra fishes' damaged hearts, but again this does not mean that the stem cells in human hearts would have the same capabilities. For scientists to work towards this end makes sense and is reasonable, but early success cannot be assumed. There are many other examples of our ignorance but the limitations of what we know and can do is no deterrent to quack doctors to offer stem cell and gene therapy to desperate patients, who will try anything if they can be persuaded there is even a small chance of success. These criminal doctors manipulate the fears of vulnerable patients to extract high fees.

The causes of most diseases and their mode of spread were quite unknown until the existence of bacteria was visualised in the late 18th century. The next step was to recognise that certain bacteria were responsible for common scourges, for example, tuberculosis, cholera and plague. Blood-borne parasites were shown to cause malaria . Very much smaller organisms called viruses were later identified as the cause of influenza, yellow fever, rabies, measles, chickenpox, smallpox and more recently several forms of hepatitis and HIV Aids. Spread of infectious diseases is sometimes by direct contact, in other cases there are insect vectors such as mosquitoes, flies, and fleas. In plague, in addition to fleas, there is an intermediate host – the rat. An understanding of the rat-flea-human spread of plague came to a young French Doctor, Paul-Louis Simond, in the 1890s who, in a plague outbreak in India, listened to villagers who told him rats came out of the sewers, coughing and vomiting blood and then died; 3-4 days later humans are struck down by Bubonic Plague. Dr. Simond suspected rat fleas were leaving the cold bodies of the dead rats and moving to the warmth of humans. At enormous personal risk he dissected affected rats and found the plague bacillus. His observations were treated with extreme scepticism by the medical hierarchy. They were later accepted and publicised by others who carelessly forgot the original brilliant work of Simond who was relegated to obscurity. Life is often sad and unfair.

Now we have unravelled the often far-from obvious trail of infection. We have developed antibiotics that will control or cure many ailments. The other mode of prevention and control of disease is to harness and enhance the body's natural tendency to battle infection by immunising with vaccines, so that antibodies and protective cells are primed and ready to eliminate infecting organisms. These few examples of important medical advances are the flowering of the scientific "seeds" identified and planted as a result of our understanding of anatomy and physiology. Hygienic concepts, antiseptic and later aseptic surgery coupled with the provision of clean drinking water, uncontaminated by sewage were important advances in reducing morbidity, mortality and misery. "Evidence based medicine" demonstrated the harm caused by smoking, alcohol, radioactive materials and asbestos, but *pari passu* with these well-researched causative associations with disease. there has been a plethora of pseudoscientific claims pounced on with delight and usually distorted by the media. Breast feeding, red wine, aspirin, statins, have each been hailed as almost miraculous causes of good health and longevity one day, and the devil's strategies for harm the next. The only defence from such confusing declamations is to stop reading newspapers, listening to radio and most difficult of all, watching television. The advice of St Benedict is wise *"all things in moderation"* including *"drinking up to one hemina of wine a day"*. Clearly since the beginning of human civilisation there has been and still is fertile soil for scepticism in medicine, especially before scientific evidence was available to determine rational practice. Peter Medawar when told of experimental results "too good to be true", commented *"curious, if it can be repeated independently it would be interesting"*. A measured sceptical response which left room for later modification if the facts demanded acceptance.

ORGAN TRANSPLANTATION

Organ Transplantation passed through a fairly long phase of criticisms. As a medical student in the 1950s we were allocated patients with whom we had a special personal responsibility. I presented my case of a boy about my age who was dying of kidney failure. The senior consultant who was presiding said *"well you must make him comfortable but sadly he will be dead in two weeks"*. Without any background knowledge I asked could he not have a graft of a kidney, thinking in terms of horticulture. I was told no, and when I asked why not I was told *"it can't be done"*. By this time my colleagues were becoming concerned for my own future welfare and I was prodded in the ribs and told to shut up and not to ask any more stupid questions. Over coffee later we discussed the surgery that would be necessary to transplant a kidney and it seemed that there would need to be plumbing junctions of three vessels, an artery, a vein and the urine drainage tube, the ureter. Surgical techniques at that time could accomplish these tasks, so I was still baffled that my suggestion of a kidney graft was condemned out of hand. I had no idea of the phenomenon of graft rejection, a very powerful biological defence evolved to protect us from infections. Unfortunately tissue grafted from one individual to another is recognised as foreign by the body and destroyed as if it was an invading virus. Medawar and his colleagues described the mechanism of rejection of skin grafts during the 2nd World War, since the subject was of great importance in the treatment of burns, particularly in aircraft crews. The main surgical skin grafting was from one part of the body to another part of the same person, an autograft, but it was also known that identical twins derived from the same egg would accept grafts from each other. The techniques of grafting skin were well established and some surgeons had looked into the feasibility of transplanting the kidney in experimental animals and showed that the kidney could withstand the surgical trauma of being removed and then transplanted with rapid restoration of its function, if the transplant operation was performed expeditiously and as with skin grafts autotransplants were accepted indefinitely.

Medawar was asked if he could distinguish between identical and non-identical cattle twins. He felt this could be determined by skin grafting; identical twins would accept the twin's skin, non-identical calf twins would reject the twin's skin. The result of reciprocal skin grafting between both identical and non-identical cattle twins was a disappointment to the scientists, since the non-identical twins also accepted the skin grafts from their twin indefinitely. In trying to understand what had happened they felt that the anatomy and physiology of the bovine placenta could be the critical factor, since it is unique in that the circulation of one twin reciprocally crosses to that of the other. It had been shown previously that non-identical cattle twins often had red blood cells of different blood groups in the circulating blood, for example in man it would be the equivalent to having some red cells group A and some group B, which does not occur. It was postulated that in the developing foetus the immune system is not able to determine between self and non-self products.

Medawar and his colleagues felt that the phenomena was worthy of further investigation. They found that exchange of tissue between incubating hens' eggs and tissue injected from one line of inbred mice into another during foetal development, rendered the animals that survived capable of accepting grafts from the donor of the tissue. The phenomena was called "specific immunological tolerance", a result of foetal or neonatal exposure to prospective donor tissue. Although there was no obvious clinical application of the work the biological observations were extremely important and raised the question "is there any way in which the immune system in adult life could be rendered similar to that in the foetus with plasticity to accept a graft, with the proviso that this would need to be only temporary so that normal immunity could protect the individual once the graft was established?" At the time that these biological experiments were underway, surgeons in Boston had in 1954 transplanted successfully a kidney between identical twins where the donor was healthy and the recipient was dying of kidney failure. This is by analogy the same as an autograft. The demonstration of successful surgical organ grafting to a patient brought the subject to the attention of physicians and surgeons worldwide. If the operation could be done, why was it so difficult to prevent the inexorable rejection of a graft that occurs in virtually all transplants that are not between identical twins? Accidents from radioactive exposure and the devastation resulting from the atomic bomb destruction of Hiroshima and Nagasaki showed that bone marrow cells that produce red and white blood cells were especially vulnerable to gamma irradiation. Deprived of the white cells that are responsible for immune protection, patients subjected to irradiation of the bone marrow usually died but could in some circumstances be rescued by injection of un-irradiated bone marrow into the blood stream. The injected bone marrow cells have a natural tendency to home from the blood to the bone marrow and if they were taken from an identical twin they would re-populate the patient's immune and blood-forming system. There was a danger that bone marrow that was not perfectly matched would react against the recipient called a graft-versus-host disease, which could be lethal but in some circumstances may be valuable in destroying leukaemia cells when bone marrow transplantation was used as therapy for leukaemic malignancy.

Surgeons wishing to develop kidney transplantation attempted to use irradiation to the whole body of the potential recipient to damage or destroy completely the immune system and then replace it with bone marrow from the potential donor. Unfortunately this led to disaster, the unprotected patient developing fatal infections and rejection of the organ graft could not be prevented. The almost 100% failure did not deter some surgeons from continuing with total body irradiation and this led to profound and justifiable scepticism from their colleagues. Only two patients were reported to have done well, and in each case they received a kidney from a non-identical twin and subsequently, as tissue typing became established, it was shown that the donor and the recipient were identically matched for the main tissue types which statistically would occur in 25% of sibling transplants. The tissue types are distinct from red blood groups which also need to be compatible. After much trial and error reliable techniques for tissue typing were established and they followed the rules of Gregor Mendel, namely that 25% would be identical, 25% would have no factors in common and 50% would be half-matched.

Since irradiation was not shown to advance organ transplantation, alternative approaches were made. 6-Mercaptopurine, a drug used to treat leukaemia was found to prolong kidney graft survival in treated animals. The first trial of this compound and a close chemical derivative "Azathioprine" in patients was not very effective, but when cortisone was added there were some long-term good results of kidney transplantation and cautious attempts were made at liver and heart transplantation as the more complicated surgical techniques were developed to transplant these organs. Some 20 years after the first use of Azathioprine and cortisone, another agent, Cyclosporine isolated from an earth fungus was shown to prolong survival of skin and organ grafts experimentally and its use in patients increased the one year functional survival from 50% to 80%. For many years a cocktail of Azathioprine, cortisone and Cyclosporine was used in most centres, Cyclosporine being a watershed, liberating the transplant surgeons from oppressive scepticism which was quite shortly inverted to reluctant acceptance and then enthusiastic advocacy. Prior to Cyclosporine there were about 10 centres worldwide seriously pursuing organ grafting but within two or three years of the introduction of Cyclosporine there were more than 1000, and good results were obtained in liver, heart and pancreas grafts. Immunosuppression is still far from perfect. There was a phase of giving doses that were too large which had serious side-effects and now the move is towards minimal immunosuppression. The goal of tolerance when no maintenance immunosuppression will be necessary has not been reached except in a few cases of liver grafting, despite the study and trial of many new agents. Monoclonal antibodies, which selectively destroy the cells that cause rejection, have been introduced to the clinic. Recently a policy to pre-empt rejection has become popular, for example giving a powerful anti-lymphocyte monoclonal antibody "Campath" at the time of surgery, followed by a really low dose of maintenance drug. The strategy has been called *"prope"* or almost tolerance. A very low dose of maintenance immunosuppression with few side effects may be sufficient for the wellbeing of the graft and the patient.

Although results are steadily improving, rejection, the side effects of the drugs, and the recurrence of the patient's original disease still cause failures. Nevertheless, patients have lived with good health and normal quality of life with the organ still functioning 40 years after kidney, liver and heart transplantation. With more than a million recipients of organ grafts worldwide, a major and increasing problem is the shortage of donor organs. The value of a life-saving organ to somebody otherwise doomed is more than any material wealth, so it is not surprising that the shortage has resulted in serious moral and ethical dilemmas, with accusations of criminal activity of stealing organs from patients having routine surgical treatment or even murder in order to obtain donors. Certainly there has been widespread exploitation by organ brokers in developing countries of poor people being paid for a kidney or a portion of the liver. Organs have been used for years from executed prisoners, especially in China.

Medical tourism is an increasing activity but a travel expedition, depending on an execution, is considered morally wrong by major international and national scientific societies; despite these condemnations the practice continues. It would seem that organ transplantation is a victim of its own success. The medical indications for an organ graft are becoming wider with older and sicker patients being considered, but the number of donors from road traffic accidents and brain haemorrhages is decreasing. Permission from their next of kin is often denied and the sceptics might justifiably claim that organ donor shortage is an insoluble problem.

GENETIC ENGINEERING AND STEM CELL THERAPIES

Genetic Engineering

It is now more than 50 years since the double helical structure of DNA was described with a clear indication of how the vital building blocks that synthesise proteins, the genes, resided in the nucleus of all cells and were replicated when the cells divided. The way in which the genetic alphabet of DNA is translated to the synthesis of complicated protein molecules is now understood, at least in principle. There is another intermediate alphabet of RNA that is essential in transmitting the signal of the gene to the manufacture of the protein. A vast array of essential participants in this process that express a gene to activity and switch it off have been identified and the whole genome of man has been described after a very laborious process, which initially was slow but now has been speeded up at an extraordinary rate. The code for individual genes can now be identified and I will discuss the goal of treating diabetes as an example of the approaches to gene and stem cell therapy.

The human insulin gene has been identified and can be isolated to reproduce in the cell of a bacterium as a so-called "plasmid" which is similar to a virus and about the same size. It is therefore possible to obtain very large numbers of copies of the gene. The plasmid can be incorporated into cells to persuade them to synthesise insulin. The plasmid may gain entrance, directly by the help of an electric current which opens up minute pores in the cell membrane or inside a virus which acts like a Trojan horse to take the plasmid into the cell in question. A liver, bone marrow or fat cell may be engineered to produce insulin but this is not enough to treat diabetes. A whole additional vital cell apparatus is required to store insulin and release it only when it is needed when the blood sugar rises, as for example after a meal or a sugared drink. Release of insulin in the presence of low sugar can result in a dangerous and potentially lethal coma. As the various molecular processes of cell biology were unravelled, at each stage there has been uncritical media hype that treatment by genetic engineering is about to transform and cure previously untreatable diseases. Despite cautious attempts in the clinic more than 20 years ago, valuable therapy on a large scale has not yet materialised. A genetically engineered cell may not behave in the way the engineer intended, it may respond inappropriately or gradually lose its function. In the case of diabetes how would the control of the release of insulin be engineered? Needless to say the sceptics have had a good time pointing to the inadequacies of not only the engineering techniques, but also the whole concept. Nevertheless some very rare diseases attributed to defects in one gene are beginning to show response to genetic engineering.

Stem Cells

The term stem cells is used loosely and often inaccurately. The perfect stem cell is a fertilised egg which will divide, proliferate and differentiate into a fully-formed foetus and eventually an adult individual. 30 years ago it was shown that at an early stage of cell division of the egg, each of the cells in an area called the blastocyst of the developing egg could be isolated and retained the capabilities of developing into a normal foetus. The cells are called "embryonic stem cells" and since they can produce any kind of tissue they are designated as pluripotent. Armed with this so-called "magic bullet" again there was speculation that embryonic stem cells, since they could in the laboratory produce cells of any type, might be used to repair and even replace damaged tissues and organs. The ability to manipulate on a minute scale cells in culture allowed the nucleus of the egg cell to be removed and replaced by the nucleus of a cell from any tissue. The nucleus itself contains all the DNA genetic material and when transferred is capable of developing into a cloned individual. The first example regained world renown, as "Dolly" the cloned sheep. Other species have also been cloned, but to date attempts to clone monkeys have failed and there is a taboo on trying to clone humans. Individuals resulted from cloning may not have a normal lifespan and developmental abnormalities can occur. The techniques are tedious and only a small number of nuclear transfer attempts are successful. The hopeful expectations led to a huge amount of money and effort to study the differentiation of embryonic stem cells and this added greatly to our knowledge of how the embryo develops from a single cell to a fully-formed foetus. Attempts have been made to nudge cells into a particular direction, for example towards the production of pancreatic beta cells, with a view to treatment of diabetes. This proved to be very difficult and only small numbers of cells have so far been produced with the characteristics of beta cells, which not only produce insulin but also store and regulate its release. If in the culture not all the cells are differentiated, following injection they can turn into tumours called teratomata and this is an important and significant danger in the use of embryonic stem cells. A very important biological observation was made in Japan by Yamanaka and his colleagues, which showed that fully developed and differentiated adult cells, for example cells found in the skin, could be manipulated to de-differentiate and revert to a state similar to embryonic stem cells. If they could be used therapeutically they would have an important theoretical advantage since, they could be derived from the patient's own skin cells and therefore they would not be liable to rejection, which is a risk with embryonic stem cells, which have foreign tissue type antigens.

The journey from an embryonic stem cell to, for instance, a pancreatic beta cell is complicated and currently the yield is low. The journey would be twice as long if the first phase is to dedifferentiate back to a state similar to an embryonic stem cell and then redifferentiate. Nevertheless this is an attractive line of research and it avoids ethical worries which have dogged embryonic stem cell research, which relies on sacrifice of a fertilised egg. A different and well-established stem cell treatment is bone marrow transplantation already mentioned. The transplantation of stem cells from the bone marrow can produce all the different types of blood-forming cells. In the laboratory using special cultural techniques it is possible to turn bone marrow cells into other types of cells such as bone, cartilage, heart muscle, nerve cells and a difficult and complicated technique can result in the production of cells that produce insulin, but so far only small numbers of such cells have been produced, nevertheless their function has been demonstrated by curing diabetic animals. The proof of principle is remarkable that certain bone marrow cells can be coaxed to produce insulin. To borrow from Dr. Johnson, the fact that a dog can be trained to walk badly on its hindlegs is unusual but it is remarkable that it can do so at all!

In all adult tissues there are probably stem cells; their role is not fully understood but may well be important in repairing damaged tissue. Much work is being done on stem cells in the brain, spinal cord and heart in attempts to mobilise them to repair and regenerate damaged central nervous or cardiac tissue. These efforts are still mainly in the experimental stage, with only cautious approaches in the clinic, often perpetrated by quack doctors interested in money and not science. This gives serious science a bad name and the sceptics a field day. There can be no doubt that safe and consistent techniques will eventually be developed. An early translation to the clinic seems unlikely but surprises occur, accidents happen which are not always harmful and eventually scepticism of these techniques will evaporate. It is up to scientists working in these areas to put the sceptics to flight, but currently scepticism encourages rigorous, repeatable scientific experiments and should discourage criminal exploitation. These optimistic thoughts would encourage the view of scepticism as a Hero in science but the role of this two-edged sword can also turn to Villain.

Chapter 8

CAN MEDICAL ETHICS SURVIVE WHEN MEDICINE IS COMMERCIALISED?

K. O. Lee
National University of Singapore, Singapore

ABSTRACT

In recent years, many countries have introduced business practices to improve efficiency and reduce health care costs. The consequences have led to an increase in the emphasis on medical ethics for the profession. This chapter will discuss the intrinsic difficulties and possible incompatibility between business practices and medical ethics.

INTRODUCTION

The commercialisation of medicine increasingly leans on doctors to by-pass traditional medical ethics. The doctor, who started as a medical student with altruistic views for caring for those in pain, fear and disability finds, in the course of medical school, internship and specialist training, that reality is rather different. In order to maintain the Hippocratic traditions in medicine, a young doctor must be prepared to recognise and resist fiscal temptations that are increasingly powerful.

To work in a prestigious institution the cost of evermore powerful equipment and staff to maintain and run the machines increases in an exponential manner. At the same time the risks of being sued and the interpretation of what constitutes the difference between negligence, malpractice and a genuine unavoidable mistake are increasingly blurred and are dealt with by medical insurance, by raising the premiums and demanding extreme and narrow specialisation so that the efficient doctor who makes few mistakes would be more a technician than the old-fashioned, professional philosopher/carer.

The long medical training may well be reduced to satisfy the needs of technology, but it is clear that improvement in understanding of disease and cures come at a price of restricted access to those who can pay. In a comprehensive healthcare system as in the UK, politicians of all persuasions are slowly having to accept that the best, most up-to-date and effective treatment just cannot be offered to every member of society. Sadly the forbidden word "rationing" that previously was avoided by politicians at all costs, may eventually return to the political scene.

On top of this big pharma companies have developed new and wonderful drugs that can control or cure previously untreatable disease. The cost of development of these drugs has also rocketed in an exponential manner. For a thousand interesting compounds in the research laboratory, the company will be fortunate if one becomes a "block-buster" and even then the initial euphoria on behalf of the shareholders may evaporate suddenly when unexpected long-term dangerous side-effects occur that had not been anticipated in experimental studies nor in early clinical trials.

When one company has an interesting-looking agent which is reaping enormous profits the other companies seek to introduce better, or least "me too" products.

The big pharma companies wield enormous power on the medical profession in designing trials so as not to prejudice their products in contrast to other agents and also to insist on how the data are analysed and what conclusions are reached. In return the powerful medical practitioners running the trials will be paid to their institution *per capita* for each patient recruited. Often generous grants are made for their research and the pharma companies have supported international meetings generously in the past, provided some sponsored symposia are included with company selected, well-paid speakers.

It is very difficult for the conscientious doctor brought up in traditional medical ethics, who is determined to practice medicine according to these ethical principles. With the advances in medicine the commercial pressure requires the would-be ethical practitioner to have the strength of character of St. Anthony in his resistance to temptation, a very difficult act to follow.

Temptation of St Anthony after Gustave Flaubert 1908 by Lovis Corinth, Tate Gallery.

MEDICAL ETHICS AND THE MEDICAL PROFESSION

The medical profession is one that is filled with privilege. Patients come to a doctor to seek help and understanding when unusual developments occur in their bodies and mind, and they seek help from one whom they regard as having greater knowledge and understanding, in the hope of assurance, comfort, care or even cure. They confide their deep fears and concerns, sometimes more than to their priests, and subject their bodies (and mind) to deep intrusions. Some of these privileges have been encoded in law, especially in Western countries. Thus, in many countries, the medical profession is the only one entrusted with legal authority to certify if someone is dead, insane, or ill and incapacitated enough to be temporarily or permanently unable to work. In most countries, it is the medical practitioner who is entrusted with the authority to give out medicines and substances that are labelled as 'poisonous' and 'dangerous', and instruct their vulnerable patients to take these 'three times a day, after meals'.

The medical profession was in turn expected to conduct itself in a way that was worthy of such privilege, confidence and trust from patients in a state of fear and vulnerability. The code of conduct was usually in a sworn oath to some higher power or deity, and these in modern times have been translated into a Medical Ethics code. Entrance into this 'higher calling' and 'noble profession' required a period of rigorous training, apprenticeship, and success in passing an examination or sometimes several examinations. After the oath had been taken to follow certain principles of conduct and practice, this 'noble' profession was then to self-regulate and discipline or expel its members that transgressed.

The most well known recorded code of medical ethics was the Hippocratic oath. The oath began with "I swear by Apollo the Physician and Aesclepius and Hygieia and Panaceia and all the gods, and goddesses, making them my witnesses, that I will fulfill according to my ability and judgment this oath and this covenant:...".[1] Modifications of this ancient oath continues to be a part of the initiation into the medical profession in the medical schools of many countries, albeit in an updated and more politically correct form. It is not unique, and similar oaths were taken in other civilisations by members of the healing profession: the Charaka Samhita Sutra (300 BC) from Ayurvedic medicine, and from Chinese Medicine, an oath from the writings of the Taoist Physician Su SiMiao (600 AD).

Despite the huge differences in origin, these oaths had many similarities, as the role of the physician-healer-confessor was similar irrespective of the cultural background. The physician healer was to respect the vulnerability of the patient who had come to seek help and healing, and not exploit it for his own monetary or other benefit. The physician was to keep confidentiality. The welfare of the patient was to be the primary direction of any advice or intervention from the physician - beneficence. The physician was to do no harm to the patient – non-malevolence. The physician was to treat all patients alike according to their need and not to discriminate according to their status in society or ability to pay. Personal gain by the physician as the main motivation for treatment of a patient was forbidden, with penalties both divine and temporal. Often the physician healers also swore to live disciplined and even ascetic lifes avoiding 'strong drink' and other vices! There was a very strong and sometimes severe dedication of their entire life to their calling. It would be difficult to imagine the bewilderment these ancients would have at the recent impostions of the 48 hour long week and shift work, for the medical profession in many of the European nations today.

One commonality of ancient times was the association of these principles with some form of higher or divine power or person(s). The association with forms of divine power are still seen in the crests of some of the medical colleges, or in the coiled serpent that some have associated with Moses in the Sinai desert (see figure 1).

In the crests of the Royal College of Physicians of London and of Ireland, there is a divine hand coming from above – presumably to guide and direct the physicians hand in the practice of comfort, care and healing.

Figure 1. The Divine hand from above in the Crests of the Royal Colleges of Physicians of Ireland and London; and the Serpent in the Royal Society of Medicine Crest.

Many of the ancient (and some modern) places of healing were located in the temples of these Gods: Aesclepius in Greece, and Taoist, Hindu and Buddhist temples in the East. The ruins of the temple of Aesclepius suggest that some hospitals had large numbers of patients from distant places, and included rest, good nutritious food, and exercise as an important part of the healing process. In tribal cultures, this association of the Divine powers with healers could be seen in the 'Witch-Doctors', although there, the benevolence of the higher powers would be less assured, and the code of ethics of the healer would similarly be in doubt.

CHANGES IN THE MEDICAL PROFESSION

Several changes have occurred over the centuries, but commercialisation of medicine has been quite a recent change in most of Europe, unlike the USA where medicine has been run as a business for much longer. In England, there has been the introduction of the principles of competition and cost recovery into the NHS.

In Holland, the provision of medical care and payment for medical services has been 'privatised' and commercialised. The introduction of 'market practices' and commercialisation of medicine has been hailed as the solution for rising health care costs: to lower these costs and improve efficiency.

Other changes have occurred. With the progress in the sciences in general, and medical science in particular, the regard and fear of modern man for supernatural and divine powers has diminished if not vanished. However, the changes taking place indicate that this has been replaced by a new faith in 'market forces'. Medical innovation and invention is increasingly dependent on large profit-driven pharmaceutical companies, whose business practices have been called into question recently.

Another major change (which has not been commented on much) is the change in the role of the physician towards the patient. Until recent times, the patient was sick, and 'those who are whole have no need of the physician'. The doctor-patient relationship was not an equal one, and the vulnerability of the patient was obvious to both. Hospitals and doctors were for the sick. This emphasis on treatment of serious disease has changed to that of health and even health enhancement, often of the 'unsick'. The World Health Organisation (WHO), in the utopian days of its foundation, defined health as 'not the mere absence of disease or infirmity, but complete physical mental and social well being'.

When someone well and healthy (no longer termed a 'patient') comes to a doctor for treatment of a 'non-disease', the relationship is that of a customer/client to a 'service provider'. There is no vulnerability on the part of the patient; the physician or surgeon is one of many 'service providers'. They are paid on a 'fee for service' basis, and compete on results, costs, efficiency and productivity, not on care and compassion. The wise, compassionate, caring, committed and selfless physician with the aim, as encapsulated in the well known quote: *Guerir quelquefois, soulager souvent, consoler toujours (to Cure occasionally, relieve often, comfort always.)*; is replaced by the 'willing buyer, willing seller' motto. The divine healing hand is replaced by the 'invisible hand'.

Of course, these changes have not come uniformly in every country, and not even within the same country. In many countries in Europe physicians equally selfless and dedicated to their profession as in the days of Galen co-exist in their temples of healing of the sick and dying with nearby places of commerce where clock-watching shift-work doctors treat their profession as 'just another job'. Doctors are still more highly regarded by the public than politicians and journalists. But the change will continue and the effects will be increasingly noticeable in the coming years. We can observe how in the USA, the excellent Veterans Adminstration (VA) hospitals, which do not have a 'fee for service' payment system, co-exist with centres that advertise their expertise and 'value for money' in face-lifts, tummy-tucks, hernias and gall-bladders.

Despite these changes, there are attempts to keep to high standards of professionalism and ethics within medicine [2], and Medical Ethics is taught in most medical schools. However, this increasing emphasis on Medical Ethics is a reflection of the increasing doubt that the Medical profession is as selfless as it was deemed to be. Scepticism and doubt increasingly abound in the public that the Medical profession will be able to self-regulate its members, and doubts have arisen that the Medical profession will even keep up to date with the advances of medicine. The lifelong learning assumed in physicians of old (Hippocrates observed that the medical art is long but our time is short. Lifelong learning and the passing on of knowledge was assumed) now require compulsion, monitoring, reexamination and recertification in many countries. Audits are now a necessary part in all aspects of medical practice, while measures of care and compassion are often neglected. A code of Medical ethics does not seem as convincing or as reassuring as before.

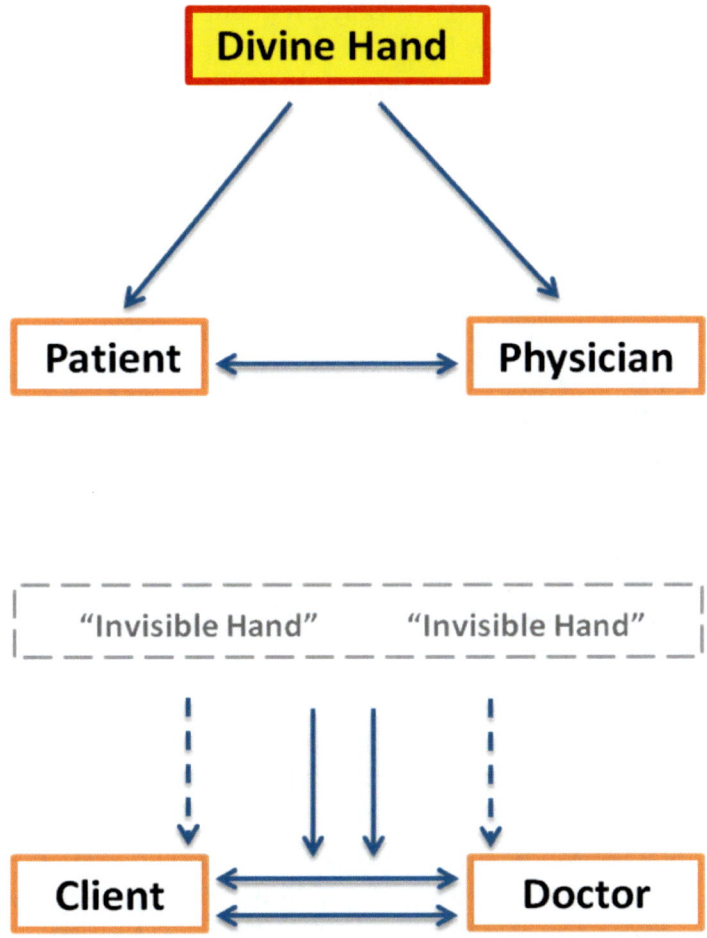

Figure 2. Change in the Doctor-Patient relationship.

THE COMMERCIALISATION OF MEDICAL PRACTICE

The transformation and commercialisation of medicine into a business has proceeded most rapidly in the USA. [3] Innovation and discovery in medicine is viewed as part of the scientific industrial enterprise, that will, with sufficient investment and research, be able to conquer diseases and get rid of all pests. The physician is seen as one who will deliver the fruits of the progress of science.

The commercialisation, which was intially more prevalent in the fringes of medicine, have moved to the mainstream of the serious diseases. Media hype have raised unrealistic hopes, and these are based frequently on poorly controlled clinical studies, which nevertheless, have persuaded desperate patients to travel long distances and pay large sums of money for 'cures'. Incentives within the system of payment, based on principles of business and the faith in market forces of competition, can and have led to more frequent tests and procedures, more visits with specialists, and more frequent admission to hospitals, most of which may be unnecessary. Patients go from one doctor or medical centre to another, and select the ones with the best and fastest service, and make their purchases. Often, more tests and more treatment are seen as better service.

Businesses have a different code of conduct. With recent financial crises, there have been some attempts to include social responsibility in commercial practices and discussions on ethics in financial institutions. 'Business ethics' is part of the curriculum of the best business schools. However, the harsh reality is that businesses must exist for profits and can only survive if profitable. [4] It is valid to question if beneficence can truly co-exist with profit making. When a business claims to 'put the customer first', does this refer to its beneficence or merely that the autonomy of the customer is important?

One of the earliest casualties in the commercialisation of medicine has been medical confidentiality. While some loss is inevitable with the implementation of electronic records, the loss of confidentiality is a requirement with the introduction of payment for particular items of service. Third party payment by Health Insurance Organisations would routinely require communication, verification, and authorisation by a number of administrators following set guidelines. These guidelines may or may not conform to principles of medical ethics and may be profit driven.

Other principles of Medical Ethics – beneficence and justice –have gone by the wayside or become secondary to the principle of autonomy – when medicine is commercialized. Centres for imaging exist in the USA for MRI's and CT Scans of any part of the body that any customer may wish – as long as they have the means to pay. A document for 'informed consent' on the risks or benefits of radiation is signed, and there is therefore a 'willing buyer, willing seller" contract of service. Medical ethics do not apply.

If medicine is commercialized, if medical institutions become businesses, it is difficult to expect medical ethics to survive when the nature of the practice has changed so fundamentally. When medical institutions get listed on a stock exchange, depend on profits supported by good quarterly reporting to financial analysts, have physician-investors as owners, is it surprising that rigid and thorough internal and external audits have to be conducted? Conflicts of interest multiply and have to be declared and regulated, and medical ethics do not apply. Surely business ethics, perhaps in a more thorough form than exists at present, should apply, with all the safeguards that do (and should) exist for businesses. It was a surprising sceptic who wrote of the necessary safeguards and regulations for businessmen: "The proposal of any new law or regulation which comes from businessmen ought always be listened to with great precaution, and ought never to be adopted till after long and carefully examined, not only with the most scrupulous but most suspicious attention. It comes from an order of men whose interest is never exactly the same with that of the public." [5] The assumptions of a noble profession, sworn to put the patient first, conscientiously following a code of Medical Ethics, should be abandoned when medicine becomes commercialised.

Atul Gawande has acknowledged and described how market driven business practices and incentives may end up being more expensive and even harmful in Medicine [6]. His contention that not-for-profit institutions without 'fee for service' incentives for individual doctors would lead to lower costs and better care is certainly valid within the context of the commercialised health system within the USA. His article (and this one also) has not addressed the relationship of the Pharmaceutical Industry with physicians and institutions – where regulation has fallen behind because of the presumption of beneficence. The fundamental problem is deeper. Perhaps there should be a separation of 'health' from serious 'diseases', such that for non-diseases, Medical ethics would not have to apply – and let the transactions between institutions and their clients/customers be treated as non-medical business, and let business ethics apply. We forget that in the days of Hippocrates there were others who sold healing potions and remedies (and snake-oil), but they did so in the agora, and not in the temples of Aesclepius. There was no confusion between the two and no naïve expectation of any noble code of ethics from these pedlars of cures, remedies and aphrodisiacs. The conflict was already noted in ancient days when Aesclepius rejected overtures from merchant minded Hermes (Figure 3). The ancient healers had faith in the Divine hand and scepticism for the Invisible hand – the reverse is true today.

Franz Joseph Ingelfinger (Editor of the New England Journal of Medicine 1967-1976, famous for the 'Ingelfinger rule' in scientific medical publication) described [7] how when he was diagnosed with a serious cancer, he lost his dispassionate scientific judgement and became a 'patient' for the first time in his life.

Figure 3. Hermes and merchant approach rejected by Aesclepius and his daughter Graces (Meditrine, Hygeia and Panacea)[Original from the then Museum Pio Clemens in Rome; *Galerie Mythologique, Recueil de Monuments* by Aubin Louis Millin, Paris 1811.].

He felt vulnerable and confused, and obtained immense relief only after he got a doctor who 'assumed authoritarian and paternalistic responsibility for his care'. For medical ethics to apply - there has to be a doctor-patient relationship that presupposes a vulnerable patient and a beneficent, dedicated and perhaps paternalistic and authoritarian doctor. This relationship must not be profit driven. Ancient faith in the Divine hand cannot be replaced by blind unsceptical faith in the Invisible hand. Medical ethics do not and should not apply in businesses. The attempts by Gawande and Pelligrino (cited above) are laudable, but as long as the two are not separated, it is difficult to avoid the confusion that will only increase, and bring undeserved scepticism for those who would still follow the path of Hippocrates.

ACKNOWLEDGMENTS

I am very grateful to Dr. John Wilson of Fife, and Dr Niall Finlayson of Edinburgh, Scotland, for helpful discussions.

REFERENCES

[1] From translation in Edelstein, Ludwig; Owsei Temkin, C. Lilian Temkin ed. *Ancient Medicine.* (Baltimore: Johns Hopkins University Press. p. 6. ISBN 0801834910, 1987).

[2] Pellegrino, Edmund D, *Professionalism, Profession and the Virtues of the Good Physicians.* (New York, Mt Sinai Journal of Medicine, Vol 69 p 378; 2000).

[3] Marcinko, David Edward (Editor), The Business of Medical Practice; Advanced Profit Maximization Techniques for Savvy Doctors. (2nd Edition, New York: Springer Publishing Company, 2004). This book, in both editions, was a best seller in the USA.

[4] Friedman, Milton, *The Social Responsibility of Business is to Increase Its Profits.* (New York Times Magazine, September 1970).

[5] Adam Smith, originator of the phrase 'the Invisible Hand' in his 1759 book, *The Theory of Moral Sentiments,* was sceptical enough to write this in his more famous book *The Wealth of Nations.*

[6] Gawande, Atul, *The Cost Conundrum. McAllen, Texas and the High Cost of Health Care. Expensive Healthcare can be Harmful.* (The New Yorker, Annals of Medicine, 1st June, 2009).

[7] Ingelfinger, Franz, *Arrogance.* (The New England Journal of Medicine, 1st December, 1980).

In: Scepticism: Hero and Villain
Editors: R. Calne and W. O'Reilly

ISBN: 978-1-62417-783-5
© 2013 Nova Science Publishers, Inc.

Chapter 9

RECOVERY FROM BRAIN DAMAGE AND PLASTICITY: NIHILISM, SCEPTICISM AND OPTIMISM

John Pickard

INTRODUCTION

How can our complex brain ever recover from injury and tissue loss? This question has challenged successive generations of neuroscientists, both basic and clinical, probably since before Hippocrates. Hippocrates was well aware of the variability of outcome in patients after head injury and 'stroke' and the difference that age makes to recovery.

Until the 1970's, most nervous system diseases posed diagnostic puzzles but were met with therapeutic nihilism. The conventional dogma was that neurones within the adult mammalian central nervous system were irreplaceable. Why then did some patients recover whilst others did not despite similar initial insults?

Is it true that the infant brain recovers more completely than the adult? If so, why is plasticity lost with age? How does the adult brain develop new skills? If remodelling occurs within the brain after injury, how does it happen? Is it possible to wear out our brains through over-use at different ages?

Why does the brain try to re-provide skills lost through injury? What are the innate drivers within the brain that 'seek' to re-provide skills lost after brain injury? How do our identities survive brain injury? Which capacities have to be stripped away to affect identity? Are our identities simply the sum total of our brain's activities? Such questions inform the mind-brain debate.

Initially, it was the scientists, both basic and clinical, who were sceptical about the dogma that regeneration did not occur in the adult brain. There is now optimism that clinical translation of novel treatments is a realistic possibility. The sceptics are now those who doubt that the brain really is sufficient explanation for who we are.

The experiments of nature with which clinicians and our patients grapple every day provide some insight in to such fundamental issues. This chapter will highlight some of the key discoveries surrounding recovery from brain injury including the role of neural plasticity. It will conclude with consideration of some ethical issues surrounding altered states of consciousness and their implications for the 'Neuromania' debate.

A Layman's Introduction to the Brain

At a physical level, the brain may be regarded as a lump of fat that almost floats on its own sea of fluid within the skull. As everybody knows who has felt a baby's fontanelle, the brain pulsates with each heart beat and becomes tense when the baby cries. However, under the microscope, this pulsating lump of fat is shown to consist of an unimaginable number of cells – the nerve cells (neurones of many types), the supporting cells (glia) and the blood vessels. Ramon y Cajal (1852-1934) used silver nitrate to stain neurones within slices of the brain. Each neurone has a body and various extensions called dendrites and axons. Neurones are grouped together in structures called nuclei (if round) and cortex (if ribbon-like around the outside of the brain). Both nuclei and cortex appear grey, hence the term 'grey matter'.

Each neurone is part of a network. The end of each axon is attached to the dendrites of the next neurone in the network. Axons are wrapped in an insulating material called myelin which is formed by one type of glia called oligodendrocytes. Axons are grouped together in bundles of cables or tracts which are white in appearance due to the myelin, hence the term 'white matter'.

Experiments on frog legs revealed that nerves act as electrical conductors. Electrical stimulation of the exposed human brain showed that the brain functions in part as an electrical machine. Electrical currents spread down the axon as pulses. In an outstanding series of experiments for which they were awarded the Nobel prize in 1963, Hodgkin and Huxley unravelled the way in which sodium and potassium ions move extraordinarily rapidly through the membrane of the giant axon of the squid to create a spike of electricity (impulse). The cycle of electrical change that generates the spike lasts only a millisecond locally but it is then able to spread down the axon. When it reaches the end of the axon, it stimulates release of chemical substances or neurotransmitters such as noradrenaline, acetylcholine, dopamine and glutamate. These neurotransmitters then stimulate the dendrites of the next neurone in the network and so on. The brain has complex mechanisms to make sure that such powerful chemical compounds do not stray from their site of action. Otherwise, mayhem and brain damage might result.

All the electrical and chemical activity within the brain demands a lot of energy which comes mainly from oxygen and glucose in the blood. Arteries take blood in to the brain and veins drain the blood back to the heart. The blood vessels within the brain are 'intelligent' and respond both to changes in blood pressure and to what the neurones and glia are doing locally. If blood pressure falls, the brain vessels dilate. If neurones are very active, the extra oxygen and glucose is supplied by an increase in local blood flow. However, the brain overdoes it! Local blood flow increases more than it has to. This results in a local increase in arterialised blood. The magnetic properties of arterial and venous blood differ (oxyhaemoglobin versus deoxyhaemoglobin). As we will see later, an MR scanner can detect this difference and use it to assess local brain activity.

This necessarily over-simplified account of the brain gives the impression of a computer composed of transistors and other components wired together in circuit boards and provided with a power supply. But how is the brain formed? Who designed it? Where is the production line for its manufacture? How is it maintained?

The brain is formed in the foetus by cells that divide many times and then move in waves towards the outside of the body in the future head and spine regions. There is not enough space for all the cells so that the human brain consists of many folds (gyri and sulci). There is enormous redundancy in this process – many more cells are formed than are needed. Modern developmental neurobiology is discovering the many complex mechanisms that control how these immature groups of cells are brought to order and redundant cells sacrificed. Such mechanisms are both the result of genetic and molecular programmes within the brain itself and the response to the outside world. Some stem cells persist in to adulthood, particularly in the hippocampus (memory) and olfactory system (sense of smell).

The brain has a highly sophisticated system for interacting with the environment, both sensing what is going on, setting goals and moving self and objects within it. One only has to see a baby making its first emotional responses and taking its first steps to appreciate what changes must be taking place in the brain. John Donne's phrase *'No man is an island entire of itself'* perfectly encapsulates the development of the brain.

In parallel with the development of the brain, sense organs including the eyes, ears, balance, joint and skin receptors are formed and wired in to the nervous system. Bundles of axons or tracts carry the sensory information in steps up the nervous system through a system of sensory pathways and nuclei until the cerebral cortex is reached. Sensory information is analysed with increasing complexity as it moves through such nuclei and adjacent brain structures informed. Once the 'brain' decides that it wants to respond, all the necessary information is gathered together in various networked areas of the brain. Electrical impulses then pass down in the motor pathways from the cerebral cortex and other nuclei to stimulate appropriate activity in, for example, the relevant muscles.

Unfortunately, there are some design flaws in the brain! There is no duplication of key areas, tracts and cranial nerves. Some arteries to essential parts of the brain are 'end-arteries' with no scope for an alternative blood supply if they become narrowed or blocked with atheroma or injury. Vital core functions such as breathing and blood pressure are grouped together in the brain stem.

One major problem is what, where and how does the 'brain' decide what 'it' wants to do – a conundrum memorably described as the *Ghost in the Machine*.

ACUTE BRAIN INJURY AND NEUROPROTECTION

Acute brain injury caused by trauma and stroke (haemorrhage or loss of blood supply) causes immediate or primary brain damage that may be followed by secondary brain damage. Obviously, prevention is always better than trying to treat a patient with a head injury or a stroke. Cycle helmets, seat belts, drink driving legislation, car design, gun law, safer playgrounds and avoidance of falls in the elderly have all played a major part in reducing the incidence and severity of head trauma. Early detection of high blood pressure, statins, transient ischaemic attacks and carotid endarterectomy have all helped to reduce the incidence of major strokes.

Secondary injury may be the result of progression of the initial injury or of so-called avoidable factors such as delays in detecting clots, low blood pressure (shock), lack of oxygen, seizures, infection and brain swelling. Success over the past 40 years has come from anticipating secondary insults through early resuscitation, brain scanning, intensive monitoring and management within dedicated major trauma and stroke networks and neurointensive care units. Evidence-based consensus guidelines are crucial to such success. Hence, the creation of neurointensive care units has improved good outcomes after head trauma by 40%, reduced mortality by 10% without increasing the number of very severely disabled survivors. Dedicated stroke and neurointensive care units have better outcomes than general intensive care units.

It was discovered 40 years ago that there is a zone with a low blood flow, the ischaemic penumbra, around areas of damage that is silent but intact. Timely use of clot-busting drugs may open up blocked brain arteries and rescue the penumbral areas. Hypothermia has been extensively assessed after children who survived near-drowning were found to be hypothermic. Brain cooling for neonatal hypoxia/asphyxia is now part of routine care. Reopening blocked brain arteries with clot busting drugs is now widely used in the first few hours after a stroke. The brain arteries may go in to spasm after bleeding over the surface of the brain caused by rupture of an aneurysm (balloon-like weakness). Secondary reduction in the blood supply may develop over the next few days, a process that can be ameliorated by the drug Nimodipine. Why are these treatments successful when all the other drugs have failed that have been trialled for head injury and stroke? Crucially, the time course of the key disease process was understood and there was sufficient time to deliver the drug in sufficient quantity to where it was required. In other words, there was a favourable therapeutic window of opportunity for the drug to be effective before the underlying processes became irreversible. The Regulatory authorities until recently have demanded that overall outcome should be improved before a new drug is licensed. What matters to an individual patient may not be overall outcome on some quality of life scale. For example, a head injured patient who survives but with no recent memory function would happily accept a drug that helped that aspect of their disability only. Surrogate outcome measures have been accepted in other areas of medicine where there is a direct correspondence between the measure and overall outcome, for example, hypertension, diabetes and glaucoma.

There has been a tension between large scale pragmatic and smaller scale exploratory trials. The story of high dose steroids for brain and spinal cord trauma is instructive. There was some experimental evidence that megadoses of the steroid methylprednisolone would reduce spinal cord injury. Another steroid dexamethasone has been used for many years to reduce brain swelling around brain tumours and make surgery safer. There followed randomised controlled trials of methylprednisolone in patients after SCI but the results have been the subject of intense controversy. This steroid is no longer recommended routinely for SCI.

A large multinational clinical trial was mounted in head injury (the CRASH trial). CRASH was stopped early because of excess deaths in the active group when compared with the placebo group. Because the pragmatic design of CRASH did not include relevant exploratory studies, we still do not know the reason for the excess deaths caused by the methylprednisolone. Furthermore, there is a wealth of data that links excess glucocorticoids to hippocampal atrophy and cognitive decline. RCT design demands as much scepticism as any other technique. Animal and tissue culture research, despite their well rehearsed limitations, remain the main source of new drug mechanisms for exploration and translation in to man.

There is now widespread scepticism within Big Pharma which has largely withdrawn from the development of new drugs for brain injury. The baton has been handed back for the moment to the universities and small spin-off companies.

WHAT HAPPENS WHEN ACUTE CARE FAILS: THE BRAIN DEATH CONTROVERSY

Death is a process rather than an event. Death has been defined as the irreversible loss of the capacity for consciousness, combined with the irreversible loss of the capacity to breathe [Academy of Royal Medical Colleges Code of Practice for the Diagnosis and Confirmation of Death 2008]. Following head injury or intracranial haemorrhage, brain swelling may be so severe that the pressure within the cranium exceeds the arterial blood pressure. When this occurs, no blood can circulate through the brain. Severe distortion of the brain stem, if unrelieved in timely fashion, will result in cessation of breathing and finally collapse of the circulation. Such patients cannot breathe for themselves and are on ventilators. The heart will eventually stop even if ventilation is maintained. It has proven possible to develop clinically based assessments of brain stem function that reliably diagnose brain death. Hence, it is now accepted in the UK that 'the irreversible cessation of brain stem function whether induced by intracranial events or the result if extracranial phenomena, such as hypoxia, will produce this clinical state and therefore irreversible cessation of the integrative function of the brain stem equates with the death of the individual and allows the medical practitioner to diagnose death'. All the cells in the whole brain do not have to be dead for death to be declared. A very careful clinical protocol was developed in the 1970's which has stood the test of time. Supplementary tests are only required where the assessment of brain stem function is obscured, for example, by multiple facial and base of skull trauma.

In 1980, the BBC Panorama programme 'Transplants – are the donors really dead' was aired and caused enormous distress with a short-term decline in donors for transplantation. That programme was a challenge to the whole concept of brain death and to the purely clinical criteria established in the UK since 1976. A Google search for 'Brain death BBC Panorama' will reveal the bitter controversy that surrounded the whole concept of brain death that continues to a minor degree to the present day. There has been no case identified of survival once the brain death criteria have been fulfilled provided that all the preconditions and testing methods have been adhered to and repeated by independent observers with the relevant training and experience. Considerable courage was displayed by Bryan Jennett and Christopher Pallis in their scholarly rebuttal of the sensationalist and ill-informed Panorama programme.

REMODELLING IN THE HEALTHY BRAIN

The cerebral cortex has an impressive ability to reassign cortical areas to changes in demands placed upon it. Over-stimulation of a body part enlarges its cortical representation (representational remodelling). The rat has whiskers which are very important for negotiating through confined spaces underground. Each whisker has its own area of cerebral cortex (barrel field) devoted to interpreting the sensations detected as the whisker is moved. If a whisker is lost, surrounding barrel fields expand for whiskers that remain intact. The sensory cortical representation of the nipples expands in rats during rearing of their pups. In humans, the sensory and motor areas of the cortex responsible for hand sensation and movement 'atrophy' after amputation but recover after successful hand transplant. Some drugs can block such remodelling.

Experience in early postnatal life shapes and stabilises key synapses and hence networks. If such experience is not gained during the correct critical period, incorrect connections may form that may be irreversible. For example, if one eye is covered soon after birth, the corresponding area of the visual cortex is taken over by connections from the other eye. This malfunction is irreversible after 3-4 months (cat), 18-24 months (non-human primate) or 5-10 years (man), even if the eye is uncovered. The visual acuity in the covered eye remains very depressed. This phenomenon explains why children whose squint is not corrected develop what is called an amblyopic or lazy eye. Patching the good eye helps to alleviate this problem. Adults may be helped by using virtual reality computer games to force the brain to use information from the amblyopic eye.

The human brain is also capable of such plastic reorganisation during adulthood with training. The technique of transcranial magnetic stimulation has been used to show that the cortical representation of the muscles used to learn the piano or a string instrument increases. When blind people start to learn Braille, the relevant area of the sensory cortex expands as revealed by recording the electrical activity in the cortex. When fingers are webbed together, either through a congenital malformation or with a bandage, their cortical representation overlaps but separates when the fingers are separated. These changes occur very rapidly (30 -120 minutes) as revealed by magnetoencephalography.

Many animals have to remember where food has been stored and how to navigate over long distances. The hippocampus is a vital part of the brain's memory circuit and expands in birds and animals during the appropriate season. Amazingly, the size of the posterior part of the hippocampus in trained taxi-drivers is larger than in control subjects matched for age and gender.

However, it is possible to 'over do' it as every athlete knows. The brain is no different. Memory traces in the hippocampus are consolidated partly in to the cortex during the phase of sleep known as REM (rapid eye movement). The REM phase is when we are dreaming. When I work too many hours for too long, I am aware that I dream less. When I go on holiday, leave the smartphone and paperwork behind and read novels, my brain relaxes and I start to dream again. 24 hours of sleep deprivation halves mental capacity including memory, reaction times and judgement.

Prolonged stress raises steroid levels and depresses the production of stem cells in the hippocampus. The internet and electronic means of communication have drastically increased the problem of information overload. Which of us, faced with inboxes that are beyond redemption, have not been aware of reduced attention span, irritability, disconnection from people and a yearning for the space to think more deeply. Drugs known as cognitive enhancers such as modafinil may improve short term performance in pilots, surgeons, students and patients after brain injury. But, what is the long term cost if their use is prolonged? Would it not be better to create filters against information overload and do as rehabilitation specialists do – tailor training sessions to the residual mental capacity and attention span of the patient after brain injury.

SIZE, LOCATION AND SPEED OF PROGRESSION (MOMENTUM) OF LESIONS, BOTH FOCAL AND TO NEURAL SYSTEMS

It is remarkable to consider that there was once debate about the existence of localisation of function within the cerebral cortex. Like all good scientific controversies, there is truth on both sides. The doctrine of equivalence of function and redundancy throughout the cortex arose in the XIXth century from removal of different parts of the pigeon's cortex which appeared to have similar effects depending on the volume removed rather than the site. Then in the 1860's, Broca contradicted this doctrine when he described how focal lesions in the certain parts of the left hemisphere of man produced speech disorders.

Fritsch and Hitzig demonstrated that the motor cortex was electrically excitable. However, Hughlings Jackson (1870's) and Goltz (1888) noted in both man and the dog that discrete cortical lesions had little or no effect on mental or behavioural capacity so that such functions must be more extensively represented in the cortex. Fast forwards to 1929 and Karl Lashley's experiments in the rat. He was searching for the localisation of learning and memory in the rat using the maze test. He concluded from lesion experiments that all areas of the cortex were equivalent and in proportion to the amount removed.

There was also recovery of motor function. However, the rat has a very small brain in proportion to that of man and the main motor pathway from the brain to the spinal cord is organised differently. Lesion experiments might be expected not to translate precisely to larger species including man. Despite the difficulties, Robbins and Sahakian have developed tests of mental function that may be used from mouse through non-human primates to man.

It is not surprising that the equivalence doctrine met with scepticism, not least from clinicians who saw the effects of disease every day. Neurosurgeons know from bitter experience that there are tunnels for access to the brainstem and through the cortex that are relatively safe but, for example, the primary cortices should never be used. Small lesions of acute onset in key areas may have devastating neurological effects. Large lesions may have little effect if they develop very slowly as with benign indolent tumours such as a meningioma (a tumour of the lining membranes around the brain). The brain has a remarkable ability to deform slowly and retain function.

The effects of depressed skull fractures and tumours led to a large number of studies of localisation including the iconic case of Phineas Gage (1823 – 1860). He was an American railroad worker who, on September 13th 1848, was using an iron bar to tamp some blasting powder in to a hole when the powder exploded. The iron bar passed through his face, up behind the left eye and exited through the top of the skull having passed through the left frontal lobe of the brain [Figure 1: Reconstruction of Gage's skull]. Remarkably, he was only briefly unconscious and still able to walk and talk coherently. There is debate about how far his personality was changed by an injury that was dramatic but only took out the left frontal lobe and did not render him unconscious. However, his case has been used with some embellishment to illustrate the relationship of the frontal lobes to higher mental function, decision making and personality. Various observations and theories led the Portuguese Neurologist Egas Moniz to suggest that severe mental illness might be the result of aberrant and fixed pathological brain circuits. With his Neurosurgical colleague, Pedro Lima, he devised the prefrontal lobotomy procedure that involves cutting the pathways between the front of the frontal lobes from the rest of the brain.

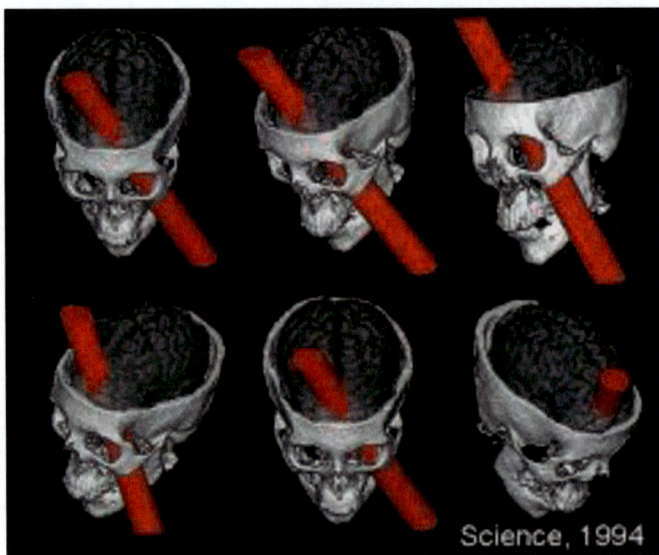

Figure 1. Reconstruction of Gage's skull. Damasio H, Grobowski TJ, Frank RJ, Galaburrda, AM, Damasio AR.

Some clinical success followed including the Nobel Prize in 1949, but only after Moniz had been shot by a disaffected patient in 1939. Unfortunately, the operation became popularised and, to meet the need for the large number of inmates in American asylums, the notorious ice pick technique was developed by Freeman and Watts. A hole was made in the thin bone above the eyeball and an ice pick-like instrument pushed upwards to cut the nerve fibres.

There was a significant incidence of bleeding and meningitis and the lesion created was variable in size. Many patients were rendered zombie-like as represented in 'One flew over the cuckoo's nest'. The procedure was slowly abandoned during the 1960's. However, lesions in general for brain disorders including tremor have been replaced by deep brain stimulation (DBS) which carries much less risk of causing harm and can be fine tuned or turned off.

The use of DBS is currently under investigation for the treatment of the severest forms of obsessive compulsive disorder and depression for which drugs have failed through lack of efficacy or severe side-effects.

Modern techniques, both experimental in non-human primates and in man, have provided an increasingly profound functional dissection of the cerebral cortex, even of the 'silent' frontal lobes, silent only because of our historical lack of insight and inability to design the appropriate experiments. Following head injury, it is now clear that the profile of cognitive deficits does not always correspond to the size and location of brain injuries – whole networks may be involved. For example, focal contusions to the underside of the frontal lobes and anterior temporal lobes do not by themselves explain the range of cognitive problems found in survivors. The advantage of modern imaging techniques is that the whole brain structure may be examined independently of any prior perception using powerful statistical methods that avoid or minimise bias. Imaging science is now the playground of some very talented mathematicians and physicists – the only problem is that their methods are not always readily presented in terms that a biologist or clinician can understand.

Serial MR scanning in patients as they recover from a head injury revealed that one specific neurochemical pathway, the cholinergic system, was damaged in different sites. Imagine the network rail from London to Manchester. It does not matter where the block in the line is, the train will not arrive. This concept helps to explain why there is a relatively stereotyped pattern of problems with higher mental function after head injury and other brain injuries despite the fact that the lesions occur at different sites in the brain.

Duffau in Paris has continued Penfield's work in Montreal by studying brain function in the awake patient after their skull has been opened under local anaesthetic:

> 'For a long time, in a localizationist view of brain functioning, a combination of symptoms called "frontal syndrome" has been interpreted as the direct result of damage involving the frontal lobe(s). Intra-operative electrostimulation mapping investigations in patients who underwent awake surgery for cerebral tumours reported in the last decade break with the traditional dogma of a modular and fixed organization of the central nervous system, by switching to the concepts of cerebral connectivity and plasticity - i.e., a brain organization based on dynamic interrelationships between parallel distributed networks. According to this revisited model, "frontal symptoms" can be generated by tumour or electrostimulation not only of the frontal lobes, but also of cortical and subcortical (white matter pathways/deep gray nuclei) structures outside the frontal lobes. On the other hand, it is also possible to perform extensive right or left frontal lobectomy in patients who continue to have a normal familial, social and professional life, without "frontal syndrome".

MECHANISMS OF PLASTICITY AND PATHOLOGICAL REMODELLING

There is considerable spare capacity in some parts of the nervous system. Cognitive reserve refers to the concept that patients with higher IQ's may be less disabled after brain injury. The circuitry of some areas of the brain such as the basal ganglia is less hard wired and more based on tonic extracellular levels of the transmitter dopamine. In Parkinson's disease, over 80% of dopamine neurones have to be lost from the substantia nigra before symptoms develop. Damage to such areas of the brain may be followed by various intrinsic strategies of the brain itself to cope including receptor supersensitivity, increased synthesis in surviving neurones, reduced reuptake and increased release per presynaptic impulse. If areas such as the basal ganglia are less hard-wired, it is more realistic to think that transplants of stem cells might work.

'Cells that fire together, wire together.' Plasticity is a normal part of brain function at all ages. Increased activity in a neural circuit leads to strengthening of synapses and increased efficiency of the circuit. Long-term potentiation (LTP) is an example of such repetitive or reverberating electrical behaviour that contributes to the formation of memory as predicted by Donald Hebb in 1949. Many new relationships are being discovered between electrical activity before and after a synapse and overall electrical rhythms in the brain such as gamma synchronisation.

In the 1980's, a series of experiments demonstrated that the areas of cortex that normally receive information from a nerve, such as the median nerve in the arm and hand, did not fall silent if the nerve was cut but immediately began to respond to stimuli from adjacent areas of skin. This must mean that normally there must be connections from adjacent cortex or thalamus that are silent but become unmasked when the messages from, in this example, the median nerve are blocked. The affected area of the hand remains numb. This process of immediate unmasking of synapses may involve the neurotransmitter GABA.

With time, even neurones which are initially silent begin to respond to stimuli in adjacent areas. Collateral sprouting of branches of neurones has now been demonstrated in the hippocampus and cortex (after cutting the nerves relaying sensation from the arm to the spinal cord), in the visual cortex and in the dorsal root entry zone of the spinal cord. Similar changes occur in the human and non-human primate motor cortex after peripheral nerve damage or nerve block or by drugs that block the effects of GABA: stimulation of the motor cortex provokes more widespread movements.

Such remapping within the cortex may help the brain to make sense of a repaired nerve. Peripheral nerves are complex cables containing many hundreds of nerve fibres. It is impossible to align all these nerve fibres accurately. However, particularly in children, cortical remapping may be able to make sense of all the misconnections. The principle is the same as the brain learning to use a transplant of neural cells – a graft of neurones will be useless without such retraining.

Various neurological problems may follow amputation of a limb. An amputee including children born without a limb may still be aware of the limb and to feel it. Phantom limb pain may be so awful as to render normal life almost impossible. The nerve endings within the stump may become involved in scar tissue and send erroneous messages back to the central nervous system. However, although excision of such scar tissue may alleviate the phantom limb pain for a short period, it returns often worse than before. Drugs often fail to control such pain. The sensory cortex changes the way in which impulses in the nerves that supplied the amputated limb are handled. Techniques are being developed that reverse these changes in the sensory cortex. Repeated touching of the skin over the stump, electrical stimulation of the adjacent motor cortex, moving the intact arm in a mirror box and imagining moving the absent limb may all help. Sensations in other systems of the body may be affected by phantom-like symptoms including a form of tinnitus. Learning to interpret the hearing signals induced by a cochlear implant probably relies on cortical plasticity.

Representational remodelling also occurs after damage to the brain itself. Removal of an area of cortex is followed by reorganisation within adjacent areas to provide a smaller cortical map for the areas of the body. Once the immediate reduction in brain blood flow and swelling have resolved after a stroke, passive movement of the paralysed limb may induce increases in blood flow in adjacent areas of cortex including the sensorimotor cortex and cerebellum on both sides of the body.

DECLINE OF PLASTICITY WITH AGE

It has been known for over 150 years that children with congenital or early atrophy of the left hemisphere were still able to understand and speak (Jules Cotard 1868). This was quite unlike the effects of a stroke in adults that affected the dominant hemisphere and rendered patients aphasic. Kennard (1938-42) showed that excisions of motor cortex in infant monkeys produced much less severe motor deficits than similar lesions in adults (Kennard Principle). Temporal lobectomy for refractory seizures is much less likely to disrupt functions associated with this brain region if performed in patients with an early age of onset of the seizures. Dendrites and synapses increase in number up to the time of adolescence. Recent advances in MR (diffusion tensor imaging, tractography) has led to a systematic assessment of white matter changes through childhood and adolescence such as sex differences in development of axonal diameter and myelination. Some sprouting of corticospinal axons may occur across the midline in the spinal cord after cerebral hemisphere damage in early life. Movement of the normal limb may be accompanied by movements of the affected side. Infants with potentially lethal status epilepticus have had complete removal of one cerebral hemisphere as a life-saving measure. This not only cured the seizures but left little functional disability despite the loss of so much brain tissue.

The loss of plasticity with age is at least partly dependent on structures within the brain called perineuronal nets (PNNs). These were first described by Camillo Golgi in the late XIXth century. Modern molecular and ultrastructural techniques have revealed that PNNs are a complex of extracellular matrix molecules interposed between a meshwork of glial processes and certain neurone cell bodies and proximal neural processes. However, scepticism surrounded their discovery and even the Nobel Prize winning Ramon y Cajal dismissed PNNs as an artefact of the staining techniques used to visualise them. Golgi and Cajal shared the Nobel Prize in 1906 but were not fond of each other.

Presciently, Golgi suggested that PNNs are a kind of corset which impeded the spread of current from cell to cell. As might be expected teleologically, the primary motor and sensory areas are more hard-wired than the associative areas. What is fascinating is that it is possible experimentally to return adult plasticity to childhood levels. Chondroitinase ABC is a bacterial enzyme that digests PNNs. Injection of ChABC into the adult rat cerebellum rapidly produces outgrowth of Purkinje neurones. Closure of the critical period described earlier in relation to amblyopia appears to coincide with the formation of PNNs which suggests that PNNs are key to synaptic stabilisation in these neurones. Injection of ChABC reactivates synaptic plasticity and the critical period. Examples include ocular dominance, fear memories dependent on the amygdala and development of bird song in the zebra finch. Traumatic injury of the brain and spinal cord results in degeneration of damaged neurones, formation of a glial scar, which contains extracellular matrix molecules, and collateral sprouting of surviving nerve cells. PNNs inhibit axonal regeneration. Fawcett's group have made the fascinating discovery that injection of ChABC enhances regeneration of axons and functional recovery after spinal cord injury in the rat.

EMERGENCE FROM COMA AND DISORDERS OF CONSCIOUSNESS

Patients in coma (Greek: deep sleep or trance) lie with eyes closed and cannot be aroused to respond appropriately even with vigorous painful stimuli. They may grimace to pain and make stereotyped withdrawal movements to pain but the movements are not targeted at the site of pain (localisation). Historically, various terms were used to describe various degrees of coma but were unusable scientifically and for assessing progress. Development of the Glasgow Coma Scale (1972) by Bryan Jennett and Graham Teasdale was the product of pragmatic studies of various features that could be reduced to three: eye opening, best motor response and verbal response. The GCS was a major step forwards that was initially viewed with scepticism by non-neurosurgeons but it then became adopted for all causes of coma.

The brain stem is key to the basic functions of consciousness as demonstrated (1890-1940's) by post-mortem studies of patients who had died in coma from diseases such as encephalitis lethargica, by neurosurgeons learning where not to go (Sir Geoffrey Jefferson's anterior and posterior critical points) and finally by experimental studies.

There are many causes of coma, some reversible and some irreversible. Remarkably little is known about the mechanisms underlying recovery from coma. Initially, there is an electrical storm and then relative silence until various distributed parts of the brain begin to work in some sort of ill-defined harmony. The great majority of patients start to eye open and respond to command within hours to days or weeks. However, there is a very small group of patients who start to eye open (awake) but do not respond to command (unaware). Such patients are described as being in the vegetative state. There are various causes of VS including trauma, hypoxia, infections and metabolic disasters. If there are no factors impeding recovery, patients will not recover from VS if still in that state after six months following severe hypoxia and twelve months after trauma. Post-mortem studies often reveal widespread loss of cerebral cortex, white matter or surprisingly limited damage to the thalamus depending on the cause. If patients improve, they go through the minimally conscious state (MCS) characterised by fluctuating but reproducible signs of awareness and responses to command. Some patients may improve further albeit with disability. Various drugs and even deep brain stimulation have been tried in an attempt to improve the level of consciousness.

In the locked-in syndrome, damage to the front of the middle part of the brain stem may stop all the impulses from the upper brain reaching the spinal cord and hence almost all the muscles of the body. However, the impulses from all the sensory organs (hearing, vision and skin) are spared. Hence, such patients are paralysed except that they may be able to breathe and can move their eyes up and down or blink. Diagnosis often takes many months because clinicians may not be aware of the syndrome and sceptical that their patient may have it. Famous patients include Julia Tavalaro and the Parisian journalist Jean-Dominique Bauby. JT became able to use a chin switch to activate a computer and write her autobiography 'Look up for yes' together with an extensive number of poems. J-D B wrote 'The diving bell and the butterfly' which later became a film.

The management and prediction of outcome of severe brain injuries in the early stages is fraught with difficulty. Families have to be made aware that prognosis may be grim.

Frequently, next of kin will say that their loved one would not have wanted to be preserved in a severely disabled state. Unfortunately, it is often not possible to be precise about the likely outcome, The vigil at the bedside can be long and arduous. Inevitably, nihilism supervenes followed sometimes by false hope when the eyes begin to open without a corresponding improvement in motor responses.

It is crucial that patients suspected of being in VS or other low awareness state are assessed for a substantial period (weeks) by an experienced team of clinicians and therapists.

Patients in a low awareness state are very vulnerable and yet should not be denied access to research provided that the latter is safe and not distressing. Over the past 15 years, major advances have been made using functional brain imaging and electrophysiology in our understanding of VS and MCS albeit against a background of considerable scepticism. The Cambridge low awareness group in collaboration with Liege and New York have developed novel methods that have shown evidence of covert awareness in a minority of patients in VS.

For example, subjects are asked to imagine playing tennis at Wimbledon or walking around their home. These motor imagery tasks activate different parts of the brain as detected by an MR scanner. Some 5-10% of VS patients will show evidence of motor imagery. Where such responses are present, the patient often improves but there are formidable technical difficulties with such studies so that the absence of a response cannot be taken as evidence of the absence of such capability. One patient was able to use motor imagery to answer yes or no to questions: for example, playing tennis for 'yes' and navigation around the house for 'no'. Interestingly, MCS patients were less able to display motor imagery than VS patients.

The issue of living wills and quality of life is often raised in the context of patients in a low awareness state. The Court of Protection in England may give permission for withdrawal of food and water in patients who are confirmed to be in VS. A recent attempt to withdraw nutritional support from an MCS patient was rejected by the Court as the patient still had some awareness and appeared to be improving.

It is often claimed that to be in MCS or severely disabled is worse than death, that living wills should be respected and that support should be withdrawn and patients allowed to die. However, the reality is that it is very difficult to know what one would want until one is in such a condition. The locked-in syndrome affords an opportunity to ask very disabled patients about their quality of life. Contrary to popular perception, a number of studies have reported that the majority of locked-in patients expressed satisfaction with life and the incidence of depression was no greater than in the general population provided that any pain was being adequately managed.

WHAT CONSTITUTES THE INNATE DRIVER TO BRAIN REPAIR AND RECOVERY OF FUNCTION?

'An Indefatigable, Immovable Striving for Adjustment Rules the Organism'

Foerster and Goldstein, a Neurosurgeon and a Neurologist respectively in the 1930's, studied recovery after brain injury, They disagreed about mechanisms of recovery - replacement of substance, redundancy, reserve capacity and change in strategy. However they did agree that the spontaneous striving of patients toward an optimal adaptation to environmental demands and satisfaction of their needs was an important factor in recovery of function. What is this force of nature, where is it located and does it function at the conscious level? When somebody is said to be fighting their illness, is there a brain mechanism involved? Far-fetched concepts but can they be formulated in to questions susceptible to experimental enquiry?

As we all know, particularly as we age, the brain cannot deal with more than one thought process at a time. The brain has developed mechanisms, particularly in the part called the basal ganglia, that funnel many input and output systems in to a final common pathway for action. The vast bulk of what our bodies and minds do is 'subconscious' – we are unaware of much of what we do. Even more impressively, Libet showed in the 1980's that our brains make decisions to act some 0.3 seconds before our conscious mind is aware of them.

To paraphrase Chris Frith, Is there an area in the brain that corresponds to 'I', a little 'me' or homunculus that is in control and makes genuinely free selections and decisions? If not a single area, are there networks of brain areas that apply constraints to make the final choice?

In one experiment using functional magnetic resonance scanning, Frith found that one area of the brain, the dorsofrontal prefrontal cortex, was more active when choices had to be made. Patients with lesions in that area were either apathetic and did little or the opposite, impulsive and with poor judgement.

There are many strange clinical conditions in which our concept of a holistic mechanism for consciousness is challenged. For example, an operation for refractory epilepsy involves division of the corpus callosum the great bundle of white matter that joins the two halves of the brain together. This renders the two cerebral hemispheres separate entities which can then be made to make contradictory decisions. For example, Michael Gazzaniga found that an apple placed in the right hand was still correctly named as such. In bizarre contrast, the patient could not recognise an apple placed in the left hand. In some other conditions, there is a mismatch between volition and the actual movement.

In the alien hand syndrome, patients complain that the hand behaves autonomously even though they retain normal sensation. Various lesions can be the cause but it is believed that the common mechanism is disconnection of the primary motor cortex controlling hand movement from areas of the brain that inform and control the motor cortex. Patients with amputated limbs may complain of painful phantom movements. Electrical stimulation of the motor cortex at operation under local anaesthetic by Wilder Penfield produced movement of the hand but the patient realised that he had not caused the movement.

Such uncontrolled experiments of nature fundamentally challenge our models of how the brain functions and hence the basis on which we try to manage our patients after brain injury. Clearly there are different levels to consciousness. Some components can be disrupted by specific lesions but what about insight and our sense of identity?

METHODS AVAILABLE FOR STUDY IN MAN – A FINAL NOTE OF CAUTION

'How can I help this patient; what can this patient teach me' to quote Sir William Osler. Many of the extraordinary phenomena described in this chapter have depended for their discovery upon the recognition and analysis by clinicians of the unusual in their patients. Patients themselves and their carers have provided invaluable insights. There have been many new techniques developed that allow us to study man directly based on insights gained from meticulous experimental studies in many different species. However, it is vital that the researcher, the public and the Courts understand the limitations and pitfalls in any new technology and retain a healthy degree of scepticism.

For example, functional magnetic resonance depends upon the BOLD effect. As described earlier, when a part of the brain becomes active, its blood supply increases more than is required. This finding was widely scorned when first published. It results in a fall in deoxyhaemoglobin and a rise in oxyhaemoglobin which changes the magnetic properties of the blood that can be then detected by the MR scanner. However, this increase in blood supply is not constant and may be reduced or absent in patients with vascular disease, after injury or who are anxious. How many of the thousands of functional MR studies have checked whether this is a problem for the interpretation of their studies? It is now becoming recognised that much is going on in the non-activated brain that is dark to functional MR scanning. Different types of scan often have to be superimposed on each other with great accuracy. One paper described how the area for anxiety was located in the lateral temporal lobe. The paper was retracted when the scrupulously honest authors realised later that the activity was a few millimetres away in the jaw muscle that is attached to the skull over the temporal lobe – nothing like anxiety to make one clench one's jaw! Enormous care has to be taken with the mathematical and statistical analyses – *'Circular analysis in systems neuroscience: the dangers of double dipping'* – to quote but one authority. There is a growing concern that current human non-invasive imaging techniques are nearing the limits of their resolving power. If the field is not to stagnate, single neurone recordings may still be necessary in non-human primates if novel concepts of higher mental function are to be explored, even if, like much curiosity-driven research, their immediate relevance to human disease cannot be easily predicted.

The time for nihilism in the treatment of patients after brain injury is over but optimism should still be tempered with constructive scepticism.

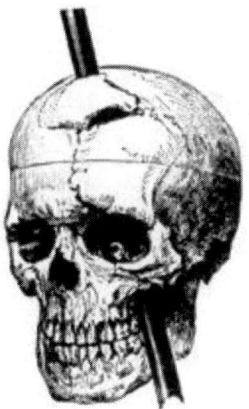

Drawing of Phineus's injury.

REFERENCES

Fawcett JW, Rosser AE and Dunnett SB. *'Brain damage, Brain Repair'*. Oxford Medical Publications, 2001.

Frith CD. *'Making up the mind. How the brain creates our mental world'*. Blackwell Publishing 2007.

Gazzaniga M. *'Who's in charge? Free will and the science of the brain'*. Dana Press 2011.

Hodgkin AL *'The conduction of the nervous impulse'. Sherrington Lectures.* Liverpool University Press 1964.

Illes J, Sahakian BJ. *'The Oxford Handbook of Neuroethics'.* OUP 2011.

Levin HS, Grafman J. *'Cerebral reorganisation of function after brain damage'.* OUP 2000.

Penfield W. *'The mystery of the mind: a critical study of consciousness and the human brain'.* Princeton University Press 1975.

Posner JB, Saper CB, Schiff ND and Plum F. *'Diagnosis of Stupor and Coma'.* 4th edition. OUP 2007.

Schurr PH. *'So that was life. A biography of Sir Geoffrey Jefferson'.* Royal Society of Medicine Press 1997.

Tallis R. *'Aping mankind: Neuromania, Darwinitis and the Misrepresentation of Humanity'.* Acumen 2011.

In: Scepticism: Hero and Villain
Editors: R. Calne and W. O'Reilly

ISBN: 978-1-62417-783-5
© 2013 Nova Science Publishers, Inc.

Chapter 10

A PRINCIPLED CLIMATE CHANGE SCEPTICISM

M. J. Kelly

*Prince Philip Professor of Technology, University of Cambridge,
Professorial Fellow, Trinity Hall, Cambridge, UK*

INTRODUCTION

Since 2000 popular discourse has focussed on a set of neo-Malthusian issues, from overpopulation, through resource depletion and environmental degradation to climate change. This last issue has risen to high levels of action in terms of the Kyoto accord to limit carbon dioxide (CO_2) emissions into the atmosphere and now even more draconian actions are being discussed. In this paper I want to express a principled and critical scepticism about the current climate science that is clearly to be distinguished from climate change denial. In the febrile space where climate change is debated, this distinction is lost in the fog of the war of words, and those who share my opinion have been compared with flat-earthers, paedophiles and holocaust deniers.

The climate of the earth has always been changing. There are many geological records of ice ages and times when the earth has been ice free. In recorded history we have warm periods in Roman and in medieval times, and the little ice age in the 1500-1700s as shown in the famous paintings by Bruegel père et fils. The level of the oceans has been both somewhat higher (by 3m 18,000 years ago) and much lower (by 120m 125,000 years ago) than it is at present. The contemporary debate about climate change focuses on the impacts of carbon dioxide released into the atmosphere due to mankind's action, principally the burning of fossil fuels since about 1800 at the start of the industrial revolution. The level of CO_2 in the atmosphere was constant over many thousands of years, but had risen by 20% above those earlier levels by 1970 and 40% now.

The average of the surface temperature over all the earth has risen since 1800, but not monotonically with predominantly downward trends between 1860-1890 and 1940-1975. There are smaller variations that track the sun spot cycles. The majority of the climate science community are convinced that the temperature rise since 1975 is predominantly due to mankind's action whereas all variation before was independent of mankind: this is based on detailed temperature data, especially since the age of satellites, and the results of computations on detailed models of the atmosphere. Given that the recent rise is still small in historical terms, it is a reasonable position to take that one wants to be convinced that there is real signal in the noise, a signal that is distinguishable from the large levels of natural climate variability that occur. This is especially so when those who take the forward projections of the climate scientists and tell us that we have to massively rearrange the way we live, at a cost of many trillions of pounds, if the earth is to have any chance of avoiding catastrophic climates in the near future.

I want to preface my own position by describing a formative moment in my education. While an undergraduate studying general relativity, the professor derived Einstein's equation of motion of the universe, and noted that it had the same mathematical structure as the equation for wave motion. He used the same techniques to solve the Einstein equation – what are the boundary conditions and what were the initial conditions? Now for a violin string or a drumhead, these conditions are clear, observable and measurable: the length of the string or the area of the drumhead, the tension in either, and how the string was plucked or where the drum was hit. For the universe the boundary and initial conditions are not clear. In cosmology, speculative and plausible, but unobservable and not directly measurable, boundary conditions are used and this means that what follows is plausible but not directly testable. Cosmology is therefore a story which could be profoundly wrong, but we do not know how to test it robustly. Furthermore it does not matter in the sense of affecting what I might do tomorrow or next year. At that point in my education, I decided that I would pursue a career in solid state physics where I could see a cubic centimetre sample, measure it, and vary all sorts of boundary conditions: shape, pressure, temperature, magnetic environment, and the exposure to light, shock or many other perturbations. From these many experiments, a robust and well-tested theory of the material is built up, which is used subsequently in the design and manufacture of vehicles, electronic circuits and many things that are safety critical in our everyday lives. Legal liability is assigned to and accepted by manufacturers on the basis of these models in respect of major failure in action.

Now consider two aspects of climate science, the level of understanding of today's climate and the projections for future climates in mid-century. First, the climate system is immensely complex. How does one deal with all the factors that impinge on the climate: the chemistry of the gases, the transfer of energy between the earth and space, and the transfer of energy and matter between the atmosphere and the oceans, and all the impacts of man's activities in changing the use of land, of building cities and of consuming fossil fuel? In technical terms any model of the atmosphere is (i) tightly coupled in that one cannot separate out or ignore some aspects without prejudicing the predictions that can be made, (ii) highly non-linear in that two small but equal sequential changes in one variable may lead to widely different impacts on the rest of the system, (iii) chaotic in being very sensitive to what is chosen as the boundary or initial conditions in trying to solve the model equations for predicting the future climate and (iv) multiscale wherein features at the 1m, 1km, 1000km and global scales are all interacting with each other. If one tried to model the behaviour of a mixture of different types of pasta in a bowl subject to a random stirring motion, one has some idea of the complexity. The attribution of *most* of the climate change of the last 40 years to the *single* factor of the increase in CO_2 since 1800, and equally strongly to associate *all* the climate change up to 1970 to random internal features of the climate system plus the impacts of solar and volcanic events offends my basic instincts about understanding complex systems.

Faced with such complexity, the underlying simplifying theory goes as follows: we assume that the increase of the globally averaged surface temperature (itself a concept of questionable relevance and never actually measured) due to a doubled concentration of CO_2 in the atmosphere can be described by $\Delta T = \Delta T_o/(1-\phi)$, where ΔT_o is the change in temperature solely due to the extra CO_2, i.e. when $\phi=0$, where ϕ is a feedback factor that takes into account all the strongly-coupled, highly-nonlinear and chaotic interactions, such as its influence on water in the atmosphere (and water is a much the most powerful greenhouse gas), or wind patterns, aerosols or many other factors. There is widespread agreement on ΔT_o, even among the critics of the global warming community that a doubling of the CO_2 in the atmosphere will lead to a 1C rise in temperature. There is no strong agreement on the value of ϕ, and even strong disagreements on its actual sign. If ϕ is negative, ΔT is less than ΔT_o and we need not worry, but if ϕ is positive and above 0.3, we should be very worried as ΔT can then be much greater than ΔT_o. No amount of modelling will narrow the range of ϕ. Some clever, repeatable, experiments, testing falsifiable hypotheses might just succeed, but I don't know of any such experiments right now. The space where solid state physicists and engineers are more comfortable in working would allow for just such discriminating experimental tests.

Well-found but complex models have been developed to predict the weather for tomorrow and next week. These put as many as possible of the relevant climatic factors into a complex computer programme which solves the equations of motion of the atmosphere. These models are tested every day as the weather is actually observed, and the models are iteratively improved so that the weather forecasts have become increasingly reliable. The weather system itself is also chaotic, non-linear, tightly coupled and multiscale, and so the computed future weathers are not always correct. Beyond about two weeks the detailed weather predictions are no longer reliable in the sense that anyone would take legal or reputational liability for the consequences of making an erroneous prediction. It is these same weather models that are run forward on computers to make predictions of the climate (which is taken to equal the (unweighted) average of the many millions of future weathers) 40 years out. As someone who has developed models of the electronic properties of such a something as simple as a single crystal of silicon (with 6-8 parameters), I know just how fraught models can be if they are not tested exhaustively against real experimental data. By definition it is not possible to do that with climate predictions, which are technically called projections precisely to acknowledge that fact. In particular, there is no convergence theorem that says that the end-point of forward simulations of complex models that approximate many aspects of the climate is even a possible 2050 climate. There is simply no question of anyone taking legal liability for the consequences of error.

Suppose I make a simple paper dart, and I arrange for it to be launched a thousand times from a given position with a given attitude and velocity. I can map out the thousand positions where it first hits the ground. None of that accumulated data can tell me where the dart will hit when I next launch it. Furthermore, I could develop a complex and sophisticated model of the dart and solve the various aerodynamic equations to predict its flight path and point of hitting the ground. If the statistics of the pattern of ground hittings from a thousand computer runs and those from the experimental runs actually agree closely, I can have some confidence in the model, but again it cannot tell me where the dart will hit the ground the next time it is launched. The same holds for many runs of the climate change models.

I could do another set of experiments: I could arrange for a drop of ink of a precise volume, colour and density of dye to be released at a particular spot on the surface of a large container of still water, and ask where the point of maximum density of ink dye concentration is one minute or one hour after the release, as measured by some optical tomography experiment. I could do that a thousand or a million times, but this data will not tell me where the next point of maximum density will occur. Again I could make a complex computer model, and I might get the statistics of the real data and the model calculation, and they might agree. Note here that the trajectory is not necessarily continuous! But no amount of modelling will tell me about what actually happens next time I release a drop. Nor do climate models tell me what will happen en route to and in 2050.

Now suppose I go back to both experiments and look more closely. I find that the room in which I do the experiments has windows that are strongly sunlit on one side and the air in the room is subject to some thermal motion caused by uneven surface temperatures. If this is not taken into account in the model, one can expect to find disagreements between the statistics for hitting points of the dart from the experiment and the computer runs. Again the sunlight on the container might induce thermal motion in the water and so one might anticipate a divergence between experiment and simulation results for the statistics of the point of maximum density of the ink dye. The thermal motion of the air or the water is a known unknown. But I am worse off in terms of asking where the next dart will land. The formation of small-scale clouds and their impact on weather and climate are comparable known unknowns in the climate models and their simulations.

Now suppose that the dart has some magnetic material in the paper filler, or that the ink dye has some magnetic character. We might analyse the response of the dart and the ink to the earth's magnetic field, and decide that the effect is too small to worry about. But suppose, unknown to me, there is a superconducting magnet in a poorly screened room on the floor above, and that it is doing a swept-field measurement while I am doing my experiments? I would then get a systematically varying disturbance imposed on what is already a chaotic trajectory each time I do an experiment. That is an unknown unknown, like the future behaviour of the sun, or the actual future carbon emissions in the climate models and their simulations.

The mathematical theory of chaos was first uncovered during primitive studies of the non-linear equations of motion of weather systems in the 1960s by Edward Lorenz. In addition to its normal description about the evolution of the weather being extremely sensitive to the initial conditions, e.g. a butterfly wing flap in Texas causing a cyclone in China, there is another important consequence. In non-chaotic systems there are theorems in the field of statistical mechanics which show when averages of many experiments do converge to a meaningful quantity. This is not necessarily so in chaotic systems.

Now let's try and project where the world's climate will be in 40 years' time with exact prescience of the actual trajectory of carbon emissions and of future volcanic eruptions. First we have no experimental data against which to compare the statistics of the computer simulations. Secondly, since we can identify many detailed aspects of the actual weather that are not in the simulations such as cloud formation on the one kilometre length scale, it is like ignoring the effects of the thermal fluctuations above. Thirdly, suppose the sun changes its pattern of behaviour over the next 40 years in a way that resembles that associated either with the medieval warm period or the little ice age, and 40 years is about the timescale on which the proxy record notes temperature changes in both those periods, that is like ignoring the magnetic field above and its polarity.

When will we know with any confidence what the climate of 2050 is to be like? The answer is on 31 December 2050, when we have the actual data, and not before. By that stage we will have the actual carbon emission trajectory to hand as well, and one hopes that the short-term climate models agree with what is observed. Suppose the solar wind on the one hand decreases cloud cover and reduces the earth's average temperature at a result. If the temperatures went down to values seen in the 1500-1700s in Europe we might expect crop failures unless genetic modification can make plants more ice-resistant. But, if the extra CO_2 we are now pumping into the atmosphere maintains the temperature to avert mass crop failure and widespread starvation among 9 billion people, the world in 2050 will regard some of today's mitigation measures with horror. The converse is true also. If a warm period returns with a rather greater than 2C rise in average global temperature today's mitigation measures will have been a godsend. No-one is sure which way the temperature will actually go. Some in the solar physics community suggest we may be in for some cooling. The CO_2 increase by itself will contribute to a temperature rise. The model simulations do not add any firm knowledge of what the climate in 20 or 40 years will actually be like, or narrow the uncertainty (and all its implications) that is associated with the feedback factor ϕ in the earlier paragraph.

For those trained in solid state physics and electronic engineering, the daily encounters with the results of controlled experiments do two things: they engender a certain humility in front of the real world, but they also give confidence that the theories are appropriate for designing aeroplanes, automobiles and electronic safety systems, for which legal liability can be assigned and assumed. It also means that looking in on other branches of science, whether cosmology or climate modelling, a principled scepticism is entirely appropriate. This is acknowledged in the primary literature of the core climate science community, but absent from the summaries for the public media and politicians. The alarmist wing of their community does not permit such a stance – we must take what they say on trust, especially on present and future impacts. It is this latter community that tells us our winters will get both warmer and colder because of climate change, that we will get both draughts and floods, etc, that the snows of

Kilimanjaro have gone forever (just before they have returned after a brief absence!). Everything is attributed to climate change and there is no falsifiable hypothesis against which to make a robust attribution. Indeed otherwise laudable efforts at attribution should be treated with deep scepticism until they become the consequence of a falsifiable hypothesis, or the direct corollary of one. Indeed there seems to be an inverse relation between reliably established facts and emotional outrage. This has led to a situation where uncertainty can be and has been exploited by individuals and organisations for political and financial gain (from both governments and the private sector), and which provides nourishment for the powerful lobbying processes. Ian McEwan's amusing novel *Solar* gives a popular insight into the ploys.

Where engineers have a real problem is in defining a measured response to the alarmism. When Governments are legislating for draconian actions on the basis of climate model projections that do not pass their test of verifiability, engineers are understandably and correctly highly critical. Engineers can also point to fact that the neo-Malthusians have a 200-year track record of total failure in their predictions. The UK did not starve (Malthus 1790s), nor run out of coal (Jevons 1860s), nor run out of oil (numerous since 1900), nor run out of half the periodic table in minerals by 2000 (Club of Rome 1960s). The arguments were all seen to be compelling in their day, why should it be different this time about climate? The millennial thinking over the last decade has been dominated by an inter-related set of Malthusian issues that start with the level of world population and locally unbalanced demographics, and proceed through energy profligacy and resource depletion more generally, environmental degradation and loss of biodiversity, to aging infrastructure and a lack of resilience to future climates. The most serious of these, namely over-population, seems to be in the process of solving itself: the fecundity of educated women and women in cities is much lower than that of uneducated rural women. In Europe and Japan, populations are declining. As more people move into cities where education is more prevalent, the estimate of the maximum world population is continuing to fall: where it was once 12B, it is at about 9B now. Some have predicted a perfect storm of climate, food, water and population in crisis 30 years from now. It is a possibility, and it may be a close run thing, but a continuation of the green revolutions and the reduction of water use in agriculture do allow a rational optimism.

It would be irresponsible to conclude this chapter without referring to two issues of national importance of real concern that are adjacent to climate change.

Engineers will point out that the real, urgent and large scale problem for the UK at present is the security of our energy supply. If 30% of our current generating capacity has to be turned off, because of agreed EU carbon emission targets in the case of coal-fired power stations and end-of-life decommissioning of first generation nuclear power plants, how will this capacity be replaced without the lights going out? Nuclear rebuild is taking a knock in the face of public over-reaction to the serious accident in Japan. At the time of writing, a few have died although no deaths are attributable to radiation poisoning, but in the much worse case, only thirty people died of radiation sickness at Chernobyl and the World Health Organisation suggests 4000 extra cancer cases (not all fatal) ensued. Since 1850, 165,000 miners have died in UK coalmines, including 16,599 in the period 1950-2000 that coincides with the availability of nuclear energy!! Wind is intermittent: while on 6 September 2010 at 5am wind produced 14% of the 23GW electricity the UK needed, on 7 December at 5.30pm, it could only produce 0.3GW when the electricity demand was 60GW. On a very cold winter day we need back-up capacity of coal and gas and nuclear power, and it does not make economic sense to have these latter facilities not operating just because the wind is blowing! My hunch is that the coal and gas will still be burning in 2020 precisely to stop the lights going out. The dominance of climate science in the public debate has distracted us from these pressing issues of energy infrastructure.

Simulations in three other contexts have had public policy consequences that should alert us to the need for robust data on which to test models. The closure of the airspace in Europe in 2010 because of zero tolerance of volcanic ash pointed to the lack of understanding of the effects of very low levels of ash on aircraft engines, something that might have been benchmarked. During the foot-and-mouth outbreak, modelling of the spread of the disease was done on the basis of different culling scenarios, and the assumed virulence of the disease. Many individual farmers had their livelihoods severely disrupted, and remain convinced that there was a serious over-reaction at the time. Similarly, models of influenza pandemics led to an overstocking of vaccines. It is right that we have the results of simulations at hand, but it still remains a matter of professional judgement how we react to those results. Over-reaction on the scale of the three examples above is even understandable. However, if the climate projection impacts turn out to have been overestimated, and trillions of pounds used less productively then was necessary, that is very serious for the whole world. Fortunately, the first steps to mitigate or adapt to future climates represent no-regrets actions associated with energy efficiency and a lesser depletion of resources. Once those first steps are complete, the case for the follow-on steps in the case of climate resilience needs to be much more robust than it is at present.

I wish to thank the several colleagues with whom I have shared this paper in draft for the helpful and insightful comments that they have made.

HUMANITIES

In: Scepticism: Hero and Villain
Editors: R. Calne and W. O'Reilly

ISBN: 978-1-62417-783-5
© 2013 Nova Science Publishers, Inc.

Chapter 11

ANCIENT SCEPTICISM AND ITS CHALLENGES

Lucia Prauscello

University of Cambridge, Faculty of Classics and Fellowe of Trinity Hall,
Cambridge, UK

'What we need is not the will to believe but the will to find out'
Bertrand Russell (*Sceptical Essays*)

INTRODUCTION

Ancient Scepticism seemingly presents us with a paradox: how can it be possible intellectually to commit oneself to the view that both human well-being and genuine philosophical inquiry should be achieved through the refusal to make intellectual commitments? Can such a life be humanly possible? And if so, is this kind of life worth living? Ancient sceptical thought saw the challenge of relentless investigation as directly relevant to one's life *as a whole*. To adopt a given cognitive stance (be it even a non-committal cognitive stance) will transform the totality of one's being. Before trying to recover some of the ways in which the sceptic way of life conceived of this transformative power of the search for truth, let us first sketch very briefly the ancient origins of sceptic thought.

The nature of reality and the nature of language, the relationship between nature and convention, cause and responsibilities, the possibility of human cognition and its limits, moral relativism and 'sceptical' doubt are all themes already largely explored by most pre-socratic thinkers. In particular, in fifth century BC Greece the so-called Sophists created a climate of intellectual debate and ferment that strongly influenced the culture of the time and left long-lasting traces in philosophical debate ever since, especially in Socrates and Plato's philosophical reflections.[1]

Ancient Scepticism is evidently an idiosyncratic upshot of this critical tradition. In its narrow definition of a given philosophical attitude to life, Ancient Scepticism is in itself an elusive aggregate of at least three distinct philosophical outlooks: that maintained by Pyrrho of Elis (ca. 365-275 BC) and his pupils (above all Timon of Phlius, ca. 325-230 BC); Academic Scepticism under the aegis of the Socratic and Platonic heritage (from Arcesilaus up to roughly Philo of Larissa, that is, from the middle of the 3rd century BC to first quarter of the 1st century BC); and the radical Pyrrhonian Scepticism of Aenesidemus (1st century BC), who tried to recover the original sceptical roots of Pyrrho's thought.

In this chapter, for the sake of clarity, we shall sacrifice a diachronic view in favour of an anachronistically synchronic approach, only occasionally pointing out the (many) differences between the various ancient incarnations of Scepticism.

We shall thus consider the different strands of the sceptic tradition as a reasonably coherent whole. Furthermore, since Sextus Empiricus (ca. 200 AD), an empiricist physician and sceptic philosopher, came *de facto* to represent *the* official face of Pyrrhonian Scepticism to the modern western world after his rediscovery and publication (in Latin translation) by Henri Etienne in the 1562,[2] our account will mainly rely on his writings, that is, the *Outlines of Scepticism* (*Pyrrhoniae hypotyposes*: hereafter *PH*) and *Against the Mathematicians* (*Adversus mathematicos*: hereafter *M*).[3]

This simplified view of the sceptical tradition, if historically problematic, has nevertheless some justification since the common denominator of the sceptical 'way of life' (ἡ σκεπτικὴ ἀγωγή) is that among the Hellenistic philosophical schools Sceptics alone, be they Pyrrhonists or Academics, distinguish themselves by having no systematic theory, and what is more, no beliefs. The only

---

[1] On the Sophists and their attitude towards traditional beliefs, see Gagarin and Woodruff 2008. For the relationship between Ancient Scepticism and Socratic thinking, see Bett 2006.
[2] For the flourishing of sceptic trends in modern philosophy in the wake of the rediscovery of Sextus' text, see the still fundamental work by Popkin (1960, 1979 and 2003). For the transmission of the text of Sextus through the ages see now Floridi 2002 and 2010.
[3] In our attempt to reconstruct the main outlines of ancient Scepticism we are obliged to rely almost entirely on secondary sources: Pyrrho, like Socrates, did not leave anything written. The biggest bulk of information on ancient Scepticism has come down to us *via* Cicero's academic writings (1st century BC), Sextus Empiricus and Diogenes Laertius (3rd century AD).

commitment they present themselves attached to is the ongoing practice of 'inquiry' (σκέψις).⁴

The Greek term σκεπτικός, a deverbative adjective from σκέπτομαι, ('to look upon or at, inspect, observe': cf. Latin *specio*, Skt. *páśyati* 'to see') means literally 'inquiring'.⁵ And inquiry about beliefs, appearances, suspension of judgment play a paramount role in Ancient Scepticism in all its various denominations. This is how Sextus introduces the Sceptics at *PH* 1.1-3:

> 'when people are investigating (τοῖς ζητοῦσι) any subject, the likely result (εἰκός) is either a discovery (εὕρεσιν), or a denial of discovery (ἄρνησιν εὑρέσεως) and a confession of inapprehensibility (ἀκαταληψίας ὁμολογίαν), or else a continuation of the investigation (ἐπιμονὴν ζητήσεως). This, no doubt, is why in the case of philosophical investigations, too, some have said that they have discovered the truth, some have asserted that it cannot be apprehended, and others are still investigating (οἱ δὲ ἔτι ζητοῦσιν). Those who are called Dogmatists in the proper sense of the word (οἱ ἰδίως καλούμενοι δογματικοί) think that they have discovered the truth [...]. But the sceptics are still investigating (ζητοῦσι δὲ οἱ σκεπτικοί)'⁶

Dogmatists⁷, among whom Sextus includes the Aristotelians, Epicureans and the Stoics, assert that they have found the truth; others (the Academics) claim that things cannot be known. The Sceptics alone persevere in their search: they self-

---

⁴ Scepticism, differently form the other Hellenistic philosophical schools, was never an institutionalized 'sect' (αἵρεσις). That Scepticism was absent from the majority of the sect catalogues (the so-called 'hairetic literature') of Hellenistic time is probably due to the fact that Sceptics presented themselves as embodying an 'attitude to life' (ἀγωγή) rather than a philosophical system proper. Only post-Hellenistic Sceptics eagerly tried to re-define their identity and enter the institutionalized *curriculum* of philosophical education: see Polito 2007.

⁵ Cf. P. Chantraine, *Dictionnaire étymologique de la langue grecque*, Paris 1999², s.v. σκέπτομαι. Was σκεπτικός ('sceptic') a self-definition of the earlier Pyrrhonists? Probably not (see Janáček 1979, Striker 1980: 54 n. 1, Sedley 1983: 20, 27-28 n. 61, Bailey 2002: 16-7, 82-3): Philo of Alexandria (1ˢᵗ c. BC/1ˢᵗ c. AD) still uses σκεπτικός in the etymologically original sense of 'enquirer' in its broader meaning (cf. *On Drunkness* 202 Wendland), without distinguishing dogmatic or sceptically oriented philosophers. Since Philo's source is probably Aenesidemus, the label 'sceptic' apparently did not originate with him. The earliest datable occurrence of σκεπτικός in its technical meaning of 'sceptic' is in Aulus Gellius (2ⁿᵈ c. AD), *Attic Nights* 9.5 (where the term encompasses both Academics and Pyrrhonists). In Sextus the word σκεπτικός is consistently used as a synonym of 'Pyrrhonist'.

⁶ The Greek text of Sextus quoted here and hereafter is that of Mutschmann (Teubner edition). The translation is, with some slight modifications, is by Annas and Barnes 2000.

⁷ I employ here the term δογματικός ('dogmatist') in the sense used by Sextus, that is, to designate anyone who makes positive or negative assertions about the nature of things on the basis of what he conceives to be the evidence.

consciously present themselves to eyes of the world as life-long inquirers. But what does this mean? At *PH* 1.8-9 we are told that:

> 'scepticism is an ability to set out oppositions (δύναμις ἀντιθετική) among things which appear and are thought of (φαινομένων τε καὶ νοουμένων) in anyway at all, an ability by which, because of the equipollence (διὰ τὴν ... ἰσοσθένειαν) in the opposed objects and accounts, we come first to suspension of judgment (εἰς ἐποχήν) and afterwards to tranquillity (εἰς ἀταραξίαν)'

According to Ancient Scepticism if, under cognitive pressure, we cannot claim any certain knowledge because of the 'equipollent nature' (ἰσοσθένεια) of the impressions produced on us by the 'appearances',[8] we should then 'withhold' from any kind of truth-claim (ἐποχή), *belief included*.

This 'ability to set out oppositions' articulated itself in 'a highly developed practice of argumentative enquiry, formalized according to a number of modes or patterns of arguments' (Burnyeat 1980: 23), which finds its fullest formulation in the so-called ten 'modes' (τρόποι) of Aenesidemus (*PH* 1.36 ff. and DL 9.79ff.).[9]

These 'modes' were conceived as dialectical weapons against the Dogmatists inasmuch as they induced suspension of judgment by prompting the withholding of assent to the results of reasoning.

At *PH* 1.7 we find a fully fledged definition of the 'sceptical way of life' in the following terms:

> 'the Sceptical persuasion, then, is also called "Investigative" (ζητητική) from its activity in investigating and inquiring; "Suspensive" (ἐφεκτική) from the feeling that comes about in the inquirer after the investigation; "Aporetic" (ἀπορητική) either (as some say) from the fact that it puzzles over and investigate everything (ἀπὸ τοῦ περὶ παντὸς ἀπορεῖν καὶ ζητεῖν), or else from its being at a loss (ἀμηχανεῖν) whether to assent or deny.'

---

[8] By 'appearances' are meant both sense-appearances (τὰ φαινόμενα) but also non-sensible appearances, i.e. objects of thought (i. e. τὰ νοητά, cf. *PH* 1.8-9 and 21).
[9] Full treatment of the sceptical 'modes' of argumentation can be found in Annas and Barnes 1985 and now Woodruff 2010. The ten modes are (i) arguments from differences among animals; (ii) arguments from differences among human beings; (iii) arguments from differences among the senses; (iv) arguments from contrasting circumstances; (v) arguments from contrasting positions, distances and places; (vi) arguments from contrasting mixtures; (vii) arguments from contrasting quantities and compositions; (viii) arguments from relativity; (ix) arguments from constant or rare concurrences; (x) arguments from contrasting ways of life, customs, myths and dogmatic assumptions.

In a sense, then, the springboard of Ancient Scepticism *is* the search for true knowledge; yet this search leads to the repeated observation that there is no reliable criterion of truth since appearances are conflicting, and hence, ultimately, to the suspension of judgment which brings with itself 'tranquility' (ἀταραξία: etymologically 'freedom from perturbation'), the sceptic vision of 'living well' (εὐδαιμονία).[10]

In its radical and systematic challenge to beliefs, we find one of the most distinctive features of ancient Scepticism when compared to other proto-sceptical or negative pronouncements about the possibility of human cognition. Pre-Pyrrhonian traces of a sceptical mind-set can be detected almost everywhere in Greek thought (not only the 5th century sophist Protagoras and Socrates have been claimed by some quarters as the Sceptics' intellectual and moral predecessors but also Homer himself[11]).

Many pre-socratic thinkers expressed some form of doubt about the possibility of human knowledge. Doubt (or straightforward denial) about the cognitive capacities of humankind to attain true knowledge is a common thread that links together intellectual figures as diverse as Heraclitus, Xenophanes, Democritus, Socrates and even (some) Plato, to mention only a few.[12] Yet there is a fundamental difference: in Pyrrho's putative predecessors doubt is always 'controlled doubt', and as such its inherent negativity is redirected such as to become a propaedeutic function to the proper search for the truth (Sedley 1983: 10; Lee 2010). In this sense, for pre-Pyrrhonian thinkers a sceptical outlook acquired a function similar to that countenanced by Kant, a 'critical' dogmatist: 'while the sceptical procedure cannot of itself yield any satisfying answer to the questions of reason, nonetheless it prepares the way by arousing reason to circumspection' (*Critique of Pure Reason* A769[13]). Sextus himself, for instance, though he recognized sceptical elements in Plato, positively rejected the image of Plato as a proto-sceptic 'in its purest sense' (*PH* 1.222 εἰλικρινῶς σκεπτικός)

---

[10] 'Freedom from perturbation' does not feature as the goal of a sceptic life in its Academic version, but it was already present in Pyrrho's teaching: cf. Aristocles of Messene (2nd c. AD) on Timon of Phlius (Pyrrho's pupil) in Eusebius, *Preparatio Evangelica* 14.18. 2-4 = T 53 Decleva Caizzi, where 'living well' (εὐδαιμονία) is identified with 'freedom from perturbation' (ἀταραξία). A word should be said about my rendering of the Greek εὐδαιμονία as 'living well', often misleadingly translated as 'happiness': differently from the English 'happiness', εὐδαιμονία is not an emotion but 'a state of life': 'to live well' means to achieve the possession of that which is deemed the highest human good (see Mikalson 2010: 7-8).

[11] For Pyrrho's alleged extreme fondness for Homer cf. TT 20-21 Decleva Caizzi.

[12] For the relationship between Socrates, Plato and Pyrrhonism, see Bett 2000: 132-39 and 2006, Annas 1992, Woodruff 1986. On Socrates' cognitive stance (his claim to lack of knowledge), see the nuanced analysis by Fine 2008.

[13] Quoted by Annas and Barnes 1985: 7.

because anyone whose writings assert some positive ideas is not 'truly' a sceptic. We glimpse here another important feature of Ancient Scepticism: its *global* dimension ('scepticism does not come in degrees— and a true skeptic is a pure and unmitigated skeptic': Bett 2006: 301).

The same proviso should be made also for the so-called sophistic enlightenment of the 5th century BC which has been seen as an important intellectual ancestor of sceptical thought. Also in this case there are some significant differences (Striker 1996). Sophists, like sceptics, do indeed share an antinomian dialectic method of investigation: they show what reasons there may be for supporting a given belief and its opposite, but the ultimate relativism of the sophists, at least in its Protagorean version, is mainly alien to the genuine Sceptic.[14] The charge of relativism against the Sceptics was indeed already ancient and Sextus (*PH* 1.127) finds itself at some difficulty in denying that Protagoras, the traditional champion of classical relativism ('man is the measure of all things') was not a sceptic. Yet in many respects this is a misguided charge: if we take sceptic in the loose modern sense, then certainly the sceptic is somehow a relativist. But if we adhere to the ancient notion of Scepticism, in its strong formulation, there is a wide gap between Ancient Scepticism and relativism in terms of both epistemological premises and practical, value-oriented behaviour. The ancient Sceptic is led by reason to suspend judgment: he does not deny that in there *is* 'out there' something to be known that he is unable to get to know, but the equal strength with which conflicting appearances strike him leads him to suspend his judgment (ἐποχή). A true relativist, on the other hand, does not suspend judgment: he actively denies that there is out there something to be known about *x* that he does not know. In a sense, then, for the relativist there is literally nothing to be sceptical about. The Protagorean relativist does indeed hold the belief that 'all appearances are true' (Aristotle, *Metaphysics* 1009a8). So, from an ancient perspective, relativism is not a form of Scepticism, since the relativist agent does hold beliefs. Let us for instance look at the sceptic version of the 'relativity' (πρός τι) criterion (the eighth mode of sceptical argumentation) as formulated by Sextus at *PH* 1.135:

> 'the eighth mode is the one deriving from relativity (πρός τι), by which we conclude that, since everything is relative (ἐπεὶ πάντα ἐστὶ πρός τι), we shall suspend judgment (ἐφέξομεν) as to what things are the case independently (ἀπολύτως) and in their nature (ὡς πρὸς τὴν φύσιν). It should be recognized that here, as elsewhere, we use "is" (ἔστι) loosely, in the sense of "appears" (φαίνεται'), implicitly saying "everything appears relative"'

---

[14] For the ambiguous relationship between Scepticism and relativism, see Annas and Barnes 1985: 97-9 and 130-5, Annas 1986: 9-11 Lee 2010: 14, 27-8.

What is interesting to note here for our purposes is that the eighth mode of argumentation *uses* relativism only as a point of *departure* to reach the suspension of judgment. Does this not turn the Sceptic into a negative dogmatist? Not necessarily: '[one] can only say how things appear to different observers or in relation to other things, not how they are in themselves, leaving it open as a good Sceptic should, whether there is a way things are in themselves' (Striker 1996: 19).

Ancient Sceptics, we have seen, reject beliefs and suspend judgment. We come here to touch upon a very important difference between ancient and modern Scepticism (Bett 2010: 1-3, Annas 1986 and 1996). That x means something different at different times is, of course, a common truism, but it is nonetheless true of the history of Scepticism, where discontinuity, more than continuity, seems to characterize its trajectory from the ancient to the modern era.

To a Hellenistic Greek to be a Sceptic and live out one's sceptical attitude meant at the same time something less (epistemologically) and more (behaviourally) than to our contemporaries.

In current parlance a minimum working definition of Scepticism which would meet with some consent is that of an epistemological stance denying the possibility of knowledge in some (or, in extreme cases, all) areas of human experience (e.g. ethics, knowledge etc.). That is, modern Scepticism often views itself as a challenge to knowledge, hence the primary importance assigned by it to issues like certainty, justified belief, and doubt.

On the contrary Ancient Scepticism, as we have just seen, targets *belief*, not knowledge (Annas and Barnes 1985: 7-10, Vogt 2010, Perin 2010). This different premise reflects an attitude about the way in which human rationality is conceived that may seem quite alien to its modern version(s).

The ancient Sceptic does not have anything to say about the ultimate nature of things ('true knowledge'), whose existence he does *not* however doubt *a priori*: at *PH* 1.19-20 we are told that

> 'when we question whether the underlying object (τὸ ὑποκείμενον) is such as it appears, we grant (δίδομεν) the fact that it appears, and our doubt does not concern the appearance itself, but the account given of the appearance (ζητοῦμεν δ' οὐ περὶ τοῦ φαινομένου ἀλλὰ περὶ ἐκείνου ὃ λέγεται περὶ τοῦ φαινομένου)'

He can only talk of 'appearances' (τὰ φαινόμενα, literally 'what is apparent, manifest' in a phenomenological sense) and to talk about 'appearances' for an ancient Sceptic is to say 'how things impress us or how they strike us, whether or not it is *via* our perceptual apparatus that the impression is made (Annas and

Barnes 1985: 27). Scepticism puts thus a strong emphasis on what has been called the 'empiricism of the mind' (Annas and Barnes 1985: 116-7). At *PH* 1.127-8 (within the treatment of the sixth mode of antinomian argumentation depending on mixtures) we are told that 'our senses (αἱ αἰσθήσεις) do not grasp (οὐκ ἀντιλαμβάνονται) what external existing object are (τὰ ἐκτὸς ὑποκείμενα) accurately like. But our intellect (ἡ διάνοια) does not do so either, especially since its guides, the senses, fail it (σφάλλονται).

That is, our intellect (ἡ διάνοια) can 'function' only through its guides, the sensorial perceptions (αἱ αἰσθήσεις): hence our intellectual capability is utterly dependent on experience.[15]

The way in which ancient Scepticism conceives of the 'appearances' explains also why the distinction between subjectivity and objectivity, so important in modern scepticism, is never really a central issue in its ancient variant: what the Sceptic undergoes when appearances strike him, is conceived by Sextus as 'affections (πάθη) of the mind' (see Fine 2000 and 2003), yet sceptics 'aim to record affections without claiming anything about the [external] world' (Vogt 2010).

But does the Sceptic forsake *all* beliefs? (Burnyeat 1983; *contra* Frede 1984). At least in the variant recorded by Sextus, there seems to be a restriction to the sceptic suspension of judgment at *PH* 1.13:

> 'when we say that Sceptics do not hold beliefs (μὴ δογματίζειν), we do not take "belief" (δόγμα) in the sense in which some say, quite generally (κοινότερον), that belief is acquiescing (τὸ εὐδοκεῖν) in something; for Sceptics assent (συγκατατίθεται) to the feelings forced upon them in accordance by appearances (τοῖς ... κατὰ φαντασίαν κατηναγκασμένοις πάθεσι) — for example, they would not say, when heated or chilled, "I think (δοκῶ) I am not heated (or: chilled)." Rather, we say that they do not hold beliefs in the sense in which some say that belief is assent (συγκατάθεσιν) to some non-evident matter investigated by the sciences (τῶν κατὰ τὰς ἐπιστήμας ζητουμένων ἀδήλων). For Pyrrhonists do not assent to anything non-evident (τῶν ἀδήλων)'

The key to the correct interpretation of this passage lies in the semantic spectrum covered by the verb δογματίζειν (Barnes 1982: 10-12). If understood in a loose sense (κοινότερον), then the Sceptic does not deny his acquiescence in the πάθη (affections) which happen to him. But the Sceptic does not dogmatize in the

---

[15] For the complex relationship between ancient Scepticism and medical empiricism, see the detailed survey by Allen 2010. Many sceptic philosophers were doctors: cf. the list at DL 1.115-6.

narrower, technical sense held by others, that is, he does not yield assent to what is 'non-evident' (Castagnoli 2000: 274-5). As put by Perin 2010: 161 'if this is right, then for Sextus a non-dogmatic belief – the kind of belief that is compatible with Scepticism – is simply a belief about how things appear to one to be.' Thus, the Sceptic on (what others would define as) a hot day, will agree that he 'seems to feel hot' — but he will withhold judgment on what that feeling might represent.

The second important difference between ancient Scepticism and its modern versions is that since ancient Scepticism attacked not knowledge but belief, this had important practical consequences on human *responses* to belief, i.e. on our *actions*, and on our motivations for acting.[16] Ancient Scepticism, differently from modern Scepticism, took very seriously the practical consequences of the suspension of judgment about beliefs (especially value beliefs: hence the hoard of anecdotes about Pyrrho's impractical and eccentric life-style). Modern Scepticism, on the other hand, tends to treat sceptical doubt as 'insulated' from everyday life (Annas 1986): modern Scepticism does not transform your everyday behaviour. The Sceptic's suspension of judgment was instead not just an intellectual exercise (the modern 'intellectual doubt')[17] but presented serious challenges to the conduct of life. In this sense ancient Scepticism lived up to Socrates' challenge, in the *Apology*, that only 'an examined life' is worth living. Hence ancient Scepticism envisages the challenge of investigation as directly relevant to the *totality* of our lives.

But how far can live 'without belief' (ἀδοξάστως), and still lead a recognizably meaningful human life, both intellectually and morally and, what is more, reach 'freedom from perturbation' (ἀταραξία)? And is this state of tranquility compatible with a truly inquiring disposition of mind? (Burnyeat 1980 gives a negative answer; *contra* McPherran 1989).[18] The charge that living without beliefs must inevitably bring one to a paralysing inability to act (ἀπραξία) is the main charge that the Stoics levelled at Scepticism in antiquity (Vogt 2010a). The sceptic answer to this charge is that the Sceptic philosopher 'lives by appearances', since human *nature* does not allow him to be totally inactive (*PH* 1.23):

---

[16] For the connections between beliefs, especially value beliefs, and actions in ancient Scepticism, see Vogt 2010a, esp. 177-8; Annas 1986 and 1996.

[17] Does an ancient Sceptic 'doubt' in the modern sense of the world? Is suspension of judgment a form of doubt? For the difference between suspension of judgment and doubt, see Voigt 2010.

[18] Burnyeat 1980: 28ff. argues at length that the radical idea that one should live without belief already goes back to Pyrrho himself (via Timon: cf. Eus. *Prep.Evang.* 14.18.2-4 = T 52 Decleva Caizzi) and was 'resuscitated' by Aenesidamus against the Academics who held 'what is persuasive' (τὸ πιθανόν) as the criterion for the practical conduct of life).

'Thus, attending to what is apparent (τοῖς φαινομένοις), we live in accordance with everyday observances (κατὰ τὴν βιωτικὴν τήρησιν), without holding opinions (ἀδοξάστως) — for we are not able (μὴ δυνάμεθα) to be utterly inactive'

In particular, 'the everyday observances of life' (βιωτικὴ τήρησις) provide the Sceptic with four guidelines among the appearances (*PH* I. 23-4): the 'guidance of nature' (ὑφήγησις φύσεως), that is, the use of the natural human capacity to perceive and reason, the 'necessity of affections' (ἀνάγκη παθῶν), that is, the drives and urges of bodily needs (thirst, hunger etc.), the 'transmission of laws and customs' (παράδοσις νόμων τε καὶ ἐθῶν), that is, the societal influence, and the 'teaching of kinds of expertise' (διδασκαλία τεχνῶν).

The 'third guide', that is, the transmission of received laws and customs has a particularly bearing on value. Let us quote here the tenth mode of sceptic argumentation (*PH* 1.145):

'the tenth mode, which especially bears on ethics (πρὸς τὰ ἠθικά), is the one depending on ways of life (ὁ παρὰ τὰς ἀγωγάς), customs (τὰ ἔθη), laws (τοὺς νόμους), beliefs in myth (τὰς μυθικὰς πίστεις) and dogmatic supposition (τὰς δογματικὰς ὑπολήψεις)'

The Sceptic, eventually, 'does what society conditions him to do' (Bett 2010a: 191-2). He acts in a given way and not another not because he holds the belief that that is the just way to conduct himself, but out of habit and environmental constraints: that is, he will be inclined to act in a certain way in given circumstances without the necessity of claiming to justify his inclination to act that given way. What is most interesting is that according to this narrative (and contrary to the modern popular opinion of the Sceptic as a prosecuted martyr of society) emphasizing the *passivity* of the sceptic agent (Burnyeat 1980: 42) it is quite unlikely that the Sceptic will turn out to be a 'social reformer'. For to be the promoter of social reforms would assume the adoption of a moral outlook at odds with the predominant one in a given society (Bett 2010a: 192). Pyrrho, in fact, far from being prosecuted, received high civic honours at Elis (DL 9.64 = T 11 Decleva Caizzi; Pausanias 6.24.5 = T 12 Decleva Caizzi) and was granted Athenian citizenship (DL 9.65 = T 13 Decleva Caizzi).

What is the role of 'tranquillity' for the true Sceptic? According to Sextus at *PH* 1.25 the 'final aim' (τέλος)[19] of a sceptic way of life (τῆς σκεπτικῆς ἀγωγῆς)

---

[19] At *PH* 1.15 Sextus defines τέλος as 'that for the sake of which everything is done or considered, while it is not itself done or considered for the sake of anything else or a goal is the final object of desire'.

is 'tranquillity (ἀταραξία: lack of perturbation, of inner turmoil) in matters of opinion and moderation of feeling (μετριοπάθεια) in matters forced upon us (ἐν τοῖς κατηναγκασμένοις)'. At *M* 11.140-61 Sextus explicitly identifies the τέλος of the sceptic life with 'living well' (εὐδαιμονία).[20] Now, to advertise 'living well' as the goal of a philosophical outlook is a completely traditional and uncontroversial feature in Greek thought: Epicureans and Stoics claimed as much. As far as the goal of its way of life, Scepticism then does not differ from the other contemporary philosophical schools (McPherran 1989: 136-40). At first sight to say that there is a τέλος, an overarching aim, for the sceptic life may seem a dogmatic posture: is a Sceptic entitled to have an aim at all? But the Sceptic might reply that in saying that *x* is the final goal, he is simply saying what *appears* to him to be the case, that is, he does not have to hold a belief about it (Annas 1993: 352). However, to a less charitable observer, he is still committing himself to *acting as if* he had a believe about it: the risk of self-contradiction is never very far from the corner: a 'goal' is neither an 'impression' nor an 'opinion'.

More importantly, at *PH* 1.26 Sextus goes to say that the Sceptic began (ἀρξάμενος) to do philosophy (φιλοσοφεῖν) in order to decide (ἐπικρῖναι) among appearances (τὰς φαντασίας) and apprehend (καταλαβεῖν) which are true and which are false, so as to be tranquil (ὥστε ἀταρακτῆσαι). But because of the equipollent nature of the conflicting appearances he could not decide and hence suspended judgment (ἐπέσχεν). And when he suspended judgment (ἐπισχόντι), 'tranquillity in matters of opinion' (ἡ ἐν τοῖς δοξαστοῖς ἀταραξία) followed 'by chance' (τυχικῶς: that is *not* causally).[21] This passage has posed many problems to interpreters, but perhaps the most crucial one is why 'freedom from perturbation' (ἀταραξία) is envisaged as the goal of a sceptic way of life. In Sextus the explanation seems to be the following: all unhappiness is the product of some 'perturbation' (ταραχή), hence well-being or living well consists in freedom from perturbation. Yet this freedom will be denied to us until we believe that what we pursue or avoid are really good or bad. Only the Sceptic lacks this belief and hence the consequent inner turmoil: he suspends judgment and this relief comes to him 'by chance'.

As formulated by Sextus then the origin (ἀρχή) of Scepticism as philosophical inquiry and way of life is the search of tranquillity (ἀταραξία) *via* the discovery of the truth, yet the Sceptic eventually achieves tranquillity, his initial goal, *via* the

---

[20] Cf. esp. *M*. 11.140 'it is proper to scepticism to secure for each person well being in life'.
[21] Cf. also *PH* 1. 29 'now the Sceptics were hoping to achieve tranquillity (τὴν ἀταραξίαν) by deciding the anomalies in what appears and is thought of, and being unable to do this they suspend judgment. But when they suspended judgment, tranquillity (ἡ ἀταραξία) followed as it were fortuitously (οἷον τυχικῶς), as a shadow follows a body'.

suspension of judgment (cf. also *PH* 1.12): a very different route from what he thought to pursue at the beginning of his search. Otherwise said, the objective of truth is *subordinate* to the ultimate objective of tranquillity (Perin 2006: 338, 342-3; Grgic 2006). And this tranquillity is said to happen to the sceptic 'by chance' (τυχικῶς), that is not causally: that is, the Sceptic 'does not seek it out, he does not believe in it: it just happen to him' (Nussbaum 1994: 300).[22] The Sceptic's disposition to ἀταραξία must thus not be seen as a value-commitment or a belief: it is best explained as a 'natural' inclination deeply entrenched in human nature (Nussbaum 1994: 305; McPherran 1989: 162-7; *contra* Machuca). But again a less charitable view might contend that the Sceptic may well say that relief comes to him 'by chance'; but yet it remains the problem that this explanation of what happens 'by chance' requires some intellectual commitment to the view on the nature of good.

Does this mean that the Sceptic is *totally* free from perturbation? Yes and no. At *PH* 1.29-30 we read that

> 'we do not, however, take Sceptics to be undisturbed in every way (ἀόχλητον πάντῃ)– we say that they are disturbed by things which are forced upon them (ὑπὸ τῶν κατηναγκασμένων); for we agree that at times they shiver and are thirsty and have other feelings of this kind. But in these cases ordinary people (οἱ μὲν ἰδιῶται) are afflicted by two sets of circumstances: by the feelings themselves, and no less by believing that these circumstances are bad by nature (κακὰς εἶναι φύσει δοκεῖν). Sceptics, who shed (περιαιρῶν) the additional opinion (τὸ προσδοξάζειν) that each of these things is bad in its nature, come off more moderately (μετριώτερον) even in these cases. This is then why we say that the aim of Sceptics is tranquillity in matters of opinion (ἐν μὲν τοῖς δοξαστοῖς ἀταραξίαν) and moderation of feeling in matters forced upon us (ἐν δὲ τοῖς κατηναγκασμένοις μετριοπάθειαν) '

Also the genuine Sceptic then, as far as external necessities are concerned, will experience some turmoil, but all the same he will be better of than the layman since he will not hold the belief that *x* is inherently good or bad.

Is the Sceptic's self-definition as an *ongoing* inquirer compatible with this state of (relative) tranquillity? Can you go on searching throughout your all life without experiencing any inner turmoil? Scholarly answers to this question have

---

[22] Is the suspension of judgment what modern Scepticism would call the result of 'inference'? The ancient Sceptic would strongly object to this (cf. *PH* 1.7, 8, 10): as expressed by Annas 1986: 6 'suspension of belief is not a conclusion of any inference; rather, pointing out differences in persuasion puts us in a position where we are led to find no more reason to hold our beliefs about value than their opposites, and hence, as a matter of fact, to suspend judgment'.

varied widely. Some have found in this attitude a sign of 'negative' dogmatism: 'the sceptic goes on seeking not in the sense that he has an active program of research but in the sense that he continues to regard it as an open question whether p or not-p is the case [...] But this should not mean that he is left in a state of *wondering* whether p or not-p is the case, for that might induce anxiety.' (Burnyeat 1980: 51-2). In principle, though, the Sceptic should remain open to the *possibility* of being persuaded otherwise, but at the same time it is difficult not to concede that he must be at least temporarily satisfied that 'no answers are forthcoming' (Burnyeat 1980: 52). And this temporary satisfaction may look like a form of belief, even if 'negative' belief. Others have argued for the compatibility of ongoing search and tranquillity of mind (e.g. Perin 2006 but if and only if we suppose that the Sceptic values the discovery of truth for its own sake and not as a means to tranquillity; for an alternative explanation cf. McPherran 1989: 165-6). Be it as it may, what is worth observing is that the Sceptic can pursue suspension of judgment as a way of achieving tranquillity *without* denying that it is impossible to discover the truth (for a critical survey see now Bett 2010a: 188-90).

But what kind of emotional inner life is left to the ancient Sceptic? To a modern sensitivity the 'detachment from oneself' (Burnyeat 1980: 37, 49-53) which is required from the true Sceptic may appear not only beyond human possibility and nature but also not exactly a desirable goal in itself.[23] According to Antigonus of Carystus (possibly drawing on Timon), Pyrrho himself complained that 'it is difficult to divest oneself entirely of one's humanity' (DL 9.66 and Eus. *Prep. Evang.* 14. 18.26 = TT 15A-B Decleva Caizzi: ὡς χαλεπὸν εἴη ὁλοσχερῶς ἐκδῦναι τὸν ἄνθρωπον).

If you divest yourself of your humanity, what space, if any, has the regard for others in the sceptic way of life? Why should a Sceptic want to argue with others? Why, once he has reached tranquillity should he care about other people being burdened by the intensity of their beliefs? Sextus' answer is the 'therapeutic model' invoked at *PH* 3.280:

> ' the sceptic, since he is a philanthrope (διὰ τὸ φιλάνθρωπος εἶναι) wishes to cure by argument (ἰᾶσθαι λόγῳ βούλεται), as far as he can, the opinion and rashness (οἴησίν τε καὶ προπέτειαν) of the Dogmatists. '

---

[23] For a more charitable view of the 'detached' sceptical self, especially on the basis of a comparative analysis with Buddhist doctrine, see McPherran 1989: 168-70. Part of the biographical tradition (DL 9. 61 = T 1A Decleva-Caizzi) links Pyrrho to the Indian 'naked sophists' and their ascetic practices (Pyrrho travelled to India with Alexander the Great): cf. also Flintoff 1980.

What follows in Sextus is a comparison of the Sceptic philosopher with the physician (a common trope in Hellenistic philosophy: Sextus himself was a physician): just like the doctor the Sceptic will apply either severe or weak purgatives as the occasion requires.

But why should the Sceptic, once he has reached his own unperturbed state, care about others? Sextus does not say anything explicit about this (and indeed this is the only passage where Scepticism and *philanthropia* are brought together so closely).

One possible answer (McPherran 1989: 164-5; Annas 1993: 244-46; *contra* Machuca 2006) might be that as long as he is surrounded by people disturbed by inner turmoil in their opinions, he himself can still be disturbed by other people's concerns: he would then benefit others mainly for the sake of his own imperturbability.[24]

Even so, ancient Scepticism, in a sense, seems to require an inner mental and emotional detachment first from oneself and then from the community one belongs to. It does not allow for any deep identification with the shared values of a community of which the Sceptic philosopher is a member: he will observe these shared values, which will have left him some inclinations or biases, but no reason to prefer. If you do away with commitment to belief, you will suspend your judgment and you will thus have done away with emotions too. What kind of person is the ancient Sceptic then? Does he contradict himself? Or is human nature itself that contradicts such a radical cognitive stance? As an ancient sceptic would perhaps have liked to hear, we moderns 'are still investigating'.

References

Allen, J. (2010) 'Pyrrhonism and Medicine', in Bett (ed.) 2010: 232-48.

Annas, J. (1986) 'Doing without objective values: ancient and modern strategies', in M. Schofield and G. Striker (eds.) *The Norms of Nature*. Cambridge: Cambridge University Press, 3-29.

— (1994) 'Plato the Skeptic', in P. Vander Waerdt (ed.), *The Socratic Movement*. Ithaca (NY): Cornell University Press, 309-40.

— (1996) 'Scepticism, Old and New,' in M. Frede and G. Striker (eds.) *Rationality in Greek Thought*. Oxford: Oxford University Press, 239–54.

Annas, J. and Barnes, J. (1985) *The Modes of Scepticism. Ancient Texts and Modern Interpretations*. Cambridge: Cambridge University Press.

---

[24] Cf. Annas 1993: 246 'perhaps the sceptic *philanthropia* lies in this, that he can never achieve full *ataraxia* while there are other dogmatic, and therefore unhappy, people around'.

— (2000) *Sextus Empiricus. Outlines of Scepticism*, 2nd edition. Cambridge: Cambridge University Press.

Bailey, A. (2002) *Sextus Empiricus and Pyrrhonean Scepticism*. Oxford: Oxford University Press.

Barnes, J. (1982) 'The Beliefs of a Pyrrhonist', *Proceedings of the Cambridge Philological Society* n.s. 28: 1-29 (reprinted in Burnyeat and Frede (eds.) 1997: 58-91).

Bett, R. (2000) *Pyrrho, his Antecedents, and his Legacy*. Oxford: Oxford University Press.

— (2006) 'Socrates and the Sceptics,' in S. Ahbel-Rappe and R. Kamtekar (eds.), *A Companion to Socrates*. Oxford: Blackwell Publishing, 298–311.

— (ed.), 2010, *The Cambridge Companion to Ancient Scepticism*. Cambridge: Cambridge University Press.

— (2010a) 'Scepticism and Ethics,' in Bett (ed.) 2010: 181–194.

Burnyeat, M. (1980) 'Can the sceptic live his scepticism?' in M. Schofield, M. Burnyeat and J. Barnes (eds.), *Doubt and Dogmatism: Studies in Hellenistic Epistemology*. Oxford: Oxford University Press, 20–53 (reprinted in Burnyeat and Frede (eds.) 1997: 25–57).

—(ed.) (1983) *The Skeptical Tradition*. Berkeley and Los Angeles: University of California Press.

Burnyeat, M. and M. FREDE (eds.) (1997) *The Original Sceptics*. Indianapolis and Cambridge (MA): Hackett.

Castagnoli, L. (2000) 'Self-Bracketing Pyrrhonism,' *Oxford Studies in Ancient Philosophy*, 18: 263–328.

Decleva Caizzi, F. (1981) *Pirrone: testimonianze*. Naples: Bibliopolis.

Fine, G. (2000) 'Sceptical Dogmata: *Outlines of Pyrrhonism I 13*', *Methexis* 13: 81–105.

— (2003) 'Sextus and External World Scepticism,' *Oxford Studies in Ancient Philosophy* 23: 341–385.

— (2008) 'Does Socrates Claim To Know That He Knows Nothing?', *Oxford Studies in Ancient Philosophy* 35: 49–88.

Flintoff, E. (1980) 'Pyrrho and India', *Phronesis* 25: 88–108.

Floridi, L. (2002) *Sextus Empiricus. The Transmission and Recovery of Pyrrhonism*. Oxford: Oxford University Press.

— (2010) 'The Rediscovery and Posthumous Influence of Scepticism', in Bett (ed.) 2010: 267-87.

Frede, M. (1984) 'The Sceptic's Two Kinds of Assent and the Question of the Possibility of Knowledge', in R. Rorty, J.B. Schneewind, and Q. Skinner (eds.), *Philosophy in History, Philosophy in History*. Cambridge: Cambridge

University Press, 255–78 (reprinted in Burnyeat and Frede (eds.) 1997: 127–51).

Gagarin, M. and Woodruff, P. (2008) 'The Sophists', in P. Curd and D.W. Graham (eds.), *The Oxford Handbook of Presocratic Philosophy*. Oxford: 365-82.

Grgic, F. (2006) 'Sextus Empiricus on the Goal of Skepticism', *Ancient Philosophy* 26: 141–60.

Hankinson, R.J. (1995) *The Sceptics*. London: Routledge.

Janáček, K. (1979) 'Das Wort *skeptikos* in Philons Schriften', *Listy Filologické* 101: 65-8.

Lee, M. (2010) 'Antecedents in Early Greek Philosophy', in Bett (ed.) 2010: 13–35.

Machuca, D. (2006) 'The Pyrrhonist's *ataraxia* and *philanthrôpia*,' *Ancient Philosophy* 26: 111–139.

McPherran, M. (1989) '*Ataraxia* and *Eudaimonia* in Ancient Pyrrhonism: Is the Sceptic Really Happy?', in J.J. Cleary and D.C. Shartin (eds.), *Proceedings of the Boston Area Colloquium in Ancient Philosophy*, 135–71.

Mikalson, D.J. (2010) *Greek Popular Religion in Greek Philosophy*. Oxford: Oxford University Press.

Nussbaum, M. (1994) 'Sceptic Purgatives: Disturbance and the Life Without Belief,' in *The Therapy of Desire: Theory and Practice in Hellenistic Ethics*. Princeton: Princeton University Press, 280–315.

Perin, C. (2006) 'Pyrrhonian Scepticism and the Search for Truth', *Oxford Studies in Ancient Philosophy* 30: 337–60.

Polito, R. (2007) 'Was Skepticism a Philosophy? Reception Self-Definition, Internal Conflicts', *Classical Philology* 102: 333-62.

Popkin, R. (1960) *The History of Scepticism from Erasmus to Descartes*. Assen: van Gorcum.

— (1979) *The History of Scepticism from Erasmus to Spinoza*. Berkeley and Los Angeles: University of California Press.

— (2003) *The History of Scepticism from Savonarola to Bayle*. Oxford and New York: Oxford University Press.

Sedley, D. (1983) 'The Motivation of Greek Skepticism', in M. Burnyeat (ed.), *The Skeptical Tradition*. Berkeley and Los Angeles: University of California Press, 9-29.

Striker, G. (1980) 'Sceptical Strategies', in M. Schofield, M. Burnyeat and J. Barnes (eds.), *Doubt and Dogmatism. Studies in Hellenistic epistemologies*. Oxford: Oxford University Press, 54-83.

— (1996) *Essays on Hellenistic Epistemology and Ethics*. Cambridge: Cambridge University Press.

— (2001) 'Scepticism as a Kind of Philosophy', *Archiv für Geschichte der Philosophie* 83: 113–29.

Vogt. K. (2010) 'Ancient Skepticism', in the *Stanford Encyclopedia of Philosophy*, available online at http://plato.stanford.edu/entries/skepticism-ancient/

— (2010a) 'Scepticism and Action', in Bett (ed.) 2010: 165–80.

Woodruff, P. (1986) 'The sceptical side of Plato's method', *Revue Internationale de Philosophie* 40: 22–37.

— (2010) 'The Pyrrhonian Modes', in Bett (ed.) 2010: 208–31.

In: Scepticism: Hero and Villain
Editors: R. Calne and W. O'Reilly

ISBN: 978-1-62417-783-5
© 2013 Nova Science Publishers, Inc.

Chapter 12

PHILOSOPHICAL SCEPTICISM: NEITHER FRIEND NOR FOE BUT FRENEMY

Fraser MacBride
Faculty of Philosophy, University of Cambridge, UK

1. INTRODUCTION

The philosophical problem of scepticism is posed by an (apparently) simple question, "How is knowledge possible?" Philosophers often take this question in a purely general way as asking "how is knowledge possible at all?" To answer the question so understood requires engagement with sceptical arguments of enduring fascination, arguments purporting to show that all knowledge is impossible.

Take, for example, the sceptical argument that runs along the following lines: knowledge requires justification, but all our reasoning must come to an end somewhere and where it ends justification must be lacking, so whatever opinions we hold, they must ultimately rely upon hypotheses or assumptions that aren't known to us at all. Since scepticism of this global variety calls all putative knowledge into question—scientific knowledge included—engaging with it cannot be a matter of scientific enquiry. This has meant that many philosophers have conceived of engaging with (global) scepticism as a peculiarly foundational endeavour, one of establishing prior to any scientific pursuit whether knowledge is possible or not.

But this does not exhaust the philosophical significance of the sceptical problem. This becomes evident as soon as we think of the variety of different ways in which the sceptical question can be posed. For example, we can ask a sceptical question about the kind of subject matter knowledge of which is being placed under the philosophical microscope: "How is knowledge of other minds possible?", "How is knowledge of mathematics possible?", "How is knowledge of God possible?", "How is knowledge of what's just and fair possible?", "How is knowledge of the meaning of our words possible?" etc. We can also be more precise in the sceptical question we pose by indicating the sort of justification that appends to the knowledge we are placing under scrutiny. For example, our knowledge of the physical world surrounding us depends upon observation and experience; it is what philosophers call 'a posteriori' knowledge. By contrast our knowledge of pure mathematics appears to be independent of observation and experience. Mathematicians don't experience numbers but prove things about them. Their knowledge is, or at least appears to be, purely rational; it is what philosophers call 'a priori' knowledge. We can accordingly distinguish between asking (e.g.) "How is a priori knowledge of God possible?" and "How is a posteriori knowledge of Him (or Her) possible?" and we will have to engage with different sceptical concerns to answer them—about whether (e.g.) purely rational reflection on the very concept of a perfect being can assure us, as St. Anselm argued, of the existence of God, or whether His (or Her) existence could be disclosed through observation of an (apparently) miraculous event.

There is, then, an extraordinary plethora of sceptical problems corresponding to all the different ways in which the sceptical question may be posed—I have suggested only a few of them. This is what has made sparring with scepticism so important an exercise for philosophers—to personalize matters, what has made scepticism neither their friend nor their foe but a 'frenemy'. Why so? Because conjuring with the different versions of scepticism has helped philosophers to investigate the structure of the sum-total of human knowledge, i.e. to appreciate the similitude and dissimilitude of the parts that compose our view of the world, the various ways in which the components of human knowledge fit together to make up an articulated body.

In the present paper I will pose a very singular sceptical question, one that's rarely considered, but will place a certain kind of distinctively philosophical knowledge under scrutiny. And then I will answer it sceptically.

But to understand the sceptical question I intend to pose we will need to bring into focus another perennial concern beloved of philosophers, the ontological problem posed by another (apparently) simple question, "What is there?" You might think this is a problem that can be dismissed lightly with the one-word answer "Everything". But that's just too general to be informative; you're none the wiser for being told so. Nor can the problem be tackled by taking on the heavy labour of listing all the individual things there are. We're woefully ill equipped as finite creatures to complete such a task—there are just too many grains of the sand on the beach, never mind all the particles strewn across the outer reaches of the universe for us to list them all. What's more, contemplation of such a compendious answer would hardly enlighten us either: our attention would merely be switched from one thing to the next as we sequentially surveyed the list. To provide an insightful answer to the ontological problem what philosophers have therefore tried to do is this: to provide a general description of the most fundamental kinds (or categories) of things there are, an account that provides, among other things, an understanding of the different ways in which these various kinds of things are related together to comprise the whole of reality. When philosophers engage in a dispute about ontology either they argue about what fundamental kinds of things there are, or they argue about how they are strung together, or they argue simultaneously about both. For example, when philosophers argue, as they often do, about whether minds are just material bodies—albeit exceptionally complex ones—or whether they are really fundamentally different in kind from their material embodiments—souls or ectoplasm—then they are engaged in an ontological dispute.

It has been an enduring concern of philosophers to lay claim to a species of ontological knowledge—a priori knowledge of the fundamental contours of reality itself, i.e. what its categories are and how they are related. But in this paper I will sketch an alternative picture of what philosophy can achieve. I will argue, sceptically, that ontological knowledge really isn't possible a priori, however venerable the tradition that traces back to the Ancient Greeks of thinking so may be. My position is this: any knowledge we have, if we have any at all, of the fundamental constituents of reality and the deep structures they exhibit is akin to scientific knowledge, a posteriori knowledge that depends upon observation and experience.

2. Two Fundamental Categories

It is a basic feature of our conceptual scheme that we are embodied creatures placed in an extended spatio-temporal world that sweeps away before us. Witness the fact that it's always intelligible for us to ask one another the question "where are you?" And however lost we may be, we expect there to be an answer, even if we don't know it. But it's no less important a feature of our self-conception that we are placed in a world that contains a potentially unbounded diversity of aspects, attributes and relations. The things and events that routinely occupy our attention and are often the subjects of our discourse, we identify as having a unique location in space and time, or as tracing a circumscribed path across it. Consider, for example, geographical landmarks and cities, governments and political crises, persons and animals. To have anything that counts as experience of such things and events it is necessary that we classify or represent them as persons, animals, cities etc. Whilst many classifications that we make are unquestionably correct, some are imperfect, others plain wrong: we're familiar not only with hitting the nail on the head with our descriptions but with sometimes discovering that our descriptions are only half-truths or straight falsehoods, based on mistaken impressions, false leads, errors of measurement. What makes it appropriate to classify things and occurrences one-way, rather than another, cannot simply be a consequence of our arbitrarily calling them one thing rather another. Something isn't a cat or an electron just because we call it one. Whether our classifications are appropriate, approximate or inappropriate depends upon the extent to which they reflect the underlying characteristics or nature of things—whether, or to what degree, they exhibit the aspects, attributes and relations that we describe them as having—whether they have whiskers and a tail or they're negatively charged etc. The development of science can be viewed as a progressive refinement of our understanding of these characteristics and the law-like connections that obtain between them—whether at the level of zoology or physics or some other science. By capturing these characteristics in the theoretical net of science we place ourselves in a position to predict and explain the occurrence of things or events bestowed with these characteristics and the effects they have upon other things.

Underlying this complex and dynamic way of thinking about the world and our place in it, philosophers have detected the sustaining influence of a binary, a priori distinction. The distinction is one between all the particulars on the one hand and all universals on the other. One route whereby we can arrive at a grasp of this distinction proceeds via elementary reflection upon some of the simple patterns of similarity and difference things potentially display. I'll lead the way.

We are familiar from ordinary experience with the possibility of many different things resembling one another, even though they differ in other respects. For example, things may share a colour whilst differing in shape and texture. We can account for this possibility by appealing to the existence of some one item of which the many resembling things partake. This is what is often called a 'one-over-many' or a universal—in this case a universal that is responsible for these things being a certain colour. So what makes it the case that many things resemble one another is that they partake of the same universal, whether one of colour or shape or texture. When things fail to resemble one another this is because they partake of different universals. [1]

This naturally suggests the parsimonious ontological hypothesis that a thing is nothing more than the constellation of the universals of which it partakes, the package of universals that accounts for the distinctive pattern of similarities, or lack thereof, it exhibits with respect to other things. But this hypothesis is confounded by reflection upon the possibility that two different things may exactly resemble one another. Since they exactly resemble—exhibit exactly the same pattern of similarities with respect to other thing—they must partake of exactly the same universals. It follows that if a thing is nothing more than a constellation of the universals then exactly resembling things are the very same constellation of universals. But then it also follows that exactly resembling things aren't many at all but really one, a recurrent exhibition of the same constellation of universals. So if we are to acknowledge the real possibility of things exactly resembling one another whilst still being different—entangled bosons may actually be like this even if the leaves of the forest or snowdrops aren't—then we must also acknowledge that things are more than constellations of universals. We need to recognize that each thing consists not only of the universals it shares but also a particular that is unique to it; an item radically different from a universal whose raison d'être is to provide the grounds for one thing's distinction from all others, however closely they resemble.

Whereas universals are used to explain how different things can be similar, particulars are used to explain how similar things can be different. Particulars and universals are thereby given to us as those fundamental categories of items that are reciprocally responsible for the emergence of similarity and difference in the world. [2]

With a few simple philosophical steps it appears that we have arrived at a fundamentally bifurcated conception of reality, a conception that—in a significant sense—is deeper than any entertained by the sciences: deeper because it tells us what is required of the world if it is even so much as to admit of the possibility of similarity and difference, whatever the actual similarities and differences detailed by the sciences may be.

3. IS OUR KNOWLEDGE OF UNIVERSALS A PRIORI OR A POSTERIORI?

We have charted a route, albeit one amongst others, whereby we may proceed on the basis of pure a priori reflection to explicit recognition of the categories of particular and universal. But how are we to identify individual instances of these categories? How can we settle just what particulars and universals there actually are?

It is usually conceded that empirical investigation is required to establish what particulars exist. Certainly this is true if we confine our attention to the particulars that are responsible for the diversity of material bodies we encounter in ordinary perceptual experience. It is a posteriori just how many of them there are. But it is less often conceded that empirical investigation is required to establish what universals exist. Philosophers have often supposed that there is an intimate communion between universals and the adjectives, nouns and verbs that we use to signify them. The connection is a natural one to make: universals are responsible for what makes different things resemble one another, and we use predicative expressions (adjectives etc.) to describe how they resemble each other. This suggests another a priori route whereby we may argue to the existence of a certain universal from a mere appreciation of the meaningfulness of the predicative expression that signifies it—from (e.g.) the meaningfulness of the adjective "square" to a corresponding universal, being square. By contrast, no such route appears to be available for particulars. "El Dorado" is a meaningful name but it doesn't follow that a corresponding particular exists; geographical exploration established that it didn't. [3]

However, many philosophers have become sceptical that we can know about the existence of universals a priori on the basis of the inspection of language. The progressive development of science provides one intellectual spur to thinking so. Take, for example, the now obsolete theory of 'phlogiston' that arose in the late 17th century when it was proposed by Johann Becher. According to this theory, 'phlogiston' is an element without colour, odour, taste or mass that is released during combustion, so when a substance burns it is 'dephlogisticated'. (Becher described phlogiston as "inflammable earth".) The theory remained dominant until a century later the unfortunate Antoine-Laurent Lavoisier discredited it (unfortunate because despite his contributions to science he was guillotined during the French Revolution). His experiments helped establish that it is oxygen, rather than phlogiston, that is the vital chemical ingredient at work when combustion occurs. The fact that the theory of phlogiston failed to predict and explain the behaviour of combustible materials suggests that the there is no such property or universal as being phlogisticated. So whilst "phlogisticated" is a meaningful expression—we can use it to say how combustible materials aren't, or what Becher believed but Lavoisier didn't—scientific investigation has revealed that "phlogisticated" no more signifies a real property than "El Dorado" signifies a real place.

Similarly, for all that we currently know on the basis of what our atom smashing hadron colliders have told us, it may turn out that the theory of the 'Higgs boson' goes the way of phlogiston theory (the Higgs boson is supposed to be a so far unobserved elementary particle predicted by the Standard Model of particle physics). The experiments that are being performed in CERN and elsewhere may establish that there are no Higgs bosons, that we should adopt a 'higgsless' model of the universe. So it may turn out that "is a Higgs boson" is an empty expression, one that no more signifies a kind of physical particle than "is phlogisticated" signifies a kind of chemical substance. Stephen Hawking even has a $100 bet on its turning out to be the El Dorado of contemporary physics.

Other scientific developments suggest cases where although a predicate is meaningful and signifies something, it does not correspond to any one property or universal. Consider, for example, the way in which the medical understanding of hepatitis (inflammation of the liver associated with jaundice) has developed. Originally hepatitis was thought to be a single disease but gradually data became available that showed hepatitis wasn't a single condition but a variety of different viral diseases of the liver (hepatitis A, B, C etc.). This suggests that whilst "is infected with hepatitis" is a meaningful predicate it does not signify a single, unique universal the partaking of which makes it appropriate to describe a patient as being infected with the disease.

Famously, Wittgenstein gave philosophers another shove towards sceptical about any a priori route between the predicative expressions we use to describe things and universals. He did so by reflecting upon the example of games. [4] Consider the enormous range of proceedings that we call "games"—board games, card games, Olympic games etc—and ask yourself: what do they all have in common? Wittgenstein declared it mistaken to proceed a priori: "Don't say: 'There must be something common, or they would not be called 'games''. For when we actually inspect what all the different activities we call "games" have in common we discover "a complicated network of similarities overlapping and criss-crossing" but no single feature that unites them—not all games are amusing, nor is there invariably a winner etc. What clearly sustains the significant use of the word "game" to describe these activities—when, as Wittgenstein insisted, we "don't think, but look!"—is the overlapping network of similarities that obtain between them. Wittgenstein accordingly described "game" as a family resemblance term: "for the various resemblances between members of a family: build, features, colours of eyes, gait, temperament, etc. etc. overlap and criss-cross in the same way.— And I shall say: 'games' form a family". Similarly, until we "look and see", as Wittgenstein enjoined us, we cannot be in a position to judge whether a predicative expression we employ—even when we are doing serious science—corresponds to a universal common to all the different things we use it to describe, or whether it is a family resemblance term too. Perhaps a posteriori medical research has shown "hepatitis" to really be a family resemblance term.

In fact a priori reflection upon what it is to be a universal itself suggests that some predicates are incapable of corresponding to universals. [5] The category of universals was introduced to us as the category of items of which things partake when they resemble one another. It was their raison d'être to confer similarity upon the things that mutually partake of them. Now consider the negative predicate "lacks a mass of 724g". Most things lack this mass but it is implausible to suggest that they thereby have something in common. Prima facie this negative predicate can be used to truly describe all these things not because they have something in common but because they don't—i.e. because they lack the mass universal in question.

Related concerns militate against the admission of universals corresponding to disjunctive predicates. Consider the predicate "is square or blue". This predicate may be used to truly describe some things that are square even though they aren't blue, whilst it may also be used to truly describe other things that aren't square but are blue. It is surely implausible to think that because all these things may be described as being either square or blue, all of them have something genuinely in common, that there's one universal they all share. The disjunctive predicate "is square or blue" applies to them not because there is one 'disjunctive' universal (being square or blue) they share, but because they partake of one or other of the universals the predicate does signify (either the universal being square or the universal being blue).

It follows that there is no simple correlation of predicates and universals to be made; no more than there is a simple correlation of names and particulars. We cannot read the structure of the world off the structure of our language. Perhaps some of our predicates correspond to a single universal, but there are others that correspond to many, whilst some predicates correspond to none. So a priori inspection of our predicates won't settle what universals there actually are; no more than a priori inspection of names will settle what particulars there are. To settle what universals exist we have to rely—no less than in the case of particulars—upon a posteriori investigation.

4. ARE CATEGORY DISTINCTIONS A PRIORI OR A POSTERIORI?

If this sketch of how we can come to know about what particulars and universals exist is correct, at least in outline, then it is also reasonable to suggest that we will need to rely upon a posteriori investigation to establish how particulars differ from universals. If we can't know a priori what particulars and universals there are, then how can we know a priori how they differ? Shouldn't we therefore be sceptical of the venerable claim that the very distinction between particulars and universals can be given to us a priori without observation or evidence?

A backward glance at the arguments we rehearsed for introducing the categories of particular and universal confirms that this sceptical suspicion is one that we need to take seriously [6]. These arguments were 'transcendental' in the sense that 'particulars' and 'universals' were introduced by them simply as those items, the xs and the ys, that would respectively solve two interrelated problems for us, viz. to reciprocally account for the possibility of similarity on the one hand and difference on the other. But there is nothing in this incredibly abstract way of introducing 'particulars' and 'universals' that guarantees these categories are genuinely distinct—that the xs and the ys don't overlap. A 'universal' is something that fulfills one theoretical role for us (accounts for similarity), a 'particular' is something that fulfills another role (accounts for difference). But nothing has been said to preclude the possibility of there being some things that perform both roles. However pure it may be, there is a gap in the reasoning that was supposed to lead us to distinguish between particulars and universals a priori.

More specifically, nothing has been done to preclude the possibility that a particular x that partakes of a universal y isn't itself such that another thing z partakes of it. The ascendancy of field theories over classical Newtonian theories in contemporary physics provides a significant indicator that this possibility is not entirely notional. [7] Field theories may be understood as assigning causal properties directly to space-time points or regions (rather than via bodies that occupy those points or regions). On this understanding the ordinary material things that we are familiar with from experience may be conceived as themselves features of the underlying spatio-temporal manifold—high-intensity zones of the overlapping fields. This at least suggests the following way of describing the denizens of the world in which we find ourselves: whilst an ordinary material thing often partakes of the same universal as other things, it itself is a universal of which different spatial regions partake—roughly speaking an ordinary material body is a universal that is common to the space-time region it traces out over the course of its lifetime.

Of course, you may think this just shows that it is space-time points or regions—rather than ordinary material things—that are the true particulars. But it's not a priori that this is so, not least because space-time itself may fail to be fundamental; in fact it's a matter of live speculation amongst physicists whether space-time isn't itself a feature of something else. Indeed it remains an open possibility—for all our a priori reasoning has shown—that there is nothing fundamental in the world we inhabit; that everything there is depends upon something else. Since human powers are finite, it is natural for us to think that there is something fundamental out there; for medical reasons our theoretical descriptions of the world have to terminate somewhere. But this doesn't mean that the things that stand at the termini of our descriptions must themselves be incapable of a deeper analysis that reveals them to depend upon other things; only that for the moment our investigations have ground to a halt, though perhaps not permanently.

The fact of the matter—for these and other reasons—is that we have no a priori reason to insist upon the world-hypothesis that there is a fundamental distinction to be drawn between all the particulars on the one hand and all universals on the other. It would be hazardous in the extreme to circumscribe the range of potentially viable theoretical descriptions of what exists in advance of inspecting the structure of our best scientific theories, the results of our a posteriori investigations. To proceed otherwise—to insist a priori that scientific descriptions are credible only if they model a certain ontological distinction— is to risk mistaking for reality what is merely a shadow cast by the accidental morphology of human cognition. [8]

REFERENCES

[1] See, for further discussion, my "Universals: The Contemporary Debate" in *The Routledge Companion to Metaphysics,* edited by R. Le Poidevin, P. Simons, A. McGonigal and R. Cameron (London: Routledge, 2009), pp. 276-85.

[2] See, for an influential statement of this position, Bertrand Russell's "On the Relations of Universals and Particulars", *Proceedings of the Aristotelian Society*, 12, 1911-12, pp. 1-24.

[3] A locus classicus of this view is P.F. *Strawson's Individuals: An Essay In Descriptive Metaphysics* (London: Methuen, 1959).

[4] See Ludwig Wittgenstein Philosophical Investigations (Oxford: Blackwell, 1953), §§66-7.

[5] This has been a persistent theme of David Armstrong's influential empiricist approach to metaphysics. See, for example, his Sketch for a Systematic Metaphysics (Oxford: Oxford University Press, 2010).

[6] See also F.P. Ramsey's influential development of scepticism about the particular-universal distinction in his "Universals", Mind, XXXIV, 1925, pp. 401-17. It is arguable that Wittgenstein's *Tractatus Logico-Philosophicus* (London: Routledge, 1922) embodies scepticism about the distinction too.

[7] Famously Whitehead urged that we should conceive of ordinary objects as recurrent features of underlying events (for reasons that stem in a large part from his critique of the Newtonian conception of space and time). See A.N. *Whitehead The Concept of Nature* (Cambridge: Cambridge University Press, 1921).

[8] I develop scepticism about the particular-universal distinction along somewhat different lines in my "The Particular-Universal Distinction: A Dogma of Metaphysics", *Mind*, 114, 2005, pp. 565-614.

In: Scepticism: Hero and Villain
Editors: R. Calne and W. O'Reilly
ISBN: 978-1-62417-783-5
© 2013 Nova Science Publishers, Inc.

Chapter 13A

INTRODUCTION TO RELIGIOUS BELIEF

Roy Calne

There is little if any evidence of a significant change in human nature from archaeology or history. There have always been individuals and communities where living in harmony has been the major pattern of life but also there has been inescapable evidence of individuals and communities where aggression has been the chief *modus Vivendi*, with a tendency to slaughter and torture enemies that existed from time immemorial and sadly continues in the present. The major change has been in killing qualities of weapons so that it is now possible to annihilate hundreds of thousands of people with one bomb. Often but not always aggressive and merciless behaviour has been fuelled in the name of religion.

In prehistoric times the hunting and gathering activities of early *homo sapiens* would be enhanced by planning, co-operation and some form of leadership hierarchy. The settlement in communities and development of agriculture must have made it essential for an efficient management of the community to establish rules and rulers in at least a semi-formal manner.

The development of abstract thought, and communication by speech enabled the leadership not only to give instructions but also to provide answers to satisfy natural curiosity to the universal questions of where do we come from, why are we here and where do we go? A strong leader would have explanations of these questions which would be developed as a credo and pattern for future generations. The leader might combine the role of ruler and mystical interpreter or shaman and also lay down the rules and a mechanism of ensuring that the rules were followed, with punishment for transgressors. In successful tribes the laws were necessary for people to live and work together, hunt in unison and divide labour in the care of crops and animals. The rules would set out the morality of dividing thoughts and behaviour into those that are good contrasting with the bad as in the example, beautifully expressed, in the Ten Commandments of the Old Testament.

The above outline has been determined from archaeological research and also observations in contemporary, primitive communities. The earliest civilisation recorded in Egypt revealed that the first Pharaohs combined the role of God who knew everything, the interpreter of God in the laying down of laws and their enforcement and the judgement and punishment of transgressors, all incorporated in one person, the almighty powerful Pharaoh. Separation of these roles occurred to varying extents in all civilisations and in Western democracies, religion, executive government and the interpretation and rule of law have acquired independence, which is regarded as essential to the wellbeing of the community.

There is evidence of a wish for religious belief and a need for answers to the universal questions in almost all societies. The separate religions became independent, powerful and each with its own interpretation of the answers to the questions. Often the individual religious beliefs were incompatible and contradictory between religions, leading to controversy, warfare and long lasting bitter hatred.

Some of these matters have been addressed in this volume. Perhaps one well-known anecdote is worthy of consideration of what is right and wrong. In 1966 a retired Marine, Charles Whitman, murdered his mother and his wife and then climbed the tower of the University of Austin in Texas and proceeded in 90 minutes with random shooting, to kill 14 people and wounded 38. The carnage ended with Charles Whitman being shot by the police. It emerged that he had suffered from terrifying and terrible feelings that he had to kill, which he could not understand. He had consulted his general practitioner who referred him to a psychiatrist who could find no psychotic abnormality. Nevertheless this obsession of a need to kill continued and he requested that when he died an autopsy should be performed to determine the cause of his disastrous destructive compulsions. At the autopsy a malignant tumour was found in the brain close to the amygdala, which is a portion of the brain that controls emotions and keeps in check violent actions. In terms of morality was this man a criminal or suffering from an incurable illness? Clearly the behaviour of mass killing cannot be accepted by society. In one way or another the individual would need to be restrained, but the presence of an organic illness makes the interpretation of the moral question extremely difficult. Society must prevent criminal activity and try to understand illness that can affect the brain and lead to disastrous behaviour.

Sudden religious conversion has been described in certain patients suffering from epileptic seizures arising in the temporal lobe of the brain. The personality of the sufferer changed dramatically from a normal sociable individual to a religious convert, obsessed with spirituality, incomprehensible to those who knew him or her before. It has been speculated that such an event in the brain may have been the cause of the conversion of St Paul, from a man previously aggressively opposed to Christianity to its most significant and effective advocate for people to follow the teachings of Christ.

I will not venture further into these matters except to speculate that a tendency to religious belief can be regarded as a consequence of abstract thought and communication and those who obeyed the rules of their own particular community in following the religious dictates would have a survival advantage over those who were sceptical and opposed the majority. Furthermore criminal, dangerous and aggressive behaviour, even if it resulted from inescapable, anatomical and physiological malfunction of connections in the brain, "my neurones made me do it", does not absolve such behaviour from constraint, which usually involves punishment. There is certainly room for scepticism of the individual religious dogmas since there are conflicting interpretations in different religions and also, if the God figure is believed to be of human form, how does this fit in with evolution? Is this belief compatible with evolutionary theories, which are now difficult to refute and if the Big Bang was the origin of the universe, who or what was responsible for the Big Bang and are there other universes in existence and if so what were their origins? These questions may be of interest and a variety of interpretations can be accepted by the faithful, but they cannot be resolved in a scientific manner.

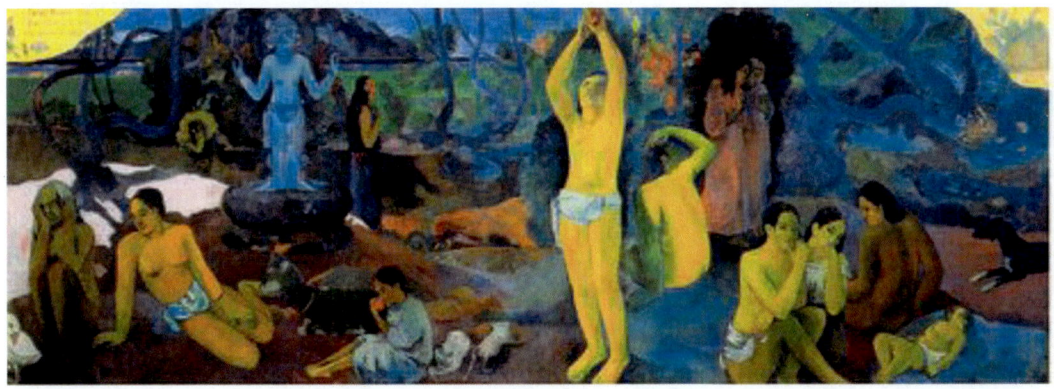

"Where do we come from? Why are we here? Where do we go" by Gauguin, Fine Arts Museum, Boston.

Chapter 13

DOUBTING RELIGIOUS FUNDAMENTALISM – THE SOCIOLOGIST AS SCEPTIC

Graham Howes
Trinity Hall, University of Cambridge,
Fellow Emeritus in Social and Political Sciences, UK

INTRODUCTION

If religious fundamentalism, within all major traditions, is clearly a contemporary global phenomenon, its academic study, especially by social scientists, has also grown from a modest cottage industry into a thriving transnational enterprise. Well-funded research projects proliferate, published monographs (and unpublished theses) now run into hundreds, and the subject area itself is increasingly perceived as a core component of many school and university curricula. Indeed within the writer's own academic lifetime, the study of religious fundamentalism has moved in from the outer margins of research and teaching towards its very epicentre. The reasons are predictable, if complex. They include both a heightened sense (especially after Nine-Eleven) of Islamic fundamentalism's political relevance, and a presumption that today, in the secular, 'post-Christian', West, religious fundamentalism can now be examined, rationally, as an interesting and meaningful, if potentially combustible, dimension of belief and behaviour. Cultural fashion, often media-induced, may also have generated a presumption, shared by teachers and taught alike, that the subject area is 'sexier' than, for example, the study of St Augustine's 'Confessions' or Max Weber's 'Protestant Ethic and the Spirit of Capitalism'. Whatever the reasons, social scientific attention (often generously funded) to religious fundamentalism continues unabated. Yet – perhaps reflecting a trajectory already familiar to many in the physical and biological sciences – such studies,although generating mountains of data,and a wide range of hypotheses and aetiologies,have yet to yield a comprehensive and convincing framework of explanation. It is this apparent shortfall that demands at least some degree of sceptical scrutiny.

To begin with, even the notionally synoptic term 'global religious fundamentalism' carries with it multiple and complex implications. It is not a unified whole, neither around the world nor within any given society. Its movements are collections of different groups with only partially shared interests. There are fundamentalist movements within Christianity, Judaism, Islam, Hinduism, Sikhism, Buddhism and Confucianism, which show substantive differences among themselves in terms of doctrine, cosmology, social composition, size, organization, and scope of influence. Therefore it is impossible to do justice to all by opting for only one all-encompassing set of explanations. Such an approach would pre-suppose, for example, that the Ayotollah Khomeni's seizure of Iran in 1979, the more recent growth of the Taliban and Al Quaida, the rise of Jewish ultra-orthodoxy in modern Israel,the emergence of the evangelical Protestant 'Moral Majority' during the 1980 U.S Election campaign,and the oppression of Hindu Tamils in Sri Lanka by Buddhist militants are all but variants of one *global* development that can be *globally* analysed and evaluated.

Such reductionism although tempting, is also over- simplistic,even absurd. What one might realistically search for, perhaps,,is at best,a common factor running through all such movements, or, falling this, at least a common 'theme', a 'family resemblance' (in Wittgenstein's phrase) that lends credence to the construct itself. At the same time, any description of global religious fundamentalism (hereafter shortened to GRF) must comprise more than the mere sum of the descriptions of X number of examples of the phenomenon.

We should also attempt to uncover a pattern that runs deeper than mere aggregation. What we need therefore, is at least some kind of formal taxonomy of features that we hold to be 'typical' of GRF, and which can serve as a basis for analysing individual case studies.

The danger of this procedure is, of course, that we assume the existence of GRF before we have tested it against a sufficient number of relevant case studies, thus imposing a homogeneity on the phenomenon that is inevitably artificial. To safeguard against this we must be equally open to examples that counter our own categories of definition as to those that elide precisely with them.

Nonetheless, with all these considerations in mind, we can still attempt to establish a preliminary, working, definition of GRF, in which four central features can perhaps be isolated:

1. Religious fundamentalists believe in certain fundamental truths: these truths are perceived as possessing absolute, objective, validity.
2. Fundamentalists believe in the existence of a historical past when these truths were universally honoured; they also believe that these truths are no longer universally honoured in their present society. Indeed they are in danger of being forgotten.
3. Fundamentalist movements tend to have charismatic leaders who define these truths by selectively interpreting both the past and the tradition of a religious system. This interpretation is understood to be the only valid interpretation of the religion in question.
4. Fundamentalists are essentially activists who engage with an 'enemy' who is associated or identified with those values of modern society that are at odds with the fundamental truths or threaten to subvert them.

To test this fourfold, essentially descriptive, definition of GRF against a variety of religious movements, perhaps the best place to start might be those evangelical churches of the United States that first gave a name to the phenomenon we are examining, and which has now itself become a global media commonplace. North American Protestant fundamentalism finds its fundamental truths in the Bible. Over and over again it propagates the 'inerrancy' of Scripture, the belief that all of the Bible is literally and absolutely true. What is puzzling to the outside observer is the fact that inspite of this assertion, not *all* parts of the Bible *are* interpreted literally, let alone given equal salience in the beliefs and practices of the congregation in question. Indeed particularly prophetic passages announcing the 'Rapture' and hence the end of time are often read metaphorically so that 'days' may come to stand for years or centuries, and the term 'armies of evil' which served to refer, in the recent past, to the atomic threat of the Warsaw Pact, now relates primarily to Iran and North Korea. Additionally, Biblical passages supporting slavery are declared to be 'indifferent to salvation', while references to certain scientific impossibilities (e.g. the world being flat) are either called 'poetic' or simply ignored. What differentiates a fundamentalist reading of the Bible from more mainstream ones is in fact only that the fundamentalists identify other (and typically more) passages to be literal truth. The question therefore arises as to who controls which parts of the Bible that are 'more equal than others', and which passages are to be either left forgotten or re-interpreted metaphorically.

This is where the charismatic leaders come in. Here it must be pointed out the individual fundamentalist churches of the United States are by no means all part of one organized movement, but rather are splintered precisely along the lines of what their individual spiritual fathers (who are almost exclusively male) have designated fundamental truth. In this context it is interesting to observe how the more potentially fissile groups tend to break up when dispute arises either about scriptural interpretation, or, for example, about what degree of compromise Biblical truths can tolerate before being contaminated. The late Jerry Falwell (1933-2007) was an interesting case in point in this context. In 1979, Falwell an evangelical Southern Baptist pastor, created the 'Moral Majority' organization that campaigned for a return to 'traditional morality' and supported the current Republican presidential candidate, Ronald Reagan, in his bid for office. Reagan succeeded, but such political involvement forced Falwell to compromise with other groups –notably the Roman Catholics - who supported his morality campaign. For some members of his own church, their leader's public cooperation with what one called' the minions of the Anti-Christ' marked him out as a betrayer of the Moral Majority's cause. Soon after, the ultra -evangelical Bob Jones branded Falwell as 'the most dangerous man in America'. Thus some fundamentalists can always decide that they are more fundamental than others.

The creation of the 'Moral Majority' also serves to illustrate two specific aspects (2 and 4) of our earlier definition of religious fundamentalism. Its foundation rested on a twofold claim. Firstly the historically dubious assertion that the United States had experienced a severe moral decline since its early Puritan days. Secondly, the suggestion that those most distressed by this decline were essentially a majority of the population that only needed to be properly mobilized. In other words, the American present had been re-interpreted in the light of a supposedly golden past,and the nation's subsequent history clearly justified present action. The campaigning techniques of the 'Moral Majority' included the use of TV for fund-raising, the publication of newspapers and the promotion of so-called 'informational' seminars on predominantly local radio and TV networks. Thus Protestant fundamentalism not only showed itself to be activist,but also very adept at using state of the art technology for the purposes of this activism: militant traditionalism pursued,as it were, with the weapons of modernity.

In stark contrast to the North American world of Protestant 'televangelism' (subsequently replicated widely in Central and South America) is that of ultra-orthodox Jews in Israel or in the culturally distinct urban enclaves to be found, for example, in New York City, London or Manchester. Worldwide there are currently about 13.5 million Jews,of whom 16% can be classified as orthodox,and within the latter less than a third can be called ultra-orthodox. The Jews call this ultra-orthodox minority'*haredim*', i.e. "those who tremble at God's word". The *haredim* themselves, however, prefer the simple term'yidu' –Jews- with the implication that all the millions of their less strict brethren have no rights to such a title. Where do these *haredim* take their truths from? Here the 'belief' dimension of our earlier, second, definition of GRF runs into difficulties. 'Doxa' (i.e. belief), is not at the centre of Judaism, and hence it is not in their dogmatic convictions that the *haredim* believe themselves to be special. Rather it is in their clothes and hair and beards that they differ from less orthodox Jews, and in their minute conformity to dietary demands and all the hundreds of other rules found in the Torah. This emphasis on 'orthopraxis' rather than orthodoxy forces us to widen the our first definition of GRF given earlier .Here truth must be understood to also include ritual. It should be pointed out here that in virtually all recent examples of Catholic fundamentalism,the creation of the movement was primarily a reaction to the changes in ritual initiated by the Vatican 11 Ecumenical Council (the change from the Tridentine Mass to the Novus Ordo Mass), and less as an overt response to doctrinal changes. Thus for certain Catholics, too, truth is embedded in movements and symbols rather than doctrine. Rabbi Elazar Shach, (1899-2001) leader of one faction of ultra-orthodox Jews, summed up the importance of ritual observance in a single sentence. 'If there is no Sabbath observance and no Yom Kippur, in what is a person to be considered a Jew?' In other words, non-adherence to practices is seen to be commensurate with the loss of religious and indeed national identity.

Our second identifiable feature of GRF –the belief in a glorious past –is equally easy to discern in the case of the *haredim*. Not only does the Biblical past as described in the Hebrew Bible (the Christian Old Testament) serve as a point of reference,but the long centuries of diaspora in which Jewish identity survived through strict observance of the laws can equally be exploited to serve as a shining example of what proper respect for God's commandments can achieve. Leaders, too, are easily found among the Rabbis who have power to decide on the precise interpretation of how and why ritual should be carried out. Again one is struck by how the different branches of Jewish fundamentalism are defined by their leaders' conflicting understandings of the past, of scripture and of ritual. Conflicts arise over such issues as who has the right to issue kosher food certificates – an issue that is both religiously significant and financially lucrative. Other divisions are social (i.e.rich versus poor), or racial (European Askanazic Jews versus non-European Sephardim) in nature. We should remind ourselves here that not all fundamentalist movements are exclusively *religious* entities!

Finally we have to ask whether the *haredim* can be classified as activists. A look at the 1990 campaign to elect the 12th Israeli Knesset shows that at least a significant proportion certainly can. The coalition between Labour and Likud, who formed the National Unity government had broken down earlier over disputes about the direction of the Middle East Peace Process, and both parties were forced to woo other, smaller, parties in an attempt to achieve a parliamentary majority. The largest single block of minor parties could be classed as *haredim*.

Hence the fate of the entire nation rested on the political stance of the individual rabbis of these minority parties. As a result of a speech made by Rabbi Shach at the Degel Ha Torah party's annual convention (part of which is quoted above) the fundamentalist party withdrew its allegiance from Labour. Other members of *haredi* parties who could not bear to collaborate with a secular Zionist party that had already been denounced as non-Jewish also defected. As a result Labour lost its narrow majority and Likud formed a government.In this sense any religious movement that actively decides who will govern a nation cannot but be classed as activist. Hence it would seem therefore that,allowing for certain minor local variations ,orthodox Judaism too,also conforms fairly precisely to our initial,fourfold, definition of GRF.

On the 29th of December, 1996, the London-based *Observer* printed an article about a phenomenon it described as 'Islamophobia' —the hatred of all things Muslim in modern Britain.This hatred is to some degree the result of popular fears concerning Islamic fundamentalism. Cross-European data (drawn from Gallup and other surveys) continues to indicate that, more than any other religion, Islam is seen as militant, anti-modern (i.e. anti-liberal, anti-woman, anti-gay, anti-democracy) and plainly dangerous. There is also some evidence to indicate that much of this negative imagery was derived less from the current NATO engagement in Iraq or Afganistan, or even from the London bombings in July 2005, but from more long-standing,and deeply embedded, folk-memories of Shi'ite activity at the time of the so-called Iranian Revolution in 1979. In the context of this essay, the question here is whether this activity, too, can be usefully described within the four 'fundamentalist' parameters outlined at the beginning of our discussion.

Shi'ite Islam has two major sources it can draw on to establish its normative truths of belief and conduct - the Koran and the Sunna (the prophet's paradigmatic life) The call to return to a strict adherence of both accompanied the resurgence of Islamic fundamentalism in Iran in the period before Khomeni's return from exile. In fact, such a return to orthodoxy,to faith fundamentals,was promised to bring about the return of social justice and international Islamic power. Return implied a time when all this was a living truth,and indeed Khomeni-style Shi'ism articulated an extraordinary re-interpretation of both the past and of Shi'ite tradition.First of all the expansionist success of early Islam was seen solely as a function of religious purity. Secondly, the Shi'ite stance towards political obedience was completely re-shaped. The Shi'ite branch of Islam had occupied a minority position for many centuries: this, and their doctrine of the return of the 12th Imam as the messianic Mahdi had brought about a quietist posture towards political hierarchy. The Shi'ites had resolved to bow to authority and wait in an attitude of martyrdom and passion for a heaven-sent saviour.

Khomeni, with the help of Western-educated Islamic intellectuals like Dr Ali Shariati set about transforming this attitude to one of revolutionary activism based around a call for social revolution in preparation for the 'second coming'. Quietism was denounced as a dogmatic misinterpretation of the tradition of Shi'ism. It should be noted that this re-reading of history added elements to the Shi'ite ideology that were blatant innovations. For example, the modern, western, concept of nationalism was exploited and the promise of 'popular political participation' made. Neither was traditional: Islam tended to be regarded as a transnational entity, and political power had always been –both *de facto* and *de jure* - strictly hierarchical and authoritarian. Again, we cannot but notice that fundamentalists are modern innovators as much as they are traditionalists. Such a transformation of Shi'ite identity, and indeed the mobilization of large sections of the Shi'ite community, required bold leadership coupled with exceptional loyalty towards that leadership. This loyalty in itself was part of Shi'ite doctrine as interpreted by Khomeni and Dr Shariati. Islamic jurists ('Faqih') such as Khomeni were publically projected as holding the status of deputies of the messianic Mahdi. In the time of his absence the loyalty towards this saviour could best be expressed by loyalty to his first disciple!

What we find in the case of Iran, then, is a subtle convergence of all four dimensions of our original definition of GRF: activism is interpreted as being part of tradition and truth, so is loyalty to the leader, and the state of affairs of a historical past is re-fashioned as the direct aim of militant nationalism. This unity of the movement, added to its appeal in non-fundamentalist circles though its agenda of nationalism and social revolution, accounts for the extraordinary success of the Ayatollah's personal bid for power. It also continues to perpetuate a powerful trace element in the negative demonology which so often features in Western perceptions of Islamic fundamentalism in general, and of what is now post-Revolutionary Iran in particular.

We have now provided a descriptive account of global religious fundamentalism in three specific historical contexts. Each relates to and reflects, in varying degrees, the operational definition of religious fundamentalism set out at the beginning of this discussion. We now have some idea what fundamentalism looks like within one comparatively uniform pattern of analysis. What remains to be done is to explain it.

One explanation is, of course, that we cannot even begin to understand the rise of GDF if we fail to understand the role of the media. Modern journalism fathered fundamentalism. This may sound excessively simplistic. Media are normally seen as entities that observe and report, rather than as creative, autonomous forces. Their power, however is the power of words, and to a lesser extent, images, and even if we do not choose to agree entirely with those philosophers who argue that all of reality is in fact just words,it seems self-evident that the media have the power to both describe and therefore to evaluate cultural-historical phenomena.

It is the media, for example, who decided that the Taliban's activities in Afganistan are to be called 'fundamentalist'. The same media decided to refer to Gandhi's political crusade in India as 'an act of liberation'. The point here is not so much to propose that Gandhi's activities in India are comparable to those of Afgan Shi'ites. The point is rather to suggest that the definition of what is fundamentalist and what is not, is not usually made by people within those movements, nor by academic experts outside, but mostly by the media - an institution that has a far wider circulation and whose public voice is thus much louder. What is interesting here is that both sides (the media *and* the religious movements) seem to understand their mutual dependency as well as the mutual benefits that can arise. The news needs headlines and stories. The fundamentalists need publicity and need to be recognized. Journalism has identified fundamentalism and thus given it a plausible identity and cultural currency. The discourse between religious movements and their perception and description in the media is thus an intrinsic part of the phenomenon we are examining.

In some ways this insight challenges much of what was suggested earlier. There we tried to develop a 'factual', historically-grounded, definition of GRF which we assumed to be somehow able to stand outside any explicit discourse between media and fundamentalism. This still has relevance, however, simply because it allowed us to gain some understanding of how individual cases of fundamentalism appear to function. One thing we discovered is the complicated relationship between fundamentalism's elevation of tradition and the practice of making selective use of both modern technology (and we may include the use made of media in this category) and of modern, secular, concepts. A brief look at Theravada Buddhist fundamentalism in Sri Lanka can help us once again to illustrate such dependency on modernity. There the nationalistic and moralistic rhetoric used by the religious leaders of Sri Lankan Buddhism smacks of phrases borrowed directly from Protestant missionaries of the colonial period,even as it denounces the values of that colonialism.One example is the injunction to 'believe not the alien who is giving you arrack, whisky, toddy, sausages'. Indeed this whole re-interpretation of Buddhism as a prohibitive moral system is both innovative *and* a result of local historical circumstance. In the movements's own rhetoric, however, it is referred to solely as a tradition that dates back two and a half thousand years. A more straightforward example can be found in North American or South Korean Protestant fundamentalists' fondness for television sermons. Here, in Gilles Kepel's telling phrase, fundamentalists reveal themselves time and again to be 'true children of our time'.

So far we have identified two factors that may help to explain –rather than merely describe – GRF. These are the media, and the dynamic of religious traditionalism encountering and utilising both modern technologies and modern ideologies. The step often taken from these two starting points is to depict fundamentalism as a function of modernity in a way that implies a necessary or even proportional relationship. The distinguished American scholar of religion, Bruce Lawrence, can to some degree be accused of such a conclusion. In his much-praised book, *Defenders of God,* he identifies two camps,one belonging to the 'modernists',the other to the 'fundamentalists –the latter being a reaction to the former.'Modernism' is held to be the ideology embraced by the vast majority of the populations of those countries where fundamentalism arises ('the modernist outlook…pervades every aspect of contemporary life') and is defined as a system that embraces technological advance and a market economy at expense of traditional values. 'At its utopian extreme' Lawrence argues 'it [modernism] enthrones one economic strategy, consumer-oriented capitalism,as the secret means to technological progress that will also eliminate social unrest and physical discomfort'. Fundamentalism, by contrast, is defined mostly negatively,i.e. as that movement which turns against modernism. Later on in his book, Lawrence goes so far as to describe the dichotomy of modernism versus fundamentalism as 'a subset of the larger, longer battle between universalism and monadism'

Two aspects of this account are particularly contestible. The first is the crude identification of that which fundamentalist movements fight against with capitalism and technological advance. While this might work reasonably well in the context of Protestant, North American, fundamentalism,it is much too generalized, and often a misleading label for the complex phenomenon of GRF.For example, fundamentalist organisations such as Opus Dei can also be politically (and economically) conservative,especially when attacking liberal relativism and possessive individualism.

Modernism, too, seems to be divided within itself. Lawrence, somewhat idiosyncratically, highlights science as one primary agent of modernism, but science is surely, by its very nature, positivist and realist in philosophical outlook, and is also challenged, within the discourse of modernism, by both anti-realism and relativism? On a more mundane level, describing capitalism as the enemy of, for example, Sri Lankan Buddhist militants, simply does'nt tell us anything at all about the ethno-religious dynamic that recently turned that island into a battle zone. Lawrence fails to offer any real explanation by merely erecting a kind of shadow theatre where two titans clash over bland clichés such as capitalism versus family values.

A second criticism might be that Lawrence's argument quickly leads to a belief that we can correlate modernism and the degree of modernity in any society with the rise of fundamentalism in that society. In short, his premise seems to be that the more modernism 'pervades every aspect of contemporary life' the more we can expect fundamentalist religion to arise. A cursory look around the world serves to disprove the thesis. Germany or Switzerland can both be classified as modernist countries both economically and in terms of ideology, yet signs of fundamentalism (save among Muslim migrants) are noticeably absent. Japan makes for an even more interesting case study.

The decades since the Second World War have not only seen it emerge as one of the paradigms of modernism in the world: they have also witnessed a major boom in new religious movements- the *shinshukyo*. Many of these sects tend to idealise a glorious, pre-War, Imperial past, yet cannot readily be identified as 'fundamentalist'. What they typically lack is any insistence on being the sole possessors of the only,exclusive truth.As the writer has frequently observed *in situ*,on any given day, *shinshukyo* members will first attend their sect's specific ritual occasions, and then stop by the local Buddhist temple or Shinto shrine on the way home from factory,farm or office. The reason for such serial religiosity is that the entire Japanese religious and metaphysical tradition is predominantly one of effortless pluralism plus credal relativism. The concept of absolute truths is not an intrinsic part of their traditional religious heritage.

The case of Japan not only shows that a high degree of modernism will not necessarily bring about fundamentalism. It also points the way to two crucial factors that have a strong influence on whether or not fundamentalist movements will arise - religious tradition, and popular cultural attitudes latent in a society.

Contrary to Lawrence's influential hypothesis, fundamentalism does *not* arise most easily in an environment that is most hostile to these,but rather in an environment that is largely sympathetic to them. Consider America: the 1985 Gallup report shows 72% of U.S citizens to believe that the Bible is the Word of God; 39% believed it should be taken literally. In Israel, the ultra-orthodox, fundamentalist, party called the Shas was,in 1990, the third biggest party in the Knesset —its rabbis remain revered as especially holy, even by those who are happy to eat pork on a Saturday!

All this points to the fact that fundamentalism prospers in those societies where a significant proportion agrees with its appeal to go 'back to basics',even if most of these are also unwilling to go along with the monopolization of one canon of truth as the sole organizational principle of their lives. Germany,by contrast with America and Israel,has no widespread normative assumption of the past having been better than the present,and here New Age sects offer an attractive antidote to the identifiable stresses of modern economic and social life. Christian Fundamentalism, however, predictably lacks serious sympathisers.

A more general conclusion to this discussion might be that while we may well acknowledge the contemporary presence of global religious fundamentalism, we will never begin to understand its specific parameters if we do not first engage with a historical analysis of its culturally specific, predisposing circumstances. On a general level, however, we should also allow ourselves to conclude that fundamentalism arises when a widely felt longing for values which are seen to be part of the past coexist with a widely based acceptance of the ideological, scientific and technological consequences of modernity.

This paradox can sometimes be seized upon by charismatic leaders who give their specific interpretation to what has to change in order to resolve the paradox and also incite their followers to actively pursue this change. The outcomes will range from war to revolution to peaceful protest, all of which we are advised to observe carefully, take seriously, but not necessarily regard as inevitable.

SELECT BIBLIOGRAPHY

Abdulaziz A. Sachedina, Activist Shi'ism in Iran, Iraq and Lebanon.
Armstrong, Karen (2000), *The Battle for God*: London: Harper Collins.
Donald K. Swearer, 'Fundamentalist Movements in Theravada Buddhism'.
Hanegraaf W.J. (1996), *New Age Religion and Western Culture*: Leiden: E.J. Brill.
Kepel, Gilles (1994), *The Revenge of God*: Oxford: Polity.
Lawrence, Bruce B. (1995), *Defenders of God – The Fundamentalist Revolt against the Modern Age*: Columbia SC: University of South Carolina Press.
Marty, Martin E. and Appleby, R. Scott (eds) (1991) *Fundamentalisms Observed*, Vol 1 of *The Fundamentalism Project* (Chicago: University of Chicago Press), and specifically articles by : Nancy T. Ammerman, 'North American Protestant Fundamentalism'.
Riesebrodt, Martin (1993), Pious *Passion-The Emergence of Modern Fundamentalism in the United States and Iran*: Berkeley, CA: University of California Press.
Samuel C. Heilman and Menachen Friedman, 'Religious Fundamentalism and Religious Jews: The case of the Haredim.
William D. Dinges, 'Roman Catholic Fundamentalism in the U.S.'
Winston Davis, 'Fundamentalism in Japan: Religious and Political'.

In: Scepticism: Hero and Villain
Editors: R. Calne and W. O'Reilly

ISBN: 978-1-62417-783-5
© 2013 Nova Science Publishers, Inc.

Chapter 14

BELIEF AND CYNICISM IN RELIGION

Robert A. Hinde
St. John's College, Cambridge, UK

ABSTRACT

In studies of religion, belief and cynicism do not form a pair of opposites. Religion contains a number of components, not all of which are equally important to all individuals or in all religions, and it is possible to accept some and not others. Where belief in a deity is an issue, the nature of the deity varies between believers and between religions, and the nature and strength of belief varies similarly. Many who do not believe in the religious stories are nevertheless comforted by religious participation. Thus cynicism can have many foci and take many forms.

In this chapter I shall present some of the reasons why that is the case. In brief, believers do not necessarily subscribe to the whole Christian story. At one extreme the fundamentalists accept every word in the Bible and believe they can guide their behaviour by what they read there. Others regard calling themselves Christians as socially convenient, but do not think deeply about what that involves. And between is a nexus of sincerities and qualities of believing. Amongst the cynics, too, there is great variety: some would sweep the whole religious system away, some merely want the right to be an atheist or agnostic to be fully recognised in society, and yet others do not believe in the Biblical stories yet feel that it has some merits. Coming to terms with this diversity needs more understanding of the nature of religion, and I shall therefore summarise some of the recent advances in the nature of religion. Because I am most familiar with it, I shall focus primarily on Christianity.

THE STRUCTURE OF RELIGIONS

In the first place, most religions have a complex structure. Christianity, for instance, can be seen as having six elements. Five of these can be discussed objectively: structural beliefs which are outside time, like God being Three Persons in One; narratives or stories which supposedly take place in the real world, like the Gospels; rituals; a moral code; and the social aspects. The sixth, religious experience, is related to all the others but, by its nature, needs more discussion.

Each of these six elements affects and is affected by others. Most obviously, the stories affect the ritual, the morals, religious experience and the social aspect, while the rituals support the structural beliefs and narratives, and so on. The beliefs affect the integrity of the community because people like others who think the same way as they do, and are especially attracted to others who share unverifiable beliefs, like those of religion (Byrne et al., 1966). Sharing the belief elements helps to make the individual feel part of the community, and feeling part of the group helps strengthen his/her beliefs (Hinde, 2010).

Religious experience is of special interest in discussions of scepticism versus belief, as for some people it has been a major contributor to belief. There are, however, three reasons why religious experience should not be interpreted in that way. First, the language used by many mystics to describe their experiences seems to resemble the language used to describe aesthetic experience. That suggests that it does not lie so far outside the everyday, or at least no further than the subjective feeling one gets from great music, great painting, the intricacies of nature or the immensity of the universe. Second, so far as I am aware, Christian mystics experience visions of Jesus, Mary, or occasionally one of the saints, but not Buddha or Krishna, and vice versa: this suggests that the vision is much influenced by the individual's past experience. Third, a vision or a subjective experience, any more than a dream, cannot be taken as evidence for a being, presence or entity of any sort: the experience may be something that we do not understand but it then requires psychological investigation (Dawkins, 2006; Hinde, 2010).

Religious experience presents an easy target for the cynic: it is based on the subjective experience of one individual. and there is no doubt that religious experiences have been faked. In general the cynic can not legitimately question the fact that the experience occurred, but can properly question its interpretation as evidence for a god or indeed for any external entity at all. We do not yet know, perhaps because we have not looked far enough, what makes our mind/brain respond in the way that it does in situations associated with religious practice.

It will be apparent that it is possible to accept the structural beliefs but be sceptical about the narratives; to be sceptical about the beliefs but believe in the value of the ritual or of the religious community; or to believe in and value the morality but not the beliefs, and so on. In other words, the complexity of religious systems makes any simple dichotomy between belief and cynicism invalid.

Of course not all religions are like Christianity in the relative importance of its components: whereas many Christians have thought that belief was the most important issue, belief is relatively unimportant in Buddhism and Hinduism, where the emphasis is more on good deeds.

In many non-scripted religions the ritual seems central, with the beliefs seemingly emerging around it.

Christian beliefs have been the principal target of cynics. Dawkins (2006), Hitchens (2007), Dennett (2006) and others have pointed to the extreme improbability of the Biblical stories. Twentieth-century minds cannot accept that the world was made in six days, that Jesus was resurrected from the dead, or even that he fed five thousand on bread and a few fishes, or turned water into wine. Non-fundamentalist believers, however, argue that such critics miss the point. The Biblical stories should not be taken literally but as metaphors, in much the same way as Bunyan's Pilgrim's Progress or Aesop's Fables have been taken as guides to how one should behave. Given the complexity of religiosity, it is perhaps useful to distinguish between belief and faith. In the sense in which I use them here, belief implies "I believe a statement to be true and potentially verifiable", while faith implies "I will act as if this statement were true". The cynic who attacks "God, all gods, anything and everything supernatural" (Dawkins, 2006, p.36) would lie in the former category, the modern believing philosopher in the latter. But belief and cynicism are not the only categories: there are many who do not accept the Biblical stories as truth yet find them useful guides in their lives, and yet others who attend religious services out of loyalty to the conventions of society.

Indeed, although "Believe and be Saved" has been a basic tenet of Christianity, not all Christian thinkers go along with that. Thus some Christian thinkers take the view that "A man is not, I think, a professing Christian unless he proposes to live according to Christian moral principles and associates his intention with thinking of Christian stories, but he need not believe that the empirical propositions presented by the stories correspond to empirical fact." (Vidler, 1963, citing Braithwaite). (In my view our moral principles are not specifically Christian, and probably had secular origins, and I regret the common assumption that religious specialists are seen to have a privileged position in discussions of ethical questions. but that is another matter (Hinde, 2002)). Many sophisticated theists argue that the "God" they believe in is a subtle concept. God, in their view, is not an entity and cannot be described, and faith is not belief in a deity but commitment to a life style and outlook that could make a difference. Armstrong (2009, 2010) insists that theologians have held such a sophisticated view of God for at least two millennia. She sees the religious texts not as factual accounts, but as opening the way to fresh insights. Such a view, however, brings further difficulties: if God cannot be described, it is not possible to discuss him. Thus the question of whether God exists becomes a non-question.

Cynics emphasize the many undesirable consequences that religion has had, like causing or supporting many bloody wars. Even small differences, perhaps especially small differences, such as those between Sunni and Shia, or between Catholic and Protestant, have been a basis for persecution, intolerance, torture and long-lasting wars. It is differences in belief that is usually the problem. If a believer believes something to be true, then anything that is contrary to his religious beliefs must be wrong, and denial of a religious belief has been taken to justify all kinds of horror. On an everyday level, unhappiness has been caused by religious pride, intolerance, self-righteousness and other personal characteristics that often stem from religious belief. In the sense used here, "Faith", as opposed to "belief", helps to evade some of these issues.

But religiosity has other consequences that are often disregarded by sceptics. Religion has done what it could to hold a line against encroaching materialism. It has spoken out against one of the greatest evils of our time, poverty, and the excessive differences between rich and poor -- though at times the clergy have been the greatest sinners in these matters. At an individual level religion has an ability to comfort, to reassure, to give strength and to "give meaning to life". There have been many records of atheists in extreme danger turning to prayer. My mother was greatly comforted by her simple religion when it was confirmed that my brother had died slowly and painfully of wounds in an open boat in World War 2. Here is an important ethical question for cynics. They may think that it is wrong to let people believe things that are not true, and in the long term as a scientist I agree with them, but at the same time is it right to take away a source of comfort until we have something better to put in its place? Would they, I wonder, tell a grieving mother that her belief that she would see her son in Heaven was nonsense?

Given that religion has consequences for the believer, do those consequences stem from any one of its six components, or is it due to a combination? That is a question that has been too little studied. What seems clear, however, is that the consequences of being a Christian, including religious experience however vivid and meaningful to the individual involved, can not be taken as evidence for a divine being, spirit or essence. Religious experience and other consequences of religiosity are phenomena still to be fully investigated.

WHAT SORT OF A GOD?

Ambiguities in the nature of gods play a great part in their acceptance. Most gods have two types of constituent: some possible and the others improbable (Boyer, 1994). To take an example from our own secular folk-lore, ghosts are seen as having certain human-like properties: they talk, they wail, they can feel unhappy. But they are also transparent and can walk through walls. The human-like properties make them understandable and acceptable, the improbable properties make them attention-getting and memorable. Ghosts, of course, are not gods: they lack, at least in recent European folklore, the ability to interfere effectively in the world. Gods must be thought to have done, do or be able to do something in the world. That is why people are so interested in them.

When a believer claims belief in God, a further question involves the nature of the god to which he/she refers. We have seen already that this is a source of debate: believers who reject the cynics' view that God does not exist go on to say God is indescribable, and differ amongst themselves in exactly what they are referring to. And even unsophisticated believers have an image of God that is less simple than appears at first sight. This is related to the way that children learn about religion.

We now know that early on children acquire the ability to distinguish between animate and inanimate entities on the basis of self-initiated movement and other movement characteristics (Gelman et al., 1995). The tendency to attribute movement to animate causes may have been of value to our ancestors: a glimpse of movement through the trees could mean danger (Guthrie, 1993). For a human child the first animate entity to be seen is almost certainly another human, and thus it is not surprising that a moving entity is likely, lacking further information, to be interpreted as human. Thus an unexplained event, like a volcano erupting or a storm at sea is likely to be explained as involving human agency. In general, novel or ambiguous stimuli tend to be seen as anthropomorphic. Given that humans dream about humans, and dreams can be perceived as real, this may also contribute to the anthropomorphic nature of gods (Dudbridge, 1993). Given that humans dream about humans, and dreams can be perceived as real, this may also contribute to the anthropomorphic nature of gods. Of course not all gods are anthropomorphic, but most are.

When children brought up in a household claiming to be Christian first hear about God, they may hear about a being who can intend to interfere in the world or respond to prayers. Or they may first hear about Jesus, who is presented as a man with similar abilities. This implies two things about the deity, that he acts as an agent and acts with intentions, that the child has come to "know" characterise animate and usually human beings (Baron-Cohen, 1997).

Actually the ability to understand these human properties takes time to develop. It is only about the age of two years that children begin to show "Theory of Mind", that is that they become aware that other people have intentions. They can then cope with statements involving propositional attitudes that express the state of the speaker with respect to the world. Other characteristics of God, such that He can be loving or angry, follow from what the child already knows about human beings, and he/she readily forms a picture of God as a special sort of Person. Given that He is said to be old and wise, and that he was pictured by Michelangelo with a beard, it is hardly surprising that He is often imagined as an old man.

It is at around this age that children have to start to come to terms with the improbable properties of God. God is Three Persons in One, He is everywhere at once, he knows everything that everybody does. The child thus acquires representations of God of two sorts. First at the basic level - God is a human being with the properties that the child knows are characteristic of humans, a little special, perhaps, but nevertheless human. But there is also the "higher level" of representation at which God has these inexplicable properties, like being able to interfere in the world by answering prayers.

These other characteristics are much more difficult to assimilate. Experiments with adults suggest that believers have two representations of God, one intuitive and inferentially rich, the other improbable and requiring teaching and effort to be assimilated. The intuitive representation is recalled easily and is used when an immediate response is required, the theological one is used in discussions about God by believers. When asked about the nature of their God or gods, believers will reply by supplying improbable properties, like the ability to be everywhere at once, but when respondents paraphrase accounts of God's activities they systematically misremember their God as having human attributes. People who reject any anthropomorphic constraints on God nevertheless use an anthropomorphic concept to understand stories. In one experiment, stories were constructed so that they could be remembered either by "theologically correct concepts" of God or by more human-like ones. The subjects affirmed the former characteristics of God when reflecting, but used human properties when reasoning about God (Barrett, 2004).

A variety of beliefs about the nature of God have been around for a long time: probably since long before the birth of Christianity. At the time of the Reformation most religious specialists had a fairly sophisticated view of God, but the peasantry, mostly illiterate, had a more fundamentalist view, seeing God as a special sort of Person.

The Three Persons of Christianity reconciled the monotheism of Judaism with Christ's teaching. It combines the Father, who is seen as the Creator, Jesus with primarily human properties but with some counter-intuitive ones that are ascribed to a Holy Spirit which lacks human characteristics.

A rigidly monotheistic religion could not have tolerated the idea of incarnation because it would have been blasphemous to identify God with a human being, but at the same time recognised his divinity. Historically the relation between the three Persons has given rise to much controversy and the emphasis has varied from seeing Jesus as scarcely god to seeing him as scarcely man.

I suggest that most people to-day who call themselves Christians do not think too much about the sort of God they believe in. For most, a concept of God was assimilated in childhood and never fully analysed. If they are church attendees, they may not be helped by the words used in Christian services. The Creeds, written in the early centuries of the last millennium, may give little clarification: even an Archbishop whom I had the opportunity to ask some years ago confessed "Well, I do have some difficulty with the Resurrection of the Dead".

As well as asking what sort of belief believers hold, it is proper also to ask what sort of god the cynics are attacking. In most cases, I suspect, it is the God as portrayed in the Bible. The more sophisticated view of those who argue that God is not an entity and cannot be described cannot be easily attacked because there is nothing to be attacked. Its description as a report of experience cannot be denied by any one except the experiencer but, as said before, it is inappropriate to see it as evidence for divinity.

THE STRENGTH OF BELIEF

Belief usually implies some knowledge of what it is one claims to believe in. In fact many of those who claim to be religious are almost quite ignorant of the substance of their belief. Many who labelled themselves as Protestants or Catholics in the USA could not name a single Old Testament prophet (Stark and Glock, 1968).

At the other extreme, religious scholars and some fundamentalists have an exhaustive knowledge of the Bible. Belief also differs greatly in its nature: it has sometimes been useful to distinguish between those who seem to live their religion (intrinsic religion) and those who use religion primarily to satisfy needs (extrinsic religion, Allport and Ross, 1967), but like all dichotomous distinctions in this area, it has only limited usefulness.

Again we must ask, at what sort of belief is the cynic's scepticism directed? Clearly in most cases it is the fundamentalist believer. Those with faith do not necessarily claim that what they believe is true, only that accepting it works for them.

CONCLUSION

So does a dichotomy between belief and cynicism have any real meaning when applied to religion? Difficulties arise because religion is not a simple entity, because believers have diverse views of God, and because the extent to which belief has a real influence on the lives of those who claim to be religious ranges from almost nothing to all-pervading.

That religion of some sort permeates every culture, that the majority of people in the world claim to be religious, is enough to show that it presents some of the most intricate problems that face us. My own bias is to believe that science, especially the human sciences, provides us with the best tools to tackle them.

REFERENCES

Allport, G.W. & Ross, J.M. (1967). Personal religion: orientation and prejudice. *J. Personality and Social Psychology, 5,* 432-43.

Armstrong, K. (2009). The Case For God: What Religion Really Means. London: *Bodley Head.*

Armstrong, K. (2010). Twelve Steps To A Compassionate Life. London: *Bodley Head.*

Baron-Cohen, S. (1997). The Maladaptive Mind. Hove: *Psychology Press.*

Barrett, J. L. (2004). Why Would Anyone Believe In God? Walnut Creek CA: *AltaMira.*

Boyer, P. (1994). The Naturalness Of Religious Ideas. Berkeley CA: *University of California Press.*

Byrne, D., Nelson, D. & Reves, K. (1966). Effects of consensual validation and invalidation on attraction as a function of verifiability. *Journal of Experimental Social Psychology, 2.* 98-107.

Dawkins, R. (2006). The God Delusion. London: *Transworld.*

Dennett, D.C. (2006). Breaking The Evil Spell: Religion As A Natural Phenomenon. London: *Viking.*

Dudbridge, G. (1995). Religious Experience And Lay Society In T'ang China. Cambridge: *Cambridge University Press.*

Gelman, R., Durgin, F., & Kaufman, L. (1995). Distinguishing between animates and inanimates: not by motion alone. In D. Sperber, D. Premack and D.J. Premack (eds). Causal Cognition. Oxford: *Clarendon.*

Guthrie, S. (1993). Faces In The Clouds. New York: *Oxford University Press.*

Hinde, ,R.A. (2002). Why Good Is Good. London: *Routledge.*

Hinde, R.A. (2010). Why Gods Persist (2nd ed). London: *Routledge.*

Hitchens, C. (2007). God Is Not Great. London: *Atlantic.*

Sands, P. (2008). Torture Team: Deception, Cruelty And The Compromise Of Law. London: *Allen Lane.*

Stark, R. & Glock, G.C. (1968). American Piety: The Nature Of Religious Commitment. Berkeley CA; *University of California Press.*

Vidler, A.R. (1964). Historical objections, In D.M. Mackinnon, H.A. Williams, A.R.Vidler & J.S.Bezzant (eds). Objections To Christian Belief. London: *Constable.*

In: Scepticism: Hero and Villain
Editors: R. Calne and W. O'Reilly
ISBN: 978-1-62417-783-5
© 2013 Nova Science Publishers, Inc.

Chapter 15

DOUBT IN RELIGION AND THEOLOGY

Brian Hebblethwaite

ABSTRACT

This chapter considers not scepticism about religion as such, but rather the place of doubt within a religious position. I discuss this from the point of view of the individual believer, from that of church authorities, and from that of the theologians. Then, in a more philosophical mode, I discuss the issues of faith and criticism, faith and knowledge, and faith and rationality. Rejecting fideism, I explore the question how far religious believers can affirm the rationality of their position, given the uncertainties revealed by biblical, historical and philosophical criticism.

INTRODUCTION

There is ... a virtue – let us call it rationality – which preserves the just mean between believing too much (credulity) and believing too little (scepticism). From the viewpoint of an agnostic both the theist and the atheist err by credulity: they are both believing something ... in the absence of the appropriate justification. On the other hand, from the point of view of theism, the agnostic errs on the side of scepticism: that is, he has no view on a topic on which it is very important to have a view.

Anthony Kenny, *The Unknown God*, pp. 108-9.

In this chapter I am not discussing scepticism *about* theism or *about* religion – the views we find in eighteenth century sceptics like David Hume or the French Encyclopaedists, in nineteenth century agnostics like Herbert Spencer and in modern disparagers of religion like Richard Dawkins. It is interesting, even amusing, to see that, according to the mild agnostic, Kenny, both believers and unbelievers err by credulity; for neither theism nor atheism is susceptible of conclusive proof. Kenny admits that, from the believer's point of view, even his mild agnosticism errs on the side of scepticism.

What I discuss here is the place, if any, of doubt or scepticism *in* religion. I shall of course, be considering Kenny's 'just mean' between scepticism and credulity, namely rationality, and its relation to religious faith and religious belief. Given the lack of incontrovertible proof in matters of religion, can the believer still claim rationality for his position, thus avoiding credulity without giving in to scepticism? And can such a position include elements of doubt or even of at least some degree of scepticism?

At first sight there would appear to be no place for doubt in genuine religious faith. 'Firmly I believe and truly, God is three and God is one' we sing in Newman's well-known hymn. 'I know that my Redeemer liveth' sings the soprano in Handel's *Messiah*, quoting Job 19.2. On the other hand 'Lord, I believe; help thou mine unbelief' (Mark 9.24) is a much used biblical text, and doubting Thomas a much loved biblical figure. Admittedly St Thomas's doubts were soon resolved, but in a highly exceptional way. Of much more common application is St Paul's declaration, in 2 Corinthians 5.7, that in this life 'we walk by faith, not by sight'. And one has only to reflect on the disagreements between believers, both within and between denominations, and on the doctrinal disputes between theologians and Church leaders throughout Christian history, to say nothing of the conflicting truth-claims of the different world religions, to realise that in religion we are far from the realm of universally agreed objective certainty. (Not that that ideal is achieved in any complex field, not even in science, as is clear from other contributions to this volume.)

FAITH AND DOUBT

Before tackling the key issues of faith and criticism, faith and knowledge, and faith and rationality, let me say something about the place of doubt where individual believers, church authorities, and theologians are concerned. Individual Christians vary greatly in the amount and degree of certainty with which they hold their Christian faith. Some Christian bodies, admittedly, insist pretty strictly on a definite list of *credenda*, subscription to which they make a condition of membership; but most churches are wiser in welcoming all who wish to be associated with their life, practice and worship, however many doubts they may have over some of the contents of the Bible or the creeds.

Peter Baelz, in his Bampton Lectures, *The Forgotten Dream* (1975), even speaks of the 'half-believer', one who is attracted by the Christian way and wants to participate in the life and practice of the Christian community, but who is not yet prepared to affirm the truth of Christian doctrine. He simply acts on the assumption that it may be true. H. H. Price, at the end of his Gifford Lectures, *Belief* (1969), suggests that such a person may seriously entertain the hypothesis of theism, meditate on its meaning and its possibility, and, perhaps, find himself just coming to believe its truth. Again, Austin Farrer, in his *Saving Belief* (1964), writes, 'To think of a possible God is to experiment in having God ... the heart goes out even to a possible God ...'.

The churches would be foolish not to welcome such 'half-believers', but clearly their position is on the fringe and not characteristic of the majority of people who subscribe to Christian belief. Without going to the opposite extremes of fundamentalism or fideism – of which more anon – most believers do hold their faith with conviction even when they allow degrees of uncertainty over aspects of the Christian faith. This distinction between subjective conviction or certitude and objective certainty, is an important theme in John Henry Newman's *An Essay in Aid of a Grammar of Assent* (1870).

Much more is required of the Church's ordained ministers, of course, than Baelz's half-belief. But it is interesting to note that, even though subscription to the teaching of the Scriptures and the Church is required of those to be ordained, a range of diverse interpretations and even elements of scepticism are not only tolerated but sanctioned in official reports and documents, certainly of the Church of England. An interesting example of this is the 1938 Report, *Doctrine in the Church of England*, set up in the wake of the controversies that arose over the 1921 Girton Conference of the Modern Churchmen's Union. On the subject of the Virgin Birth, the Commission explicitly conceded that belief in the Incarnation did not require literal belief that our Lord was born of a virgin. Some decades earlier, this very issue was at the heart of the controversies surrounding the consecration of Dr Hensley Henson to the see of Hereford. While affirming without doubt the doctrine of the Incarnation, Henson admitted to a degree of 'Christian agnosticism' over the Virgin Birth.

But of course much greater differences exist over the interpretation of much more central Christian doctrines in the minds of Church members, ministers and theologians. Belief in the resurrection of Jesus Christ is central to mainstream Christianity, but interpretations of its meaning differ widely, as may be seen in the dialogue between Professors Lampe and MacKinnon in the book, *The*

Resurrection (1966), Lampe taking the 'objective vision' view, MacKinnon insisting on a mystery confronting the disciples from beyond themselves, to which the empty tomb bears witness.

FAITH AND CRITICISM

This takes us into the sphere of theology, where, throughout Christian history, the interpretation of doctrine has led to bitter disputes, and where, since the rise of biblical and historical criticism, greater and greater degrees of scepticism and doubt are to be found. University teachers of theology will be well aware of the sometimes devastating effect of this on students coming from a traditional church background and encountering biblical criticism for the first time.

One of the best treatments of this problem is to be found in Basil Mitchell's book, *Faith and Criticism* (1994). Mitchell emphasises the fact that practising Christians, whether brought up in the faith or converted to it, are participating in a long tradition of faith and practice which sustains them in their membership of the Church and makes sense of their lives. But he goes on to show how such faith is quite compatible with critical reflection and open dialogue with persons of other views. Firm commitment is not incompatible with honest recognition of difficulties or with fairness to others' arguments. He points out that this is just as true of science and the humanities in general as it is of religion and theology. 'Criticism', he writes, 'requires a strong tradition whose claims to truth are seriously advanced and will not readily be surrendered. Faith requires that the tradition which is being upheld should be tested in the fires of criticism.' And he goes on to ask 'which attitude shows the greater trust in God, that which refuses to submit our traditional formulations of belief to criticism, or that which is confident that, if we put them to the test of reason and experience, we shall be led in the end to a fuller understanding of them and a firmer conviction of their truth?'.

Mitchell is concerned here with the believer's openness to criticism and debate. His theologians are church theologians operating from within the community of faith. But it is an implication of what he says that theology is not restricted to believers. The subject is open to students and teachers of any faith or none. I shall return to this issue in discussing fideism below.

It is beyond the scope of this chapter to explore the question what difference is made to the assessment of evidence in the critical study of the Bible by approaching the issue from the perspective of belief or from that of unbelief. Certainly what is claimed as background knowledge does make a difference. A purely secular perspective may distort the picture. But this question too can be discussed and pondered by all parties to the debate.

FAITH AND BELIEF

In the discussion so far I have tended to conflate the notions of faith and belief, but clearly there is much more to Christian faith than belief in the doctrines of the creed. What attracts even the 'half-believer' is the life and worship of the Christian community, with its long tradition of faith and practice. As I say, the place of such a tradition is stressed by Mitchell in his treatment of faith and criticism. But there is no denying the belief element in religious faith and, whatever doubts about the details of church doctrine may be entertained, commitment to Christianity includes conviction of its basic truth. This is what the 'half-believer' may come to find through sympathetic participation; it is what church members profess in saying the creed; it is what church ministers are required to teach; and it is what church theologians critically explore and defend. It is the core element in religious faith under discussion here.

FAITH AND KNOWLEDGE

But how far is the believer justified in claiming knowledge for his or her position? A good treatment of this question is to be found in John Hick's early book, *Faith and Knowledge* (2nd ed. 1966). Hick suggests that, in saying 'I know that my Redeemer liveth', the believer is not so much claiming propositional knowledge as knowledge by acquaintance, i.e. personal knowledge. This leads us to consider the epistemology of religious experience. By far the best analysis of this topic is William P. Alston's *Perceiving God* (1991), in which the author compares what he calls 'mystical' perception to sense perception. In both cases, he argues, alleged experiential awareness is held to provide *prima facie* justification, subject to certain conditions, viz., support from background beliefs, absence of factors suggesting alternative explanations, and practical efficacy in ways one might expect if the perception were valid. The fact that sense perception is universal, while mystical or religious experience is not, does not effect the issue, since special conditions, such as participation in a specific tradition, may well have to obtain. In any case religious experience is quite a common phenomenon. Its diversity compared with sense perception is admittedly a major problem, but there remain sufficient grounds, including explanations for such diversity, for trusting experience that has not been shown to be illusory.

Reasons supporting the validity of religious experience will be considered in a moment, but it is worth pointing out that, *if*, say, Christianity is true, then the believer does indeed stand in a personal relation to God and enjoy knowledge by acquaintance with the divine, whatever doubts he or she may entertain over the details of church teaching.

FIDEISM

Fideism is the view that faith is the precondition of Christianity's intelligibility. Important strands in Christianity, admittedly more Protestant than Catholic, hold that the fallen nature of humanity renders natural human reason quite incapable of assessing the meaning and truth of Christian faith. Only from within the circle of faith and practice can the truth of Christian doctrine be appreciated and assessed. In what follows I shall be endorsing the criticism of this position by Terence Penelhum in his book, *God and Scepticism* (1983). This book is not so much concerned with scepticism *in* religion – the subject of the present essay – as with the fideist's scepticism about reason. Penelhum argues that such scepticism is quite unjustified. Debate between believer and unbeliever is perfectly possible; and natural theology, the attempt to provide, from neutral ground, some rational support for theistic belief, is a tenable and useful enterprise.

Notwithstanding this rejection of fideism, there is much to be learned from scholars who adopt and defend a basically fideist position. Fideism is not to be confused with fundamentalism - an uncritical, even bigoted, insistence on literal acceptance of the Bible and certain allegedly key doctrines. Fundamentalism may be a species of fideism, but profound fideists - theologians like Karl Barth and Thomas F. Torrance, and philosophers like Alvin Plantinga - are not fundamentalists. Barth's *Anselm: Fides Quaerens Intellectum* (1930) illustrates the inner rationality of faith seeking understanding, and indeed his whole monumental literary output exemplifies this project. Similarly, Torrance's *God and Rationality* (1971) rightly insists on theological thinking being controlled by the nature of its object, namely God, and not by some alien scheme of thought. Plantinga's much discussed essay, 'Reason and Belief in God', to be found in *Faith and Rationality*, edited by Alvin Plantinga and Nicholas Wolterstorff (1983), defends the idea that, for the Christian, belief in God is simply basic to his whole world view, its rationality being open to rigorous exploration and defence from within. As I say, much can be learned from these explorations of the inner rationality of Christian faith. What I do not accept is the view, expressed most explicitly by Torrance, that faith has its own logic, inaccessible to those outside. As Basil Mitchell shows, it is perfectly possible to discuss matters of doctrine across the borders of belief and unbelief and, given sufficient sympathy and imagination, to put oneself in the shoes of people of different persuasions. And it is perfectly possible to consider and debate, for example, reasons for and against belief in God.

FAITH AND REASON

This brings us to consider, finally, Kenny's 'just mean' between credulity and scepticism, namely rationality, and its place in relation to religious, and specifically Christian, faith. In addition to Christianity's inner rationality, already mentioned in connection with the work of profound fideists like Barth and Plantinga, there is much to be said in favour of natural theology, that is, the provision and defence of arguments in support of a theistic world view. The long series of Gifford Lectures, founded in 1885 in the four ancient Scottish universities, exemplifies the strength and variety of such support for theism. Two other studies of the relation between faith and reason may be recommended here, Richard Swinburne's *Faith and Reason* (1981), and Roger Trigg's *Rationality and Religion* (1998). It is important to realise that these defenders of natural theology are not suggesting that religious faith stands or falls by the success or failure of their arguments. As already stressed above, religious faith is more a matter of experience and participation in a long tradition than just the result of rational reflection. But supporting arguments play their part in sustaining such participation, as indeed do the internal explorations of faith's rationality.

There is not space here to set out and discuss these arguments, as I have attempted to do in my own book, *In Defence of Christianity* (2005). My point here is simply to draw attention to the possibility and actuality of serious rational exploration and defence of, for example, the doctrines of the Christian creed. In the course of such exploration, there is, of course, much room for criticism and indeed scepticism about details of the tradition and about different interpretations of its tenets. Many doubts and reservations will be entertained and admitted without necessarily leading to any loss of faith. Some people do lose their faith, admittedly. But I suspect this is more likely in the case of the fideist than in that of the believer who remains open to the tests of reason as well as of experience.

CONCLUSION

I hope I have shown that men and women of faith, including church theologians, are quite justified in participating in the life and worship of the

Church, and indeed of claiming knowledge by acquaintance of God their Creator and Redeemer, while at the same time subjecting the Church's teaching to criticism and debate. In the course of these debates different degrees of doubt and scepticism are likely to be entertained. There are, of course, limits to such scepticism. One may find oneself only on the fringe of half-belief, ceasing to be sustained by that combination of tradition, experience and reason that has given conviction to the full participant. Or one may lose faith altogether, as my friend and colleague, Don Cupitt, has done at the end of his long journey from *Taking Leave of God* (1980) to *The Fountain. A Secular Theology* (2010). Let me sum up the conclusions of this chapter hypothetically, with reference to Anthony Kenny's 'just mean' of rationality between the extremes of credulity and scepticism. If Christian doctrine is true, then the believer does not err by credulity. As noted above, he enjoys knowledge by acquaintance with the divine. This applies, of course, to the fideist, and even to the fundamentalist, deficient in rationality though the latter may be. On this hypothesis, many of the believer's reasons, both in terms of faith seeking understanding and in terms of natural theology more generally, may well be valid, though there is plenty of room for doubt over details and over interpretations. If Christian doctrine is false, then it is the unbeliever who does not err by credulity and is justified in his scepticism. The difference between believer and unbeliever, however, is not just a matter of the validity or non-validity of each party's reasoning. The unbeliever lacks the traditional and experiential support of participation in the life and worship of the Church. Each accuses the other of credulity, but it could be argued that the believer has a more solid base for his conviction.

Kenny's mild agnosticism can hardly be accused of credulity. It is certainly over-sceptical if Christian doctrine is true, though not sceptical enough if Christian doctrine is false. Much does depend on the respective rationality of the believer's and the unbeliever's positions.

Chapter 16

SCEPTICISM AND HISTORY

*William O'Reilly**
Centre for History and Economics, University of Cambridge, UK
Early Modern History and Fellow and Tutor, Trinity Hall, Cambridge, UK

Writing in 1748, David Hume in his *Enquiry concerning Human Understanding* put forward the unsettling idea, not for the first time, that there was and could not be any logical security in cause and effect. As in his philosophical writings, so too Hume's historical readings were faced with this sceptical view: science and reason were the watchwords of the age and cast the world in a more rational light, but there could be no guarantee that cause would always result in the same effect just because it had, until now, seemingly always done so. "Our conclusions from that experience are not focussed on reason or any process of the understanding. […] We believe solely because our day-to-day experience confirms us in a certain habit of belief. […] After the constant conjunction of two objects... we are determined by custom alone to expect the one from the appearance of the other." [1]

For Hume, the relationship of cause and effect was not misplaced, or ridiculous; neither was it certain or the result of inherent laws of thought. His scepticism was grounded on his belief in confluential change, the growing possibility that outcome would likely be different given the proclivity for variation: input of a kind would not necessarily, and certainly not desirably, result in outcome of a known or established form simply because it had once before

---

* He has been visiting professor in History at Harvard University, 2008-9, and visiting fellow of the Hungarian Academy of Sciences and the Austrian Academy of Sciences, and at the universities of Graz, Hamburg and Kiel.

done so. Hume's sceptical views are those of the Historian, or certainly should inform best practice for scholars engaged in a study of change over time, including historians. At its most popular level, History is understood to be that which teaches us the errors of the past that we might best avoid them in the future. However naïve this may appear, History as an academic discipline has long served as the custodian of fact, the repository of certainty and the arbiter of debate. Had Hitler learned the lessons of history, we are told, he would have invaded Russia earlier in the season, heeding the failures of Napoleon (who might, in turn, have learned his lesson from Charles XII of Sweden). History, in this iteration, informs, but it also educates: it serves a semi-religious purpose by showing the 'sins' of the past and how one can avoid sinning in the future. Positive pasts, those seemingly rare occasions on which things worked well, offer an alternative future, but no Historian would ever advocate that a positive past might be repeated if its lessons were to be learned and repeated. Rather, popular belief is that History is prophylactic, permitting an enjoyable encounter with the past while prohibiting an unwanted outcome. It is the act of encounters which is the historian's act; not the production of outcome, but the qualified and experienced act of intellectual engagement with a revealed and revealing past. Of course, History in the Academy does not cast itself, partly or at all, in such terms. History has birthed sub-fields that focus with expert intent on economy in the past, on social processes, on cultural encounter and a whole raft of areas, which allow for a more nuanced and balanced understanding of people in context in the past. Context, then, is the adhesive that holds together a set of past moments and it is context that, ultimately, preoccupies the professional Historian. The range of Context determines: in Hume's words we "expect the one from the appearance of the other".

Since the end of the eighteenth century, scepticism has come to be associated with disbelief and particularly with disbelief in Christianity; yet it is strange that the sceptics of the early modern age and after, so important in locating the origins of the academic discipline of History, from Savonarola to Luther and beyond, stressed their belief in Christianity. For them, scepticism was a philosophical method and belief that cast doubt on the utility and reliability of evidence offered to justify any proposition. Arguments for sceptics should show and suggest that evidence, reasons and proofs were never entirely satisfactory as a foundation for belief. Judgement, sceptics suggested, should be suspended on the question of whether beliefs were true or not; hence beliefs could be maintained even in the absence of all persuasive factors so long as the believer did not mistake persuasive factors for adequate evidence that the belief was true.

It is important, then, to remind that a 'sceptic' and a 'believer' are not opposing classifications: while a sceptic raises doubts about the rational or evidential merits of the justifications given for a belief, the sceptic doubts that necessary and sufficient reasons either have been or could be discovered to show that any particular belief must be true and cannot possibly be false. The sceptic may still accept and hold various beliefs, religious or metaphysical. Faith, or any form of 'fideism', of course is or at least is likely to be at variance with what is reasonable or even believable; writing of his Christian faith, Pierre Bayly's colleague Pierre Jurieu famously wrote 'I believe it because I want to believe" ('Je le crois parce que je veux le croire'). Dogmatism, then, is the antithesis of scepticism and even writers like St Augustine, who insisted that reasons could be given for faith, but only after one has committed to that faith. In this way, Augustine and later thinkers like Kierkegaard share views as fideists, holding beliefs of a religious or metaphysical bent [2]

Elsewhere in this volume, we have read of the origins of scepticism in Greece. It was in the age of revival of interest in the Greek and Roman past in the West, in the long fifteenth century and after, that a renewed interest in the writings of the sceptics, especially Sextus Empericus (? $2^{nd}/3^{rd}$ cent. BCE) emerged and led to a questioning of the criterion of truth. [3] In an age known to History as the Renaissance, scholars reflected on the nature of truth and fact first in the context of religion, entering into theological disputes that would birth Christian reform in the Latin Church, and later moved from theology into the arena of natural knowledge.

It was the Florentine Dominican friar Savonarola (1452-98) in his protestations against Rodrigo Borgia (1431-1503), pope Alexander VI, who in 1497-8 first cast doubt in Italy on the surety of religious truth and the authority of the papacy. In suggesting that Greek sceptical methods should be published in Latin and thereby made more readily available to a western Christian readership, Savonarola predated Luther in seeking to use sceptical treatises to defend a reading and defence of true religion. Certainly, other sceptics were read with renewed interest in the fifteenth century and thereafter, not least Cicero (106 BCE-43 BCE) and Diogenes Laertius (3rd cent. CE), but it was Savonarola's application of sceptical views to religious belief and the papacy which led to his execution in 1498.

Scepticism found new voice and a welcome audience in the cities and academies of Renaissance Europe. At this time of renewed interest in the Roman and Greek past, the writings of the ancients came under scrutiny, enlightened by the avant guard of the *studia humanitatis*. A unifying feature of the varieties of ancient scepticism as understood in the Renaissance is that, all are concerned with promoting, in some manner, the benefits of recognizing epistemic limitations, not least on an understanding of truth in and of the past. The ancient sceptics nearly had something to say about how one might live, and live well, in the absence of knowledge. Sceptics and the new adherents of scepticism in the Renaissance cast doubt on the ability to gain knowledge of the world and by extension to form and propagate a 'history' of the past. The renewed interest in epistemological systems and the role and relevance of the past in the present which came to occupy the scholarly interests of so many Renaissance thinkers means, scepticism lies at the core of modern historical theory and practice.

As we have read above in the chapter on the classical origins of scepticism, from the time of Plato's Academy during its sceptical period (c. 3rd-1st BCE) to Pyrrho (c.365-270 BCE) and on to Sextus Empericus and his outline of scepticism, *Hypotyposes*, two strands of scepticism, the Academic and Pyrrhonian, emerged and exerted influence on the Academy and its views of truth and the readability of the past. From the Greek noun *skepsis*, meaning consideration, examination, inquiry, scepticism casts doubt on what one should or might believe. Nearly every variety of ancient scepticism includes a thesis about our epistemic limitations and a thesis about suspending judgment. As such, scepticism casts doubt on the ability to construct a view of the past that claims to be complete or near complete; the whole notion of History as a site of information about the past is thrown on its head.

Yet the application of a sceptical approach to the Historian's method, or even the very idea of History itself, is not without its challengers. Two frequently made objections to scepticism target its weakness. The first is that the sceptic's commitment to our epistemic limitations is inconsistent. A sceptic cannot consistently claim to know, for example, that knowledge is not possible; neither can a sceptic consistently claim that we should suspend judgment regarding all matters insofar as this claim is itself a judgment. Either such claims will refute themselves, since they fall under their own scope, or the sceptic will have to make an apparently arbitrary exemption. The second variant of objection is that the alleged epistemic limitations and the suggestion that we should suspend judgment would make life unliveable. [4] The business of day-to-day life, after all, requires that we make choices and this requires making judgments. Similarly, an individual's apparent success in interacting with the world and each other entails that we must know some things. As such, some form of judgement, or opinion forming, of view of the past in-context is at least desirable, at best necessary and at most essential for human existence.

Scepticism was revived in the work of Renaissance scholars in large part due to the revival of interest in Sextus Empericus, a philosopher of the third century BCE of whom very little is known. It is Sextus who first distinguishes three fundamental types of philosopher or thinker and whose categorisation informed the humanist scholars of the fifteenth century who came to reflect on the merits and demerits of History. Sextus, in his typology, saw Dogmatists, those men who believe they have discovered the truth; Academics (negative Dogmatists), who believe the truth cannot be discovered; and sceptics, who continue to investigate, believing neither that anyone has so far discovered the truth nor that it is impossible to do so. Although his characterization of Academics is probably polemical and almost certainly unfair, the general distinctions he makes are important and held great sway in Renaissance thought. For Sextus, then, the sceptic was one who by suspending judgment determines nothing, and enjoys tranquillity – which was the apogee of the human condition - as a result. It is only through a general sense of unease, he agues, that the scholar stumbles upon scepticism: one is not born a sceptic nor can one unwittingly become one. The motivation for working out the way the world works is to become tranquil; to remove any disturbance from confronting incompatible views of the world. As any proto-sceptic attempts to sort out the evidence and discover the privileged perspective or the correct theory, he finds that for each account that purports to establish something true about the world there is another, equally convincing account, that purports to establish an opposed and incompatible view of the same thing. Being faced with this challenge, he is unable to assent to either of the opposed accounts and thereby suspends judgment. Of course, this is not what he set out to do, but by virtue of his intellectual integrity, he is simply not able to arrive at a conclusion and so he finds himself without any definite view. What he also finds is that the tranquillity that he originally thought would come only by arriving at the truth follows upon his suspended judgment as a shadow follows a body.

Sextus develops his thesis further through the use of an explanatory story. A certain painter, Apelles, tried to represent foam on the mouth of the horse he was painting. Each time he applied the paint to his canvas, he failed to attain the effect he desired and, growing frustrated, he flung the sponge on which he had been wiping off the paint at the canvas, inadvertently producing the effect he had been struggling to achieve. The analogous point in the case of seeking the truth is that the desired tranquillity only comes indirectly, not by giving up the pursuit of truth, but rather by giving up the expectation that we must acquire truth to get tranquillity. In this sceptical view, it becomes clear that one cannot intentionally acquire a peaceful, tranquil state but must let it happen as a result of giving up the struggle. Giving up the struggle for the sceptic, however, does not mean giving up the pursuit of truth. The sceptic continues to investigate in order to protect himself against the deceptions and seductions of reason that lead to our holding definite views. So for the Historian, in this methodological framework, it is the act of engaging in a conversation with histories, not with History *per se*, which is the act of being an Historian. History must seek to investigate *why* certain views are purported and held, *not* to seek to form a view of the past. In essence, sceptical

History becomes a history of historiography, and has echoes of the post-modernist call-to-arms that seeks to reduce everything to a condition of equality, irrespective of scale, form or intentionality.

Arriving at definite views, be it of the past or of any postulation or event, is not merely a matter of intellectual dishonesty, the sceptic Sextus argues, but more importantly, it is the main source of all psychological disturbance. Anyone who believes that things are good or bad by nature, are and will always be perpetually troubled. When they lack what they believe to be good or truthful, their lives must seem seriously deficient if not outright miserable, and they struggle as much as possible to acquire those things or those views. But when they finally have what they believe to be good or true, they spend untold effort in maintaining and preserving those things and live in fear of losing them. Sextus did not limit his theory of scepticism to evaluative beliefs alone. Rather, he provides extensive arguments against physical and logical (scientific and epistemological) theories, too. How, then, do such beliefs contribute to the psychological disturbances that Sextus seeks to eliminate? The most plausible reply is that any such belief that we find the sceptic Sextus arguing against is one that will inevitably contribute to one's evaluations of the world, of the past and of the place of the past in the present and the future and thus will contribute to the intense strivings that characterize disturbance. An examination of a sample of the logical and physical theses that Sextus' discusses bears this out. Many of these beliefs played foundational roles in the Epicurean or Stoic systems, and thus were employed to establish ethical and evaluative beliefs; they came to have significant value in the reform of History in the Renaissance and thereafter, influencing the discipline to the present day. Believing that the physical world is composed of invisible atoms, for example, would not, by itself, produce any disturbance since we must draw inferences from this belief in order for it to have any significance for us with respect to choice and avoidance. So it is more appropriate to look past the disturbance that may be produced by individual, isolated beliefs, and consider instead the effect of accepting a system of interrelated, mutually supporting dogmatic claims. In this understanding, scepticism becomes an ability to discover opposed arguments of equal persuasive force, the practice of which leads first to suspension of judgment and afterwards, fortuitously, to tranquillity. This makes Sextus' version of scepticism dramatically different from other Western philosophical positions, for it is a practice or activity rather than a set of doctrines. Indeed, insofar as the sceptic is supposed to live without belief, he could not consistently endorse any philosophical doctrine.

Yet, is it possible to live without beliefs? Is it possible to accept a multitude of approaches to a shared view, of a shared event or a shared past? More than any other question, this is the one that occupied the greatest minds of the Renaissance and on to the Enlightenment and thereafter: singularity of practice and belief, or relativism. And how one cast the runes of the past and read the story of development lay at the heart of this struggle. The short answer is that one may simply follow appearances and withhold judgment as to whether the world really is as it appears, or was as we hold it to have been: History becomes negotiable in a way in which it had never been. While a previous telling of the past focussed on the 'truth' of a Judeo-Christian narrative, for example, not all was negotiable, all was questionable, and all could be cast into doubt. This seems plausible with respect to physical perceptions, but appearances for Sextus include evaluations, and this creates a complication. For how can the sceptic say, "this appears good (or bad) to me, but I don't believe that it is really good or bad"? It seems that there is no difference between evaluative appearances and evaluative beliefs. One possible response to this problem is to say that, Sextus only targets sophisticated, philosophical theories about value, or about physics or logic, but allows everyday attitudes and beliefs to stand. On this view, scepticism is a therapy designed to cure the disease of academics and theoreticians. It seems that Sextus intends his philosophical therapy to be quite widely applicable. The sceptical life, as he presents it, is an achievement and not merely the recovering of a native innocence lost to philosophical speculation.

Any answer to the question about how the sceptic may live without beliefs will depend on what sort of beliefs we think the sceptic avoids. Can a sceptic live, enjoy life, without an understanding of the past, an understanding of History? An elaboration on living in accordance with appearances comes in the form of the fourfold observance. Rather than investigate the best way to live or even what to do in some particular circumstance, Sextus remarks that the sceptic will guide his actions by [1] nature, [2] necessitation by feelings, [3] laws and customs, and [4] kinds of expertise. Nature provides us with the capacity for perception and thought, and we may use these capacities insofar as they don't lead us to dogmatic belief. Similarly, hunger and thirst will drive us towards food and drink without our having to form any explicit beliefs regarding those physical sensations. One need not accept any nutritional theories to adequately and appropriately respond to hunger and thirst. Laws and customs will inform us of the appropriate evaluations of things. We need not actually believe that the gods exist and that they are benevolent to take part in religious ceremonies or even to act in a manner that is (or at least appears) pious. But note that the sceptic will neither believe that the gods exist nor that they do not exist-he is neither a theist nor an atheist, but agnostic in a very robust sense. And finally, the sceptic may practice some trade or profession without accepting any theories regarding his practice. For example, a carpenter need not have any theoretical or geometrical views about doors in order to be skilful at hanging them. Similarly, a doctor need not accept any physiological theories to successfully heal his patients. Does the sceptic merely avoid sophisticated, theoretical beliefs in employing these observances, or avoid all beliefs whatsoever?

It is impossible to estimate the significance of sceptical thought, in the form of Sextus and others, on the emergence and development of modern historical method and practice. One might write volumes on Luther alone, for example, in an attempt to measure the influence. Let us take one example of a scholar who came to engage with Sextus views and who has come to exert influence on the method and practice of History. In the age of societal and religious reform which saw History dissected by scepticism, Michel Eyquem de Montaigne (1533-92), born in the decade of Jean Bodin, Etienne de La Boétie, Henri Etienne and other influential intellectuals of the age, is remembered by posterity for one question, if nothing else: *Que sais-je?*, 'what do I know?'. Embossed on a medal in the 1570s in his honour, this sceptical question became his very motto; just like the mottos painted on the beams of his study, 'All that is certain is that nothing is certain' and 'I suspend judgement', the latter a phrase he borrowed directly from Sextus. [5] Like Sextus, and indeed like Cicero, Erasmus, Guy de Bruès, Agrippa and many other authors whose works adorned his shelves, Montaigne did not reach his sceptical views in isolation; rather, he built on William of Ockham's (c.1300-49) separation of the realms of reason and faith. Erasmus reflections on scepticism in *In Praise of Folly* likely also influenced Montaigne, at least in so far as it brought together classical themes and Christian traditions. Montaigne certainly used scepticism as a rhetorical device and seems to have been personally burdened by the weight of doubt: *raison universelle* was, for him, acceptable, while *raison humaine* ought best be rejected. Sceptics "use their reason to enquire and debate", he wrote, but did not choose, and this was wise. [6] It is in this light that Montaigne's views of religion and politics must be seen, and indeed the scholars in a western tradition who followed him drew greatly on his views. And it is on History that his sceptical influence was perhaps greatest.

Montaigne was an avid student of the past, citing with greatest frequency the works of Plutarch, Livy, Tacitus, Herodotus and Caesar, especially the latter's *Commentaries*. As has been pointed out, Montaigne's interests in History stretched from the global to the local, from González de Mendoza's *History of the Great Kingdom of China* to Bouchet's *Annals of Aquitaine*. [7] Believing History to be at the heart of a boy's education, Montaigne noted that a study of the past cast the reader into the company of "the worthiest minds, who lived in the best ages."[8]

Studying the past, he continued, allowed one learn virtue, not to learn dates or details; a good teacher of History will "imprint in his pupil's minds not so much the date of the ruin of Carthage, as the morals of Hannibal and Scipio". [9]

More important for Montaigne, was that History taught psychology as well as virtue; recalling René, Duke of Lorraine weeping for his dead enemy Charles the Bold, Montaigne noted "how we weep and laugh for the same thing". [10]

History revealed the human condition; "It is one and the same nature rolling by. Anyone who has judged the present accurately may draw valid conclusions about the future and the past." [11] So while change is ever present for Montaigne – "Instability is the worst thing I find in our state; our laws can no more take a stable form than our clothes" – he is more concerned with casting doubt on the presumed story of the past, and concerns himself with process, with decay more than with certainly. [12] Everything changes, for Montaigne; "The beliefs, judgements and opinions of men…have their revolutions, their seasons, their births and deaths, like cabbages." [13] His deep concern with time is almost certainly new; just as he saw change in the world, he saw that he himself and others were in a state of flux, and as such their reading of the past cast into doubt the belief that a 'correct' view of the past was ever possible.

His scepticism, his belief in the uncertainly of belief, formed his view of the past and his understanding of what History as a theory and in practice might be. And like all Historians who have come in his wake, he struggled with the sceptical dilemma: to seek to know a truth, or to seek to explain why the human condition seeks to know. Unlike all other sentient beings, humans gaze at the stars not because we learn from them, but because we can and because we enjoy so doing.

To conclude where we began: "Our conclusions from that experience are not focused on reason or any process of the understanding." At times, it is enough to seek to know, without seeking to explain why.

REFERENCES

[1] For more on Hume and scepticism and the historical method, see: Markus Völkel, 'Pyrrhonismus historicus' und 'fides historica': die Entwicklung der deutschen historischen Methodologie unter dem Gesichtspunkt der historischen Skepsis, Frankfurt am Main, Peter Lang, 1987.

[2] For a balancing view, see: *Anthony Kenny,* Wittgenstein, London, Allen Lane, 1973, ch. 11, 'On scepticism and certainty'.

[3] See, inter alia, Dorothy Gabe Coleman, Montaigne's 'Essais', London, Allen Lane, 1987, ch. 3, *'Intellectual and Philosophical Background'*.

[4] See, inter alia, Barry Stroud, The Significance of Philosophical Scepticism, Oxford, Clarendon Press, 1984, esp. ch.II, 'Philosophical scepticism and everyday life'.

[5] Peter Burke, Montaigne, Oxford, O.U.P., 1981, p. 14.
[6] *Montaigne, Essais,* book 2, ch. 12.
[7] Peter Burke, Montaigne, Oxford, O.U.P., 1981, p. 52.
[8] *Montaigne, Essais*, book 1, ch. 26.
[9] *Montaigne, Essais*, book 1. ch. 26.
[10] *Montaigne, Essais*, book 2, ch. 38.
[11] *Montaigne, Essais*, book 2, ch. 12.
[12] *Montaigne, Essais*, book 2, ch. 17.
[13] *Montaigne, Essais,* book 2, ch. 12.

In: Scepticism: Hero and Villain
Editors: R. Calne and W. O'Reilly
ISBN: 978-1-62417-783-5
© 2013 Nova Science Publishers, Inc.

Chapter 17

GOTCHA:
THE POETICS OF LINGUISTIC SCEPTICISM

Drew Milne
The Judith E Wilson Lecturer in Drama and Poetry,
Faculty of English, University of Cambridge, UK

'CLOV: Do you believe in the life to come?
HAMM: Mine was always that. [*Exit* CLOV.] Got him that time!' [1]

'What is poetry and if you know what poetry is what is prose.
There is no use in telling more than you know, no not even if you
do not know it.' [2]

The world and its dog queue up to pore buckets of sceptical disbelief over the self-styled *science* of linguistics, without so much as denting its various institutional paradigms. It seems almost too easy to find any formal science of language wanting in the face of the copious informality and grammatical liberties of language use: viz, *gotcha*. [3] Lent on, nevertheless, to help out with applied and theoretical forms of knowledge from machine translation, artificial intelligence, language acquisition, psychology and speech therapy to the philosophy of language, there is an evident variety of needs for linguistics. Gotcha journalists, despite regular skirmishes with sub-editors and copy police, express surprise at widespread interest in books such as Lynne Truss's *Eats, Shoots and Leaves: The Zero Tolerance Approach to Punctuation*. [4] Professional linguists, with their strong sense of the priority of facts over values, of description over prescription, appear no less wrong-footed. Desires for grammatical standards, stylistic rules and prescriptive linguistics suggest yearnings for ethical, even regulative ways of understanding language, engaging with precisely those hierarchies of value and ethics largely eschewed by modern linguists. Beyond the intellectual demands and necessary technical difficulties of its articulation, then, linguistics more often disappoints all but those most committed to its institutional reproduction. Needs for poetry are evident too, but poetry is not so much lent on for its knowledge of language, as given up to the role of feeble ornament for the world of prose, neglected as if 'twere some residual idol come idle fancy of mere imagining. Even modern linguistics now scarcely finds poetry an object of language warranting the exercise of its philological scepticism or disbelief.

Perhaps the most striking evidence of the intellectual isolation of academic linguistics is the comparatively recent evolution of its separation from the historical and comparative study of literature, above all poetry. Modern linguistics comes out of what is often thought of as a golden period of philology in the nineteenth century, not least in the understanding of Indo-European language systems. Despite the pioneering and pivotal role of linguists such as Roman Jakobson, who was profoundly interested in literature and poetics, modern linguistics has turned against historical questions, comparative philology and poetics. The modern paradigm of linguistics, dominated by Noam Chomsky's models of universal grammar, pursues a concept of language whose thinking is defined against literary, cultural and anthropological thinking about language. There have been many criticisms of the development of linguistics and its claims to scientificity, with more literary-minded critics and philosophers suggesting deep problems in the paradigms of language pursued by modern linguistics. Despite revisions of Noam Chomsky's programme that respond to difficulties articulated from within Chomsky's paradigm, literary-critical and philosophical objections are largely dismissed as amateur or prescientific, while rival models of linguistics are kept at bay, out of the funding queue. In 'Could Chomsky Be Wrong?', Timothy Mason sketches a number of relevant counter-positions, including disagreements from among Chomsky's students. Despite Chomsky's apparent dominance in English-speaking linguistics, he notes that the French 'are far more sceptical' and offers this summary of paradigm protectionism: 'One beef I have with Chomsky is the way he airily declares out of court any work which is not within his own domain.' [5] But where to take your beef if the supermarket chains are so powerful? In *The New Grammarians' Funeral: A Critique of Noam Chomsky's linguistics* (1975), Ian Robinson took book length issue with Chomsky. [6] Robinson's book is nevertheless unusual in being an argument with and against linguistics, but written from outside the professional academic consensus governing publications in linguistics, a consensus for which Cambridge

University Press remains an important publisher. The question of public and published authority with regard to language and linguistics runs right through the structure of Cambridge University Press, as it does through Oxford University Press, with significant gaps and critical frictions between the academic publication of professional studies in linguistics, and more commercial or educational books in language teaching, including grammars and dictionaries. Part of the difficulty, however, is that anyone interested in questions of language who turns to linguistics for specialist help will discover that professional linguistics defines itself against historical, comparative and literary types of philology. Robinson offers specific objections to Chomsky, including some striking counter-assertions: 'The study of language cannot be a science, in the sense of *science* consistently intended by Chomsky, and all his friends and all his enemies within linguistics, because language is inherently metaphysical.' [7] Beyond such high level objections, Robinson also expresses sceptical scorn:

> 'Why linguists disdain the study of the written language I have never been able to understand, especially as even when they are reporting speech the examples in linguists' books always happen to be written down, not spoken. In the case of the study of syntax, the disdain of writing is worse than mere dogma, for syntactic analysis is always of the written language.' [8]

Especially? Always? Are these not examples of *gotcha* objections, rather than developed arguments? Such surprise points to peculiarities in the writing of linguistics, but not with the force of the questions brought to the priority of speech over writing developed by Jacques Derrida. [9] Robinson's book is dedicated to F.R. Leavis and, for Robinson, it is imaginative literature that provides the central historical material for any understanding or judgment of language: 'Poets have the deepest working knowledge of language...' [10].

Robinson's alternative model of knowledge for language through imaginative literature and criticism is explicitly opposed to the reduction of thinking about language to the claims of 'exact science'. In this, Robinson is sceptical about the very project of linguistics, and yet his own scepticism, as well as reflecting the professional interests of a lecturer in English language and literature, generates a kind of Leavisite disciplinary grand-standing that is in the end more dogmatic than critical: 'Judgment of literature is ordinary judgement, not specialist judgement, for the sufficient reason that the centre of language is not propositions but poetry. Hence linguistics is an underlabourer of criticism (of literature or language) not a super-language' [11]. Does language have a centre, and what is poetry when it is so centred? With the power of such a 'hence' it is perhaps not surprising that Robinson has not succeeded in persuading linguistics to think again. The critical investment in poetry he proposes has, moreover, met sustained scepticism within literary studies: literary studies has almost succeeded in removing specifically *literary* criticism from the academic study of poetry and writing, in favour of various kinds of theoretical, historical and cultural research. Robinson's provocations all too easily invite the perception that they are opinions, public musings of a man of letters, professionally grounded in literary criticism, [12] but not provocations of a kind likely to provoke paradigm change from within Chomsky's linguistics or for the poetics of a more sceptical linguistics.

Robinson's book dramatises both the futility of criticising the paradigms of linguistics from outside those paradigms, while suggesting too the widely felt lack of contemporary linguistics germane to literary studies. Scepticism on opposing sides appears mutually reinforcing rather than productive. While linguistics remains dogmatically well-defended against Robinson's scepticism, literary studies have become sufficiently sceptical as to the value of what might seem like its principle focus – literature or poetry – as to seem continually in search of some new object or model, any object or model so long as it isn't the kind of thing imagined by Chomsky. Robinson observes that: 'Chomsky has never to my knowledge betrayed the slightest public interest in imaginative literature.' [13] Literary criticism has not shown much more interest in Chomsky's linguistics. The once shared disciplines of university language *and* literature departments, held together partly by a shared interest in the *history* of language, notably in departments of English, have diverged, leaving the question of language curiously homeless, more likely to be taken up by philosophers of language than as an object of historical or literary study. The question of language is perhaps at its most critical for understanding poetry and its histories, but poetics, especially poetics willing to entertain such speculative problems as the metaphysics of language, often struggles to constitute itself as a research paradigm, in part because the models of language in play are resistant to scientific modelling. If language is nevertheless necessarily a shared preoccupation of academic studies in language *and* literature, there is no dialectical fudge that might allow some synthesis between the claims of poetry and linguistics as a science. It is possible, however, to recognise the consequences of such different types of scepticism and the way scepticism also entails exclusions hardening into opposing dogmatisms.

The comedy of fruitlessly opposed scepticisms is evident from a reprise of Robinson's critique of Chomsky. Writing in 2006 in *Times Higher Education*, Robinson restates his critique by reviewing shifts in Chomsky's paradigm for linguistics as it has modulated through Chomsky's *The Minimalist Program* (1995), taking issue both with Chomsky's biological conception of universal grammar and with what Chomsky calls the 'Language Acquisition Device'. Robinson resorts to something resembling sceptical satire:

"The child has," Chomsky writes in *Architecture* [*The Architecture of Language* (2001)], "a repertoire of concepts as part of its biological endowment and simply has to learn that a particular concept is realised in a particular way in the language. There is overwhelming reason to believe that concepts like, say, climb, chase, run, tree and book and so on are fundamentally fixed." The tree concept will be found even in the brains of children who live in places where there are no trees, and the book concept where there is no written language. There must surely then be a universal concept of television, and liberalism and feudalism.' [14]

This broaches significant historical problems for any account of the universal grammar of the human brain, whether the argument is understood at the ontogenetic level as a problem of human evolution, according to some more universal mind-brain biology, or with regard to historical phenomena, such as technology or democracy, which might be claimed to have rewritten the grammar of human conceptuality. But the arguments offered do not quite have the power of glitch recognition worth of a *gotcha*. Robinson's scepticism is characterised, rather, by a weary recognition that the arguments are here performed for a journalistic public rather than engaging linguistics. [15] He even conflates his sceptical disagreement with the tired old chestnut that the claims of Chomsky are scarcely original:

'I cannot see that in grammar (the only context in which the discussion has any sense) universal grammar means any more than that a skeleton grammar can be adapted to all "natural" languages. That is very remarkable, but it is not a new idea.'

This kind of admonition never goes down well, but is perhaps deserved in the face of Chomsky's own maximalist and scepticism-inducing announcements regarding his supposedly minimal programme.

Robinson himself cites some remarkable instances, such as the claim made by Chomsky in *On Nature and Language* (2002), that: 'I think it is fair to say that more has been learnt about language in the past 20 years than the preceding 2,000 years.' True to his own earlier stated sense of the greater importance of the history of literature, Robinson cites Wordsworth against Chomsky: 'The real status of the Language Acquisition Device within linguistics is as an exclamation of wonder. Children do begin to talk. But the Language Acquisition Device is not Wordsworthian enough to fulfil this role and is debilitated by offering itself as explanation.' One imagines Chomsky spluttering into his morning coffee with disbelief. And yet, such is the wonder of the internet, such disbelief can be read, rather than imagined, in the form of a reader's comment added by John Torr to Robinson's piece some five years later. Torr's comment is worth quoting from at length because it exemplifies the way self-styled scepticism of one supposed discipline for another can turn into prejudicial rant:

> 'Ian Robinson, not everyone wants to study language in the kind of wooly, subjective and pretentiously sentimental way that most literary critics do. Some of us derive great intellectual satisfaction from contemplating objectively observable phenomena in our research, not just reaching deep within ourselves to produce yet another pointlessly subjective interpretation of what Chaucer and Shakespeare may or may not have meant when they said such and such... [...] if only literary critics would wake up and realize what has made WIll's [Shakespeare's] work so appealing and enduring is the LANGUAGE, the metaphors, similes, exquisite turns of phrase... it would not be a sin to mention these for their own sake from time to time, you know... it is not compulsory to tie them in with another idle speculation about Shakespeare's socio-political-marxist-feminist-existential state at the time of writing, as per the reams of mumbo jumbo spouted by literary critics down the centuries.. [....] This has been a rant and you may feel that I have been rudely discussing your profession in a manner which indicates my thorough lack of understanding of it. [...] Linguistics is a proper discipline, but literary studies, as they stand currently, have the same status as religion as far as I can see... [...]' [16]

With the turn to faith versus knowledge, the rhetoric of what are presumably meant to feel like *gotcha* objections only reveals ungrounded faith in the objective value of 'our' research and in modern linguistics, a faith that can only gesture at rather than explain the enduring appeal of Shakespeare's language as poetry. Shakespeare, it might be replied, is a radical grammarian whose flexibility with syntax is both exemplary for any account of grammar and defining for the history of English as a language. That Torr's response takes the form of a *bump* or *necrobump* [17] more than five years after initial publication suggests both an immediacy of irritation generating belated heat, and a curiously performed counter-argument in which Robinson himself is an unlikely recipient of what is addressed to him. Scepticism as to the merits of literary study can take more subtle forms, but Torr's rant has the merit of making explicit some of the potential dogmatism of the hostility. Linguistics, the literary critic might reply, behaves more like a religious orthodoxy, a cult faithful to founding fathers such as Chomsky, than the lively plurality of literary studies, in which neither subjectivity nor the socio-political dynamics of class and gender can be excluded by fiat from the understanding and democratic judgment of literary language. A brief trawl on the internet reveals that Ian Robinson is no Marxist-feminist, indeed rather the opposite, a UK Independence Party activist, a committed Christian, and a conservative defender of traditional literary values. [18] The oppositions of subjectivity and objectivity, of faith and knowledge, find here some feeble echoes even within their articulation – note the ambiguity of 'sin' in Torr's flights of scorn – but such scepticism is surely symptomatic rather than acute or critical. Understood as a deeper dynamic, the descent of scepticism into new dogma might be said to be constitutive too of Chomsky's own most speculative claims. Chomsky's conception of the innate capacity for acquiring language can be understood as a sceptical, perhaps even necessary riposte to behaviourism and behavioral psychology, but then Chomsky's scepticism too quickly hardens into an anti-behaviourism, a metaphysical, ahistorical set of presuppositions about univeral nature and language as an 'organ'.

The difficulty of going beyond faith and knowledge in bringing scepticism to linguistics, and especially to Chomsky's linguistics, is also evident in the life and work of Daniel Everett. Everett trained as a field linguist and worked as a Christian missionary intent on translating the Bible. On the basis of this work, and on his subsequent linguistic and anthropological research into the culture and language of the Amazonian people known as the Pirahã, Everett became sceptical as to the validity of his metaphysical orientation and his linguistic training. He describes, for example, how the Pirahã have no numbers, no fixed colour terms, no perfect tense, a different language of temporality and memory, and no words for 'all', 'each', 'every', 'most', or 'few'. For Everett, the distinctive grammar of Pirahã reflects their cultural constraints and conditions, and coexists with the resistance of Pirahã people to various attempts to teach them other languages, Christianity, farming techniques, numeracy and a variety of conceptual abstractions. As John Colapinto puts it in a profile piece on Pirahã and Everett's work:

> 'Inspired by Sapir's cultural approach to language, he hypothesized that the tribe embodies a living-in-the-present ethos so powerful that it has affected every aspect of the people's lives. Committed to an existence in which only observable experience is real, the Pirahã do not think, or speak, in abstractions—and thus do not use color terms, quantifiers, numbers, or myths...' [19]

The possibility that the grammar of abstract conceptuality might reflect culture and be determined through construction and praxis opens up sceptical perspectives on the claims of universal grammar and of grammar or language as something 'hard-wired' in the human brain. Such are the critical implications, the details of Everett's claims have been disputed, notably in discussions of colour terms. [20] Directly contesting a central presupposition of Chomsky, Everett further claims that Pirahã displays no evidence of recursion. For Everett, despite having earlier completed a doctorate that offers a 'strictly' Chomskyian analysis, the language culture and grammar of the Pirahã people offers living refutation of Chomsky's conception of universal grammar. [21] The break with a tenet central even to Chomsky's 'minimal' program takes on the quality of a conversion narrative. [22] Indeed, a striking feature of Everett's account is the way rejection of his earlier belief in Chomsky's linguistics is paralleled by Everett's rejection of his earlier Christianity: both become unsustainable faiths. The resistance of the Pirahã language to missionary Christianity, to bible translation, and to Chomskyian linguistics forces Everett into sceptical recognition of the cultural anthropology of language, into a sceptical linguistics. It is perhaps characteristic of the seemingly closed shop or faith community around Chomskyian linguistics that from having been a supporter of Everett's earlier academic career, Chomsky has dismissed Everett while other Chomskyians have sought to discredit or refute both the substance and the implications of his work. [23] Whereas Robinson offers a critique of Chomsky from the perspective of literary criticism, Everett works through and out of Chomskyian linguistics into a perspective that involves reanimating the Sapir-Whorf traditions of American anthropology and linguistics. Part of the interest of Everett's work is the way his cultural anthropology demonstrates just how deeply beliefs in grammar can come to seem universal, natural, theological even, while at the same time sustaining scepticism as to the deeply held conceptions of grammar held by others. There is much that is thought-provoking in his examples, not least in the attempt to make concrete how peculiar our grammatical presuppositions seem in the eyes of a quite different language.

Everett's work confirms the suggestive power of Nietzsche's remark: 'I fear we are not getting rid of God because we still believe in grammar.' [24] Nietzsche knew well the difficulties involved in assessing and thinking against the authority both of philology [25] and of grammar, and his attempt to shake the self-evidence of the inherited categories of Western thought prefigures what has widely been understood as the linguistic turn in modern philosophy. In part Nietzsche achieves his own linguistic scepticism through a deep understanding of ancient scepticism, and through the Pyrrhonian tradition of scepticism revived by Montaigne and Pascal. [26] The specific turn suggested by Nietzsche has, moreover, an implied set of responses to the account of scepticism suggested by Hegel. [27] Hegel discusses the modes of Pyrronhism, suggesting ways in which ancient scepticism's suspension of judgment will become the central to his own account of thinking. [28] For Hegel, the superiority of ancient scepticism over modern scepticism bears in part on the difference between scepticism as a procedure engaging the doubts of subjective or sensory consciousness, whereas:

'By contrast, ancient scepticism "is found on a developed and thought out annihilation [*Zunichtemachung*] of everything held to be true and existent, so that everything is made unstable." This instability extends, as we saw in Hegel's discussion of the five modes of late Pyrrhonism, to the very categories with which we think.' [29]

Part of the power of ancient scepticism is just this willingness to suspend the very grammar of thinking. Sextus Empiricus explicitly brings Pyrrhonian arguments to bear on grammar and grammarians, [30] although the modes and workings of his arguments only with difficult translate into a sceptical account of modern linguistics. Some sense of the difficulties involved is suggested by Emile Benveniste's remarkable essay exploring the extent to which Aristotle's categories depend on Greek grammar and Derrida's subsequent critique. [31] Coming to terms with Everett's work suggests the necessity for further research, not least in trying to find ways to reconsider the extent to which Indo-European grammar embodies historically evolved cultures rather than a universal grammar. Everett's experience of the culture of Pirahã language and its implications for his own linguistic understanding has something of this quality of instability, and even if Everett's readers inevitably lack both his experience and his contextual understanding of the language, his work nevertheless implies a poetics of linguistic scepticism that might be shared and extended beyond his particular experience. Such a poetics can scarcely say *gotcha* of any language.

Read as a poetics of linguistic scepticism, one response to Everett might suggest that he need not have embedded himself in Pirahã language and culture, but could have experienced comparable linguistic disorientatons by reading modernist literature and poetry. From Gertrude Stein through James Joyce's *Finnegans Wake* to Samuel Beckett, John Cage and beyond there are many examples of modernist writing which turn grammar back on itself, bringing language into relations of resistance and scepticism. One of the historical features of poetry is the way it has articulated different parameters and formal constraints -- such as verse conventions, sound patterns, metre, but also constraints of function associated, for example, with music, or with religious, spiritual or meditative practices such as prayer, chanting and worship. The articulation of some such parameter often brings grammar into strained relief as a competing formal constraint: even the simplest nursery rhymes can break grammatical rules for the sake of a good rhyme. Understood as a problem germane to the diversity of poetics, the variety of linguistic and social parameters explored through poetry make poetry especially sensitive to and culturally attuned to the artifice and construction of grammar and syntax. Poets remain sceptical with regard to the claims of universal grammar, perhaps because their own practice is deeply concerned with exploring the possibility of making langauge anew in ways not dreamt of by existing grammatical rules. Modernist poetry and poetics have been especially interested in exploring the limits of speech-based conceptions of grammar and associated grammatical rules. Many modern poems mark themselves as poems by the way in which they suggest linguistic scepticism as regards inherited categories of speech and prose discourse.

As Jean-Jacques Lecercle suggests, 'a theory of the structure of language, no matter what level it is situated at, which ignores the literary use of language or is incapable of accounting for it, is a problematic theory to say the least.' [32] And to say the most?

Might it become evident that modern thought – whether in modern science, philosophy, linguistics or literary theory – constitutes part of its truth and scientificity precisely by ignoring the thought of poetry? Lecercle offers his own critique of Chomsky, and also of the philosophy of language suggested by Jürgen Habermas, but his attempt to revivify Marxist traditions in the critical philosophy of language ends with a discussion of political 'spin', rather than developing a poetics of linguistic scepticism that might account for modernist poetry. The chorus of modern thought's scepticism in the face of poetry and poetics extends well beyond the apparent triumph of rational prose as the language of reasoned expression.

One of poetry's many unacknowledged claims to think through and against the power of language, especially the language of power associated with prose, is to suggest a poetics of linguistic scepticism in relation both to language and to the culture which shapes language. But who among us would not raise a sceptical eyebrow when presented with the claims put forward by a poet such as J.H. Prynne: 'poetic thought is brought into being by recognition and contest with the whole cultural system of a language, by argument that will not let go but which may not self-admire or promote the idea of the poet as arbiter of rightness.' [33] Claims made on behalf of poetic thought or the *idea* of 'the poet' inevitably lack the appeal and quality of poems themselves.

A poetics of lingistic scepticism needs to account for the sense in which poems challenge languages of description to acknowledge their limits. For those sceptical of the claims and explorations of modernist poetry, modernist poems can seem ungrammatical, unintelligible, or nonsensical rather than both critical and self-critical as investigations into the authority of sense. Understood in this light, the resistance of modern linguistics to the claims of poetry is perhaps not surprising, but the shared need for a poetics of linguistic scepticism is also thereby made clearer: *gotcha?*

REFERENCES

[1] Samuel Beckett, *Endgame*, from *The Complete Dramatic Works* (London: Faber, 1986), p. 116.

[2] Gertrude Stein, from 'Poetry and Grammar', *Look at Me Now and Here I Am: Writings and Lectures, 1909-45*, ed. Patricia Meyerowitz (Harmondsworth: Penguin, 1971), pp. 125-147 (p. 125).

[3] Wikipedia's entry on *gotcha* suggests some of the variousness of its use and grammar: <http://en.wikipedia.org/wiki/Gotcha>; see also *urban dictionary*.

[4] Lynne Truss's *Eats, Shoots and Leaves: The Zero Tolerance Approach to Punctuation* (London: Profile, 2003).

[5] Timothy Mason, 'Could Chomsky be Wrong?', <http://www.timothyjpmason.com/WebPages/LangTeach/CounterChomsky.htm>

[6] Ian Robinson, *The New Grammarians' Funeral: A Critique of Noam Chomsky's linguistics* (Cambridge: Cambridge University Press, 1975).

[7] Robinson, p. 170.

[8] Robinson, p. 174.

[9] Jacques Derrida, *passim*, but especially in *De la grammatologie* (Paris: Les Éditions de Minuit, 1967), translated as *Of Grammatology* (Baltimore and London: Johns Hopkins University Press, 1976, trans. Gayatri Chakravorty Spivak).

[10] Robinson, p. 183.

[11] Robinson, pp. 180-1.

[12] Robinson's other publications include *Chaucer's Prosody: A Study of the Middle English Verse Tradition* (Cambridge: Cambridge University Press, 1971); and *The establishment of modern English prose in the reformation and the Enlightenment* (Cambridge: Cambridge University Press, 1998).

[13] Robinson, p. 180.

[14] Ian Robinson, 'The false prophet's promise of apples', *Times Higher Education (T.H.E.)*, 4th August, 2006. [<http://www.timeshighereducation.co.uk/story.asp?storycode=204690>, accessed 23rd January, 2012.]

[15] On the performance of scepticism, see Drew Milne, 'The Performance of Scepticism', *act 3: Endgames*, eds. Juliet Steyn and John Gange (London: Pluto, 1997), 50-76.

[16] John Torr, <http://www.timeshighereducation.co.uk/comments.asp?storycode=204690>, dated 15 June, 2011; accessed 23 January, 2012.

[17] For some sense of the energy of these terms, see the Wikipedia entry on 'Bump', esp. 'Bump (Internet)': <http://en.wikipedia.org/wiki/Bump_%28Internet%29>, accessed 23 January, 2012.

[18] See, for example, Ian Robinson, *Prayers for the new Babel: a criticism of the Church of England Alternative Service Book* (Retford: Brynmill, 1983).

[19] See John Colapinto, 'The Interpreter', *The New Yorker*, April 16, 2007: <http://www.newyorker.com/reporting/2007/04/16/070416fa_fact_colapinto #ixzz1jzsNOpl8>.

[20] Terry Regier, Paul Kay, Naveen Khetarpal, 'Color naming and the shape of color space', *Language: Journal of the Linguistic Society of America*, 85:4 (December 2009), 884-892.

[21] Everett's initial controversial paper was published as, 'Cultural Constraints on Grammar and Cognition in Pirahã: Another Look at the Design Features of Human Language', *Current Anthropology*, 46:4 (2005), 621–646.

[22] See Daniel Everett, *Don't Sleep, There are Snakes: Life and Language in the Amazonian Jungle* (London: Profile, 2008).

[23] For critical discussion of Everett's work and his reply, see Andrew Nevins, David Pesetsky, and Cilene Rodrigues, 'Pirahã exceptionality: A reassessment', *Language: Journal of the Linguistic Society of America*, 85:2 (June, 2009), 355-404; Daniel L. Everett, 'Pirahã Culture and Grammar: A Response to Some Criticisms', *Language: Journal of the Linguistic Society of America*, 85:2 (June, 2009) 405-442; Andrew Nevins, David Pesetsky, and Cilene Rodrigues, 'Evidence and argumentation: A reply to Everett (2009)', *Language: Journal of the Linguistic Society of America*, 85:3 (2009), 671-681.

[24] Friedrich Nietzsche, *Twlight of the Idols*, chapter 2.

[25] See, for example, James I. Porter, *Nietzsche and the philology of the future* (Stanford, CA.: Stanford University Press, 2000).

[26] Jessica N. Berry, 'The Pyrrhonian Revival in Montaigne and Nietzsche', *Journal of the History of Ideas*, 65:3 (July, 2004), 497-514.

[27] Although his account of skepticism is also represented in *The Phenomenology of Spirit* and in the lectures on the history of philosophy, see especially G.W.F. Hegel, 'Relationship of Skepticism to Philosophy' (1802), *Between Kant and Hegel: Texts in the Development of Post-Kantian Idealism,* ed. George Di Giovanni and H.S. Harris (Albany: SUNY Press, 1985), pp. 313-362.

[28] On the modes, see Julia Annas and Jonathan Barnes, *The Modes of Scepticism: Ancient Texts and Modern Interpretations* (Cambridge: Cambridge University Press, 1985). See also Richard Popkin, *The History of Scepticism: From Savonarola to Bayle* (Oxford: Oxford University Press, 2003).

[29] See Will Dudley, 'Ancient Skepticism and Systematic Philosophy', chapter 5, in *Hegel's History of philosophy: new interpretations*, ed. David A. Duquette (Albany: SUNY, 2003), pp. 87-106 (p. 98).

[30] See, for example, Sextus Empiricus, *Against the Grammarians (Adversus mathematicos I)*, translated with introduction and commentary by D.L. Blank (Oxford: Clarendon, 1998).

[31] See Emile Benveniste, 'Categories of Thought and Language', *Problems in General Linguistics*, trans. Mary Elizabeth Meek (Coral Gables, Fla.: University of Miami Press, 1971), pp. 55-64; and Jacques Derrida, 'The Supplement of Copula: Philosophy before Linguistics', *Margins of Philosophy*, trans. Alan Bass (Brighton: Harvester, 1982), pp. 175-205.

[32] Jean-Jacques Lecercle, *A Marxist Philosophy of Language*, trans Gregory Elliott (Chicago, Illinois: Haymarket, 2009), p. 54.

[33] J.H. Prynne, 'Poetic Thought', *Textual Practice*, 24:4 (2010), 595-606 (596).

Chapter 18

LOVE, SEX, PROSTITUTION AND HYPOCRISY

Roy Calne

Each species from bacteria and fungi to plants and animals must reproduce or perish. The reproductive process involves transfer of the nucleic acids (DNA) building blocks of life from one generation to the next.

This may be achieved by a budding process of cell division without any sexual process, however the majority of plant and animal species have male and female sexes, which in the process of reproduction convey approximately half of the DNA from the male to a similar DNA portion in the female to form a fertilized egg which has the potential to develop into the next generation (Figure 1).

Humans propagate the species by fusion of the male sperm with the female ovum to produce a fertilised egg and this is incubated over a long period in the womb until the baby is ready for existence in the outside world but still requires years of tender care, food and drink, and protection from environmental heat, cold and predators.

With such a vital function as reproduction it is not surprising that the biology has evolved with extreme complexity but there is an enormous waste of sperm and ova that are never fertilised. The human reproductive anatomy has been studied and reasonably well understood but the brain's participation in the process is more mysterious and, with modern techniques of imaging, some aspects are becoming clarified but the actual physical process of mating is controlled by complex neurological circuits.

There is little evidence of sexual activity in the human child until secondary sex organs undergo development and this is associated with the beginnings of a powerful urge to mate. At puberty the hormones involved in sexual arousal and activity are secreted in large amounts and the usual pattern of behaviour is strong attraction to the opposite sex, which is likely to blossom into a state of love which has been the centre of attention of poets, artists and musicians during the whole of recorded history and presumably long before.

Being in love especially between teenagers makes the participants focus all their attention and care on each other in a very possessive manner, almost like a mental disease as perceived by bystanders.

Figure 1. Explicit sexual image of 'Poppy Love' – demure shy buds on the right will in turn blossom into a full flower, with striking markings to attract bumble bees, which collect pollen and nectar and in the process will convey male pollen grains from the stamens to fertilize the female stigma of other poppies to produce the fertilized eggs in the pods on the left, from which seeds will germinate to repeat the cycle and ensure survival of this species.

Nevertheless this highly-focussed attraction is biologically important in providing a mutual interest in parents to take care of children resulting from the act of love. Of course falling in love can occur at any age, but in the young it is particularly intense and tends to be regarded as selfish by other family members and any potential threat is rapidly countered by hostility and jealousy. Couples in love tend to be unaware of any blemishes in their loved one and certainly do not criticise any aspect of their appearance or behaviour. The apparently irrational behaviour is encapsulated by Juliet's speech when she tries to persuade her loved one to leave his family and if he will not do that and she will change her name:

> "O Romeo, Romeo! Wherefore art thou Romeo,
> Deny thy father and refuse thy name;
> Or, if thou wilt not, be but sworn my love,
> And I'll no longer be a Capulet".

As we know, the tribal hatred between Montagues and Capulets ended up in tragedy for the lovers.

The extreme, almost pathological, state of love with frequently physical requiting must change with time and usually pregnancy and birth of the first child is a major event that requires the couple to readjust their relationship. The change tends to be more gradual if there are no children. Their mutual love may be undiminished, but they start to notice other things happening in the world and return to family contact and friendships. The urge for sexual satisfaction may be critically balanced between the lovers who are now parents or the balance may shift and physical and behavioural defects, previously unnoticed or ignored, can become apparent with a more realistic appraisal and often deeper understanding of the loved one.

In the Western world marriage was, until recently, the acceptable basis for rearing children and creating a family, bound together across different generations. In the last 30 years it has become acceptable for lovers to live together without the formality of a marriage contract and this has proved to be a less stable relationship than marriage.

The sexual drive and appetite varies greatly, being minimal in some throughout a lifetime, but strong and even pathological in others. To seek sexual satisfaction elsewhere than the marital bed may be abhorrent to many people but the fact remains that infidelity is frequent and a powerful distinguished status does not render the individual immune to these tendencies. Catherine the Great was said to have had countless lovers from among the handsome guardsman that were there to protect her. Cleopatra was irresistible to both Julius Caesar and Mark Anthony. The attitude to marriage has varied considerably throughout history, there have been a few polyandrous tribes where women are permitted more than one husband, polygamy is far commoner and is enshrined in the Islamic religion where up to four wives at a time are permitted provided the man can take care of them all. Polygamy was practised by the Mormons in North America but in recent years, in Western countries, polygamy has been officially frowned upon and instead there has evolved a pattern of divorce and one at a time sequential monogamy with different spouses which seems to be tolerated. In Iran a "Temporary Wife" can be obtained for travellers.

My discussion arose from a consideration of the biological need to reproduce but it is clear that in *homo sapiens* there is often a desire that will seek out sex with or without love. Acknowledged mistresses have been common in many societies and are still accepted behaviour for some prominent French politicians.

Viewed from the moral high ground there should be no pornography nor extra-marital sex, but the sexual pornography industry is huge, the profits enormous and there are millions of "hungry" consumers confirming a sceptical assessment of the articulated wishes of the Establishment. There are very important and significant financial considerations. The pornography industry was large and has increased exponentially when pornography became easily accessible through the Internet. Besides the financial turnover of pornography there are also important considerations of money being paid for sex. A mistress providing love and sex will expect to be kept in reasonable comfort. Woody Allen commented that "the most expensive sex is free sex".

There is a hinterland between pornography and crime which has become very prominent recently in the use of Internet contact for criminal abuse of children. This has proved to be very difficult to prevent since most children have independence in the use of the computer for networking. Another area of terrible abuse of children has been in institutions, particularly Church establishments run by teachers who have taken the oath of celibacy. The worldwide scandal in the Catholic Church has been publicised extensively, the Pope has apologized on behalf of the Church and efforts have been made to prevent future abuses. Deviations of what is considered to be normal sexual behaviour are common and some are harmful and dangerous. At the other extreme there are many people who have little interest in sex from an early age or lose interest at different stages in their lives.

Scepticism of widely expressed views of normality and what is acceptable would seem to have justification in a comparison of the high moral stance articulated on the one hand, and the actual practices that are widespread on the other. Modern biological and medical science have enabled humans to separate the act of copulation from the necessity for the species for reproduction.

A courtesan, a prostitute or a gigolo demand hard cash for their services. It may be difficult to draw the line between different relationships as the demarcations are not clear and can change. A young, beautiful model who is prepared to marry an aged and ill millionaire may be regarded by the community as a "gold-digger" but technically she is not a prostitute.

A reasonable citizen may be sceptical of the whole scene. Prostitution is the oldest profession and was recorded in ancient history. Prostitutes may ply their trade under a repressive, illegal environment which is dangerous for them and their clients, provides wealth to their pimps and avoids contributing tax to the Exchequer. A high-charging courtesan may be in less danger of being assaulted or acquiring disease with few but more wealthy customers and also avoids paying tax. The physical attractiveness of those selling sex is strongly related to the fees they can charge.

There is remarkable agreement in all races that have been studied and of different age groups, both male and female, as to what constitutes a beautiful face in a man and a woman, so this gives one gauge of attractiveness. However other important factors include charm, fitness and the operating environment which are relevant to the desirability of both female prostitutes and gigolos.

There are still other aspects of attractiveness besides facial beauty, for example physical strength, family and business connections, the size of a bank balance, expertise in sexual techniques and in some cases an opportunity to blackmail, which has featured in legal injunctions imposed by the courts in the UK.

George Bernard Shaw at a dinner party suggested to the woman sitting next to him that "everyone would agree to do anything for money if the price was high enough". *"Surely not"* she said. *"Oh yes"* he said. *"Well I wouldn't"* she said. *"Oh yes you would"* he said. *"For instance would you sleep with me for a million pounds?"*. *"Well"*, she said, *"maybe for a million I would yes"*. *"Would you do it for ten shillings?"* said GBS, *"certainly not"* said the lady, *"what do you take me for, a prostitute!"*. *"We have established that already"* said GBS, *"we are just trying to fix your price now"*.

This example of Shavian wit of course has more than a grain of truth running through the anecdote.

Another factor that is very important is the danger of transmission of disease through sexual contact. Before venereal diseases were understood, syphilis and gonorrhoea were commonly encountered in all strata of society, from the aristocracy to the very poor and killed thousands. Once the mode of transmission was understood and controls put in place with hygiene, the use of condoms and antibiotics, sexually transmitted diseases became a relatively minor problem then the whole medical field and society in general was thrown into panic when a deadly viral disease – acquired immunodeficiency (AIDS) suddenly appeared. For many years this was universally and rapidly fatal, with horrible, painful complications prior to death. There are now effective methods of treatment but often not available to the poorest communities and again money has raised its ugly head. Huge sums have been collected by nations and international organisations to combat HIV AIDS, by education, the use of condoms, hygiene and early and effective treatment. However, as with so many human activities, money has frequently mysteriously failed to reach the areas where it was intended to do good and dishonest, bureaucratic criminals have diverted much of the funds to their own pockets. Again one does not need to look far to justify a sceptical assessment.

The subject of this chapter began with love and has now reached an impasse of disease and crime. Is there a possible solution, bearing in mind human nature shows no sign of changing, but the urge for sexual gratification by both married and unmarried individuals will continue to exist and there are people who are prepared to sell sexual services in most countries. Unregulated prostitution is a bountiful source of income for criminals who coerce and traffic young people of both sexes for prostitution and reap the benefits, usually avoiding severe penalties for their illegal behaviour. The alternative would be to have a regulated sex trade with compulsory medical examination, hygiene checks and financial accounting so that taxes are paid from the very considerable earnings involved in the commerce. In countries where there are licensed brothels, the mental and physical health of the sex workers and indirectly their clients and clients' families are likely to be improved, but society in general does not like the idea and in particular there will be serious disputes as to the location of the bordellos, which are likely to bring unsavoury characters into the district and may increase local crime and certainly constitutes a bad example for children growing up in the neighbourhood.

These matters are important but not insoluble. Special areas could be designated, policed and controlled, with health checks, hygiene and registering of the sex workers to make it difficult for criminals to benefit from illegal trafficking. The motives of sex workers varies from those who are forced into prostitution because of poverty, drug addiction, coercion and trafficking, but there are others who recognise that if they adopt this profession in a suitable environment for a few years, they can become very wealthy, even if they do not like what they are doing. At the upper end of the scale there are some sex workers who appear to be happy in their work, especially with the rewards, provided they are protected from exploitation and danger. Perhaps sceptics can contribute in the dialogue as to how to handle these complex and difficult problems that are unlikely to go away spontaneously.

BOOKS FOR FURTHER READING

"The Wisdom of Whores " by Elizabeth Pisani, pub. Granta Books, London
"Sex at the Margins: Migration, Labour Markets and the Rescue Industry" by Laura Maria Agustin, pub. Zed Books

In: Scepticism: Hero and Villain
Editors: R. Calne and W. O'Reilly
ISBN: 978-1-62417-783-5
© 2013 Nova Science Publishers, Inc.

Chapter 19A

INTRODUCTION TO ART

Roy Calne

Although as a hub for international travel Atlanta airport must be among the worst in the Western world, it holds one redeeming attribute. If you miss the train link from terminal T to terminal A and walk underground you will be presented with a wonderful exhibition of sculptures from Zimbabwe, beautifully executed and a joy to lift the spirits from the misery of contemporary air travel. The authorities have put together a substantial sculpture collection for the public to enjoy and the chance to see this exhibition should not be missed. When rich Western nations become interested in art from developing nations it is not long before commercial considerations intrude on the original aspirations of the artist. In her chapter on Inuit art Dr. Tippett outlines the pattern that is probably inevitable. A similar fate overtook art of the Haida people in North West of Canada, the Aboriginal art in Australia and native art from all parts of Africa. Images are now ubiquitous and the market can disseminate fine art to a huge audience but sadly the aesthetic aspect of art can be irrelevant in pursuit of the mighty dollar.

A unique attribute of *homo sapiens* is the ability to communicate in language. This facility required complex evolution of the brain and larynx so that speech can be conceived and articulated. Language gave early man an important survival advantage, allowing planning and cooperation. To communicate language in a written form was an advance of extreme importance, allowing records to be made and the establishment of a history. The earliest findings of written language would suggest that pictures or ideograms were used as a form of conveying information probably relating to important topics such as where to find food, water and warning of danger. Some of the earliest images preserved in caves are extremely beautiful and were executed approximately 30,000 years ago, using natural earth pigments and charcoal. Most of the images are of animals, hunting or being hunted and they have often been found in remote locations only reached by crawling through narrow tunnels. Their significance is unknown but the highly developed skills would suggest that they were important, probably in a religious role. Images can fulfil three roles, practical, aesthetic and religious. Initially as a practical plan for mapping, constructing buildings, boats and imparting information. The aesthetic side is difficult to define, but has been a feature of image making throughout history. Ideograms have been found engraved in bronze, etched on bones and drawn in charcoal-based paint. In the diagram figure 1, the word 'dragon' is represented with standard Chinese writing, in modern simplified Chinese and as a calligraphy with an added poem. The aesthetic component of the calligraphy contrasts markedly with the more practical depictions yet all three images mean "Dragon".

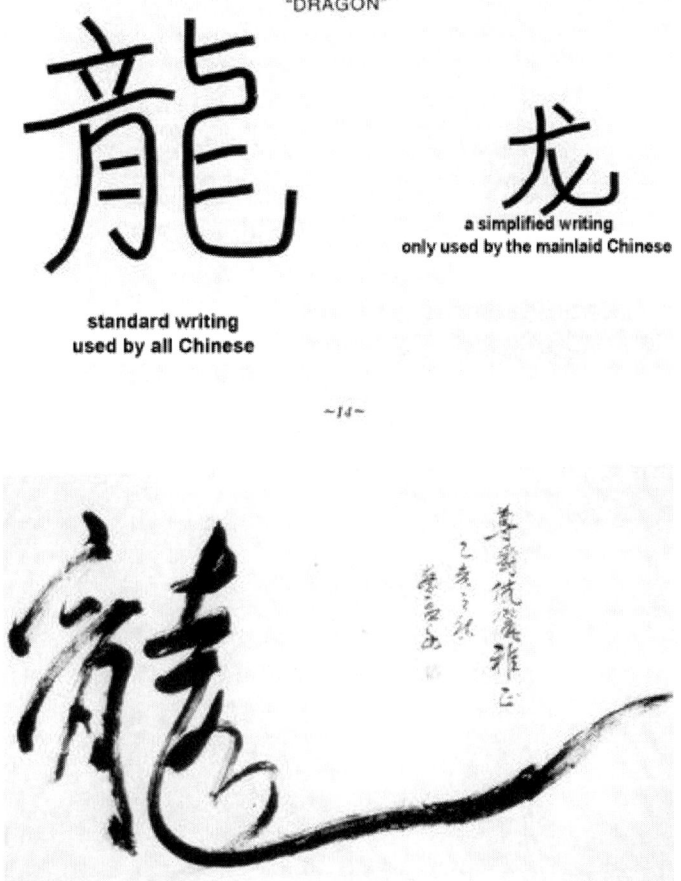

Figure 1. Chinese Calligraphy "Dragon" by Dr. Tsai, presented to RYC with poetry dedication.

Introduction to Art

Image-making can be regarded as part of the general cultural instinct present in all human beings, which includes music, dancing, singing, sculpture, painting and drawing. They probably confer survival advantage in the hierarchical organisation of early tribes and have in common the establishment and practice of religion, the seeking of a mate, the staking out of territory, warning of danger and mobilisation of group effort in avoiding or defeating an enemy. The importance of images and sculpture in religion have been apparent since the earliest recorded history, enthusiastically accepted by some communities and regarded as being most evil of practices by others, as exemplified by the wrath of Jehovah when the Israelites started to worship craven sculptured images.

To date there has been no convincing evidence of aesthetic behaviour and appreciation in any mammals including our closest relatives, the Chimpanzees. However birds have evolved behaviour which can be easily understood by modern man as artistic. Many avian species have characteristic song and dance courtships and some have elaborate displays, particularly Birds of Paradise and Peacocks. The most convincing illustration of artistic ability is practised by Bower birds of which some twenty species are found in Northern Australia and New Guinea. The male constructs an elaborate archway or bower with twigs and on occasion even adds to the display coloured berry juice or charcoal. He arranges an arena in front of the bower in which he performs his dance, often decorating the whole area with shells, dead beetles, feathers from Birds of Paradise and brightly coloured objects taken from human dwellings. The purpose of the bower is solely to attract a mate, it is not a place for nesting, shelter or refuge. The most elaborate and beautiful bower is likely to attract the most sought-after female as a mate.

Originality in art is difficult to define and can lead to endless controversies. To some extent all art is derivative, many of the most famous Western artists of the last 200 years have been influenced by oriental art, especially Japanese woodblock images and also by paintings and sculpture from primitive communities. Much of the skilled work in sculpture has been executed by artisans. Many famous sculptors in Victorian times, including Rodin, modelled in clay and then sent the plaster cast or mould to Carrera, where the carvers in marble produced the beautiful, highly polished final works. The original maquette or clay model was responsible for the artist's fame but the arduous, skilful carving and grinding work was performed by the artisans.

Now instant imagery is available, and easy to distribute worldwide. Images are everywhere and at all times. So there has been much debate as to what constitutes art and what is commercial illustration. The jury is out as to where this dividing line should be drawn. The perceived wisdom of the art critics, those who patronise artists and the views of prominent artists themselves became established as the accepted "school" in different epochs and when challenged by sceptics incurred hostility or were ignored. Van Gogh, now revered as one of the most significant and innovative artists of the past 200 years, could not earn a living from his art, selling in his lifetime only one painting, kindly purchased by his brother. Evanescent fashions in art often create markets leading to extraordinarily high prices being paid for abstract images, sculptures and "installations" that are incomprehensible to the majority of people and long textual explanations frequently do little to clarify the supposed significance of the art work, which may receive extravagant praise and achieve temporarily elitist status but has little chance of longevity. A short period of hyped prominence, engineered by critics, dealers and often the artists themselves can lead to huge fortunes. An example of this trend was publicised a few years ago when an inexpensive toy model to display anatomy to children was purchased by an artist, who instructed a bronze foundry to copy the mannequin on a large scale and then sold it as an original artwork for around one million pounds. The doll-maker maintained that the idea was his, but the artist argued that the transformation in size was a true aesthetic artistic innovation. Can enlargement of a 14in toy to a 20 ft copy be regarded as a manifestation of artistic originality? Would doubting the justification of this claim be regarded as sceptical or merely a commonsense assessment of the story?

Figure 2. "La Liberte" by Delacroix. The Louvre, Paris.

In addition to the aesthetics and financial gain, art has been a powerful tool for political purposes, as propaganda to attack or support politicians and other celebrities. Sculpture and paintings designed to depict history from a biased political standpoint have been an important component of all civilisations. Delacroix's "La Liberté" is one of the best known examples, Fig 2. Cartoons can be extremely effective instruments in praising, but more often denigrating personalities and policies. A clever cartoon often has more influence than a textual polemic. The visual image is a fertile hunting-ground for those sceptical of the art establishment, which defends contemporary trends as the epitome of high aesthetic art.

Figure 3. Two images together - "The Commissar of water walking with Stalin" and in the second image, he vanishes.

Chapter 19

'ART MADE FOR STRANGERS': RE-THINKING INUIT ART

Maria Tippett

'I don't know much about art but I know what I like,' is a cliché that contains a significant truth. It is a truth not about the merits of what people like but about the nature of what they know. For most Westerners have no difficulty understanding European art forms. They are like Moliere's Monsieur Jourdain, to whom it came as a revelation that he had been speaking prose all of his life. An implicit knowledge of the mode of production, the history of the artists, the origins of styles and the various ways in which art has been disseminated all contribute to meaning. Westerners have been carrying this baggage around with them all their lives without often realizing it. But does this baggage travel well?

The fact is that it is a bigger challenge than they appreciate when Westerners confront non-European forms of art. This is not to say that formal Islamic script on a mosque, the jagged rocks and furrows of sand in a Zen Buddhist garden or the deep carving of an Ashanti mask cannot be appreciated on a purely aesthetic level – providing they conform to Western ideas of beauty and symmetry. But is art really a universal language, as the philosopher John Dewey suggested more than seventy-five years ago in his 1934 publication *Art As Experience*? Should we be sceptical of our response if we have no knowledge of the historical, social and religious context in which these non-European art forms were created? Sceptical, also, about the cultural baggage that we bring to these non-European art forms? And sceptical, above all, about why we wish to display them in our galleries and in our homes? Certainly the extent to which we should be sceptical is crucial when it comes to the production, reception and validation of Inuit (or Eskimo) art.

It took a long time for the National Gallery of Canada to collect Inuit art. One mid-1970s director pejoratively called it "bingo art." This arose from the assumption that the stone carvings were hastily produced on a Saturday morning and sold to a government official in the afternoon in order to earn the cost of admission to that evening's bingo game. Others felt that the "primitive", "unsophisticated" and "crude" nature of contemporary Inuit art qualified it for display in an ethnographic museum not in a public art gallery. Still others pronounced Inuit art static, time-warped and not adaptable to Western standards of art criticism where change and "progression" were the goalposts. A smaller group of art specialists questioned the authenticity of an art form that had been "created" largely for the southern Canadian market place.

The irony is, of course, that while the art establishment was quibbling over where and how Inuit stone carvings should be exhibited, whether they should be acquired for their permanent collections and whether they were art or artifact, Canadians had embraced them as their national art.

From the 1950s a stone carving or a stone-cut print of a stalking bear, a supine seal or an Inuk hunter was the most socially acceptable gift one could receive. This was perhaps because Inuit carvings and prints linked southern Canadians to their resource-rich hinterland and to the expansive yet little-explored northern frontier. They offered an alternative to the difficult-to-understand modernist paintings and sculptures championed by professional curators and art historians.

Produced by a people who were thought to live close to the land, Inuit carvings were untainted by decadent Western ideas and values. Subsidized initially by the Department of Mines and Resources and after 1952 by the Department of Northern Affairs and National Resources, they were evidence of the Canadian government's liberal-minded policy towards the country's indigenous peoples. And above all, in a country where national symbols have always been in short supply, Inuit carvings, prints and drawings served as a testimony for urbanized Canadians that they were a northern people and therefore different from their American neighbors to the south.

There is no word in Inuktitut for art. Yet ever since the Inuit first inhabited the Eastern Arctic in c. 2000 BC (or Nunavut as this area has been called since 1999) they had been carving utensils, amulets and grave goods from tusk, bone and stone as well as "drawing" or "building" two and three-dimensional ephemeral maps in the snow or sand. It was not, however, until the early part of the nineteenth century, when American and Scottish whalers as well as Hudson's Bay Company fur traders appeared in the Eastern Arctic, that Inuit men and women adapted these skills to the production of curios and souvenirs. One hundred years later the market for these items expanded exponentially with the arrival of RCMP officers, missionaries, adventurers, then teachers, government officials, tourists and construction workers. The work that the Inuit sold to or traded with these newcomers had little connection with the traditional carvings that their ancestors had created for domestic or religious reasons, for hunting and amusement. The fact that they now produced ashtrays and cribbage boards in addition to model kayaks, sleds and animals underlines this point.

The Canadian government recognized the economic potential of what they referred to as 'Eskimo handicrafts' as early as the 1920s. They also feared 'that an increase in demands for curios and souvenirs, coupled with a changing material culture would soon lead to the disappearance of native articles.' The non-profit Montreal-based Canadian Handicrafts Guild, which had been devoted to the preservation of indigenous arts and crafts since 1906, was equally concerned about the fate of Inuit handicrafts. They mounted the first exhibition of "Eskimo" arts and crafts in 1930. The artifacts and contemporary small ivory carvings on display duly caught the attention of the *New York Times*. The Hudson's Bay Company also collected curios in its Eastern Arctic outposts and sold them through its stores in the South. Along with Roman Catholic oblate priests, Company officials also attempted to encourage the Inuit to make more. However producing curios and souvenirs "for strangers" did not become an integral part of the Inuit economy until after the Second World War.

The Inuit had long been subjected to Canada and Europe's fluctuating market cycles, to changing company policies and to trends in fashion. But they had coped with these fluctuations and incursions while remaining on the land. Towards the middle of the twentieth century, however, their lifestyle, which blended subsistence with trade, was threatened – as it had been since the early part of the century - by the collapse of the white fox industry and falling prices for Atlantic hair seal skins. Added to this was the decline of the caribou population. In search of alternative forms of employment, a few Inuit men took on construction jobs at newly established weather and radar stations. Others helped build airstrips. And a smaller number worked in the newly established mines. Even so, many families went hungry; many starved to death.

In an effort to address this situation, to ensure Canada's sovereignty over uninhabited regions of the High Arctic, and to comply with Canada's nationalist sentiment to expand northward, the government moved several communities substantially further North. Government officials assumed that the Inuit could *enjoy* a better standard of living if they were returned to their *natural state*. The colonization of the High Arctic was a disaster. There were few caribou. New hunting and trapping methods had to be learned. Darkness came months earlier –

and left months later - than in the Southern Arctic. As a result, many died of starvation in their new home. Unable to cope, some even committed suicide.

With the introduction of the Northern Federal Day School system in the early 1950s, the Canadian government's efforts to incorporate the Inuit into the social, economic and political sphere took another form. Children were forced to live in residential schools far from their homes. They were prohibited from speaking Inuktitut or practicing their customs and beliefs. They were even more susceptible to disease – particularly tuberculosis. (Illness moved them to sanatoriums in southern Canada.) Many children were also subjected to sexual abuse at the hands of their Anglican and Catholic teachers. A few Inuit families moved close to the residential schools in order to be near their children. Most families could not afford this luxury and remained on the land.

It was against the government of Canada's clumsy attempt to bring the Inuit into the ambit of southern Canada that Inuit art was "created" in the late 1940s. Many people – the schoolteacher Marjorie Hinds, RCMP officer R.D. Van Norman, the missionary Father Henri Tardy along with Hudson's Bay Company personnel Jim Bell and Peter Murdoch – were involved. But it was the Canadian Handicrafts Guild to whom most of the credit must go for developing the Inuit art industry.

In 1948 the Guild hired Toronto-born artist James Houston to travel to the Eastern and Central Canadian Arctic in order to purchase Native crafts. The following year Houston shipped several crates of curios to Montreal in time for the Guild's annual sale. The show was an instant success.

It was while working for the Guild that Houston attempted to raise the status of Inuit crafts and souvenirs to fine art by producing *Sanajaska: Eskimo Handicrafts* in 1951. The manual consisted of simple line drawings. Although some were derived from the graphic images that appeared on recent Inuit carvings, others were clearly inspired by the work of the British sculptor, Henry Moore, and the totem pole carvings of Canada's northwest coast First Nations' People. Whatever their origin, Houston's drawings showed the Inuit what sort of carvings would be 'useful and acceptable to the white man.' Carvings with a pedestal, Houston indicated in both English and Inuktitut, made them suitable for display on a mantelpiece or in an art gallery's glass showcase. A favored viewpoint was preferable to sculptures that were carved in the round. Smooth stone surfaces were more likely to appeal to the White buyer than carvings with rough ones. (Inuit carvers were given sandpaper for this purpose.) And the most highly sought-after motifs, in order of preference, were people, walrus, bears, seals, caribou, birds and fish.

Houston not only encouraged the Inuit to carve objects that would be attractive to non-Inuit people. He helped mount exhibitions of Inuit carvings in and outside of Canada. One notable exhibition held in 1953 at the Gimpel Fils gallery in London introduced Inuit sculpture to the Europeans. Its success prompted the Canadian government's greater involvement in the production of contemporary Inuit art.

That year Houston was appointed crafts officer for the Arctic Division of the Department of Northern Affairs and National Resources. And, after convincing the government that he would be in a better position 'to encourage a new and exciting field of Canadian art' if he were permanently based in the Arctic, Houston was made the Northern Service Officer for West Baffin Island, covering an area of 65,000 square miles, in 1956.

It was from Houston's base in Cape Dorset (*Kingait*) that he and his wife Alma introduced a new art form to the Inuit: print-making. The first stone and lino-cut prints were made in what was soon to be called "The Florence of the North" in 1957. Often based on simple pencil drawings, they owed as much to the iconography of comic books as to contemporary Japanese prints an art form that Houston would study in Japan for three months in 1958-1959. Within a few years Inuit men and women were drawing directly on the stone. And when Terry Ryan took over the workshop, following Houston's departure from Cape Dorset in 1962, they were producing stencil prints, etchings, mezzotints as well as lithographs. Ryan also encouraged the making of jewelry, appliqué wall hangings and clothing – all destined, of course, for sale in the South.

The stone-cut prints were an instant success when they were exhibited in southern Canada in 1959. This was an art form – albeit alien to the Inuit - that was acceptable to southern Canada's art specialists and gallery officials. Prints were more affordable to the expanding art-buying public than stone carvings. With the founding in 1961 of the Canadian Eskimo Arts Committee (from 1969 the Canadian Eskimo Arts Council), a price as well as a rigorous selection process was imposed on every print. As their role as gatekeepers, the Canadian Eskimo Arts Committee were thus able to control what kind of prints went on to the art market.

In his numerous articles and books produced during the 1950s and early 1960s, Houston extolled the virtues of Inuit art as 'primitive,' 'emotionally stimulating' and 'intellectually rewarding'. Speaking on lecture tours across Canada and in the United States he told his audiences that contemporary Inuit art had an unbroken link with prehistoric art.

With an eye to promoting quick sales, he reminded his audiences that Inuit art was vulnerable to extinction. This line of thinking was popular among audiences who clung to the romantic idea that the so-called *primitive* art of the Inuit was untainted and, above all, ephemeral. It was good for sales as evidenced in the emergence of galleries that dealt only with Inuit art. And it reinforced James Houston's much deserved standing as the impresario of Inuit art.

Houston always insisted that Inuit art was 'created for the artist's satisfaction, not just for commercial ends.' But not everyone agreed. As early as 1958, the Winnipeg-based Inuit art scholar George Swinton argued that the government was turning the Inuit into 'a bunch of cultural phonies.' 'The good Eskimo carvers don't care any more. They're even making ashtrays and bookends because of the white man's buck. And the Handicrafts Guild is imposing its taste.' The result, in Swinton's view was 'doing irreparable harm to the Eskimo's dignity.' He also fired a salvo at Houston when he said that 'Northern Affairs officers are not only making the Eskimo dependent on the white man by carving, but are telling him what to make.'

By 1963 even James Houston, who was now working in New York as assistant director of design for Steuben Glass, had mixed feelings about his earlier activities in the Arctic. 'Eskimo prints have been so successful and the price-rise so steep that there is a danger they may price themselves out of the market.' This was the penalty of success. 'If buyers require high standards, that's what they'll get,' he told a reporter, but his worry was that the opposite would occur. 'If on the other hand they encourage the Eskimo to make thousands of prints and carvings,' Houston continued, 'they'll get them, with resultant deterioration and quality.' He warned: 'I want them to make their money through quality not quantity.'

The making, collecting, marketing and exhibiting of Inuit art was as foreign to an Inuk man or woman as art schools, art patrons, art critics and galleries. Yet whether they were carving, drawing, sewing or printmaking, Inuit artists quickly caught on to the tricks of the White trade. They produced larger carvings because they sold better than the traditionally smaller ones. When heavy duties were imposed on the export of stone carvings, they carved non-taxable whalebone.

They showed no false pride in their work. Hollywood's star system was alien to them since the Inuit favor group over individual effort. So when they discovered that the work of some artists fetched higher prices than that of others, this prompted one celebrated print-maker, Kenojuak, to sign drawings that had in fact been produced by her husband, Johnniebo. Nor were the carvers averse to using sandpaper. 'The Qablunaat (white man) likes shiny finish, while the Inuit like to see a rough finish.' And, as stone carver Simon Tookoome continued, 'If I took such a carving to you, you would pay less because it wasn't highly polished and you would tell me if I do more work and make it look [the way you like], you'll pay me more.' Inuk carvers were, above all, not naïve. George Akikuluk from Baffin Island's most northern settlement, Artic Bay, was not alone in wondering whether Inuit art was being used 'to make a lot of profit for a lot of people' in the South.

There can be no doubt, however, that many Inuit artists enjoyed a higher standard of living from the early 1950s. By 1967 seventy per cent of the population in Cape Dorset were carving or making prints thus providing the community with half of its annual income. By 1978 Inuit artists had established their own co-operative, the West Baffin Eskimo Co-operative. Their Toronto-based distribution service earned them substantially more money for their work. And by 2000 Inuit art was fetching higher prices, on the international art market, than most work produced by non-Inuit Canadian artists.

Clearly making art for strangers complemented the Inuit lifestyle. Drawings could be made on the land, then deposited in the co-op where other hands would usually turn them into prints and market them in the South. Carvings could be done between hunting excursions on the land. As Kenojuk observed: 'In times of need, and when hunting was poor, we carved.'

Making money was not, however, the only motive for making art. Carving and printmaking did enable many to recapture an earlier way of life. 'When I carve, I try to convey what it was like for Inuit in the early 1940s,' reported stone sculptor, Uriash Puqiqnak, in 1991. Many agreed. The biggest concern for another stone carver, Manasie Akpaliapik, was 'to record the legends. These are important to us because we use them as guide posts to the old days.' However the irony of being asked to recapture the past was not lost on one artist from Baker Lake who observed in 1976 that: 'Years ago all the *qallunat* (white men and women) who came here told us to get rid of *angakut* (shamans) and all the beliefs in *turngat* (evil spirits), and we did. Now the *qallunat* asks us all the time, "Where are the *angaku* and *turngat* among your people and your art"?'

It was a double-edged process. James Houston found himself given the Inuit name, Sowmik, meaning left-handed one. He could feel gratified that making prints and stone carvings had given many Inuk men and women more confidence. 'After Sowmik came there were many changes,' Peter Pitseolak recalled. 'You could very easily notice that people started being their own bosses. They didn't listen any more to what was the right or wrong thing to do. They following their own ideas.' Others remained fiercely independent: 'I make what the white man wants,' one artist said in 1986, 'but I make it *my* way.' And Paulosie Sivuak remembered seeing Houston's instruction manual but 'didn't follow his advice because I didn't like those drawings at all.'

But not everyone had as much confidence as Paulosie Sivuak. Manasie Akpaliapik recalled that 'Lots of times the Hudson's Bay Company and co-op managers might not know about art at all. They might be good at paper-work and managing, but a lot of times they tell people what to carve: "We need 10 polar bears".' The demand for assembly-line carvings did not encourage creativity it stunted it. According to Akpaliapik many younger carvers felt that 'If they do something different, it might not sell.'

It can, of course, be argued that western artists have always worked to the demands of the marketplace, just as they have been known to copy their own and other people's work. But how many of them have been encouraged to recreate a past that they only know from hearsay? Or to portray a way of life that no longer exists? Or to make art that will be acceptable to an untutored foreign audience? Or to make work for display in galleries and homes of a kind that they have never seen?

As early as the mid 1970s Inuk artist George Akikuluk had wondered how southern Canadians, who possessed a limited knowledge of his culture, could understand his art. He suggested that 'the carvings could be accompanied by stories or explanations' when they were put on display. Twenty-five years later Inuk artist Gary Baikie made the same point when he insisted that '"You only see how we used to live and not how we live today".' Like many in the new generation of Inuit artists, Baikie explores themes that attempt to come to grips with the oppressive school system, the re-location programs, not to mention the problems that the Inuit face today. These are challenging works.

But this is not the kind of art that sells. Few want to know about the residential schools, the relocation programs, the starvation and the epidemics that swept, at regular intervals during the twentieth century, across the Arctic. Moreover, even fewer want to acknowledge that Inuit art been created, judged, sifted by non-Inuit gatekeepers. Worse still, almost no one wants to recognize that this *untainted* art has been influenced by comic books, contemporary British sculpture and Japanese prints.

Southern Canadians are more confortable embracing the mythic version of their fellow countrymen and women in the Arctic. Government and company officials have found an uncontroversial art form that makes suitable presentation gifts and public display. And, above all, collectors have derived a great deal of satisfaction from possessing an art that they believe has sprung from untutored hands and is now in short supply.

No one should know this better than art dealers. The welcome success of Inuit carvings and prints certainly made Duncan McLean at Waddington Galleries in Toronto 'really glad' that he got involved with Inuit art. 'It's unique to the world. There is no other Arctic,' he was quoted as saying in 1987. 'You can buy so many other kinds of art and not care at all about the culture or where it came from. With Inuit, you buy the art and you want to know the people and you want to know the story.'

But how many really want to know the full story – one that might be rather different from what such words may suggest? Should we not, in the end, be sceptical about making Inuit art stand proxy for the not-so-romantic history of the Inuit Peoples in the twentieth century? Perhaps, in short, we need a measure of scepticism.

In: Scepticism: Hero and Villain
Editors: R. Calne and W. O'Reilly

ISBN: 978-1-62417-783-5
© 2013 Nova Science Publishers, Inc.

Chapter 20

'I SAW IT WITH MY OWN EYES' SCEPTICISM AND PHOTOGRAPHY: A MARRIAGE MADE IN HEAVEN

Kiloran Howard

"A deception that elevates us is dearer than a host of low truths"

Marina Tsvetaeva (1892–1941)

INTRODUCTION

(Copyright difficulties prohibit inclusion of images except my own)

Although the camera never lies, the photographer does. Digital Photoshop can manipulate a photographic image beyond recognition. For nearly every portrait for which I am commissioned, I am asked if I will, on the side, also do a little nip'n tuck.

What used to be the curio of a few is nowadays accessible and practiced by the masses. Photography promised realism that other arts could not deliver. It is this promise that has been corrupted providing such fertile grounds for deception. One must be sceptical about everything. We have altered the way we project ourselves. However, distortion of the truth in photography is nothing new. Perhaps the promise was never really there.

PLASTICIZATION

The word photography derives from the Greek words *phōtós* meaning light and *gráphein* to write. The revered realism photographer Ansel Adams, [see www.anseladams.com] confided: "Dodging and burning are steps to take care of mistakes God made in establishing tonal relationships". In a traditional photographic darkroom you could dodge, burn, blur, tone – effectively the print could be endlessly manipulated. This was, however, labour intensive by comparison to the modern alternative: photoshoping, or just 'shopping' as it aficionados call it. Photoshop is the modern sophisticated software that gives its user the tools to dismantle and recreate any image.

Portrait photography has changed radically in just a few years. Shearer West points out: "Portraiture plays with ideas of identity as they are perceived, represented and understood in different times and places'.[1] What has not changed is our ongoing fascination with ourselves. This, in conjunction with the omnipresent mobile phone camera and ease with which the results they produce can be manipulated, has rendered today's photography a sham. Elliot Erwitt said "Digital photography has made every man, woman, child and chimpanzee a photographer of sorts and consequently has numbed down the general quality of photographs..."[2] He is rightly sceptical of the digital revolution. It would be hard to visit the website 'www.portrait professional.com' and not share his sense of scorn. Even casual portraits are today more a representation of how we want to view ourselves and be viewed than an honest representation of what we are actually like. Images are succumbing to a type of perceived beauty. We are using a visual language that is recognisable to the viewer. Ironically, Erwin Panofsky (1892 - 1968) in his analysis of individuality captured the essence of present day portraiture: "a portrait aims by definition at two essentials…On the one hand it seeks to bring out whatever it is in which the sitter differs from the rest of humanity and would even differ from himself were he portrayed at a different moment or in a different situation; and is what distinguishes a portrait from an 'ideal' figure or 'type'. On the other hand it seeks to bring out whatever the sitter has in common with the rest of humanity."[3] Amongst women, there is a taste for bulbous lips and satin smooth brows. These can be plumped and ironed out respectively to their heart's content. Many of today's portraits are simply a record of the re-chiselled surface of a person. We are turning into effigies. No visible signs of wear and tear seem the rather suspicious-making aim. As Walter

---

[1] Shearer West 'Portraiture' p.ll (Oxford Press 2004)
[2] Elliott Erwitt - On the question: "How do you feel about the digital photography explosion?" Interview with Elliott on photoshopsupport.com
[3] Erwin Panofsky Early Netherlandish Painting New York & London (1971) Vol 1 p.194

Benjamin observed, to live means to leave traces, but the unruffled, highly touched-up images of today evince a disturbing sense of clinical perfectionism. John Singer Sargent warned: 'every time I paint a portrait I lose a friend.'[4] These days we clearly want to keep our friends!

Digital manipulation [see, for example, the Bulgari Advertising Campaign featuring Julianne Moore] allows the photographer to incorporate what the human eye sees with the limited monocular vision of the camera. The intention need not necessarily be to deceive but instead to add expression. Hockney elegantly describes this process: '...we all know our eyes move constantly, and the only time they stop moving is when we're dead – or when we're staring. And if we're staring, we're not really looking. That is the problem with the single frame photograph: all you can actually do is stare at it. Your eyes cannot wander around it, because of its inherent lack of time.'[5]

Digitally created images are impressionist representations. According to ancient etymology, the word *image* derives from *imitari*. The images work on our senses. An unadulterated photograph relies on the viewer's recognition of the object represented: a nose looks like a nose. Electronic media's systematic pixelation implies a similar lack of human artistry. And yet Pointillism was also just a series of dots. Digital manipulation allows the photographer to imply what the camera cannot 'see'. Francis Bacon [www.francis-bacon.com] argued that we are not about physical attributes but instead about essence. He always wanted to work from a photograph when painting a portrait – it encouraged his ability to conjure the spirit of his sitter without the necessity of being in their physical presence. His logic was clear: "I've had photographs taken for portraits because I very much prefer working from photographs than from them. It's true to say I couldn't attempt to do a portrait from a photograph of somebody I didn't know. But, if I both know them and have photographs of them I find it easier to work than actually having their presence in the room. I think that, if I have the presence of the image there, I am not able to drift so freely as I am able to through the photographic image. This may be just my own neurotic sense but I find it less inhibiting to work from them through memory and their photographs than actually having them seated there before me."[6] Bacon prefers to be "totally alone with their memory."[7] He is relying on photography as the product of, as Voltov the Russian film director put it, a "truth machine".

Interestingly, Lucian Freud eschewed any help from a photograph to achieve his brutal candour. His work is the epitome of a 'warts and all' approach. In the

---

[4] The Oxford Dictionary of Quotations p.644 no.17
[5] Marina Vaizey 'The Artist as Photographer' p.167
[6] David Sylvester 'Interviews with Francis Bacon' p.39
[7] David Sylvester 'Interviews with Francis Bacon' p. 37

Sunday Times (24th July 2011) A.A. Gill reminisced about his time as Freud's pupil at the Slade School of Art. Gill recounts about his mentor: "I don't think he said a word to me in the four years I was there, but I do remember once painting away and my canvas started moving and I looked round and he was stroking the back of it. I was a very bad painter so I bought very expensive canvas and he was just stroking it." The flatness, in both the physical and spiritual sense of the word, of a photograph was unlikely to hold much comfort for someone so tactile.

A photographer can now 'paint' his photographs and can seek to achieve what Archile Gorky tried to convey in his painting. His daughter Maro once told me that when his wife, Magoush, asked why the forest he was painting had no trees, he replied he was depicting the space in between them.

Deception, however, does not necessarily need to be perpetrated electronically. Thomas Demand asserts that 'truth' has been called into question because photographs can be used to deconstruct, or is that actually to construct, the very reality they are supposed impartially to record. His pictures [www.thomasdemand.info] are genuine photographs – not digital images. But they are still a type of lie. Indeed, they are the embodiment of a sceptical view of the world. Demand contends that 'things just enter reality through photographs'. He explores the powerful and subliminal process by which we perceive information. His work is motivated by events in the press, the images of which are culled and are subsequently used as the basis for his basic tenet that, in photography, things are not what they appear to be. He begins by sourcing an image from visual media. He then copies it, using paper and card, to build a life size replica. His work is immaculately crafted and looks 'real'. The installation is then photographed using a 10" x 8" camera with telescopic lens which paradoxically creates the effect of the subject matter being far way whilst simultaneously bringing it closer (an old Hitchcockian trick). The image is then laminated under Plexiglas. By this point the image has been removed from reality three times.

Demand's photograph titled 'Office' 1995 [http://katyatylevich.com/pdf/demand] is specifically seeking to provoke a sceptical reaction in the viewer. It is derived from pictures he found showing the ransacked offices of the East German Secret Police, the Stasi, after the fall of the Communist regime. Papers, files and folders are strewn about the room. The papers are in fact blank and the folders empty. The photograph is barren of details, and it is this evasion that depicts a failure of a photograph to impart the truth. Despite the chaos, there is an implied sense of controlled anarchy. Demand is alerting us that the eye is easily deceived. This is the ultimate plasticized image.

REALISM – DON MCCULLIN AND THE BRUTAL TRUTH

We expect the truth from photography. It is a dependable medium to 'capture' a model not only "from life" but also "in life".

Elliott Erwitt's photographs [www.elliotterwitt.com] are witty, informal views of everyday life. The supposed merit of reportage photography is that it portrays reality, albeit subjectively. The content depicts a story or conveys a message. Nothing but the truth counts. Any artifice would render the image a lie.

Prince Malik Atta of Awan Pakistan: Kiloran Howard, 1996.

Prince Malik Ata of Awan, a fierce warlord in Northern Pakistan, looks imposing and his portrait looks all the more impressive because it is clearly genuine. I shot it when I stayed with Malik on his enormous remote estate. I survived a terrifying ride on his fiercest, most highly-strung stallion to win his respect before he would allow me to shoot this picture. Were the dusk or his sartorial attire to have been digitally enhanced, or worse created, the portrait would lose its vitality. He is one of a dying breed of regional rulers with feudal control over thousands of subjects. Everything in the photograph is as it was.

The acclaimed war photographer Don McCullin work is synonymous with the Vietnam War. He worked on location - not from the comfort of his study. The hallmarks of his work are his endurance and empathy; neither of these could have been conveyed digitally. In his book "Unreasonable Behaviour", McCullin says '... I found I was able to share other people's emotional experiences, live with them silently, transmit them. I felt I had a particular vision that isolated and homed in on the essence of what was happening, and could see the essence in light, in tones, in details. I had a powerful ability to communicate. What I hoped I had captured in my pictures was an enduring image that would imprint itself on the world's memory.' A large part of his photographs' power relies on the viewer trusting that his images are a genuine testimony of what he saw. In the early 2000, John Tusa interviewed Don McCullin who apparently has "the balls of a commando, the cunning of a rat, the eye of an artist, the anger of a man with his eyes open, so that anger finally threatened to consume him"! This assessment is easy to understand given McCullin's own explanation of his craft: "Photography isn't looking, it's feeling. If you can't feel what you're looking at, then you're never going to get others to feel anything when they look at your pictures". McCullin's work is about being physically present and confronting head on the ravages of war. He is as remote from any digital manipulation as his locations are from the comforts of home. He does have misgivings about his role as photographer, admitting to feeling 'very ashamed of doing that really, because maybe it's a big intrusion'. He is painfully aware of his immediate predicament: that his presence as a photographer is not at that moment helping the injured when 'they would be much happier if you were standing in front of them as a doctor'. However, these anxieties help him deliver his painful and memorable images, evocative images of life and death on the front line [google images: Don McCullin].

McCullin was also sent to cover the famine in Biafra. He is still haunted by the image of an emaciated albino boy clutching his empty French corned beef tin. Unlike most of McCullin's images, the boy is not looking up to us, but instead gazes down bewildered. 'It is difficult to associate the word "dignity" with conditions such as I photograph, yet dignity is what I try to show. I find it most in the people who suffer the most, they seem to marshal the energy of dignity, because they will not surrender.'

McCullin's intentions are always honorable. To use any form of digital enhancement would be an anathema to him. He is, however, acutely aware of his own human failings - of being, by his own admission, an apologist for working in media. He says 'I am a compassionate person... working for media involves manipulation. I have been manipulated, and I have in turn manipulated others, by recording their response to suffering and misery. So there is guilt...' He has tried to work alone in the field, not only to get a better picture, but also because he cannot otherwise give his images the 'dignity' he so reveres. McCullin describes with this need with graphic honesty: 'there is no way of being dignified with dozens of newsmen around, pushing and shoving and punching each other over one injured soldier, shouting to another "you spoilt my picture", while almost depriving the wounded man from oxygen around him. I looked at them and thought: "Who are these people?" At night, in Beirut, they used to meet at the bar, talking about day-rates. Or someone would say to another one: "if you get the cover, you buy us the champagne".' McCullin is remorseful in conceding that his images are of people that have been exploited. He remembers showing his pictures in the office of a prospective editor and hearing: "God, that's terrible; make it a double page spread!" McCullin feels his subject-matter's pain and transmits it to himself. In an interview with Frank Horvat, he elaborates on this exchange by articulating the dynamic between photographer and subject: 'when people look at me as if to say: "help me" and they can't speak because their jaw is shattered, I try to respond with my eyes, I make my eyes say: "I hear you, I see you, I wish I could help you". But at the same time I am photographing them and I feel shabby, I know that, instead of helping, I am an unnecessary burden to them.' He usually presses the shutter the moment they look up.

McCullin denies that he deliberately sets out to shock. The tension between his integrity and his tormented soul used to drive him on. Success was not the determining factor in his career. He was essentially compelled to photograph by an inner quest to come to terms with the tragedy in his life. It is deeply ironic that his own suffering brought him praise, especially as he believes that suffering belongs to life and that, therefore, misery should be accepted as inevitable. He felt an imperative to shoot his pictures, acknowledging a power greater than him that put him 'in the right place at the right time'. Although fundamentally an atheist, he has mused on theological matters in recognizing the energy of the universe. Sure of it, he would wait for the right light to enhance the pathos in his pictures. In Beirut, he photographed the aftermath of the shooting by Christian Phalangists in the Sabra and Chatilla Palestinian refugee camp. It was alleged the Israeli army turned a blind eye to the massacre. In McCullin's pictures the sun light streams through the destroyed make-shift camps creating an almost biblical atmosphere. Although arguing he has no right to practice 'creativity at the expense of human suffering', in shooting his pictures to the best of his ability, that is exactly what he has done. McCullin's images represent the true interpretation of the world as he saw it but still they are his creations. It is not surprising that he has never posted his exposed film at the end of a shoot, insisting instead on carrying it back 'cradled' like a baby to be developed. He has even described his time in the darkroom as giving birth. Surely this must beg the question: has even the arch realist dramatized the moment for maximum effect?

By the late 1980s, Don McCullin's life fell apart. His wife, whom he had loved since they were childhood sweethearts, but with whom he could not stay because of his compelling need to roam, was dying of cancer. He now regards his photography as one of the ruinations of his life and blames it for his wretched loneliness. If he had had the ability to convey the humanity in his work digitally, would it be reasonable to suggest he may have saved his marriage? He was married to his work, faithful to it alone and, thus, he lost his relationship with his beloved wife. This led to the revelation that his photography has been a series of self-portraits. He decided to stop photographing war and instead started photographing peace. Beauty is his new truth and he has never taken up digital imaging. He has said he wants to bring energy to his peace pictures (although, despite himself, he still prefers to photograph at night. His new work gives him pleasure because it is about life and not death.

Though McCullin has turned his back on war reportage, this does not mean that it was all in vain. On the contrary, he now feels he has won his battle. He now just 'sees' differently. Mark Haworth-Booth described McCullin's images as '...like candles that no-one will put out, or stains that cannot be removed'. McCullin's work, suffused with the suffering of his subjects and thus able to reveal their innate dignity, can be trusted. If there is artifice, it is perhaps unconscious, and serves only to heighten the viewers' comprehension of the terrible truths recorded for posterity. McCullin's pictures are indictments of man's inhumanity to man. This is the fundamental truth he never glosses over. The camera has not lied; rather it has revealed the essence of an awful reality.

If Oliviero Toscani's images had been digitally created they would not have been scandalous. His aim was to provoke but this could only be done through the content being 'real'. Toscani was immersed as a child in the power of pictures. His father photographed the famous image of Mussolini's corpse suspended upside-down from a meat hook. In an interview for the Independent Magazine (31st July 1993) Toscani almost ranted: "Today's culture is images, and I don't draw any distinctions between them.... pasta advertising or tampon advertising or Red Cross information are all the same. They are images pertaining to the way the world behaves. Probably a spaghetti picture might be in a way more right, more important, and more interesting than editorial picture of the Bosnian war. The way people eat pasta is very important, how much they eat, what kind of shape they eat and what they are looking for. Every picture has an effect on somebody; some people don't want to be disturbed by what they see. But I think that, today, language is dying and the language of images is the new language.... There is a reality, a truth in pictures that we don't get any more through the traditional language". Toscani's billboards created uproar when they came out starting in 1986. Had they been created digitally, we would have walked passed without noticing [google images: toscani de benetton].

CONCLUSION

Photography is a vehicle of consciousness. A classic film noire, for example Double Indemnity, is imbued with tension and energy by its gritty, dark look. It is devoid of computer-generated imagery and relies on the performances, camera work and directorial editing to generate is atmosphere of foreboding. The contrast with a modern CGI reliant blockbuster is striking. I know which I prefer. The same comparison can be made between a genuine photograph and a 'shopped' digital image. Digital manipulation requires the suspension of disbelief and engages us in a rhythm of recognition and misrecognition. Put another way, digital images set traps for us. We look but do not really see. The plasticization we see is now rooted in our expectations. No matter how apparently sensational the effect, it is rendered banal. We have all become so sceptical we no longer believe or trust anything we see. And yet we accept it happily. Photography has become a fascination but it is dependent on its knowing audience – we all know that an actress really looks ten years older, yet we will buy the age-reducing lotion her unreal image is representing. We have been duped and have become unshockable. We assume images have been artificially created. We are complicit in their creation.

However, digital trickery is not always the culprit. There exists photograph of a tiger feeding what she believes to be her cubs [google images: piglets with tiger] In reality, her real cubs had died so the zoo substituted piglets wrapped in their pelts. It seems trickery can even be perpetrated on the animal world!

Photographers and digital manipulators have yet to surpass the expertise with which the nature can enhance and camouflage itself. The grasshopper in Doug Aghass' image [www. Amazing Insect Camouflage.com] is barely discernable. The natural world has its own in built Photoshop: phyllium giganteum's eyes and antennae barely reveal the whereabouts of its head. Early botanists believed that leaf insects actually incorporated the foliage they mimicked. As Royal Society Fellow Richard Bradley wrote in 1759: "The insect is nourished by the juices of the tree … and at the fall of the leaf, drops from the tree with the leaves growing to its body like wings, then walks about."

Digital imaging distils the world's multifarious textures, along with human blemishes, into smooth façades. Sceptically we are no longer satisfied with the unsettling truth of our physical shortcomings. We have standardized and diminished ourselves into a muted homogeneity. We have betrayed our trust in photography and in ourselves.

Yet duplicity has been practised almost since photography was invented – we just have got much better at it. Sir Conan Doyle fell under the spell of what became known as the Cottingley Fairies [www.cottingley.net]. As a spiritualist, he interpreted them as evidence of psychic phenomena. He was commissioned to write an article on fairies for the Christmas 1920 edition of The Strand Magazine and even went so far as to ask both Kodak and Ilford to verify the images were genuine. Amazingly, it was only in the 1980s that Elsie and Frances publicly admitted their famous fairies had been faked.

Today we are masters at deception. It is not a question of liking or disliking digital phenomena- it is part of our lives. Perception and recognition are highly subjective; beauty as ever is in the eye of the beholder. Lucian Freud called Rembrandt's portraits "brown and disgusting"![8] The spectator need only be circumspect or, at least, be willing to suspend disbelief. There is nothing new under the sun, and if there is, a photographer can be relied upon to make it appear commonplace. It is, perhaps, no longer sceptical to suspect that this is how we like things. The truth, the whole truth, and nothing but the truth – that is, of course, unless you can improve upon it…

REFERENCES

David Sylvester 'Interviews with Francis Bacon' p. 37
David Sylvester 'Interviews with Francis Bacon' p.39
Erwin Panofsky Early Netherlandish Painting New York & London (1971) Vol 1 p.194
http://www.photoquotes.com/showquotes.aspx?id=17&name=Erwitt,Elliott>
 Elliott Erwitt - On the question: "How do you feel about the digital photography explosion?" Interview with Elliott on photoshopsupport.com
Marina Vaizey 'The Artist as Photographer' p.167
Shearer West 'Portraiture' p.11 (Oxford Press 2004)
The Oxford Dictionary of Quotations p.644 no.17

---

[8] William Feaver 'Lucian Freud' p.13.

Chapter 21

SCEPTICISM AND THE ARMY

*Nigel Chancellor**
Research Associate at the Centre of South Asian Studies,
University of Cambridge, UK

INTRODUCTION

The link between a sceptical truth based only on the certainty of human experience, and a cynical disbelief in the sincerity of human motives has been proved in history, and no less by military history. 'Rude and licentious soldiery' may, like the ancient cynic Diogenese of Sinope (c.412- 323BC) dream of living in a bath tub and of shameless excess in the street, especially after days and nights fighting a ruthless enemy determined to drive them from a mud fort in central Helmand. Yet, for the professional soldiers in today's British Army, the life they have chosen is one of true Cynical 'virtue'; isolated from opportunities for greed and power by service to the common good; the strict practice of 'mens sana in corpore sano', and for officers, both commissioned and non-commissioned, an authority which is never less than fulfilling the covenant of care for those who must obey their orders. In the modern idiom, there is also a tangible connection between the Army and Cartesian scepticism concerning anything or anybody who has not passed the test of empirical experience. It is not just a subjective view looking outwards to the Army's political masters, it also suggests a raft of

---

[*] Nigel Chancellor is a Research Associate at the Centre of South Asian Studies, University of Cambridge, former Domus Bursar and Staff Fellow in History at Trinity Hall, Cambridge, and current Director of the Jawaharlal Nehru Memorial Trust. His area of research is state formation and political development in the State of Mysore, 1700-1920.

divisions and fissures within the immutable ethos of British military practice forged over three hundred years. This chapter draws on the experiences of a former Guards officer of the '60s, and reflects on the generic scepticism that exists to-day within what Blanning calls, the state's agency of 'legitimate force'. [1].

A first encounter with military scepticism as a new officer cadet at the Royal Military Academy Sandhurst (motto 'Serve to Lead') was the realisation that so far as the Non-Commissioned staff were concerned not a minute should pass without reminding the cadets that their aspiration to lead men into battle was at best a waste of valuable time, and at worst an insult to a proud service; 'You call me 'Sir' because I tell you , I call you 'Sir' because I have to', summed up the poorly disguised distain with which this powerful cadre regarded the officers of the future. The system gave Sergeant Instructors considerable license to first break down and then rebuild personalities to a predetermined model; those who had an excuse to be outside this process were never forgiven. Thus, the established Church of England was the official religion. Every Sunday the whole academy was paraded and marched to Church with a band, except for declared 'Roman Catholics and others (Muslims and practicing Jews)' who were ordered to leave the parade as public dissenters from the system, whose patriotism appeared questionable, or at least in some doubt. Cadets filed into the Academy chapel, their studded boots clattering on the marble slabs. Should any cadet forget to remove his cap, a terrifying voice would quickly appear at his ear in a stage whisper that could be heard by all present, 'Take yer 'at orf in the 'ouse of God - PILLOCK!'. Officer Cadets from Commonwealth or defence treaty countries such as Jordan, Ghana, or Somalia often received special treatment. 'Now pay attention, we shall now march in three ranks from Victory College to the Headquarters building, and because it is dark and we have no lights, we'll ask Mr Musa to march at the front of the column so that his teeth will reflect the headlights of oncoming vehicles'. Officer Cadet Gunnawardana from Sri Lanka was asked a question on Sandhurst intelligence during a pause in a drill parade, 'What is the name of the Commandant?' failure to give the correct answer would see the diminutive cadet marching at full speed with arms flailing across several playing fields to a statue of Queen Victoria where he would halt, salute and after a pause salute again, about turn about and quick march back to the drill squad. 'Well ', said the Sergeant, 'What did she say?' Failure to give the correct answer could result in a second trek to interrogate the Queen Empress.

At another level, officer instructors regarded potential recruits to their own world as a polyglot of social variants who must be moulded into the physical and mental persona of a 'Sandhurst officer'. Cadets were 'encouraged' and occasionally instructed to dress in a particular style of 'plain clothes' consisting of knife edge pressed trousers made from fawn cavalry twill cloth, highly polished brown shoes, a tweed jacket with Sandhurst tie, a long regulation army riding mackintosh of rubberised cotton, brown leather gloves, the whole bizarre image topped off by a brown felt trilby hat set on top of a head shorn of hair for two inches above the ears. For those who enthusiastically embraced this stylistic model, points were awarded towards the 'Character Grading' element of the final order of merit from which selection for posts in regiments and corps was subsequently made. Hordes of such mutant clones could be seen every Saturday after 1200hrs, crowding onto the London trains at Camberley station. Alternatively, serious sceptics in contemporary clothes could be spotted heading out of the academy grounds by obscure side exits on bicycles to where ancient and barely roadworthy cars were hidden deep amongst the rhododendron bushes of Surrey. Once loaded up and the riding macs disgarded, these chariots headed up the A30 to basement flats in South Kensington or nurses hostels in Pimlico for a few hours 'rest and recuperation'; the whole process being reversed to report back by 2359hrs. For hard core sceptics who were being punished by 'Restrictions', confined to barracks in uniform, the loss of visits to London could be inverted with the help of a loyal girlfriend who would travel to Camberley against the flow, then to be smuggled into the cadet's small room for a day on a narrow iron bedstead interrupted every four hours when he went off to be inspected or drilled.

It became clear that there were two sorts of officer instructors at the Royal Military Academy, those who subscribed wholeheartedly to the cloning process of 'Character Grading', and those who did not. The first group largely represented officers in the technical and service corps who were products of the system, and the officers of the 'teeth arms' made up of infantry and cavalry regiments who by and large did the fighting; in the middle were engineers and artillery regiments who were both technocrats and combat soldiers. In other words, Sandhurst revealed the first major systemic fissure associated with scepticism, that the Army's officer corps was and still is divided by class, both sides mutually suspicious of the other, with that suspicion becoming more focussed as it translates into the senior ranks of the chain of command. At its heart, the class issue was embedded in the regimental system which marked every officer with a distinctive 'family' identity from the moment he joined his battalion as a new Second-Lieutenant. From the outset, this new identity was defined by the regiment's distinctive uniform with all the historic references to its foundation and subsequent battle honours. For example, the Cameronians or Scottish Rifles carried their weapons into church and placed guards around the building to restate their origins as the Covenanters who had forcibly rejected the Church of England in favour of the Church of Scotland; or the Grenadier Guards who were awarded the unique right to wear the bearskin cap as a battle honour for defeating Napoleon's bearskin capped Imperial Grenadiers at Waterloo; or, the Gloucestershire Regiment who wear their badge both in the front and at the back of their caps to recall being surrounded by a Chinese Division at the battle of the Imjin River in the Korean War of 1956; the list goes on....

Customs in uniform which reflect a regiment's origins play a part in defining group identity. For example, many older county regiments have contrasting histories arising from their origins in the English civil war depending on whether they fought for the King or were part of Cromwell's New Model Army against the monarch. Similarly, kilted Highland regiments reflect the clan origins of their founders with all the associated implications for the Cameron Highlanders (Cameron of Lochiel) and the Seaforth Highlanders (Mackenzie) who fought for Charles Stewart in the rebellion of 1745; alternatively, Campbell's Argyles and the Black Watch were raised to police the highlands, and fought for King George against the Pretender's loyal clans. It is the prevailing custom in one highland regiment for the Commanding officer to have priority in front of the Mess fire with kilt raised to warm his naked buttocks; a privilege denied to the 'trewsered' officers of the King's lowland regiments. Consequently, drinking 'the loyal toast' to the reigning sovereign took on special significance and became mandatory in Officers' Messes of all regiments of the line from Charles II onwards. Guards regiments were excluded from this order because they were the Sovereign's Household troops whose loyalty, in theory, was not in question. Loyalty to the Crown for a line regiments was defined by the Union flag forming its 'Regimental Colour'. The Colours represent the heart of a regiment's identity and were carried into battle by two Second Lieutenants or Ensigns defining the centre of a regiment's line in the face of the enemy. Although the Crimea War saw the last battles in which colours were carried, they still accompany a regiment on operational duty, as in the Helmand province of Afghanistan today where soldiers fight and die under those colours. In other words, the British regimental system contains many historical elements which provide a very strong identity for those who join that family; 'once a Fusilier, always a Fusilier!' But, for those not of that family, it is a short hop to sceptical judgements and cynical expressions of another unit's fighting worth.

The army as a reflection of historic class differences was never more on show than at the outbreak of the 'war to end all wars'. The men of the British middle class responded to Kitchener's call to enlist and do their duty for King and Country. When the whistle blew on the morning of 1st July 1916 to signal the start of the First Battle of the Somme, 290,000 British infantry soldiers were committed to the attack. The 55,000 who died were led out of their trenches by 3,000 officers, a revolver in one hand and an ash walking stick in the other. They marched steadily across 'no-man's land'to their deaths from the withering fire of the German machine guns. The ordinary soldiers came from rural and industrial communities across Britain; the officers represented a middle class long privileged by social and economic conventions for whom the war was the ultimate test of their unchallenged right to lead and govern British society. Failures of courage, or withdrawal through moral scruples brought personal shame, public disgrace and occasionally death to those who failed to live up to their class responsibilities for national leadership in time of war. Regimental and personal histories of horrific experiences confirm the ethos of regimental solidarity and the venomous scepticism with which collective memory seeks to find someone to blame, normally the top brass who ask soldiers to go forward to die on badly prepared strategies, ill-equipped, and badly led. What was true for the Somme in 1916, was equally true for the Helmand province of Afghanistan in 2006/7.

During the horrific battle of Passchendaele in 1917, a young staff officer returned to his Divisional Headquarters to report to the Guards General. He arrived just in time for dinner and found himself placed next to the great man at a table covered with a white linen cloth and regimental silver. During dinner, the General listened to what the young officer had to report of the terrible hardships being experienced by the men in the front-line trenches after three weeks of continuous rain. The officer was so engrossed in his narrative that he failed to notice the General's rising blood pressure as the port decanter remained firmly stuck at the junior officer's right elbow, until with an outburst the General exploded, ' Never mind the weather, the men have their ground-sheets , PASS THE PORT!' It has become an invariable custom of the Grenadiers that this shameful disregard for the first responsibility of officers for their soldier's welfare should be remembered to the present day by the table conversation turning to 'ground-sheets' every time the port becomes stuck at someone's elbow (junior Fellows please note!).

From a soldier's perspective, degrees of scepticism or the lack of it towards life in the Army depends on task and location, whether he is married , other members of his squad, immediate superiors(non-commissioned officers), and finally officers. One certainty for infantry soldiers is that no officer can be trusted with a compass to lead a night march across country. Active service operations such as Northern Ireland or in Afghanistan are generally regarded as 'Corporal's wars' because the majority of tasks, such as passive or aggressive patrolling, and road blocks are led by non-commissioned officers with commissioned officers usually providing tactical direction and essential logistic support; of which the most important task of all is to ensure that the soldiers receive their mail from home. But, in the Afghanistan campaign of 2006/07, aggressive action against Taliban compounds by one Guards company resulted in just one commissioned officer out of five being classified as fit for duty after a month of continuous fighting. [2]. For the soldiers, reliance on the support of the next man is crucial, whether it is knowing that if you go out the night before a parade in London, when you get back all your kit will have been cleaned and laid out by your mates, or in an action where you need covering fire before moving over open ground in the face of deadly enemy fire, you know without question that support will be there to answer the lurking personal scepticism of fear. The bonds formed by performing well as a team within a regime of the strictest discipline can carry a soldier through the Queen's Birthday parade in front of millions or in a vicious fire-fight, are strong and lasting. When the body-bags and paraplegics return, the ranks close no less tightly to support the families; death and maiming applies indiscriminately to officers and men alike.

On joining the 1st Battalion of the 'First, or Grenadier Regiment of Foot Guards', a young Second-Lieutenant, or Ensign, must immediately report to the Adjutant. Acting on directions I entered a detached two storied building expecting to find the Adjutant's office on the ground floor. I pulled open the swing doors to the corridor, and was confronted by the largest man I had ever seen in uniform who was holding the second largest man by the lapels of his uniform jacket so that his boots were clear of the ground. The two men swayed from side to side in a rhythmic dance with the suspended man's head bouncing off the corridor walls in time to the larger man's intonation, 'You- are- a lazy- idle- guardsman', then catching sight of me added, 'Adjutant- up-stairs'. Earlier than anticipated, I had just encountered the Battalion Regimental Sergeant-Major. Some months later this peacetime colossus conducted the annual ritual of 'spring drills', in which a Guards Battalion is generally sharpened up by two weeks of unremitting drill parades for every member of the Battalion including all officers except the Adjutant and the Commanding Officer. After three days of sweaty hell, the colossus suddenly stopped the proceedings and in a fog horn voice announced that, 'two thirds of the battalion is workin' 'ard, but the other two thirds is - BONE IDLE !'. In 2007, a successor Regimental Sergeant Major carried a critically wounded guardsman who had lost a leg and most of his stomach in an IED explosion for over two kilometers at night to the rescue helicopter. In 2009, during his second tour, the same Sergeant Major was shot dead by a rogue Afghan policeman he was training in Helmand Province.

Amongst those mandarins in the civil service who believe there is always a better way of doing things, there is a former Permanent Secretary and Master of an Oxford College who used to walk daily down Birdcage Walk, past Wellington Barracks and Buckingham Palace on his way to the then Ministry of Education. Through the railings of the barracks he could see the drill rituals that had moved battalions of infantry a thousand strong around battle fields in close formation from the time of Marlborough, Wellington, and the Crimea; 'surely', he sceptically suggested to me,' in this modern day and age, there must be a better way of training soldiers to fight?' And of course he was right if drill was the only element in the process. What he didn't see was the exhaustive training of a modern infantryman in all the technical and weapon skills necessary to succeed in Northern Ireland, Iraq, and Afghanistan. Like the Royal Marines and the Parachute Regiment, the Guards have an extra dimension to their self belief and collective cohesion as elite fighting units. As 'Household' troops, the Guards hold a unique position through their part in every state occasion and in most aspects of royal ceremonial. The Queen's (or King's) Company of the Grenadiers provides the bearer party for the late sovereign's coffin at the state funeral; the Company's camp colour is the only item laid on the coffin at interment. The selected bearer party is always ready to be called upon, and may be encountered in barracks or camp quietly rehearsing, including 'adopting a mournful aspect' while lowering the 'practice coffin' into a vehicle inspection pit. Selected officers move on to hold positions in the court, organizing and planning state occasions, royal weddings, jubilees, and state funerals. Some are appointed as personal staff and private secretaries to members of the royal family. These military courtiers bring a respectful scepticism to their work, suggesting that at one level the considerable personal power of the Royal Family must be mediated by advice against behaviour which might otherwise harm the public image of the monarchy or threaten the institution itself.

It is said, that following a series of ineffective personal staff officers, the Prince of Wales was counseled by some of the senior military courtiers to invite a brilliant young Guards General to resign from the army and join his staff as Private Secretary. For these courtiers, the agenda was simple, the Prince of Wales's affair with the wife of a prominent serving officer in the court was becoming the cause of public embarrassment, with the potential to become a constitutional issue. He must be persuaded to end the affair. The General resigned from the army and took up his duties at St James's Palace, where in due course the sensitive issue was raised by the new secretary. The consequence was an immediate and heated outburst, at the end of which the General was told to clear his desk and leave the palace immediately; he has remained unemployed ever since. In a less serious reminiscence, the Irish Guards officer employed as the Private Secretary to Prince Andrew and the Duchess of York felt he had no option than to resign when Fergie's use of her royal position to promote 'Budgie the Helicopter' became a public relations disaster. His exit from Buckingham Palace was halted before he reached the main gate when a messenger ran up asking him to urgently reconsider his decision as it had been overlooked that there would be no-one left to look after Prince Edward; he duly returned to the Palace. At the other end of the spectrum, so to speak, protracted periods of peacetime ceremonial duties created boredom for the ordinary soldier. Tall, good looking men in uniform found that life in London offered unusual ways of making some extra money. When a Conservative MP was charged with an act of indecency in St James's Park, one sceptical wag was prompted to comment, 'there are Tories at the bottom of my guardsman!'

The ultimate act of military scepticism is mutiny. Throughout its modern history British soldiers have mutinied, rarely in the face of the enemy but more frequently in the face of bureaucratic insensitivity and ineptitude. In 1956, the Third Battalion of the Grenadiers was dispatched to Malta as part of the Anglo-French expeditionary force tasked with regaining control of the Suez Canal following Egyptian nationalisation. Prior to this emergency operation, the battalion was in the process of running down its establishment to a skeleton formation known as 'suspended animation'; consequently, the majority of its officers and guardsmen were on demobilization leave; many had found new civilian jobs. With the call up for Suez, the running down process went into reverse as the battalion was hurriedly reconstituted. The Grenadiers were given a reserve role and found themselves in July 1956 encamped on a disused Maltese airfield in canvas tents where they slept on straw filled sacks on the runway. The Commanding Officer took the view that the 'demob' culture he judged pervaded the battalion must be reversed by a programme of exhausting field exercises from one end of the island to the other. In the event, the disastrous Anglo-French' Operation Musketeer', which started on the 29th October, was over when all allied forces were withdrawn by 22nd December. The Grenadiers in reserve were not called upon to fight. None the less, they remained on the Maltese airfield long after outraged international reaction to the whole Suez debacle made it abundantly clear there would be no further military action. For these recalled reservists, every day away from their newly found civilian jobs put their post Suez livelihood at risk. As the weeks of inaction passed from December into the spring of a new year, the Grenadiers felt increasingly sceptical about the government's strategy and the Whitehall bureaucrats who kept them isolated from their civilian jobs on a far off runway. Eventually, enough was judged to be enough and as one, the battalion's straw bedding was set on fire. A Guards' mutiny finally concentrated the minds of the bureaucrats, and the Suez reservists were quickly on their way home.

The wiff of mass dissent was also in the air ten years after Suez, when rumours spread that Harold Wilson, then Prime Minister, was considering using the army against the white minority government of the Southern Rhodesia colony led by Ian Smith, who proclaimed a 'Unilateral Declaration of Independence' from Whitehall in 1965. There were some officers who had made lasting friendships with white Rhodesian cadets during their time together at the Royal Military Academy. These white supremacy sympathisers didn't take kindly to the prospect of being ordered to kill their old chums and in conversation at least had the bravado to suggest a refusal to obey any such order. In the event, force was not used to recover the recalcitrant colony, but recent research suggests a real concern in the Ministry of Defense that the issue of loyalty should not be put to the test.

The largest mutiny of British military officers ever recorded also concerned a bureaucracy unable to connect the institution of government with the long established association of personal honour in the performance of military service.

In 1809, over one thousand British officers of the East India Company's Madras Army mutinied by refusing to take an oath of loyalty to the civilian governor of the Presidency. They were immediately relieved of their commands and ordered to proceed to various coastal stations to await trial by courts martial. As a consequence, an army of over a quarter of a million Indian troops which then maintained only a tenuous British control over southern India, was deprived of 95% of its European officers for almost nine months, until the belated intervention of the Governor-General. During this time any serious uprising could have changed the subsequent history of the British in India. The issue concerned the introduction of bureaucratic controls over the East India Company army by a civilian Governor who believed that power over the army, including officer appointments should be vested in him, in spite of the customary practice that the Commander in Chief should be a member of the Madras Council of Government with responsibility for all military matters. Instead of justifying these changes as necessary bureaucratic reforms, the Governor falsely claimed that some senior military appointments carried private financial benefits for the holder which defrauded the public purse. Thus the 'White Mutiny' became a highly charged issue of honour between the officer corps and the new forms of bureaucratic government associated with the burgeoning British Empire in India. An earlier confrontation between a Madras Governor and the then C-in-C had been settled in 1786 by a duel in Hyde Park. The confrontation was regarded as a matter of corporate honour, the one-legged General defending the honour of the Madras Army against an implied charge of corporate cowardice in the face of the enemy by the civilian Governor. In the event, the latter was wounded and honour was seen to be satisfied and recorded for public consumption in a precise account by the seconds and published in the *Gentleman's Magazine*. There would be no duel to settle the expatriate mutiny of 1809, but the confrontation with the governor over loyalty to state institutions marked a watershed between personal ethics and public service, and between public service and the state's responsibilities to its servants.

Some might argue that ever since the development of the modern state, the relationship between its core institutions and the state itself has become a matter of mutual scepticism, and never more so than with those who form 'the legitimate force' by which the state defends itself. The modern governments of Thatcher and Blair manipulated expectations of military capability beyond what was practically possible because they knew that their military commanders once presented with 'the challenge' would try to achieve 'the impossible' at minimum extra cost. They also knew that an overstretched military poses less of a political threat and a diminished financial liability. On the other hand, ordinary soldiers believe they are invariably under paid and under resourced; if the Generals can be managed successfully by their political masters, the soldiers claims will go largely unnoticed, unless and until their grievances become a matter of public concern and consequently a political issue in its own right. The understated military case for rearmament in 1938 set against the sceptical case for political appeasement reflects the first, as much as the flow of paraplegics and body bags from Afghanistan represents a very public issue to-day. Since 1918, there has never been a greater degree of scepticism in the Army than now through the government's failure to honour 'the military covenant' it drew up in 2000, but has refused until now to make law. The covenant declares 'that those who are called upon to die in the service of their country should expect the state to provide fair treatment for themselves and their families, and that they should be sustained and rewarded'. The reality has been a Treasury driven campaign to reduce the cost of rehabilitation care and personal injury claims from seriously wounded soldiers and their families; leading to national charitable campaigns such as 'Help for Heroes', or single regiment campaigns such as the Grenadiers' who have raised over £2m for their own list of wounded and bereaved to meet the cost deficit.

CONCLUSION

Scepticism in the army threads its way through the fabric of this ancient profession, appearing at times as barely disguised disdain for the objects of its criticism, frequently other soldiers who are judged to be weak links in a system of profound mutual support, or political masters who have no empirical understanding of what they require the army to achieve. As this chapter has shown, not far below the surface of the army's official veneer runs a rich vein of black humour through which many of these sceptical and frequently deeply cynical sentiments are expressed.

The explanation for this invariably ironic comedy lies in the brutality of violent death that is the context of a soldier's life. Humour is part of the mechanism which helps to reconcile a life of ethical behavior with actions of extreme brutality. At its deepest level, scepticism in the army relates to the reality of killing another human being and a soldier's capacity to carry this out as a deliberate act. While the capacity to kill defines the individual soldier, control of its initiation and the level of its proportionality invariably rests with the hierarchy of a combat unit. Clearly, a great deal depends on the circumstances of combat, but the ability to act with extreme brutality and violence as a function of soldiering is a self-evident truth, it is what soldiers 'do'. The evolution of Libya's civilian revolutionaries into a semi-cohesive force of organized brutality is a recent graphic example of this process. Evidence taken from those returning from combat in Afghanistan reveals both the fear of facing a skilled and cunning enemy, and the 'enjoyment' of killing individual Taliban in large numbers on a daily basis. The mindset for brutality is frequently enhanced by the death or maiming of comrades. Thus an ability to kill, a sense of proportionality in its execution, and the resilience to absorb the death of close friends, informs the degree of scepticism with which individual soldiers and regiments experience the realities of combat. Of course, the British public should be shocked and outraged by incidents such as the brutal killing in detention of the Iraqui hotel receptionist by soldiers of the Queen's Lancashire Regiment in Basra, but they should not be surprised that the capacity for such brutality exists; it is essential that it does, but deployed in combat and with proportionality and discipline.

The need to reconcile the dichotomy of ethical violence also begs some historical analysis. At its most basic level, the performance of soldiering has always been a brutal business, often practiced by men of high principle and sensitivity. In his upcoming magisterial work on the life of Descartes, Timothy Reiss shows the impact of Descartes' four years of military service in the armies of Maurice of Nassau and Maximillian of Bavaria on his search for truth. [3]. Reiss suggests that the values of virtuous soldiering; working for the commonwealth, exclusion from opportunities for wealth and power, adhering to a strict personal regime of abstinence and physical fitness, the application of mathematics, and a commitment if necessary to die for the head of state, provided some of the empirical certainties of Descartes' life and by extension the direction of his philosophical thought. There is much in his experience of military values in the early seventeenth century which sits comfortably with the ethics of British military leadership to-day, extending as they do from Cromwell's New Model Army of 1645. Equally, there are enough examples from current and recent conflicts such as Iraq to support a healthy scepticism of British military behaviour, especially under fire and in the treatment of suspected insurgents. In the most effective units, managing the dychotomy of controlled and uncontrolled brutality is acknowledged as the foundation of active service training. At its best, the soldiers' life provides a compelling virtuous circle; protecting its members from the scepticism associated with failure to perform in action, the fear of death or maiming, the random logic of who will die, and the guilt of those who return safely. Of course, it helps if all this takes place within the context of 'a just war' defined by Parliament or the United Nations; but, that must be the subject of another chapter....

REFERENCES

[1] TWC Blanning, *The French Revolutionary Wars, 1787 -1802* (London, 1996), p. 82.
[2] Patrick Hennessey, *The Junior Officers Reading Club: Killing Time and Fighting Wars* (London, 2009), p. 303.
[3] Timothy J Reiss, *'Descartes, Philosophy, and the Public Sphere: Archaeology of an Epochal Transition'*. Timothy Reiss is Emeritus Professor of Comparative Literature in the University of New York.

ECONOMICS, LAW AND POLITICS

In: Scepticism: Hero and Villain
Editors: R. Calne and W. O'Reilly

ISBN: 978-1-62417-783-5
© 2013 Nova Science Publishers, Inc.

Chapter 22

ECONOMIC SCEPTICISM

Andrew Verity
BBC Financial Presenter and Correspondent, Manchester, UK

INTRODUCTION

Right now the leaders of the world's most advanced economies are struggling to avert what threatens to become the second global economic shock in less than four years.

The Eurozone debt crisis is proving difficult to contain and continually threatens to cause a new banking crisis which could pitch the world into a slump even deeper than the last. What I will argue is that both the current crisis in the Eurozone and the credit-fuelled boom and bust that led to the banking crisis of 2008 were caused by a failure, on a colossal scale, of scepticism.

It is only in these crises, and because of them, that we have learned just how much money was riding on unwarranted economic assumptions. International investors, politicians, central banks, ratings agencies, mortgage lenders and thousands of ordinary members of the house-buying public, all failed to be appropriately sceptical, in spite of vast financial commitments running into trillions of dollars.

It was the realisation that those economic assumptions were unwarranted that set off the panic in financial markets. These giant financial crises are best understood, in other words, as a re-assertion of scepticism. And I want to venture an explanation as to why, on both a personal and political level, we suspended our scepticism for so long – based on something economic theory is not so great at understanding: our less rational, more emotional side.

TOO LITTLE SCEPTICISM

Here are some of the assumptions that led to the Eurozone crisis and the global economic shock of 2008, starting with the latter. During the late 1980s and throughout the 1990s, politicians in the US and the UK de-regulated their financial services sectors. In the US, a key provision of the Glass-Steagall Act was repealed, allowing retail banks to diversify into investment banking activities - which, since 1933, had been forbidden. In the UK, banks were released from regulations that limited the type of activity they were involved in and the amount of borrowing and lending they were allowed to do. The policy makers who approved that de-regulation knew that it meant banks would be able to borrow and lend far more, and to take on greater risks.

Central bankers also knew, when they cut interest rates dramatically in the wake of the dotcom bust and the September 11th attacks, that there was a risk of an upsurge in cheap credit that might cause an asset bubble – for example, in house prices – with all the risks that it might burst, as it had in the past with unpleasant consequences. But those who agreed with the likes of Alan Greenspan, chairman of the board of the US central bank the Federal Reserve from 1987 to 2006, assumed that trying to limit the risks banks were allowed to take would only hold them back and constrain economic growth: the market knew best. They assumed that the banks would, in accordance with the Darwinian law of the free market, ensure their own survival first and foremost – and therefore contain the amount of borrowing they did, and the risks they took on to their balance sheets. They assumed that they would do so not least because if they took too many risks the bank would be allowed to fail and go bust, and with it their livelihoods. They assumed bankers were responsible, and not the sort to cave into the temptation to ramp up their bonuses by ramping up the risks they were taking with other people's money.

International investors, from hedge funds to pension funds, assumed that it was possible to buy an investment that consistently beat the returns on other investments without taking on any extra risk. They knew that these too-good-to-be-true investments, known as collateralised debt obligations (CDOs), would give them a stream of income which came out of mortgage repayments, and that some of the mortgage repayers were "subprime" ie borrowers with poor credit ratings. But they assumed that their money was safe, because CDOs were designed by clever people with big mathematical brains. Oh – and the ratings agencies (who were assumed to know what they were doing), had given them a triple A rating. So they poured billions into them. So confident were investment banks about the soundness of CDOs that they offered investors the chance to get a superior return just like the one on CDOs, without linking them to actual mortgages. Instead, they would simply mimic the performance of the CDOs without buying the underlying mortgage-backed securities, assuming there was no extra risk in that. Companies like the US insurer AIG assumed that they could sell hundreds of billions of dollars-worth of insurance against these CDOs defaulting (credit default swaps) and collect the resulting premiums, without jeopardising their company's future or their own. And the banks assumed they could create off-balance sheet vehicles, or "shadow banks", borrowing and lending each other billions with synthetic CDOs as security, without jeopardising the integrity of the banking system and with it the whole world's economic future.

The ratings agencies rarely examined the quality of the underlying portfolio of mortgage loans, and the repayments therefrom, on which CDOs were based. Instead they assumed that, because the subprime mortgages were only a small part of the portfolio of mortgages supporting a CDO, that even if they defaulted, the CDOs would remain secure. The companies that lent the mortgages that were securitised into CDOs assumed that the subprime borrowers would be able to repay even if interest rates went up. They assumed that if interest rates rose and their monthly payments jumped after the initial discount period ended, they would be able to re-mortgage. Separately, many homebuyers both prime and subprime assumed that house prices would continue, broadly, to rise, so it was ok to stretch to that giant mortgage.

Trillions of dollars was riding on these assumptions. As we have learned at great cost, every one of them proved false. As mortgage default rates rose in 2007, the penny dropped: many if not most of the CDOs were worthless.

Suddenly, scepticism was everywhere - in the shape of an excruciating credit crunch. Alan Greenspan and other devotees of the free market had their faith (for that is what it turned out to be) shaken. Banks had no idea how much they had lost, nor how much other lenders had lost – so they became reluctant to lend to each other. That forced through a properly sceptical, realistic assessment of the true value of CDOs and other financial instruments. That assessment kicked a massive hole in banks' balance sheets. That led to the banking crisis of the autumn of 2008, which forced taxpayers to step in and rescue the banks. at great cost, from their own folly.

Trillions of euros was also riding on a set of dubious assumptions in the Eurozone crisis. In the early 1990s, the criteria set out in the Treaty of Maastricht for member states to enter the Euro *seemed* to acknowledge an important economic reality: a currency union could only succeed if its member states had one attitude (and not 17) to managing government finances and to stewardship of the economy. Limits were set on the acceptable size of trade and budget deficits, overall indebtedness and other economic indicators. The European authorities in Brussels assumed that when Greece said it had met the entry criteria, nothing untoward was going on. They also assumed that Italy meant what it said when it promised to cut its national debt in the coming years rather than let it grow. They assumed that, if an emergency cropped up in future, the European institutions such as the European central bank would have the financial muscle to deal with it; or, if they needed more firepower, Germany and France would be prepared to support that.

You might have thought that losing billions in the credit crunch would have made international investors and bond traders more sceptical – less inclined to listen to their star traders and more inclined to listen to their risk management teams. But in many cases, the same banks, brokers, bond funds, hedge funds and sovereign wealth funds that had invested in CDOs had also invested heavily in bonds issued by heavily indebted Eurozone governments like Portugal, Ireland, Italy, Greece and Spain (collectively known on the bond markets as "the Pigs"). They assumed, crucially, that they deserved their triple-A ratings from the rating agencies, meaning they could borrow at cheaper rates. After all, Greece might lack fiscal discipline. But, they assumed, if it ran into trouble, they would always get their money back, because this peripheral European country had the might of the great German economy behind it. They assumed that if Greece threatened to default, Germany and France would step in. And because of these unquestioned assumptions, countries like Greece were able to borrow at far cheaper rates, and therefore to sustain unsustainable debts for far longer, then they would have done outside the euro.

Again, all of these assumptions were false. Scepticism has now re-asserted itself in the sovereign debt markets, where traders are no longer so sure that if they lend money (by buying bonds) to the Greek, Italian, Portuguese or Spanish governments, that they will get all of it back. As I write they have become so sceptical of the Italian government's ability to manage its debts that markets imply that Italy would have to pay more than 7 per cent to borrow new long-term funds – a higher rate than it can sustain. That rate would be lower if markets were not so sceptical about the capacity of European institutions to calm the crisis. If they could believe that there would always be a buyer of the bonds in the shape of a viable monetary authority, they might relax. But that would require a massive expansion of the role of the European Central Bank and other institutions. So long as Germany is unwilling to countenance that, the bond market's scepticism about the euro will deepen.

The result of the adoption of all these assumptions, and the lack of rigorous questioning of them, has been two giant financial crises, both of them threatening recession or worse, in less than four years. Why were so many clever people, in charge of so much money, so unprepared to be duly sceptical *before* these crises took hold? After all, there were thousands of people employed in both the private and the public sector whose job it was to be sceptical: civil servants, regulators, central bankers, risk managers, legal advisers, even "bears" on the trading floors who bet against a certain asset class. Some of them were indeed sceptics. Why, when so much money was at stake, did their views go unheeded?

I believe the answer lies in factors which you might loosely group together as the "human factor". The failure to be duly sceptical in these crucial matters was down to aspects of human nature that, economists acknowledge, play a vital role in the way economic developments unfold, even though they defy any attempt to measure, quantify or predict them. That human factor includes of course what Keynes called "animal spirits" – mass sentiments like greed and fear, optimism and anxiety, which find expression in the ups and downs of the financial markets. For example, an investor's desire for a great return, (and therefore a great bonus) may lead them not to press too hard to learn the provenance and mechanics of the CDO, or a Greek government bond, before committing sizeable funds to it. In this particular instance, scepticism is trumped by a form of wishful thinking caused by greed. But by the "human factor" I do not just mean greed and fear.

It also includes the desire among politicians to be re-elected or to make history; the effect of corporate lobbying on policymaking; the natural reluctance of analysts, central bankers and politicians to challenge the prevailing view; and the inclination of too many ordinary consumers and borrowers to entertain flawed economic ideas not because they are true but because they make them feel better off: for example, that rising house prices are "good news".

POLITICS VS ECONOMICS

In the 1990s, the German and French governments wanted monetary union – a big economic change. But it was every bit as much a political goal as an economic one. They did not allow countries to enter the Euro *only if* they met a strict interpretation of the Maastricht criteria for entry. It is now clear that they were quite happy to welcome with open arms those countries that met those criteria only loosely. The rigour of the economic analysis was subordinate to what would really enable Europe's leaders to change history: the higher goal of a larger and more closely united Europe. And behind that lay the desire to move on from the past and strengthen Europe's role in the world.

It is only human. Politicians have to get re-elected, and they hope to leave politics having achieved something they can look back on. In a clash between political and economic priorities, the political imperative may trump the economic.

That mattered little while the Eurozone remained free from crisis. The Euro's international reception was, for years, a great success. The pound sterling was marginalised even more than before. The euro was even talked of as a challenger to the dominance of the US dollar, a potential new reserve currency for the world, as governments from China to Brazil started selling dollars and buying into the euro.

But in the euro crisis of 2011 to 2012, that clash between the political and economic imperatives has been thrown into sharp relief. Among some of the more significant moments of the crisis have been the following: the then Greek prime minister George Papandreou threw months of careful international negotiation into doubt, threatening his own country with bankruptcy by the apparently innocent act of asking it to hold a vote. In a similar vein, the German chancellor Angela Merkel dismissed a plan to hold the Eurozone together by turning the European Central Bank into an effective monetary authority – because German voters fear they would be writing a blank cheque (it would require a referendum she could never win). The British prime minister David Cameron has refused to hold a referendum on EU membership, saying that it was in no-one's economic interest.

At the summit of leaders of the world's 20 largest economies in November 2011, leaders of west European democracies were furious about Greece's decision to hold a referendum. Stop for a moment and absorb that: democratic leaders were livid with the Prime Minister of the birthplace of democracy, for proposing to ask a democratic question.

In a Socratic spirit, let us ask an ancient question: why? Why should it be that the Greek prime minister should throw the Eurozone and indeed the entire financial world into a panic by the simply act of offering his electorate the chance to vote? After all, the effect on their lives will be profound. In exchange for billions of Euros in bailout money to keep their country inside the Eurozone and solvent, millions are being asked to accept deep cuts in salaries and pensions. And many have lost their livelihoods altogether.

Similarly, if Angela Merkel has come to believe it is right to fork out to save the Eurozone, why can't she persuade her voters? And if David Cameron believes it is right to stay in the Europe Union in spite of its troubles, why does he have no faith in his ability to persuade the electorate that what he believes is right?

The answer, of course, is that even if Merkel or Cameron believe there is a rational economic case to make, they fear they might not persuade their electorates, and the vote might not go their way.

Why? For two potential reasons. One is rational: what is in the interest of the economy as a whole may not be in the interest of the individual or their family. Therefore voters might not vote for it. Although austerity may be in the interest of the Greek economy as a whole, Greeks facing higher taxes and lower salaries might feel like turkeys voting for Christmas.

But it goes deeper than this. Even if it *is* demonstrably in a voter's rational economic self-interest to vote for something, they may not be thinking rationally at all. They may be thinking, as we all do, under the influence of their emotions - individual or collective.

Angela Merkel was urged by economists to support a change to the constitution of the European Central Bank so it could use monetary policy to alleviate the pressure on economies in the euro zone.

The proposal to expand the ECB's role would have allowed it to effectively print money – as other central banks can. Some leading economists think that in the context of a threat of deflation and recession, that is a rational thing to do. But Ms Merkel knew very well how hard it would be to make that rational case to German voters. Printing money is perceived as inflationary; and German attitudes to inflation are dictated less by economic analysis and more by the collective memory of the hyperinflation of 1923 (and all that followed).

To a German electorate that craves few things more than to be rid of its past, inflationary policies, economically rational as they may be, are profoundly unappealing. Similarly, even if David Cameron is convinced that the case for keeping the UK in the European Union is the only rational course, he is contending with anti-European sentiment, driven by a certain sense, drawn from history, of what it is to be British.

In the case of Germany or Greece that emotion may be rooted in history – a history of revolt against colonial powers perhaps, or indeed a history scarred by memories of inflation and war. Politicians know that emotions like this, writ large in the political arena, are far more crucial to winning elections than rational economic argument. And that can be another reason why they ignore what is economically sensible in favour of what is politically feasible. The clash between economics and politics, in other words, is also a clash between the rational and the emotional.

EMOTION VS RATIONALITY

It is not merely macroeconomics that is swayed by the human factor. In relation to microeconomics, too – including our own personal finances - our emotions are at often at odds with rationality. Take house prices. In 2005, an exasperated BBC economics editor, Evan Davis, entered the BBC newsroom and cried: "Can we *please* stop saying 'Good news for homeowners – house prices have risen by 2 per cent in one month'? It is *not* good news for homeowners! It is only good news if you're going to move somewhere cheaper or go abroad, or live on the street!"

He was right of course, and was merely reminding the rest of the BBC's team of a basic economic point. But the implications, in the context of the times, were profound. Between 1996 and 2007, nominal house prices in the UK trebled. Millions of people became convinced they had "done well" on the back of an asset that seemed to enrich them, even without any improvement or investment on their part. They might for example, have bought their modest house for £100,000 and it was now worth £300,000. A £200,000 enrichment, more than they could ever possibly save and more than decades of pension contributions might yield. Partly on the back of that hope for easy money, a whole culture of enthusiasm for house and home took off as never before. Highly successful TV series fed the assumption that if you were a little bit clever you could make rapid profits simply by buying and improving more property. Companies sprang up offering motivational seminars encouraging amateur landlords to overcome their fear and borrow more to enrich themselves faster. I have met a number of people who really listened to that message – people who began on average incomes of less than £20,000 who succeeded in buying more than 100 properties. One I came across had borrowed £19 million pounds to do so. The lenders, including the likes of Northern Rock and Bradford and Bingley, were not very sceptical of his applications – in fact, Northern Rock alone extended him more than 20 mortgages. All the lenders wanted to know was that the rent the property could fetch would cover the mortgage, with a little bit to spare. They never asked, or seemingly cared, how many other mortgages they had lent him. This was the true meaning of loose credit (his property empire later went bust).

But the idea that rising house prices had enriched homeowners was, for the vast majority, an illusion – and one that could be exposed with only a modest amount of scepticism. What was crucial to remember was your next likely move in the housing market. You may have bought your house for £100,000 in 1996 and your neighbour's identical property may indeed just have sold in 2007 for £300,000 – a "paper gain" of £200,000. But – unless you were going to leave the country or give up home ownership - how would you realise that gain? What was your next move? If it was UP the housing "ladder" to a larger or more valuable property, it may *feel* like the price rise had made you better able to do so. But the price of the place you wanted to buy would *also* have trebled – from, say £200,000 in 1996 to £600,000 in 2007. So in 1996 you would have needed to borrow another £100,000 more to step up to that larger house of your dreams. But now, in 2007, you would need to borrow £300,000 more, quite possibly putting that move beyond your means.

To use that favourite phrase of economists "all other things being equal", the same pattern is repeated for anyone whose next move will be to a more valuable property. It is not just first-time buyers who are hurt by rising prices. Existing homeowners whose next move in the housing market is to "upsize" will be made not better off, but worse off, by rising house prices. For those who plan to stay put for the rest of their lives, the paper gains on their equity will never be realised – so it makes little difference to them (apart from increasing their capacity to borrow). In fact the only homeowners who benefit from rising house prices are those whose next move is to "downsize" to somewhere smaller or cheaper. Except for them, house price rises diminish, not increase, a homeowner's capacity to buy a necessity of life. Put simply, they diminish your wealth.

The converse is also true. A fall in house prices only harms those who were planning to downsize and take some money OUT of the housing market. For those whose next move will be to up-size (to buy more property or a larger one) a fall in house prices helps them – they can buy more for their money and they will save more on the place they are buying than they will lose on the place they are selling. And for those never planning to sell it makes little difference.

That was the rational way to think of it. But it was not the way that unsceptical homeowners, enthused about their potential profits, *felt* about it. To them, property was simply a marvellous investment, and worth going into debt for. Politicians knew house price rises made homeowners feel prosperous, which had two advantages. One was that it gave them a better chance at the ballot box. Another was that that "feelgood" factor – that comforting knowledge of how much equity they had made - was encouraging homeowners to borrow more against their homes, and to spend more.

In 2003-2006 there were some sceptical voices, such as the UK think tank Capital Economics, who were warning that house prices were way out of line with historic norms: loose lending was causing a house price bubble that was bound, at some point, to burst. If they had been listening, policy makers such as the members of Bank of England's monetary policy committee might in theory have sought to tame that house price inflation in 2004 before it really got out of control, by, for example, raising interest rates. Yet imagine what the UK government's reaction would have been. A rise in interest rates causing house price rises to flatten out or fall, just a year before a general election? What would happen to the feelgood factor then? The Bank of England would almost certainly have been attacked for damaging the feelgood factor and with it the economy, jeopardising its newly won independence.

A modestly rigorous economic analysis shows, with house prices, millions thought they had got rich when they hadn't, and feared a crash when they needn't. For most homeowners, to feel that rising house price rises make us better off, or that a crash would make us worse off, is irrational. Yet what counts when setting policy isn't the rationally analysed effect on people's wealth. It is how, we assume, they "feel" about it.

OPEN TO INFLUENCE

A defender of economics might point out that the sceptical view of the effects of house price rises on wealth comes from economists. It was not then, that economists failed to spot the problem – nor was it a failure of economics as such. It was more that politicians and the voting public were not always listening. Why does it happen this way with economics, that the correct, sceptical view may be put forward, but won't make it on to the policy agenda?

Economics is not a science, not even a dismal one. It does not seek to interrogate its subject as a science would, with scepticism built in.

In macroeconomics at least there is no opportunity for controlled experiment; there is no scientific method, no control group, no null hypothesis that you seek to prove. Instead, like other "social sciences", it seeks to make sense of a morass of complex and sometimes contradictory data and form the best theory it can. That theory will then only be tested by future events. If it is wrong, we will all learn the hard way.

The facts may be clear enough – although arguments abound about the accuracy of data on inflation, GDP and unemployment. But the interpretation is so wide open that it throws up a problem. A monetarist and a Keynesian, for example, can live in the same world and look at the same facts and have completely different conclusions about those facts – and therefore different policy recommendations. The facts are too indeterminate to allow either to refute the other. Therefore policymakers have to make crucial economic decisions not on the force of economic evidence, but on the basis of choosing an interpretation of the facts. And this is the crucial difference between economics and the natural sciences. In physics or biology, a shallow theory, based only loosely on highly selective facts and guesswork, can, in knowledgeable academic circles, be comfortably dismissed. In economics, it might well become government policy.

What becomes crucial, then, is which interpretation of the facts the policymakers are drawn to. Large corporations, especially those who spy a great business opportunity which requires legislation, can afford to employ impressive and persuasive lobbyists, who know how to pitch a policy to a politician. They will seek to show that a policy that is evidently in their own self-interest is nevertheless in the interests of the public as a whole. On the one hand, the lobbyists will dangle the carrot of an anticipated economic benefit, should the policymakers adopt the reform they seek. On the other, they will warn of disaster should their reform not be implemented.

This was exactly what led to the financial de-regulation, without which the debt crises we have been going through would not have happened. The banking lobby knew that banks could expand their business rapidly (and therefore ramp up dividends and pay) if they could succeeded in convincing central banks and regulators in New York and London that the rules were holding them back. Those rules, harking back to earlier crises, required them to set aside a certain amount of capital for every lending activity they were involved in. So, for example, a bank might be prevented from lending or deploying any more than 17 times what they kept in reserve in case something went wrong. The banks wanted those rules to be relaxed.

In London and New York in the 1990s, the lobbyists succeeded. The consequences we now know all too well. The relaxation of capital requirements allowed RBS, for example, to expand rapidly on the back of borrowed money. After de-regulation, this modestly sized regional bank took over the much larger NatWest, then went on to take over the Dutch banking giant ABN Amro, turning itself into a global banking behemoth. But by the time the acquisition was completed, it was massively overborrowed; its borrowings were more than 30 times the amount it set aside in reserve, leaving its finances so stretched it was highly vulnerable to any economic shock that came along. Without de-regulation, the taxpayer would never have had to fork out more than £40 billion pounds to rescue RBS.

The case for de-regulation in the 1990s was also the more convincing because it fitted in to the then contemporary economic consensus - a consensus which now looks distinctly shakey and is being questioned not just by the Occupy protestors in Wall Street and the City of London, but by the likes of the world's most successful investor Warren Buffett.

This includes for example, the idea that one must keep taxes on the wealthiest individuals light, in order to attract those individuals who are likely to create wealth (Mr Buffett objects to the fact that he now pays a lower rate of tax than his secretary). It includes the idea that corporations do nothing wrong if they increase executive rewards far faster than that of ordinary employees - faster, if necessary than any improvement in shareholder returns. It also includes the idea that meddling bureaucrats never improve a free market: the market always knows best.

The benefits of scepticism about the prevailing consensus, and about reforms promoted by vested interests, can be immense. In Canada in the 1990s the banks, just as they had in the US and UK, set up what one person close to events at the time describes as a "furious lobby" pressing for Canadian banks to be allowed to merge and expand just as RBS had done. They also wanted to "gear up" - to borrow more and deploy more capital, than Canada's regulations would allow (the higher the gearing, the faster the profits grow, the bigger the bonuses). Lobbyists held out the prospect of economic benefits to Canada if regulations were relaxed. If the authorities resisted, they warned, the financial services sector would be uncompetitive and the Canadian economy would suffer.

But Canada had gone through a banking crisis relatively recently - in 1984 when a home-grown oil boom came to an end. Second-tier banks failed with painful economic consequences and a system was set up designed to prevent a repeat. As one central bank insider put it: "We had had quite a serious crash in the mid 1980s and the people that were in charge had grown up with that crisis burned into them and didn't want to repeat it." The Prime Minister of Canada at the time, Jean Chretien, was duly sceptical of the lobbyists' claims and said 'non'. "He was very clear. We were not going to open this thing up. We were not going to let our banking sector be a New York-style casino." As a result, in 2008, Canadian banks, modestly borrowed and carefully regulated, needed no bailing out. For decades Canada's economy was growing only modestly and the US dollar was far stronger. But, apart from inevitable and manageable knock-on effects from other countries, it escaped the crisis of 2008. And now, relative to the US or UK, Canada's economy, and the Canadian dollar, are stronger than they have been in decades.

Here are some constructive suggestions for a well-intentioned policymaker (they do exist) who wants to avoid succumbing to pressure from lobbyists and adopting an economic policy that leads to disaster.

First, they should be sceptical of policies that have more to do with emotion than economic rationality (eg trying to ensure house prices stay high and rise further). Second, they should be sceptical of policies that fit too glibly into the prevailing economic consensus of their times. Third, it should be at precisely those moments when the lobbyists are pressing their case hardest that the policymakers should be most sceptical. Traders in the City are highly sceptical of fellow traders who may be "talking their book" - promoting what they have bought so the price goes up. Policymakers should similarly ask if lobbyists are talking their book - promoting their narrow economic self-interest. And if the lobbyists claim their goal is also in the public interest - the policymakers must demand truly convincing evidence.

Few events could demonstrate better than the eurozone crisis that if due economic scepticism is blocked by wishful thinking, the price, an expensive price, will be paid in the future. And nothing could demonstrate better than the credit crisis that the policy-making process needs to be freed from undue influence by corporate lobbying. The interests of, for example, the banking sector are not the same as that of the public – and, as we learned in 2008, they can be opposed. Due scepticism towards the banking lobby in the 1990s could have done much to avert our current economic trouble.

As the Canadian story shows, scepticism, and therefore economic rationality, prevails when the fear of what might go economically wrong is stronger than the blithe assumption that it will all work out fine. It also illustrates the point that our capacity to be duly sceptical in economic matters is far greater when something has recently gone wrong. In economics, given the scale of our recent crises, scepticism should prevail for quite some time.

In: Scepticism: Hero and Villain
Editors: R. Calne and W. O'Reilly

ISBN: 978-1-62417-783-5
© 2013 Nova Science Publishers, Inc.

Chapter 23

IS MONEY GOOD OR EVIL, DOES IT REALLY EXIST AT ALL?

Marcus Johnson[*]
Chief Executive of NW Brown Group
and Regional President of the Chartered Institute
for Securities and Investments, Cambridge, UK

INTRODUCTION

All social animals require trust to exist alongside other individuals in a society. Modern nations only exist because we have invented money. It is the foundation of all exchange systems beyond barter and allows trust and language to function over time and distance in ways which have created the worldwide interchange of goods and services we know and benefit from today. If trust and language are the foundations of society, money is what translates them into civilisation.

Everything we regard as civilisation has its roots in the extension of our inborn capability to labour with hands and minds into exchange systems where we can produce more than we need and freely give it to others in the knowledge that what we receive from them will allow us to consume other goods and services made by completely unrelated third parties at a place and time of our choosing. If we only produce what we need or can store, exchange systems based on barter are possible but very inefficient in time use, and (pre-internet) geography.

---

[*] The views expressed in this article are personal and should not be attributed either to NW Brown or to the Institute.

It was only at the point that the introduction of a common standard of exchange usually based on a metal - lead, copper, silver and gold being favourites, that free markets could be established and trade expand over thousands of miles on a multi lateral basis.

The history of currency is fascinating - both in the wide variety of forms of money, and in its interaction of government, power and currency. The History of Money (E V Morgan), gives a highly readable account of the former, whilst for the latter Benjamin Franklin gives an insight into how the ebb and flow of power is reflected in currency. Did a stable currency form the basis of the Roman Empire and its debasement destroy it? Was the Spanish Empire destroyed by the silver it stole from the Americas? The interplay of money and power, the emergence of banking in medieval Italy, the repeated failures of banks and nations as credibility waned, suggest that the history of money is the history of the World.

But what exactly is money? Like "i" (the square root of -) it is entirely imaginary but extremely useful. It is similar in concept to the lowest common denominator - the whole number which can be multiplied to give a selection of the other - numbers which allow you to add fractions. But because it is the common denominator for all goods and services in the world, the meaning of "one dollar" is not constant over time - and any attempted definition is likely to be partial. It is the time element which is so liable to change - and yet also the single most productive use of money. As a measure of the number of screws I should expect to exchange for a length of timber, or of the number of hours I should labour to buy my food, money is hugely useful and saves immense effort, therefore making everyone better off. The consequence of having money in a properly governed state, where laws are applied, is that capital accumulation can be rewarded. So that if I can believe in money I can work today for reward tomorrow - if I spend time improving my land, building a house or making machines, I can expect to earn money by selling those services in future - I can build capital. So money allows me to set aside real resources today ("saving" in economic terms "investment") in the belief that I will be adequately rewarded for doing so tomorrow. When money fails, or rather belief in money ebbs, investment in capital which will produces an income in future years falls to near zero. Hoarding and acquisition of stocks of real goods become the only sensible ways of holding wealth, and ultimately when paper money loses all value it will be burned to prevent freezing to death. Ultimately the value of modern paper (Fiat money, from the Latin "let it be") is only as good as the instruments of government which lie behind it - the legal system, the police, the army and the Central Bank cannot save a government which has no system of the tax collection to ensure its revenues will over time meet its expenses. All of these require faith and belief - and if its citizens no longer believe in their government's ability to meet its obligations, then their faith in its currency and all its other arms will disappear very fast.

A stable strong currency (one which retains its value overtime) does not create strong government or establish a mighty empire, but is in effect an excellent measure of how good a government is and there is a mutually beneficial reinforcement mechanism. When people talk of the 'Almighty Dollar', they are really talking about the worldwide credibility established by the USA; this means international trade can take place between countries which have no special reason to trust each other but can happily deal with each other in dollars because they know that the Dollar will still have value tomorrow. This power of the Dollar has allowed American firms to buy into industries worldwide; it has allowed the US government to promote trade worldwide and it has enabled military influence to be bought in almost all quarters of the globe. China is the biggest beneficiary of the free international trade system established on the back of the credibility of the dollar. A universally accepted means of exchange encourages trade, production and investment so internationally the existence of the US $ has allowed the exploitation of natural resources, the specialisation of production and the creation of real capital in the form of power stations, factories, transport facilities etc. Billions of people have been brought from poverty to living standards above those in the United States 100 years ago at a time when it was widely considered to have delivered prosperity to all its people!

Such is the power of a shared belief that a piece of paper with a picture of an eighteen century English gentleman on it is a guarantee of value today and into the future! But what money will our children's children be spending in their retirement. Will the 'Almighty Dollar' remain the universal monetary index of value for a hundred years? The value of the dollar is the result of hundreds of millions of entrepreneurs making their capital and labour available in the market place, and when any one of them withdraws his support the value of the dollar falls, and when any new supply becomes available the value rises. This is the process of inflation and deflation, which we try to measure by indices (Cost of living, Retail Price Index, etc). The value has a steady downward bias (inflation) because of the existence of 'government' which can be regarded as a consumer of goods and services; but in the particular context of 'money' it also acts as supplier in that the debts of the US government are ultimately indistinguishable from the currency it issues, the Dollar. Can we invent a currency which is better - more stable, more predictable and independent of governmental authority? Through the ages many have proposed alternatives - in the UK we still talk of 'coppers' for our pennies, silver for the more valuable change and make our £1 coins look like gold - but metals are imperfect substitutes as they all have real uses and involve significant storage and transport costs if used for exchange. Their relative values can change quite markedly. Many people, not all of them certifiably mad, believe that the World should use a gold standard (see Ayn Rand, 'The Fountainhead' for a wonderful fictional argument in favour) and probably the most widely read/watched/performed treatise on money traces the emotional fault line which was for over a decade the most bitter political debate in the United States as liberals argued for both silver and gold to be legal tender (See the Wizard of Oz ....). if William Jennings Bryan had won (if the lion was braver), what would have happened when silver suddenly became relatively more expensive with the advent of photography, a major consumer for 100 years. British silver coins disappeared from currency because their intrinsic value rose above their face value.

For anything to have value you need a market in which you can exchange it and markets require laws, policy and Public Order, so you are back to the fact that currency only has value as long as the government can rule. Today we live in a world where instant communication worldwide has become possible and where infinite amounts of data can be stored and manipulated. Is it possible to imagine a world where Marx's labour theory of value becomes workable? Could we actually 'sell forward' all our working hours in exchange for all goods and services we would need? The Labour theory of value does not allow for different talents, abilities, state of health let alone technical changes or discoveries. All of these remain even if at any one time rapid data processing could allow me to exchange my going into the office for the postman's time in delivering my mail, the journalist's time in writing the news I read, and the farmer's time in supplying my breakfast. There is a huge conceptual problem of trust left as to who guarantees that if I perform the work today the postman will deliver tomorrow. In the absence of an exchange system between currencies, a worldwide exchange system would need to have a global enforcement system for contracts, for instance a World Bank or International Monetary Fund with the power to overrule governments. To keep track of income and expenditure, for raising taxes, for assessing the cost and benefit of consuming tomorrow rather than today ('interest rate') it would be sensible to translate all the trillions of bilateral exchanges into a 'Universal credit' - perhaps the standard hours of the average worker? - which sounds like a currency unit.

So in conclusion the future of money seems pretty secure - it is a wonderfully cheap and convenient way of organising economic activity and allowing Adam Smiths' invisible hand (see 'The Wealth of Nations') to raise everyone's living standards. We can expect governments to keep on debasing their currencies, but with more open borders the freer market's becomes more difficult, and if these trends continue perhaps stable currencies will become more usual. If governments gave up their right to debase their own currency, then common currency areas may become more usual. Money is not the root of all evil (St Paul's letter to Timothy says), its existence, and particularly a stable currency is proof of a system of law and governance which works. Money is neither good or evil - but evidence that people believe in it is a sensitive indicator of trust and honesty in every society. It is a necessary condition for stability and its value is a sensitive indication of social stress and governance.

REFERENCES

Adam Fergusson – *'When Money Dies, The Nightmare of the Weimar Hyper-Inflation'* – published 1975. This provides the best description of what happens when a government completely loses credibility. The 1923 Weimar inflation still affects German attitudes to money.

Adam Smith – *'The Wealth of Nations'* – published 1776. The Invisible Hand of his seminal work is often thought of as a paean to selfish self-interest translating into social responsibility but the efficient allocation of resources is impossible without price signals and price signals can only be read because of the translation mechanism afforded by money.

Ayn Rand *'Atlas Shrugged'* – This is a critique of the New Deal and illustrates the loss of government credit in a fictional account of economic breakdown. A distinctly libertarian view! But a good read.

Benjamin Franklin - *'A Modest Enquiry into the Nature and Necessity of a Paper Currency'* – Philadelphia, April 3, 1729.

E. Victor Morgan - 'A History of Money' - published 1965.

Karl Marx Vol. 1 – *'DAS KAPITAL'* - Marx – published 1867 has a polemic on the nature of money and why labour is the only proper measure of value.

L. Frank Baum – *'The Wizard of Oz'* – published 1900. The Wizard of Oz is an allegorical play about the popular nostrum of the late nineteenth century when American political debate centred on 'bimetallism". This was, as all political campaigns, more about form than content and generated more heat than light. Essentially it was the same thesis (and as false) as that propounded by Franklin 160 years earlier – that increasing the quantity of money would increase the wealth of the country. Perhaps not dissimilar to the C21st debate on the merits of "Quantitive Easing". Marx thus argues that money should be an index of the labour value input into any good - Benjamin Franklin in 'A Modest Enquiry', as quoted above, makes the case that empirically, "the riches of a country are to be valued by the quantity of labour, its inhabitants are able to purchase, not by the quantity of a silver and gold they possess", which is slightly different.

The Bible – Timothy 6, Verse 10 – "For the love of money is the root of all evil: which while some coveted after, they have erred from the faith and pierced themselves through with many sorrows" (King James' version)

Chapter 24A

INTRODUCTION FOR TEACHING SCEPTICISM

Roy Calne

The best education in the UK is probably as good as or better than that to be found in other Western countries but there is a real crisis in education in some deprived areas. Research by the University of Sheffield in 2009 showed that 17% of English 15-year olds are functionally illiterate and 22% are functionally innumerate. Because of this, these youngsters are unemployable even in relatively menial occupations.

Many reasons have been put forward for such failure. Undoubtedly, one problem is that of behaviour. A minority of disruptive children can monopolise the teachers' efforts and deprive the majority who wish to learn from the education to which they are entitled. Some 64% of staff recently surveyed by the recruitment company, TLPA Education, said they had been verbally threatened in the past 12 months and 20% had been physically attacked.

The experienced teacher Katharine Birbalsingh has blamed the breakdown in some sections of society where children were no longer guided by their parents as to what is right and wrong and some parents behave like children. She has linked educational failure in the classroom to a wider failure of adult authority in society at large. Some parents who try to discipline their children fail because the children threaten to call the police and cry abuse. There have been well-publicised cases of parents handcuffed in their own houses, hauled away by the police, their children put into social care for a night, all because of some made-up story. In the absence of such adult authority, the results are predictably tragic. Katharine Birbalsingh explains that she has had many conversations with young women who think getting pregnant is an appropriate means to get a flat because the State subsidises rental expenses for single mothers. She also points out that some young men think it is best not to live with their girlfriend and child because it means they will lose out on benefits.

In an article in The Sunday Times, 14.8.11 Katharine Birbalsingh writes "It's white-flag Britain were kids rule all. Children are never held to account for what they do. Is it any wonder they decide to show the police that they're in charge? They've been in charge of some of our schools and even buses for years. Why not the streets too?" The recent riots in London and other English cities erupted suddenly and resulted in deaths and widespread destruction. Many of the perpetrators have previous convictions.

In this chapter, Daisy Christodoulou looks specifically at the ways in which the weakening of adult authority has affected the nature of teaching in schools, and the material that is taught in them. She suggests that a misguided notion of scepticism has led schools to relegate the importance of the teacher and the teacher's knowledge. Instead, she argues that truly sceptical and questioning citizens must rely on a bedrock of knowledge and information which is most efficiently acquired from a knowledgeable and well-informed teacher.

Although the educational approach she favours will be considered to be traditional, she adduces some startling new evidence from the field of cognitive science about the nature of the brain and how it learns. There are strong scientific as well as moral arguments for restoring the teacher to a position of authority.

In: Scepticism: Hero and Villain
Editors: R. Calne and W. O'Reilly

ISBN: 978-1-62417-783-5
© 2013 Nova Science Publishers, Inc.

Chapter 24

HOW DO WE TEACH SCEPTICISM?

Daisy Christodoulou
University of London, UK

ABSTRACT

This chapter surveys the place of scepticism within education. It argues that scepticism is one of the most important attitudes of the modern world, but that its importance has been misinterpreted within education. Many modern educators argue that teaching knowledge to children is potentially dangerous, as it risks indoctrinating them. Instead, it is argued, more emphasis should be given to instilling sceptical attitudes and all-purpose questioning skills. Such ideas have been enormously influential within the US and the UK over the past half-century. However, recent research shows that such ideas are flawed. It is impossible to teach skills such as 'questioning' or attitudes such as 'scepticism' in the abstract. Bodies of knowledge are fundamental to learning. Paradoxically, these abstract attempts to promote sceptical thinking have in fact led to the proliferation of pseudoscientific theories of learning within classrooms. For true learning to take place, teachers must teach knowledge. This will not hinder the development of sceptical attitudes in pupils, but is in fact the best method of achieving that goal.

HOW DO WE TEACH SCEPTICISM?

Scepticism is one of the central attitudes of the modern world. The skills of thinking critically, questioning everything and approaching all ideas with an open but critical mind are the bulwarks of modern western thought. It is by questioning received ideas that science has been able to make such startling progress over the last five hundred years, whilst sceptical attitudes towards repressive traditions have delivered greater freedom for many human societies.

The fact that scepticism seems to be so vital for human progress poses some problems for education, though. A large part of education is about the transmission of knowledge and tradition. How can we ensure that we educate pupils without stifling their critical faculties? Is it possible to have an education based around the transmission of knowledge that does not at the same time sanctify that knowledge and place it beyond criticism? How can we educate children to be sceptical and questioning, rather than simply filling their minds with facts?

From the 18th century onwards, humanist and progressive philosophers wrestled with these issues. Jean-Jacques Rousseau advocated education that focussed on developing the reasoning faculties and developing the innate ability to learn, and considered that the transmission of knowledge through books and teachers stifled such faculties. [1] In the 19th century, Charles Dickens created in Thomas Gradgrind one of the most famous criticisms of the unthinking transmission of knowledge. Gradgrind's attempts to fill his pupils' heads with 'imperial gallons of facts' turns them into unthinking robots who lack the capacity to act intelligently and autonomously. [2] At the end of the 19th century, and the beginning of the 20th, the American educator John Dewey agreed, arguing that placing the transmission of knowledge at the heart of education turned the children into passive, unthinking receptacles. Instead, education should concern itself more with the development of the child's innate potential [3]. And in the 1930s, the Swiss child psychologist Jean Piaget developed some similar ideas. For him, education's aim was not to transmit knowledge, but to equip children with the critical faculties to be able to thrive in any situation. [4]

The ideas of both Dewey and Piaget were extremely influential. In the UK, the 1967 report *Children and their Primary Schools* (known as the Plowden Report) was explicitly influenced by the theories of Piaget, whilst a number of popular educationalists of the 1960s developed similar ideas about the aims and methods of education. [5]

In practice, these theories often required a very substantial redesign of the typical classroom. In the progressive classroom, the teacher was not a wise, all-knowing figure who stood at the front of the class, but more of a 'facilitator', standing on the sidelines and constructing knowledge alongside the pupils. Rather than the teacher designing the curriculum and choosing the material to be studied, pupils should be allowed to pursue the things that interested them, and to move on at their own pace rather than when the teacher or school thought was right. Pupils were encouraged to work independently or in groups, to ask questions, to go where their imagination took them and to learn by doing things rather than being told things. The importance of grammatical rules and technical accuracy were downplayed. The important thing was to get pupils to think creatively for themselves, so it was a mistake to bog them down with pettifogging conventions like correct spelling. As the Plowden Report put it: 'Teachers must not burden their pupils with the observance of out-worn conventions. Correctness should be sacrificed rather than fluency, vigour or clarity of meaning.' [6]

In the 1980s, in the UK at least, there was a backlash against such practices. Progressive education, as the above collection of beliefs was termed, became a dirty word. It was associated in the minds of politicians and the public with a lack of rigour and an 'anything goes' culture. Newspapers outraged their readers with stories of schools where pupils were unable to read, write or count because the schools had allowed them to choose their own course and develop at their own pace.[7] In 1989, the Conservative government introduced the National Curriculum, a state-mandated curriculum which was intended to ensure that all pupils would have to study certain topics and content.

What I want to argue here is that the attitudes and beliefs of progressive educators did not die with the National Curriculum, or indeed become any less influential. Instead, very similar beliefs and practices have persisted down to present day, albeit with different rationales. Progressive educators in the 60s and 70s were particularly exercised by political concerns. But over the last 30 years, many similar ideas have been advocated but with an economic and technological rationale rather than a political one.

For these modern educationalists, there are new reasons why we have to worry about the transmission of knowledge being at the heart of education. Firstly, modern technology has eliminated the need for you to remember and memorise vast quantities of knowledge. Secondly, modern technology and the rate of modern development mean that a lot of knowledge will quickly become obsolete. We need to 'future-proof' education by teaching transferable skills which can apply in a range of situations, not knowledge which may soon be irrelevant. The importance of developing scepticism and critical thinking skills remains, just with a different justification. The phrase '21st century skills' often stands as a catch-all term for this set of beliefs.

We can see the main outlines of the '21st century skills' movement in many publications and proposals of the last two decades. When Labour came to power in 1997, their education secretary David Blunkett promised a traditional approach to education. But he also commissioned a report from the National Advisory Committee on Creative and Cultural Education who argued in 1999 that:

'We live in a fast moving world. The foundations of the present education system were laid at the end of the nineteenth century. They were designed to meet the needs of a world that was being transformed by industrialisation. We are publishing this report at the dawn of a new century. The challenges we face now are of the same magnitude, but they are of a different character. The task is not to do better now what we set out to do then: it is to rethink the purposes, methods and scale of education in our new circumstances.' [8]

In 2003, the Department for Education and Skills, the Department for Trade and Industry, the Treasury and the Department for Work and Pensions published a joint white paper called *21st century Skills: Realising Our Potential: Individuals, Employers, Nation*. It too took the line that the changing nature of the modern economy meant that our education system needed to focus on transferable skills rather than set bodies of knowledge. It stated that: 'the global economy has made largely extinct the notion of a '"job for life". The imperative now is employability for life. that is dependent on raising our skills game.' [9]

These theories provided an unlikely point of agreement between New Labour modernisers and the unions. The Association of Teachers and Lecturers (ATL) produced a pamphlet called *Subject to Change*, which stated that: 'A twenty-first century curriculum cannot have the transfer of knowledge at its core for the simple reason that the selection of what is required has become problematic in an information rich age'. [10]. It drew on research from the OECD which looked at different types of knowledge and predicted that:

'As access to information becomes easier and less expensive, the skills and competencies relating to the selection and efficient use of information become more crucial. Capabilities for selecting relevant and disregarding irrelevant information, recognising patterns in information, interpreting and decoding information as well as learning new and forgetting old skills are in increasing demand.'

Russell Hobby, head of the National Association of Head Teachers, argued in a blog that 'demand in the workplace for "routine cognitive skills" – based on easily digestible knowledge (like lists of kings and queens) – is in decline, as these tasks are automated and outsourced the future lies in problem solving and interpersonal skills.'[11]

The Royal Society for Arts, one of the UK's most prestigious think tanks, is a keen supporter of these ideas, particularly those about blurring subject boundaries. It has designed its own curriculum, called Opening Minds, which is used in over 200 schools. Instead of organising the curriculum through subjects, the Opening Minds curriculum is organised 'round the development of five key competences:

1. Citizenship
2. Learning
3. Managing Information
4. Relating to people
5. Managing Situations'[12]

But the most significant and far-reaching way in which these beliefs were implemented came in the 2007 curriculum reforms. In an information pack accompanying the new curriculum, the Qualifications and Curriculum Alliance made it clear that there 'is less prescribed subject content' and more of a focus on 'key concepts and processes that underlie each subject' than there was before.[13] For example, the English curriculum, instead of providing a prescribed list of writers or a set of important grammatical terms, was organised around four key concepts – competence, creativity, cultural understanding and critical understanding. Within the last concept were the following subcategories: 'Forming independent views and challenging what is heard or read on the grounds of logic, evidence or argument' and 'analysing and evaluating spoken and written language to explore their impact on the audience.'[14] Likewise, the History curriculum did not include a list of the dates of battles and kings and queens, but was organised around the three key processes of historical enquiry, using evidence, and communicating about the past. [15] Science's core processes were data, evidence, theory and explanation; practical and enquiry skills, communication skills and application and implications of science. [16]

In the US, such ideas are similarly prominent. To show how these ideas have drifted into the mainstream, we can look at a video designed by an American school teacher called 'Shift Happens'. This video makes the case for the curriculum and schools to be reorganized to take account of the rapid changes in technology. It has been viewed five million times on YouTube and has gone through several different versions. [17] The Arizona-based organization Partnership for 21st Century Skills (P21), which is sponsored by a number of multinational corporations, has the following mission statement: 'To serve as a catalyst to position 21st century readiness at the center of US K12 education.' [18] Its aim is to promote what it calls the four important 21st century skills – 'critical thinking and problem solving; communication, collaboration; and creativity and innovation.'

The types of classroom activities promoted by P21 and many of the other organisations mentioned above are remarkably similar to those of the 1960s and 1970s progressive educators. They want independent and group work, a reduction in the transmission of knowledge, the teacher as facilitator rather than sage, active and discovery learning and greater pupil control over the content and pace of the curriculum. For example, the RSA Opening Minds programme is designed so that 'children plan their work, organise their own time and explore their own ways of learning,' whilst Partnership for 21st century Skills recommends 'inquiry-driven, project-based' approaches to learning. [19] The author of the ATL's report into the curriculum, Martin Johnson, argued that the school curriculum should prioritise life skills such as walking rather than 'totalitarian' knowledge:

> 'There's a lot to learn about how to walk. If you were going out for a Sunday afternoon stroll you might walk one way. If you're trying to catch a train you might walk in another way and if you are doing a cliff walk you might walk in another way. If you are carrying a pack, there's a technique in that. We need a nation of people who understand their bodies and can use their bodies effectively.'[20]

Measuring the success or otherwise of these changes is difficult. Whilst the newest incarnation of the knowledge-light curriculum was only in 2007, as I have shown it was really just a continuation of a series of changes dating back to at least the 1960s. Supporters of this style of education would say that despite this, their plans have never been implemented properly due to funding constraints and an atavistic focus on exam results. Others would claim that these methods have been successful. If we do look at pupil performance over this time, the picture is mixed. Certainly, there is evidence to suggest a very significant absence of knowledge amongst many young people.[21] But of course, the advocates of the sort of ideas I have described would not see this as a problem, because pupils can easily look up this information. For them, the important piece of evidence is rising scores in exams which test these modern 21st century competences such as critical thinking and creative problem solving. Against this, there is one study by Michael Shayer of KCL, who found that 11 year olds' ability to solve problems had declined over the last thirty years. [22]

In general, trying to establish a link between pedagogical changes and pupil performance is a fraught area. I would like now to propose a new way of evaluating the success or otherwise of these styles of education. Instead of looking at pupil performance, we can consider the attitudes which predominate inside the educational establishment. If a system is to try and instil sceptical, critical attitudes, then it would seem important for the system itself to embody these attitudes. And yet what we see in education is precisely the opposite. In important and far-reaching ways, the English education system as a whole is remarkably susceptible to faddish and unproven innovations.

Two minor but very illuminating examples are those of Brain Gym and learning styles. Brain Gym is a programme developed by an American educationalist called Paul Dennison who 'found that learning was most easily accomplished when it was "embodied" - experienced in the body rather than solely on a mental level.'[23] The programme consists of 26 proprietary exercises which claim to help pupils to boost their brainpower. In 2008, the doctor and journalist Ben Goldacre stated that 400 UK schools mentioned the programme on their website, whilst he also noted that it was promoted on the Department for Education and Skills website.[24] Goldacre also highlighted some of the more ridiculous exercises it encouraged:

> 'Make a 'C' shape with your thumb and forefinger and place on either side of the breastbone just below the collarbone. Gently rub for twenty or thirty seconds whilst placing your other hand over your navel. Change hands and repeat. This exercise stimulates the flow of oxygen carrying blood through the carotid arteries to the brain to awaken it and increase concentration and relaxation. Brain buttons lie directly over and stimulate the carotid arteries.' [25]

In 2007, research by the Economic and Social Research Council criticised the programme for being unscientific. [26] In the same year, a scientific paper concluded that 'a review of the theoretical foundations of Brain Gym® and the associated peer-reviewed research studies failed to support the contentions of the promoters of Brain Gym®.'[27] In 2008, the UK organisation Sense about Science concluded that Brain Gym depended on 'pseudoscientific explanations' of how the body works and wrote to every local authority in the country warning them about it. Three years on, Google searches of government and school websites suggest many are still using the programme. [28]

Learning styles are slightly harder to pin down than Brain Gym, as there are several different theories, and many more ways of implementing such theories. [29] But put simply, the basic learning style theory argues that people have a specific style in which they learn. In perhaps the most common way the theory is implemented in UK schools, pupils are classified as one of three types of learner – visual, auditory or kinaesthetic, or VAK. [30] This theory is less obviously absurd than Brain Gym, and indeed it does seem to have an intuitive appeal to it. We've all met people who are fantastic at dismantling and repairing a car engine, say, but who couldn't clearly express how they did so in prose. The learning styles theory appeared to explain this phenomenon.

Whilst the theory itself is not so ridiculous, like Brain Gym it has been responsible for some fairly inane classroom practice. One of the foremost learning styles theorists, Howard Gardner has admitted to being 'uneasy' at the way his ideas have been adapted for use in the classroom. On a visit to Australia, he learnt that:

'An entire state had adapted an education programme based in part on Multiple Intelligence theory. The more I learned about this programme, the less comfortable I was. Much of it was a mishmash of practices - left brain and right brain contrasts, sensory learning styles, neurolinguistic programming and multiple intelligences approaches, all mixed with dazzling promiscuity.' [31]

Its implementation in UK schools has also been criticised, perhaps most chiefly for the tendency teachers have to use the theory rigidly to classify children into learning styles categories, perhaps by wearing badges or labels. [32]

Perhaps, therefore, this is an example of a good theory being poorly implemented? Not quite. Over the past few decades, no evidence has been found to back up the idea that pupils have different learning styles. [33] The learning styles theory confused a learning style with a learning ability – perhaps this was the reason why it was so persuasive. The friend we know who can dismantle a car engine but can't draw you a diagram to explain is not a kinaesthetic learner. He simply has high kinaesthetic ability. For the learning styles theory to have meaning beyond the fairly obvious idea that we are all good at different things it has to have a predictive power – it has to be able to predict that someone with learning style A will learn something better when it is presented in style A. It isn't enough to say that Jack is very good at dismantling car engines and is therefore a kinaesthetic learner. We have to say that because Jack has a kinaesthetic style of learning the best way for him to learn a list of spellings, say, or a good French accent, is by moving around while he does so or manipulating the words with his hands. And that is what every single piece of research on learning styles has failed to prove. [34] As those examples of the spellings and the French accent show, the way that we present material should depend not on the spurious learning style of the individual, but on the nature of the material itself. As well as this fundamental flaw, much of the research into learning styles theory has noted the unreliability of the self-diagnosis test used to establish a person's learning style and the overall incoherence of many of the theories and their practical implementation. [35]

What are the educational implications of such pseudoscience? Some would argue that it isn't such a significant issue. For all that they were based on flawed theories, Brain Gym and learning styles theories had some positive outcomes. Brain Gym encouraged pupils to do regular exercises, take breaks and drink lots of water. Learning styles encouraged teachers to vary their teaching style and pupils to think about the way they learnt. These are all clearly good things. So, if the overall impacts of learning styles theory and Brain Gym were positive, surely it is therefore OK to carry on with them? There are a couple of objections to this, I think. Firstly, there is a wider philosophical point. If we know that something isn't true, we really shouldn't be using it as the basis for action. We most especially should not be teaching it to pupils. As Goldacre notes, 'authority figures who fill [children's] heads with nonsense are sowing the ground, I would say, for a lifetime of exploitation.' [36] Finally, and to return to the point I began with, what does it say about the education system that it not only falls prey to pseudoscientific fads, but that it is unwilling to give them up even when they are categorically proved to be fads? More specifically, how can we possibly claim to be instilling pupils with the sceptical attitudes and critical thinking skills they need for life when we ourselves are signally failing to display such skills? How could the 2007 curriculum claim to be promoting 'critical understanding' when a significant number of its accompanying case studies uncritically promoted a scientifically invalid theory of learning? [37]

In the case of Brain Gym and learning styles, the scientific proof refuting these theories has been relatively well publicized in the UK. But there is a similarly convincing body of evidence that shows most of the educational theories about the dangers of the transmission of knowledge are false – only in this case, the evidence is not well-known in the UK, and the theories about transferable, 21st century skills still reign as an unchallenged orthodoxy. In short, many educationalists have failed to apply sufficient critical thinking skills and scepticism to their own pet theories of how to encourage critical thinking and scepticism. I am not suggesting that critical thinking skills and scepticism are bad things. Indeed, I think they are very good things, which is precisely why I am so worried that the methods that have been used to try and inculcate them over the last fifty years have been fundamentally flawed and counter-productive. The persistence of such methods into the modern day is proof of a remarkable lack of scepticism and knowledge within the educational establishment.

Perhaps the most fundamental way in which these methods are flawed is in the way that they marginalize the transmission of knowledge and instead promote a form of education based on developing skills. In reality, skills and knowledge are not nearly as discrete as this model suggests. As the cognitive psychologist Dan Willingham puts it:

> 'Data from the last thirty years lead to a conclusion that is not scientifically challengeable: thinking well requires knowing facts, and that's true not just because you need something to think about. The very processes that teachers care about most – critical thinking processes such as reasoning and problem solving – are intimately intertwined with factual knowledge that is stored in long-term memory (not just found in the environment).'[38]

It isn't enough to just look something up on Google. It isn't possible to outsource memory. We need that factual information in our long-term memories in order to be able to apply it, evaluate it, synthesise it and criticise it.

As Willingham intimates, the body of research backing up the importance of knowledge is significant. Over the last thirty years, developments in the field of cognitive science and artificial knowledge have deepened our understanding of how humans learn. One of the pioneers of artificial intelligence, the Nobel Laureate Herbert A Simon, conducted research that has profound implications for education. The American educationalist E.D. Hirsch summarised his findings as follows:

> 'Simon and his colleagues have cast doubt on the idea that there are any general or transferable cognitive skills. All cognitive skills depend on procedural and substantive schemata that are highly specific to the task at hand. Once the relevant knowledge has been acquired, the skill follows. General programmes contrived to teach general skills are not effective.' [39]

A series of fascinating experiments with chess players by the Dutch psychologist Adriaan de Groot confirms this. Again, Hirsch summarises:

> 'In one experiment, de Groot displayed for five to ten seconds a chess position from an actual game in which twenty-five pieces were left on the board. The subjects were asked to reproduce this position from memory. Grand masters performed this feat with 100% accuracy, masters with 90% accuracy. Weaker players were lucky if they could correctly place five or six pieces. Then de Groot varied the conditions of his pieces in one respect. Instead of placing the twenty five pieces in positions from an actual game, he placed them on the board randomly. The results were unexpected. All his subjects – grand masters, masters, class A players and class B players – performed the same as novices did, placing only five or six pieces correctly. This experiment has been duplicated in several different laboratories, and structurally in several other fields, including algebra, physics medicine, always with the same striking results. When the configuration of a task is significantly changed, past skills are not transferred to the new problem. In normal circumstances, of course, elements from past problems appear in present ones, and experts perform well with duplicated elements. But beyond similar or analogous circumstances, skill is not transferred.' [40]

This flies directly in the face of curricula like the RSA's Opening Minds and the 2007 National Curriculum, which try to minimise or even abolish subject boundaries on the grounds that important skills cut across subject domains. One of the RSA's organising principles is 'Managing Information'. But the way you manage the information contained in a maths problem is very different from the way you manage the information contained in a history problem. Your skills are bound up with the content you work with. If we really want to ensure that pupils have sceptical, questioning attitudes, we need to make sure they have a firm, detailed foundation of knowledge in a range of important areas. This knowledge will allow them to formulate insightful and probing questions and see the flaws in weak and shoddy arguments.

The other main argument of the 21st-century skills advocates is that traditional bodies of knowledge are obsolete in the modern world. This argument relies for its force on the fact that it seems to agree with something we all intuitively know to be true. Modern life *does* change remarkably quickly, modern technology *is* extraordinarily fast-moving, the economy *is* subject to rapid structural alterations. But the advocates of a skills curriculum take these undeniable and obvious facts and extrapolate from them some extremely dodgy conclusions. A good example can be seen in the video called 'Shift Happens', which I spoke about above.[41] It tells us that 1.5 exabytes of unique new information are generated each year, and that the amount of new technical information is doubling each year. And while you're reeling at such huge numbers, it slips in the dodgy conclusion – that this flow of new information means that for students starting a four year college or technical degree, half of what they learn in their first year will be outdated by their third year of study. This is simply not true. Of course people make new discoveries all the time, but a lot of those new discoveries don't disprove or supersede the old ones – in fact, they're more likely to build on the old discoveries and require intimate knowledge of them. The fundamental foundations of most disciplines are rarely, if ever, completely disproved. Universities can turn out as many exabytes of information as they like – they are unlikely to disprove Pythagoras's theorem or improve on Euripides's tragedies.

And there are very many such ancient, fundamental ideas and inventions which have stood the test of time: perhaps more than we are willing to admit. The alphabet and the numbering system, for example, are two of the most valuable inventions we have. As far as we know, these were invented in about 2000 BC and 3000 BC respectively. So far they show no signs of wearing out or being superseded. All of the most modern and advanced technological devices depend on them in one way or another.

The irony, of course, is that if the idea that in the 21st century we should be sceptical about teaching our kids content has any validity, it is actually that the newer the idea, the more likely it is to become obsolete. If something has proved itself valuable over 5000 years, it's a good bet it'll be useful for the next 100; if something has only been valuable for the last 50 or 20, then we cannot be nearly so certain. Microfiche readers and minidisk players have more chance of becoming obsolete than the alphabet and the numerical system. So the newer the idea, the more sceptical we should be about teaching it, and the older the idea, the more likely it has stood the test of time. Yet of course, the 21st century skills movement draws exactly the opposite conclusion. Its mantra is about being constantly new, constantly up-to-date, always on the cutting edge. But nothing dates so fast as the cutting edge.

It is also remarkable that these ideas, which so fetishise technology and the new, are so incredibly ignorant of the new research into how the brain learns. Many of these ideas about the development of skills are dependent on research done before the war by people like Jean Piaget. The research which proves that knowledge and skills are intertwined and that we cannot outsource memory to Google is research that was carried out in the last few decades by the pioneers of artificial intelligence. One of those pioneers, Herbert Simon, expressed his surprise at the lack of evidence for so many curriculum theories.

> 'New "theories" of education are introduced into schools every day (without labeling them as experiments) on the basis of their philosophical or common-sense plausibility but without genuine empirical support.' [42]

The more we learn about the brain, the more we learn how much knowledge and memory matters. The more we learn about how we learn, the more we realise the value of apparently old-fashioned methods such as learning by heart and frequent repetitive practice. [43] In contrast, it is the unthinking advocates of '21st century skills' who are the true reactionary stuck-in-the-muds, refusing to learn from evidence and experience. The popular buzzword '21st century skills' suggests that it is a forward-thinking, modern concept. But in fact, as I have shown, its intellectual underpinnings are neither new nor true. Instead, the 250-year-old progressive attempts to promote scepticism have left us with an education system peculiarly susceptible to fads and snake oil.

REFERENCES

[1] Rousseau, Jean Jacques. *Émile, or, Education*, trans. Barbara Foxley. (London: J.M. Dent, 1911).

[2] Dickens, Charles. *Hard Times*. (Harmondsworth: Penguin, 1969), p.48.

[3] Dewey, John. *Democracy and Education: an Introduction to the Philosophy of Education*. (London: Collier Macmillan, 1966).

[4] Piaget, Jean. *The Origins of Intelligence in the Child*, trans. Margaret Cook. (London: Routledge and Kegan Paul, 1953).

[5] Plowden, B.H. *The Plowden Report: Children and their Primary Schools: a report of the Central Advisory Council of Education, England*. (London: HMSO, 1967); for evidence that Plowden was influenced by Piaget, see Halsey, AH and Sylva, K. 'Plowden: history and prospect', *Oxford Review*

of Education, 31:1, 3–13, 1987; for evidence of popular pedagogical texts of the 1960s and 1970s, see Freire, Paulo. *Pedagogy of the Oppressed*, trans. Myra Bergman Ramos. (Harmondsworth: Penguin, 1972) and Postman, Neil. *Teaching as a Subversive Activity* (Harmondsworth: Penguin, 1971).

[6] Plowden, p.230.

[7] Haigh, Gerald. *Times Educational Supplement*. 7 July 2006. 'Flutterings from the Tyndale affair' http://www.tes.co.uk/article.aspx?storycode=2259514 Accessed 19 July 2011.

[8] National Advisory Committee on Creative and Cultural Education. *All Our Futures: Creativity, Culture and Education.* 1999. p.16. < http://www.cypni.org.uk/downloads/alloutfutures.pdf> Accessed 19 July 2011.

[9] *21st Century Skills: Realising Our Potential*. HMSO, 2003. p.11.

[10] Association of Teachers and Lecturers. *Subject to Change: New Thinking on the Curriculum.* London, 2006. http://www.atl.org.uk/Images/Subject%20to%20change%20-%20curriculum%20PS%202006.pdf Accessed 19 July 2011.

[11] Hobby, Russell. 'Russell Hobby stops biting his tongue with the CBI.' 10 September 2010. http://www.naht.org.uk/welcome/resources/blogs/russell-hobby/?blogpost=362 Accessed 25 February 2011.

[12] Royal Society for Arts Opening Minds. *What is RSA Opening Minds?* http://www.rsaopeningminds.org.uk/about-rsa-openingminds/ Accessed 19 February 2011.

[13] *The New Secondary Curriculum: What has changed and why*. QCA, 2007. p. 4. http://www.tgsonline.co.uk/assets/files/why%20the%20curriculum%20has%20changed.pdf Accessed 19 July 2011.

[14] English: Programme of study for key stage 3 and attainment targets. *QCA*, 2007. < http://curriculum.qcda.gov.uk/uploads/QCA-07-3332-pEnglish3_tcm 8-399.pdf> Accessed 19 July 2011.

[15] History: Programme of study for key stage 3 and attainment targets. *QCA*, 2007. < http://curriculum.qcda.gov.uk/uploads/QCA-07-3335-p_History3_tcm8-189.pdf> Accessed 19 July 2011.

[16] Science: Programme of study for key stage 3 and attainment targets. *QCA*, 2007. < http://curriculum.qcda.gov.uk/uploads/QCA-07-3344-p_Science_KS3_ tcm8-413.pdf> Accessed 19 July 2011.

[17] 'Shift Happens', http://www.youtube.com/watch?v=ljbI-363A2Q Accessed 19 July 2011.

[18] 'Partnership for 21st Century Skills: Our Mission'. Partnership for 21st Century Skills <http://www.p21.org/index.php?option=com_content andtask=viewandid=188andItemid=110> Accessed 19 July 2011.

[19] Royal Society for Arts Opening Minds. 'RSA Opening Minds competence framework'. <http://www.rsaopeningminds.org.uk/about-rsa-openingminds/competences/> Accessed 20 July 2011; Partnership for 21st Century Skills. Curriculum and Instruction: A 21st Century Skills Implementation Guide http://p21.org/documents/p21-stateimp_curriculuminstruction.pdf Accessed 20 July 2011.

[20] Andalo, Debbit. *The Guardian*. 30 March 2007. 'Teachers' union calls for lessons in walking'. <http://www.guardian.co.uk/education/2007/mar/30/schools.uk> Accessed 19 July 2011.

[21] Matthews, Derek. *The strange death of history teaching: (fully explained in seven easy-to-follow lessons)*, p.33. http://www.cardiff.ac.uk/carbs/faculty/matthewsdr/history4.pdf; *Times Educational Supplement*. 19 January 2001. 'What did Hitler do in the war, miss?' <http://www.tes.co.uk/article.aspx?storycode=342835>; The Independent. 10 November 2001. 'Don't know much about history? You are not alone, says questionnaire' <http://www.independent.co.uk/news/uk/home-news/dont-know-much-about-history-you-are-not-alone-says-questionnaire-747612.html>; BBC News. 5 August 2004. 'Britons 'ignorant of UK history' http://news.bbc.co.uk/1/hi/3537162.stm All accessed 19 July 2011.

[22] Shayer, Michael, Denise Ginsburg and Robert Coe. *Thirty years on – a large anti-Flynn effect? The Piagetian test Volume and Heaviness norms, 1975–2003. British Journal of Educational Psychology* (2007), 77:1, 25–41.

[23] Brain Gym. 'About Educational Kinesiology and Brain Gym in the UK'. http://www.braingym.org.uk/about/about.htm

[24] Goldacre, Ben. *Bad Science*. (London: Fourth Estate, 2008), p.14.

[25] Ibid, p.14.

[26] Economic and Social Research Council. 'ESRC Neuroscience and Education: Issues and Opportunities: A Commentary by the Teaching and Learning Research Programme.' <http://www.tlrp.org/pub/documents/Neuroscience%20Commentary%20FINAL.pdf>

[27] Hyatt, Keith J. 'Brain Gym - Building Stronger Brains or Wishful Thinking?' *Remedial and Special Education,* (2007), 28:2, 117–124.

[28] Google searches of websites ending in sch.uk that feature the words 'Brain Gym': http://www.google.co.uk/search?q=inurl%3Asch.uk+%22brain+gym%22andstart=0andie=utf-8andoe=utf-8andclient=firefox-aandrls=org.mozilla:en-US:official; Google searches of websites ending in gov.uk that feature the words 'Brain Gym': <http://www.google.co.uk/search?num= 100andhs=2Ajandhl=enandclient=firefox-aandrls=org.mozilla%3Aen-US%3 Aofficial andq=inurl%3Agov.uk+%22brain+gym%22andbtnG=Searchandmeta=>

[29] Coffield, F., D. Moseley, E. Hall, and K. Ecclestone. 'Should we be using learning styles? What research has to say to practice' (London: Learning and Skills Research Centre, 2004).

[30] Sharp, J., R. Bowker, J. Byrne. 'VAK or VAK-uous? Towards the trivialisation of learning and the death of scholarship', *Research Papers in Education*, (2008) 23:3, 293-314, p.293.

[31] Demos. 'About learning: Report of the Learning Working Group' (London: Demos, 2004), p. 15.

[32] Sharp, p.311.

[33] Willingham, Daniel T. *Why Don't Our Students Like School?* San Francisco: Jossey-Bass, 2009, p.153.

[34] Ibid, pp.147-167.

[35] Coffield, pp.44-45.

[36] Goldacre, p.18.

[37] Qualifications and Curriculum Development Alliance. 'Case Studies: History Matters.' http://webarchive.nationalarchives.gov.uk/201008 23130703/http://curriculum.qcda.gov.uk/key-stages-3-and-4/case_studies/ casestudieslibrary/case-studies/History_matters.aspx; 'Case Studies: Personalisation and Relevance.' http://webarchive.national archives. gov.uk/20100823130703/http://curriculum.qcda.gov.uk/key-stages-3-and-4/ case_studies/casestudieslibrary/case-studies/Personalisation_and_ relevance. aspx; 'Developing 3D drawing skills (improving the performance of boys)'. http://curriculum.qcda.gov.uk/key-stages-1-and-2/assessment/nc-in-action/ items/design-and-technology/6/2068.aspx;'Case Studies: Cutting exclusions through personalisation' http://webarchive.nationalarchives. gov.uk/ 20100823130703/http://curriculum.qcda.gov.uk/key-stages-3-and-4/case_ studies/casestudieslibrary/case-studies/Cutting_exclusions_through_ personalisation.aspx All accessed 20 July 2011.

[38] Willingham, p.28.

[39] Hirsch, E.D. *Cultural Literacy: What Every American Needs to Know.* (Boston: Houghton Mifflin, 1987), pp.60-61

[40] Ibid, p.61

[41] Fisch, Karl. 'Shift Happens'. http://www.youtube.com/watch?v=ljbI-363A2Q Accessed 21 January 2011.

[42] Anderson, John R., Lynne M. Reder, and Herbert A. Simon. 'Applications and misapplications of cognitive psychology to mathematics education', Texas Education Review (Summer 2000), p.19

[43] Kirschner, P. A., J. Sweller, and R.E. Clark, 'Why Minimal Guidance During Instruction Does Not Work: An Analysis of the Failure Of Constructivist, Discovery, Problem-Based, Experiential, and Inquiry-Based Teaching.' *Educational Psychologist* (2006) 41:2, 75-86; Karpicke, J. D., and J.R. Blunt, 'Retrieval practice produces more learning than elaborative studying with concept mapping', *Science* (2011), 331, 772-775.

Chapter 25

SPORT

Stephen Chittenden
Reporter for BBC News, London, UK

ABSTRACT

This chapter examines the origins of organised sport and attitudes towards the apparent benefits that come from sport. It looks at some examples of the claims which have been made on behalf of sport, including how it can replace warfare; how sport can unite a nation and whether large sporting events have wider health benefits for society. The chapter also examines several examples of cheating, match-fixing and corruption in the sports of sumo wrestling, cricket, athletics and rugby. It suggests that the huge financial rewards may have caused some malpractice in sport, and asks whether this should make a sceptic of the spectator.

INTRODUCTION

Since its earliest forms the apparent benefits of organised sport have been manifest. It has been seen as a substitute for battle, a means to a healthier society and for a few sport has become a route to riches. But cheating is as old as sport itself. So long as there have been rewards for sporting endeavour, there have been attempts to gain those rewards by unfair means. Sometimes it only takes the actions of one person to ruin the reputation of all his fellow competitors. The sceptic may ask this; can I always trust that what I am seeing on the sports field is genuine?

One of the earliest records of organised sport comes from the ancient Greek Olympic Games of around 776 BC. The games were held at Olympia in honour of the god Zeus and formed part of a religious festival. Ancient Greece could be a dangerous place, with city states often at war. A direct benefit of the sporting event was the 'sacred truce', a message of peace that went round the Greek world ahead of the games to ensure safe passage for participants and spectators alike.

The links between spiritual observance and physical exercise remain to this day, especially in the case of football, which has become a new type of religion for many. Where the ancient Greeks venerated Zeus or Apollo, today's football fans literally bow in obeisance to players like Manchester United's Rooney or Messi of Barcelona. Any churchgoer watching league football for the first time would be entirely familiar with the ritual of chanting and singing, if a little shocked by some of the content. And just as religious observance passes down the generations, so does sporting allegiance. It is a kind of baptism for a child to be taken to their first match. When Arsenal fan George Carey was enthroned as Archbishop of Canterbury, he likened Christianity to football by quoting the great Liverpool manager Bill Shankly:

"Some people think football's a matter of life and death. I can assure them it is much more serious than that." [1]

Nearly three thousand years ago war would stop so that Olympic sport might take place. But the similarities between war and sport are obvious; the undying tribal loyalty of football supporters, the teamwork of both fighting and sporting units, and the plain war-like aggression required for victory on the rugby pitch.

The Duke of Wellington is said to have thanked school sports for a famous British victory in 1815. Whether or not he actually said, 'The Battle of Waterloo was won on the playing fields of Eton', the sentiment is clear.

As the world entered the age of horrific industrial warfare in the early twentieth century it dawned on some scientists that perhaps sport might take the place of fighting. Dr Walter B Cannon, Professor of Physiology at Harvard claimed to have unearthed startling proof; an island tribe of Filipinos who rejected warfare after the American occupation and now embraced sportsmanship.

'The fierce Igorrotes of Bontoc, once constantly at war with neighbouring tribes now show their prowess not in head-hunting but in baseball, wrestling and the tug-of-war.' [2]

The New York Times approved of the new work, and its editorial advanced the idea that athletics be substituted for war.

'Athletics not only satisfy the demand of young men for the clash of strength against strength in opposition,' the newspaper said,

'But also produce valour, fortitude, self-control and obedience to command – the virtues which are lauded by the militarists as the virtues bred by war.' [3]

Mercifully for the modern spectator a hard-fought match is as close as they will ever get to witnessing war. Aside from actual pugilism, tennis is perhaps the most gladiatorial of sports. The participants enter the arena alone and slug it out face to face until one of them is victor. The longest ever match took place at Wimbledon in 2010, when American John Isner defeated France's Nicolas Mahut after more than 11 hours of play which took place over three days. At the climax of battle Mahut hung his head; his body slumped, while the victor lay on his back wiggling his legs in the air. Today there is a plaque on the wall of the court to commemorate the match, much like a battlefield sign marking some conflict from the past.

Isner versus Mahut proved another claim about the benefits of sport; that it reveals character. Many commercial deals are sealed on the golf course not just because businesspeople like the sport, but they see it as a place to discover their opponent's strengths and defects. A golfer's response to a wobbly putt that just misses the hole can be revealing; was it bad luck or a bad putt, a treacherous green or a dodgy technique? In short, do they take responsibility for their actions or not?

The best and funniest writer on golf PG Wodehouse certainly believed a round on the links was the surest route to reveal a person's nature. He called it the infallible test.

'The only way of really finding out a man's true character is to play golf with him. In no other walk of life does the cloven hoof so quickly display itself',

he wrote,

'The man who can go into a patch of rough alone, with the knowledge that only God is watching him, and play his ball where it lies, is the man who will serve you faithfully and well.' [4]

For the individual there is overwhelming evidence of the benefits of sport. Regular physical activity has been shown to help prevent cardiovascular disease, diabetes and cancer. [5]

The human spirit can benefit too, and that is not a new idea. The Latin 'Mens sana in corpore sano' (a sound mind in a sound body) is thought to come from the

Roman poet Juvenal in the first century AD. It is a motto adopted by sports clubs and organisations around the world, and has even helped sell millions of running shoes made by ASICS (Anima Sana in Corpore Sano).

But the beneficial claims of sport go way beyond the individual. As the great Indian batsman Sachin Tendulkar strode out to the middle of London's Oval in August 2011, he carried on his shoulders the hopes of hundreds of millions of cricket lovers back home. In a glorious career he had accumulated 99 international centuries (scores of 100 runs or more), and they all wanted to see him make history with his hundredth hundred. On that occasion he fell just short, leaving his millions of fans united in disappointment. As so often in sport, there was to be another chance.

Watching Tendulkar from high in the pavilion was the Commonwealth Secretary General Kamalesh Sharma, who reflected on how only sport can unite such a diverse country as India; a nation of 1.2 billion souls, but one sporting hero.

> "Cricket is integral to Indian cohesiveness and unity", he said, "It is a passion that is shared all over the country." [6]

The domestic news that summer had been dominated not by sport, but crime. Riots and looting had broken out apparently spontaneously in towns and cities across England. But at the end of the worst week of criminal activity, sport once again managed to nudge the bad news off the front pages. England's cricketers had beaten India to become officially the world's number one team. The veteran British journalist Michael Parkinson said the win had 'lifted the spirits of the country in an otherwise terrible week'. [7]

I have witnessed first hand how a sporting victory can bring a nation or at least a city together. At Murrayfield in 1990 Scotland won a famous Grand Slam decider against favourites England in Rugby's Five Nations tournament. England were led by ex-public schoolboy Will Carling, and had been accused of arrogance before the game. Whether right or wrong, it made the win all the sweeter for the Scots. That night there was an extraordinary buzz on the streets of Edinburgh; such singing, drinking and jubilation that even this dejected England fan could not fail to appreciate how a simple game of rugby could lift people.

Yet amid all the happy celebrations, some Scottish fans indulged in a little anti-Englishness. The odd comment, some less good-natured than others served to remind that sport does not always bring out the best in human beings and that there are always grounds for scepticism about its myriad benefits. Let us examine some.

In 2005 London won the bid to host the 2012 Olympics. This prompted celebrations in the capital, and also triggered an avalanche of optimistic claims by politicians to help justify the ever-rising price tag, not least how the event will benefit the health of the nation.

Shortly after winning the bid, the Labour government's health secretary Patricia Hewitt said: "The real legacy of the Olympics and Paralympics will be all of those people who are encouraged to get involved in sport and physical activity, and improve their health." [8]

England's chief medical officer Sir Liam Donaldson not only supported her view, he went on to predict how the Olympics could stop children getting fat:

> "Winning this bid will give a huge boost to improving the health and wellbeing not just of Londoners but of people across England. It will encourage people to get involved in sport and physical activity. Encouraging children to get active will reverse the upward trend of childhood obesity." [9]

It must have seemed obvious to them that a massive sporting event like London 2012 would have widespread healthy consequences for the general population.

Unfortunately what seems obviously right at the time can turn out just wrong. Researchers in Glasgow who examined the impact of major sports events on the wider public found little or no evidence to support those claims.

They concluded: "Events such as the 2012 Olympic Games or 2014 Commonwealth Games cannot be expected automatically to provide benefits it is unclear how the costs of major multi-sport events can be justified in terms of benefits to the host population." [10]

In time even the politicians came to realise this. In March 2011 the Olympics secretary Jeremy Hunt dropped the government's aim of getting a million more adults to play regular sport.

While the truth dawned, the costs went up. Less than two years after winning the right to host the games the government announced that the budget had risen somewhat from the original £2.4 billion. It now stood at £9.35 billion.

The Olympic Games are a massively expensive business. Only a sporting event such as the games could allow the construction of London's £42 million basketball arena that will be used for just a few weeks before being taken down and sold off.

The cost of an Olympics has risen significantly over the years. Recent games cost an estimated $3.4billion for Sydney in 2000 and at least 10 billion Euros for Athens four years later. The true budget for Beijing 2008 remains a Chinese state secret, but is reckoned to run into the tens of billions of dollars. [11] With so much money at stake and the choice of host city in the hands of so few, it was surely only a matter of time before a corruption scandal broke, as was to happen in 1998.

Bribes had been accepted by members of the International Olympic Committee, that select and tiny club who choose host cities. A Swiss IOC member, Marc Holder told how fellow members had promised their votes to Salt Lake City in exchange for college scholarships, money and holidays. The city went on to win the vote and hosted the 2002 winter Olympics.

As a result six IOC members were expelled and ten were warned. The IOC promised to clean up its act by changing the bidding process and setting up an ethics commission. But any organisation, be it sport or business, which puts decisions worth billions into the hands of an unaccountable few will open itself to accusations of corruption. It happened to the IOC, and now it has happened in football.

The head of football's world governing body FIFA, Sepp Blatter came under huge pressure to reform his organisation by addressing allegations of corruption in the same way as the IOC was forced to do. The accusations centred again on how one place had emerged victorious in the contest to host a big sports event, this time the gulf kingdom of Qatar allegedly 'buying' the right to host 2022 World Cup. FIFA officials were suspended pending investigation; sponsors grew nervous; but still Blatter fought the idea of reform, claiming there was no crisis in FIFA. One IOC official, speaking anonymously, said football had to be cleaned up just like the Olympics:

> "FIFA knows exactly what it needs to do. It just has to look at what happened to the IOC, and how far-reaching the consequences can be."[12]

Eventually Blatter's resistance crumbled and in August 2011 he promised to deliver a set of anti-corruption reforms. It was welcome news to any sports-lover concerned about corruption in the world's most popular game, and familiar with the saying that a fish rots from the head down.

The modern Olympics are often contrasted with the simplicity and purity of the ancient games of Olympia. But even they saw cheating, bribery and match-fixing, according to contemporary witness Pausanias.

> 'During the 98th Olympics (in 388 BC) a boxer named Eupolus bribed his three opponents to let him win. The Hellanodikai fined all four men. The fines paid for a row of bronze statues of Zeus with inscriptions explaining what happened.' [12]

Pausanias also records incidents of competitors being bribed to switch allegiance between city states. However the punishments for those caught cheating could be harsher than today, taking the form of exile, fines and flogging.

The ancient games were a religious festival, but now as then a religious connection is no guarantee of a clean and fair sporting contest.

In Japan the national sport of Sumo wrestling is wrapped in traditions that are 2,000 years old. Before each bout the wrestlers or 'rikishi' scatter salt in the ring; it is a ritual from Shinto religion. The sport itself and its participants are venerated by followers. The sport is a fundamental part of Japanese identity and tradition, yet this was not enough to protect it from scandal.

Japanese society was understandably shocked when claims of illegal gambling by wrestlers emerged. But when an investigation into the betting allegations unearthed even more serious evidence, this time of match-fixing, things looked even worse for the ancient sport.

Prime Minister Naoto Kan virtually accused the guilty parties of treason:

> 'Sumo is our national sport. If match-fixing has occurred, it is a very serious betrayal of the people.' he said. [13]

One theory is that lower-tier competitors were allegedly bribing their opponents to lose, thus allowing the victors promotion to higher-paid levels.

On examining text messages sent between wrestlers, it seemed the Japanese police had uncovered instructions on how they planned not to throw each other, but to throw a whole contest for money. One texted: 'I'll hit my opponent head on.'

Another outlined the price to be paid for losing: 'For 20 more I will concede. After the meet I need to make at least 50 or I'll be in serious trouble.' [13]

The chairman of the Japan Sumo Association Hanaregoma walked into a packed media conference and bowed low in apology; a symbolic gesture that showed how a sport wrapped in traditions of athletic purity and religious tradition had been brought down by common greed. 'I feel great indignation and sorrow', he said, 'I want to apologise from the bottom of my heart. This problem shakes the very foundation of our sport.' [14]

The Association's investigators concluded that match-fixing probably had taken place but could not say how widespread it was. Three sumo wrestlers had reportedly confessed, and in March 2011 the Grand Tournament in Osaka was called off. This was a truly serious measure; the first cancellation since the Second World War.

Like Sumo for the Japanese, cricket is supposed to embody all that is right about Englishness; fair play, honesty and lots of handshakes. Its intricacies have become metaphors that are now part of the English language: A 'sticky wicket' is a tricky situation that may leave you 'stumped'. Above all if something is 'just not cricket' then it must be jolly wrong. The implication then is that cricket must be jolly right.

Unfortunately even this paragon of sporting rectitude has faced its share of scandals and controversies. In the 1990s, if one man could be said to embody cricket's virtues it was Hansie Cronje, the captain of South Africa who had helped lead the side out of the wilderness of the apartheid years when they were banned from the world stage. Cronje was the uncomplicated straight-talking face of the game, described by the head of South African cricket Dr Ali Bacher as 'a man of unbending moral resolve, particularly as a practising Christian.' [15]

So cricket lovers refused to accept it when Indian police claimed to have tape recordings of phone conversations between Cronje and Delhi bookmakers in which he agreed to fix the outcome of a one-day match against India.

And they could still scarcely believe their ears when Cronje, who had initially denied the allegations, confessed to taking $140,000 from the bookmakers. He had even hidden the money from his wife at home.

Cronje begged forgiveness and admitted that he had 'taken his eyes off Jesus' when Satan approached him.

> 'There is no forgiveness and I have let the United Cricket Board, the team, the fans and the game down', he said. [15]

Cronje received a life ban which was to last only two years as he died in a plane crash in 2002. His tragic legacy was to be remembered not as the man who brought South Africa glory on the world stage, but shame upon the game of cricket.

More recently came allegations of so-called 'spot fixing' by members of the Pakistan test side in 2010. Following a classic newspaper sting operation, the News of the World alleged that Pakistan players Mohammad Amir and Mohammad Asif took payments to bowl no-balls during the Lord's test match. Both players protested their innocence but were subsequently banned from the sport by its ruling body.

The BBC's cricket correspondent Jonathan Agnew identified the key problem when such allegations surface:

> 'This is not necessarily match fixing.' He wrote,
> 'Although what it does do if these allegations are true – or even if they're not, frankly – you do wonder what you are watching in front of you.'

He continued: 'This is the danger to any sport in which there is any question of match fixing or betting within it – you do wonder if what you have been watching here over the last few days is real or not. And that is the damage to the integrity of the game that these allegations have.' [16]

The point Agnew makes is universal in sport; once the accusation has been made the damage is done. It does not matter whether the players are guilty or not; once the spectator is no longer sure he is watching a true contest and instead casts a sceptical eye on proceedings, the magic of sport evaporates in an instant and the activity becomes utterly devoid of meaning.

When Canadian Ben Johnson blasted his way to Olympic 100 metre gold in 1988 with a breathtaking 9.79 second dash, the world saluted him. But his glory lasted only so long as his feat was believed. His positive test for steroids days later made the achievement worthless and Johnson was sent home empty handed. But the shadow cast by his behaviour remained hanging over the sport. Rightly or wrongly, many spectators continued to wonder if what they were seeing was real or not. Similar questions hung over cycling's Tour de France for years until the ruling body tried to tackle the problems of doping in the sport. In one bizarre episode an attempt was made to deceive an entire stadium with a sleight of hand that might have come straight from a magician's handbook. It happened when one of England's finest and most respected rugby forwards Dean Richards became entangled in the so-called Bloodgate affair.

Richards, a former policeman resigned as coach of Harlequins and later received a three year ban from the game for his role in the use of a fake blood capsule by winger Tom Williams to feign an injury during a crucial European cup match in April 2009. The ploy allowed a tactical substitution and might never have been discovered had the player not been spotted on TV winking as he was led off the field, the 'blood' pouring from his mouth. Williams' lip was deliberately cut later to allay suspicion, which only added injury to insult.

Harlequins' chief executive Mark Evans accepted that although a departed coach and money lost could be replaced, it would take much longer to regain their good name:

> 'We lost in terms of our reputation and a lot of money' he said,
>
> 'You would be incredibly naïve to think the stigma will ever disappear completely. Things like that don't, they become part of history.' [17]

Before Bloodgate, rugby's record was relatively clean. The episode reminded fans that few sports are beyond a little devious manipulation, so long as the price is right. And in sport the price is very often right because the rewards for success can be huge.

Here are just three examples of how much money is to be made in sport.

In just one year golfer Tiger Woods earned an estimated $90 million in prize money, sponsorship and other earnings. [18]

In 2007 baseball player Alex Rodriguez signed a ten year contract for $275 million with the New York Yankees. [19]

In 2010 England's Premier League football clubs reportedly sold the domestic TV rights for £1.8 billion and the foreign rights for £1.4 billion, a total of more than three billion pounds. [20]

CONCLUSION

Sport derives its popularity from its unpredictability. That is where the excitement comes from; the shock defeat of a favourite or a last-minute goal to win a title. If the outcome were known beforehand, none of the millions who pay to watch sport live or on TV would bother. So any attempt to undermine the unpredictability by fixing a result or gaining unfair advantage will, once it becomes public knowledge, drain any event of its magic. We are assured most sport is clean and fair. But now there are such massive rewards for success, who would not be sceptical about some of the things that happen both on and off the field of play?

REFERENCES

[1]   'Matches made in heaven' BBC News online 22 June 2004.
[2]   Walter B. Cannon, 'Bodily changes in Pain, Hunger, Fear and Rage' D.Appleton and Co, New York 1915.
[3]   New York Times archive April 25 1915.
[4]   'From The Clicking of Cuthbert' by P G Wodehouse, published by Arrow Books. Reprinted by permission of The Random House Group Limited
[5]   'Health benefits of physical activity: the evidence'Darren E.R. Warburton, Crystal Whitney Nicol, Shannon S.D. Bredin *Canadian Medical Association Journal.*
[6]   Test Match Special interview with Kamalesh Sharma. BBC Radio 20th August 2011.
[7]   Sunday Times 14th August 2011.
[8]   Society Guardian 6th July 2005.

[9] 'The Health and socioeconomic impacts of major multi-sport events' Gerry McCartney and others. *British Medical Journal* 20 May 2011.
[10] Citymayors.com July 2003.
[11] Reuters.com 1st June 2011.
[12] 'Crime and Punishment in Greek Athletics' Clarence A. Forbes. *The Classical Journal* vol 47 No.5.
[13] CNN.com Feb 4 2011.
[14] Guardian.co.uk 3 Feb 2011.
[15] BBC Sport website/Cricket 1 June 2002.
[16] Jonathan Agnew blog BBC Sport 29 Aug 2010.
[17] BBC Sport/rugby 26 March 2010.
[18] Sports Illustrated 'The Fortune 50' July 2010.
[19] ESPN.com Dec 13 2007.
[20] Independent 23 March 2010.

In: Scepticism: Hero and Villain
Editors: R. Calne and W. O'Reilly

ISBN: 978-1-62417-783-5
© 2013 Nova Science Publishers, Inc.

Chapter 26A

INTRODUCTION TO THE LAW

William O'Reilly
University Lecturer, Cambridge, UK

Perhaps in the Law more than in any other field of encounter. Scepticism has exercised a healthy influence on the part of both litigant and bench. From the very act of arrest and charge to trial and sentencing, in the criminal and in the civil law, doubt can and has been cast on the exercise of the law. In the following series of essays, we view the law in its many applications, from the causes and effects of growth in increase in the severity of punishment and the administering of punishment; to the use of lynching as a radical extra-legal; tool in the illegal armoury of the state, serving as a revenge for intolerable crime; to the sceptical principle of the infinite regression of justification and how courts prefer the empiricist dogma of observation justification over the absolutist position of the sceptics; to the prison as site of 'performance improvement'. In a wide-ranging and impressive survey of the law and scepticism, our four expert authors cast new light on the subject, calling into doubt established views of the law as a universally and wholesale agent of positive change.

In: Scepticism: Hero and Villain
Editors: R. Calne and W. O'Reilly

ISBN: 978-1-62417-783-5
© 2013 Nova Science Publishers, Inc.

Chapter 26

BETWEEN BLIND JUSTICE AND SCEPTICAL JUSTICE: LYNCHING IN BRAZIL

Jose de Souza Martins
University of Cambridge, UK

ABSTRACT

Brazil is among the countries with the largest number of lynchings in the world, a practice that has been growing in the last half century. Several factors underlie this social anomaly and the discredit of formal and official justice. The longstanding Brazilian tradition of private justice, linked to the slavery system abolished in 1888, along with the elitism of the judiciary branch have contributed to the scepticism that leads to executions in lieu of what one might properly refer to as justice. Lynching is a radical revenge for an intolerable crime, such as the rape of a child or of a young woman, inexplicable homicide and even theft devoid of the motivation of social inequality. The assumption is that there are good people and bad people among both the rich and the poor. In the case of such crimes, it is assumed that evil cannot be redressed by conventional justice, as the agent of evil presumably lacks the human condition. This is why lynchers feel that lynching is licit. The most significant evidence of this notion is found in lynchings within prisons: lawfully condemned criminals who lynch the authors of crimes such as those mentioned above, because they refuse to be seen as equal to such individuals or to share cells with them. Lynchings are crimes carried out in the name of society, but of an archaic idea of society, and in the name of social values rather than against them, which therefore distinguishes them from common crime. They result from a belief that the punishment inflicted by conventional justice falls short of the severity of the crimes driving the lynchings.

It is inevitable that in a study on violence in Brazil, centered on the issue of scepticism about the rule of law and institutions, it becomes necessary to separate what belongs specifically to the theme of lynchings from other, different manifestations of the infringement of the rights of the individual, in particular police violence. Brazil is among the countries in the world that lynch the most, with an average, today, of four lynchings or attempted lynchings per week in the several regions of the country.

There are strong indications that one of the causes underlying this state of affairs is scepticism about the efficacy of official, formal justice. Nevertheless, anomalous police violence cannot be explained by the hypothesis that it is due to the said scepticism. To the contrary, these two forms of violence are sociologically antagonistic. Evidence indicates that, to some extent, the population lynches because it does not believe in the efficacy of police repression of criminality. On the other hand, the police, especially the military police of the various states, is involved in a high number of actions that lead to the death of civilians, because it has a distorted and archaic view of its functions. According to data from the Center for Studies of Violence of the University of São Paulo, from 1980 to 2004, the number of cases of police violence per week fluctuated between 3 and 5.7, figures slightly above the average number of lynchings and attempted lynchings.

Although the so-called public opinion of the middle class tends to be favorable to police violence, the cultured and politicized population does not condone it. This differs, in this case, from the reaction of the poorer population, which fears the police, mainly because it knows that police violence tends to target the poor, the blacks and the young. In both cases, the intensity of the occurrences indicates that Brazilian society is a violent one. However, it does not necessarily indicate that the same factors elucidate both phenomena: one is explained by lack of confidence in the police; the other, by an excess of confidence of the police in its own actions. Basically, because the violent policeperson is driven by a distorted notion of his or her entitlement to tyrannical authority and to a personal and arbitrary interpretation of the law and of what it dictates. The police prepotency that arises from time to time in Brazil has clear historical roots, being tied to the tradition of personal authoritarianism, a vestige of the slavery that gripped the country for almost four centuries.

Likewise, not all lynchings are driven by the same factors. Some are motivated by the thirst to avenge a wrongdoing. Others result from disbelief in justice when it comes to crimes for which the population is unwilling to live with impunity. Alternatively, there may be a fear that the sentence likely to be passed by the law upon a criminal for a given crime might be inadequate in the light of the perceived seriousness of the said crime, according to values that seem commonsensical but that clash with the law. It is not uncommon for evidence to show that lynchings combine these two motivations. In addition, many people take part in them merely because the opportunity to do so arose, because they were at the time and place of a violent collective reaction to a given crime.

This is precisely one of the factors underlying the eventual lynching of innocents. Out of the 2,028 cases of lynching and attempted lynching considered in this analysis, 54 of the individuals killed, or 2.7% of the total, were innocent. Among those who were hurt or killed, 159 were innocent, or 7.8% of the total. The impulsive nature of the participation of the aggressors in these violent acts is evidenced by the fact that in 56.6% of the cases of innocent death, the motivation and cause of aggression were relatively banal. Only in 35.9% of the cases did the motive involve physical aggression or the murder of the alleged victim of the person lynched. This finding is further confirmed by the fact that, of those who died in lynchings, 59.2% were killed by groups or gangs that were merely occasional, i.e., the identity of which was occasional and that dissolved promptly after the event, while 26.5% were killed by diffuse and occasional mobs. In other words, 85.7% of all lynched innocents were the victims of anonymous groups and mobs with no bonds with the family or the community of those persons that the lynching was meant to avenge. What usually occurs is that once a situation likely to incite lynching is unleashed, a range of motivations come together. This makes it impossible for one to tell what is specifically an expression of scepticism from what is specifically an expression of vengeance (which lies at the opposite end of the spectrum of reasons for lynching) and what is merely an opportunity to give vent to personal and collective tensions.

Thus, one must also understand scepticism within the context of the added, complementary motivations connected with it. In lynchings in Brazil, it is unlikely that scepticism about justice and the rule of law alone would fuel such violent reactions.

In an entirely different sphere, but one that is also an expression of the survival of archaic conduct, and for the purposes of comparison, one cannot define the persistent practice of slavery tied to indebtedness in Brazil as an expression of scepticism. This form of slavery erupted again as from the 1970s, when tens of thousands of laborers were brought into the workforce used to fell forests in order to establish new cattle ranches in the Amazon region. Forced labor resulted from the very rationale underlying the expanded reproduction of capital in areas in which there was no prior, structured labor market. There are areas that can only be taken over for economic activity if the costs of the workforce are competitive with those of the more prosperous and up-to-date sectors of the economy. Slavery is one way to cut such costs in areas where there is a shortage of labor when there is a peak of demand for workers. Infringing the labor laws is far easier in the isolated geography of such work places. Their physical distance from the government agencies that oversee labor relations and that can inflict penalties upon the transgressors undoubtedly fuels scepticism about the strictness of inspections. Indeed, a highly active and very efficient special inspection group in the government charged with repressing forced labor was only able to partially reduce the number of occurrences.

Therefore, the factors underlying persistent slavery are broader than merely scepticism about the risk of being caught for a breach of the labor laws, a risk that is supposedly low. Likewise, on the side of the victims, it is relatively commonplace to find individuals, in the clandestine work teams in the jungle discovered by labor inspectors, who refuse to be released or to sue their bosses for labor law violations. They claim that they have the moral obligation to settle their debt, built up through cash advances for their family's subsistence at their homeplace and the supply of food for their own subsistence on the job. A debt that is, however, the tool for their enslavement. This is a system internationally known as "debt-bondage." In this case, it is obvious that these workers are not skeptical about the effectiveness of the law and the respect for their rights: their subservience is part of a moral entanglement of social values that keeps them from becoming aware of what their rights actually are vis-à-vis the law. These are people who were socialized within a culture of rights and duties, of silence and obedience, that still smacks of the black slavery abolished in 1888.

Likewise, the repeated episodes of political corruption in Brazil are not the result of disbelief in the rule of law and the rights of people, but of the persistent notion that a political mandate does not dissociate what is public from what is private in the relation of patronage of the politicians and their electorate in the more politically backward regions. A cultural lag permeates the entire tissue of social relations in Brazil. This is undoubtedly what gives rise, in the more modern sectors of society, to so much scepticism, to a certain disbelief in all that is formal and contractual. The assumption that the backward part of Brazil is blocking the modern part of Brazil is one of the more deep-rooted notions of Brazilian society. However, it also gives rise, in the more backward segments of the population, to a comparable level of scepticism as to the efficacy of modern institutions in making social relations be fair. This also applies to the conduct of those whose behavior should in theory be governed by the rules of impersonality and of respect for individual rights.

This widespread frailness of the country's institutions has led to social conditions that can foster the recrudescence of archaic forms of law. One can witness this in several areas of reality. The iniquity of property rights, linked to the chronic concentration-oriented tendencies of land ownership in Brazil, is reinvigorating in the popular movements the notion of useful ownership of land as the moral basis for its economic use. This actually resumes the colonial notion of property rights, based on the assumption that the right of ownership stems from human labor. The right of those who work on the land. A denial of land ownership based on a merely commercial notion of property rights, of rights that stems from a land purchase deed rather than from the labor that makes the land productive.

Frequent lynchings, even for banal reasons, indicate a resumption of very ancient legal practices that stemmed from the various traditions that formed what one may call Brazilian popular culture. A blend of traditions drawn both from the many centuries of Arab influence in the Iberian Peninsula and from the notion of justice disseminated by the Roman Catholic Inquisition, active in Brazil up to the eighteenth century. These lynchings reveal that as soon as some room for popular and anti-legal violence materializes, notions of punishment now banished from Brazilian law re-emerge and come to life, such as physical punishment and the death penalty itself.

The practice of lynching, in Brazil, has been rising in the last 50 years. Several factors underlie this social anomaly and the discredit of formal, official justice that goes hand-in-hand with it. Not only Brazil's longstanding tradition of private justice, tied to the slavery abolished in 1888, but also the quagmire of red tape and the elitism of the Judiciary Branch of government have fueled the scepticism that leads people into taking the law into their hands rather than resorting to what is actually justice. Lynching is a radical way of taking revenge for a crime that the lynchers believe is intolerable, such as the rape of a child or of a young woman, inexplicable homicide, or even theft.

Those who take part in lynchings tend to disregard social class distinctions. The assumption is that there are good people and bad people among both the rich and the poor. Therefore, lynchers take the law into their own hands not only in relation to the poor population, although there is a tendency for the poor to be more heavily identified with the traditions and the social values of the past. It is not uncommon, especially in lynchings in small and even relatively prosperous towns of the inner-state areas, for middle class individuals to be involved in this violence, or for members of the elite to be in the roll of the victims of lynching attempts. In these cases, the assumption, based on the evidence, is that conventional justice will not redress the evil done. The agent of evil is seen as a being devoid of the human condition. Thus, the lynchers feel that the lynching is licit, rather than a crime against the human species itself. The most significant evidence of this notion is found in prison lynchings: legally condemned criminals lynch other criminals, such as those mentioned above, in particular the rapists of children, because they refuse to be seen as their equal or to share cells with them.

Lynching is a crime committed in the name of society, albeit an archaic idea of society, in the name of social values rather than against them, which therefore sets them apart from regular crimes. They are fuelled by the belief that the punishment inflicted by conventional justice is inadequate in the light of the seriousness of the crime, leading the involved parties to lynch the criminal. One must keep in mind that Brazil, when it comes to criminal law, was subject for almost its entire colonial period to the Ordinances of King Philip II of Spain, instituted at the time when the kings of Spain also sat on the Portuguese throne (1580-1640). According to these ordinances, in certain cases, such as marital betrayal and blood crimes, avenging the crime took precedence over normal justice. Thus, the cheated husband's or the offended family's honor took precedence over the law and its courts. In these cases, the right to direct vengeance for an offense to one's honor came before state-applied justice. Likewise, several characteristics of present-day lynchings are a clear legacy of the torture and punishment procedures that typified the Roman Catholic Inquisition.

In this chapter, I analyze certain aspects of those lynchings in Brazil. Scepticism is one of their evident triggers, to judge from the 2,028 cases of a database that I organized during the last few years, covering the 1945 to 2010 period. These data concern not only lynchings, but also lynching attempts. In Brazil, one encounters the same difficulties that researchers have stumbled upon in the United States, where studies of this kind are now divided into two groups: those based on a major statistical database organized back in the 1930s, drawn on newspaper narratives, with information provided by local correspondents; and case studies whose numbers have been slowly rising in recent years. In Brazil, there is only a few case studies on the subject and what few quantitative studies do exist are also based on newspaper information.

My database is not a probability sample of the occurrences, as the newspaper information in the subject is random. Therefore, it is not statistically representative. One can, nevertheless, interpret trends and, above all, the characteristics of the lynchings, by comparing the series of cases of actual lynchings with those that were only attempted lynchings, or the series of cases that concern different reasons for lynching.

My database differs from the reference database of the American studies, which is limited to basic information, with a few classification elements, such as the data of the event, the place and the name of the victim. My record sheet for each lynching (successful or otherwise) has fields for 189 items, ranging from the date of the sources to a long list of details. Based on the reference material found in newspapers (generally more than one publication per lynching), I broke down the descriptions, whether of the act of lynching or of the composition of the lynching mob, the characteristics of the victim and the reasons for attacking this person. Thus, I obtained a longer list of comparison items and therefore a more in-depth description and interpretation of the phenomenon, which would have been impossible using the US database. This is a methodological tool that provides me with a better sociological understanding of this type of violence.

One of the results is an index of the endurance of hate, a means of finding out for how long a human group is likely to have the impulse to lynch a person for a given cause. In 68.5% of the cases, the violent act of lynching occurs immediately after the crime that triggers it. However, in 17.9% of the cases, hate persists throughout the same day, until the lynching is accomplished. In 5.2% of the cases, there is still a willingness to lynch on the day after the occurrence of the driving event. And in 8.4% of the cases, hate persists beyond two days, there being some cases in which it lasted more than one year after the driving event, when, the opportunity having arisen, the hated person ended up being lynched. Therefore, in 31.5% of the cases, the lynching impulse does not wear out in the first few minutes after an event such as a murder, rape or theft.

Prompt lynchings and attempts can be ascribed to the impulsive and irrational conduct of the crowd. In principle, they cannot be imputed solely or decisively to scepticism about legal punishment of the author of the violent act that spurred the collective crime. Still, one can talk about a predisposition to lynching and the impulsive act in the face of the reiterated information disseminated by the media about the slow workings of the legal system and laws that tolerate crimes that the population tends to consider far more serious than the judicial system does. In this case, even the 68.5% of cases of a sudden and impulsive attack upon someone potentially subject to lynching contain an element of scepticism in their motivation. Nonetheless, this scepticism is tied to a general frame of reference rather than to an immediate motivation; it is the scepticism of predisposition to a violent act, rather than scepticism properly connected with motivation.

When one groups the reasons for consummated or attempted lynching, new motivation components surface. I have created four motive classification categories: a reaction to a trifling cause (such as when a car drives through a puddle in the street and splashes water on those who are standing at a bus stop); personal attack (which includes murder and rape); personal attack coupled with an attack upon property (such as wounding in order to steal), and property crimes (such as theft). The lynching stimulus is more immediate both in the case of trifling causes (86.3%) and of property-related crimes (88.4%). As for the more serious crimes against individuals, the bulk of lyncher motivation is limited to the moments immediately following the event (60.1% when the crime was against a person and 55.7% when it was against a person and property). However, in both cases, the endurance of the hate that drives lynching is far greater, extending beyond the day of the triggering factor in 18.3% of the cases of crimes against individuals and in 22.7% of the cases of crimes against individuals and property. When the motivating event is a trifle, only in 4.5% of the cases does hate extend beyond the day of the crime and in the case of crimes against property alone, hate endurance is limited to 1.4% of the cases.

These data suggest that not all lynchings are an expression of scepticism or, at least, that scepticism is distributed unevenly across the different types of lynching and their drivers. Scepticism is at play when the reason for lynching is a crime against the person. As from the occurrence of the triggering event, a widening time window opens for the possibility of police intervention to arrest and even to protect a person accused of a crime that might lead to lynching. In 91.9% of the cases in which lynching was not promptly consummated, the police was able to save the victim. This corresponds to half of all the occurrences, if we include in this those people who were actually lynched and killed, cases in which there was not the slightest possibility of saving the victim. The few documented cases of attempts to save the person being lynched show that those who engage in such attempts run the serious risk of also being lynched or, at least, severely battered.

Another index that I have developed measures the delay in the execution of the victim of successful lynchings. It is very unusual to get any information about the number of minutes it takes to perform the lynching. However, one can establish an indirect time indicator by listing the procedures of the mob at the lynching and by ascribing a numeric figure to the sum of the items. A lynching generally starts with the search for and pursuit of the criminal, then unfolds into stoning and hitting the person with sticks and beating this individual. It then proceeds to physical mutilation (such as ripping out the eyes or extirpating the penis) and to burning the person's body, sometimes while the individual is still alive. This is the entire cycle of the typical Brazilian lynching, a sort of unconscious script followed by the lynchers, though not all stages are always performed. Thus, a typical lynching is an act of collective cruelty, inspired by a notion of vengeance.

In attempted lynchings, i.e., those that are not completed, in which the victim is only wounded or in which the victim is saved, the lynchers' drive wears out fast. In 47.4% of the cases, only one item is performed, such as battering the victim; in 24.8%, two; in 14.7%, three; in 6.5%, four; and in 6.3%, more than four. In successful lynchings, the drive is greater, as indicated by the range of procedures applied to conduct the lynching: persecution, stoning, battering, mutilation, etc. In only 1.4% of the cases do the lynchers resort to a single element of lynching to kill the victim; in 12.8%, they resort to two; in 18.7%, to three; in 18.9%, to four and in 48.12%, to more than four. Even when an individual is promptly lynched following an act that awakens the wrath of the mob, the unfolding of the lynching stages, as evidenced by the number of procedures involved, suggests that here too a high degree of scepticism is at play. This is what the diversification of the means and instruments of violence and the notorious sequence of choices indicates. One can state that the greater the number of items or moments of the act, the greater the likely scepticism, because the closer the lynchers are to archaic patterns of justice. Hence, the greater their rejection of the modern notion of justice.

My analysis is based on the hypothesis that scepticism alone does not explain the lynchings. However, this scepticism can range from weak to strong, its being impossible to talk about scepticism as a uniform attitude with the same intensity in this mode of collective violence. Scepticism itself depends on a variable set of factors involved in the occurrence. Based on this hypothesis, I found that there are frequent assumptions in Brazil against young people, involving increasing objections to and prejudice against them. It seems that in this country there is widespread scepticism about the possibility of youngsters from a given social background to be on "the right track" toward becoming valid adults, especially in those sectors of society that identify more closely with the precedence of order and of work in the organization of social life. In the last 50 years, the protection of children and of adolescents has risen, even when these minors engage in wrongdoings. The resistance to child labor and actions to combat it have also increased, the State having put in place measures that define as illegal the early recruiting of new generations into the workforce. Nonetheless, these measures clash with the popular notion that work educates and that failure to work encourages delinquency and vagrancy. Parents themselves generally have their doubts about the government policies that prohibit their children from working. Thus, society has been left with no tradition-based references in order to accept and understand youth, but has instead a context that some look upon as being more of a preference for laziness than preparation for life.

I have tried to find out whether the lynchings and lynching attempts reflect these notions via a greater incidence of the lynching of youths. It is sometimes impossible to include in the database information on the age of the victims of this kind of violence, which makes it difficult to draw up comparisons. This information is lacking for 32.5% of the victims of lynching and attempts. However, one can analyze the data on lynching victims separately, in particular those cases in which the mob took violent action, versus those in which the victims were only the target of attempted lynching, when the thirst for vengeance is lower.

I grouped the ages that were known into four groups: minors (under 18), young adults, adults, and the elderly. No significant difference was noticeable among those who were victims of attempted lynching, the relatively more mild form of violence, and those who were actually killed. In the first case, minors and young adults comprise 51% of all victims of the two levels of intensity of the aggression. In the second case, this category accounted for 55% of those who were killed. Therefore, one cannot state that the scepticism of the population is greater if the author of the crime is young, when it comes to the strictness of punishment.

However, the data do show that scepticism is strong when one takes into account the racial variable. Lynchers are willing to accept that Justice will be harsh enough for a white person, but not for a black one. This actually conceals the greater complicity of the crowd with a white person's crime than with that of a black person. Whites deserve tolerance and even a pardon, but this is not true for blacks. Hence the option for the direct violence of vengeance when the object of hate is black.

Even serious crimes committed by white people can be judged by the crowd with relative mildness as compared to the strictness that the lynchers expect for the same crime when committed by a black. In the set of victims of lynchings and attempts, 48.1% are white and 51% are black and of mixed race. Here too, as the database lacks information on the race of all the victims, so that one can only compare the ratio of successful and unsuccessful lynching attempts for those victims whose skin color is known. Again, the difference is highly significant. Among those who die at the hands of lynchers, only 29.2% are white, whereas 70.1% are black or of mixed race. Thus, in the overall set of lynchings and attempts, the ratio of white victims to black victims is about the same, but in the case of deaths by lynching the proportion of blacks and people of mixed race is almost double that of whites.

The different reaction of the lynchers to blacks and whites still reflects the widespread notion that blacks do not deserve equal rights, this being an expression of the historically old idea that transgression forms part of the temperament of blacks, a notion typical of Brazil's persistent racial prejudice. This state of affairs suggests that the likelihood of a black person being lynched for a given crime is twice as great as it is for a white person. Therefore, scepticism is even greater in this case, indicating that the skeptical posture is not the same for the same people, scepticism varying in accordance with other factors that intervene in social relations in the face of violence. Scepticism is not an *a priori* and absolute phenomenon. To the contrary, this study on lynching clearly shows that it fluctuates according to the circumstances, the factors and the target.

Scepticism also varies depending on who is doing the lynching. I have grouped the data on 1,756 victims of lynching and of attempted lynching based on the social characteristics of the group of lynchers. The first group comprises people who belong to the family of the victim of the crime that motivated the lynching. This accounts for 6.7% of the sociologically identified cases. The second group consists of friends and neighbors and accounts for 17.1% of the cases. The third group, which accounts for 34.2% of the cases, is made up of people in general and those who live in the area, who are geographically close but are not neighbors, generally people who do not know the victim of the crime. Finally, there is the fourth group, accounting for 42% of the total, comprising anonymous people, passers-by, who occasionally happen to find themselves near an occurrence that drives the crowd to violence. They too do not know the victim and in general they are only occasionally at the site of the occurrence, being drawn to the lynching by induction, going along with the so-called collective behavior, which can be irrational and impulsive. Sociologically, this group forms the characteristic crowd. The first group tends to be numerically small, usually far less than 50 people. The second group tends to be a little bigger, about 50 to 60 people. The third group ranges from 60 to 100 people. The last group generally has at least a hundred people, more often 400 to 500 people, and it may even exceed 1,000 people.

In this order, scepticism as one of the reasons for lynching tends to be greatest in the first group and weakest in the last. One can measure this by taking into account the higher ratio of dead people in the first group (39.9%) and the lower ratio of dead people in the last group (28%). The same scale can be observed concerning wounded victims (16.9% and 13.6%). However, if one considers those who were saved (37.3% and 52.4%, respectively) or who escaped from the hands of the lynchers (5.9% and 6%), the order is reversed. The larger groups, the true crowd, which lacks affective bonds with the victim of the original crime, seem to be less skeptical about justice and the law than those groups that are affectively closer to the victim of the target of the lynching, whether the latter was killed or not.

Descriptive data for each case do not suggest that the size of the group is decisive for lynching success. In theory, though, an irrational mob tends to be more dangerous than smaller groups. Therefore, one should expect the last of the four groups to be responsible, proportionately, for a larger number of killings than the first. However, the data show that the opposite is what actually occurs. Lynchers from the family of victim of the crime that is giving rise to the lynching apparently have a weaker belief in the effectiveness of formal, official justice. Still, the evidence does indicate that this group is driven not only by the duties of a relative (which they could fulfill by turning to the police), but mainly by the rights of family ties, especially blood rights. The ritual adopted in one of the lynchings is a good indication of this. One morning, an adolescent killed, in order to steal, an impoverished adolescent girl that was minding her family's small bar. He then fled, but was pursued by the neighbors, who caught him and dragged him back to the front of the place where the murder had taken place. Here they tied him up. Before killing him, they called the family members that were closest to the dead girl, including her mother, to exercise their right of precedence by striking the lynched adolescent first. Only then did the crowd finish killing the murderer, beating and stoning him. There have been other similar cases.

This is the type of lynching that is part of a vengeance culture, with a defined target, for a precise reason. This is not true, however, in lynchings carried out by a veritable mob, when people's relations with the cause and the target of violence tend to be diffuse and imprecise. This characteristic of some emblematic lynchings reflect the remote influence of the aforementioned Ordinances of King Philip, which defined certain crimes, even some that involve blood shedding, as a matter of private interest of the parties involved. Scepticism, in this case, is relative, because the revenge, though illegal, is based on tradition, on a popular culture that is still loaded with social values from former, pre-modern times.

However, I cannot fail to mention one feature of the lynchings that reinforces the interference of scepticism in their occurrence. If one examines the 24 hours of the day of the occurrence of the lynchings and attempted lynchings by type of group of lynchers, there is a clear tendency for the first group (members of the family of the victim that generated the lynching reaction) to lynch more at night (58.5%) than in daytime (41.5%). As for the last group, the true mob, it lynches mainly in daytime (55%) rather than at night (45%). Daytime lynchings result in fewer fatal victims, whereas nighttime ones generate more. At night, the level of violence is greater and the violent act takes longer. One can only surmise that the lynchers are more careful during the day than at night, when they can be harder to identify. Thus, they act less violently in daytime.

This is a good indication that even a group that is affectively motivated to lynch due to hate and the thirst for revenge, by revealing its stronger scepticism about law and justice, has a more relative interpretation of scepticism at night, even though it may seem that the opposite is at play, when the crowd shows an awareness that there is a conflict between habits and the law, between what it is doing and what the law would do. It is therefore less skeptical than it might seem at first, tormented by the risks of its dilemma: to take justice into its own hands or to delegate the punishment of a criminal to the neutral hands of institutional, official justice.

Overall, there is no doubt that scepticism about Justice is at play, to varying degrees, in lynchings and attempted lynchings. However, this scepticism is not entirely independent from a certain degree of cowardice in the choice of revenge, as evidenced by the lynchers' reluctant determination to lynch: they are braver when cloaked in the darkness of the night than in the light of day; and they are more violent in the identifiable complicity of the affective group, of those who are close and recognizable, than in the solitude of an anonymous crowd, even though, in this case, these individuals become more dangerous, their behavior being more unforeseeable.

There is no indication of what the individual and subjective effects of taking part in lynchings carried out by anonymous mobs may be. However, there are two proven types of consequences and outcomes of lynchings. One consists of the social effects of the lynchings in the sites where they occur. First, a small tendency for lynching to be repeated, even in the neighborhoods of a metropolis such as São Paulo. The occurrences are clearly tied to a popular notion of keeping the social order or of establishing order in new neighborhoods, where neighboring relations are yet to be consolidated. Second, in small communities, concerns with personal safety and nervousness can follow a lynching, there being cases of lynchers fleeing and even relocating their home to avoid the ensuing social stigma. This notwithstanding, these groups affirm what they believe is a socially altruistic motivation to lynch, in the sense of taking action to defend their social values.

These consequences can be observed in two cases. One concerns a community lynching that took place in the southern region of Brazil in 1987. Ten years later, 23 of the lynchers were tried based on the testimony of the victim (who had murdered a young man from the community at a dance). Before dying, he gave a deposition to the police, saying he could recognize them from their voices during the lynching, which took place at night and in the dark. Tried by jury in that place, all were absolved, other than the poorest of them all, who was turned into something of a scapegoat in order to meet the requirements of legal, formal justice.

The second case concerns the lynching of three thieves and assassins of a taxi driver in the Central region of Brazil, in 1998. The case is yet to be solved and a new attempt to try 59 accused people was under way in September 2011. The partiality of the local jury during the first attempt to try the accused caused the court to transfer trial to a different legal district. Furthermore, witnesses refused to identify the accused, making the progress of the trial and the work of the accusers, of the prosecution, difficult.

Ultimately, all these cases, including the lynchings carried out by a typical mob, indicate that the scepticism that forms part of public vengeance is an expression of the strong survival of the values and of the mentality of archaic communities, united by blood or by neighborhood. Even large cities and an urban lifestyle have been incapable of modifying certain habits and traditions, which can be explained, to a substantial extent, by the major importance, in the areas of modern Brazil, of the continuous and frequent migrations of populations from remote and rural locations.

REFERENCES

José de Souza Martins (1991). Lynchings - life by a thread: street justice in Brazil, 1979-1988.

José de Souza Martins (1996). Linchamento, o lado sombrio da mente conservadora. *Tempo Social - Revista de Sociologia da USP,* Vol. 8, Number 2, p. 11-26.

José de Souza Martins (2002). A justiça popular e os linchamentos no Brasil. In Isaura de Mello Castanho e Oliveira, Graziela Acquaviva Pavez e Flávia Schilling (Eds.), *Reflexões sobre Justiça e Violência*, p. 139-157. São Paulo, Educ – Editora da Puc-SP/Imprensa Oficial-SP.

José de Souza Martins 1995). As condições do estudo sociológico dos linchamentos no Brasil. *Estudos Avançados*, Vol. 9, Number 25, p. 295-310.

Martha K. Huggins (Ed.), Vigilantism and the State in Modern Latin America (Essays on extralegal violence), p. 21-32. New York, Praeger Publishers.

In: Scepticism: Hero and Villain
Editors: R. Calne and W. O'Reilly

ISBN: 978-1-62417-783-5
© 2013 Nova Science Publishers, Inc.

Chapter 27

SENTENCING AND PUNISHMENT OF OFFENDERS

David A. Thomas
Trinity Hall, Cambridge, UK

ABSTRACT

This chapter provides an overview of the growth of the law of England and Wales relating to the sentencing and punishment of criminal offenders, highlighting the frequent tensions between judges and legislators.

For centuries lawmakers have been preoccupied with the punishment of criminals. Three themes constantly recur in the debates. For legislators, a continuing increase in the severity of punishment has been a dominant purpose, based on the belief that severe punishments deter potential offenders, and in modern times by the often misplaced belief that the voting population wishes to see offenders dealt with more and more harshly. For judges, the ability to adjust punishment to meet the circumstances of the individual offence and offender and to exercise discretion has been a priority. For those administering punishments, the high cost in both human and economic terms of administering a system of severe punishment has proved a challenge. The interplay of these themes has produced throughout recent history a series of conflicts, often resolved only in a way which satisfies none of the interested groups.

Processes leading to the award of criminal punishments differ greatly in different societies. The formal structure of criminal justice systems frequently reflects the fundamental social principles on which a particular society is based.

More democratic societies allow members of the general public to participate in the system, usually as jurors, although the role of juries and the extent of their authority differs considerably from one country to another. In some contexts juries are strictly limited to determining whether the guilt of an accused person has been proved; in others the jury may have a role in determining the details of the penalty to be inflicted. In more authoritarian societies, there is no room for participation of the general population, and the principle that the judiciary should be independent of government is less important. Despite the formal differences between legal systems, almost all urbanised countries are faced with the same problem - that of dealing with a larger numbers of cases than the system can process, while remaining loyal to its basic principles. The need to accommodate large numbers of cases leads either to enormous delays in bringing cases to their conclusion, or a variety of compromises, typified in most English speaking countries by rewarding those who admit their guilt with a lesser sentence than they would receive if convicted after a full formal trial. Plea bargaining, as it is generally known, takes many forms but it is probably a universal if hidden feature of all criminal justice systems.

The second area of compromise is in the administration of punishment. Few modern urban societies do not suffer from prison populations which far exceed the capacity of the prison system to accommodate them in decent and constructive conditions. This problem invariably leads to systems designed to contain the growth of the prison population without apparently undermining the superficial rhetoric of the system, with the result that there is a often a wide gap between sentences imposed and sentences actually served.

These problems are demonstrated by the evolution of the English criminal justice system. As long ago as the seventeenth century, the severity of English criminal law, which appointed death as the punishment for any felony, was mitigated by a combination of judicial and executive devices. The judicially devised way of avoiding the obligation to impose a death sentence was the bizarre concept of benefit of clergy. The theory behind the concept was that anyone who was a priest – a clerk in holy orders – should not be subject to secular sanctions, but should be handed over to his Bishop to be dealt with within the framework of ecclesiastical discipline. As there was no reliable record of who was and who was not a clerk in holy orders, the courts devised an instant test of literacy to be applied to an offender who had been convicted of felony and who was likely to be sentenced to death. The convicted felon would be asked to read from the Bible – psalm 51, verse one –which became known as the "neck verse". If the convict made a reasonable attempt to read the verse, it was assumed that he was a clerk in holy orders and he was released without punishment on the misplaced understanding that he would surrender himself to the Bishop. Many offenders who were not priests would try to learn the neck verse by heart, so that when the time came they could make a pretence of reading it and thus avoid being sentenced to death. This practice, which led to many convicted offenders escaping any punishment, continued with modifications throughout the 17th and 18th centuries, although it was much curtailed in the 18th century, but it was not finally abolished until 1827.[1]

The economic aspects of the excessively severe system of punishment led to a different procedure. During the 17th century, it became apparent that what were then the American Colonies were badly in need of labour, and that convicted felons who might otherwise be executed could be useful in fulfilling the needs of the Colonies. This led to the introduction of a system of transportation. A convicted felon would be sentenced to death, but the judge had the choice of leaving him for execution, in which case he would be executed within a very short time, or granting him a reprieve, a temporary stay of execution to allow the offender or his friends to petition the King for him to be pardoned. Pardon was normally on the condition that the convict submitted to being transported to the American Colonies for a period to be specified.[2] This system operated in an arbitrary manner, as the choice of which convicts were to be left for execution and which were to be granted the chance of a conditional pardon was entirely in the hands of the individual judge, with no appeals or other kind of guidance. It operated into the early years of the 19th century and was described by Samuel Romilly in his "Observations on the Criminal Law of England" as the 'lottery of justice'.[3]

Transportation did not come to an end with the loss of the American Colonies in the late 18th century. Instead, attempts were made to find other territories to which convicts could be transported and the discovery of Australia by Captain Cook gave transportation a new impetus. The growth of transportation as a means of dealing with convicts during the 18th and early 19th centuries led to the development of another aspect of the sentencing of offenders which is a recurring theme of current debates. This is the gap between the sentence pronounced by the judge in court and the punishment actually experienced by the offender. By the beginning of the 18th century, Parliament had begun to close off the concept of benefit of clergy and numerous statutes were enacted which provided that the sentence for the offence concerned was death without benefit of clergy. This development simply gave more significance to the procedure of transportation under conditional pardon. Many offenders sentenced to death were in fact

---

[1] 7 and 8 Geo 4 c. 28.
[2] See Radzinowicz, A History of English Criminal Law (1948), Vol. 1.
[3] Observations on the Criminal Law of England as it relates to Capital Punishment and on the mode in which it is administered (1810).

pardoned and transported, first to the American Colonies and later to Australia. During the same period, transportation itself evolved as a sentence which courts were empowered to impose without going through the mechanism of a conditional pardon, but very frequently the sentence of transportation passed by the court was not carried into full effect. Many offenders ordered to be transported for a particular period were granted a ticket of leave and allowed to return to England before the transportation period had expired, and many others sentenced to transportation never left their home country, instead serving out their sentences in hulks moored in the Thames and other rivers.

Until the early 19th century the idea that judges should exercise discretion and determine the precise term of the sentence to be passed on a particular offender had little formal place in English criminal law. The penalty for felony remained in most cases death, to be mitigated by the process of conditional pardon. Judicial discretion occurred only in relation to the lesser offences of misdemeanour, for which statute did not appoint any maximum penalty and the judge could at least in theory impose a sentence of any length whatsoever. The idea that judges should be empowered to determine the length and a nature of a sentence really came about almost by accident. By the 1820s, parliament was beginning to dismantle the grotesquely severe penal system which had been established in the 18th century, and transportation was being substituted for death as the penalty for many offences. Some statutes fixed transportation for a specified period as the penalty for the offence –transportation for life or 14 years might be fixed. In some cases legislators could not agree on what the fixed period of transportation should be, and compromised on a formula such as "transportation for any period from seven years to life", which left the judge to determine the period of transportation. It was in this way that the modern concept that judges should determine the details of the sentence to be served became established in English criminal law[4]. By curious coincidence, the Criminal Law Commission which was attempting to codify the criminal law was opposed to the idea of extensive judicial discretion in sentencing. Their idea was that sentencing should be closely regulated by detailed statutory provisions and that judicial discretion should be limited to making very fine adjustments within a highly prescriptive legislative scheme[5]. The ideas of the Criminal Law Commission did not prevail, although in modern times there is an increasing tendency to move in the direction of the scheme imagined by the Commission.

The decline of transportation during the mid 19th century created the need for a system of dealing with offenders within the country and the inevitable

---

[4] See Thomas, The Penal Equation, (1979).
[5] See Seventh Report of the Criminal Law Commissioners (1843).

acceptance of the fact that offenders would returned to normal society after completing their sentence. Transportation was replaced by a new sentence known as "penal servitude". Courts were empowered to sentence offenders to terms of penal servitude, chosen by the judge in the exercise of his discretion, but the offender did not necessarily or even normally serve the period specified by the judge. Penal servitude always involved various schemes by which the offender could earn early release by good behaviour and hard work while serving a sentence. The principle that the sentence pronounced by the court was not carried into full effect was by now well established. Allowing offenders to earn early release from a sentence of penal servitude had two advantages – it allowed some control over the size of the captive population, and it provided a powerful incentive for good behaviour while in custody.

The decline of transportation and the substantial reduction in the use of the death penalty gave rise to another problem which had not previously troubled the system. This was the problem of the persistent offender. In the days when the death penalty and transportation were widely used, a persistent offender would normally either be executed, or transported overseas without much realistic prospect of ever returning to take his place in normal society. Once it became the general practice for an offender to serve out a sentence in England and to be released back into the community, the problem of persistent offenders and how to deal of them became highly visible. One judge referred to the end of transportation as "the stoppage of that great sewer which for so many years carried away the dregs of our population.[6] "

One solution, which has found echoes in more modern thinking, was what became known as the "cumulative principle", invented by a magistrate, Barwick Lloyd Baker. His principle was simple; he pointed out that it was necessary for sentencing to be organized in a way which was easily understood by those who were likely to be sentenced, whom he described in the politically incorrect language of the time as "that weak and unreasoning class who are to form our future criminals" . Under his cumulative principle, a convicted offender would expect on a first conviction, a short sentence of imprisonment, perhaps of a few weeks; on a second conviction the sentence would be 12 months; but on a third conviction, however trivial the offence, the sentence would be seven years' penal servitude[7]. This principle, Baker argued, would avoid the necessity to make difficult judgments about the culpability of the offender, but would allow a consistent approach to be adopted which everyone could understand. The cumulative principle was enthusiastically adopted by many judges and led to

---

[6] Matthew Davenport Hill, Charge to the Grand Jury of Birmingham of October 1851, in Suggestions for the Repression of Crime (1857) p. 185.
[7] See War with Crime (ed Phillips and Verney) 1889, pp. 27-91.

sentences of enormous length, often for what would now be considered relatively minor offences. Many other judges refused to follow the cumulative principle and argued that sentences should be related to the gravity of the offence committed by the offender, however many other offences he had previously committed. This led inevitably to enormous disparity in sentences and pointed to the need for some system to provide consistency in sentencing, so that the sentence imposed on any offender would be determined by the gravity of his offence rather than by the accident of which judge sentenced him.

By the end of the 19th century, a series of problems confronted the designers of the sentencing system. First, it was necessary to find some system which would ensure a reasonable measure of consistency in sentencing between different judges. Second, it was essential to develop a satisfactory method of dealing with persistent offenders. Third, a new principle had begun to emerge – the principle of the rehabilitation. It came to be recognized that the protection of society from the depradations of criminals might be avoided if young offenders in particular could be dealt with in a way which equipped them to lead a law abiding life in the future, rather than by severe punishment premised on the assumption that they and their contemporaries would be deterred from future offending by fear of being exposed to the same severity. Finding a place for this principle in the scheme of things required attention.

The method of securing consistency in sentencing which was eventually adopted was the creation of a Court of Criminal Appeal. Until the early years of the 20th century, there was no formal system of criminal appeal of any kind in the sense in which that term would now be understood. Occasionally, a convicted offender might persuade the judge to reserve a question of law for consideration by all the judges, and this system was eventually formalised as the Court for Crown Cases Reserved in 1848. Over a period of many years, bills to create a system of criminal appeals were introduced into Parliament, but they were rejected on the grounds that a system of appeal would weaken the sense of responsibility of jurors. The idea that an appellate court with jurisdiction to review sentences might contribute towards the harmonising of sentencing began to emerge in the last decades of the 19th century[8], but the Court of Criminal Appeal was not established until a series of miscarriages of justice involving Adolf Beck, who had the misfortune to be twice wrongly convicted, gave new urgency to the need to create a better system of appeals. The provisions of the bill allowing the new Court of Criminal Appeal to review sentences were of secondary importance. The Court of Criminal Appeal was eventually established in 1908 with power to increase as well as to decrease the sentence on an appeal by

---

[8] See Thomas, Constraints on Judgment, (1979) p. 75.

a convicted offender, and the existence of this power proved for many years to be a powerful deterrent to an offender considering whether or not to appeal. The judges who constituted the Court of Criminal Appeal were not eager to develop a new jurisprudence of sentencing; early judgments were extremely short, with little attempt to relate the decision in the particular case to any general principle. It seemed that the court was more concerned to deter appeals than to encourage appellants to bring forward issues for resolution. While the court did identify a few relatively broad principles of sentencing, its impact on sentencing in the trial courts was limited. Decisions of the court on sentencing matters were not systematically reported and academic and other legal commentators showed little interest in the problems of criminal law in general and sentencing in particular.

The study of sentencing as a judicial process became a more popular after 1960, and the first detailed analysis of the principles on which the Court of Criminal Appeal acted was published in 1970[9]. A critical development was the appointment of Lord Lane as Lord Chief Justice in 1980. Faced with the growth of the prison population and the need to stabilise sentencing, he took the initiative in delivering a series of what became known as "guideline judgments" setting out general guidance to judges on sentencing in various types of case, such as the importation and distribution of drugs and rape. The production of guideline judgments was not systematic, and often was a response to particular episodes. The guideline judgment on sentencing in rape was the result of a particularly controversial case in which a man convicted of rape received a suspended sentence[10].

At about the same time, the systematic reporting of selected decisions of what was now the Court of Appeal Criminal Division began[11], and an encyclopaedia collecting the reported decisions under relevant headings appeared in 1982[12]. Decisions of the Court of Appeal on sentencing were now much more readily accessible to the judges who sentenced in the lower courts, and citation of previous decisions of the Court of Appeal in sentencing matters, previously rare, now became accepted and normal practice. The power of the Court of Appeal to increase the sentence on an appeal by a dissatisfied offender had been removed in 1966, and there was now no powerful deterrent to an appeal, although in a few cases of unmeritorious appeals the court retained and used the power to order that part of the time spent by the defendant in custody awaiting a hearing of his appeal – normally a few weeks - should not count against his sentence. (Offenders

---

[9] See Thomas, Principles of Sentencing (1970).
[10] Roberts (1982) 4 Cr.App.R.(S.) 8, later amplified in Billam (1986) 8 Cr.App.R.(S.) 48.
[11] The Criminal Appeal Reports (Sentencing).
[12] Current Sentencing Practice.

seeking to appeal against conviction or sentence were not normally granted bail pending the outcome of the appeal.).

Another important development of the same period was the institution of formal seminars on sentencing for judges sitting in criminal courts, organised by the Judicial Studies Board (now known as the Judicial College). All judges except those who sat in the High Court were expected to attend seminars at which matters of sentencing were discussed, and take part in sentencing exercises in which hypothetical cases, based on real cases, were considered. The introduction of judicial studies (the words "judicial training" were not acceptable) was at first highly controversial. Some commentators took the view that judges were necessarily possessed of all human knowledge and that no person could possibly tell them anything that they did not already know. There was also concern to that a system of judicial training would allow persons other than judges to influence the way judges performed their duties and this might threaten the hallowed principle of judicial independence. Once the system of judicial studies had passed through its early years, it became apparent that most judges welcomed help with the performance of their role and the system of judicial studies expanded beyond sentencing into other areas of judicial activity.

While the increased activism of the Court of Appeal in sentencing matters, the greater accessibility of its judgments and the introduction of judicial training promised much for the development of greater consistency in sentencing, a countervailing force was the growth in the frequency of legislation affecting sentencing. The statutory framework of sentencing in post- war years was provided primarily by the Criminal Justice Act 1948, a relatively short piece of legislation written in clear language which remained virtually unchanged for 20 years. From the late 1960s, driven partly by concern over the growth of the prison population, and partly by political agendas unrelated to the real problems of criminal justice, Parliament began to legislate with greater and greater frequency on sentencing, without necessarily paying much attention to the practical consequences of the legislation enacted. After 1982, hardly a year passed without at least one new piece of legislation on sentencing; the legislation itself became more and more complex and interventionist.

Increasingly, the legislation began to intrude into the area which judges had come to regard as the proper sphere for the exercise of judicial discretion. General criteria, often so vague as to be meaningless, were laid down in statute. A statute of 1991[13] provided that a custodial sentence could not be passed unless the offence was "so serious that only a custodial sentence could be justified." This provision left to the judiciary the decision how serious an offence had to be before

---

[13] The Criminal Justice Act 1991.

it was "so serious," and the judges soon came to the conclusion that just about any offence could be "so serious" if the judge considered it to be so. Despite the failure of legislation of this kind to have any impact, for good or ill, on the sentencing process, politicians began to realise the potential political value of interventionist legislation. Until the final years of the 20th century, the administration of criminal justice had been treated by both major political parties in a politically neutral manner. Electoral capital was seldom sought from criminal justice legislation. This came to an end in 1997, when a failing Conservative government introduced the Crime (Sentences) Act 1997, introducing mandatory minimum sentences for certain offences. Minimum sentences had disappeared from the criminal law in the 19th century, except for murder. The Act introduced minimum sentences of seven years' imprisonment for offenders convicted on a third occasion of trafficking in class A controlled drugs (in fact, such offenders would be lucky to receive a sentence as short as seven years for such offences), minimum terms of three years for those convicted on a third occasion of domestic burglary, and most controversially a mandatory sentence of life imprisonment (known as an "automatic life sentence") for offenders convicted of one of a list of serious offences, who had previously been convicted of an earlier "serious offence." The Bill was passed into law shortly before the 1997 general election, at which the Labour Party was returned to power. Although the new Labour government was not obliged to bring the mandatory sentencing provisions of the Act into force, it did so.

The automatic life sentence produced some of the most bizarre sentences ever passed in history of English criminal law. One was a life sentence passed on a man who robbed a small shop at the point of a banana, which was treated for the purpose of the Act as an imitation firearm[14]. Another was a man who went into a bank and handed over a note signed in his own name saying "this is a robbery - give us the money - I have a gun." He had a plastic toy pistol in his pocket. He was sentenced to life imprisonment, as he had done something similar on an earlier occasion. Happily in this case the Court of Appeal was able to find grounds for quashing the sentence[15].

Undeterred by the experience of the automatic life sentence, whose application the judiciary were eventually successful in controlling by adopting an interpretation derived from the Human Rights Act 1998, Parliament pressed on with mandatory sentencing provisions which frequently had results opposite to those which were intended.

---

[14] The case of Howard Allen, reported in the Sunday Mirror, December 26, 1999.
[15] Buckland [2000] 2 Cr.App.R.(S.) 217.

One example is provided by the provisions requiring courts to treat "racial aggravation" as an aggravating factor[16]. There was no need for such legislation, as the Court of Appeal had already stated in unambiguous terms that the fact that an offence was motivated by hostility on racial grounds was to be treated as an aggravating factor. The legislation created a new series of racially aggravated offences based on existing offences. For example, to the existing offence of common assault, punishable in the magistrates' courts with a maximum sentence of six months' imprisonment, there was added the offence of racially aggravated common assault, punishable with two years' imprisonment. This gave rise to two practical problems. Those who designed the legislation overlooked the fact that in proceedings in the magistrates' court a defendant can be convicted only of the offence charged, and not of what is known as a "lesser included offence", an offence all of whose ingredients are contained within the graver offence specified in the charge. The result was that if a defendant charged with racially aggravated common assault, admitted the assault itself but disputed the allegation that the offence was racially aggravated, which might mean simply that he used words of racial abuse at the time of the assault, he was acquitted not merely of the racially aggravated common assault, but of the underlying assault itself, even though there was no doubt that he had committed that offence. A further complication was the fact that as racially aggravated common assault was punishable with more than six months' imprisonment, a defendant charged with that offence had the right to insist on trial by jury in the Crown Court. Faced with the possibility that a defendant charged with racially aggravated assault might exercise this right, with the result that the Crown Court might be called upon to try, at great public expense, an allegation which amounted to little more than a drunken minor assault accompanied by words of racial abuse, prosecutors would decide to abandon the charge of racially aggravated assault and proceed on a charge of simple common assault. The result of this manoeuvre was that the defendant had to be sentenced on the basis that the offence was not "racially aggravated," as it is a fundamental principle of sentencing that an offender must not be sentenced on the basis that he is actually guilty of an offence more serious than the offence of which he has been convicted.

The increasing the volume of legislation on sentencing, together with its complexity, inhibited attempts by the judiciary to secure a consistent and logical approach to sentencing. Inspired by developments in the United States of America, Parliament became attracted by the idea of a Sentencing Council which might lay down general rules for sentencing. Such bodies, usually known as Sentencing Commissions, had been created in many criminal jurisdictions of the

---

[16] See the Crime and Disorder Act 1998, sections 29 to 32.

United States in response to a particular development. For decades, the majority of American jurisdictions relied heavily on the indeterminate sentence. A judge passing a sentence of more than 12 months' imprisonment would not normally decide on the term of the sentence; the sentence might be expressed as one year to 10 years in the state penitentiary. Partly for this reason, American appellate courts took no significant interest in sentencing, and no jurisprudence of sentencing developed. Public confidence in the indeterminate sentence evaporated in the late 1970s and it was necessary to fill the vacuum left by the abolition of the indeterminate sentence with formal rules laid down in statutory or quasi-statutory form by a body established for the purpose[17]. Some academic commentators in England supported the introduction of a similar body, and by a series of stages Parliament established what is now the Sentencing Council , with the duty to formulate and publish guidelines on sentencing. While in the United States, the sentencing guidelines formulated by the various sentencing commissions filled a vacuum, the English Sentencing Council and its predecessor the Sentencing Guidelines Council, are effectively in competition with the Court of Appeal Criminal Division, and there is increasing confusion about which will predominate.

An underlying concern of all those involved in managing the sentencing of offenders during the second half of the twentieth-century was the continuing growth of the prison population. The prison population had declined dramatically over a period of about 40 years, from 1880 until the end of the First World War, and remained relatively stable until the end of the Second World War. From about 1945, the prison population began to increase steadily, and was approaching 40,000 by the mid-sixties[18]. By 2011 it was more than 80,000. Some of the legislation introduced during this period was designed to discourage judges from passing custodial sentences, either by attempting to restrict the power to do so or by the provision of what were hoped to be attractive alternative forms of sentence to be served in the community.

The most significant set of changes involved the introduction of procedures under which offenders sentenced to terms of imprisonment might be released before completing the sentence pronounced by the court. There was nothing new in the idea that the sentence of the court would not necessarily be served in full, and by 1948 a relatively simple and straightforward system had evolved. Anyone sentenced to a term of imprisonment (penal servitude had by this time been abolished, and all custodial sentences imposed on adults were designated "imprisonment") would normally expect to serve two-thirds of the sentence

---

[17] See Frankel, Marvin E, Criminal Sentences, Law without Order , 1972.
[18] See Report of the Committee of Inquiry into the United Kingdom Prison Service (1979).

pronounced by the court and then be released on remission. A prisoner who misbehaved in prison might be ordered to lose part of the one-third remission, as a result of internal disciplinary procedures.

In 1967 a new parole system was introduced. Under this system offenders serving sentences of at least 21 months might be released, at the discretion of the Parole Board, after serving at least 12 months or one third of the sentence, whichever was the greater. Release was discretionary and considered a privilege rather than a right. A prisoner released under this scheme was on licence and could be recalled to prison if his licence was revoked, usually but not necessarily as a result of misbehaviour following his release. Prisoners who were not released under the discretionary system continued to be entitled to the remission of one third of the sentence pronounced by the court, and those whose licences were revoked would also be released after serving two-thirds of the sentence.

The pressure to contain the growth of the prison population led to numerous changes being made to the parole system, with the result that it became ensnared with anomalies which could operate in an extremely unfair manner. In 1991, Parliament replaced the original parole system with a second system. Under this system, prisoners were divided into three categories - those serving sentences of less than 12 months were released after serving half the sentence, but could be required to serve the remaining part of the sentence if they committed a further offence. Those sentenced to 12 months and less than four years were also entitled to release after serving half of the sentence, but release for them was subject to a licence which lasted until the end of the third quarter of the sentence. If they committed a further offence during the whole term of the sentence they could be ordered to serve the remaining part of the original sentence in addition to the sentence imposed for the new offence. Those sentenced to four years' imprisonment or more were not entitled to release halfway through the sentence, although they became eligible for discretionary release at that point. If they did not achieve discretionary release, they were entitled to release after serving two-thirds of the sentence and would in all cases remain on licence until the end of the third quarter of the sentence.

This system, although apparently complicated, worked reasonably well but again Parliament could not leave well alone. In 1998 legislation introduced a system of release on "home detention curfew, " at the discretion of the governor of the institution where the offender was detained, without any formal procedure. Under the original legislation, an offender could be granted release on home detention curfew 35 days before the date on which he would otherwise become entitled to release, but this period was gradually increased to its present level of 135 days.

In 2005 yet another parole scheme was introduced[19]. Under this scheme, all prisoners would be released on licence halfway through their sentence, irrespective of the length of the sentence. The new scheme applies only to offenders convicted of offences committed after 4th April, 2005, and the old scheme continues to apply to those sentenced for offences committed before that date, whenever the sentence is imposed. This dual system gives rise to cases where a defendant is sentenced for two or more offences, some committed before and some committed after 4th April, 2005, with the result that he is subject to both parole systems simultaneously. The extension of "home detention curfew" means that offenders sentenced to relatively short terms of imprisonment - less than two years – may find that they are required to remain in custody for only one quarter of the term pronounced by the judge. An offender sentenced to 18 months' imprisonment is entitled to release after serving one half of the sentence or nine months, but may well qualify, at the discretion of the prison governor, for release on home detention curfew after serving only 4 1/2 months.

The lesson to be learned from the recent history of the English sentencing system is that constant change and political intervention will produce a system which lacks all credibility. Achieving consistency in the approach to sentencing adopted by a large number of judges - over 2000 full or part-time judges are entitled to pass sentence in the Crown Court, and almost 30,000 lay magistrates in the magistrates' courts - is inevitably a gradual process which takes time to accomplish. Changing the basic framework at frequent intervals, as has happened in the last 30 years, obstructs this process. Changes in the rules which determine what proportion of a custodial sentence must be served in custody leads to confusion on the part of sentencers and sentenced alike. While no system of sentencing could operate on the principle that all sentences must be served in full, the gap between the sentence pronounced by the judge and the sentence actually served is now so great in many cases that the system lacks credibility in the eyes of the public. There is a desperate need to simplify the framework of sentencing, to allow judges to develop their own means of achieving consistency without constant legislative interference, and to restore some stable relationship between the sentence pronounced and the sentence served which can be understood by all concerned.

Any proposal for change in the administration of criminal justice deserves to be greeted with a healthy degree of scepticism and subjected to rigorous analysis before being adopted. All too often, what is proposed as a new and exciting departure is in fact a return to practices which have been tried and abandoned in the past, sometimes the distant past.

---

[19] By the Criminal Justice Act 2003.

REFERENCE

Ashworth, *Sentencing and Criminal Justice* (fifth edition, 2010). Contains an extensive bibliography.

In: Scepticism: Hero and Villain
Editors: R. Calne and W. O'Reilly

ISBN: 978-1-62417-783-5
© 2013 Nova Science Publishers, Inc.

Chapter 28

THE PRISON AND THE PERFORMANCE REVOLUTION: 'VIRTUAL' OR VIRTUOUS IMPROVEMENT?

Alison Liebling
Institute of Criminology, University of Cambridge, UK

ABSTRACT

The prison has been found to be, on balance, 'criminogenic': making crime more rather than less likely. Prison sentences deprive children of their parents, offenders of their livelihoods, and many prisoners of the few resources they have to survive legitimately in the community. Prisons are better at achieving their symbolic and political aims: expressing rage, soothing anxiety, and winning public political support, than they are at changing lives for the better. So how do we evaluate the quality of a prison? Have prisons improved since the 'performance revolution' of the late 1980s and early 1990s? What are their main purposes? This chapter explores the application of a broad set of public service management changes aimed at improving and modernising the public sector to the case of the prison, addressing the question of performance measurement in particular. There may be other institutions (such as schools, families, and communities) and interventions which are better placed to achieve a reduction in crime.

INTRODUCTION

If management reform really does produce cheaper, more efficient government, with higher-quality services and more effective programmes, and if it will simultaneously enhance political control, free managers to manage, make governments more transparent and boost the images of those ministers and mandarins most involved, then it is little wonder that it has been widely trumpeted. Unfortunately however, matters are not so simple (Pollitt and Bouckaert 2000: 6).

I think prisons have to be values driven. I'm not personally fascinated by Performance Management. I recognise that a degree of it is necessary, but I think some of the worst Governors are the ones who believe that their job is to deliver all their Key Performance Targets by hook or by crook and it doesn't really matter how. So I would much rather have a prison that misses some of its targets but is doing right by people than the other way round.

(Prison Service Senior manager, pers. comm. 2009)

Have prisons improved in quality since the 'performance revolution' of the late 1980s and early 1990s? Does it make sense to describe prisons as 'successful'? Put in more contemporary language, do modern prisons achieve their objectives? What *are* their main purposes? Do prisons work, and if so, what do they accomplish? This chapter looks at the application of a broad set of public service management changes aimed at improving and modernising the public sector to the case of the prison, addressing the question of performance measurement in particular. Can performance targets be trusted in the deeply complex environment of the prison?

MANAGERIALISM AND PRISON QUALITY MEASUREMENT

Managerialism - a process of public sector transformation involving the specification of organisational objectives, the use of performance targets and regular measurement, and the introduction of clear lines of accountability and work specification - can be characterised as the search for more efficient, effective output-oriented techniques for organising and improving public services, or as an 'ideology of total, finely calibrated control' (Nellis 2001: 33). The process began under the Conservative Government of the early 1980s, continued under New Labour, and has continued with the added vigour of intense financial restraint under the Conservative-Liberal Democratic Alliance. The aim of managerialism was to overcome the deficiencies of the bureaucratic traditions of the machinery of government by introducing private sector practices and mechanisms into well meaning but inefficient organisations. Prisons are often used as an example of the success of the public sector 'modernisation' project as there has been a clearly visible management revolution in the prisons world. Up-and-coming Governors tend to be graduates of management studies and accountancy rather than the social policy and sociology scholars they once were. They know precisely how their prisons are performing, and share this information with prison officers at monthly full staff meetings. Managerialism brought with it close attention to budgets, target setting, strategic plans, competition, best practice, performance measurement and the concept of 'value for money' but, many have argued persuasively, a move away from any serious discussion of purpose and ethics, in part because of its tendency to focus on 'what is easily measurable'.

Critics argued throughout the 1990s that managerialism was displacing older moral concerns and rehabilitative ideals in criminal justice. It represents a departure from an 'old way of life': the welfare state compromise between capitalism (the free market) and socialism (public provision through the state), ameliorative aspirations, and an ethos of 'public service'. A clear value base had once been embedded in notions of rehabilitation, bureaucracy and professionalism. This framework was de-stabilised during the 1980s in the face of complex pressures of public spending restraint, shifting government ideologies and the exposure of bureaucratic inefficiencies in the public sector. The state was seen as acting as an inhibitor of innovation and efficiency – whereas the market would increase and enhance consumer choice. Bureaucrats were the enemy of the people. Professionals were self-interested and had become too powerful.

This critique of bureaucracy and professionalism was applied wholesale to prisons. They were poorly managed, increasingly expensive, wasteful, bureaucratic, and shamefully out of date. Regimes were impoverished, although nobody knew this with any accuracy until prison scholars King and McDermott published an article in the *British Journal of Criminology* in 1989, showing this to be the case. There were major concerns about ineffectiveness, lack of accountability and brutality. The Prison Officers' Association (POA) had far too much power and led the resistance to modern management practices.

Two decades later, with a powerful performance framework in place, increased management control, and powerful private sector competition, have prisons improved?

The Chief Executive of the Prison Service (now subsumed under the National Offender Management Service, incorporating the Probation Service) argues that they have. Compared to the 1980s, when prisons were unstable, unhygienic, beset by industrial relations disputes and suffering from frequent escapes, prisons are more ordered, stable, and survivable. The workload of the Prison Service has grown rapidly: the average prison population rose by 29% between 1999/2000 and 2009/10 (from 65,153 in 1999/2000 to 83,970 in 2009/10). The cost per prisoner is almost the same, despite better service provision and facilities. New prisons have been built, to a modern (and more efficient) design. Official performance has improved substantially. The most important success - the ability to protect the public - has also improved dramatically: There have been no Category A (the highest security category) prisoner escapes since 1995/6; in the decade and a half preceding there were 27. There has been an 87% decrease in all escapes from prisons and prison escorts between 1999/2000 and 2009/10, dropping from 38 to 5. There has been a 70% decrease in absconds (failures to return to, or escapes from open prisons) between 1999/2000 and 2009/10, dropping from 907 to 273[1]. There has been a 73% reduction in escapes from contractor escorts to courts and hospitals between 1999/2000 and 2009/10, dropping from 1 escape per 22,251 movements in 1999/2000 to 1 escape per 81,416 movements in 2009/10. The number of offenders convicted of serious further offences whilst subject to statutory supervision continues to be low – around 0.4% of the overall caseload.

These figures show significant improvements in *security*, which are in turn linked to improvements in the way prison officers carry out basic procedural aspects of their work. Since a series of dramatic escapes from two high security prisons in 1994/5, prisons are now audited on most of the 'process' dimensions of their work (such as following the numerous 'compliance baselines' for security and other procedures). There is no question that staff, including prison governors, are more accountable for the delivery of basic standards in their prisons, and that procedures are more clearly specified. They are audited regularly on these aspects of their work.

Inside prison, and turning to regime quality, the Prison Service has also increased the number and quality of offending behaviour programmes provided to prisoners. These programmes are aimed at tackling their offending, thinking and self-control. So there were three times as many Offending Behaviour Programme, Sex Offender Treatment Programme and drug treatment programme completions delivered in prisons in 2009/10 than in 1999/2000 (16,441 compared to 5,024). These programmes are research-based, empirically validated, cognitive-behavioural interventions thought to reduce the likelihood of reoffending by specific groups of prisoners, who are appropriately risk-assessed for a place. Note

---

[1] The number of absconds rose in the middle of this period, peaking at 1,310 in 2003/4 (Spurr 2011).

that the number and variety of programmes available compared to the size of the prison population (around 85,000) is still relatively small. Some improvements to reconviction rates among prisoners serving between 1 and 4 years (those most likely to be placed on such programmes) have been demonstrated in recent years. Reconviction rates for prisoners serving under 12 months remain high, at around 68 per cent.

The growth in population has been managed by the provision of more than 7,900 prison places built since a well orchestrated Prison Capacity programme began. The rate of overcrowding has still increased by 4.6% over the last 10 years, as sentences become longer and the population continues to rise above most predictions, and the capacity to build. Prisons have expanded in size (from around 500 prisoners each, on average, to around 1200 each), as space within prison sites (such as sports fields) are used to house quick build extensions and nearby prisoners are clustered together under one 'super-Governor'. New prisons are designed with a much larger capacity than old traditional prisons. A fierce debate about so-called 'Titan prisons' (expected to house 3000 prisoners each when originally proposed) was resolved in favour of somewhat less ambitious prison sizes: prisons currently under construction aim to house around 1500 prisoners each. This is still significantly larger than used to be the case, or the figure recommended by Lord Justice Woolf and others in reviews of penal order (around 3-500).

This increase in population build up has occurred 'without any adverse impact on the safety of prisoners or staff'. So, for example, the rate of suicide, and the rate of murder, have both declined up to 2011 (but there are signs of upward movement as 2011 draws to a close). There were 60 self-inflicted deaths in each of 2008 and 2009. This was the lowest number of self-inflicted deaths since 1995 and, at 86 per 100,000 prisoners, the lowest three year average rolling rate since the three years ending 1988. There were three prisoner-on-prisoner homicides in 2008 and none in 2009. The 10 year rolling average homicide rate fell to 1.9 per 100,000 prisoners and remained at this level in 2009. This represents the lowest since the 10 years ending 1990. It is unusual to have more than one prisoner homicide per year. This is considerably lower than in some other penal systems. On the other hand, there have been planned murders (as well as serious assaults) committed by prisoners, often against offenders convicted of sexual offences, who are strongly disapproved of by the rest of the prisoner community.

Though the proportion of the prison population serving sentences for violence has increased from 20% in 2000 to 27% in 2008, prison violence, as measured by 'offences of violence punished per 100 prisoners', has remained fairly constant at 23 per 100 prisoners. The rate of assault on staff in 2009 was 4%, down from a peak of 5% in 2005. Rates of positive mandatory drug tests (prisoners found to have used drugs in compulsory urine tests) have fallen by 5.5 percentage points from 13.4% in 1999/2000 to 7.8% in 2009/10. Between 1990 and 1999 there were 13 of the most serious acts of concerted indiscipline (riots), falling to four in the decade 2001 to 2010.

Prisons are, then, more *ordered* as well as more secure. Some of these gains can be attributed to better design (for example, clearer sight lines, with gated areas separating individual wings and landings), better intelligence (staff anticipate and proactively manage threats to order), and improved legitimacy: that is, a well-publicised 'decency agenda' requiring staff to address and treat prisoners respectfully, a well established complaints system, the use of prisoner representative committees, the establishment of a prisons ombudsman, and a more judicial approach to internal prison discipline. Many of these improvements followed the most serious and widespread series of disturbances seen in prisons in England and Wales – the Strangeways and other disturbances – in 1990, among the causes of which were, according to Lord Justice Woolf, legitimate grievances by prisoners about the nature of their treatment.

Other improvements to regimes have occurred. 'Purposeful activity' has increased since 1999/2000 from an average of 23.2 hours per week to 24.5 hours per prisoner per week in 2009/10. This means that most prisoners are unlocked for a higher proportion of the day, that they have somewhere to go, and some have jobs to do. Work and education constitute a significant part of the prison day in most prisons, for at least a proportion of prisoners.

Security, order and regime provision have all increased. Staff are, and feel, more accountable, and receive regular visits from the Audit and Assurance team, the Prisons Inspectorate, the Regional Custodial Manager, and interviewers from the Prisons Ombudsman team, inquiring into specific complaints. Prisons have their own Independent Monitoring Boards, who report annually. Prisons are far more transparent than they once were, a fact aided by the availability and proliferation of information technology. A colleague and I, who spend all of our research time studying prisons, recently agreed that were we ever to find ourselves in this position, we would prefer to be in a prison of today than a prison of the 1980s. They are more materially decent and purposeful places.

So all is well in prison. Or is it? There are at least four main problems with the account outlined above: critics suggest that the performance measures used are inappropriate and set at far too low a standard, and that audit and performance measurement are distorting activities aimed at 'legitimation' (presentation) rather than substance; secondly, the aims and objectives of imprisonment have transformed and become unrealistic and politicised (as well as out of proportion to the role legitimately played by the prison in society); and thirdly, all roads have led to privatisation as a solution to the management and other 'problems of imprisonment'. This is a risky and inherently expansionist option. Finally, there are important but less measurable indicators of life in prison missing from the official performance framework.

PERFORMANCE MEASUREMENT AND AUDIT

Senior Officer: 'Have we got any ticks in any of the boxes yet?'
Auditor: 'Only little ones.'[2]

First, the measures themselves. Critics often point out that whether in the Prison Service or in other organisations, 'Key Performance Indicators' (KPI's: targets the organisation must reach) do not always reflect the declared strategic direction of the Service (for example, they reflect security as a bottom-line goal but not 'humanity'). Those KPIs which do measure a relevant goal (such as security, order, safety or decency) often measure only one aspect of it, and this they may do ineffectively, despite constant refinement. Meaning is lost when 'rehabilitation' has as its key measure, 'average amount of purposeful activity' delivered (an 'input' rather than an outcome), and 'safety' is measured as 'number of serious assaults'. The figures used refer only to recorded findings of guilt at adjudication for assault and so fail to take account of both the separate charge of fighting and of assaults which staff ignore or fail to see. Other indications of safety which staff and prisoners may judge relevant but which are not reflected in performance measurement include levels of bullying, minor and major disorder, the approachability of staff ('trust in the environment'), use of Incentives and Earned Privileges schemes or other methods of informal discipline, and so on.

KPIs are a limited way of measuring performance, although they can, to some extent, measure change over time. They can, however, have important distorting effects on organisations. A recent Chief Inspector of Prisons suggested that they create a 'virtual prison system' far removed from reality (New Statesman 2002: 16). Targets tend to be set in areas that are amenable to measurement, rather than in areas that 'matter'. As one commentator put it, they measure 'progress through the jungle', but they do not necessarily indicate whether this is 'taking them further into or out of the jungle' (Sinclair 2002: 11). Wormwood Scrubs has been used as an example of a prison that was 'failing', and brutal, and yet apparently effective according to its KPI performance (see HMCIP 2000; 2002; and on similar findings in Wandsworth, see HMCIP 2011). These shortcomings are

---

[2] The Senior Officer is commenting on the ongoing audit visit his establishment is undergoing. See further Liebling, assisted by Arnold 2004.

contrary to the declared spirit of the managerialist ethos, whereby greater control over important organisational goals is being sought.

A study of the role of KPIs in the management of prisons and their performance concluded that what they bring to prison management is clarity or direction (Sinclair 2002). Some indicators are deliberately 'target-stretching', and others are lowered when they prove impossible to meet. As Sinclair argued, the Prison Service does not have control over its environment (for example, population size, which impacts on regime delivery); and KPIs do not take into account different populations and their propensity to assault, for example. There are significant omissions, so that, for example, health care, important personnel matters, and the perceived legitimacy of increasingly long and indeterminate sentences, with complex routes out, are not included in these measures. Senior managers are aware that 'we still measure what we do, rather than what we *should* be doing' (Prison Service Senior manager, pers. comm.).

Some governors have commented that the introduction of KPIs constituted the single most important transformation in the role of governor and in the way the Service is managed. They clarify objectives and can be used to demonstrate to staff where the strengths and weaknesses are in their own organisation (as well as how they are 'performing' in relation to like establishments). Because they are quantitative, and provided that individual governors believe in them, the introduction of KPIs 'for the first time gave staff confidence that they knew what they were being asked to deliver' (Sinclair 2002: 4). Whilst they constitute an imperfect measure of 'what is going on', they focus attention on performance generally. The can bring about a form of 'governing-at-a-distance', however: governors locked in offices poring over figures, rather than out and about on their wings, alert to the mood of prisoners and staff. Governors are well aware that their competence is judged by whether or not they succeed in meeting KPI and KPT (Key Performance) indicators and targets, the latter of which are more numerous, and represent 'inputs' or processes intended to deliver the KPI's. They have reduced idiosyncracy, but also, arguably, charisma and innovation; and they arise from a mechanistic image of organisations. There is considerable debate about whether KPIs constitute distracting outputs rather than outcomes:

> When managers are enjoined to concentrate on concrete outputs (training courses completed) they tend to lose sight of outcomes and, therefore, to stress efficiency rather than effectiveness...when, alternatively, managers are asked to concentrate on outcomes and effectiveness, it is hard to hold them responsible and accountable, for several reasons. This is because the attribution of outcomes to the actions of individual units or organisations is frequently obscure or doubtful, and also because, for many public programmes, measurable outcomes manifest themselves over such extended

time periods that they cannot provide a sensible basis for annual accountability exercises anyway (Pollitt and Bouckaert 2000: 166-7).

Performance *measurement* has been privileged over performance *management*, so that expertise in creating league tables is more developed than expertise about how to turn around failing prisons. But on balance, it has to be said that KPIs have precipitated a cultural change within the Prison Service, from an input (staff-led) organisation, to an outputs-focused Service, with some apparent improvements in regime delivery as well as in the kinds of measures in use. Governors and staff 'care about how my prison is doing on those charts' (Sinclair 2002: 57) almost regardless of whether or not the charts are measuring the right thing.

Linked to the phenomenon of performance targets is another new management tool: the auditing of process compliance. This is now a familiar practice in schools, hospitals, universities and prisons. A practice originating in the world of finance, the process of auditing is now applied to non-financial practices and systems and is used to scrutinise them closely. Auditing, like performance measurement, represents a 'new rationality of governance', whereby central control reaches deeply into organisations, bringing with it expectations of self-control, individual accountability and unprecedented levels of knowledge about internal organisational arrangements (Power 2001). The 'audit explosion' is related to a distinct 'phase in the development of advanced economic systems' (Power 2001: 14).

The level at which audit standards are set is, arguably, relatively low with most prisons achieving acceptable ratings most of the time[3]. Some argue that the audit process serves as a 'stimulus to professional strivings to improve practice' and make relevant changes (e.g., Scrivens 1994: 95). Others are more cynical, believing that performance *and* audit figures are irrelevant, meaningless, and systematically fabricated. Power has suggested that the excessive checking involved in 'the audit society' is pathological. He describes auditing as a 'ritual of verification' which is rarely based on a solid understanding of what practices matter. It is related to a deeper set of issues about 'the organisation of trust in developed societies' (Power 2001: xvi). The need to check suggests doubt, mistrust, risk and danger. Power suggests that auditing systems are primarily about 'reaffirming order' rather than constituting a true system of accountability and that:

---

[3] Rex and colleagues found, in a study of the accreditation process for offending behaviour programmes, that the Prison Service gained accredited status with apparent 'ease' compared to the Probation Service. See Rex et al. 2003.

Institutionalised pressures exist for audit and inspection systems to provide comfort and reassurance, rather than critique (Power 2001: xvii).

This yearning for order via control, without trust, may have unintended consequences. As O'Neill argued:

Perhaps the culture of accountability that we are relentlessly building for ourselves actually damages trust rather than supporting it (O'Neill 2002: 19).

Inappropriately precise and rigid measurement systems used in complex organisations can lead employees to 'conclude that they are not valued or understood as professionals' (Sitkin and Stickel 1996: 210) and can lead to a reaction of distrust and non-compliance (Braithwaite 2001). Audit is, as Power argued, a 'sociologically significant activity', with important and barely understood effects on prison life. It may bring with it evasions and fabrications. New generation senior managers are often experts in constructing the most surprising activities (for example, intelligence interviews with prisoners) as 'purposeful' (hardly the spirit of the original indicator). The alternative to checking is *trust*. Few policy-makers are currently reflecting on how trust might be built in organisations. Perhaps this is regarded as too difficult, and too risky, but research suggests it is an important aspect of effective organisational behaviour.

THE PURPOSE AND OBJECTIVES OF PRISON

It was failure to deliver acceptable standards of daily provision in most prisons, that led King and Morgan to favour the potentially achievable 'humane containment' goal for the Prison Service in their submission to the May Committee Inquiry at the end of the 1970s over the hopelessly unrealistic, aspirational, 'good and useful life' statutory formulation of the Prison Service's aims.[4] Human warehouses are surely preferable to *inhuman* warehouses? What use are 'good intentions' for the prison, if they are 'devoid of real meaning' and not aimed at 'specifying achievable objectives' (King and McDermott 1995: 9)? Industrial relations disputes, poor systems of managerial control, an increasing prison population and deteriorating prison conditions made for impoverished regimes and a lack of justice. So what we saw under managerialism, was the substituting of lofty but unachieveabole aims for the Prison Service, with less

---

[4] Rule 1 of the 1964 Prison Rules, now preserved at Rule 3 of the current Prison Rules.

ambitious but more achievable aims (so, delivering 16,441 accredited programmes to a population of 85,000 prisoners rather than an abstract but un-evidenced general rehabilitation aim). Achieving this target is constructed as 100 per cent success. This is a modest, as well as indirect, achievement.

Meanwhile, public and political discourse about the prison has changed. Liberal and humanitarian values of individual transformation and reintegration into the community have been discredited and all but abandoned in criminal justice practice. This is so in prisons in particular, in the wake public outcry at serious offences committed by prisoners on home leave and early release schemes throughout the 1990s as well as a general public anxiety about crime. Some important changes to the penal landscape have taken place in the public sphere, according to recent political pronouncements, which shape the values and targets expressed, practised and aimed for in prison. Punishment has returned as one of the main purposes of prison.[5] Population size has increased enormously as sentence lengths have increased, and new crimes have been introduced. It is harder to engage in moral dialogue about the uses of imprisonment when lack of clarity about its purpose and proper limits exists, and the main focus is on 'public protection' and the symbolic expression of punishment. The current mood in relation to the prison is contradictory. On the one hand, prisons should punish and deter; on the other, they should reform. Achieving both simultaneously is, in practice, extremely difficult. Demanding but legitimate sanctions can be effective. Punitive or degrading sanctions are counter-productive, creating resentment and defiance. The evidence for the effectiveness of deterrence as an objective is negative.

The new penal framework revolves around the concept of 'effectiveness' – making sentences 'work' – and requires prisoners to 'engage fully in the process of their own incarceration': attending offending behaviour courses, complying with the requirements of their sentence plan, and voluntarily avoiding the use of drugs. It is a deeper and tighter form of imprisonment than formerly, cutting deeply into the prisoner's soul (Crewe 2009: Liebling et al 2011). Prisoners can no longer passively undergo imprisonment but must work strategically towards goals set by the institution. In return, the prison should be decent. Effective prisons are capable of following their own rules, delivering reasonable (but not excessive) standards, securing compliance by a mixture of control, incentives, disincentives and legitimate (but not indulgent) treatment, and offering a menu of accredited offending behaviour programmes increasingly tailored to particular populations and criminogenic needs (only those needs related to offending

---

[5] Alexander Paterson famously said that, 'people are sent to prison as not for punishment. Jack Straw, on the other hand, pronounced in 2009 that prisons are places of 'punishment and reform'.

behaviour), and designed to challenge thinking and behaviour (rather than 'understand' it).[6] There have been new attempts to replace recreational education with evidence-based basic skills courses (against some significant opposition). This mixture of better standards, adherence to process, control over 'privilege-drift', intervention in criminal attitudes and lifestyles and a more robust approach to performance on public safety issues (that is, more emphasis on outcomes), has become the 'new legitimacy' of the early 21st century. Prisoners tend to find this 'new penology' somewhat illegitimate (for example, they tend to prefer the older designed prisons, which sometimes express the paternalistic, rehabilitative aspirations of an older generation of prison managers and policy makers). It is a narrow, aggregate and responsibilised (neo-liberal) vision of the function of the prison in contemporary society.

PRIVATISATION AND PERFORMANCE

Finally, we come to privatisation, the logical conclusion of managerialism applied to the prison. The use of private companies to build, manage and eventually finance prisons was originally conceived as 'an experiment' (Home Affairs Committee 1987) and was to be restricted, in the first instance, to facilities for prisoners on remand. Monopoly had led to complacency and a failure to innovate. A competitive bid was held for the management of Wolds Remand Centre in 1989, and shortly afterwards for several additional prisons holding both sentenced and remand prisoners. Wolds was soon able to house both remand and sentenced prisoners. These newly built, modern prisons would offer 'value for money' and 'humane, challenging and purposeful' regimes (Windlesham 1993: 300). This move would pave the way for a broader programme of institutional and penal reform. England and Wales now has 11 prisons (of 135) operated by three private companies (Serco, Sodhexo Justice Services, formerly Kalyx, and G4S). This development has had major effects on the operation of public sector prisons, who have to compete to 'win new contracts' or increasingly, to retain their existing work. The contract to manage Birmingham prison, a traditional local prison in the Midlands, was recently 'awarded' to G4S and has been operated by them since October 1 2011. This wholesale transfer of public sector work to the private sector is almost unprecedented in prisons in the UK (it has been achieved in New South Wales, Australia, with one prison: Parklea, and Buckley Hall in Rochdale has been operated by both the private and the public sector). The performance of private prisons, compared to public sector prisons is, however,

---

[6] As Bottoms observed, this agenda is very 'correctionalist' (Bottoms 2002).

varied. Staff turnover is high, experience and expertise is low, and policing and safety tend to be weaker than in the public sector. The better private prisons are more open to innovation, and can sometimes forge creative partnerships with external agencies willing to work with ex-prisoners in the community. Their managing companies are hungry for business, and so incentivised to adapt to the Government's new 'payment by results' agenda, promising success and driving their prison Directors hard to deliver it. This is highly complex and deeply contested territory. One evaluation suggests limited success to date, and some fight back on formerly weak areas – cost and culture – by the public sector; see Liebling and Crewe 2011).

Criminologist Richard Sparks suggested that privatisation was offered as a weak solution to the legitimation problems of the modern penal system (Sparks 1994). Privatisation, and experiments with market testing, form part of a pragmatic, 'control model' approach to the delivery of penal services. 'The delivery of penal services' is an instrumental notion with little relevance to the ethics or purposes of imprisonment. The type of quantification, and the regime aspirations, arising out of these developments leave crucial questions of moral responsibility, penal purpose and individual transformation untouched.

Private sector competition has reached a new level of intensity, with seven further prisons announced for 'competition' as this book goes to print. Without detailed empirical scrutiny, a clearer grasp of the prison's main purpose, and some reflection on the proper limits to prison use, and the role, training and employment conditions of prison officers, the Prison Service is entering new and unchartered territory.

PRISON LIFE AND MEASUREMENT

Many aspects of prison life remain difficult to measure, and stand in conflict with the positive instrumental purposes inherent in official goals. The culture and atmosphere in prisons can be fraught, complex and dangerous. Drug taking is higher than suggested by official performance measures, as it is not always possible to detect, despite compulsory testing programmes. Some prisoners are introduced to drugs in prison, or step up their drug of choice, an unintended fact of prison life exacerbated by its pains and frustrations, and the relative ease with which drugs can be smuggled in to prison, via prisoners returning from home leave (sometimes under threat), visitors, or sometimes, prison staff. The threat of violence is felt keenly by many, especially vulnerable, prisoners and vendettas arising from 'the street' may be imported into establishments. Religious conflict or intolerance, increasing features of late modern society, can lead to discrimination, disputes over codes of conduct in living areas (for example, the cooking of bacon in communal kitchens in long term prisons), and coerced 'conversions' (for example, to the Muslim faith, in some prisons) orchestrated by powerful 'gangs' that might offer protection from violence to (for example) unpopular and 'at risk' sex offenders in exchange for 'conversion' (in this sense, meaning belonging to a numerous new power base in the prison).

The prison has been found, in systematic reviews of the evidence, to be on balance, 'criminogenic' (making crime more rather than less likely). In one high security prison, towards the end of 2011, a sex offender was 'disembowelled' by two prisoners, in an act of violence prisons are intended to prevent. Witnessing violence (including hearing its effects) is one of the unintended consequences of imprisonment many ex-prisoners talk about on their release as they begin to digest and assimilate this part of the trauma associated with their experience. Prison sentences deprive children of their parents, offenders of their livelihoods, and many prisoners of the few resources they have to survive legitimately in the community. Prisons are better at achieving their symbolic and political aims: expressing rage, soothing anxiety, and winning public political support, than they are at changing lives. There are other institutions (such as schools, families, and communities) and interventions (for example, intensive supervision, restorative justice, and drug treatment programmes) which are better placed to achieve those objectives.

REFERENCES

Bottoms, A. E. (2002) 'Morality, Crime, Compliance and Public Policy', in A. Bottoms and M. Tonry (eds.), Ideology, Crime and Criminal Justice: A Symposium in Honour of Sir Leon Radzinowicz, Cullompton, Devon: Willan.

Braithwaite, J. (2001) Restorative justice and responsive regulation, New York: Oxford University Press.

HMCIP (2000) 'Report on an unannounced inspection of HMP Wormwood Scrubs', London: HMIP.

HMCIP (2011) 'Report on an unannounced follow-up inspection of HMP Wandsworth', London: HMIP.

Committee, Home Affairs (1987), 'Contract Provision of Prisons, Fourth Report from the Home Affairs Committee, Session 1986-87', (London: HMSO).

Liebling, A. and Crewe, B. (2012) 'Prisons beyond the new penology: the shifting moral foundations of prison management', in Jonathan Simon and Richard Sparks (eds.), Handbook on Punishment and Society (London: Sage Publishing).

Liebling, A. assisted by Arnold, H. (2004) Prisons and their Moral Performance: A Study of Values, Quality, and Prison Life, Oxford: Clarendon.

Liebling, A., Crewe, B. and Hulley, S. (2011) 'Conceptualising and Measuring the Quality of Prison Life', forthcoming in D. Gadd, S. Karstedt and S. F. Messner (eds) The Sage Handbook of Criminological Research Methods, London: Sage Publishing.

King, R. D. and McDermott, K. (1995) The State of Our Prisons, Oxford: Oxford University Press.

King, R. D. and McDermott, K. (1989) 'British prisons 1970-1987: The Ever-Deepening Crisis', *British Journal of Criminology*, 29, 107-28.

Nellis, M. (2001) 'Community Penalties in Historical Perspective', in A. E. Bottoms, L. Gelsthorpe, and S. Rex (eds.), Community Penalties: Change and Challenges, Cullompton, Devon: Willan Publishing.

New Statesman (2002) 'The Chief Inspector of Prisons fears that Squalid Conditions and Overcrowding breach the Human Rights of Some Inmates', New Statesman, 15/718: 783-91.

O'Neill, O. (2002) A Question Of Trust, Cambridge: Cambridge University Press.

Pollitt, C. and Bouckaert, G. (2000) Public Management Reform: A Comparative Analysis, Oxford: Oxford University Press.

Power, M. (2001) The Audit Society: Rituals of Verification, Oxford: Clarendon.

Rex, S., et al. (2003) 'Accrediting Offender Programmes: A Process-Based Evaluation of the Joint Prison/Probation Services Accreditation Panel', Home Officer Research Study 273, London: Home Office.

Scrivens, E. (1994) Accreditation: Protecting the Professional or the Consumer? (Buckingham: Open University Press).

Sinclair, A. (2002) 'A Study of How and the Extent to Which KPIs Drive Performance in the Prison Service', unpublished M.St thesis, Cambridge: Institute of Criminology, University of Cambridge.

Sitkin, S. B. and Stickel, D. (1996) 'The Road to Hell: the Dynamics of Distrucst in an Era of Quality', in R. M. Kramer and T. R. Tyler (eds.), Trust in Organizations: Frontiers of Theory and Research, Thousand Oaks, California: Sage.

Sparks, Richard (1994) 'Can Prisons be Legitimate?', in Roy D. King and M. McGuire (eds.), Prisons in Context, Oxford: Clarendon Press.

Spurr, Michael (2011), 'Perrie Lecture: reducing costs and maintaining values', *Prison Service Journal*, 198, 12-16.

Windlesham, D (1993) Responses to Crime Volume 2: Penal Policy in the Making (Oxford, Clarendon Press).

In: Scepticism: Hero and Villain
Editors: R. Calne and W. O'Reilly

ISBN: 978-1-62417-783-5
© 2013 Nova Science Publishers, Inc.

Chapter 29

THE REASONABLENESS OF DOUBT: SCEPTICISM AND THE LAW

Ian Winter[*]
Cloth Fair Chambers, London, UK

ABSTRACT

Most people think that the ambition of law is the ascertainment of truth. In fact its obsession is proof. A court is not asked to conclude that a proposition is a true proposition; it is required only to find that it has been proved. A fact is proved if notwithstanding the existence of doubt as to the actuality of its occurrence that doubt does not exceed the level stipulated by the forum in which the fact requires to be proved. Truth is, as the sceptics identified over two and half millennia ago, strictly speaking impossible to establish. It would therefore be extremely problematic for courts to be required to establish the truth. In such a world scepticism would be the villain responsible for the total failure of law to reach conclusions. The sceptical principle of the infinite regression of justification (that each purported justification itself requires justification) would send the tribunal of fact on an endless voyage of alternative possibility exclusion. Courts as a result have preferred the empiricist dogma of observation justification over the absolutist position of the sceptics.

This result however can produce disturbing incongruity. The innocent person convicted as a result of the lack of doubt producing evidence is conclusively and for all purposes guilty of the crime. In lay terms the "truth" of his/her guilt was established by the legal process. When some time later

---

[*] E-mail: ianwinter@clothfairchambers.com.

the doubt producing evidence emergences, such as scientific advances in deoxyribonucleic acid analysis, resulting in acquittal on appeal: innocence is re-established. A person is innocent until proven guilty, not innocent until the truth of his guilt is established. Thus it is possible for a person to be conclusively and for all purposes guilty of a crime whilst subsequently being innocent of it. Since the person was innocent of the crime until he/she was found guilty of it and innocent of it after acquittal on appeal it is obvious that the law has nothing to do with truth and is only concerned with proof.

This result is highly unsatisfactory and makes empiricism the villain. No scepticism based legal process could produce such mutually inconsistent results. Likewise a legal process that involved no scepticism at all would be vulnerable to accusations of gullibility or naivety. The empiricist would accept the evidence of the eye witness who saw the murderer, whom he recognised, commit the felony. The sceptic would ask; does the murderer have an identical twin? That the evidence must be tested is an essential principle of any established legal process and is particularly so in an adversarial process such as ours. Ultimately it is a question of degree. What is the reasonableness of the doubt in any fact specific equation? The answer is arrived at by the application of empiricist observation justification tempered by common sense constrained scepticism that produces the most reliable practical conclusion as to whether a particular fact has been proved to have occurred. This must not however be confused with a determination of the truth.

TRUTH AND THE REASONABLENESS OF DOUBT

"As for certain truth, no man has known it,
Nor will he know it; neither of the gods,
Nor of all the things of which I speak.
And if by chance man were to utter
The final truth, he would not himself know it;
For all is but a woven web of guesses."

>[Xenophanes 530BC as translated by Popper *Conjectures and Refutations: The Growth of Scientific Knowledge* 1962 London: Routledge and Kegan Paul].

Woven or otherwise constructed webs of guesses are of no use to a legal system that has to arrive at an established standard of proof. Neither is the ultimate sceptical axiom that since all knowledge is based on perception and all perception is subjective the intrinsic, objective properties of truth or knowledge are impossible to ascertain. This essential thesis of sceptic philosophy underpins however the decision of legal systems to seek proof rather than the truth. Once one has accepted that truth is beyond reach the only question is how close to truth does one have to get before one can issue judgment as to the occurrence of an asserted fact.

The English civil law requires merely that the fact in question be more likely to have occurred than the asserted alternative. What this actually means in practice depends on the nature of the asserted fact. The more inherently improbable the asserted fact is the stronger the evidence will have to be in practical terms. It can immediately be seen therefore that judges in English civil law cases are concerned only to identify the evidence that makes a particular relevant fact more likely to have occurred than not, whilst bearing in mind that some asserted facts are inherently unlikely to have occurred. This has very little to do with where the truth lies although most judges would be anxious to assert that their essential function is to do justice: where is justice if it is not aligned with truth?

This gives rise to an interesting epistemologically focused jurisprudential question; if justice requires knowledge of the truth can a legal system that by definition does not exist to identify the truth do justice? A judicial system by definition does not identify truth where its standard of proof is satisfied merely by balancing the probabilities of fact occurrence. The English civil law is one such judicial system. The English criminal law is another albeit that the standard required is that the tribunal of fact must be sure of the existence of an asserted fact beyond reasonable doubt. It can therefore be argued that the standards of proof in the English legal system necessarily exclude truth from their processes and as such are inherently unjust. The mere fact that by accident truth might accompany proof does not render a system just. In such cases justice would have been achieved by the accidental coincidence of proof and truth. The police officer who buries the evidence that would give rise to the reasonable doubt might achieve proof of guilt but he/she does not achieve justice.

Once however one accepts that the sceptical thesis that knowledge or truth is impossible is a wholly impractical basis upon which to reach conclusions as to the occurrence of an asserted fact, justice can only be done by the setting of practical standards upon which basis to resolve disputes. Otherwise one is in a condition of paralysis unable to reach a decision. This practical response to the philosophical problem has been approached in different ways. Pyrrho relied on his friends to save him from the undecidability of nature by protecting him from the consequences of the suspension of his judgment as to the dangers that nature occasionally presents. Cratylus opted simply to move his finger and to do and say nothing else since he could not know that what he would otherwise be doing or saying amounted to the truth. Arcesilaus argued that the consequence of the suspension of judgment was that the sceptic could do no more than to regulate his actions in accordance with *"the reasonable"* [*to eulogon* in the Greek]. This of course immediately begs the question as to what is *"the reasonable"*.

If *"the reasonable"* is defined according to the *"axioma"* that its tendency to be true is greater than its tendency to be false (as scholars tend to understand it to mean) it appears that practical scepticism is not so far away from the English civil law standard of proof. In other words whilst it might be logically correct to assert that absolute truth cannot be known, practical truth and therefore practical justice can be achieved by balancing the probabilities of the occurrence of asserted facts (where liberty is not at stake) and by requiring the exclusion of reasonable doubt where life or liberty is at risk. This means that the commonly understood concept of justice is achieved by arriving not at the truth but only at a practically established truth. This downgrades justice from an absolute to a balancing exercise between conflicting assertions of fact: hence the scales in the hand of the Roman goddess, Justitia.

Very few witnesses of course live their lives, these days, according to Pyrrhonian sceptical principles. Very little testimony is presented on the basis that the witness does not know what occurred because of the sceptics' infinite regress of justification. Most witnesses are more than happy, indeed often eager, to express their certain knowledge of the occurrence of an alleged fact. Take the following exchange between the empiricist pathologist and the sceptic US Attorney,

> "Attorney: Doctor, before you performed the autopsy, did you check for a pulse?
> Witness: No.
> Attorney: Did you check for blood pressure?
> Witness: No.
> Attorney: Did you check for breathing?
> Witness: No.
> Attorney: So, then it is possible that the patient was alive when you began the autopsy?
> Witness: No.
> Attorney: How can you be so sure, Doctor?
> Witness: Because his brain was sitting on my desk in a jar.
> Attorney: I see, but could the patient have still been alive, nevertheless?
> Witness: Yes, it is possible that he could have been alive and practicing law"

In such circumstances the tribunal of fact would hesitate little before excluding the technical but unreasonably remote possibility that the subject of the autopsy was alive. It would either conclude that there was no doubt as to the fact that the subject was dead or that any doubt in that regard could not be regarded as being reasonable. What however if the pathologist were the accused? His failure to establish that the subject was dead before commencing the autopsy would radically affect the reasonableness of the doubt as to whether that was the case. It can be seen therefore that in any given case the tribunal of fact will have numerous decisions as to the existence of reasonable doubt with regard to asserted propositions of fact, the outcome of each of which will in turn affect the overall decision as to the existence of a reasonable doubt as to guilt or innocence.

The resolution of those issues will ordinarily involve an essentially empiricist analysis of the evidence with the application of a common sense confined scepticism. It will often however also involve an assessment of whether a witness is telling the "truth" or not. What is meant by "truth" in this context? Whereas the philosophical definition of "truth" is an unresolved argument between sceptics and dogmatics millennia old it is much easier to tell whether someone is telling the "truth" or not. To the philosopher a person only tells the truth when he states a fact that i) he believes to be a fact, ii) is a fact, and iii) can be shown to be or is justified as a fact. A tribunal of fact however is entitled to and frequently does introduce the subjective concept of disbelief. A witness X might state a fact that he genuinely believes to be true, which is in fact true and which he can show is true: D assaulted me in the presence of witness Y. The tribunal of fact may disbelieve both X and Y because it is shown that X is an inveterate liar with a reason to frame D and Y received a payment from him to bolster the case.

The reasonableness of the doubt in such a case is established not by showing that the witness X did not tell the truth in the philosophical sense of the word but by inducing a subjective element of disbelief in the mind of the tribunal of fact. This subjective element can give rise to practical difficulties. Take the following example from a libel case. A newspaper printed an article that C had at different times sexually assaulted a number of young women, all of whom worked in different capacities for the same company for whom C was a senior manager. C sued the newspaper for libel. In libel law the burden of justifying the words complained of lies on the newspaper on the balance of probabilities: is it more likely than not that the words complained of were true? The women did not all know each other but each women knew at least some of the other women. There was no evidence that the women had conspired to invent the story against C but there was evidence of the communication of allegations of assault such that each of the women (bar the first) could have known of the existence of other allegations.

Two of the women did not testify, their evidence was read to the jury. The other women were cross examined and the detail of their testimony tested. All were found wanting in terms of the reliability of the peripheral facts surrounding the allegations but all maintained that the core allegations of assault were true.

The jury found in favour of C on the basis that they did not believe the women because of their lack of credibility or reliability in relation to the peripheral facts. As is usual in such cases it is only the peripheral facts that are capable of being tested: where they went before the assault, the time or place of the assault, what was said when others were still present, for example. The core asserted fact, the nature of the intimate touching, is rarely susceptible of independent testing.

The jury relied on their own subjective judgment that the women were not telling the truth. The judge, in such cases not the tribunal of fact, indicated privately that he would have found for the newspaper on the basis that whilst the witnesses were unreliable in relation to the peripheral details they were consistent with regard to the core allegations. The case demonstrates that the existence of the subjective element of disbelief in the tribunal of fact's decision making process can give rise to diametric judgments based on the same evidence dependent upon the subjective characteristics of the instant tribunal of fact. One person may give more weight to unreliability over peripheral details, another may give more weight to the inherent unlikelihood that a number of women would invent allegations of assault where there is no evidence of a conspiracy to do so. This reduces justice and the ascertainment of practical truth to the lottery of who the tribunal of fact is.

The alternative however would be to devise an objective test for assessing the truthfulness or otherwise of a witness. Is such an objective test for assessing truthfulness possible? Most philosophers agree that for a statement by a witness to be true the witness must at the very least believe it to be true, in addition to it in fact being true and with that belief being justified. A statement that D stabbed V is, not a true statement if the witness does not believe the statement to be true. This is so, even if D did in fact stab V. The philosophical test as to the meaning of a true statement does not therefore assist in establishing whether any particular statement is actually true. Any such exercise will inevitably return to whether it is true that the witness believed that his testimony was true. Further, if the requirement for accepting the witness' assertion that D stabbed V is independent proof that D did stab V, then no fact could be established on the evidence of a single witness.

It appears therefore that it is not possible to establish a practically acceptable, objective test for whether a witness is telling the truth about a fact in respect of which only that person can give evidence. In earlier times English law required there to be corroboration of certain evidence such that conviction could not depend upon the evidence of only one witness. This of course did not resolve the problem of the subjective element in assessing truthfulness it merely required there to be more evidence that would need to be subjectively assessed. The requirement for corroboration in English law has been abolished, rightly so, because it prevents a tribunal of fact from relying upon the evidence of a single witness, however reliable that evidence may be. Since it is not possible to determine whether a witness is telling the truth in respect of a fact, about which only he/she can give evidence, other than by the application of the subjective belief or disbelief of the tribunal of fact it follows that justice and the ascertainment of practical truth in such cases is incapable of objective verification.

The position is not restricted to those witnesses who give evidence about facts unique to their knowledge. Many witnesses in a case have to be assessed so that a decision can be made about their honesty. The individual decisions in that regard make up the jigsaw puzzle of factual determinations as to whether the elements of doubt exist to the standard prescribed by the legal proceedings in which the evidence is given. It follows therefore that in most cases the wholly subjective assessment of the truthfulness of a witness will determine the levels of doubt that will resolve the case. This means that not only does the English legal system not aspire to the ascertainment of truth it is fundamentally dependent upon subjective judgment calls that cannot be verified.

Hence the importance in criminal cases where liberty is at stake of the requirement for there to be a jury of peers whose collective subjective judgment will determine the case. The fact that the subjective judgment of at least ten jurors (nine in certain reduced juror cases) must coincide before guilt can be established is an important safeguard against a malicious, prejudiced, incompetent or perverse tribunal of fact.

SCEPTICISM AND THE EXPERT WITNESS

So far we have considered only the application of scepticism to the ascertainment of asserted facts. Not all evidence however falls within that category. In certain circumstances evidence of a witness' opinion may be given. For opinion evidence to be admissible it must be the opinion of a competent and properly qualified expert in a recognised field of expertise which is likely to be outside the experience and knowledge of the tribunal of fact. So long as the opinion evidence is admissible the opinion may extend even to the ultimate issue that the tribunal of fact is to determine. Thus evidence of a facial mapping expert was admissible to prove that D appeared in the CCTV video recordings of two bank robberies [see R v Stockwell, 97 Criminal Appeal Reports page 260]. Given that this was a matter for the jury to decide the expert opinion went to the ultimate issue in the case. Notwithstanding that in such cases the tribunal of fact must be careful to ensure that such opinion is not blindly followed, given that by definition the expert opinion is only admitted because the field of expertise is outside the experience and knowledge of the tribunal of fact, it would be a rare case in which such opinion would not be determinative of that issue.

This means that in a case where the opinion evidence of an expert is central to the outcome of a case, such as it was in Mr Stockwell's case, it will be the subjective judgment of the expert which is decisive and not that of the tribunal of fact. In such cases justice and the ascertainment of practical truth will depend not upon the judges of fact who will have heard all of the evidence and assessed the reliability of it but upon the opinion of a witness called by one of the parties to advance that adversarial position.

As is made clear elsewhere in this book science is not concerned with whether a proposition of fact is *"reasonable"* it is concerned with what is the empirical basis for the proposition. A facial mapping expert will therefore be concerned to ensure that the match between D and the questioned video recordings pass sufficient of the scientific bases to justify the opinion that D is shown in the video recordings. As in fingerprint science there are an established number of matching characteristics that have to appear before a scientific match is shown. These necessarily require the subjective judgment of the expert and what he sees. Once a sufficient number of matching characteristics are present the expert will feel able to opine that D is shown in the videos. Since the video recording of a bank robbery is very strong evidence that there was a bank robbery the only live issue for the tribunal of fact will be whether D was party to it. The opinion of the expert, outside the knowledge and experience of non-experts, is effectively conclusive of this issue and thus the case. The expert opinion does not however establish that it is true that D was in the video recordings all it establishes is that in the subjective opinion of the expert, D's face shared the scientifically accepted number of matching characteristics with the face in the video for the opinion to be one that a responsible expert can give.

The sceptic would immediately ask; does D have a matching twin? But in this case the sceptic would also ask; does D share the characteristics that matched the face in the video with any number of other people with those characteristics? Whereas a person cannot share all facial characteristics with a person other than his/her matching twin he/she may well share the selected number relevant to the facial mapping exercise. The science involved appreciates this of course and states that the number of matches required is scientifically established to exclude the random possibility of an erroneous identification. That test is by definition however dependent upon the samples upon which it is based. Since the expert will not have access to a data base of persons who share the facial characteristics of D that match the face in the video recordings, the expert is not in a position to opine that it was D in the video recordings as opposed to one of the unknown persons who share the characteristics that D shared with the face in the video recordings.

At least with an expert witness however these points can be put in cross examination and if there is serious dispute as to the opinion alternative expert evidence can be called by the opposing party. This is not possible where the expertise is applied by the tribunal of fact itself. Juries, of course, possess no expertise and must take any expert opinion from the expert witnesses called by the parties. Likewise judges, whatever private expertise they may possess, must decide the case on the basis of the expert testimony. The situation is very different however in the case of specialist tribunals. The General Medical Council regulates the conduct of medical practitioners. Its disciplinary panels contain medical practitioners and will often contain experts in areas relevant to the case in question. Those practitioners draw on their knowledge and expertise in questioning the witnesses called and in determining the case. In such cases it is not just the subjective judgment of the tribunal of fact that determines the case it is the subjective expertise of the tribunal of fact. That expertise cannot be cross examined or the basis for it tested. At least however those medical practitioners are qualified and the expertise is additional to that called by the parties before the disciplinary panel.

This is not so in other specialist tribunals such as sports tribunals. Before the British Horseracing Authority, for example, whether a jockey rode a horse on its merits or deliberately failed to do so is usually determined by the members of the disciplinary panel. Ordinarily no expert evidence in this regard is adduced; reliance is placed instead on the private experience of the members of the panel. Experience is of course not the same as expertise. More importantly however the experience of the members of the panel cannot be tested since they are not witnesses and cannot be cross examined. Worse still, it is impossible to know which asserted facts were established by the operation of empirical observation from the primary evidence such as the video footage of the race and which were established from the internal, subjective *"know-how"* of the members of the panel.

The sceptic in such a case would rightly want to know how it is that the panel can *"know"* that a jockey was deliberately not trying on his mount. Is it from something that can be *"seen"* to have occurred by the application of not-expert sense observation? Is it from something that can be rationalised, i.e. something that must have happened because of the observation of some other event? Is it from something that experience has told the panel will have occurred notwithstanding that it cannot be seen or otherwise rationally assumed to have occurred? The application of scepticism in such circumstances is critical since if it is the latter then guilt will have been established not from any empirically ascertainable fact, not from any rationally inferable fact but from the inherent knowledge of the tribunal of fact. This is the same as saying *"I know it occurred because I know it occurred"*.

No philosophical axiom could justify such a conclusion. It is not possible to conclude that something happened on the sole basis that someone believed that it did without any justification for that belief. The believer must at least be able to state why he/she holds that belief. In the example above the stated justification for the belief would be *"my experience tells me that it occurred"*. This is not justification it is mere assertion. In such a case therefore not only is truth not ascertained neither is proof. The jockey is subject to the whim of the untestable, private, subjective thought processes of the tribunal of fact. Neither sceptics, empiricists, rationalists or frankly any philosophical thought process would support such an approach as an acceptable route to the ascertainment of an asserted fact.

CONCLUSION

It can be seen therefore that whilst the ascertainment of truth may be the aspiration of judges and jurors, and whilst for practical purposes judicial determinations must be regarded as having established it, the English legal system is in fact only concerned with proof. If absolute sceptical principles were to be applied the infinite regress of justifications would ensure that no case was ever decided: scepticism would be the villain. If purely empiricist principles were to be applied however the law would be at risk of being hijacked by sense perceived testimony that might actually be the product of fraud or dishonesty: scepticism would be the hero. The balance is required between the blind acceptance of empirical proof and the sceptical understanding that such proof may be unreliable. No system of justice could operate however without the application of subjective judgment as to the essential honesty or believability of the witnesses. A mature legal system therefore melds elements of empiricism, scepticism and subjective judgment in assessing the strength of the evidence for any asserted proposition and more importantly the reasonableness of any doubt about the existence of an alternative factual proposition. Once it is acknowledged that certain truth is unascertainable we must content ourselves merely with the proof.

In: Scepticism: Hero and Villain
Editors: R. Calne and W. O'Reilly

ISBN: 978-1-62417-783-5
© 2013 Nova Science Publishers, Inc.

Chapter 30

'AN IMPOSSIBLE SENSE OF EXPECTATION': LIES AND DISAPPOINTMENT IN BRITISH POLITICS

Ross Hawkins

BBC, Westminster, London, Britain

ABSTRACT

Members of Parliament are widely regarded as dishonest by voters. Their leaders accept politics needs to be 'cleaned up'. Yet while many British politicians have been proved dishonest, those who lie take risks. Scrutiny, aided by a series of initiatives designed to increase transparency, is considerable. Parties and leaders seeking election are often cautious in their manifesto pledges.

However, their campaigning language inflames voters' expectations, downplays the implications of difficult economic decisions and risks disappointment, not least because modern consumers are used to seeing promises honoured. The changes that a modern British Prime Minister can effect are limited by constitutional checks, and by the waning powers of an individual state in a globalised world. It would be neither desirable nor possible to strip electioneering of its colour and rhetoric. However, those concerned about a breakdown in public confidence may wish to examine not only misbehaviour, but also the promises implied in ordinary electioneering and the disillusion created when governments fail to deliver.

INTRODUCTION

'Scepticism' fails, by a considerable margin, to adequately convey public distrust of the political class. The majority of British voters think Members of Parliament are liars. One survey suggests a mere fifth believe all or most MPs tell the truth.[1]

The causes of this malaise are well documented and little doubted. A series of stories about personal misconduct (dubbed 'sleaze') by leading politicians in the Nineties, the failure to find the weapons of mass destruction central to the case for British involvement in the 2003 Iraq conflict, and the publication of expenses claims - some fraudulent, many ridiculous - of every member of the House of Commons towards the end of the last Parliament, are all blamed for the common perception that MPs cannot be trusted.

There is no shortage of proof that politicians lie. In 1999, the former Conservative cabinet minister Jonathan Aitken was jailed for perjury and perverting the course of justice. Two years later the former Conservative deputy chairman Lord Archer suffered a similar fate for the same offences. In 2011 six politicians (four previously Labour, two previously Conservative representatives) were imprisoned over their parliamentary expenses claims.

The political elite has long since capitulated, in public at least, to claims of systematic dishonesty. During the 2010 election campaign the need to clean up politics was widely accepted;[2] its filth regarded by many as settled fact. Few active politicians would question the charge, or note the UK has not seen a spectacle quite like that of the Italian Prime Minister Silvio Berlusconi, or the former French president Jacques Chirac, facing corruption charges (which both denied), or the Monica Lewinsky scandal in the US. Few rush to remind voters that the police investigation into an allegation that honours were sold by Tony Blair's government failed to result in charges.

SCRUTINY AND THE PERILS OF LYING

The former Labour MP Chris Mullin, a junior minister under Tony Blair, and no longer standing for election, argues that to be downright dishonest in British politics is to take a great risk. He says: "Politicians, on the whole they don't (lie), not because they're better human beings but because any statement by a

---

[1] Grasso, M. (2011). Survey of public attitudes towards conduct in public life 2010. http://www.public-standards.gov.uk/Library/CSPL_survey_Final_web_version.pdf.
[2] This language featured in the Conservative, Liberal Democrat and Labour manifestoes.

prominent politician is subject to such scrutiny that any lie will be exposed almost instantaneously."[3] That scrutiny is considerable, and to an extent state subsidised. More than 400 journalists are accredited to report on Parliament from within the Palace of Westminster, those working for the BBC funded by the licence fee. They are supplemented by online journalists and analysts. The official opposition receives direct government funding, currently worth more than £6m a year[4] in addition to the pay, staffing and support due to its own members, and access to resources like the researchers of the House of Commons Library. Within Parliament, questions, oral and written, can prompt information and evasion in roughly equal measure. Select committees of MPs are growing in power.

The effectiveness of this corps of critics is contested by those who accuse the media of being overly reliant on government briefings, and mitigated by a rival group containing government MPs and ministers, civil servant press officers - facing cuts now but numbering 372 in 2009[5] - and political advisers.

Successive Prime Ministers have simultaneously directed considerable resources, attention and ministerial time towards controlling the media, while legislating to the opposite end. Both Blair[6] and his Downing Street chief of staff Jonathan Powell[7] rue the creation of the Freedom of Information Act, an indication perhaps that for all its flaws and frustrations it has aided scrutiny. As Powell notes,[8] in the Information Commissioner Blair created both an arbiter of the act's implementation and an enthusiast for greater openness, a combination never likely to limit its application. A new Statistics Authority with a robust chair began its work under Gordon Brown's premiership, putting the critique of massaged figures on a statutory footing. A drive by David Cameron's government to publish details of individual items of expenditure by national and local government, and by 'arm's length' bodies known as Quangos,[9] has been thus far an effective way of generating stories about the alleged profligacy of the previous administration or civil servants. It will, inevitably, be turned against the sitting government in time.

---

[3] Interview.
[4] Kelly, R. (2011) Short Money. http://www.parliament.uk/documents/commons/lib/research/briefings/snpc-01663.pdf.
[5] Khan, U. (2009). Number of Government press officers jumps by three-quarters under Labour. http://www.telegraph.co.uk/news/politics/labour/4337393/Number-of-Government-press-officers-jumps-by-three-quarters-under-Labour.html.
[6] Blair, T. (2010). *A Journey*. London: Random House.
[7] Powell, J. (2010). *The New Machiavelli*. London: The Bodley Head.
[8] Ibid.
[9] (2011). Eric Pickles: Blazing a trail on spending transparency. http://www.communities.gov.uk/news/corporate/ 1685198.

In his tremendous compendium of political deceit Peter Oborne[10] called for the creation of a monitor not unlike the Statistics Authority, and a body to check politicians' facts not unlike services that now exist online.[11] None take exactly the form he prescribed, but the need he identified has, to an extent, been recognised and met.

Taken as a whole, the tools available to interrogate politicians' claims are imperfect, frustrating to use and often frustrated by those paid to take the side of government; but when wielded by savvy journalists and political opponents they are powerful.

Voters' Revenge

Lying, therefore, risks exposure, and exposure in turn risks political failure. An apology in the House of Commons can, for all the bluster of the modern politician, prove damaging for the MP confessing error or omission. Oborne rightly points out that the then transport secretary Stephen Byers received conspicuous support from Blair in 2002 after he expressed his regret to the Commons for a misleading television interview,[12] but it is worth noting that three months later Byers' ministerial career was over. His woes were, by then, legion but the business of being caught out helped drain his already dwindling political capital.

When whole parties are accused of misleading voters the consequences are inevitably greater. During the 2010 election campaign the Liberal Democrats promised to vote against any proposed rise in fees for university tuition by signing up to a student union pledge campaign. After the party took its place as a junior partner in a coalition government with the Conservatives, a vote allowing fees of up to £9,000 to be charged by English universities arrived, and almost half the Liberal Democrat parliamentary party backed the measure. Their leader Nick Clegg, now Deputy Prime Minister, argued that as he failed to win a majority he could not deliver his entire manifesto, although he conceded he should perhaps have been more circumspect in his promises.[13] Some of his fellow MPs certainly

---

[10] Oborne, P. (2005). *The Rise of Political Lying*. London: Simon & Schuster.
[11] fullfact.org was created partly in response to Oborne's book. Channel 4 runs a similar site: blogs.channel4.com/factcheck/.
[12] Oborne, P. (2005).
[13] (2010). Nick Clegg regrets signing anti-tuition fees pledge. http://www.bbc.co.uk/news/uk-politics-11732787.

with a warning it contained "no magic formula or lavish promises". Blair recalls re-reading his 1997 manifesto pledges during his second winter in government: "I laughed at their modesty. The challenge wasn't meeting them. The challenge was: so what?"[20] But most voters do not sift the detail of manifestoes.

These were the words of the Liberal Democrat leader Nick Clegg at the opening of the first television debate:

> "You're going to be told tonight by these two that the only choice you can make is between two old parties who've been running things for years. I'm here to persuade you that there is an alternative. I think we have a fantastic opportunity to do things differently for once."[21]

His pitch was predicated on an unlikely outcome; the breaking of the duopoly of Labour and Conservative governments (which he dubbed the "old politics"), and his own outright victory. His party had never boasted any more than 62 MPs in its current form, a number that fell to 57 following the 2010 contest. There had not been a Liberal Prime Minister since David Lloyd George left office in 1922, and a Liberal Prime Minister had not governed without the support of other coalition parties since Herbert Asquith's cabinet fractured in May 1915. Clegg's chances of providing a standalone alternative to the other two parties, capable of implementing his manifesto commitments (including his tuition fee pledge) without compromise, were extremely slim.

Neither Brown nor Clegg did anything particularly unusual. The former sincerely believed he was better qualified to make economic decisions than the other men. Clegg could hardly have done anything other than present himself as a possible leader of a Liberal Democrat majority government. Neither stands accused of dishonesty; and both framed their openings as descriptions of the possible rather than as guarantees. Yet viewers may have been left with the impression they had been offered universally improved living standards and prosperity, or the fruits of an outright Liberal Democrat victory. Both men risked sowing seeds of disappointment.

The Conservative leader David Cameron, who would become Prime Minister, said:

> "Britain can do much better; we can deal with our debts, we can get our economy growing and avoid this jobs tax, and we can build a bigger society."[22]

---

[20] Blair, T. (2010).
[21] Ibid.
[22] Ibid.

Dealing with debt by reducing the deficit was the key policy theme of the campaign. An analysis by the Institute for Fiscal Studies[23] (IFS) considered the areas in which each party had pledged to protect spending and the cuts to which it was publicly committed, then assessed the scale of extra, unannounced savings needed to fulfill their economic plans. It concluded the Conservatives had announced measures totaling 17.7% of the cuts they would need, leaving a shortfall of £52.4bn. Labour announced measures covering 13.1% of necessary cuts leaving a £44.1bn shortfall. For the Liberal Democrats the figures were 25.9% and £34.5bn respectively.

Any Conservative would argue their party was much more explicit than Labour about the need for savings in the run up to the election, perhaps citing Darling's frustration in his memoirs about: "Gordon's insistence on the line 'investment versus cuts'".[24] Come the third Prime Ministerial debate all three candidates were clear that cuts were needed. The IFS suggests none were explicit about the scale of the task, or how they would complete it.

This was unsurprising. Peter Riddell notes a long history of politicians failing to warn voters about the full scale of tough budgetary measures that will follow an election.[25] New Labour stuck to its pre-election commitment in 1997 not to raise the basic or higher rates of income tax, but compensated the exchequer with other measures, and paid a political price. As Riddell notes "one of the Conservatives' few telling attacks of this period" concerned 'stealth taxes'".[26] Darling suggests he had to see off the risk of similar circumstances in 2010:

> "Ed Balls [then a cabinet minister, now shadow Chancellor] and Gordon [Brown] wanted to make a virtue of us not increasing VAT by ruling it out for the whole of the next parliament. They then wanted to challenge the Tories to do the same. Nice electoral politics, but economic madness was my view. No Chancellor can tie his hands on tax."[27]

My aim is not to suggest the 2010 election claims (of which I have presented a tiny slice in a brief study) were unusually hyperbolic or overblown. If anything, in the wake of the expenses scandal, and in anticipation of spending cuts, the protagonists were, by and large, cautious in their claims. Instead, I suggest the protagonists – like a great many of their predecessors – gave the impression they could guarantee outcomes that were either difficult or impossible to deliver.

---

[23] Chote, R. Crawford, R. Emmerson, C. Tetlow, G. (2010). *Filling the Hole,* London : Nuffield Foundation.
[24] Darling, A. (2011) *Back From the Brink*, London: Atlantic Books.
[25] Riddell, P. (2011). *In Defence of Politicians*. London: Biteback Publishing.
[26] Ibid.
[27] Darling, A. (2011).

I might just as well have cited Harold Wilson, who during his famous "white heat" speech of 1963, said there would be "no place for restrictive practices or for outdated methods on either side of industry"[28] in his vision of Britain (an ambition well beyond the fiat of a Sixties PM), or Blair in the 2001 campaign who both pledged to create full employment, and to make Britain a place "where we break down every barrier, every impediment to our big idea - the development of human potential".[29] Electors later had cause to question whether all the promises made to them had been kept.

There are reasons though to suppose such shortcomings are less easily endured by the electorate of 2005 or 2010 than by those who went to the polls in 1964. Arguments can be mounted that a more vigorous and better-armed media, and a populace shorn of deference, are less willing to forgive political shortcomings. Twenty first century citizens are used to getting what they are promised. In the normal course of events where goods fail, they expect replacement or refund, whatever the cost; consider the many millions of cars recalled by Toyota between 2009 and 2011. If frustrated by powerful interests they expect protection from regulators, and will pool grievances and speak in groups. In this setting the politician's habit of appearing to promise much and deliver comparatively little appears anomalous; the excuse that fuller versions of their promises, complete with caveats, are available in manifestoes seems weak.

THE LIMITS OF POWER

In his opening remarks to the first televised debate Cameron made a claim vital for any serious aspirant for power in a Western democracy: "we can get our economy growing". Once again this was couched in the language of aspiration rather than pledge, and for good reason. Like many of the things voters most desire, politicians cannot legislate for economic growth; just as they cannot pass laws to create strong communities or make vulnerable people feel safe on the streets at night. Prime Ministers can change structures and provide incentives, attempt to offer moral and social leadership, and seek to guide through praise or criticism. They may also venture more subtle change, as the current government would argue it is doing in seeking to stimulate greater civic involvement by making it easier for charities and others to provide services previously delivered

---

[28] Pimlott, B. (1992) *Harold Wilson*. London: HarperCollins.
[29] (2001). Tony Blair's first keynote speech of the campaign. http://www.guardian.co.uk/politics/2001/may/13/ labour.tonyblair.

by the state. None of these measures give a Prime Minister the power to craft society, or the economy, at will.

Indeed, even the changes they should be able to effect, in laws and governing structures, are often frustrated. The proper checks and balances of the British constitution, that group of professional critics in opposition and media, and the resistance of other opponents (inevitably dubbed 'special interests' by frustrated Prime Ministers) all serve to resist change. Many political practitioners feel the weaknesses of Downing Street as keenly as its strength. Powell writes: "In truth, political power does not reside in Number 10 but is instead widely diffused in the British elite, not just in government but outside it as well. The only way a Prime Minister can govern is by persuading that elite, by building coalitions of support and by carrying his colleagues with him."[30]

In economics and foreign policy, the job of addressing global forces invariably requires action on an international stage. British leaders can attempt to direct these; consider Blair agitating for a NATO air offensive against Slobodan Milosevic in 1999, Brown attempting to cohere international opinion and finance behind a stimulus programme before and during the 2009 G20 meeting in London, and Cameron securing a UN Security Council Resolution against the Libyan leader Muammar Gadaffi and forming an alliance for its enforcement. Such moves in economic and foreign policy can be successful; but inevitably they require multilateralism, often with state and non-state actors alike. They are not in the gift of the Prime Minister alone.

None of this belittles the position of Prime Minister, one that still allows its incumbent to go to war or launch a nuclear weapon on his or her personal authority. It does, however, suggest a premier's ability to deliver the sort of change voters demand is heavily constrained, and the restrictions on his or her power are rarely highlighted.

Reviewing his time serving within these limitations, Blair makes an argument that may sound more boast than analysis. Interpreted unkindly, he appears to suggest his charisma was so profound, he lost control of its consequences:

> "You quickly realise that though you are the repository of that hope and have in part been the author of it, it now has a life of its own, a spirit of its own, and that spirit is soaring far beyond your control. You want to capture it, tame it and harness it, because its very independence is, you know, leading the public to an impossible sense of expectation."

That expectation did not arise by accident at his election in 1997. It was carefully conjured and Blair's successors dream of emulating it.

---

[30] Powell, J (2010).

CONCLUSION

In the wake of the expenses row there has been much talk about trust and politics, a great deal of it acknowledging the fact MPs are considered liars. The political reaction to this centres on measures designed to constrain misbehaviour, such as the creation of an independent regulator for MPs' expenses or a proposed right of recall.

Yet this approach assumes public mistrust derives from political dishonesty. As we have seen, this is a feature of political life, but to argue it is somehow endemic to the British system is to overstate a case.

In short: voters distrust politicians not just because they lie, but because they fail.

This is not to argue for a desiccated politics shorn of inspiration. Philip Blond, whose ResPublica think tank has been considered influential on the Conservative leadership, says: "There's a disconnect between if you will very specific policy pledges and the rhetoric people employ... That's not how people operate in our society through politics. People deal in vision and it's vision that they believe in."[31] If politicians do, to use that now hoary cliché, campaign in poetry and govern in prose, they do so for a reason. Voters wish to project their dreams. Candidates wish to inspire. Change has its own allure. This is the stuff of democracy.

Yet politicians may want to reconsider what deal they strike with an electorate that pays only passing attention to the caveats that surround their pledges, and the documents in which those caveats are set out.

Do their modes of electoral communication - from manifestos to speeches - properly convey to an audience at large what they can hope to achieve? Are they overselling the influence of the leader of a modern, moderately-sized constitutional democracy? Do they sufficiently explain the limitations - economic, political and international - on their freedom to achieve change?

And if they were clearer about their promises and their powers, might voters be more inclined to accept honest failures, and less ready to charge them with dishonest practice?

---

[31] Interview.

In: Scepticism: Hero and Villain
Editors: R. Calne and W. O'Reilly

ISBN: 978-1-62417-783-5
© 2013 Nova Science Publishers, Inc.

Chapter 31

THE REVIVAL OF ARAB SCEPTICISM: FROM PRIVATE TO PUBLIC

Farah Dakhlallah[1] and Adam Coutts[2]

[1]Department of Politics and International Studies, Cambridge University, UK
[2]Affiliated research Department of Sociology, University of Cambridge, UK

ABSTRACT

The recent Arab uprisings have defied those sceptics who thought that revolutionary change was impossible in the Middle East and North Africa. But it also marks the revival of an altogether different – more constructive – genre of scepticism that authoritarian governments thought they had successfully weaned their subjects off after decades of systematic state repression.

A BRIEF HISTORY OF THE SCEPTICAL ARAB

Scepticism has long been integral to Arab culture, particularly during the early centuries of the Islamic Empire, when Islam acted as a site of perpetual public contestation between the proponents of various sects and traditions vying for supremacy.[1] The late 7th century AD witnessed the development of the Arab

---

[1] For a discussion of the major movements of Muslim theology include the Khawarij, the Murji'a, the Qadariyya, the Mu'tazila, the Ash'ariyya and the Maturidiyya, see: Akhavi, Shahrough, *The Middle East: The Politics of the Sacred and the Secular* (London: Zed Books, 2009), 22-28.

Sciences such as rhetoric, lexicography, grammar and literary theory, in order to establish the authoritative text of the Quran, as well as theology, jurisprudence, and the study of the life of the prophet Mohammad, in order to provide guidance for everyday life. The Muslim expansion by conquest in the seventh and eighth centuries, particularly westwards to the Levant and eastwards to Iran, provided encounters with long-established traditions of advanced learning grounded in Reason such as Medicine, Mathematics and Philosophy that would soon be appropriated by and assimilated into Muslim culture. Greek texts that had been translated into the Syriac and Pahlavi languages made their way into Arabic and sparked debate about how sciences that were grounded in Reason, such as Logic, could be reconciled with Islam, which was grounded in Revelation.[2]

The Sceptical Philosophers

Various schools of thought emerged as Muslim thinkers sought to bridge science and religion. This critical approach is epitomised by the epistemological debates that would span the breadth of the Muslim world, from Avicenna in Central Asia to the Averroes (Ibn Rushd) in the Iberian Peninsula, and persist across several centuries through the works of philosophers such as al-Kindi, al-Farabi, al-Ghazali and others. With the exception of al-Ghazali, these thinkers viewed Logic as a vehicle for the attainment of genuine knowledge and, ultimately, as a route to salvation. Their methodological scepticism[3] scrutinised knowledge claims with the goal of acquiring a firm foundation for genuine knowledge. Centuries later, Arab translations and treatises on Aristotle and Plato would help bring Europe out of the Dark Ages and hasten the coming of the Italian Renaissance with a healthy dose of scepticism towards received dogma, especially of the religious sort.[4]

However, the Muslim world's most prolific sceptic was also scepticism's greatest detractor. After having overcome his own profound personal crisis of scepticism by embracing Mysticism, al-Ghazali sought to debunk the notion that human Reason, through Logic, could lead to the attainment of Truth. Al-Ghazali maintained that salvation could only be attained through faith and through

---

[2] Gaskill, Thomas, *Avicenna and Medieval Muslim Philosophy* (Blackstone Audio, 2006).

[3] Methodological scepticism is distinct from philosophical (also known as radical or systematic) scepticism, which is a form of agnosticism or disbelief in any claims of ultimate knowledge. Scepticism is understood as a specific form of critical thinking that questions prevailing/received dogma. It is understood here as a tendency to habitually doubt accepted beliefs – not as a form of agnosticism or disbelief in any claims of ultimate knowledge.

[4] Lewis, Bernard, *The Middle East: 2000 Years of History from the Rise of Christianity to the Present Day* (London: Phoenix Press, 1995), 264-265.

following the precepts of the Quran and the traditions of the life of the Prophet. Discursive reason should be subordinate to faith and not be practised by those whose conviction might be troubled by it.[5]

A century later, al-Ghazali's assault on scepticism faced a firm rebuttal by Averroes who maintained that philosophy was sanctioned by specific Quranic verses and therefore could not contradict the Holy text. Averroes argued, instead, that apparent contradictions between the literal meaning of Quranic verses and the truths arrived at by philosophers through the exercise of reason could be resolved through a metaphorical interpretation of those verses. However, these interpretations should be restricted to an elite who could accept them, while the literal meanings of the Quran would suffice for the masses.[6]

Such debates continued within the ranks of the philosophers, as well as between the philosophers and the more traditional schools of moral and legal interpretation (such as the Shafi'is, Malikis, Hanafis and the Hanbalis), but they would gradually recede from the public sphere with the ascendancy of more uncompromising thinkers such as Ibn Taymiyya during the Mamluk dynasty in 13th century Syria, who sought to reassert the middle path of the Hanbalis as the dominant religious doctrine. Later, during the 18th century, Ibn Taymiyya's writings would influence the rise of another even stricter religious doctrine in the Arabian Peninsula, Wahhabism, which would lead to the creation of the Saudi state.

The ebb and flow of public scepticism in the Arab world continued in the ensuing centuries in its habitually disparate and contextually contingent manner; to attempt to construct a chronological narrative of its development would only be misleading. The experience of living and thinking in the Arab world, with its cultural, geographical, ethnic and linguistic diversity is – to borrow from Aziz al-Azmeh's formulation[7] – as diverse as the situations that sustain it. However there are particular periods or debates that illustrate this dynamic of sceptical resurgence and retreat such as that of the Arab philosophical debates and the 19th century cultural renaissance movement known as *al-Nahda* or Arab Renaissance.

---

[5] Hourani, Albert, *Arab Thought in the Liberal Age: 1789-1939* (London: Oxford University Press, 1962).
[6] Ibid.
[7] "There are as many Islams as there are situations that sustain it". See: Al-Azmeh, Aziz, *Islams and Modernities* 3rd Edition (London: Verso Books, 2009), 1.

The Sceptical Arab Renaissance

Another period of Arab history that witnessed a resurgent public scepticism was that of the intellectual movement known as *al-Nahda* which flourished in the late 19th and early 20th centuries in major Arab cities such as Cairo, Beirut and Damascus. The Napoleonic Expedition to Egypt (1789-1801), with its unusually large contingent of *savants* (French mathematicians, inventors, scientists, artists and writers), is often credited with inspiring this Arab Renaissance by demonstrating Western military, technological, and organisational superiority and introducing inventions, such as the printing press, and ideas such as liberalism and nationalism. This spurred reformist programmes on European models led by two modernising dynasties in Tunisia and Egypt, as well as the Ottoman *tanzimat* reforms culminating in the first Ottoman constitution.[8] This period was characterised by the emergence of a new Arab bourgeoisie of clerks and tradesmen; the proliferation of foreign missionary schools with modernised educational curricula; increased cultural exchange with Europe through trade, study abroad and cultural and scientific expeditions; the modernisation of the Arabic language; the widespread adoption of the printing press; the proliferation of newspapers particularly in Cairo and Beirut; and the formation of various Arab societies, the precursors to political parties.[9]

Although they continued to engage in theological-epistemological debates, the architects of *al-Nahda* were more concerned with the reordering of social and political life. *Al-Nahda* was inspired by the European Enlightenment and espoused modernisation and Arab nationalism. Its vanguards included liberal thinkers such as Francis al-Marrash, Shibley Shamil and Farah Anton, Muslim reformers such as Jamal al-Din al-Afghani, Rifa'a al-Tahtawi and Mohammad Abduh, and nationalists including Najib Azouri, Boutros al-Boustany and Adib Ishaq.[10]

This newfound scepticism of the prevailing Ottoman order played a pivotal role in subsequent Arab revolts and the rise of Arab nationalism, an idealistic doctrine that would be ravaged in the coming decades by the forces of imperialism, sectarianism and authoritarian government.[11] The spirit of *al-Nahda* persisted in the interwar period as an outlook and in the works of public intellectuals such as Taha Hussein, Tawfiq Hakim, Ahmad Shawqi and Amin

---

[8] Cole, Juan, *Napoleon's Egypt: Invading the Middle East* (New York: Palgrave Macmillan, 2007).

[9] Nsouli, Anis, *Asbab al-Nahda al-Arabiya fi al-Qarn al-Tasi' 'Ashar* [Causes of the Arab Renaissance in the 19th century] (Beirut: Dar al-Jadeed, 2010[1926]).

[10] Kassir, Samir, *Being Arab* (London: Verso Books, 2006), 43-52.

[11] Ajami, Fouad, The Arab Predicament: Arab Political Thought and Practice Since 1967 (Cambridge: Cambridge University Press, 1992).

Rihani, but this would prove a brief interlude on the road towards the consolidation of Arab nationalism as dogma.[12]

ANTI-SCEPTICAL ARAB STATE FORMATION

With the formation and consolidation of the Arab nation state, scepticism would enter a period of retreat from the public sphere as the newly independent Arab polities grappled with pressures of de-colonisation, the Arab-Israeli conflict (particularly the 1948 and 1967 defeats) and the competing claims exacted upon them by the doctrine of Arab nationalism on the one hand, and the requirements of state sovereignty on the other. From the mid-twentieth century onwards, these new Arab countries would not only have to contend with the difficulties associated with state building and social change in an inequitable international system, but also with the insistent ideological challenges to their institutional legitimacy posed by supra-state identities – such as pan-Islamism, pan-Syrianism and pan-Arabism – which, in their maximalist versions, denied the legitimacy of extant state boundaries altogether and became a force for undermining state institutions.[13] The spread of radical left-wing movements after the establishment of the state of Israel in 1948 led to a wave of Arab nationalist coup d'états in countries such as Egypt, Libya, Syria and Iraq. Egypt, Syria and Iraq even shared versions of the same flag between 1963 and 1972 to symbolise their desire for unity; and Egypt and Syria became the United Arab Republic for three years, until Syria's secession in 1961.

During this period, Arab ruling elites – whether of the radical Arab nationalist flavour or the conservative monarchies such as Jordan or the Gulf countries – successfully deployed and consolidated coercive power domestically, and developed their governing capabilities through state bureaucracies, the armed forces, state security agencies, education curricula and other instruments of nation building. This period witnessed the spread of state-sponsored education, particularly in the quasi-socialist 'populist authoritarian' states,[14] and the provenance of state mass media (newspapers, radio and television) that sought to inculcate unquestioned allegiance and the near-deification of the ruler. The rise of these paternalistic quasi-fascist cults left no room for scepticism, for even the slightest expression of doubt, in the public sphere.

---

[12] For more on Arab thought during the 'liberal age' from the French Revolution in 1789 to 1939, see (Hourani 1962).

[13] Barnett, Michael, "Sovereignty, Nationalism and Regional Order in the Arab States System", International Organization 49(3), 1995, 479-510.

[14] Hinnebusch, Raymond, Syria: Revolution from Above (London: Routledge, 2002).

This is not to say that Arab citizens were empty vessels waiting to be filled with state propaganda; they practised manifold forms of resistance, both individual and collective. The contention, rather, is that they had abandoned public scepticism, resorting to what could be described as social and political *Taqiyya* or Dissimulation – concealing their true beliefs in order to safeguard their lives.[15] Indeed, were it not for the daily acts of resistance practised by their subjects, Arab governments would have had little need for an ever-expanding state security apparatus and perpetual reification of the ruler.[16]

The choking of public scepticism was not uniform across the region but two archetypes would emerge: the Arab monarchies and the national security states. While the former, with their abundant natural resources, were held together by a social contract of sorts between the dynasties and the societies they ruled through massive state subsidies and a policy of buying off the disgruntled; the national security states relied on 'entirely different foundations: political terror, a primitive cult of personality and an unyielding notion of the state as a virtual possession of the man at the helm. After all the pamphlets and the ideological smoke screens, it came down to the rule of the soldier and the despot'.[17]

Faced with systematic regime oppression, many of the techniques of which were borrowed from allies in the Soviet bloc, scepticism had to go underground as governments and their associated religious establishments banned books such as Sadeq Jalal al-Azm's *Critique of Religious Thought*[18] and intimidated their authors. For the first time, public intellectuals would be rounded up in droves for questioning this or that government policy, or even for proposing alternative forms of government or social organisation. The post-colonial modernisation project required constant reaffirmation through disciplinary technologies such as the printed press, radio and television. However the mass media also had the power to magnify the voices of dissent, and the modern Arab prisoner of conscience is born. The role of cassette tapes and leaflets in propagating Ayatollah Khomeini's message and the subsequent fall of the Shah of Iran in 1979 has been expounded in the book *Small Media, Big Revolution*.[19]

---

[15] Although traditionally practised in a religious context, *Taqiyya* is essentially the practice of concealing one's beliefs for fear of retaliation by the purveyors and protectors of the prevailing dogma.

[16] Wedeen, Lisa, *Ambiguities of Domination: Politics, rhetoric and symbols in contemporary Syria* (Chicago: University of Chicago Press, 1999).

[17] Ajami, Fouad, *The Arab Predicament: Arab Political Thought and Practice Since 1967* (Cambridge: Cambridge University Press, 1992), 27.

[18] http://www.aljadid.com/content/40-year-old-classic-remains-influential-sadiq-jalal-al-azm's-'-critique-religious-thought' Accessed 22 August 2011.

[19] Sreberny-Mohammadi and Mohammadi, *Small Media, Big Revolution: Communication, Culture and the Iranian Revolution* (University of Minnesota Press, 1984).

In the West, the term 'prisoner of conscience' first gained international currency as a result of advocacy efforts by Amnesty International in 1961. Amnesty defined the PoC as 'any person who is in jail or any other detentions centre, or who is physically restricted by the authorities (for example, under house arrest or banning order, or in internal exile), because of beliefs, colour, sex, ethnic origin, language, or religion, as long as he or she has not used or advocated violence'.[20]

Dictators Don't Do Scepticism

Egypt under Gamal Abdel Nasser (1956-1970), the paragon of Arab nationalist dictators, would offer a template that was soon to be duplicated across the region. The luminaries of the Muslim Brotherhood were among the first prisoners of conscience of this period, notably Sayyed Qutub, as were the Arab Communists. In Syria, President Hafez al-Assad pioneered the practice of locking up non-violent dissenters for decades,[21] and an entire generation of activists would soon spend large parts of their adult lives in 'the school of prison'. Upon their release, they would be marked by the security forces for frequent visits, stripped of their civil rights such as pensions and access to public sector employment as well as the right to vote, and suffer near total social exclusion due to fear of the repercussions of associating with them, in addition to the disastrous consequences for their health, families and personal lives. Some remained firm in their commitment to scepticism, to their right to question prevailing dogma, and, like Egypt's irreverent musician Sheikh Imam, paid dearly for it[22]. Others migrated to Europe where they attempted to reconcile their desire for freedom with efforts to influence their countries through writing books and articles such as Bahraini dissident and academic Abdulhadi Khalaf[23], or setting up newspapers such as the pan-Arab al-Quds al-Arabi[24] in London.

Such practices gradually became the norm across the Middle East and North Africa; what's more, they became enshrined in national legislation. An Amnesty International report published in 1998 states that: "Prisoners of conscience are in

---

[20] Kaufman, Edy, "Prisoners of Conscience: The Shaping of a New Human Rights Concept", *Human Rights Quarterly* 13(1), 1991, 343.
[21] In Syria, the Muslim Brotherhood suffered at the hands of the authorities after successful participation in the political process, with Presidenti Shishakli closing down their offices in Damascus and imprisoning their leaders.
[22] http://mondediplo.com/2006/05/20prison Accessed September 1, 2011.
[23] Abdulhadi Khalaf's blog http://jaddwilliam2.blogspot.com/ Accessed August 20, 2011.
[24] Based in London, al-Quds al-Arabi is widely perceived to be populist and critical of Arab governments. See http://www.alquds.co.uk/ Accessed 20 August 2011.

jail in virtually every country in the region. They have been targeted solely for expressing their views or on suspicion of opposing the government. They have not used or advocated violence. The fact that so many have been convicted in courts of law is a damning indictment of both the laws and practices in the region. In many states, including Algeria, Egypt, Iraq, Jordan, Libya, Morocco/Western Sahara, Saudi Arabia and Tunisia, national laws allow for people to be punished for exercising peacefully their fundamental human rights. Such laws include those that unduly restrict freedom of expression and association and ban certain opinions or beliefs."[25]

It is no coincidence that, in 2011, there have been unanimous calls across the region for the repealing of such laws and the lifting of decades long states of emergency. Regardless of the political orientations of their rulers – pro- or anti-Western – these national security states have thrived on crushing public debate and discouraging scepticism. Algeria was one of the first such states to appease protesters with the approval of a draft ordinance repealing the country's 19-year state of emergency on 22 February 2011, only to replace it with anti-terrorism laws and a ban on protests in the capital, Algiers. Syria's Baathist rulers have embarked on a similar strategy in efforts to allay public outrage but to little effect.

The Arab monarchies have proved more stable and tenacious thus far, largely due to their ability to tap into vast national resources to fund handouts, to rely on foreign and regional support, and their willingness to appease their populations with concessions. They also tend to enjoy greater legitimacy with their citizens, who have mainly called for reform rather than regime change. In Morocco, for example, limited reforms and a referendum on a new constitution were offered early on to pre-empt and constrain bottom up demands, a strategy that has by-and-large succeeded. Faced with an unprecedented frequency of small-scale protests across the country this past year, Jordan's monarch has resorted to piecemeal appeasement measures such as changing Prime Ministers, cabinet reshuffles and the appointment of committees to review the electoral law and consider constitutional reform.[26]

MEDIATING SCEPTICISM

It was not until the spread of Arab satellite television that 20th century intellectual pluralism became available to the masses. Low Arab literacy and

---

[25] (Amnesty 1998: 16).
[26] http://carnegieendowment.org/2011/12/16/arab-monarchies-chance-for-reform-yet-unmet/8kfo Accessed 15 December 2011.

readership rates have meant that television and radio are the media of choice, not newspapers or books, and a satellite dish offers alternatives to state-sanctioned discourse. Through the proliferation of television networks with competing political agendas beaming into their living rooms from London, Cairo, Dubai or Beirut, Arab publics became routinely exposed to alternative modes of thinking, and to criticism of their rulers. It took several years before satellite technology was affordable in low- and middle-income households and countries such as Syria and Yemen, but the tide was soon unstoppable. Al-Jazeera TV is the most widely known such channel, but there were many established before and after it, and the Arab mediascape continues to expand and offer a plethora of political, social and religious options for Arab audiences across the world. Moreover, television news channels have been the tool of public diplomacy of choice for nearly a decade, deployed by foreign governments to appeal to the hearts and minds of Arabs, as evinced by the launch of the BBC Arabic Service, France24 Arabic, al-Hurra Television (US), Russia Today Arabic, Al-Alam TV (Iran), CCTV Arabic (China) and so forth.

Twenty-four-hour Arabic language news channels reintroduced Arab publics to one another, after they had been locked into hermetically sealed nation states feeding on state propaganda for decades. Images of life elsewhere – and not in the distant West but in countries inhabited by 'Arab people like us' – became available for public consumption and comparison. Live coverage showed Arabs joining worldwide protests against the Iraq war in 2003, allowing a collective affirmation of public sentiment across national borders regardless of government policy. This was taken a step further in Lebanon in 2005, when Arabs witnessed 24-hour coverage of protests culminating in the withdrawal of Syrian troops after decades of effective occupation. Despite the Lebanese divisions and complications that would ensue, and without wanting to overestimate the significance of Lebanon's events as an antecedent to the Arab Spring, here was an Arab country showing – live – that it could achieve independence through street power. Once again, the old sceptics who had doubted that public protest could be successful were debunked, and powerful inroads were made for the emergence of a new public scepticism that challenged the old logic of citizens as mere pawns on the chessboard of geopolitics.

The rapid spread of the Internet and associated social network media has only further expanded these possibilities, especially by allowing for an interactive process in which users can engage in debates, share experiences and mobilise to action across distances and national borders as well as circumvent established internal security networks. According to the Arab Social Media Report, the total number of Facebook users in the Arab world increased by 78 per cent between January and December 2010. Interestingly, Internet freedom indicators do not correlate to Facebook penetration, as some countries with stringent controls over web usage have relatively high Facebook penetration.[27] Young Arabs are also increasingly active on the blogosphere, despite intimidation and arrest by the authorities in countries such as Bahrain, the UAE, Morocco and Saudi Arabia.[28]

It is ironic that in their drive towards social development and economic liberalisation without accompanying political reform, Arab states have equipped youth with the very tools with which to challenge them, namely literacy, telecommunications and the Internet. That said, social networks such as Twitter and Facebook were not the primary facilitators of the Arab Spring. The revolution was not Facebooked! But new media certainly acted as facilitators amongst many other mechanisms of protest – satellite television and mobile phones being among the most important.

The Arab uprisings, particularly Tunisia, Libya and Egypt, seem to have done away with that haunting sense of powerlessness, of impotence, that was the badge of the 'Arab malaise'.[29] But perhaps one of the greatest marks of our initiation into the Arab sceptical era is the ongoing Syrian uprising. For even after the fall of the West's favourite lackeys in North Africa – Ben Ali and Mubarak – many remained sceptical of Syria's capacity for change, arguing that Syria was different because of its resistance to Israel and doubting the Syrian people's resolve for freedom. Indeed, the Syrian President himself expressed such old-school scepticism in his now-famous interview with the Wall Street Journal in January 2011[30], only weeks before his people took to the streets. But Arab publics have clearly rejected this false choice between a 'moderate' and 'steadfastness' camp at the expense of their civil rights.[31]

The explosion of insurrectionist zeal fed by a long-fomenting scepticism that the Arab populist authoritarian state is the only option has arisen from the combined failures of economic liberalisation, arrested social development, the

---

[27] Arab Social Media Report, Facebook Usage: Factors and Analysis, 1(1), January 2011.

[28] http://www.jadaliyya.com/pages/index/3643/pioneer-bloggers-in-the-gulf-arab-states Accessed 28 December 2011.

[29] Kassir, Samir, Being Arab (London: Verso Books, 2006), 43-52.

[30] http://online.wsj.com/article/SB10001424052748703833204576114712441122894.html Accessed 21 August 2011.

[31] This schism arose with Egypt's signing of the Camp David accord in 1979 that led to peace with Israel. Initially, the Steadfastness Front (jabhat al-mumana) was mainly composed of the Arab 'republics' such as Algeria, Libya and Syria – while Moderate Front (jabhat al-itidal) countries tended to be the conservative 'traditional' Arab monarchies as well as Egypt. It is widely accepted that Syria, Hezbollah and Hamas have come to represent the Steadfastness Front – in their insistence that the military option is the only way to achieve a resolution to the Arab-Israeli conflict that is just or favourable to Arabs. The split also had roots in what Malcolm Kerr has referred to as the 'Arab Cold War'. See Kerr, Malcolm, The Arab Cold War 1958-1967: A Study of Ideology in Politics. 2nd Edition (London: Oxford University Press, 1967).

world's highest regional unemployment rate[32], regional insecurity, the persistence and entrenchment of the Arab-Israeli conflict, the occupation of Iraq and its bloody sectarian outcome, and the near global demonisation of Arab cultural and religious values. This has been topped off by the almost endless saga of humiliations that have been experienced by two generations of Arabs and the increased access to knowledge of the possibilities of life elsewhere through migration and transnational media. These conditions have given rise to new dynamics of dissent and empowerment, and placed the region on the verge of a new era of public scepticism.

SUGGESTED READINGS

Ajami, Fouad, The Arab Predicament: Arab Political Thought and Practice Since 1967 (Cambridge: Cambridge University Press, 1992).

Hitti, Philip. *History of the Arabs* (London: Palgrave Macmillan, 2002) 10th Edition.

Hourani, Albert, Arab Thought in the Liberal Age: 1789-1939 (London: Oxford University Press, 1962).

Kassab, Elizabeth Suzanne, *Contemporary Arab Thought: Cultural Critique in Comparative Perspective* (New York: Columbia University Press, 2010)

Kassir, Samir, Being Arab (London: Verso Books, 2006).

Khalaf, Samir and Khalaf, Roseanne Saad, *Arab Society and Culture: An Essential Reader* (London: Saqi Books, 2009)

Perthes, Volker, Syria Under Bashar al-Asad: Modernisation and the Limits of Change (Oxford: Oxford University Press, 2005).

Sreberny-Mohammadi and Mohammadi, Small Media, Big Revolution: Communication, Culture and the Iranian Revolution (University of Minnesota Press, 1984).

Wedeen, Lisa, Ambiguities of Domination: Politics, rhetoric and symbols in contemporary Syria (Chicago: University of Chicago Press, 1999).

---

[32] ILO, Global Employment Trends 2011: The challenge of a jobs recovery (Geneva: International Labour Office, 2011).

In: Scepticism: Hero and Villain
Editors: R. Calne and W. O'Reilly

ISBN: 978-1-62417-783-5
© 2013 Nova Science Publishers, Inc.

Chapter 32

ISRAELI DUAL SCEPTICISM

Yonatan Mendel and Ronald Ranta

He was very sceptic. Even before they arrived he was sceptic. And also she was sceptic. They were a sceptic family. Even in Europe he was sceptic. He was a young sceptic man. But when they arrived here… Oh, how sceptic was he. And they lived here in terrible poverty… just terrible poverty. And I remember that when they announced on the radio, he was very sceptic about it. And she then made him dinner, and sounded also very sceptic herself. Both of them were very sceptic. And it was very difficult to watch… just very difficult. Especially as he was a person with a vision…. and as his vision was such a sceptic one…[1]

This quote is taken from one of Israel's most famous television sketches. Composed by *Ha-Hamishiya Hakamerit* (*'Chamber Quintet'*) in the mid-1990s, this segment is told by an old couple to an unknown interviewer who sits with his back to the camera. The couple sit together outside by a table and drink orange juice. The scenery around them is kibbutz-like, and the woman speaks Hebrew with a strong Polish accent. These features suggest that the couple immigrated to Palestine in their adolescence, and were members of the Zionist movement, and that today – as retired people – they are being interviewed about their arrival to the country and their memories of that period. The story is told mainly by the woman, while the man next to her mostly nods and repeats after her. By doing so he so contributes to the meaninglessness of the story about the sceptic man and his sceptic wife.

---

[1] Quoted in: Yonatan Yavin [in Hebrew] "So what did we have there? Israeli comedy shows and their contribution to modern Hebrew slang", *Ha'aretz*, 19.8.2011 (our translation).

The sarcasm in this scene is rooted in the way the story hangs in the air, and in the impossibility of us, the viewers, to understand who is the 'sceptic man', what was announced on the radio, or what was his vision all about. However, there is something deeper than this, which probably made Israeli spectators find this scene so hilarious: it is the word 'sceptic', or even the concept of 'scepticism'. Through this short scene, the centrality of this notion in the Israeli-Jewish discourse is uncovered: the viewer suddenly realises that the 'sceptic' and 'scepticism' mentioned over and over again are not a mere description of a particular person but a state of mind of a nation, a generic portrayal of Israeli-Jewish society at large and, more particularly, of its Zionist-European worldview.

This realisation brings to the fore a number interesting questions and contradictions regarding Israeli-Jewish society, which were our points of departure for the writing of this article. Firstly, we pondered, if indeed at the heart of the Zionist project during the pre-state period was a sceptic 'sting' - especially regarding the ability of the Zionist movement to overcome the obvious political difficulties - how come a serious debate about the local Arab-Palestinian population, or the 'Arab question', was postponed to such a very late stage?;[2] Secondly, with regards to Israeli-Jewish society nowadays, we were puzzled how, on the one hand, there is so much scepticism regarding the chances of Israel to live peacefully in the Middle East and, on the other hand, an instinctive rejection of critics who uncover Israeli aggressive policies and wrongdoings?;[3] Thirdly, and stemming from the last question, we asked ourselves how come Israeli academia has excelled in scientific research, in which a 'sceptic engine' drives the researcher to challenge his or her initial beliefs, while at the same time academic fields such as Middle Eastern Studies, Israeli international relations, or the history of Zionism, lacked a similar challenging 'engine'?;[4] Lastly, and as we marched in summer 2011 in the biggest Israeli demonstration of all times under the banner of 'Israel demands social justice', we tried to comprehend how come Jewish-Israelis

---

[2] See, for example, how in 1936, following the Arab Revolt, Zionist critics highlighted that the movement has until then almost totally ignored the existence of the Arab-Palestinians, their interests and national aspirations. In: Walter Laqueur, *A History of Zionism* (New York: I.B. Tauris, 2003), 209-210.

[3] See, for example, the following article that analyses the majority attitude of Israeli public towards journalist Gideon Levy, who writes weekly columns on the Israeli occupation. See: Johann Hari, "Is Gideon Levy the most hated man in Israel or just the most heroic?", *The Independent*, 24.9.2010.

[4] See, for example the critique of Israeli academic departments of sociology, Middle Eastern studies and Jewish history, in: Uri Ram, *Israeli Nationalism: Social Conflicts and the Politics of Knowledge* (London: Routledge, 2010); Gil Eyal, *The Disenchantment of the Orient: Expertise in Arab Affairs and the Israeli State*, (Stanford: Stanford University Press, 2006); Shlomo Sand, *The Words and the Land: Israeli Intellectuals and the Nationalist Myth* (Cambridge MA: MIT Press, 2011).

were indeed sceptic about their government's policies, but only if those were related to the state budget, the lack of adequate welfare programmes, and growing privatisation, and not when related to others – such as the Israeli occupation, the discrimination against Palestinian citizens of Israel, or the dominance of Israeli military establishment?[5]

We therefore felt it apt to analyse scepticism not only as a philosophical concept, but in relation to modern politics, and embarked on a rather unfamiliar journey in which we decided to look at the place and affects of scepticism on Israeli-Jewish society and its political decision-making. We hoped that by so doing we would provide a sceptic angle to the Israeli-Arab conflict.

Acknowledging that the Israeli case study contains very different and at times even confusing attitudes, we realised that we first needed to differentiate one 'scepticism' from another – at least in so far as perceived by Israeli-Jewish society. We found two dominant strands that are note-worthy, and which we discuss and analyse in this article. On the one hand, we are talking about a scepticism that encompasses a scientific-empirical-rational worldview. This strand is rooted in positivism and seeks to explain the world around us through testable scientific methods.[6] This kind of scepticism is driven by a desire to find evidence to different phenomena, but also with a yearning for a deep understanding of why things – animals, countries, people, ideas – are the way they are.[7]

On the other hand, we are talking about a second form of scepticism which is rooted in a general disposition towards doubt and reluctance to accept anything that threatens or even challenges previously held belief or ideas.[8] According to this analysis of scepticism, there is no need to explain different phenomena as

---

[5] See also: Dahlia Scheindlin and Joseph Dana, "The tent protest: neither social justice, nor revolution", *972 Magazine*, 1.8.2011.

[6] See, for example: Ruth, Weintraub, *The Sceptical Challenge* (London: Routledge, 2002), 32. See also the website of the Skeptic Magazine for a classic definition of scepticism: http://www.skeptic.com/about_us/

[7] This definition of 'scepticism' probably describes many of the modern sceptic societies and organisations worldwide.

[8] With relation to the case study analysed in this article, a representative Israeli example of this form of scepticism is the presupposition that people would try to take advantage of one another if only given the chance. Therefore, being 'naïve', trusting someone you don't know or being generous for no obvious reason, is considered a badge of shame. Its most famous articulation is in the Israeli colloquial expression 'don't be a dupe' ('*al tihiye freier*') which has become synonymous with Israeli-Jewish culture. See: Luis Roniger and Michael Feige, "The social construction of self-interest: From pioneer to freier - The changing models of generalized exchange in Israel", *European Journal of Sociology* 33, 1992, 280-307; Yoram Peri, *Telepopulism: Media and Politics in Israel* (Stanford: Stanford University Press, 2004), 219-221; Orit Kamir [in Hebrew] *Israeli Honour and Dignity* (Jerusalem: Carmel, 2004), 99-101.

some things are just the way they are. This form of scepticism is based on axioms constructed in a specific society that make all other explanations perceived as false and, in more acute situations, not to be perceived at all. This 'type' of scepticism is characterised by interests – which can vary from self-interests to national or ethnic interests – and an over-riding concern for personal security and survival. As such, this scepticism does way with the positivist world view; it does not seek to question the a-priories; it lacks the desire to apply scientific-empirical methods; and does not challenge the central beliefs, especially with regards to issues of identity, politics, and religion. In other words, this 'type' of scepticism chooses to feed the sacred cows rather than slaughter them.[9]

The Israeli-Jewish prevailing myth that 'the Arabs do not want peace' is an example which highlights the political dimension of this second 'type' of scepticism. According to this myth, despite Israel's best efforts to bring about peace with its Arab neighbours (a given for most Jewish-Israelis) there has been a recalcitrant response by its Arab neighbours. This prevailing myth has persisted among the Israeli-Jewish public, media and political debate even though numerous examples have proven the contrary.. Among some of the most prominent examples one can find is Egyptian President Anwar Sadat's 1971 peace initiative,[10] which Israel's Prime Minister at the time Golda Meir claimed not to have understood;[11] King Hussein's attempts to reach a peace agreement with Israel during the years 1968-1985, which were eventually rejected by Israel;[12] the 2002 Arab peace initiative, which was not even discussed;[13] and the 2008-2009 secret talks between Israel and the PLO, which proves that Israel was not willing to reach a settlement to the Israeli-Palestinian conflict even after Palestinian have given up almost all of their principles.[14] Despite

---

[9] The dominance of this 'type' of scepticism within Israeli-Jewish society can be explained by its very conversion to modern Hebrew: Interestingly, the Hebrew translation for the adjective 'sceptic' is 'safkan', a word that originates from the Hebrew word safék, which means 'doubt'. This linguistic linkage, we believe, can help explain the rather simplistic resemblance made by Hebrew speakers between being 'sceptic' and 'doubtful'.

[10] See, for example: Gideon Rafael, *Destination Peace: Three Decades of Israeli Foreign Policy* (New York: Stein and Day, 1981), 258; See also: Gad Yaacobi, [in Hebrew] *On The Razor's Edge* (Tel Aviv: Edanim Publishers, 1989) Pages 66-67.

[11] See, for example: Shlomo Ben Ami, *Scars of War, Wounds of Peace: The Israeli-Arab Tragedy* (Oxford: Oxford University Press, 2006), 135.

[12] For more information, see: Avi Shlaim, *Lion of Jordan: The Life of King Hussein in War and Peace* (London: Allen Lane, Penguin Books, 2007); See also: Ronald Ranta *The Wasted Decade* (Unpublished PhD dissertation, 2009, UCL), 117-118, 161-162, 211-215, and 229.

[13] See, for example: Ghazi Walid-Falah, "Peace, deception and justification for territorial claims: The case of Israel." In: (ed. Colin Flint) *Geographies of War and Peace* (Oxford: Oxford University Press, 2005), 297-320.

[14] For more information, see: 'The Palestine Papers', *Al-Jazeera's official website*, http://english.aljazeera.net/ palestinepapers/

the fact that serious and genuine Arab peace offers have been made – and the literature/documentation related to them is, as shown here, very accessible – the Israeli axiom among the general public and among considerable part of the experts is that Israel's hand has been always outstretched for peace, but that there was just 'no one to talk to'.[15] This myth is and has been based on a general fear of the Arab 'Other' and on an unwillingness to engage with or understand the Arab people.[16]

Despite the prevalence of this sceptic notion within the Israeli-Jewish society, it is interesting to reveal how it can go side-by-side with the former, more scientific, 'type' of scepticism. This phenomenon might be, to an extent, a product of the perception that the application of scientific-empirical methods is useful and encouraged with regards to certain issues (biology, economics, statistics, etc) but not regarding others (politics, state security, Jewish-Zionist identity, etc). This realisation helps explain Israel's dual desire and endeavour: to be technologically advanced with regards to many fields by applying an approach based on critical and visionary thinking,[17] while keeping other fields, most notably national-security, as a matter beyond criticism or doubt.[18] The famous quote by Israeli Minister of Defence Ehud Barak, according to which Israel needs to stay militarily strong because it is a "villa in the jungle",[19] probably captures Israel's two-fold scepticism at its best: it implies that Israel is the only country in the region advanced enough to establish a 'villa', and also that it needs to remain suspicious of its neighbours who still live in a 'jungle'.

The evident lack of critical thinking in Israel regarding security issues, or basic assumptions regarding Israeli foreign affairs, could well be a product of Zionist and Israeli history and ideology, where the emphasis is and has been placed on security and survival in a region often described by Israeli-Jewish

---

[15] See, for example: Avi Shlaim, *The Iron wall: Israel and the Arab World* (New York: W.W. Norton, 2001); See also: Amal Jamal, "The Palestinians in the Israeli peace discourse: a conditional partnership", *Journal of Palestine Studies* 30 (1), 2000, p. 40; Dalia Gavrieli-Nuri, "If both opponents 'extend hands in peace' — Why don't they meet?: Mythic metaphors and cultural codes in the Israeli peace discourse", *Journal of Language and Politics* 9 (3), 2010, 449-468.

[16] For more information on Arab-Israeli peace negotiations and missed opportunities, see: Zeev Maoz, *Defending the Holy Land: A critical Analysis of Israel's Security and Foreign Policy* (Ann Arbor: University of Michigan Press, 2006), 386-498.

[17] This corresponds with the Zionist self-perception and desire to "make the desert bloom". See: Derek Jonathan Penslar, *Israel in History: The Jewish State in Comparative Perspective* (New York: Routledge, 2007), 95.

[18] See, for example: Gabriel Sheffer and Oren Barak (eds.) *Militarism and Israeli Society* (Bloomington: Indiana University Press, 2010). See also: Dan Horowitz and Moshe Lissak, *Trouble in Utopia: The Overburdened Polity of Israel* (New York: SUNY Press, 1989), 195-231.

[19] Quoted in: Akiva Eldar, "The price of a villa in the jungle", *Ha'aretz*, 30.1.2006.

politicians as "a tough neighbourhood".[20] This viewpoint could explain the general aversion many 'declared' Israeli sceptics have from engaging in politics.[21] And this can also help to explain the peculiar situation where Jewish-Israelis who define themselves as 'secular' (or 'sceptic') are willing to apply the use of scientific methods for the examination of the origins of the bible and the existence of God (seen by them as an 'acceptable' use) but not to the perceived Jewish right to the land (an 'unacceptable' use). Israeli scholar of Jewish history, Amnon Raz-Krakotzkin, recapitulated this even better when he summarised the Zionist-secular perception of Judaism with 'There is no God, but he promised us the land'.[22] This, as we argue, has led to a situation where the advancement of scientific reasoning and a strong scientific community has been paralleled with the growth of Israeli nationalism and xenophobia.

With this clarification in mind, one can better 'decode' the Israeli double standards of scepticism. One can actually argue that Israeli-Jews are trapped in a rare sceptic *Catch-22*, in which they are pressed between the scepticism that demands new gains and inventions and the scepticism that is driven by the fear of losing existing 'gains', tangible and psychological alike. We therefore argue that a sceptic angle, or even a sceptic drive, is always 'out there' in Israeli-Jewish society and only the *kind* of scepticism that is 'used' is unfixed. This 'kind', as will be demonstrated hereafter, is conditioned by the given topic.

An example from the work of Israeli security agencies sheds light on this 'conditioning' phenomenon. During the second *Intifada* (Palestinian uprising) Israeli Intelligence forces were very *sceptic* about the intentions of the Palestinian President at the time, Yasser Arafat. They did not believe he wished to stop the violence and were very pessimistic with regards to a possible change in his policies. Their general evaluation of the situation was that President Arafat was orchestrating an armed struggle against Israel and was not willing to stop the fights. However, when Israeli Intelligence received information according to which Arafat spoke with some of his subordinates and ordered them to 'cut the

---

[20] See, for example the use of this expression by Israeli Prime Minister Binyamin Netanyahu, in: Clive Jones, "The Foreign Policy of Israel". In: Raymond A. Hinnebusch and Anoushiravan Ehteshami (eds.) *The Foreign Policies of Middle East States* (London: Lynne Rienner Publishers, 2002), 123.

[21] For example, looking at the Israeli Sceptic Community's website one notices the complete lack of any debate or discussion on matters of politics. See: The official website of the *Israeli Sceptic Society*: http://www.skeptics.org.il/

[22] Amnon Raz-Krakotzkin [in Hebrew] "There is no God, but he promised us the land", *Mita'am* 3 (2005), 71-76.

hands' of the Palestinians who provoked the violence, the Israeli confusion was evident.[23]

At that moment, a sceptic 'conditioning' took place, with one 'kind' of scepticism replacing another. The Intelligence officers were again *sceptic*, not about the unknown but rather about the new information they had. What followed was a re-evaluation of their prevailing assumptions. They re-examined and re-assessed their analysis based on the new information they obtained, striving to uncover the 'truth'. Eventually, in a special report they reached a straightforward 'conclusion' according to which the violence from the Palestinian side is going to continue, and that Arafat is no longer in control of events and therefore there is no significance to what he says or does not say.[24]

The following example demonstrates even better this Israeli sceptic 'syndrome' and its fluid nature. In July 2011 an Israeli social-protest movement was born. This movement symbolised the Israeli-Jewish public's rejection of the old socio-economic system of the state and its demand for fundamental changes in the structure of Israeli social policies. Israeli activists, driven by ongoing scepticism of previous political promises to reduce the cost of living and provide cheap housing, took to the streets. For the first time in years, and in light of the protest movement, many Israelis started to question the perceived wisdom of the state's economic system. The daily papers were filled with rigorous economic discussions and analyses, and it seems that there was no one component of the government's economic legislation and policies which was not thoroughly dissected and scrutinised. A few weeks into the protest, two competing committees, one established by the Israeli government and the other by the protest movement, held public consultations and delivered their conclusions in September 2011. Their analysis, they promised throughout the whole process, which was bound to be a product of a scientific-empirical approach, attempted to account and explain the need for policy change through meticulous scientific analysis.

But lo and behold, side by side this scientific approach a more worrying trend continued. Neither the protest-movement leaders nor those opposing it have shown any particular willingness to examine some of the underlining issues of the economic situation. For example, the examination of the basic prices of food in Israeli supermarkets was seen as a legitimate area for discussion and analysis, and even for a thorough comparative research of the food prices in the UK, US, and Australia. However, a critical analysis of the economic cost of the Israeli

---

[23] Information taken from: Raviv Drucker and Ofer Shelah [in Hebrew], *Boomerang: The Failure of Leadership in the Second Intifada* (Keter: Tel Aviv, 2005), 234-235.

[24] Ibid. A famous Israeli metaphor that spread out at the time said that the violent clashes with the Palestinians will continue as 'at times Arafat rode the "tiger" [meaning here - "violence"] and at times the "tiger" rode Arafat'.

occupation, or an examination of Israeli investments in projects such as the Separation Wall or the construction of new settlements in the West Bank, were perceived as issues which were neither debatable nor worthy of serious study. Strikingly, at the heart of the Israeli protest for 'social justice' it was practically impossible to find a serious economic analysis of Israel's diplomatic and security policies, nor a serious debate regarding the discrimination of one fifth of Israel's population - the Palestinian citizens of the state. It seems that one may be a true sceptic and apply scientific and critical methods of analysis in certain matters, and at the same time ignore and exhibit no scepticism whatsoever regarding other policies, which are at least as controversial, if not more.

This 'conditioning' is of course not an Israeli patent, but it seems to reach some disturbing heights among the majority of the population of the strongest military country in the Middle East. Furthermore, in our view, this unwillingness to challenge the prevailing Zionist narrative and discourse, and the refraining from adopting a *sceptical* critical-thinking attitude towards the most burning issues of Israeli society, have taken a more worrying turn in the last couple of years. The passing, by the Knesset, of the Boycott-ban law;[25] the proposed parliamentary investigation into the conduct of left-wing NGOs;[26] and the newly-proposed bill to "enshrine Israel's Jewish nature" in law,[27] are all examples of this radicalisation. Another living proof to this development is a recent campaign by '*Im Tirzu*' ('*if you will it*'), a popular right-wing extra-parliamentary movement, calling for a "second Zionist revolution... and the renewal of the Zionist discourse, Zionist thinking and Zionist ideology".[28] This movement is not only busy advocating for the 'renewal' of Zionist thinking but also for purging post-Zionist material and academics from Israeli universities.[29]

With this academic McCarthyism in mind, one should take into consideration that academic freedom is almost a holy principle in Israeli academia, for example

---

[25] The law bans Israeli citizens from advocating an economic or academic boycott of Israel, including 'territories under its control'. This means that Israeli citizens can boycott tourist packages to Turkey, support an economic boycott of the Gaza Strip, and also boycott buying cottage cheese in their supermarkets, but they can be taken to court if they sign a petition that calls customers not to buy products made in the Occupied Territories. For further information, see: Harriet Sherwood, "Israel passes law banning citizens from calling for boycott" *Guardian*, 11.7.2011.

[26] See, for example: Jonathan Lis, "Knesset nears final hurdle in forming panels of inquiry into left-wing NGOs", *Ha'aretz,* 2.2.2011.

[27] See, for example: Moran Azolay, "Knesset mulls 'Jewish state' bill", *Ynetnews*, 8.3.2011.

[28] See the official website of '*Im Tirzu*', in: http://en.imti.org.il/

[29] See, for example: Or Kashti, [in Hebrew] "Im Tirzu to Ben Gurion University: fire Left-wing lecturers or we will scare away donors", *Haaretz*, 17.8.2010.

This movement also advocated calling the Palestinian *Nakba* (national catastrophe of 1948) as *kharta* (a fib). See, for example: Roy Arad, [in Hebrew] "Im Tirzu: dangerous fascists or geeks with good intentions?", *Haaretz*, 16.05.2011.

in its science departments, but that this principle is easily desecrated when research questions the official history of Zionism and the political-security policies of nowadays Israel. As a matter of fact, the ability to utilise scepticism and science in the pursuit of knowledge and technological advancement is and has been almost a hallmark of Israeli society. It is a well known fact that Israel, in its short history, has made tremendous progress in the fields of science and technology, with a recent article described its "Silicon Wadi" (based around Tel Aviv) as maybe "the closest international rival to California's iconic Silicon Valley".[30] The same scientific zeal associated with scepticism, however, cannot be attributed to other fields, as is the case with the national-security approach. As a result, some prominent Israeli critics have gone all the way to label Israel's national security decision-making process as nothing less than 'amateurish', 'based on improvisation', 'decisions taken [by the leadership] on a spontaneous basis' and 'relying on personal intuition'.[31]

As we see it, this aversion from adopting a sceptic attitude has, time and again, led Israeli military and political leaders to misunderstand and misinterpret events and to follow an especially pessimistic approach towards the Arab world.[32] It seems that more than establishing a 'villa', the scepticism of Israeli-Jewish society has contributed to the construction of the 'Jungle' around it. As such, and considering the current climate of increasing ethnocentric, nationalist, non-critical and fundamental fervour, the political and military visions of the state of Israel make us extremely *sceptical* about its long-term future.

REFERENCES

Ben Ami, Shlomo (2006) *Scars of War, Wounds of Peace: The Israeli-Arab Tragedy* (Oxford, Oxford University Press).

Ben-Meir, Yehuda [Hebrew] (1987) *National Security Decision-Making: The Israeli Case* (Tel Aviv, Hakibbutz Hameuchad).

Drucker, Raviv and Shelah, Ofer [in Hebrew] (2005) *Boomerang: The Failure of Leadership in the Second Intifada* (Keter, Tel Aviv).

Eyal, Gil (2006) *The Disenchantment of the Orient*: Expertise in Arab Affairs and the Israeli State, (Stanford, Stanford University Press).

---

[30] David Baker, "Europe's hottest startup capitals: Tel Aviv", *Wired*, 15.8.2011.
[31] Yehuda Ben-Meir, [Hebrew] *National Security Decision-Making: The Israeli Case* (Tel Aviv: Hakibbutz Hameuchad, 1987), 85-86.
[32] See, for example: Yonatan Mendel, 'Thank you, dictator', *LRB blog*, 21.2.2011.

Gavrieli-Nuri, Dalia (2010) "If both opponents 'extend hands in peace' — Why don't they meet?: Mythic metaphors and cultural codes in the Israeli peace discourse", *Journal of Language and Politics* 9:3, pp. 449-468.

Horowitz, Dan and Lissak, Moshe (1989) *Trouble in Utopia: The Overburdened Polity of Israel* (New York, SUNY Press).

Jamal, Amal (2000) "The Palestinians in the Israeli peace discourse: a conditional partnership", *Journal of Palestine Studies* 30:1, pp. 36-51.

Kamir, Orit [in Hebrew] (2004) *Israeli Honour and Dignity* (Jerusalem, Carmel).

Jones, Clive "The Foreign Policy of Israel". (2002) In: Raymond A. Hinnebusch and Anoushiravan Ehteshami (eds.) *The Foreign Policies of Middle East States* (London, Lynne Rienner Publishers), pp. 115-140.

Laqueur, Walter (2003) *A History of Zionism* (New York, I.B. Tauris).

Maoz, Zeev (2006) *Defending the Holy Land: A critical Analysis of Israel's Security and Foreign Policy* (Ann Arbor, University of Michigan Press).

Penslar, Derek Jonathan (2007) *Israel in History: The Jewish State in Comparative Perspective* (New York, Routledge).

Peri, Yoram (2004) *Telepopulism: Media and Politics in Israel* (Stanford, Stanford
University Press).

Rafael, Gideon (1981) *Destination Peace: Three Decades of Israeli Foreign Policy* (New York, Stein and Day).

Ram, Uri (2010) *Israeli Nationalism: Social Conflicts and the Politics of Knowledge* (London, Routledge).

Ranta, Ronald (2009) *The Wasted Deacde* (Unpublished PhD dissertation, UCL).

Raz-Krakotzkin, Amnon [in Hebrew] (2005) "There is no God, but he promised us the land", *Mita'am* 3, pp. 71-76.

Roniger, Luis and Feige, Michael (1992) "The social construction of self-interest: From pioneer to freier - The changing models of generalized exchange in Israel", *European Journal of Sociology* 33:2, pp. 280-307.

Sheffer, Gabriel and Barak, Oren (eds.) (2010) *Militarism and Israeli Society* (Bloomington, Indiana University Press).

Sand, Shlomo (2011) *The Words and the Land: Israeli Intellectuals and the Nationalist Myth* (Cambridge MA, MIT Press).

Shlaim, Avi (2001) *The Iron wall: Israel and the Arab World* (New York, W.W. Norton).

Shlaim, Avi (2007) *Lion of Jordan: The Life of King Hussein in War and Peace* (London, Allen Lane, Penguin Books).

Walid-Falah, Ghazi (2005) "Peace, deception and justification for territorial claims: The case of Israel." In: (ed. Colin Flint) *Geographies of War and Peace* (Oxford, Oxford University Press), pp. 297-320.

Weintraub, Ruth (2002) *The Sceptical Challenge* (London, Routledge).
Yaacobi, Gad [in Hebrew] (1989) *On The Razor's Edge* (Tel Aviv, Edanim Publishers).

NEWSPAPER ARTICLES

Arad, Roy [in Hebrew] "Im Tirzu: dangerous fascists or geeks with good intentions?", *Haaretz,* 16.05.2011.

Azolay, Moran "Knesset mulls 'Jewish state' bill", *Ynetnews*, 8.3.2011.

Baker, David "Europe's hottest startup capitals: Tel Aviv", *Wired*, 15.8.2011.

Eldar, Akiva "The price of a villa in the jungle", *Ha'aretz*, 30.1.2006.

Kashti, Or [in Hebrew] "Im Tirzu to Ben Gurion University: fire Left-wing lecturers or we will scare away donnars", *Haaretz*, 17.8.2010.

Lis, Jonathan "Knesset nears final hurdle in forming panels of inquiry into left-wing NGOs", *Ha'aretz,* 2.2.2011.

Mendel, Yonatan 'Thank you, dictator', *LRB blog*, 21.2.2011.

Scheindlin, Dahlia and Dana, Joseph "The tent protest: neither social justice, nor revolution", *972 Magazine*, 1.8.2011.

Sherwood, Harriet "Israel passes law banning citizens from calling for boycott" *Guardian*, 11.7.2011.

Yavin, Yonatan [in Hebrew] "So what did we have there? Israeli comedy shows and their contribution to modern Hebrew slang", *Ha'aretz*, 19.8.2011.

WEBSITES

Al-Jazeera's official website, http://english.aljazeera.net.
'Im Tirzu' official website, http://en.imti.org.il.
Israeli Sceptic Society, official website: http://www.skeptics.org.il.
Skeptic Magazine: http://www.skeptic.com.

In: Scepticism: Hero and Villain
Editors: R. Calne and W. O'Reilly

ISBN: 978-1-62417-783-5
© 2013 Nova Science Publishers, Inc.

Chapter 33

CORRUPTION: EVIL OR NECESSITY OR HOW I LEARNT TO LOVE HUMAN NATURE

Paul Ffolkes Davis
Bursar of Trinity Hall, University of Cambridge, UK

'Some years ago I interviewed the chief executive officer of a successful Thai manufacturing firm as part of a pilot survey project. While trying to figure out a good way to quantify the firm's experience with government regulations and corruption in the foreign trade sector, the CEO exclaimed: "I hope to be reborn as a custom official." When a well-paid CEO wishes for a job with low official pay in the government sector, corruption is almost surely a problem.'

Jacob Svensson, in 'Eight questions about corruption',
Journal of Economic Perspectives, Vol.19, No.3 Summer 2005, p.19-42

'Corruption is like a tango: it is a dance for two. If there is a corrupt customs official, it is because there is a businessman who is rewarding him; if there is a serious tax-evader, it is because there is a bureaucrat who is being bribed.'

Nicanor Duarte Frutos, President of Paraguay,
Financial Times, 14 August 2006

When the esteemed editor of this volume approached me to contribute a chapter on corruption, I was both flattered and immediately wary. Why, I asked him, had he thought of me? "Well, you were a banker in the City for twenty-five years, weren't you?" came the disconcerting reply. Something serious has happened in the public imagination. How have bankers gone from being corpulent, dull, bowler-hatted gentlemen for whom 'their word is their bond' to sleazy pond-life driven only by greed and the need for self-aggrandizement? Since when was being in the City axiomatic with being corrupt? And stranger still, why would a Cambridge college want one of these dreadful creatures of Mammon as its Bursar? Is it a question of 'if you can't beat them, join them?' Something must explain this paradox.

Banks and banking have always had an importance to the British economy unmatched by the financial sector of any other developed country, with the possible exception of Wall Street's vital contribution to the US. In the mid-nineteenth century the houses of Rothschild and Barings had far more influence over national and, indeed, international prosperity than ever Lehman Brothers or Goldman Sachs has had in our times. The great merchant houses were certainly resented by princes and governments as they were the only source of the loans and bond issues by which the great leap forward through industrialisation and the creation of transport infrastructure could be funded. The Rothschilds were even on both sides at the Battle of Waterloo, with Baron James helping Bonaparte from the Paris house, while his brother Nathan Mayer in London paid for Wellington's troops. Was this corruption or realpolitik?

For all the resentment of the wealth of the great merchant banking families there was very little doubt that they were part of the Victorian social pact, that they stood for progress and helped make the country stronger and richer for the greater good. The City was the engine of Empire and Britain's rightful hegemony. As a child in the 1950s, I remember the monthly report on television news about the level of what were termed our 'invisibles' – the contribution to national earnings made by the City and all the activities of the financial sector. It was assumed that although the average citizen might not understand the arcane goings-on in the Square Mile, nevertheless and in an era where manufacturing was still an important part of economic output, the bankers, brokers, insurers, even corporate lawyers, were still a force for good, to be respected. There was never any doubt that they looked after themselves, that they were better paid than most, but the Victorian ideal still held – what was good for the bankers was good for the country. When the mysterious 'invisibles' were down, we all suffered.

What happened to break this understanding? The answer has a lot to do with changes in governmental regulation and the resultant alteration in public perception of the role and usefulness of financiers. It was not that bankers have suddenly, or even gradually, become corrupt. In 1986, the Big Bang opened the way for the amalgamation of previously separate financial activities. Commercial or high street banks could become merchant or investment banks and stockbrokers too. They all did. Everything in the City was for sale and the previous demarcation lines that had determined centuries of professional behaviour were lost within a generation. Now the relationship of the bank manager with his customers on the local high street was broken: a wall of money overran the sense of hierarchy that had sustained old City customs. Commercial bankers started paying themselves like investment bankers but for doing their usual essentially simple lending business. As the order of the day under successive British governments was to spur on domestic retail consumption to keep alive economic growth, mortgages and loans were foisted on the public like never before. This fever of credit expansion reached its apex under prime ministers Blair and Brown. I know of one family living in a four-bedroom house in West Acton, a London suburb, that contains twelve flat screen televisions, all wired up to satellite and broadband internet, and all paid for by bank credit.

It was always going to end in tears. Still, it is ironic that it was investment banks, Baer Stearns and Lehman Brothers, which were allowed to go bust, although it was the commercial or lending banks that had initiated the crisis by their careless, over-generous mortgage lending. Was the City to blame for what happened? Hardly. In Britain it was the collapse of Northern Rock, a former Newcastle-based mutual building society, which precipitated the crunch. In the painful aftermath of the credit orgy, it has become popular to vilify the evil bankers who were the cause of so much hardship and a recession that will last longer than any since the 1930s. However, it is obvious that, much as we would like it to be, this was not Fred the Shred's[1] fault or that of any of his rapacious cohort. They were guilty of an exaggerated form of what many in the City have traditionally indulged in: greed. But greed is not corruption and the two should not be confused. Bankers have always been greedy, though admittedly it reached epic proportions in the decade before the meltdown. This was only the obvious exploitation of a previously accepted social anomaly (that financiers are by definition rich): it is not the same as some moral or ethical depravity.

The credit crunch was not the result of corrupt practices, rather it was the consequence of the blind following of the dictates of politicians Through their misguided reform of the City regulatory regime and desperate encouragement of everyone to borrow and the banks to lend, they effectively rigged the system to blow. In most countries where corruption is acknowledged as widespread, people have no hesitation in identifying its source as their political rulers. In Britain, we do not tend to see ourselves as corrupt (as will be demonstrated in a moment) and it has taken us some while to work out what has happened. Bankers are a convenient cipher but, as they are constantly lamenting, politicians have never

---

[1] Fred Goodwin, former Chief Executive of the Royal Bank of Scotland.

been held in such low esteem - for very good reason. 'Power corrupts' maybe a commonplace but perhaps we should remember the whole quote:

> "Power tends to corrupt, and absolute power corrupts absolutely. Great men are almost always bad men."

Lord Acton's second sentence is at least as perceptive as his first. The disaster that has befallen the world's economy has as much to do with politics as it does with money. Or is that the banker in me talking – is self-deception a form of corruption? Maybe the editor knew what he was doing after all.

> 'Corruption is a problem that all countries have to confront. Solutions, however, can only be home-grown. National leaders need to take a stand. Civil society plays a key role as well.'
>
> James D. Wolfensohn, President of the World Bank,
> 1996 Bank-Fund Annual Meetings Speech

> If Bangladesh were to improve the integrity and efficiency of its bureaucracy to the level of that of Uruguay its yearly GDP growth rate would rise by over half a percentage point.
>
> Mauro. P, 'Corruption and Growth',
> *The Quarterly Journal of Economics*, Vol.110, No., Aug 1995, p.681-712

> 'Corruption is a subject talked about a lot where I live, as it is the cause of many of the ills and injustices in society'.
>
> BBC Global Minds - Thailand

9th December 2010 was United Nations Anti-Corruption Day. It was also the day the BBC Global News's annual poll The World Speaks was published. This poll, in its second year and the result of extensive research in twenty-six countries by the GlobeScan organisation, identified corruption as the most talked about global issue of all those measured. As a hot topic, corruption beat climate change, extreme poverty, rising costs and human rights. Interestingly, if the question asked is what are the greatest concerns facing the world, corruption falls to second behind 'economic crisis and extreme poverty'. However, it came first in developing nations, including regional giants like China, Russia and Nigeria. It was second in another five, including the US, while, notwithstanding the MPs expenses scandal, it only rated a lowly seventh in the UK. In Japan, where people obviously believe their rulers are institutionally incapable of graft, it came in fifteenth! What is clear is that these two issues are inextricably linked in the public mind. As the report says: "The blame heaped on bankers for the recent global economic turmoil may have widened the normal sense of 'corruption' among the general public to encompass a whole industry". Those poor old bankers are in the frame again!

Everybody has a word for corruption: from 'baksheesh' in the Middle East to talk of 'eating' in Africa. But do we all agree on what it is? Corruption takes many forms. Transparency International UK talks of wholesale 'rottenness' in Nigeria and quotes a BBC estimate of 2002 that throughout the African continent corruption costs $148 billion a year representing 25% of the region's GDP. Put another way, it raises the cost of goods by up to 20%. African corruption is, therefore, brazen and endemic. More surprising perhaps is the calculation that German companies lose more than EUR 6 billion a year due to corruption, embezzlement and fraud[2]. Is this likely?

When working as a Mergers and Acquisitions advisor, it was never hard to spot when an Italian or Spanish counterparty was telling me something they knew not to be true; their eyes and gesticulations gave the game away. This was not really deceitful; it was deliberate, part of a process, of a dance, we all bought into. The Germans and Swiss, on the other hand, would look you straight in the eye and never have allow the slightest suggestion that there already existed a side-letter that specifically contradicted every assurance they were at that moment giving you. Racial stereotyping is always going to be foolish and dangerous, there are always going to be exceptions, but I came to know whom I could trust and whom I could not. One is entitled to be sceptical about accepted but lazy-minded perceptions of how and where corruption operates: in my experience, Northern Europeans have not demonstrated their expected rectitude in business dealings but instead an entrenched turpitude of the worst kind.

People conceive corruption in different ways and to different degrees. An article by Andrew Hill in the Financial Times on 5th April 2011 discussed his guilt at having both taken and offered bribes. This was the disingenuous hook for an elegant piece about the UK's new Bribery Act – an attempt to tidy up various disparate existing rules into a comprehensive whole of politically correct behaviour. Before the act came into force there was much concern about the need to rationalise the shades of grey covering a favourite British pastime: corporate hospitality. Would taking prospective clients to Wimbledon or Covent Garden be an acceptable inducement to commerce while a three-week all expenses paid trip

---

[2] GermanMartinLutherUniversity of Halle-Wittenberg, PricewaterhouseCoopers and Germany's TNS-Emnid, 2007.

to Barbados would not? When does gracious hospitality degenerate into a bribe? Who is to judge? Clearly a code of good conduct is needed. But the judicious application of common sense can turn one man's sensible code into another's straightjacket. Hill points out that under its own rules Merck of the US would regards invitations to Centre Court as 'excessive' and concludes that perhaps the best test (and the FT's own) is whether one would be embarrassed to see a specific conduct written about in a newspaper. At this point, I am tempted to ask whether the newspaper in question might be owned by Rupert Murdoch's News Corporation or not? Next stop the Caribbean…

Alex Masterley, the cartoon creation of Russell Taylor and Charles Peattie whose strip runs in the Daily Telegraph, conforms completely to the now popular image of the feisty investment banker. He is a manipulative chancer of the worst sort. He has an angle for overcoming all obstacles placed in his way in his relentless pursuit of profit for Megabank and bonuses for himself. Yet his own moral serenity is utterly untrammelled and his readers (the largest for any broadsheet in the UK) are inexorably drawn to him out of a secret sense of recognition and association. Is Alex corrupt or merely resourceful? He has certainly never baulked at whatever was necessary to secure his attendance at a major sporting event, including whole test series in the West Indies as the seasons have rolled around over the years, but then gradations of grey are not his thing. He is clearly black and white.

> Corruption undermines political, social and economic stability and damages trust in institutions and authorities. It also fuels transnational crime. Terrorists and organized criminals are aided in their illegal activities by the complicity of corrupt public officials.
>
> Interpol Website

> "Corruption is any course of action or failure to act by individuals or organizations, public or private, in violation of law or trust for profit or gain."
> Definition of Corruption by Interpol Experts

> "There's corruption and there's just the way things get done"
>
> The Chicago Code - 2nd Episode FOX/SKY 1

> "When you see that trading is done, not by consent, but by compulsion – when you see that in order to produce, you need to obtain permission from men who produce nothing – when you see money flowing to those who deal, not in goods, but in favors – when you see that men get richer by graft and pull than by work, and your laws don't protect you against them, but protect them against you – when you see corruption being rewarded and honesty becoming a self-sacrifice – you may know that your society is doomed."
>
> Ayn Rand: Atlas Shrugged (1957)

In a paper published at the Chicago Business School[3], Maxim Mironov analysed the effect of corruption on economic growth in 141 countries from 1996 to 2004. Having defined corruption as use of public office for private gain, he goes on to distinguish between bad corruption, or corruption associated with poor institutions which has a negative effect on GDP growth, and residual corruption, which is uncorrelated with other governance characteristics and is positively related to GDP growth in countries with poor institutions. He goes on to create a mathematical model to explain his empirical results, which, without repeating the component parts of the formula, is able to represent 'the bribe in equilibrium' as:

$$B* = \frac{(C\gamma * + F\_p\ (\gamma *))\ (NG + NB)}{2}$$

Mironov concludes: 'The paper shows that different types of corruption differently affect economic development. Bad corruption, or corruption which is associated with poor institutions, has a negative impact on economic growth and capital accumulation. However, residual (idiosyncratic) corruption, or corruption which is uncorrelated with other governance characteristics, has a strong positive effect on development in countries with poor institutions… For policymakers, this might imply that curbing corruption without improving other institutions would have a negative effect on economic development. Another interesting finding is that residual corruption has a different effect on development in different countries: a positive effect in countries with poor institutions and negative effect in countries with developed institutions. An analysis of companies' financial data

---

[3] Bad Corruption, Good Corruption and Growth: Maxim Mironov. Graduate School of Business, University of Chicago 14th November 2005. (http://home.uchicago.edu/~mmironov1).

gives similar results: residual corruption is positively related to capital accumulation and productivity growth in developing countries.'

What Mironov has proven 'empirically', if rather dryly, is what we really already know about corruption: that it is not always a bad thing. There can be no doubt that endemic corruption damages economic development – it is the principal reason the Third World stays Third World – but if you are unfortunate enough to live under a regime where graft and bribery are rife, embracing the system and playing the game may provide the only way forward. When dealing with corrupt officials in a state that has no other norm, what Mironov terms a county with poor institutions, then bribing or using influence will just be the legitimate method of getting things done. In this situation, the use of corruption in a low quality environment, does no further harm, indeed, it actually improves things by allowing them to move forward. Mironov gives the example of the use of 'speed money' to lead to an efficient outcome. In order to open a jewellery store in Novosibirsk, one must comply with the police's security diktat that windows be covered by a steel net, while the fire department requires them to be accessible as emergency exits as part of its health and safety policy. 'Fortunately for jewellers – and Police and Firemen – these regulations can be overlooked with the help of a few bribes. If the jeweller internalises the costs of burglary or the death of her clients in a fire, nothing is lost'. I am tempted to add nothing is lost except money and lives, but, as can be seen from the example, this deemed to be a price worth paying to enable business to go on.

Mironov's central tenet is that corruption is only useful, only aids economic development, is only 'good', in regimes with 'poor' (i.e. corrupt) institutions. Even if this was ever true, which I doubt, surely it is so no longer. The effect of sustained economic and population expansion in the wealthy but upright democracies of the West since the end of the Second World War has been an accompanying explosion in the plethora of state-sponsored regulation. This has been especially evident in the last twenty to thirty years since the collapse of the Cold War threat. While the good times continue to roll, this intervention in and curbing of the creative process by politicians (yet again!) may be absorbed and incorporated into the system. It is the 'price of doing business' in a country with 'good institutions', what the entrepreneur might term a necessary evil. But now, post the 2008 credit crunch and in the environment of a stalling global economic recovery, all this regulation and control is only doing one thing – dragging us further into the mire.

Graft and corruption have always existed in successful economies. The British Empire could never have prospered without it. It is deeply embedded in the human psyche; either aligned with or actually part of the ambition and competitive instincts that drive the most achieving people. To the extent that we have come to accept that corruption is bad, Acton's maxim must be right. Whether good or bad, its classification is ultimately irrelevant, a certain level of corruption is necessary. The human race will not move forward without it. If it is regulated out of existence, all we will face is stasis initially and then decay. Graft is the oil that allows the engine to run. It may be a truism but if there is no money in it, no chance of getting ahead, no obvious gain, then the brightest and most able will not bother to overcome the obstacles placed in their way.

We should not forget the evident truth of the first line of Acton's maxim. There is no doubt that previous condemners of corrupt practices tend to be seduced as soon as they get their hands on the levers of power. Indeed, corruption does not need to be financial. It can be moral too. From Tony Blair's self-righteous justification of the origins of the Iraq War to Gordon Brown's delusional references to his moral compass as the Son of the Manse. The hypocrisy of these two leaders is staggering. When in office they may not have been driven by personal gain (though they have both done pretty well out of it subsequently), but their egos and ability to deceive themselves or believe they could deceive others, are evidence of the most profound intellectual corruption. The consequences of their actions, in terms of loss of life and destruction of wealth, rival all but the most spectacular African despots.

Good old fashioned graft is not beyond the ken of the Western political caste either as the operation of American municipal regimes has always shown. The House of Commons expenses scandal proved to a sickened but always suspicious British nation that the traditional notion of the probity of elected officials was misplaced. A politician who is too corrupt, too lacking is self-awareness and possessing the inability to recognise the impurity of his or her motives, is clearly damaging. However, one that is whiter than white (probably a creature than does not exist) would be too trusting and would never get anything done. In Italy nobody has seriously doubted the existence of 'Bunga Bunga', yet Silvio Berlusconi's career has extended over an unconscionably long time. In a country with less than 'good institutions', he is seen as a 'great' and 'bad' man who can get things done. The realisation that this apparent effectiveness is not real is a gradually forming disappointment, but not a surprise, as the crisis in the Eurozone spreads and Italy's morally (but not financially) bankrupt leadership is revealed. Sadly, it is the cant and hypocrisy of the political class generally that has both caused the current crisis and is now, through an exaggerated but inadequate response, erecting the obstacles barring the way to recovery.

Corruption is nature's way of restoring our faith in democracy.

Peter Ustinov

> It is well enough that people of the nation do not understand our banking and monetary system, for if they did, I believe there would be a revolution before tomorrow morning.
>
> Henry Ford

> The modern banking system manufactures money out of nothing.
>
> Josiah Stamp

> I am opposed to millionaires, but it would be dangerous to offer me the position.
>
> Mark Twain

On 20th November 2009 the 'Climategate' scandal broke. The server at the Climatic Research Unit of the University of East Anglia was hacked into two weeks before the much anticipated Copenhagen Summit on climate change, and thousands of emails and files were sprayed across the internet. In the ensuing controversy everybody got involved: from the Association for the Advancement of Science, the American Meteorological Society and the Union of Concerned Scientists to every pundit and news columnist around led by the Daily Telegraph's James Delingpole. At stake was the very probity of scientific research. The climate sceptics had a field day. The accusation was clear: UAE scientists had manipulated data to exploit their assertions about the danger of global warming and had suppressed other results that inconveniently seemed to contradict them. As Newsweek put it the sceptics alleged that "global warming is a scientific conspiracy".[4]

The fact that various committees set up to investigate the allegations have mostly exonerated the scientists, suggesting they were guilty of disorganization rather than fraud, has done little to take the sting out of the debate. And yet, despite continued widespread suspicion of the science driving the academic consensus asserting mankind's responsibility for global warming, to be an open sceptic renders the individual vulnerable to ridicule, and worse, the charge of being a denier. Why does this matter? Because it implies that even the precious academics may not be pure as the driven snow (damaging for what can appear to be their rather smug self-image). Even more importantly, the debate reeks of dogma and this is anathema to change and independent thought. Orthodoxy holds us back as surely as too much regulation. Political correctness, one of the most

---

[4] Ravi Somaiya, 7th July 2010.

disingenuous and regrettable features in modern society, has given an enviable weapon to be wielded by the bastions of moral rectitude and liberal approbation. I know that as a right-wing, cigar-smoking, champagne-drinking, climate change-doubting, old school cynic, I am in big trouble. However, I am equally certain that for the next decade or so, the 'civilised' world is going to go backwards; its peoples' wealth and living standards are going to decline, even as their aspirations and their house prices do, and my greatest pleasure is the unshakeable knowledge that this is not my fault.

> The beast for me is greed. Whether you read Dante, Swift, or any of these guys, it always boils down to the same thing: the corruption of the soul.
>
> Ben Nicholson

> The problem of social organization is how to set up an arrangement under which greed will do the least harm, capitalism is that kind of a system.
>
> Milton Friedman

Corruption has become an excuse. Indeed, it has become THE excuse. It is the thing we blame for anything we do not like or trust. Since we no longer trust bankers (did we ever like them?), they must be corrupt. Politicians profess to be worried that our political coconut shy is held in such contempt at a time when they have done nothing so much as to indiscriminately hurl missiles at the coconuts, the barker and each other. Society sees corruption where it wants, and right now it sees it everywhere. Normally, this might not matter, but we are facing the greatest challenge to our way of life in the modern age, and a culture of blame-mongering and finger-pointing will only exacerbate the problem.

The global financial conflagration of 2008 has initiated an economic crisis unknown since the Great Depression. To deny bankers played their part, to free them of all culpability, is clearly not credible. To condemn them as its sole architects is similarly naïve. My own view is that politicians are largely responsible and it is in the political class that corruption and graft is vested to the largest extent. It must be becoming obvious however, even to the most PC do-gooder, that ascribing blame will not start to lift us out of the mess. The recovery is already painfully slow, making the wrong choices now will make it disastrously so.

Gordon Gekko famously defended his actions by asserting that 'greed is good'. He was right. No country, whether possessed of 'good; or 'bad' institutions, can operate without a certain level of graft or influence to lubricate the wheels of commerce, political activity or, as we have seen, even academic discovery. In times of plenty, it makes sense to try to control and regulate this behaviour, to crack down on something that tends to discriminate against the common good. Ethics seem to require going through the motions, even as we remain sure that it will not be eradicated. Now, however, when we are facing economic Armageddon this is precisely the wrong response. We cannot and should not deny human nature; trying to will only prolong the present downturn. To expedite recovery we must slice through bureaucracy and subvert the political imperative to stop people operating freely. When face with panic in the markets, we should cut the entrepreneurs and the bankers free and get out of their way. If anyone wants a pay rise in the foreseeable future or even just to keep their jobs, governments and society must let the wealth creators start recreating wealth. It is time to let the sceptics and doubters have their run of the place. Let those evil financiers get on with it or we will all be in the ordure and we will have thrown away the shovel.

POSTSCRIPT

This volume has looked at scepticism in its many different guises in the sciences and humanities. Scepticism would seem to be relevant to some aspects of almost all human activities and clearly we had to be selective and not comprehensive. The eclectic result is extremely varied but we asked the chapter writers to consider a readership of the average reader of The New York Times, with a wide interest and curiosity. Inevitably some of the subjects considered are highly specialised and unfamiliar concepts may be difficult reading for the non-specialist. The views expressed in the chapters are those of the chapter authors and not necessarily of the editors. They are diverse, coming from separate political approaches and some are controversial, but we hope the reader will find these essays interesting and capable of provoking discussion, debate and in certain cases, criticism and disagreement. We hope the reader will agree that scepticism is important and can be both "Hero and Villain."

INDEX

#

20th century, xix, 3, 15, 57, 348, 351, 402
21st century, 301, 302, 303, 304, 307, 309, 310, 368

A

abolition, 353
abuse, 232, 297, 352
access, 78, 83, 100, 119, 126, 302, 380, 385, 388, 401
accountability, 358, 359, 365, 366
accreditation, 365
acetylcholine, 113
acquaintance, 201, 202, 204
activism, 178, 181, 350
actuality, 203, 373
adaptation, 127
adjustment, 27
administrators, 106
adolescents, 337
adulthood, 113, 117
adults, 34, 38, 76, 79, 123, 192, 319, 337, 338, 353
advocacy, 95, 401
aesthetic, xviii, 25, 188, 237, 238, 239, 240, 241, 243
affirming, 199
Afghanistan, xix, 266, 267, 269, 272, 273
Africa, 237, 423
age, xvi, 19, 21, 38, 41, 44, 92, 111, 118, 123, 124, 127, 131, 132, 136, 192, 205, 206, 207, 212, 230, 232, 233, 261, 269, 302, 316, 337, 399, 429
agencies, 277, 278, 279, 332, 369, 399, 412
aggregation, 176
aggression, xvii, 171, 316, 331, 338
agriculture, 137, 171
AIDS, xii, xviii, 233

Algeria, 402, 404
alternative medicine, 89
Alzheimer's disease (AD), 5, 61, 62, 63, 102, 318, 395
ambiguous stimuli, 191
amblyopia, 124
amphibia, 90
amplitude, 11, 20
amputation, 90, 117, 122
amygdala, 124, 172
anatomy, 67, 68, 74, 75, 76, 79, 81, 82, 83, 89, 91, 93, 229, 240
ancestors, 191, 245
aneurysm, 115
anger, 258
annihilation, 223
anthropology, 222
antimatter, 24
antithesis, 207
anxiety, 39, 43, 57, 129, 281, 357, 367, 370
apex, 421
appeasement, 272, 402
appetite, 231
Arab countries, 399
Arab world, 397, 403, 415
Arabian Peninsula, 397
architect(s), 90, 398, 429
Aristotle, 4, 5, 6, 28, 50, 89, 223, 396
armed forces, 399
arousal, 230
arrest, 13, 327, 336, 401, 404
artery(ies), 92, 114, 115, 305
articulation, 90, 216, 221, 223, 409
artificial intelligence, 215, 308, 310
asbestos, 91
aseptic, 91
asphyxia, 115

aspiration, 264, 382, 391
assault, 352, 361, 363, 364, 377, 378, 397
assessment, xx, 32, 35, 40, 60, 116, 123, 200, 232, 234, 240, 258, 279, 313, 377, 379
atheists, 31, 190
atmosphere, 9, 131, 132, 133, 134, 136, 259, 261, 369
atoms, 17, 210
atrophy, 116, 117, 123
attitudes, 32, 34, 42, 184, 192, 211, 283, 295, 299, 301, 304, 307, 308, 315, 384, 409
attribution, 133, 137, 364
authenticity, 244
authoritarianism, 330
authorities, 115, 197, 198, 237, 279, 288, 401, 404, 424
authority, 12, 29, 52, 54, 101, 129, 180, 207, 217, 222, 224, 263, 280, 293, 297, 298, 305, 307, 330, 344, 392
autonomy, 106
autopsy, 172, 376
aversion, 412, 415
avian, xviii, 239
avoidance, 114, 210
awareness, 125, 126, 201, 340
axons, 112, 114, 123, 124
Azathioprine, 94

B

bacillus, 91
background radiation, 18, 33, 41
backlash, 301
bacteria, 91, 229
bacterium, 96
Bahrain, 404
balance sheet, 278, 279
ban, 322, 323, 402, 414
Bangladesh, 422
Bank of England, 285
bankers, 278, 420, 421, 423, 429, 430
banking, 277, 279, 287, 288, 292, 420, 428
banking sector, 288
bankruptcy, 282
banks, 278, 279, 280, 287, 288, 292, 420, 421
Barbados, 424
bargaining, 344
basal ganglia, 121, 127
Beijing, 319
Belarus, 37
benefits, 10, 32, 42, 52, 57, 58, 106, 182, 207, 234, 271, 287, 298, 315, 317, 318, 319, 324
benign, xiii, 24, 59, 119

bias, 59, 60, 62, 121, 194, 293
Bible, 12, 177, 179, 184, 187, 193, 199, 200, 202, 221, 222, 296, 344, 412
Big Bang, 18, 19, 20, 21, 173, 420
bioavailability, 35
biodiversity, 137
biological evolution, 72
biological sciences, 176
biomedical scepticism, 63
birds, xviii, 77, 118, 239, 246
birth control, xviii
births, 213
blackbody radiation, 18
blame, 267, 421, 423, 429
bleeding, 115, 120
blogs, 56, 311, 386
blood, 33, 76, 89, 90, 91, 93, 94, 96, 98, 112, 113, 114, 115, 116, 123, 128, 267, 305, 323, 334, 340, 341, 376
blood circulation, 89
blood flow, 113, 115, 123
blood group, 90, 93, 94
blood pressure, 113, 114, 116, 267, 376
blood stream, 94
blood supply, 114, 115, 128
blood transfusion, 90
blood vessels, 76, 89, 90, 112, 113
bond market, 280
bonds, 268, 280, 331, 339
bone(s), 33, 36, 69, 76, 77, 78, 79, 85, 90, 93, 94, 96, 98, 120, 238, 244
bone form, 33
bone marrow, 93, 94, 96, 98
bone marrow transplant, 94, 98
borrowers, 278, 279, 281
boson(s), 163, 164
boxer, 320
Braille, 117
brain, xvi, 89, 95, 98, 111, 112, 113, 114, 115, 116, 117, 118, 119, 120, 121, 122, 123, 124, 125, 126, 127, 128, 129, 130, 172, 173, 188, 219, 229, 237, 298, 305, 306, 310, 376
brain activity, 113
brain damage, 113, 114, 130
brain functioning, 121
brain functions, 112, 128
brain stem, 114, 116, 125
brain structure, 114, 121
brainstem, 119
brainwashing, xvi
Brazil, ix, 282, 329, 330, 331, 332, 333, 334, 337, 338, 341, 342
breakdown, 18, 295, 297, 383

breast cancer, 33, 38
breathing, 114, 116, 376
bribes, 423, 426
Britain, xix, 73, 180, 267, 298, 383, 387, 389, 391, 420, 421
Brownian motion, 16
brutality, 272, 273, 359
Buddhism, 176, 182, 185, 189
budding, 229
budget deficit, 279
building blocks, 78, 81, 89, 96, 229
bullying, 363
bureaucracy, 271, 359, 422, 430
business ethics, 107
businesses, 106, 108
bystander effect, 40, 41

C

cables, 112, 122
Cairo, 398, 403
calculus, 13, 49, 50
Camp David, 404
campaigns, 272, 295
cancer, 35, 37, 39, 40, 41, 107, 138, 259, 317
cancer death, 39
candidates, 52, 390
capillary, 89
capital accumulation, 292, 425
capitalism, 183, 359, 429
carbon, xvii, 43, 131, 135, 136, 137
carbon emissions, 135
carcinogen, 39
cardiovascular disease, 317
carotid arteries, 305
carotid endarterectomy, 114
cartilage, 98
cartilaginous, 78
cartoon, 241, 424
case study(ies), 176, 184, 307, 334, 409
cash, 232, 332
casting, 213
catalyst, 303
catastrophes, 85
category a, 338
Catholic Church, 8, 9, 12, 232
Catholics, 179, 193
causation, 60
cell biology, 75, 81, 96
cell division, 97, 229
cell membranes, 81
Central Asia, 396
central bank, 277, 278, 280, 281, 283, 287, 288

central nervous system, 111, 121, 123
cerebellum, 123, 124
cerebral cortex, 114, 117, 118, 120, 125
cerebral hemisphere, 123, 128
CERN, 164
chain of command, 265
challenges, 62, 182, 302, 399, 409
chaos, 135, 256
charities, 391
checks and balances, 392
chemical, 67, 94, 113, 164, 165
Chernobyl accident, 35, 43
Chicago, 30, 84, 85, 185, 227, 400, 405, 425
chicken, 78, 79, 80
Chief Justice, 349
child labor, 337
child mortality, xviii
childhood, 19, 35, 75, 123, 124, 193, 259, 319
children, xvi, 34, 36, 37, 38, 41, 43, 115, 117, 122, 123, 182, 191, 192, 219, 230, 231, 232, 234, 240, 246, 293, 297, 299, 300, 304, 306, 307, 319, 334, 337, 357, 370
chimpanzee, 254
China, 95, 135, 194, 212, 282, 293, 403, 422
cholera, 91
Christianity, 3, 173, 176, 187, 188, 189, 192, 199, 201, 202, 203, 206, 221, 222, 316, 396
Christians, 187, 189, 193, 198, 200
circulation, 89, 93, 116, 182
citizens, 37, 184, 293, 298, 391, 400, 403, 409, 414, 417
city(ies), 133, 137, 161, 178, 207, 287, 288, 298, 318, 320, 341, 398, 419, 420, 421
civil law, 327, 375, 376
civil rights, 401, 404
civil servants, 281, 385
civil service, 268
civil war, 266
clarity, xiii, 78, 301, 364, 367, 387
classical mechanics, 13
classification, 16, 334, 335, 427
classroom, 297, 300, 303, 305
clients, 107, 233, 234, 423, 426
climate(s), xiii, 43, 55, 56, 67, 71, 74, 131, 132, 133, 134, 135, 136, 137, 138, 415, 422, 428, 429
climate change, 131, 133, 134, 136, 137, 422, 428, 429
climatic factors, 134
clinical application, 93
clinical trials, 59, 100
clone, 97
cloning, 97, 265
clusters, 19, 20

CNN, 325
CO2, 131, 133, 136
coal, 44, 53, 137
cochlea, 77
cochlear implant, 123
codes of conduct, 370
coercion, 234
cognitive deficits, 120
cognitive development, 37
cognitive process, 73
cognitive psychology, 313
cognitive science, 298, 308
cognitive skills, 302, 308
cold dark matter, 20
Cold War, 404, 426
collaboration, 126, 303
collateral, 124
color, 221, 226, 338
coma, 8, 96, 124, 125
commerce, 104, 234, 423, 430
common sense, xii, xvi, 374, 377, 424
communication, 106, 118, 171, 173, 294, 303, 377, 393
communication skills, 303
compassion, 104, 105
competition, xvii, xviii, 103, 106, 353, 359, 369
competitors, 315, 321
complexity, xvii, 72, 114, 133, 189, 229, 352
compliance, 360, 365, 366, 367
complications, 233, 403
composition, 81, 82, 176, 335
compounds, 100, 113, 267
comprehension, 82, 83, 260
compulsion, 105, 425
computer, 24, 26, 52, 58, 113, 117, 125, 134, 135, 136, 232, 261
computer simulations, 136
computer software, 58
concept map, 314
conception, 73, 163, 168, 218, 221, 222
concordance, 21
conditioning, 412, 413, 414
conduction, 130
confabulation, 24
confidentiality, 44, 102, 106
conflict, xviii, 107, 317, 340, 369, 384, 399, 404, 405, 410
conformity, 179
confrontation, 271
Confucianism, 176
connectivity, 121
consciousness, 43, 112, 116, 125, 127, 128, 130, 222, 261

consensus, xii, xiii, 24, 32, 41, 52, 53, 55, 114, 216, 287, 288, 428
consent, 425
conspiracy, 378, 428
constituents, 35, 161
construction, xviii, 78, 221, 223, 245, 319, 361, 414, 415
consulting, 57
consumer choice, 359
consumers, 232, 281, 383
consumption, 45, 271, 403, 421
contamination, 35
contradiction, 26, 52
control group, 286
controlled trials, 115
controversial, 36, 44, 61, 226, 349, 350, 414
controversies, xiii, 118, 199, 239, 322
convergence, 134, 181
conversations, 55, 297, 322
conviction, 54, 199, 200, 201, 204, 347, 350, 378, 397
cooling, 18, 115, 136
cooperation, 178, 237
copulation, 232
corporate hospitality, 423
corpus callosum, 127
correlation, 166
corruption, xix, 315, 320, 332, 384, 419, 420, 421, 422, 423, 425, 426, 427, 429
cortex, 112, 114, 117, 118, 119, 122, 123, 128
cosmos, xiii, 19
cost, 32, 33, 42, 64, 83, 99, 100, 103, 118, 132, 244, 272, 279, 294, 319, 343, 360, 369, 391, 413, 423
cost of living, 413
cotton, 265
covering, 36, 51, 247, 268, 334, 390, 423
cranial nerve, 114
cranium, 116
craving, xiv
creationism, 68
creative process, 426
creativity, 65, 249, 259, 303
credentials, xiii
credit rating, 278
crimes, 329, 331, 334, 335, 338, 340, 367
criminal activity, 95, 172, 318
criminal attitudes, 368
criminal justice system, 343, 344
criminality, 330
criminals, 234, 329, 334, 343, 347, 348, 424
crises, 106, 162, 277, 280, 287, 289
critical analysis, 413
critical period, 117, 124

critical thinking, 301, 303, 304, 307, 396, 411
criticism, xii, xvii, 8, 183, 197, 198, 200, 201, 202, 203, 204, 217, 218, 222, 226, 244, 272, 300, 391, 403, 411
culture, 57, 59, 97, 116, 194, 221, 223, 224, 245, 250, 260, 270, 284, 301, 332, 333, 340, 366, 369, 395, 409, 429
cure(s), 91, 96, 100, 101, 106, 107, 211
currency, 182, 279, 292, 293, 294, 401
curricula, 175, 308, 398, 399
curriculum, 106, 300, 301, 302, 303, 304, 307, 309, 310, 311, 313
customers, 107, 233, 414, 421
cycles, 132, 245
cycling, 323

D

damages, 366, 424, 426
dance, xviii, 239, 268, 341, 419, 423
danger, xviii, 12, 94, 97, 176, 177, 190, 191, 233, 234, 238, 239, 248, 323, 365, 428
dark energy, 21
dark matter, 20, 21
Darwinian evolution, 72
Darwinism, vii, 71, 72, 80, 81, 82, 83, 86
database, 334, 337, 338
David Hume, 198, 205
death penalty, 333, 347
deaths, 39, 42, 115, 138, 213, 267, 298, 338, 361
debts, 280, 293, 389
decision-making process, 415
decontamination, 36
deductive reasoning, 4
deep brain stimulation, 120, 125
defects, 38, 60, 96, 231, 317
defence, 10, 13, 51, 92, 202, 203, 207, 264
deficiencies, 359
deficit, 272, 388, 390
deflation, 283, 293
degenerate, 424
delinquency, 337
democracy, 54, 180, 219, 282, 391, 393, 427
Democrat, 384, 386, 387, 389
demonstrations, xvi
dendrites, 112, 113
denial, 131, 190, 333
Denmark, 9
density fluctuations, 20
deoxyribonucleic acid, 374
depressed skull fracture, 119
depression, 120, 127
destruction, 88, 93, 298, 427

detention, 273, 354, 355
deterrence, 367
developing brain, xvi
developing countries, 95, 426
developing nations, 237, 422
developmental process, 79
diabetes, 96, 97, 115, 317
dichotomy, 183, 189, 194, 273
diet, xiii
diffusion, 123
dignity, 248, 258, 260
diplomacy, 403
disability, 99, 115, 124, 125
disabled patients, 126
disappointment, 17, 93, 318, 383, 389, 427
disaster, 94, 245, 269, 287, 288, 422
discomfort, 9, 183
discontinuity, 27
discrimination, 370, 409, 414
disease models, 63, 64
diseases, 35, 37, 43, 60, 61, 62, 88, 89, 91, 96, 106, 107, 111, 125
disorder, 61, 120, 363
displacement, 14
disposition, 409
distress, 116
distribution, 9, 14, 17, 20, 37, 38, 64, 249, 349
divergence, 5, 135
diversification, 337
diversity, 74, 83, 161, 163, 187, 201, 223, 397
DNA, xix, 38, 40, 41, 42, 60, 62, 67, 88, 96, 97, 229
doctors, 57, 58, 60, 65, 88, 91, 98, 99, 104, 107
dominance, 124, 138, 216, 282, 409, 410
donors, 95, 116, 414
dopamine, 113, 122
doping, 323
double helix, 67
drawing, 68, 239, 244, 247, 248, 313
dream, 118, 188, 191, 263, 392
dreaming, 118
drinking water, 91
Drosophila, 63
drug addiction, 234
drug discovery, 61, 62
drug targets, 62, 63
drug treatment, 360, 370
drugs, 95, 100, 115, 116, 117, 120, 122, 125, 349, 351, 362, 367, 369
duality, 28, 29
duopoly, 389

E

early universe, 20, 21
earnings, 234, 324, 420
economic activity, 294, 332
economic change, 281
economic consequences, 288
economic crisis, 422, 429
economic development, 281, 425, 426
economic growth, 278, 391, 421, 425
economic indicator, 279
economic policy, 288
economic systems, 365
economic theory, 277
economics, xiii, 283, 286, 289, 392, 411
ectoplasm, 161
educated women, 137
education, 43, 44, 68, 75, 132, 137, 212, 234, 297, 299, 300, 301, 302, 303, 304, 306, 307, 308, 310, 312, 362, 368, 399
educators, 299, 301, 303
egg, 80, 92, 97, 98, 229
Egypt, 172, 398, 399, 401, 402, 404
elaboration, 40, 211
election, 383, 384, 386, 387, 388, 390, 392
electric current, 96
electricity, 112, 138
electromagnetism, 23
electron, 162
electronic circuits, 132
electrons, 18, 41
elementary particle, 164
embryology, 69, 75, 76, 81
embryonic stem cells, 97
emergency, 270, 280, 402, 426
emission, 12, 14, 19, 136, 137
emotion, xvi, xvii, xx, 43, 44, 283, 288
emotional experience, 258
emotional responses, 113
empathy, 257
empirical methods, 410, 411
employability, 302
employees, 287, 366
employment, 245, 369, 401
empowerment, 57, 405
encephalitis, 125
encouragement, 421
endurance, 257, 335, 336
enemies, 87, 171, 217
energy, 16, 18, 21, 33, 34, 39, 41, 42, 44, 45, 113, 133, 137, 138, 225, 258, 259, 260, 261
energy density, 21
energy efficiency, 138
energy supply, 44, 137
enforcement, 172, 294, 392
engineering, xiii, 96, 136
England, 9, 103, 126, 199, 226, 264, 265, 285, 310, 318, 319, 323, 324, 343, 345, 346, 347, 353, 362, 368
enlargement, 240
enslavement, 332
entrepreneurs, 293, 430
environment, 35, 113, 132, 184, 233, 234, 307, 358, 363, 364, 426
environmental degradation, 131, 137
enzyme, 124
epilepsy, 127
epistemology, 29, 201
equality, 210
equilibrium, 425
Estonia, 76
ethical issues, 112
ethics, 58, 99, 100, 102, 103, 104, 106, 107, 108, 216, 271, 273, 320, 359, 369
eugenics, 72
euphoria, 100
Europe, xvii, 7, 8, 33, 35, 37, 39, 41, 49, 69, 103, 104, 136, 137, 138, 207, 245, 281, 282, 396, 398, 401, 407, 415, 417
European art, 243
European Central Bank, 280, 282, 283
European Union, 283
everyday life, xi, 213, 257, 396
evil, 88, 177, 239, 249, 295, 296, 329, 333, 421, 426, 430
evolution, xvi, xvii, 18, 19, 21, 42, 69, 72, 79, 81, 83, 84, 85, 135, 173, 216, 219, 237, 273, 344
exaggeration, 50
examinations, 101
excision, 123
exclusion, 273, 373, 376
execution, 95, 207, 273, 336, 345
exercise, 24, 61, 103, 160, 216, 305, 327, 340, 343, 346, 347, 350, 352, 376, 378, 380, 397
exile, 180, 321, 401
expert systems, 58
expertise, 78, 104, 211, 233, 261, 365, 369, 379, 381
exploitation, 26, 88, 95, 98, 234, 293, 307, 421
exposure, 32, 33, 34, 35, 36, 37, 38, 40, 41, 42, 93, 132, 359, 386
extinction, 247
extracellular matrix, 124
extreme poverty, 422
eye movement, 118

F

Facebook, 403, 404
facilitators, 404
factories, 33, 293
factual knowledge, 73, 307
fairness, 200
faith, xv, xvi, xviii, 12, 13, 32, 51, 57, 68, 88, 103, 106, 107, 108, 180, 189, 190, 193, 197, 198, 199, 200, 201, 202, 203, 207, 212, 220, 221, 222, 279, 282, 292, 296, 370, 396, 427
families, xviii, 61, 234, 245, 246, 268, 272, 357, 370, 401, 420
family members, 60, 231, 340
famine, 258
farmers, 138
farming techniques, 221
farms, 45
fat, 96, 112, 319
fear, 29, 38, 45, 88, 99, 101, 103, 124, 210, 222, 268, 273, 274, 281, 282, 284, 289, 331, 348, 400, 401, 411, 412
fears, 41, 91, 101, 180, 330, 371
feelings, 172, 211, 248
financial data, 426
financial institutions, 106
financial markets, 277, 281
financial sector, 420
financial support, 32, 75
finite speed, 14, 19
fires, 200
first generation, 138
fish, 68, 80, 90, 246, 320
fishing, 37
flaws, 52, 53, 54, 114, 309, 385
flexibility, 220
floods, 136
fluctuations, 20, 136, 245
fluid, 112, 413
Flynn effect, 312
folklore, 191
food, xvii, 103, 118, 126, 137, 179, 211, 229, 237, 292, 332, 413
football, xix, 316, 320, 324
force, xviii, 13, 44, 117, 127, 210, 217, 264, 270, 271, 272, 273, 286, 309, 350, 351, 399, 420, 423
forecasting, 36
foreign affairs, 411
foreign language, 45
foreign policy, 392
formation, 20, 78, 122, 124, 135, 136, 263, 268, 270, 398, 399
formula, 16, 346, 389, 425

fossils, 68
foundations, 4, 14, 16, 18, 291, 302, 305, 309, 370, 400
foxglove, 89
France, 15, 280, 317, 323
fraud, 84, 382, 423, 428
freedom, 300, 393, 401, 402, 403, 404, 414
Freud, 255, 262
frontal lobe, 119, 120, 121
fruits, 62, 106, 389
full employment, 391
funding, 44, 216, 304, 385
funds, xvii, 234, 278, 280, 281
future scientific communities, 65

G

GABA, 122
galaxy(ies), 14, 15, 16, 17, 18, 19, 20
Galileo, 9, 11, 12, 13
gambling, 56, 321
gamma radiation, 33
gamma rays, 33, 34
gangs, 331, 370
Gauguin, 173
Gaza Strip, 414
GDP, 286, 422, 423, 425
gene therapy, 91
general election, 285, 351
general practitioner, 89, 172
General Relativity, 55
generation of data, 59
genes, 40, 62, 63, 90, 96
genetic engineering, 89, 96
genetic study, 62
genetics, 62, 79
genome, 62, 96
genome wide association study (GWAS), 62, 63
genomic instability, 40, 41
genre, 395
geography, 291, 332
geology, 54
geometry, 4, 10, 16, 48, 49, 50
Germany, 44, 86, 184, 280, 283, 423
gestation, 88
gland, 37
Glass-Steagall Act, 278
glaucoma, 115
glia, 112, 113
global economy, 302
global forces, 392
global scale, 133
global warming, xvii, 56, 133, 428

globalised world, 383
glucocorticoids, 116
glucose, 113
glutamate, 113
God, 8, 10, 54, 160, 172, 173, 178, 179, 183, 184, 185, 188, 189, 191, 192, 193, 194, 195, 197, 198, 199, 200, 201, 202, 204, 222, 254, 259, 264, 317, 412, 416
good deed, 189
goods and services, 291, 292, 293, 294
google, 258, 260, 261, 312
governance, 295, 365, 425
government policy, 286, 400, 403
governments, xix, 43, 137, 161, 272, 280, 281, 282, 294, 358, 383, 389, 395, 400, 401, 403, 420, 421, 430
governor, 271, 354, 355, 364
grants, 100
gravitation, 13, 16, 17, 27
gravitational field, 16
gravitational force, 21
gravity, xv, 9, 11, 13, 16, 20, 348
Great Depression, 429
Greece, xv, 4, 103, 207, 279, 280, 282, 283, 316
greed, 263, 281, 321, 420, 421, 429
Greeks, 4, 5, 7, 47, 48, 161, 283, 316
green revolution, 137
greenhouse, 133
greenhouse gas, 133
group identity, 266
group work, 303
growth, xvii, 20, 80, 176, 327, 343, 344, 345, 349, 350, 353, 354, 361, 388, 412, 422, 425
growth rate, 422
guardian, 312, 391
guidance, xiii, 345, 349, 396
guidelines, 60, 106, 114, 353
guilt, 258, 274, 344, 363, 373, 375, 377, 379, 381, 423
guilty, 9, 321, 323, 352, 373, 421, 428
Guinea, 239

H

habitat, xvii
hair, 179, 245, 265
half-life, 33
Hamas, 404
harmony, 125, 171
hazards, 42
head injury, 111, 114, 115, 116, 120, 121
head trauma, 114
healing, 32, 102, 103, 104, 107
health care, 99, 103, 364
health care costs, 99, 103
health effects, 34, 39
health risks, 42
heart failure, 89
heart transplantation, 94, 95
hegemony, 61, 65, 420
helium, 18
hemisphere, 35, 123
Henry Ford, 428
hepatitis, 91, 165
hepatitis a, 91
Hezbollah, 404
Higgs boson, 164
high blood pressure, 114
highlands, 266
hippocampus, 113, 118, 122
Hippocratic tradition, 99
historical reason, xix
history, xx, 3, 4, 9, 25, 44, 49, 68, 73, 76, 80, 82, 84, 85, 87, 131, 171, 178, 181, 198, 200, 206, 208, 210, 218, 219, 220, 226, 230, 231, 233, 237, 239, 241, 243, 251, 263, 270, 271, 281, 283, 292, 308, 310, 312, 318, 323, 343, 351, 355, 390, 398, 408, 411, 415
HIV, xii, 91, 234
home ownership, 284
homeowners, 283, 284, 285
homicide, 329, 333, 361
homogeneity, 18, 176, 261
honesty, 52, 258, 295, 321, 379, 382, 425
hormones, 230
hospitality, 424
host, 91, 94, 253, 319, 320
host population, 319
hostility, 79, 220, 231, 240, 352
house, 324, 384, 385, 386, 427
housing, 284, 285, 413
hub, 237
human activity, xix
human agency, 191
human body, 34
human brain, xvi, 112, 113, 117, 130, 219, 221
human cognition, 168
human condition, 209, 213, 329, 333
human existence, 208
human experience, 263
human health, 41, 43
human nature, 171, 234, 281, 430
human right, 402, 422
human rights, 402, 422
human sciences, 194
human subjects, 63

hunting, 171, 238, 241, 245, 249, 316
husband, 32, 231, 248, 334
hydrogen, 18, 19, 36
hydrogen atoms, 18
hydrogen bomb, 36
hygiene, 33, 233, 234
hyperinflation, 283
hypertension, 115
hypocrisy, xix, 427
hypothesis, xv, xvi, 6, 14, 15, 18, 26, 27, 62, 87, 137, 162, 168, 184, 199, 204, 330, 337
hypothyroidism, 36
hypoxia, 115, 116, 125

I

iconography, 247
ideal, 8, 15, 73, 79, 198, 254, 359, 420
identical twins, 92, 93
identity, 73, 111, 128, 179, 181, 182, 254, 265, 266, 321, 331, 410, 411
ideology, 181, 183, 184, 358, 411, 414
idiosyncratic, 425
illusion, 284
image(s), 77, 181, 191, 230, 238, 239, 240, 241, 246, 253, 254, 255, 256, 257, 258, 259, 260, 261, 262, 265, 269, 358, 364, 424
imagery, 126, 180, 239, 261
imagination, 203, 301, 420
Immanuel Kant, 14
immune system, 93, 94
immunity, 93
immunodeficiency, 233
immunosuppression, 95
imperialism, 398
implicit knowledge, 243
imprisonment, 347, 351, 352, 353, 354, 355, 362, 367, 369, 370
improvements, 360, 361, 362, 365
impulses, 59, 114, 123, 125
impulsive, 127, 331, 335, 339
in vitro, 65
incarceration, 367
incidence, 35, 40, 43, 114, 120, 127, 337
income, 234, 249, 278, 292, 294, 390, 403
incompatibility, 99
incongruity, 373
increased access, 405
incus, 77, 78, 79
independence, 172, 220, 232, 270, 285, 350, 392, 403
India, 91, 182, 271, 318, 322
Indian Ocean, 68
indigenous peoples, 244
individual development, 80
individual rights, 332
individualism, 183
individuality, 254
individuals, 52, 60, 62, 137, 171, 187, 234, 287, 291, 329, 331, 332, 333, 335, 341, 424
indoctrination, xvi
indolent, 119
Indonesia, 68
induction, 339
industrial relations, 360
industrial revolution, 14, 131
industrialisation, 302, 420
industry(ies), 39, 42, 43, 65, 175, 232, 245, 246, 293, 391, 423
ineffectiveness, 359
inequality, 329
inertia, 13
infection, 91, 114
inferences, 210
inflammation, 165
inflation, 21, 283, 285, 286, 293, 295
influenza, 138
information technology, 362
informed consent, 106
infrastructure, 137, 138, 420
ingestion, 32, 33, 36
ingredients, xix, 352
inheritance, 67
inhibitor, 359
initiation, 102, 273, 404
injury claims, 272
innocence, 211, 322, 374, 377
instinct, xvi, xviii, 239
institutions, 9, 60, 106, 107, 232, 271, 272, 280, 330, 332, 333, 357, 370, 399, 424, 425, 426, 427, 429
insulin, 96, 97, 98
integrity, 188, 209, 259, 279, 323, 387, 422
intellect, xii
intelligence, 264, 362, 366
intensive care unit, 115
intentionality, 210
interest groups, 43
interest rates, 278, 279, 285
interference, 340, 355
International Atomic Energy Agency, 37
international meetings, 100
International Monetary Fund, 294
International Olympic Committee, 320
international relations, 408
international trade, 293
internship, 99

interpersonal skills, 302
interstellar dust, 15
intervention, 102, 271, 336, 355, 368, 426
intimidation, 404
intonation, 268
intrinsic value, 294
intrusions, 101
inventions, xv, 309, 398, 412
inventors, 398
invertebrates, 82
investment, 106, 217, 278, 284, 285, 292, 293, 390, 420, 421, 424
investment bank, 278, 420, 421, 424
investments, 278, 414
investors, 107, 277, 278, 280
invisible hand, 104, 294
iodine, 35, 36, 37
ionising radiation, 40
ions, 112
Iran, 176, 177, 180, 181, 185, 232, 396, 400, 403
Iraq, 180, 185, 269, 273, 384, 399, 402, 403, 405, 427
Iraq War, 427
Ireland, 15, 102, 103, 280
iron, 119, 265
irony, 244, 249, 309
irradiation, 36, 93, 94
irritability, 118
Islam, 176, 180, 395
Islamism, 399
Islamophobia, 180
islands, 37
isolation, 212, 216
isotope, 33
Israel, 176, 178, 184, 399, 404, 407, 408, 409, 410, 411, 412, 414, 415, 416, 417
Israeli-Arab conflict, 409
issues, xiii, 26, 31, 112, 131, 137, 138, 179, 190, 197, 198, 293, 300, 349, 365, 368, 377, 410, 411, 413, 414, 420, 423
Italy, 207, 280, 292, 427
iteration, 206

J

Japan, 35, 37, 40, 97, 137, 138, 184, 185, 247, 321, 422
jaundice, 165
Jews, 178, 179, 185, 264, 412
joints, 90
Jordan, 264, 399, 402, 410, 416
journalism, 181
journalists, xiii, 104, 215, 385, 386
judiciary, 329, 344, 350, 351, 352
Jupiter, 9, 10, 12
jurisdiction, 348
justification, 159, 160, 197, 201, 232, 240, 301, 327, 373, 374, 376, 382, 410, 416, 427

K

Keynes, 281
Keynesian, 286
kidney, 92, 93, 94, 95
kidney failure, 92, 93
kidney transplantation, 94
kill, xviii, 33, 172, 271, 273, 337

L

labor market, 331
labor relations, 332
lack of confidence, 330
landscape, 367
language acquisition, 215
languages, 219, 221, 224, 396
larynx, 237
Latin America, 342
laws, 11, 13, 14, 27, 73, 88, 171, 172, 179, 205, 211, 213, 292, 294, 332, 335, 391, 392, 402, 425
lawyers, 54, 420
lead, xv, xvii, xix, 3, 8, 24, 27, 29, 31, 39, 43, 47, 52, 65, 107, 133, 162, 167, 172, 209, 211, 239, 240, 245, 264, 267, 281, 292, 307, 322, 330, 336, 348, 366, 369, 396, 397, 426
leadership, 33, 171, 181, 267, 273, 391, 393, 415, 427
learning, xiv, 49, 58, 105, 119, 122, 125, 299, 302, 303, 304, 305, 306, 307, 310, 313, 314, 396
learning styles, 304, 305, 306, 307, 313
Lebanon, 185, 403
left hemisphere, 118, 123
legislation, 114, 286, 350, 352, 353, 354, 401, 413
legs, 112, 317
lending, 278, 279, 285, 287, 421
lesions, 118, 119, 120, 121, 123, 127, 128
liberalisation, 404
liberalism, 219, 398
liberation, 182
liberty, 376, 379
life cycle, 80
life expectancy, 33
lifelong learning, 105
lifetime, 55, 71, 73, 167, 175, 231, 240, 307

light, xiii, xvi, 14, 15, 16, 17, 18, 19, 28, 29, 48, 54, 60, 81, 132, 178, 205, 212, 224, 254, 258, 259, 287, 295, 304, 327, 331, 334, 341, 412, 413
linguistics, 215, 216, 217, 218, 219, 220, 221, 222, 223, 224, 225
Lion, 410, 416
literacy, 344, 402, 404
lithium, 18
liver, 94, 95, 96, 165
loans, 279, 420, 421
lobbying, 137, 281, 288
lobectomy, 121, 123
local government, 385
locus, 168
loneliness, 260
longevity, 34, 92, 240
long-term memory, 307
love, xix, 230, 231, 232, 234, 296
loyalty, 181, 189, 266, 271, 316
luminosity, 15
lung cancer, xii
Luo, 79, 85
lying, 27

M

Maastricht criteria, 281
macroeconomics, 283, 286
magnetic field, 135, 136
magnetic properties, 113, 128
magnetic resonance, 127, 128
magnetoencephalography, 118
magnitude, 20, 302
maiming, 268, 273, 274
majority, xv, xix, 41, 42, 44, 54, 73, 125, 127, 132, 173, 178, 179, 183, 194, 199, 229, 240, 267, 270, 284, 297, 353, 384, 386, 389, 408, 414
malaise, 384, 404
malaria, 91
malignancy, 94
manipulation, 90, 255, 258, 261, 323
mapping, 121, 238, 379, 380
market economy, 183
marketing, 248
marketplace, 250
marriage, 231, 260
marrow, 94, 98
Mars, 5, 7, 10
Marshall Islands, 35, 36
Marx, 294, 295
mass, 11, 18, 19, 21, 44, 136, 164, 166, 172, 270, 281, 399, 400
mass media, 44, 399, 400

material bodies, 161, 163
materialism, 190
materials, 32, 91, 164
mathematics, 4, 5, 16, 26, 48, 49, 51, 52, 160, 273, 313
mathematics education, 313
measure of value, 295
media, 43, 44, 89, 91, 96, 136, 175, 177, 181, 182, 183, 255, 256, 258, 321, 335, 385, 391, 392, 403, 405, 410
medical, xiii, 38, 42, 57, 58, 59, 60, 65, 74, 83, 89, 91, 92, 95, 99, 100, 101, 102, 103, 104, 106, 107, 108, 116, 165, 167, 232, 233, 234, 319, 381
medical care, 103
medical reason, 167
medical science, 103, 232
Medicare, 60
medicine, xiii, xviii, 32, 37, 58, 59, 88, 91, 99, 100, 102, 103, 104, 105, 106, 115, 308
membership, 199, 200, 282
membranes, 119
memory, 53, 87, 113, 115, 118, 119, 122, 221, 255, 258, 267, 283, 307, 308, 310
memory function, 115
memory loss, 87
meningioma, 119
meningitis, 120
mental capacity, 118
mental illness, 119
mental power, xii
mentor, 76, 256
mentoring, 75
Mercury, 5, 7, 10, 16, 25, 27
messages, 122, 123, 321
meta-analysis, 59, 60
metabolism, 36
metals, 293
metaphor, 413
methodology, 39, 74
methylprednisolone, 115
Miami, 227
mice, 63, 64, 93
microeconomics, 283
microscope, 112, 160
microscopy, 67, 78, 89
middle class, 266, 330, 333
Middle East, 179, 395, 396, 398, 401, 408, 412, 414, 416, 423
migrants, 184
migration, 405
military, xix, 34, 75, 263, 264, 269, 270, 271, 272, 273, 293, 330, 398, 404, 409, 414, 415
Milky Way, 12, 14, 15

Ministry of Education, 268
minors, 337, 338
mixed economy, 23
mobile phone, 254, 404
model system, 63, 65
models, 3, 10, 21, 50, 63, 64, 65, 128, 132, 134, 135, 136, 138, 216, 218, 398, 409, 416
Modern Age, 185
modern science, 11, 224
modern scientists, 68
modern society, 177, 369, 429
modernisation, 359, 398, 400
modernism, 183, 184
modernity, 178, 182, 183, 185
modifications, 27, 345
molecular medicine, 60
molecules, 96, 124
momentum, 29
monetary authority, 282
monetary policy, 283, 285
monetary union, 281
monoclonal antibody, 95
Moon, 5, 6, 7, 9, 10, 11, 12
moral code, xvi, 188
morale, xviii
morality, 172, 178, 189
morbidity, 42, 91
Morocco, 402, 404
morphology, 72, 168
mortality, 91, 114
mortgage-backed securities, 279
Moscow, 39
Moses, 102
motivation, 102, 209, 329, 331, 335, 341
multilateralism, 392
multinational corporations, 303
murder, 95, 331, 335, 340, 351, 361
muscles, 114, 117, 125
music, xviii, 188, 223, 239
musicians, 230
Muslims, 264
myelin, 112
mythology, 4

N

narratives, 188, 189, 334
nation building, 399
nation states, 403
national borders, 403
national debt, 280
National Health Service, 60
national identity, 179
national security, 400, 402, 415
nationalism, 181, 398, 399, 412
nationalists, 398
NATO, xx, 180, 392
natural resources, 293, 400
natural science, 74, 83, 286
natural sciences, 286
natural selection, 72, 74, 80, 84
nematode, 63
nerve, 98, 112, 120, 122, 123, 124
nervous system, 111, 114, 121
nervousness, 341
Netherlands, 85
neurobiology, 113
neuroscience, 129
neurotransmitter, 122
neurotransmitters, 113
neutral, 18, 202, 340, 351
neutrons, 34, 36
New Deal, 295
New England, 107, 109
new media, 404
New South Wales, 368
Newtonian physics, 28
next generation, 229
NGOs, 414, 417
Nietzsche, 222, 226
Nigeria, 422, 423
Nobel Prize, 120, 124
non-linear equations, 135
North Africa, 395, 401, 404
North America, 177, 178, 182, 183, 185, 232
North Korea, 177
Northern Ireland, 267, 269
Norway, 37
nuclear weapons, 32, 35
nuclei, 112, 114, 121
nucleic acid, 69, 229
nucleus, 81, 82, 96, 97
null, 286
null hypothesis, 286

O

obedience, 180, 317, 332
obesity, 319
objectivity, 221
obstacles, 81, 424, 427
oceans, 131, 133
OECD, 302
offenders, 343, 344, 345, 346, 347, 348, 351, 353, 354, 355, 357, 360, 361, 370
officials, 245, 247, 250, 320, 426, 427

oil, 58, 107, 137, 288, 310, 427
oligodendrocytes, 112
openness, 44, 200, 385
operations, 42, 267
opportunities, 263, 273, 411
oppression, 176, 400
optimism, 90, 112, 129, 137, 281
orbit, 6, 10, 11, 12, 13, 14, 15, 16
organ, 77, 88, 93, 94, 95, 221
organelle, 82
organism, 61, 63, 78, 80
organs, 43, 88, 89, 90, 94, 95, 97, 114, 125, 229
originality, 240
ossicles, 71, 79, 85
overlap, 62, 165, 167
overpopulation, 131
oxygen, 113, 114, 164, 259, 305

P

pain, 99, 123, 124, 127, 259
painters, 33, 34
Pakistan, 257, 322
Palestinian uprising, 412
pancreas, 95
paper money, 292
paradigm shift, 27
Paraguay, 419
parallel, 50, 114, 121
paralysis, 23, 375
parasites, 91
parents, 38, 42, 230, 231, 297, 357, 370
Parliament, 36, 274, 345, 348, 350, 351, 352, 354, 383, 384, 385
parole, 354, 355
participants, 57, 96, 230, 316, 317, 321
particle physics, 21, 164
pasta, 133, 260
pathologist, 376, 377
pathways, 61, 63, 114, 119, 121
patriotism, 264
peace, xviii, 34, 260, 316, 404, 410, 411, 416
penalties, 102, 234, 332
penicillin, 89
perfectionism, 255
performance measurement, 357, 358, 359, 362, 363, 365
perpetrators, 298
personal responsibility, 92
personality, xii, 71, 119, 172, 400
phantom limb pain, 123
philosophical knowledge, 160
photographs, 254, 255, 256, 257, 258

photons, 18, 28
physical activity, 317, 319, 324
physical aggression, 331
physical attractiveness, 233
physical exercise, 316
physical fitness, 273
physical health, 234
physical laws, 50
physicians, 93, 102, 104, 105, 107
physics, xvi, 5, 7, 11, 16, 20, 21, 25, 28, 41, 132, 136, 162, 165, 167, 211, 286, 308
physiology, 68, 89, 91, 93
planets, 5, 6, 8, 9, 10, 13, 27
plasmid, 96
plasticity, xvi, 93, 111, 112, 121, 123, 124
plasticization, 261
platform, 89
Plato, 5, 6, 208, 396
plausibility, 310
playing, 60, 126, 264, 316, 426
pleasure, xviii, 260, 429
pluralism, 184, 402
plutonium, 36
poetry, 215, 216, 217, 218, 220, 223, 224, 238, 393
polarity, 136
police, 172, 215, 266, 292, 297, 298, 321, 322, 330, 336, 339, 341, 375, 384, 426
policy, 31, 44, 45, 95, 244, 278, 285, 286, 288, 294, 366, 368, 390, 392, 393, 400, 413, 426
policymakers, 31, 286, 278, 285, 288, 368, 425
political leaders, 415
political participation, 181
political parties, 351, 398
political power, 181, 392
political system, xvi, xix
politics, 44, 212, 281, 283, 383, 384, 385, 386, 389, 390, 391, 393, 409, 410, 411, 412, 422
polygamy, 231
population, xvii, xviii, 34, 35, 36, 37, 38, 39, 40, 44, 45, 60, 127, 137, 178, 245, 249, 319, 330, 331, 332, 333, 335, 338, 343, 344, 347, 349, 350, 353, 354, 360, 361, 364, 366, 408, 414, 426
population growth, xvii
population size, 364
portfolio, 279
portraits, 254, 255, 262
Portugal, 280
positivism, 409
poverty, 190, 234, 293, 407, 422
power generation, 43
praxis, 221
prayer, 190, 223
predators, 229

predicate, 165, 166
prefrontal cortex, 127
prejudice, 60, 100, 194, 337, 338
prevention, 91, 114
price signals, 295
prima facie, 201
primate, 117, 122
principles, 4, 27, 44, 53, 67, 73, 100, 102, 103, 106, 189, 308, 343, 349, 376, 382, 410
prisoners, 95, 354, 355, 357, 360, 361, 362, 363, 364, 366, 367, 368, 369, 370, 401
prisons, 329, 357, 358, 359, 360, 361, 362, 364, 365, 366, 367, 368, 369, 370, 371
private sector, 137, 359, 368
probability, 12, 56, 334
problem solving, 302, 303, 304, 307
productivity growth, 426
professionalism, 104, 359
professionals, xii, 59, 366
profit, 103, 106, 107, 108, 245, 248, 424
prognosis, 57, 58, 126
project, xii, 21, 51, 83, 135, 202, 217, 253, 304, 359, 393, 400, 408, 419
proliferation, 299, 362, 398, 403
propaganda, 241, 400, 403
property crimes, 335
property rights, 333
prophylactic, 206
proportionality, 273
proposition, xv, 29, 49, 206, 373, 380, 382
prosperity, 293, 388, 389, 420
protection, 40, 94, 229, 337, 348, 367, 370, 391
protectionism, 216
proteins, 61, 62, 63, 67, 90, 96
Protestants, 193
protoplasm, 82
psychiatrist, 172
psychologist, 43, 300, 307, 308
psychology, 213, 215, 221
public concern, 37, 272
public health, 36, 40
public interest, 218, 288
public life, 384
public officials, 424
public opinion, 32, 43, 330
public policy, 138
public safety, 368
public sector, 281, 357, 358, 359, 368, 388, 401
public service, 271, 357, 358, 359
publishing, 8, 16, 67, 302
punishment, 171, 172, 173, 327, 330, 333, 334, 335, 338, 340, 343, 344, 345, 348, 367
purity, 180, 320, 321

Q

qualifications, 59
quality of life, 95, 115, 126
quantification, 369
quantum field theory, 28
quantum fluctuations, 21
quantum theory, xvi, 16, 25, 27
quasars, 19
questioning, 23, 38, 61, 87, 207, 280, 298, 299, 300, 308, 381, 400
questionnaire, 312

R

race, 47, 60, 338, 381, 427
radar, 17, 245
radiation, vii, 18, 31, 32, 33, 34, 35, 37, 38, 39, 40, 41, 42, 44, 106, 138
radio, 19, 92, 178, 399, 400, 403, 407, 408
radioactive isotopes, 32
radium, 32, 33
rainfall, 37
random errors, 9
randomised controlled trial (RCT), 59, 115, 116
rape, 329, 333, 335, 349
rapists, 334
rating agencies, 280
rationality, xvi, 29, 197, 198, 202, 203, 204, 283, 288, 289, 365
reaction time, 118
reactions, 331
readership, 207, 403
reading, xii, 49, 59, 72, 82, 84, 92, 177, 181, 207, 213, 223, 345, 389
real property, 164
realism, 183, 253, 254
reality, 6, 8, 23, 24, 27, 28, 64, 99, 106, 117, 126, 161, 163, 168, 182, 256, 257, 260, 261, 272, 273, 279, 307, 333, 363
reasoning, 47, 48, 49, 50, 51, 53, 54, 75, 159, 167, 192, 204, 300, 307, 412
recall, 53, 266, 393
recalling, 213
reception, 69, 73, 74, 84, 85, 244, 282
receptors, 114
recession, 17, 280, 283, 388, 421
recognition, 34, 71, 83, 128, 163, 200, 219, 222, 224, 253, 255, 261, 262, 424
recovery, 103, 111, 112, 119, 124, 125, 127, 405, 426, 427, 429, 430
recruiting, 337

red blood cells, 93
red wine, 92
reductionism, 176
redundancy, 113, 118, 127
reference system, 16
reform(s), 8, 207, 210, 212, 271, 287, 303, 320, 358, 367, 368, 371, 387, 398, 402, 404, 421
reformers, 398
regenerate, 98
regeneration, 90, 112, 124
regenerative medicine, 90
regional unemployment, 405
regression, 327, 373
regulations, 107, 278, 288, 419, 426
rehabilitation, 118, 272, 348, 359, 363, 367
rejection, 4, 27, 52, 58, 92, 93, 94, 95, 97, 202, 222, 337, 408, 413
relative size, 10
relativity, xvi, 13, 16, 17, 18, 21, 24, 27, 132
relaxation, 287, 305
relevance, 129, 133, 175, 182, 208, 313, 369
reliability, 43, 206, 377, 380
relief, 108, 223, 282
religion, xvi, 3, 29, 31, 57, 171, 172, 177, 180, 183, 184, 187, 188, 190, 191, 193, 194, 197, 198, 200, 202, 207, 212, 220, 231, 239, 264, 316, 321, 396, 401, 410
religiosity, 184, 189, 190
religious beliefs, 4, 5, 6, 29, 172, 190
REM, 118
Rembrandt, xix, 262
remodelling, 111, 117, 123
renaissance, 10, 397
repair, 90, 97, 98
repression, 330, 395
reproduction, 216, 229, 232, 331
reputation, 76, 315, 323
requirements, 287, 341, 367, 399
researchers, 334, 385
resentment, 367, 420
reserve currency, 282
resilience, 137, 138, 273
resistance, 8, 9, 100, 221, 222, 223, 224, 320, 337, 359, 392, 400, 404
resolution, 349, 377, 404
resources, xvii, 65, 138, 292, 295, 311, 357, 370, 385, 402
response, 6, 92, 96, 113, 125, 126, 135, 137, 179, 192, 211, 220, 223, 243, 258, 317, 349, 353, 375, 386, 410, 427, 430
restoration, 93
restrictions, 392
retail, 278, 421

retaliation, 400
retirement, 293
rewards, 234, 287, 315, 324
rhetoric, 56, 58, 65, 182, 220, 344, 383, 387, 393, 396, 400, 405
rhythm, xviii, 261
rights, 178, 324, 330, 332, 333, 338, 340
risk management, 280
RNA, 96
Roman Catholics, 178, 264
Royal Society, 103, 130, 261, 302, 311, 312
rugby, 315, 316, 318, 323, 325
rule of law, 172, 330, 331, 332
rules, xiii, 48, 50, 51, 52, 94, 171, 173, 179, 216, 223, 287, 301, 332, 352, 355, 367, 423
rural women, 137
Russia, xix, 34, 75, 206, 403, 422

S

safety, 32, 37, 38, 39, 41, 45, 132, 136, 341, 361, 363, 369, 426
sanctions, 344, 367
sarcasm, 56, 408
satellite technology, 403
Saturn, 5, 7, 9, 10, 12
Saudi Arabia, 402, 404
schemata, 308
scholarship, 74, 75, 76, 313
school, xvi, 4, 5, 37, 53, 54, 75, 99, 102, 104, 106, 175, 240, 246, 248, 250, 298, 300, 301, 302, 303, 304, 305, 306, 310, 312, 316, 357, 365, 370, 396, 397, 398, 401, 404, 429
school performance, 37
science, xi, xii, xiii, xiv, xv, xvi, xvii, xviii, xix, 3, 11, 23, 24, 25, 26, 27, 28, 29, 31, 44, 53, 56, 58, 62, 71, 73, 75, 80, 98, 106, 121, 129, 131, 132, 133, 136, 138, 162, 164, 165, 183, 194, 198, 200, 205, 215, 217, 218, 286, 300, 303, 380, 396, 415, 428
scientific knowledge, xiii, xv, 159, 161
scientific method, xv, 4, 286, 409, 412
scientific progress, xix
scientific theory, 24, 26, 28, 53
scientific understanding, xii, 24, 27
scope, xii, xiii, 74, 114, 176, 200, 208
sculptors, 239
Second World, 184, 245, 321, 353, 426
secondary education, 75
sectarianism, 398
security, 57, 137, 205, 279, 360, 363, 370, 399, 400, 401, 403, 410, 411, 412, 414, 415, 426
security forces, 401

self-assessment, xii
self-awareness, xvi, 427
self-concept, 161
self-conception, 161
self-confidence, 27
self-control, 317, 360, 365
self-image, 428
self-interest, 283, 286, 288, 295, 359, 409, 410, 416
self-portrait, 260
seminars, 178, 284, 350
sense perception, 201
sensitivity, xvii, 273
sentencing, 327, 343, 345, 346, 347, 348, 349, 350, 351, 352, 353, 355
Sentencing Guidelines, 353
September 11, 278
services, 103, 189, 193, 232, 234, 278, 288, 292, 358, 369, 386, 391
set theory, 51
sex, 123, 229, 232, 233, 234, 370, 401
sex differences, 123
sex offenders, 370
sexual abuse, 246
sexual activity, 229
sexual behaviour, 232
sexual contact, 233
sexual offences, 361
sexually transmitted diseases, 233
sham, 254
shame, 267, 322, 409
shock, 114, 132, 259, 277, 278, 287, 324
short supply, 244, 250
shortage, 88, 95, 332, 384
shortfall, 176, 390
showing, 23, 27, 34, 206, 256, 259, 359, 377, 403
Siberia, 76
sibling, 94
side effects, 95
signs, 125, 184, 254, 309, 361
Silicon Valley, 415
silver, 112, 267, 292, 293, 295
simulations, 20, 134, 135, 136, 138
Sinai, 102, 109
Singapore, xv, 99
skeleton, 219, 270
skin, 32, 34, 90, 92, 93, 94, 97, 114, 122, 123, 125, 338
skin grafting, 92, 93
slavery, 177, 329, 330, 331, 332, 333
sleep deprivation, 118
smallpox, 55, 89, 91
smoking, xii, 91, 429
social care, 297

social change, 399
social class, 333
social construct, 409, 416
social contract, 400
social development, 404
social exclusion, 401
social justice, 180, 408, 409, 414, 417
social life, 184, 337
social network, 403, 404
social order, 341
social organization, 429
social policy, 359
social relations, 332, 338
social responsibility, 106, 295
social sciences, 286
social stress, 295
social upheaval, 38
socialism, 359
society, xvi, xviii, xix, 9, 42, 54, 58, 59, 61, 100, 102, 172, 176, 177, 183, 184, 187, 189, 233, 234, 267, 291, 295, 297, 315, 321, 329, 330, 332, 334, 337, 343, 347, 348, 362, 365, 368, 389, 392, 393, 408, 409, 410, 411, 412, 414, 415, 421, 422, 425, 430
sociology, xiii, 359, 408
solar system, 14, 15, 27, 73
solid state, 132, 133, 136
solidarity, 267
solitude, 341
solution, 17, 32, 67, 88, 103, 234, 347, 362, 369
Somalia, 264
South Africa, 68, 322
South America, 178
South Asia, 263
South Korea, 182
sovereignty, 245, 399
sowing, 307, 389
Spain, 280, 334
spare capacity, 121
special relativity, 16, 23, 26
specialisation, 100, 293
specialists, 106, 118, 189, 192, 244, 247
species, xvii, 55, 68, 80, 83, 84, 90, 97, 119, 128, 161, 202, 229, 230, 232, 239, 334
speculation, 21, 73, 74, 79, 97, 167, 211, 220
speech, xix, 118, 171, 180, 215, 217, 224, 231, 237, 391
spelling, 301, 387
spending, 293, 359, 385, 390
sperm, 229
spin, 116, 224
spinal cord, 98, 115, 119, 122, 123, 124, 125
spinal cord injury, 115, 124

spine, 113
spiral galaxy, 15
spirituality, 173
Spring, 403, 404
sprouting, 122, 123, 124
Sri Lanka, 176, 182, 183, 264
stamens, 230
Standard Model, 164
standard of living, 245, 249
stars, 4, 5, 6, 7, 8, 9, 12, 14, 15, 16, 19, 213
starvation, 136, 246, 250
stasis, 427
state of emergency, 402
status epilepticus, 123
statutes, 345, 346
statutory provisions, 346
stem cells, 88, 90, 97, 98, 113, 118, 122
stereotyping, 423
steroids, 115, 323
stigma, 230, 323, 341
stimulation, 112, 117, 122, 123, 128
stimulus, 335, 365, 392
stock exchange, 106
stress, 118, 364
stretching, 18, 364
stroke, 8, 111, 114, 115, 123
strontium, 35, 36
structure, xiii, xix, 14, 15, 19, 20, 21, 26, 67, 69, 88, 96, 132, 160, 166, 168, 188, 217, 224, 343, 413
style, 16, 48, 180, 190, 264, 288, 304, 305, 306, 342
subjective experience, 188
subjectivity, 220
subsistence, 245, 332
substitutes, 293
substitution, 323
suicide, 29, 246, 361
Sun, 5, 6, 7, 8, 9, 10, 11, 12, 13, 14, 16, 22, 27
supernatural, 4, 103, 189
supervision, 360, 370
suppression, 35, 65
surgical technique, 94
survival, xviii, 94, 117, 173, 230, 237, 239, 278, 331, 341, 410, 411
survivors, 40, 115, 121
suspense, 57
Sweden, 37, 206
swelling, 114, 115, 116, 123
Switzerland, 184
symmetry, 243
sympathy, 203
symptoms, 63, 89, 121, 122, 123
synapse, 122
synaptic plasticity, 124
syndrome, 121, 125, 126, 128, 413
synthesis, 5, 67, 96, 122, 218
syphilis, 233
Syria, 397, 399, 400, 401, 402, 403, 404, 405

T

Taliban, 176, 182, 267, 273
target, 40, 61, 88, 188, 189, 208, 330, 337, 338, 339, 340, 359, 364, 367
tax collection, 292
taxes, 234, 283, 287, 294, 390
taxonomy, 176
taxpayers, 279
teachers, 175, 200, 232, 245, 246, 297, 299, 300, 306, 307
technological advancement, 415
technological progress, 183
technologies, 183, 400
technology, 34, 35, 100, 128, 178, 182, 219, 301, 303, 309, 310, 313, 415
telecommunications, 404
temperament, 165, 338
temperature, 18, 19, 20, 132, 133, 136
temporal lobe, 120, 129, 172
tension, 115, 132, 259, 261
tensions, 331, 343
territory, 63, 239, 369
terrorism, 402
testing, 35, 36, 37, 40, 48, 117, 133, 369, 378
testing program, 369
Thailand, 422
thalamus, 122, 125
theft, 329, 333, 335
therapeutic approaches, 88
therapeutic strategies, 61
therapeutic targets, 61, 63
therapeutics, 58
therapist, 58
therapy, 88, 94, 96, 211, 215
thermal history, 18
Third World, 426
Thomas Kuhn, 27
thoughts, 52, 53, 98, 172
thyroid, 35, 36, 37, 38
thyroid cancer, 35, 36, 37, 38
thyroid gland, 37
thyrotoxicosis, 38
time periods, 6, 365
time use, 291
tinnitus, 123
tissue, 32, 67, 81, 92, 93, 94, 97, 98, 111, 116, 123, 124, 332

torture, 13, 171, 190, 334
trade, xix, 63, 211, 233, 234, 245, 248, 279, 292, 293, 398, 419
trade-off, 63
traditionalism, 178, 183
traditions, 175, 212, 222, 224, 300, 321, 333, 342, 359, 395, 397
trafficking, 234, 351
training, 74, 75, 99, 100, 101, 117, 118, 221, 268, 269, 273, 350, 364, 369
trajectory, 135, 136, 176
transactions, 107
transformation, 105, 181, 240, 358, 364, 367, 369
transgression, 338
translation, 88, 98, 109, 112, 116, 215, 222, 295, 407, 410
transmission, 233, 300, 301, 303, 307
transparency, 383, 385, 387
transplant, 88, 92, 94, 117, 122
transplantation, 88, 89, 94, 95, 98, 116
transport, xv, 293, 294, 386, 420
transport costs, 294
transportation, 345, 346, 347
trauma, 93, 114, 115, 116, 125, 370
treatment, 32, 36, 37, 57, 59, 88, 89, 92, 95, 96, 97, 98, 100, 102, 104, 106, 120, 129, 201, 233, 264, 272, 273, 362, 367
trial, 59, 60, 94, 115, 271, 327, 341, 344, 349, 352
triggers, 334, 335
true belief, 400
tuberculosis, 91, 246
tumours, 33, 97, 115, 119, 121
Turkey, 414
tympanic membrane, 78

U

Ukraine, 37
unhappiness, 190
unification, 13
uniform, 5, 6, 7, 8, 16, 18, 181, 265, 266, 268, 270, 337, 400
universe, xvi, 3, 4, 5, 6, 7, 8, 9, 10, 12, 14, 15, 16, 17, 18, 19, 20, 21, 25, 29, 55, 132, 161, 164, 173, 188, 259
universities, 44, 116, 203, 205, 365, 386, 414
urban, 178, 225, 341, 344
urban life, 342

V

vacuum, 353

validation, 63, 194, 244
variations, 20, 62, 132, 180
varieties, 207
Vatican, 179
velocity, 17, 27, 134
ventilation, 116
Venus, 5, 7, 10, 11, 12
vertebrates, 71, 76, 77, 78, 79, 80
vessels, 92, 113, 400
vested interests, 287
victims, 331, 332, 333, 337, 338, 339, 340
videos, 380
violence, 273, 330, 333, 335, 337, 338, 339, 340, 342, 361, 369, 370, 401, 402, 412, 413
viral diseases, 165
viruses, 91
vision, 50, 125, 188, 200, 255, 258, 368, 391, 393, 407, 408
visions, 188, 415
visual acuity, 117
vote, xx, 282, 283, 320, 386, 387, 401
voters, 282, 283, 383, 384, 386, 389, 390, 391, 392, 393
voting, 52, 283, 286, 343, 387
vulnerability, 101, 102, 104
vulnerable people, 391

W

Wahhabism, 397
Wales, 45, 269, 343, 362, 368
walking, 126, 241, 266, 304, 312
war, xix, 18, 34, 43, 131, 185, 257, 260, 266, 274, 283, 310, 312, 316, 317, 350, 392, 403
war years, 350
Warsaw Pact, 177
warts, 255
waste, 42, 75, 229, 264
waste disposal, 42
watches, 33, 53
water, xvii, 32, 126, 133, 134, 135, 137, 189, 237, 241, 306, 335
watershed, 94, 271
wavelengths, 19
weakness, 115, 208
wealth, 95, 116, 233, 273, 280, 285, 286, 287, 292, 295, 420, 427, 429, 430
weapons, xvii, xviii, xx, 34, 35, 36, 37, 171, 178, 265, 384
weapons of mass destruction, 384
wear, 111, 254, 266, 335
web, 61, 82, 374, 384, 404
websites, 305, 312

welfare, 92, 102, 267, 359, 409
welfare state, 359
West Bank, 414
West Indies, 424
Western Australia, 26
Western countries, 101, 232, 297
white matter, 112, 121, 123, 125, 128
wholesale, 327, 359, 368, 423
wilderness, 63, 322
withdrawal, 124, 126, 267, 403
witnesses, 102, 341, 376, 378, 379, 381, 382
workers, 33, 38, 234, 245, 332
workforce, 331, 337
working hours, 294
World Bank, 294, 422
World Health Organisation (WHO), 39, 104, 138
worldview, 408, 409
worldwide, xiii, 35, 42, 88, 93, 95, 232, 239, 291, 293, 294, 403, 409
worry, 133, 135, 248, 301
wrestling, 315, 316, 321
wrongdoing, 330

X

xenophobia, 412
x-rays, 32

Y

yellow fever, 91
Yemen, 403
yield, 36, 98, 176, 284
young adults, 38, 338
young people, 234, 304, 337
young women, 32, 33, 297, 377

Z

Zimbabwe, 237
zoology, 162